United States Foreign Policy and World Order

United States Foreign Policy and World Order

Fourth Edition

James A. Nathan
James K. Oliver
University of Delaware

HarperCollins*Publishers*

Library of Congress Cataloging-in-Publication Data

Nathan, James A,
    United States foreign policy and world order / James A. Nathan,
  James K. Oliver. — 4th ed.
       p.   cm.
    Includes index.
    ISBN 0-673-39689-4
      1. United States — Foreign relations — 1945-   2. United States —
  Foreign relations administration.   I. Oliver, James K.   II. Title.
  E744.N265   1989
  327.73 — dc19   88-38134
                                                        CIP

      95   96   97   CWI   10   9   8   7

Printed in the United States of America

Acknowledgments

Portions of the Introduction are published by permission of Transaction Publishers, from *Society*,
Vol. 11, No. 6. Copyright © 1974 by Transaction Publishers.

Excerpts from Dean Acheson, *Present at the Creation*, are reprinted by permission of W.W.
Norton & Company, Inc., and Hughes Massie Limited. Copyright © 1969 by Dean Acheson.

Portions of Chapter 6 are from James A. Nathan, "The Cuban Missile Crisis: His Finest Hour
Now," *World Politics* 27, No. 2 (January 1975). Copyright © 1975 by Princeton University
Press. Reprinted by permission of Princeton University Press.

Portions of Chapter 8 are from James A. Nathan, Commitments in Search of a Roost: The
Foreign Policy of the Nixon Administration," *The Virginia Quarterly Review*, Vol. 50, No.
3 (Summer 1974). Reprinted by permission.

Portions of Chapter 9 are from James A. Nathan, "Zbigscam: The Carter Administration's
Foreign Policy, 1976–1980," *The Virginia Quarterly Review*, Vol. 57, No. 2 (Spring 1981).
Reprinted by permission.

Portions of Chapters 10–13 are from James A. Nathan, "Decisions in the Land of Pretend:
U. S. Foreign Policy in the Reagan Years," *The Virginia Quarterly Review*, Vol. 65, No. 1
(January 1989). Reprinted by permission.

Preface

In the last days of the Reagan tenure, there was more than the usual feeling of expectancy associated with the end of a president's term. It was as if more than an administration was ending; many observers thought they were seeing the close of the postwar era. Ronald Reagan, perhaps the most strident cold warrior since John Foster Dulles, seemed to concur. His summit meeting with Soviet General Secretary Gorbachev in Moscow was emblematic of the deep shifts that had taken place. Indeed, by 1988, hopes for resolution of hitherto intractable conflicts and enormous changes in the terms of other problems were apparent in almost every region of the world. There seemed to be a great sprouting of democracy throughout East Asia. From Taiwan to South Korea to the Philippines, previously authoritarian regimes relaxed their grip. Even the truly hermetic regimes of Burma and North Korea seemed ready to at least consider joining the community of nations.

Nowhere was change more flabbergasting than in China. A regime that had suffered a paroxysm of revolutionary zealotry gave way to one that oversaw a process of decentralization and encouraged individual initiative. In Southeast Asia, Vietnam appeared ready to end its ten-year adventure in imperialism in Cambodia. In Southwest Asia, Gorbachev took steps to heal what he called a "running sore"—the protracted effort to subjugate Afghanistan—by withdrawing Russian troops. Peace even appeared to break out in the Persian Gulf, when Iran, diplomatically isolated and bereft of two generations of young men, finally agreed to negotiations after eight years of near-total war with Iraq.

In southern Africa, negotiations between South Africa, Angola, and Cuba, mediated by the United States, produced an agreement in principle on a Cuban withdrawal from Angola, linked to the exit of South Africa from Namibia. Skeptics noted, however, that this was not the first time the announcement of such an agreement coincided with a U.S. election campaign. Moreover, although the agreement was a welcome sign of reduced tension in the area, it left unanswered the great question of the future of South Africa: How long could a tiny white minority rule a huge black population? And while the question remained open, the violence of resistance continued to match the escalation of repression.

In the midst of all this promising change, the Soviet-American relationship also improved dramatically. For years Reagan had characterized the Soviet system as an "evil empire." However, beginning in late 1985, there was a dizzying metamorphosis. The two superpowers reached an arms control agreement, including a workable scheme of mutual inspections, that exceeded any arrangement even dreamed of during the heyday of detente. New Soviet proposals on the reduction of conventional forces, along with a less rigidly doctrinaire approach to the talks by their negotiators, seemed to signal a significant break with the past.

Not surprisingly, the Reagan administration claimed much of the credit for these changes, both in East-West relations and in other foreign policy areas. Former National Security Council official Geoffrey Kemp argued that Reagan-era policies had been "redeemed by events." He was talking specifically of the Iranian decision to accept a U.N.-mediated cease-fire, which came just days after a U.S. guided missile frigate incorrectly identified an Iranian commercial airliner with 290 passengers aboard as a hostile fighter plane and shot it down. The refusal of other nations to join Iran in condemning the U.S. action made clear to Iran's leaders the country's isolation. Perhaps this realization opened some eyes in Iran, but what really lead the country, however reluctantly, to the peace table was the loss, after eight years of the most brutal fighting, of over half a million young men. The Reagan administration has also claimed that its sometimes embargo of war goods to Iran — Operation Staunch — dried up Iranian arms. But it was not the embargo that gave Iraq the advantage in air power (a superiority gained well before the ban), caused Iran's logistical inadequacies, crippled its oil industry, or led Iraq to the use of poison gas — all key determinants of the war's outcome.

The United States' aid to the Afghan rebels, especially outfitting them with Stinger missiles, was instrumental in driving the Soviets from the country. However, supporting the insurgents — Islamic fundamentalists sympathetic to the Ayatolla Khomeini — had its cost, including the displacement of about eight million Afghans, nearly half the population. In addition, many of the U.S.-supplied arms destined for Afghan freedom fighters ended up in other hands. In the late 1980s there were disturbing reports that one of the most effective antiaircraft weapons in the world, U.S. Stinger missiles, were traded freely from Northeast Asia to North Africa. Finally, in exchange for Pakistan's provision of a rebel redoubt, the Reagan administration turned a blind eye to the Pakistani-Afghan heroin traffic as well as ignoring (and thus tacitly approving) Pakistani development of an atomic bomb. In short, while the Soviets may have been balked in their conquest of Afghanistan, the region has been dangerously destabilized.

The United Nations was essential in each of the accords that brightened prospects for peace in the last days of the Reagan administration. And yet the United States under Reagan was anything but an ardent supporter of the United Nations. Indeed, in response to a U.N. complaint that without the payment of U.S. dues (withheld by the Reagan administration) the organization could not afford to operate in New York, one senior U.S. representative to the United Nations said he himself would be pleased to stand on the dock and "wave a fond farewell." At the last minute there was a budgetary reprieve when the United States paid part of its arrearage. Much of the U.N. operating costs were picked up, for the first time, by the Soviet Union.

In Nicaragua, after eight years of war, the Sandinistas seemed willing to deal with the U.S.-backed rebels, contras, but it was hardly U.S. arms that changed the Nicaraguan government's stance. The contras never controlled or administered even so much as a village for more than twenty-four hours. Soviet or Cuban unwillingness to save the Nicaraguans from the results of their repression and economic bungling seem a more likely explanation for Sandinista willingness to attend to some of the peace proposals developed by Costa Rican President Oscar Arias. Peace may come in Nicaragua, but the United States has been no friend to the peace process. The State Department's Elliot Abrams has spoken of the Arias plan with consistent contempt and apparently advised the contras to harden their demands after the Sandinistas had satisfied the initial contra agenda. Perhaps the long U.S. association with the unsavory contras and the costly effort to reconfigure Central America in support of the anti-Sandinista fight was worth it. We now know, however, that one price was the uncontrolled growth of cocaine traffic in the region. Drugs have become one of the two thin spindles that prop U.S.-backed military regimes from the isthmus through the Caribbean. When U.S. military support recedes, as assuredly it will, only the drug business will remain.

An ocean of obstacles was traversed during the Reagan years. United States proposals crafted under Secretary of State Haig—who believed that the United States' positions in arms control negotiations were so lopsided in favor of the United States that the Soviets would never accept them—have been embraced by Gorbachev. Indeed he has become more enthusiastic about verification than the U.S. Joint Chiefs. The initial U.S. plan may have been, as one high American official forthrightly told one of the authors, to "spend the Soviets into the ground." On the other hand, U.S. military budgets may have been raised not by policy but by inadvertence. David Stockman once asserted that the rise in defense spending was, in part, the result of a midnight "calculator error," when he in his weariness underestimated the Carter defense programs by 56 percent.

In any case, the Soviets decided to rejoin the West not because they were pauperized by Reagan, but because Gorbachev, like Peter the Great, believes that the Soviets have been too backward and too isolated for too long. President Reagan, moreover, did not select Gorbachev. Former KGB and Communist party chief Andropov spearheaded that move. The Reagan hagiographers may claim success for the old cold warrior, but his program has been salvaged by events that his administration's policies often touched only tangentially, if at all. The truth is that the Reagan administration had meandered like some weary hobo to a place, in Mathew Arnolds' words, between two worlds, one not yet dead, and the other still unborn. The great danger, however, is that the wrong lessons will be drawn from success attributed to wrong policies. The cock that crows at dawn may well believe that he brought up the sun. But the United States cannot afford such a superficial analysis of its recent good fortune.

This book has been dramatically redone in order to take into account the many significant changes in the international system over the last eight years. Three new chapters were added, and a significant pruning of the rest of the manuscript was necessary to keep the length manageable. We have integrated into the text a great deal of new scholarship, especially on the Eisenhower years and Vietnam. Overseeing this edition were Cynthia Chapin at Scott, Foresman/Little, Brown and Ralph Zickgraf at Editing, Design and Production, Inc. John Covell maneuvered this book through some stormy waters. We have become accustomed to his calm support.

Contents

United States Foreign Policy and World Order

Introduction

The chapters that follow trace the attempt by the United States to fashion and apply its conception of world order in the increasingly turbulent and interdependent post–World War II world. The task involves more, however, than a simple recitation of events, for any survey of events as complex and controversial as those under examination here inevitably entails, either explicitly or implicitly, the adoption of an analytical perspective so that one might choose, weigh and *understand* the significance of the events.

THINKING ABOUT
AMERICAN FOREIGN POLICY

The student of international relations and foreign policy is confronted with different conceptions of the structure and dynamics of world politics in the late twentieth century. On the one hand there is "realism," a framework that emphasizes the interaction of nation-states in a quasi-anarchical environment in which the preparation for and use of force are the dominant and controlling realities for foreign policy makers and the societies within which they act. In contrast, there is the notion of "interdependence." This "transnational" perspective acknowledges the continuing importance of the nation-state and its strategic concerns, yet nonetheless emphasizes the new salience of political economic forces and conditions. A transnational perspective gives weight to new actors and forces now constraining the foreign policies of even the most powerful of states.[1] We suggest in the discussion that follows that American foreign policy since World War II can be understood, in part, as the attempt by American policy makers to control and order a world politics that is moving from an approximation of the traditional world politics to an international environment that today is a mix of the traditional and the transnational.

The analyst of American foreign policy has to acknowledge still other analytical debates and choices. One of the most intense arguments during the last several decades is between those who see the course of American foreign policy determined by a bipolar struggle between an America intent on establishing an open, liberal capitalist world order

1

and, on the other side, an aggressive, expansionist Soviet Union determined to establish a closed, totalitarian communist world state. This "orthodox" or "traditional" view of the motivation of American foreign policy contends that American behavior since the end of World War II has been essentially a defensive reaction to the unremitting expansionism of the Soviet Union. In contrast, the "revisionists" tend to view American policy and behavior as largely responsible for the cold war. In one of its manifestations, revisionism sees in American foreign policy the operation of institutional imperatives growing out of capitalism and its purported need for international dominion to secure markets, raw materials, and cheap labor.[2]

In a variant of revisionism somewhat closer to the position adopted in the analysis that follows, greater emphasis is placed on the sense of moral, social, cultural, and historical — as well as economic — "exceptionalism" that has informed so much of the American view of itself and its role in the world. Extending back to the colonial and revolutionary experience, and certainly a tangible force by the beginning of the twentieth century, exceptionalism was most eloquently and forcefully articulated by Woodrow Wilson. This belief tends to define American security interests in terms of a world order that excludes virtually all other notions of security. But then, at the the end of World War I, there arose an alternative and no less exclusive conception of world order: Soviet communism. Because the Soviets' vision of a global order was defined by not only communist revolution but also authoritarian rule, cultural isolation, periodic invasion resulting in a historical sense of insecurity, and pride in having persevered in its position on the "edge" of Europe, bipolar conflict over the shape of the future was virtually inevitable.

The analytical approach adopted in this study is eclectic. We have no desire to demonstrate the truth or error of the many philosophical and analytical perspectives. Where the traditional or orthodox analysis seems valid, we employ it; where a revisionist perspective appears reasonable and warranted by documentation, we are not averse to bringing such analysis to bear. In any event, at every turn we have tried to make our analytical posture explicit within the range of possible interpretive positions.

Similarly, we have tried to use, where appropriate, various models of policy making and the other accoutrements of contemporary political science policy analysis. Here again, the analyst has several distinct horizons to survey. One might, for example, simply dismiss foreign policy "processes" and view decision making as a kind of black box from which "policy" emerges and interacts with the international political system.

From this perspective, the United States can be regarded as a "rational actor" seeking to devise courses of action that maximize its interests and minimize the costs associated with pursuing the national interest. Conversely, much contemporary analysis of American foreign policy insists that one must shift the "level of analysis" to the black box, that is, the U.S. political system. But here one encounters still more levels or potential foci of analysis.[3]

"Bureaucratic politics," for instance, have gained much attention among students of foreign policy in the last decade. In this view, foreign policy is best understood as the outcome of a complex bargaining process involving career bureaucrats, political appointees, and, of course, the president. Each of these individuals seeks to maximize both personal interests and organization interests. The *national interest*, therefore, emerges as the result of the pulling and hauling between bureaucrats and the president. A variant of this approach concentrates on the group dynamics of close presidential advisers and their interplay with the president.[4] A more focused analysis is one that concentrates on the psychology and the cognitive and administrative styles of presidents and high officialdom.[5]

Another approach suggests that concentration on bureaucratic politics, personal psychology, or small-group dynamics ignores the societal context.[6] Thus, it is argued, foreign policy is bounded by executive–legislative relations, electoral politics, and the interplay of public attitudes and the decision-making process.

We have not applied, because we have not located, a single framework, model, perspective, or level of analysis that encompasses these many dimensions and implications of American foreign policy. The careful student will observe, however, a tendency for analysis to focus on the perceptions (insofar as these can be determined), actions, and rationalizations of presidents and their chief advisers.

Inasmuch as the process whereby these perceptions are translated into policy has focused on the president and the presidency during the period under study, this focus seems warranted. At the same time, however, we find it essential to place such analysis in the rich context of bureaucratic and executive–legislative politics, public opinion, the exercise of private power, and, ultimately, the interaction of American policy with the constraints imposed by a dynamic international system. This approach has as its objective an understanding of the origins of the American image of international reality, the resultant policies, and the global consequences of these policies. Finally, we hope to shed some light on the extent to which the dominant perceptions of America's interests and policy have reached the outer limits of utility.

THE CONTEXT
OF WORLD POLITICS AND
THE COURSE OF AMERICAN POLICY

For over four decades, American foreign policy has sought to build an international order predicated on American military and economic superiority. From the outset of the postwar period, American policy makers postulated a relationship between American national security and some form of world order. In late 1945, American policy makers faced the tasks of reconstructing a world order shattered by three decades of global war, economic dislocation, depression, and political and social revolution. The United States possessed seemingly limitless military power with its monopoly of atomic weapons. Moreover, it was the only national economy of significance to have weathered World War II intact. Despite apprehension about inflation and postwar adjustment, the American economy had grown and even prospered as the arsenal for the wartime alliance. The European economy, however, lay in ruins.

But the postwar international system has been resistant to American political, economic, and military sculpting. The cold war between the Soviet Union and the United States concerning the political, military, economic, and social structure and dynamics of Europe immediately took the place of World War II. The origins of the cold war lie in the chaotic end of World War I and the American, European, and Japanese attempts to crush the Russian communist revolution of 1917. The Western intervention failed to overcome Lenin and his associates, but the resultant Soviet perceptions of the capitalist world and the Western preoccupation with Soviet designs festered throughout the interwar period. This mutual distrust was not completely suppressed even when the Soviets and the West fought against a common enemy in World War II (see Chapter 1).

In the West, the greatest threat to international order after World War II was the political and economic chaos of Western Europe. The severe economic dislocations of the war seemed to provide the opportunity for Soviet expansion beyond their Central European hegemony, gained through the defeat of Nazi power in 1944 and 1945. Because the immediate postwar European problem was deemed to be primarily economic, economic remedies seemed most appropriate (see Chapter 2). However, because American economic assistance was predicated on the twin necessities of a strong, essentially capitalist Europe and a reconstructed Germany (see Chapter 2), the Soviet fear of capitalist encirclement and renewed German aggression was exacerbated (see Chapters

1 and 2). The mix of brutal Soviet administration of the territories from which they rolled back Germany and superior postwar American arms and economic strength directed toward an open, liberal world order resulted in a sustained crisis. Beginning in 1946 and more plainly with the Berlin Blockade of 1948–1949, crisis followed crisis. The apparent necessity for using in some fashion—either by threat or demonstrations of "will"—the instrumentations of force combined with the American sense of responsibility for the military imperatives of world order came to override an earlier interest in the international economic order and the economic instrumentations of the Marshall Plan (see Chapter 2). That a successful diplomacy had to be predicated on military power was a lesson subsequently confirmed by the Korean War (see Chapter 3).

The psychological and material burdens of the Korean conflict seriously eroded domestic support for American conventional military interventions in furtherance of U.S. global activism. The Eisenhower administration successfully deflected this frustration, however, and built an even larger structure of international obligations. Massive retaliation, the dependence on the ultimate threat—nuclear force—was for the Eisenhower administration the means of upholding far-flung commitments at a reduced cost (see Chapter 4). During the late 1950s and early 1960s, the Soviet Union's apparent acquisition of a global nuclear capability and nationalist upheaval throughout the Third World seemed to neutralize this conjoining of nuclear force with an American desire to establish a cogent global order (see Chapters 4 and 5). By the mid-1960s, a coalition of scholars and analysts concurred: nuclear weapons had robbed the United States' threats of force of their credibility. The problem, wrote Henry Kissinger in the late 1950s, was that "since diplomacy which is not related to a plausible employment of force is sterile it must be the task of our military policy to develop a doctrine and capability for the graduated employment of force."[7] A great edifice of strategic theory on how to make military force relevant to diplomacy was subsequently incorporated into the Kennedy administration's concepts of "flexible response." The upper ranges of this strategic doctrine were employed in Cuba in 1962 (see Chapter 6), and the lower ranges were used throughout the Third World—especially in Vietnam from the mid-1960s until the end of the decade (see Chapter 7).

By the mid-1960s "graduated response," in the Defense Department's argot, became an article of faith. The *Pentagon Papers* show the Joint Chiefs of Staff and civilians in the executive branch debating varieties of "squeezes" on Vietnam. Intervals of "pain" were proposed, each with "pauses" that varied in tempo from "low" through "moderate" and proceeded to a fast "full squeeze" and then to a "blitz" or a "crescendo."[8] But by the 1970s, it was still an open question whether enormously expanded military power, no matter how "flexible," could be effectively managed to support American security interests (see Chapter 8). American policy had been predicated in large measure on the assumption that force could be productively wedded to diplomacy. But it was apparent, however, that this vast undertaking was perhaps too simple in formulation and too complex in execution.

In the meantime, the conditions of world politics changed significantly. Prior to the mid-1960s, the traditional image of world politics, with its emphasis on military security, was at least plausible. By the mid-1960s, however, newer forces had begun to emerge, although in the mid-1970s security concerns were never eclipsed. The Soviet Union's approaching strategic parity with the United States changed a thirty-year precondition of American national security policy. At the same time, however, new problems—the oil embargo of 1973–1974, the persistence of global inflation, and the appearance of vast concentrations of economic power outside the traditional framework of the industrialized world—confronted American foreign policy of the 1970s and early 1980s with challenges for which the lessons of the cold war seemed inappropriate (see Chapter 9).

By the late 1970s and early 1980s, students of American public and elite opinion discerned only fragments when delving into the belief systems about America's role in the world.[9] One set of beliefs kept the central elements of the old cold war consensus and applied them to the world of the 1980s. These "cold war" or "conservative" internationalists believed that the world remained essentially bipolar and was dominated by the strategic threat to American interests and world leadership posed by an aggressive and expansionist Soviet Union. In this view the "new forces" in world politics were ultimately secondary to the "old" realities of the cold war era.

A second set of beliefs and attitudes constituted a "liberal" or "post–cold war" internationalism that rejected the traditional emphasis on a bipolar cold war dominated by the threat and use of military instruments. For this group, Soviet–American strategic parity, international political economics, Third World nationalism and upheaval, and diminished capacity for American leadership composed the essence of world politics. New conditions required no less international commitment and activism than the conditions of cold war; but the interests and objectives of American policy were seen as both different and necessarily more restrained than those of policies applied before the mid-1960s.

A third position—that of the "noninternationalists" or "neoisolation-ists"—was itself split. On the one hand, a belief was prevalent, largely on the part of mass publics, that the United States should avoid and minimize the interdependencies of world politics, seek "peace," but also retain American "strength." Others, for the most part within the policy elite, went even further and doubted the efficacy and utility of military force and preferred a concentration on domestic economic, environmental, and social priorities.

The Carter administration tried and failed to straddle all three positions in its approach to the world of the late 1970s. By 1980, Carter had reverted to the strenuous commitments of cold war internationalism (see Chapter 9), but it was a late conversion that could not stave off the ascendancy of a Reagan administration. Reagan rarely strayed from the verities of the cold war approach to international relations (Chapters 10, 11 and 12). By the end of the second Reagan administration, the appropriateness and efficacy of its conservative internationalism remained open to question, however, for neither American strategic superiority nor economic hegemony—the essence of the original American primacy—had been reestablished or seemed within reach. Indeed, as the turn of the century came into view, the United States was faced with adjusting to a Soviet Union under younger and seemingly more creative leadership and making its way as a more "normal" nation. The Gorbachev challenge was the most novel since Lenin—and perhaps the most welcome.

NOTES

1. The literature explaining, comparing, and arguing over these perspectives is vast. Seminal works include the following: Seyom Brown, *New Forces in World Politics* (Washington, D.C.: The Brookings Institution, 1975); Robert O. Keohane and Joseph S. Nye, *Power and Interdependence: World Politics in Transition* (Boston: Little, Brown, 1977); Kenneth Waltz, *Theory of International Politics* (Reading, Mass.: Addison-Wesley, 1979); Robert Gilpin, *War and Change in World Politics* (New York: Cambridge University Press, 1981); Keohane, *After Hegemony: Cooperation and Discord in the World Political Economy* (Princeton: Princeton University Press, 1984); and Brown, *New Forces, Old Forces, and the Future of World Politics* (Glenview, Ill.: Scott, Foresman, 1988). For a survey of the debate between the perspectives as it developed in the scholarly literature, see Keohane, ed., *Neorealism and its Critics* (New York: Columbia University Press, 1986). For a good revisionist synthesis see Robert A. Pollard, "Economic Security and the

origins of the Cold War: Bretton Woods, the Marshall Plan, and American Rearmament, 1944–1950," *Diplomatic History*, Vol. 9 (Summer 1985), pp. 271–289.

2. Perhaps the most straightforward statement of this thesis remains that of Harry Magdoff in *The Age of Imperialism: The Economics of U.S. Foreign Policy* (New York: Monthly Review Press, 1969). The most comprehensive developement of this thesis is to be found in Joyce and Gabriel Kolko, *The Limits of Power: The World and United States Foreign Policy, 1945–1954* (New York: Harper and Row, 1972).

3. The most important exploration of these levels of analysis as well as the original exposition of the "bureaucratic politics" approach to analyzing foreign policy is Graham Allison, *Essence of Decision: Explaining the Cuban Missile Crisis* (Boston: Little, Brown, 1971). See also Morton H. Halperin and Arnold Kanter, eds., *Readings in American Foreign Policy: A Bureaucratic Perspective* (Boston: Little, Brown, 1973); Morton Halperin, *Bureaucratic Politics and Foreign Policy* (Washington, D.C.: Brookings, 1974); and Allison and Halperin, "Bureaucratic Politics: A Paradigm and Some Policy Implications," in Richard Ullman and Raymond Tanter, eds., *Theory and Policy in International Relations* (Princeton: Princeton University Press, 1972). For a more critical view of this approach, see: Stephen D. Krasner, "Are Bureaucracies Important? (Or Allison Wonderland)," *Foreign Policy*, No. 17 (Summer 1971) and Robert Art, "Bureaucratic Politics and American Foreign Policy: A Critique," *Policy Sciences*, 40 (1973). For the authors' critique of this approach see, James A. Nathan and James K. Oliver, "Bureaucratic Politics: Academic Windfalls and Intellectual Pitfalls," *Journal of Political and Military Sociology*, Vol. 6 (Spring 1978), pp. 81–91.

4. Irving Janis, *Groupthink*, 2nd ed. (Boston: Houghton Mifflin, 1982).

5. James David Barber, *The Presidential Character*, 2nd ed. (Englewood Cliffs, N.J.: Prentice-Hall, 1977); see also Alexander George, "Assessing Presidential Character," *World Politics*, Vol. 26 (January 1974), pp. 234–282.

6. See the present authors' *Foreign Policy Making and the American Political System*, 2nd ed. (Boston: Little, Brown, 1987). A good recent anthology of readings on these many domestic factors and levels of analysis is Charles W. Kegley, Jr. and Eugene R. Wittkopf, eds., *The Domestic Sources of American Foreign Policy: Insights and Evidence* (New York: St. Martin's Press, 1988).

7. Henry Kissinger, *Nuclear Weapons and Foreign Policy* (New York: W. W. Norton, 1969), p. 54.

8. Neil Sheehan, Hedrick Smith, E. W. Kenworthy, and Fox Butterfield, *The Pentagon Papers* (as published in *The New York Times*) (New York: Bantam Books, 1971), pp. 365–371, especially documents nos. 85 and 87.

9. Ole Holsti and James Rosenau, "Vietnam, Consensus, and the Belief Systems of American Leaders," *World Politics*, Vol. 31 (October 1979), pp. 1–56; "U.S. Leadership in a Shrinking World: The Breakdown of Consensus and the Emergence of Conflicting Belief Systems," *World Politics*, Vol. 35 (April 1983), pp. 368–392; and "Consensus Lost. Consensus Regained?: Foreign Policy Beliefs of American Leaders," *International Studies Quarterly*, Vol. 30 (December 1986), pp. 375–409. For a critique of Holsti and Rosenau's analysis, see: Thomas Ferguson, "The Right Consensus?: Holsti and Rosenau's New Foreign Policy Belief Surveys," *International Studies Quarterly*, Vol. 30 (December 1986), pp. 411–423; Eugene Wittkopf, "On the Foreign Policy Beliefs of the American People: A Critique and Some Evidence," *International Studies Quarterly*, Vol. 30 (December 1986), pp. 425–445; and Wittkopf, "Elites and Masses: Another Look at Attitudes toward America's World Role," *International Studies Quarterly*, Vol. 31 (June

1987), pp. 131–159. See also William Schneider, "Conservatism, Not Interventionism: Trends in Foreign Policy Opinion, 1974–1982," in Kenneth Oye, et al., *Eagle Defiant: United States Foreign Policy in the 1980s* (Boston: Little, Brown, 1983), pp. 33–64 and John Reilly, "America's State of Mind," *Foreign Policy*, Vol. 66 (Spring 1987), pp. 39–56.

Chapter 1
Prelude to the
Cold War

Just before World War I, Woodrow Wilson[1] identified American ideals and aspirations with those of all mankind:

> My dream is that as the years go by and the world knows more and more of America it . . . will turn to America for those moral inspirations which lie at the basis of all freedom . . . and that America will come into the full light of day when all shall know that she puts human rights above all other rights, and that her flag is the flag not only of America, but of humanity.
>
> I do not know that there will ever be a declaration of independence and of grievances for mankind, but I believe that if any such document is ever drawn it will be drawn in the spirit of the American Declaration of Independence, and that America has lifted high the light which will shine unto all generations and guide the feet of mankind to the goal of justice and liberty and peace.[2]

There was more to this vision than patriotic rhetoric, for it was part of a larger conception of world order that continues to shape American foreign policy.

To Wilson, the internal order of states was a major determinant of state behavior and, hence, world peace. If a state's domestic politics were not marked by democratic institutions and processes, that state was a potential threat to world peace because such states almost invariably turn to aggressive behavior for the aggrandizement of their rulers or to deflect the attention of the ruled from their domestic plight. Wilson's beliefs about world politics supported an interventionist policy in two ways. First, the exceptional purity of the American purpose and power allowed the United States to contribute to the creation of an international order among states. But, second, the Wilsonian vision was necessarily concerned with the undemocratic internal order of those states that might become a threat to the larger international order. Both dimensions are captured in Wilson's famous statement at the time of World War I:

> We are glad . . . to fight thus for the ultimate peace of world and for the liberation of its peoples . . . for the rights of nations great and small

and the privilege of men everywhere to choose their way of life and of obedience. The world must be made safe for democracy. Its peace must be planted upon the tested foundations of political liberty.[3]

However, an important paradox is implicit in this vision. Although people were "to choose their way of life and obedience," the strong implication existed that unless the outcome of this act of self-determination conformed to Wilsonian standards, intervention would follow. How could it be otherwise if one believed that those "moral inspirations which lie at the basis of all freedom" were somehow uniquely American? Denial of what was to Wilson a self-evident truth necessarily placed the offending state in the camp of the enemy. Wilson, moreover, was prepared to use force in pursuit and protection of his vision. In the case of the Mexican intervention in 1916 and again in World War I, Wilson fought — presumably for some higher notion of the "ultimate peace." And in his conception of the League of Nations after World War I, force was deemed essential to the maintenance of world order,[4] only now it was to be the "concerted force of the combined action of mankind through the instrumentality of all the enlightened governments of the world."[5] But through all the rhetoric, however, one assumption remained constant and unchallenged: "The tested foundations of political liberty" were self-evident, and they were "drawn in the spirit of the American Declaration of Independence." To deny this — to deny that America's flag was indeed "the flag of humanity" — marked a state as one of the unenlightened and, therefore, the legitimate target of intervention.

The Soviet view of international politics and Russia's place in the international system that emerged from the Bolshevik Revolution in 1917 challenged Wilson's vision. Yet, curiously, Lenin's understanding of world politics paralleled some features of American foreign policy. For instance, the Leninist view of world politics carried traces of the traditional Russian sense of mission, which was similar to the American and Wilsonian vision. The sixteenth-century idea of Moscow as a "third Rome" and the nineteenth-century Pan–Slavic movement saw Russia as possessing a destiny and a duty larger than the mere frontiers of Great Russia. But whereas Wilson viewed consensus as the natural scheme of things, Marxism saw class conflict as the path of social and political development. Where democracy was seen in the liberal tradition as a means for giving expression to the people at large, Marxists thought democracy in the West only an expression of dominant economic and class interest.

Lenin, moreover, believed that his regime was not secure while capitalist values flourished in Europe. He and his followers thought that European leaders would be profoundly hostile to a Soviet Russia. The

Soviet Union stood for social revolution; the West stood for orderly progress. As the West questioned the very validity of the political, moral, and intellectual foundation of the Soviet state, the Soviets denied the validity of the Western order. Furthermore, Lenin and his followers believed that the West would attempt, in Churchill's metaphor, to strangle the Soviet infant in its crib (he called it a "monster"); and therefore the best protection for the October Revolution was an expanding system of states based on the revolutionary principles propounded by the Bolsheviks. As Lenin said in March 1919:

> We live not only in a state, but in a system of states, and the existence of the Soviet Republic side by side with the imperialist states for a prolonged period of time is unthinkable. In the meantime a series of frightful collisions will occur.[6]

Wilson's reaction to the Bolsheviks was predictable—they had established, he thought, an illegitimate government. As Wilson proclaimed in July 1919, "The men who . . . control . . . the affairs of Russia represent nobody but themselves. . . . They have no mandate from anybody. . . . [A] group of men more cruel than the Czar himself is controlling the destinies of that great people."[7] The loathing of the West for the kind of regime that had come to power in 1917 was intensified by Lenin's successful extrication of Russia from World War I and Trotsky's negotiation of a quick peace favorable to the Germans. The most fundamental source of Wilson's antipathy, however, was the communist vision of humanity's political, economic, and social order that emerged from the revolution of 1917. Wilson therefore sought to interpose American military and economic power against the Communists even as they, and all of Russia, were engulfed in civil war.

INTERVENTION IN
THE RUSSIAN CIVIL WAR

Some seventy thousand Czechoslovak soldiers,[8] deserters from the Austrian army, were left in the Soviet Union after the Bolsheviks signed the Treaty of Brest-Litovsk ending hostilities with the Germans. The Czechs, though isolated in Siberia, retained their discipline and organization and represented an important organized military force in Russia during the chaotic civil war that followed the revolution and Russia's departure from World War I. The plight of the Czechs helped fuel anti-Bolshevik sentiment in the West and served as a rationalization for Wilson to contribute to the intervention by Allied troops ostensibly to aid the Czechs to reach the European front.[9] But the Czechs had been joined by Russian anti-Bolshevik forces, so the decision to intervene was known to support the anti-Bolshevik factions in the Russian civil war. In Wilson's words, the intervention would "steady any efforts of the Russians at self-defense, or the establishment of law and order."[10] Wilson's motives were complex, but any "self-defense" assistance to aid the Russians regain "self-government" left little doubt that the dispatch of troops to help the brave Czechs who had attracted so much attention would also buttress anti-Bolshevik factions.

In the end, two American interventions occurred in alliance with with the British and French, who were as appalled by initial Bolshevik successes as was Wilson. One was in European Russia, in the north, above the Arctic Circle. In the summer of 1918, five thousand men went to Murmansk and Archangel to see that the vast Allied stores of war goods might not fall into German hands. The American troops were to join an Allied expedition that had already battled Bolshevik troops in an attempt to gain authority over the two important port cities. On arrival, the American troops, plagued by dysentery, confused leadership, and clothing ill-suited for the harsh climate, were placed in the position of defending White Russians and breakaway Bolsheviks against Lenin's regime. As temperatures fell to − 50°F and casualties rose to more than five hundred, the Americans neared mutiny.[11] A second American troop contingent entered Siberia in 1918 at just about the same time that the troops destined for Murmansk and Archangel had arrived. More than nine thousand men were in Siberia under the command of General Graves, who divided his loathing for Russian politicians equally between Whites and Bolsheviks. The American presence in Siberia was related to Japanese designs on Siberia.[12] But once American troops were in place in Siberia, their presence tended to favor the reactionary anticommunist forces. Indeed, the Russian embassy in Washington, representing the provisional White Russian government, campaigned vigorously to get the American people to support the intervention, including sending speakers on tour in the United States and even suggesting logistics to the State Department.[13]

The Intervention and Its Consequences

Although Wilson reached his decision to intervene in the Soviet Union because of his wider image of American interests, he had support from large sections of public opinion. When the Bolsheviks seized power, "most Anericans reacted as if the impossible had happened."[14] The Bolsheviks were considered, in Secretary of State Robert Lansing's words, a "usurping gang" of lunatics, anarchists, and Jews. Because they were considered illegitimate in every sense by Americans, general predictions were that they would not last. In one study by Walter Lippmann, the demise of Soviet rule was predicted ninety-one times in the years from 1917 to 1919.[15] If the impossible had happened, it was comfortable to predict that it would soon cease happening. The vilification of the new regime in the press was intense. The *Saturday Evening Post* was typical of journalistic response. It editorialized that German despotism was at least practiced by an elite, whereas Bolshevism was a "despotism by all the lowest."[16] The Bolsheviks came to be characterized as veritable freaks and monsters. *The New York Times*, for instance, reported that in Soviet areas, every eighteen-year-old girl had to register at a "bureau of free love" and was then given a husband without her consent.[17]

Thus American involvement in the intervention had enormous consequences domestically. It froze American attitudes toward the Soviet Union into a kind of hostility that can be described only as bizarre. The famous journalist Lincoln Steffens wrote privately that "Bolshevism means chaos, wholesale murder, the complete destruction of civilization."[18] Senator Henry Lee Myers of Montana spoke for many Americans:

> They have utterly destroyed marriage, the home, the fireside, the family, the cornerstones of all civilization, all society. They have undertaken to destroy what God created and ordained. They defy alike the will of God, the precepts of Christianity, the decrees of civilization, the customs of society. It is hard to realize that such things exist and are tolerated by the civilized world."[19]

The atheism of Bolsheviks repulsed most Americans. The influential *Literary Digest* reported that the Soviet government had sponsored ceremonies in which young men dressed as devils and danced about bonfires containing effigies of Jesus, Moses, and Mohammed.[20]

It is important to note the degree of isolation and disruption the Soviets experienced in this period. Their only port, Petrograd, was blockaded by the Allies; foreign trade was reduced to smuggling; even gold was embargoed. In 1919, the only foreign official in the Soviet Union was a Danish representative of the Red Cross.[21] It is not, therefore, hard to see how the intervention confirmed the suspicion of the Bolsheviks that the West was implacably hostile to the Soviet regime. The nature of these interventions and America's involvement in them are well remembered by Soviet historians. Yet they are all but ignored by Western scholarship. The scholarly former U.S. ambassador to the Soviet Union, George F. Kennan, confessed that he did not understand the reasons for the contempt and resentment borne by the early Bolsheviks toward the Western powers until he unearthed the details in his own research.[22]

In the American and Allied intervention, Lenin and the Bolsheviks saw the fulfillment of the communist prophecy of capitalist enmity and aggression. It did not matter that Wilson's aims in the intervention, although undeniably anti-Bolshevik, were pursued with some reluctance. The Americans were clearly part of the range of forces arrayed against the Bolsheviks. Huge sums of money were spent on this adventure. But its cost continued to mount long after Western troops had left. Very probably this intervention aided the coup d'état of October 1917 in becoming a permanent regime, for as the Russian civil war and the intervention coalesced, the communist leaders played the role of national leaders fighting foreigners. During the struggle, the Communists were able to forge an army, a police force, and a party apparatus that enabled them to expand from a weak base. This power was to become so early entrenched that soon the Soviet regime was able to undergo the tremendous strain of social transformation under the brutal leadership of Stalin. And the early isolation and encirclement of the new communist state became absorbed in the Soviet mentality. The heroic theme of being subjected to the onslaught of world capitalism and repulsing it was a useful forge on which to build the foundations of a new Soviet order.

The intervention failed because of pro-Bolshevism in much of the Russian population and because the cost of imposing a Western solution was disproportionate to any immediate security interest. Troops in the Russian intervention never quite understood what their purpose was, and by mid-1919 outraged parents who had sent their sons to fight the Kaiser caught the ear of Congress, and the troops were withdrawn. But the expansive Wilsonian concept of world order based on a comprehensive political capitalism was a precursor of later years and later administrations and, as such, forms the opening phrases of the dialogue of distrust that characterizes the cold war.

Nonrecognition

Throughout the 1920s, Soviet–American relations were frozen by an American policy of nonrecognition of the communist regime. Wilson's secretary of state, Bainbridge Colby, explained that

> the existing regime in Russia is based upon . . . the negation of every principle of honor and good faith upon which it is possible to base . . . relations. . . . [S]pokesman of this power have declared . . . the maintenance

of their role depends . . . upon the occurrence of revolutions in all other great civilized nations . . . and set up Bolshevist rule in their stead . . . [w]ith a Power whose conceptions of international relations are so entirely alien . . . so utterly repugnant . . . we cannot hold official relations.[23]

The United States pressed for Soviet acknowledgment of Czarist debts. It was clear, however, that the Soviet conception of world order and the internal regime of states were the dominant bones of contention. Even as Russia experienced a terrible famine in the spring and summer of 1921, the emergency relief organized by Secretary of Commerce Herbert Hoover was tied to preconditions. "It was his view that the Allies should insist, as part of the price [for food] . . . that the Bolsheviki cease hostilities against their opponents in Russia and stop their propaganda abroad."[24] These conditions, concluded Kennan, although "moderate and reasonable," would be such as to place before the Soviet government the choice of falling in with the general Western desideratum or accepting the onus of denying food to the Russian people.[25]

Despite Lenin's death and Stalin's break with Trotsky (over, in the dictator's words, "the idiotic slogan, 'The World Revolution'"[26]), lurid reports of Soviet activity in China and Britain — as well as the beginnings of Latin American revolutions purported to be Soviet inspired — were sufficient cause for restricting contact with the Bolshevik regime. Thus, in spite of the emerging "peace offensive" of Soviet foreign minister Maxim Litvinov and the expulsion of Trotsky, the Russians were not invited to sign the Kellogg–Briand agreement, which outlawed war as an instrument of state relations. Only global economic depression brought the United States to a reversal of more than a decade of nonrecognition. In 1933, Litvinov was reportedly talking of placing orders of more than an incredible $1 billion with the West.[27] Whereas American editors appeared five to one to oppose recognition in 1931, a poll in late 1933 showed editors almost three to one favoring relations.[28] Objections arose when Roosevelt and Litvinov exchanged terms of agreement in November 1933, but the view of most Americans had become, according to the *Literary Digest,* an agnostic willingness to "see how it all works out."[29]

THE COMING OF WORLD WAR II

American and especially Western European cooperation with the Soviet regime never moved beyond these tentative contacts. The United States remained preoccupied with the Depression, and the Europeans, especially the British, persisted in a distrustful, even hostile ambivalence toward Stalin. Nowhere was this posture more evident and of greater consequence than regarding the rise of Adolf Hitler in Germany.

Stalin was initially ambivalent—perhaps believing that Hitler was not much more than the anti-Western "national socialist" he (Hitler) proclaimed himself to be. Moreover, Hitler's natural adversaries in Germany, the Social Democrats, were not pro-Soviet in their sentiments. Indeed, they seemed sympathetic to similar regimes in the West, thereby raising the possibility of a formidable alliance against Russia. Stalin was, therefore, passive toward, if not actually supportive of, the Nazi's destruction of the Social Democrats.

It became increasingly difficult to ignore, however, that the Nazis were a real menace to the Soviet Union. German officials had begun to advocate giving Germany "space for the settlement of its vigorous race" in Russia where "war, revolution, and internal decay had made a beginning" and must be stopped.[30] Words like these and the increasing militarization of Germany led Stalin to seek allies in the West, as in the Franco–Russian mutual assistance treaty in 1935. Furthermore, when the Spanish civil war broke out in 1936, Stalin attempted to enlist the West in aiding the Republican forces against the Fascists led by Franco and equipped by the Italians and Germans. Stalin's intervention in the Spanish civil war resulted, in part, from communist ideology; but Stalin also sought to induce Britain and France to intervene and thus join in containing Germany. The British, however, feared antagonizing the Fascists and hoped for a Western settlement that, by implication, would have thrown Hitler against the East and Russia. The unsuccessful effort to enlist the West to aid antifascist forces in Spain and the emerging Western policy of appeasement convinced Stalin that he should make preparations to deal independently with Hitler.[31] If collective security had not tempted the West, neither was it apparent that Hitler would be interested in a deal; thus, in Kennan's view, Stalin's diplomacy was increasingly one of "watchful waiting."[32]

Further evidence of Russia's isolation was recorded in Moscow when Hitler moved on Austria in March 1938, raising an obvious security threat to Central Europe. France, however, declined to consult with its nominal ally, Russia. Hitler next denounced the Czech government as a staging area for Bolshevism in Central Europe and charged that Germans living in Czechoslovakia were being oppressed by the Czechs. But when the Soviets urged a multilateral "firm and unambiguous stand," Neville Chamberlain, the British prime minister, told the House of Commons that such a "mutual undertaking" was unacceptable because it would handicap the British government's freedom to maneuver. Paris and London seemed more interested in accommodating themselves to a German plan for partitioning the Czech state than in entertaining the Russian suggestion of concerted resistance to German expansion. Only when Hitler demanded an "international guarantee" of the new Czech boundaries and German occupation of Czechoslovak districts did Chamberlain become alarmed. His response was continuation of past policy.

"How horrible, fantastic, and incredible," he told a British radio audience, that "we should be digging trenches and trying on gas masks here because of a quarrel in a far-away country between people of whom we know nothing."[33] Hitler gave respite to Chamberlain by inviting him, Mussolini, and the French premier, Edouard Daladier, to confer at Munich. The Czechs and the Soviets were noticeable by their absence even as Chamberlain agreed to all of Hitler's demands. The Soviets protested the Munich agreements as "monstrous," knowing that the remaining Czech state would be a virtually indefensible vassal of Hitler. The British prime minister knew, however, that the Munich settlement pointed Hitler eastward and he declared that the agreement signaled "peace in our time."[34]

When the German army moved to occupy all of Czechoslovakia in March of the next year, Chamberlain finally became aroused. Chamberlain had staked his reputation on divining the dark corners of Hitler's mind, but now he was convinced that he would have to be more forceful. When it appeared that Poland would be the next victim of Hitler's aggression, Chamberlain, together with Daladier, guaranteed Polish independence. The Poles, however, did not want the Soviets included in this declaration, harboring a historic anti-Russian and recent anticommunist orientation. The exclusion of Russia once more from Western security arrangements was hardly encouraging to Moscow and moved Stalin to pursue actively his own arrangement with Hitler. His short-run objectives were not unlike those of Lenin at the end of World War I — to gain a territorial buffer in Eastern Europe and, hence, time.

Russia initiated feelers to Germany while continuing attempts to make security arrangements with the West.[35] In May 1939, London and Paris languidly made an overture to Moscow to discuss a tripartite security pact. But the formula submitted for negotiation contained such caveats as excluding the invasion of the Baltic states by Germany as sufficient cause for France and England to come to the aid of the Soviet Union.[36] On the other hand, Russian demands for transit rights through Poland in the event of war were understandably rejected by the Poles, and the talks stalemated. Moreover, it was known that Stalin was now in formal contact with Hitler. In sum, the Allies were less than forthcoming and the Russian negotiating style was ponderous and opaque as Stalin sought to extract the best terms possible from the negotiations.

Finally, in the last days of August 1939, the courtship of the West ended as Stalin wired Hitler to send Foreign Minister Joachim von Ribbentrop to Moscow, where a Nazi–Soviet pact was announced and the Anglo–French mission sent home. Through the agreement, Hitler sought to dissuade the West from standing by Poland, now wedged between the so-called German and Soviet allies. This assumption was, of course, Hitler's major miscalculation — the miscalculation that brought on the war. In the short run, however, he had prevented the Soviet opposition to his pending move into Poland. The price was a Soviet sphere of influence in eastern Poland and Soviet control of the Baltic states under the guise of Moscow as their guarantor. In addition, the two dictators agreed that the Balkan states were to be viewed in a a disinterested manner. To the extent that Stalin believed that Hitler would allow him a free hand in this area, he miscalculated as grievously as Hitler concerning Western intentions. In the meantime, however, Stalin thought that he had bought time to prepare for any future German aggression whether the West assisted or not.

The degree of animosity in the West stemming from the blinding shock of the Nazi–Soviet pact cancelled whatever marginal improvement Soviet–Western relations might have gleaned during the Litvinov period of diplomacy. The Russians were blamed, with justification, for encouraging the Nazi attack on Poland that brought on the full measure of World War II. Finally, the image of a cynical Soviet Union was fixed in the Western mind — an image that was confirmed as Stalin hastily embarked on a course of strategic consolidation that involved the occupation of the Baltic states of Latvia, Lithuania, and Estonia. Similar moves were initiated against Rumania (with the consent of the Nazis) and, rather clumsily, Finland. By November of 1940, Stalin was demanding Hitler's formal recognition of Soviet control of these areas. No doubt Stalin was buoyed by the success of the British in the air battle of Britain and the possibility that the Germans would be preoccupied in the West until well into 1941. Stalin probably figured that even if Hitler, not wanting to fight on two fronts, would not concede a Southeastern European buffer to the Soviets, the Germans would at least proceed cautiously with their claims in the area. But Stalin miscalculated. Instead of continuing the air assault on Britain, Hitler turned to planning a strike on Britain's Mediterranean lifelines. This stratagem required German pressure in the Balkans and an absence there of Hitler's ally, the Russians. By attempting to give himself more of a buffer in the Balkans,

Stalin may have hastened Hitler's preparation of his attack on the Soviet Union, which eventually came in 1941.

The German attack on Russia in the spring of 1941 was greeted with disbelief by the Russians and relief by the West, especially the British, who had stood alone since the collapse of continental resistance after Dunkirk. Roosevelt's personal reaction to the German attack on Russia was equally unambiguous. He was delighted and told Churchill that he would support "any announcement that the Prime Minister might make welcoming Russia as an ally."[37] But Roosevelt's policy had considerable opposition in the American government, especially among the foreign service officers who had watched the unpleasant paroxysm induced by Stalin's purges in the 1930s and did not want to be associated in the same moral universe as Stalin.[38] Nevertheless, Roosevelt promised more than $1.5 million to Russia by the fall of 1941 and succeeded in the not inconsiderable feat of moving a balky bureaucracy and garnishing Congressional consent to the extension of "lend–lease" aid to Russia.[39] In his letter to the lend–lease administration, Roosevelt confirmed that "the defense of the Union of Soviet Socialist Republics is vital to the defense of the United States."[40]

The emergence of the common enemy in the spring of 1941 was not, however, a sufficient basis for overriding the dismal history of distrust of the previous twenty-five years. Russia and the West fought a common enemy simultaneously, and tens of millions of dollars in assistance and materiel were extended to the Russians by the West, but the diplomacy of East–West interactions during the war reveals a continuation of the misunderstandings and real differences that separated Russia and the West before Hitler struck across the Niemen in June 1941. Stalin's objectives and diplomacy during the war were consistent with his efforts before 1941 in that he sought from his new allies what he had sought from Hitler: Soviet influence and control in Eastern Europe and the Balkans.[41] But during and after World War II, Stalin's efforts to construct and gain legitimacy for a Soviet presence in Central Europe were resisted by the West, and Western resistance to Soviet consolidation of their objectives in Europe was to be the central politico-strategic issue of the early cold war.

CONFLICTING STRATEGIC CONCEPTS

The slaughter of World War I seared the memories of the British. They had lost a generation in Flanders, the Marne, and the Somme in a ghoulish holocaust that drained Britain's treasury and enervated its society.

A repetition of such sacrifice would not be countenanced by Churchill. He favored, not surprisingly, the use of Britain as if it were a massive aircraft carrier to launch Allied bombers at German industry. Indeed, 50 percent of British production was allocated to the bomber command. Yet he knew that wars are won and lost on the ground.[42] At the first meeting of the combined chiefs of staff, Churchill presented his view of a gradual encirclement of Germany; then, when Germany was bled white, the last dagger would be inserted in a continental assault from the west. Churchill pushed for a landing in French North Africa in cooperation with a large American expedition. Germany was to be engaged at a distance in 1942, in a classic grid that guarded historic British interest in the Mediterranean and India while eventually wrestling the weakened Germans to defeat.[43]

Churchill's attention to the periphery of battle was prompted by the bogey of a Japanese–German division of India and the Middle East as a mortal peril, "a measureless disaster." Roosevelt was skeptical of such joint action by the Axis powers,[44] and the American military questioned Churchill's strategy. General George C. Marshall thought that Churchill's policy was fraught with risk and was never convinced that the Russians could withstand Hitler unaided by Allied reinforcements. Furthermore, if the Russian army of eight million were defeated, then the war would be lost. Even if the Russian army withstood the formidable Wehrmacht, Marshall believed that the war would drag on until 1944 or 1945 if a second front were not launched, and the result would be higher, not lower, Allied costs.

Clearly, these two conceptions of how to proceed with the war were incompatible. It fell to Roosevelt to resolve the issue, because it could be only with American assistance that any strategy would succeed. Roosevelt's decision was in favor of the British concept, and therefore the invasion of Europe was deferred. Among the factors influencing Roosevelt were British opposition and his own views concerning the as yet incomplete American mobilization and the inevitability of very high casualties resulting from a frontal assault on Germany's continental bastion. The Russo–German theater of the war remained, therefore, disconnected from the Anglo–American engagement of German power on the periphery of Europe for more than two years. However, the eventual Soviet victory in the struggle between the two former totalitarian allies was to be the central factor in the postwar configuration of power in Central Europe. The nature of the victory no doubt intensified Soviet conviction that they alone should structure politically and economically what had been largely their conquest — namely, of the eastern portion of the Nazi empire. In the meantime, the issue of Anglo–American assistance to the Soviets by way of a second front poisoned East–West diplomacy.

The Issue of the Second Front

Even before Pearl Harbor, when Britain was weathering a furious air onslaught, Stalin pressed Churchill to open a second front. Churchill turned the pleas aside,[45] perhaps believing that Russia could not hold out and that a second front would make little sense if he had to face the full might of the German army alone. British military intelligence concurred with the German estimates that Russia would be beaten before the onset of the famous Russian winter. The Germans had fielded 175 divisions and soon raised the number to 232. But they had badly miscalculated, for although Germany gave an initial appearance of success, it was more apparent than real. Hitler's supply lines were badly extended; and when the Russians stood their ground and mobilized remarkable numbers, German casualties assumed staggering proportions. Nevertheless, the Russian situation was grave. By October, the Germans stood at the bus stops in the outer suburbs of Moscow only five miles from the city center.[46] The effect of the initial joyous proclamation of Churchill that the British and Russians were partners in the same glorious enterprise was shaken. But a number of factors combined to vitiate the effect of Churchill's obvious reluctance to commit troops to the Russians. First, the vicious Russian winter overtook German troops ill equipped for temperatures that reached $-40°F$.[47] Second, the Western allies committed themselves to substantial military aid for the Soviets by the middle of the next year.[48] Finally, the Japanese attack on Pearl Harbor and the consolidation of their conquests in Southeast Asia diverted their attention from the Soviets' Asian front and allowed for the transfer of Russian forces to the European front.

Perhaps as important, Roosevelt did not have the abiding dislike of the Soviets that Churchill maintained. He believed that his own personal winning charm could bridge great historic and ideological cleavages. He wrote somewhat arrogantly to Churchill, "I know you will not mind my being brutally frank when I tell you I think I can personally handle Stalin better than either your Foreign Office or my State Department. Stalin hates the guts of all your top people. He thinks he likes me better, and I hope he will continue to do so."[49] Nor did Roosevelt have the same history of anti-Bolshevik efforts and statements that had motivated Churchill since his days as First Lord of the Admiralty in World War I. While many Americans shared Senator Harry

Truman's view, "If we see that Germany is winning we ought to help Russia and if Russia is winning we ought to help Germany and that way let them kill as many as possible . . . ,"[50] Roosevelt had somewhat daringly proclaimed: "I think the Russians are perfectly friendly; they aren't trying to gobble up all the rest of Europe or the world."[51]

On the other hand, Churchill's conception of how to proceed with the war ultimately won over Roosevelt; hence, the United States was inevitably a target of Soviet distrust during and after the war as a result of the issue of the second front. This distrust was deepened by what must have appeared to the Russians to have been Churchillian duplicity in 1942. When Soviet Foreign Minister Molotov came to Washington in May 1942, he elicited a joint declaration that "full understanding was reached with regard to the urgent task of creating a second front in Europe in 1942."[52] Churchill reluctantly endorsed this document and handed Molotov a memorandum that claimed that Britain was "making preparations for a landing on the continent in August or September, 1942."[53] But by July 1942, the British had vetoed the idea of a second front in favor of a North African one followed by an Italian invasion. Marshall threatened to resign; Eisenhower feared that a North Africa campaign would "not materially assist the Russians in time to save them,"[54] and concluded that this decision could go down as "the blackest day in history."[55]

Roosevelt, understandably, suggested that Churchill himself relate the change of plans to Stalin.[56] Churchill complained, "It was like carrying a large lump of ice to the North Pole."[57] Churchill again promised Stalin that there would be a second front in 1943. But Stalin was skeptical and claimed to an associate after Churchill's departure, "A campaign in Africa, Italy . . . they want us bled white in order to dictate to us their terms later on. . . ."[58]

The landings in North Africa allowed, by Stalin's estimate, more that 27 German divisions — confident that the Allies would not invade that year in Europe — to move to the Eastern front.[59] By Churchill's own embarrassed estimate in early 1943, the West was engaged with, at the most, 12 German divisions, the Russians with 185.[60] The net effect of the North African campaign was to limit the amount of material that could be conveyed to the Soviet Union[61] and to increase Soviet suspicions of the West. The rearrangement of manufacturing in preparation for the desert campaign cut into the production of landing craft and artillery shells, prerequisites for a large landing in France, and the West did not regain its 1942 production levels for this materiel until 1944. In short, the North African campaign precluded the 1943 landing in France that had been promised.

Stalin was enraged. He noted that there was not a single German division in France of any value, a fact confirmed by British intelligence. The German policy was to station those in the West who suffered disabilities and could not be sent East.[62] Against this rather motley effluvia of the German war machine, Churchill unconvincingly related to Stalin that the British guns and aircraft were keeping the "Germans pinned in Pas de Calais" across the English Channel.[63] Stalin's lack of appreciation was evident in his reply: "That, I hope, does not imply a renunciation of your Moscow promise to open a second front in Western Europe in the spring of 1943."[64] But the North African campaign could not lead to a landing in France as the West had promised.[65] Instead, the invasion was directed at Italy by the way of Sicily. The net result of the landings in Sicily and southern Italy — predicted by Eisenhower — was an early Italian surrender; but the Germans stayed on doggedly in central and northern Italy, and the Allies were bogged down in Italy for almost two more years.[66]

The invasion of France would not come until June 1944, less than one year before the war ended and well after a Russian victory in Central Europe became inevitable. Of more immediate importance, it would not come until the Russians were convinced that it was Allied policy to bleed them white. The Allies, for their part, saw themselves as moving with all prudent speed. The gap in mutual perceptions became an open breach by late 1943 as Stalin withdrew his ambassadors from London and Washington.

Fears of a Separate Peace

Exacerbating the distrust generated by the second front issue were persistent rumors and occasional indications that one side or another would seek a separate peace with Hitler. Stalin may have deliberately manipulated the situation in his eagerness to encourage more Anglo–American assistance. On the other hand, in view of the Molotov–Ribbentrop Non-Aggression Pact, one can understand that the Americans and British were not prepared to place the best interpretation on Soviet maneuvering. Furthermore, during 1942 and 1943 low-level contacts were reported between German and Soviet agents concerning a break-off in the fighting and some form of frontier agreement. And in June 1943, according to some historians, a meeting of foreign ministers Molotov and Ribbentrop was held behind German lines to discuss a separate peace and the postwar Russian–Polish frontier.[67] However, all talks were broken off in late 1943 after the Soviet successes at Stalingrad and at Kursk had signaled the beginning of the Soviet offensive that would end the war in the East.

From the Soviet standpoint, the most suspicious developments were at the end of the war when German, British, and American intelligence and military officers met in early 1945 in Berne, Switzerland, to negotiate the surrender of remaining German troops in Italy. The talks expanded to include all German troops in Western Europe. The Russians, however, were not invited to these talks, and they reached the conclusion that the Western Allies were conspiring with the Germans so as to allow rapid movement of Anglo–American forces to the East. The American ambassador to Moscow, Averell Harriman counseled against letting the talks be broadened. Harriman, with long and bitter experience in negotiating with Russians, thought that such a stand would teach the Russians a salutary lesson that they could not always get what they asked for.[68]

Churchill himself was later to admit that these talks treaded close to actual negotiations. While confirming Churchill's observation, Allen Dulles (former head of OSS and CIA) noted in his memoirs also that the full extent of these conversations was not at all clear to Roosevelt.[69] Roosevelt, faced with harsh Soviet suspicions,[70] promised that if details of a surrender were discussed, Soviet leaders would be invited. These were, he emphasized, preliminary discussions and not negotiations.[71] Nevertheless, Russian fear of a separate peace or settlement primarily or even exclusively beneficial to the West ran throughout the war and was particularly intense at its end. Soviet suspicions intensified and poisoned the atmoshpere in which important substantive issues were coming to a head, most notably the interrelated questions of Eastern Europe and the postwar disposition of Germany. In the disputes surrounding these political and strategic issues, we find the immediate antecedents to the cold war.

POLAND AND EASTERN EUROPE: THE TURN TOWARD COLD WAR

Eastern Europe and Poland were the incubus in which old distrusts festered. The issue of Poland was, perhaps, the most critical in the wartime and immediate postwar dialogue between the West and the Soviet Union. Poland provided the sharpest challenge to Allied unity because of the seemingly unreconcilable ambitions and interests—a conflict that anticipated and contributed to what was to follow.

The Poles had suffered great privations under the czars and the Soviets. They had suffered partition, absorption, and various efforts at colonization and, of course, the Soviets had attempted to extinguish Poland in league with the Nazis in the Molotov–Ribbentrop pact. In the West, sympathy was high for the Poles; many refugee Poles fought bravely with the British, and about 20 percent of the pilots who fought the battle of Britain were Polish.[72] Moreover, urban Polish–Americans were an influential minority that merited considerable attention in American electoral politics. For example, there were and are more Polish-speaking persons in Chicago than in Warsaw, and more Polish radio stations and newspapers in the United States than in Poland. For the United States at the end of the war, the Polish question had become a factor in domestic politics and a symbol of Soviet–Western cooperation.[73] The Soviets' claims in Poland had an entirely different justification. As Stalin noted:

> In the course of twenty-five years the Germans twice invaded Russian via Poland. . . . The invasions were not warfare but like incursions of the Huns. . . . Germany had been able to do this because Poland had been regarded as part of the *cordon sanitaire* around the Soviet Union and previous European policy had been that Polish governments must be hostile to Russia. In these circumstances either Poland had been too weak to oppose Germany or had let the Germans come through. . . . Poland's weakness and hostility had been a great source of weakness to the Soviet Union and had permitted the Germans to do what they wished in the East and also the West. . . . It is therefore in Russia's vital interest that Poland should be both strong and friendly.[74]

Thus the postwar political future and a territorial configuration of Poland, based on 1941 borders, was a central concern of Russian wartime diplomacy. Soviet insistence on a different geography for Poland also strained their delicate, newly formed relationship with the London-based Polish government in exile. The London Polish government was recognized by the Soviet Union in July 1941, but the London Poles were in a precarious position. Except for whatever influence they might have with the British or Americans, they were practically powerless. Moreover, the British were less than completely supportive, as the Polish question stood between the Soviets and the British in reaching other understandings and was therefore something of an embarrassment.[75] Yet the Poles refused tenaciously to yield their eastern territories to the Russians. They harbored little good will for the Russians in view of the 1939 pact with the Nazis. The fate of some fifteen thousand captured officers and more soldiers as well as about 1.5 million Poles deported from the zone the Soviets occupied after the Molotov–Ribbentrop pact greatly concerned the exile government.

The West, not able to deliver a second front and watching the rapid advance of the Soviet army, began to waver in their support of the London Poles. As the West began to waver in support, the Poles felt abandoned[76] and became increasingly unyielding toward Soviet claims in the face of the ever-apparent Russian designs in Poland. The actual break between the London Poles and the Russians occurred in April 1943, when the Germans discovered the graves of fifteen thousand Polish officers in the Katyn Forest of Poland. The Germans claimed they were slaughtered by Russia in 1940 – a claim accepted by the London group. Stalin's fury at this immediate Polish acceptance of the Nazi version of the massacre prompted him to break diplomatic relations with the London Poles.

By now, two distinct issues were involved. One was the future composition of the Polish government; the second was the geographic boundaries of Poland. The Soviets argued for an eastern limit of Poland that coincided with the frontier of 1941 resulting from the Molotov–Ribbentrop pact. At Tehran in late 1943, Churchill and Eden initiated a proposal that this line be adopted in the east and Poland be compensated in the west out of former Prussian territory to the Oder River. Roosevelt did not demur in the massive territorial or population adjustments that Stalin had conceded. But, he added, "he could not publicly take part in any such arrangement" because he could not prejudice the "six to seven million Polish–American votes in the upcoming election."[77] Roosevelt's concern about his domestic flank was well taken, for the Republicans would build much of their campaign around charges that Roosevelt's labor support tied him to communist influences. Such Republican "Red-baiting" would become commonplace and more effective over the next decade. But even in 1944, its effect was sufficient to undercut Roosevelt's seemingly impregnable position to the point that his electoral margin would be one of the smallest in decades.[78] To have associated himself publicly with the Polish boundary decision, therefore, might well have been disastrous. Probably no alternative was available to Roosevelt and Churchill, but by this action they conceded to Stalin both the dominant voice in the future government of Poland and the territorial aggrandizement he desired.

The Tehran plan envisaged a population movement involving at least six million people who would have to find homes in Germany. The territory to be taken from Germany stretched 200 miles into Prussia. A future government that displaced so many Germans and held such a vast tract of former German territory could not be but fearful of German claims in the future and dependent on Moscow. As for the new regime to be established in postwar Poland, Stalin now demanded that it comprise primarily those Poles acceptable to the Soviet Union. As Soviet troops were marching into Poland, Stalin created the Polish Committee of Liberation that was clearly the prototype government of Poland. When Soviet troops entered Lublin, this group was installed, and Lublin was made the administrative center for all of Poland.

The meaning and full consequences of Soviet policy became clear as the Soviet military action in Poland established a kind of record for cynicism. As the Russians reached the banks of the Vistula within sight of Warsaw in August 1944, Moscow radio urged the Polish underground (or home) army to revolt. The Poles did, yet the Russians did not advance to drive out the Germans; rather, they watched until January 1945 as the Nazis liquidated the last vestiges of any potential opposition to Soviet domination of the future government of Poland. A quarter of a million Poles were to die in Warsaw fighting Nazis, and the city was destroyed, blown up block by block. Stalin even refused Western planes landing rights to drop supplies to the beleaguered Poles.

The Allies were horrified but could do little more than tacitly support the Soviet territorial claim in Poland legitimized earlier at Tehran. The British and the Americans had been presented with an accomplished fact of Soviet power in Poland, signaled by Soviet recognition of the Lublin government despite protestations that the decision to recognize a Polish government be left until the summit conference at Yalta in February 1945.

Yalta

At the Yalta Conference, Roosevelt extracted vague and ambiguous assurances from Stalin concerning reorganization of the Lublin government and free elections in Poland. Similar weak commitments were made by Stalin concerning all of Soviet-controlled eastern Europe. The overseeing of these elections was left vague and elastic, and when the Soviets later interpreted matters to their advantage, many in the United States would denounce the Yalta agreements as a sellout. But Roosevelt's biographer James McGregor Burns has concluded otherwise:

> He had reached the limit of his bargaining power at Yalta. His position resulted not from naivete, ignorance, illness, or perfidy, but from his acceptance of the facts: Russia occupied Poland. Russia distrusted its Western allies. Russia had a million men who could fight Japan. . . . And Russia was absolutely determined about Poland and always had been.[79]

Moreover, Roosevelt believed — and he may have indulged his vanity to the point of self-deception here — that his personal charm could cut through the ideological differences, accumulated distrust of the preceding decades, and the historic Russian interests in Central Europe to capture Stalin's trust and cooperation. If successful, the Wilsonian ideal of an institutionalized world order might yet be fulfilled in the new United Nations, in which case the compromises of Yalta would be mere footnotes on the opening pages of a new era.

The presentation of the Yalta accords to the American people led most Americans to believe that free democratic elections would be held in Eastern Europe. At the same time, Roosevelt understood enough of the realities of the situation to know that in the free hand he had allowed the Soviets in Poland since 1943, and in his acceptance of the "friendly" governments — no matter how cloaked in electoral procedure — he had acknowledged the Soviets their ambitions. Also, he must have known that the military realities of the postwar situation conflicted with what the American people had been led to expect in terms of a new liberal order promised to arise out of the ashes of the war.[80]

It was Harry Truman who was to try to resolve the dilemma of public and private expectations in favor of America's aspirations, rather than acknowledge what increasingly seemed inevitable in the face of Soviet guns and tough interpretations of their security interests. Truman and his advisers were to argue the issue as a breach of faith.[81] There was never explicit agreement, however, on the procedure or meaning of free elections or international supervision. These items were kept ambiguous because it was apparent that the declaration of Yalta concerning Poland satisfied different purposes for the West and Stalin. To the West, it helped keep up appearances, and to the Russians, it confirmed the obvious. As Stalin was to remark: "This war is not as in the past; whoever occupies territory also imposes his own social system as far as his army can reach. It cannot be otherwise."[82]

THE ADMINISTRATION
OF LIBERATION

The issue of the administration of former enemy and enemy-occupied states in Europe was a consistent element of the growing distrust between Russia and the West. It is commonly held that the cold war was a contest between a Western vision of an open, liberal political order and a narrow Soviet definition of security in terms of spheres of interest.[83] But the West accommodated itself to having its own security spheres when military convenience allowed it in Europe or when historical ambition demanded it in Latin America. The first evidence of a lack of deep Western commitment to its liberal rhetoric and aspirations was in North Africa, where the United States and the British worked out a surrender deal with the anti-Semitic, collaborationist commander of the Vichy French forces. In return for his surrender, Admiral Jean Darlan was allowed to maintain his political position.[84]

The squalid arrangement with Darlan was viewed as an unfortunate expediency. Unhappily, it was repeated in the Western action in Italy of negotiating with the rightist regime of General Pietro Badoglio. By dealing with the leader of Italy's brutal Ethiopian campaign and leaving much of Mussolini's governmental structure intact, the West indicated the possibility that the Allies would deal with anyone when the time came. Just as important, by managing to arrange for a sphere of influence in areas in which Western troops were placed, the West became poorly positioned to argue against the harsher but functionally equivalent strategy that the Soviets employed in Eastern Europe.

In Greece, German withdrawal touched off fighting between communist and left-wing partisans on the one hand and collaborationists and monarchists on the other. The British army supported the rightists, actively attempted to root out the leftist opposition, disbanded the partisan resistance by extreme methods, and tried to reinstate the king; reportedly, 80 percent of the population was opposed to such moves.[85] It was a blatant and unpopular exercise in reclamation of the British Empire, which brought protest to the House of Commons and from some Americans who saw liberal principles desecrated. Nevertheless, Roosevelt acquiesced in Churchill's attempt to impose a British solution on Greece.[86]

Although the British army was aimed at the "communistic elements in Greece [who] plan to seize power by force,"[87] not a word of reproach was uttered by the Soviet press, and Stalin was completely silent on the subject. In this, Stalin was conforming to the agreement worked out between Churchill and himself in October 1944, in which Rumania and Bulgaria were conceded to the Soviet sphere of influence and Greece to the British. Yugoslavia and Hungary were to be divided equally. Churchill wrote appreciatively, "I am increasingly impressed, up to date, with the loyalty with which . . . Stalin has kept off Greece in accordance with our agreement."[88] The Russians did nothing to help their ideological brethren in Greece and everything possible to discourage them. Stalin even aided the British occupation by offering Soviet recognition of the British-reconstituted monarchist Greek government in December 1945. The move caused extreme consternation among the left in Greece; but it was impressive evidence that the Soviets understood the language of power and interest. They had, after all, their own going concerns in Germany and Eastern Europe.

In Greece, Italy, and North Africa, the Soviets had precedent for their conduct in Eastern Europe. But the West would not concede that spheres of interest could cohabit the same planet. If they had, the Soviets and the West might not have undergone the frightful postwar tension that was rapidly strangling the slim neck of wartime amity. But the Western powers were unable or unwilling to reciprocate Stalin's behavior regarding Greece. The harsh Soviet interpretation of their own security needs and Anglo–American resistance to this interpretation (while pursuing a similar policy wherever practicable) became, therefore, the focus of dissension and distrust from which other issues proliferated.

Americans emerged from the war in Europe supremely confident. Although planning for the postwar period had not been systematic, the State Department envisaged a world where the judicious use of postwar rehabilitation loans would break down trade barriers and establish a prosperous global economy free from imperialism and revolutionary socialism. By late 1944, Ambassador Harriman was suggesting that postwar economic reconstruction aid be used to influence Soviet behavior in Eastern Europe. The U.S. Air Force and military planners saw a world where American military power would be so imposing that threats to the peace would have little choice but to yield.[89] The Soviet vision was clearly different. Although the Soviet Union was in ruins, with three quarters of its industrial plant destroyed and twenty million dead, it nonetheless possessed an immediate challenge to the American vision by the presence of its troops in the heart of Europe and by the affinity of armed partisans for collectivist principles. This, in Stalin's view, could become the basis of a Soviet-controlled Central European barrier to further aggression from the West.

TRUMAN AND THE ORIGINS OF THE COLD WAR

In this context, Harry Truman came to power following President Roosevelt's death little versed in foreign affairs and, in contrast to Roosevelt, heavily dependent on his advisers. Indeed, given Roosevelt's personal diplomacy, Truman had been excluded from major decisions and was relatively ignorant of what had transpired previously. His closest foreign affairs advisers had long and bitter distrust of Soviet ambitions and chafed at Roosevelt's view that good will and yielding to the strong-

est of Soviet security claims in Eastern Europe could beget a condominium of great powers. They had witnessed the purges and the undeniable excesses and dark features of Soviet life and Stalin's character
for too many years.[90] Most of these officials concurred with Kennan's
analysis that the Soviets were "Never—neither then nor at any later
date . . . a fit ally or associate, actual or potential."[91]

Ambassador Averell Harriman left the Moscow embassy to George
Kennan's care and returned to Washington to advise Truman. Harriman had spent months attempting to resolve the question of which parties actually constituted "democratic and anti-Nazi parties"[92]—those
agreed to by the Soviets at Yalta as acceptable in a new Polish government. Neither Roosevelt nor Churchill had frankly faced up to the fact
that truly free elections might have returned governments manifestly
unfriendly to the Soviet Union, and the Soviets were reluctant to provide a structure on which all parties whom the West supported might
stand. Harriman was exasperated and told Truman that Russia confronted Eastern Europe with a "barbarian invasion." They could be
responded to firmly for, he held, they needed reconstruction credit for
their decimated industry. The tough approach to Russia was seconded
by most of Truman's foreign affairs advisers, although some broached
the fear that too unyielding an attitude over Poland would break Soviet–American relations completely and endanger the entrance of Russia into the Pacific war.

Truman responded to Harriman that he understood "the Russians
need us more than we need them," and though we cannot "expect 100
percent of what he proposed," he did think "we would be able to get
85 percent."[93] The first step in the march toward 85 percent of U.S.
claims was to be taken with Molotov, who was coming to San Francisco in a gesture of good will to the fledgling United Nations Conference and the new American president. In meetings with the Soviet
foreign minister, Truman pointed out in "words of one syllable" the
American desire for immediate free elections. Truman stated that Poland had become the symbol of U.S. foreign policy. The terse but correct conversation turned into a very undiplomatic diatribe. Truman spoke
to the foreign minister as if he were a simple-minded recruit, demanding that elements of the London Poles join the Polish government and
that elections be held immediately. When Molotov protested, "I have
never been talked to like that in my life," Truman snapped, "Carry out
your agreements and you won't get talked to like that."[94]

Stalin seemed both puzzled and bitter. In a letter following Truman's April 23, 1945, meeting with Molotov, the Soviet premier protested that "Poland, unlike Great Britain and the United States, had

common frontiers with the Soviet Union. . . . 'I do not know whether a truly representative government has been set up in Greece or whether the government in Belgium is truly democratic.' The Soviet Union was not consulted . . . and claimed no right to interfere, 'as it understands the full significance of Belgium and Greece for the security of Great Britain.'"[95]

Truman did not see his policy as the reversal of previous agreements. Instead, he seemed to fear that the political closing of Eastern Europe would presage its economic closure. In the view of Truman and his advisers, such a political and economic division of East and West would threaten economic chaos in Europe. Moreover, Truman's most fervently held belief was that a "breach of peace anywhere in the world, threatens the peace of the entire world."[96] In contrast, the Russians concluded that the West, because of its concern and claims in Eastern Europe, was involved in a resurrection of the old course of encirclement.

Security did not necessarily mean expansion for the Russians. To the contrary, momentous difficulties were inevitable in holding the areas where their armies stood. The "iron curtain" was a protective shell masking Stalin's concern that the relaxation of ideological control Russia experienced in the "great patriotic war" would accelerate. Moreover, it was feared that if the extent of the internal devastation were known, it would be an invitation for the West to press its claim. Had the Russians been ready to advance, they would not have demobilized nor torn out the rail connections between the Soviet Union and Germany that ran through Poland. The extent of the Soviet military standdown is even more impressive if one considers the very considerable state of tension in Central Europe in this period and the enormous amount of police supervision required. Yet the West interpreted the Soviets' fierce defense of their acquisitions and political tactics as preparation for expansion.[97]

Truman increased the pressure. Shortly after Truman's decision to search for 85 percent Soviet agreement with the American understanding of the political future of Eastern Europe, lend–lease was abruptly cancelled. Ships already unloading cargo were packed up and others in the mid-Atlantic turned around in an effort to use economic leverage against the Soviets. As the assistant chief of lend–lease observed, this "decision was taken deliberately and probably was a part of a general squeeze now being put on the USSR."[98] Stalin protested, "the American attitude toward the Soviet Union . . . had perceptibly cooled once it became obvious that Germany was defeated. . . ."[99] Although the decision was partially reversed,[100] the damage already done was exacerbated by Truman's decision to implement a "more realistic policy": an approach minimizing financial help to the Russians while agreements were yet to be reached on Eastern Europe to Truman's satisfaction—a satisfaction that demanded a great deal from the Soviets.

THE ATOM BOMB, ASIA, AND EUROPE

Economics were only one part of the strategy of convincing the Russians that they needed to cooperate in Eastern Europe. Another element was the potential of the atomic bomb, which Secretary of State James F. Byrnes told Truman "might well put us in the position to dictate our own terms."[101] Or, as Truman himself explained just before the news of the first test reached him, "If it explodes . . . I'll certainly have a hammer on those boys."[102] The Polish issue and the atomic bomb were conjoined, if not, as some have argued, "inextricably bound together."[103]

In the meantime, Truman called on Harry Hopkins, well known as an associate of Roosevelt and a symbol of more cordial times, to go to Moscow, although Hopkins was gravely ill. In Moscow, Hopkins made a substantial concession that granted that the Lublin Poles be formally recognized as the basis for a postwar government in Poland in return for the admittance of a few London Poles. On July 5, 1945, pleased with Stalin's promise to install five independent Poles and the Poles from London into a nucleus of a Warsaw (Lublin) cabinet and pleased with Stalin's reaffirmation of his pledge to hold free elections, Truman extended diplomatic recognition of the Polish provisional government. Nevertheless, this agreement over the composition of the Polish government was not considered final by Truman and his advisers.[104]

Indications existed that Stalin, having received a Polish government compatible with Soviet interest, relaxed some controls in most of Eastern Europe. Concessions were granted to the West in the Allied commissions of Hungary and Rumania, and in Hungary the West was even given a veto in the Allied Control Commission. Coalition governments were accepted in Hungary and Czechoslovakia. Stalin probably pursued this policy for three reasons. First, it was a conciliatory gesture toward the West. The territory in which he was interested was under the control of Soviet troops, Poland had been accorded recognition, and he thought he could now turn to other matters in Central Europe and of economic assistance. Second, he had no desire to provoke the further ill will of the West. Third, administrative limits impeded the Soviets' achieving effective control over such a vast area—if indeed that was their strategy. The nature of that control became quite harsh; but the most unpleasant features of Eastern European life were not established until after the defection of Yugoslavia in 1948. Whether or not totalitarian domination was the long-range vision of Stalin, the immediate tactics of gaining Soviet control were gradualist and unprovocative to center leftist parties in Eastern Europe and conciliatory of Western sensibilities. Stalin requested that Truman recognize leftist regimes in Eastern Europe, but the Americans refused, stating that the governments were neither representative nor responsive to the will of the people.

Truman and Churchill arrived in a devastated Berlin for their meeting with Stalin at Potsdam, a suburb of Berlin, on July 16, 1945. Truman said that his "immediate purpose was to get the Russians into the war against Japan as soon as possible."[105] The need to substitute Russian casualties for Americans became less apparent when a message arrived from the heat-fused desert of Alamogordo, New Mexico, that the atom bomb had been tested successfully. The success at testing the bomb signaled to the West, in Churchill's words, that "we should not need the Russians. . . . We had no need to ask favors of them."[106] Truman became both confident and visibly more rigid with Stalin after the news of the New Mexico test arrived. He no longer negotiated with the Russians; rather, there occurred a sharply barbed exchange of views. As Churchill recalled, "[Truman] stood up to the Russians in a most emphatic and decisive manner, telling them as to certain demands that they absolutely could not have and the United States was entirely against them. . . . He told the Russians just where they could get off and generally bossed the whole meeting."[107] In short, the bomb buoyed the West, for as Churchill told the House of Commons, "we possessed powers which were irresistible."[108]

Truman, his advisers, and Churchill determined that the bomb could have several diplomatic and military purposes. First, if it was used quickly, the shock might prompt an immediate surrender of the Japanese and thus be, in Churchill's words, "a merciful abridgement of the slaughter."[109] Second, it could keep Russian participation in the Asian war and, hence, postwar claims against Japan and China to a minimum. As Navy Secretary James Forrestal recalled in his diary, "Byrnes [the secretary of state] said he was most anxious to get the Japanese affairs over with before the Russians get in. . . . Once in there, he felt, it would not be easy to get them out."[110] Third, a significant Russian voice in the internal order of the postwar Japanese government by means of the occupational control agreement might not come into force if Japan could be forced to surrender before Russia managed a meaningful participation in the war. Truman recalled: "I would not allow the Russians any part in the control of Japan. . . . I made up my mind that General MacArthur would be given complete command and control of Japan."[111]

Finally, it was hoped, especially by Secretary of State Byrnes and probably by President Truman as well, that the bomb could be exploited to political advantage in Eastern Europe. As Byrnes explained in relation to Eastern Europe in late July, the "New Mexico situation had given us great power, and that in the final analysis, it would control."[112] After the bomb was dropped, Byrnes became increasingly rigid, as Henry L. Stimson's diary relates:

> I took up the question . . . how to handle Russia with the big bomb. I found that Byrnes was very much against any attempt to cooperate with the Russians. . . . He looks to having the presence of the bomb in his pocket.[113]

The official American justification for dropping the bomb has always been in terms of a calculus of military necessity and humanitarian concern. President Truman explained that the bomb was dropped "to shorten the agony of war, in order to save the lives of thousands and thousands of young Americans."[114] But historical evidence suggests that there were alternatives to dropping the bomb. First, was the bomb necessary to save lives? The Japanese may have wanted to surrender anyway. In mid-June 1945, Foreign Minister Hideki Tojo approached the Russians "with a view to terminating the war if possible by September."[115] These overtures became more intense throughout the summer, others were intercepted, and still others were being made directly to the West.[116] The Americans, who had broken the Japanese code years earlier, had easy access to Japanese communications, which were alive with efforts to convince the Russians to intercede on their behalf. In fact, Hopkins advised that these peace overtures be explored, but they were not. Instead, on July 26, 1945, only thirteen days before Russia was scheduled to enter the war, China, the United States, and Britain issued an ultimatum to the Japanese to surrender unconditionally or face "prompt and utter destruction."

This insistence on unconditional surrender in the face of Japanese attempts to quit if only the future status of the emperor were clarified is confusing in view of Truman's contention that his sole motive was to end the war with the least bloodshed. If the complete humiliation of Japan was desired, one can only note that the terms finally offered and accepted did allow for the retention of the emperor and were the same as an important faction of the deeply divided Japanese cabinet was prepared to accept in mid-summer 1945. If the minimization of human suffering alone was the motive, those terms could have been at least explored; instead, they were ignored until after the bombs were dropped.

Moreover, the bomb was not universally perceived as a military necessity. The fire raids on Tokyo destroyed as much life. American air strikes came and went with no interference, imposing fire storms that incinerated up to one hundred thousand human beings a raid. Much American military analysis was in agreement with Air Force Chief of Staff General Curtis LeMay that "even without the atomic bomb and the Russian entry into the war, Japan would have surrendered in two weeks. . . . The atomic bomb has nothing to do with the end of the war." The authors of the U.S. Strategic Bombing Survey concluded that

> it is the Survey's opinion that . . . in all probability prior to November 31, 1945 Japan would have surrendered even if the atomic bomb had not been dropped, even if Russia had not entered the war, and even if no invasion had been planned or contemplated.[117]

Finally, contemporary critics of the decision to use the bomb have noted that other options were available to the president, the use of which — either alone or in combination — could have brought Japanese surrender. These included: 1) diplomatic negotiations especially on the terms of surrender; 2) a naval blockade; or 3) the Russian action of declaring war. The use of force, including the bomb itself, could have taken a different form as well. For example, conventional air strikes could have continued given total American air superiority. It has been suggested that Truman might have threatened its use or even demonstrated the bomb rather than use it on civilians with no warning.[118] In each case, of course, these options would have required time and thus increased the possibility or even ensured greater Russian participation and presence in the structuring of postwar Asia. Historian and participant Herbert Feis has concluded:

> It is likely that Churchill, and probably also Truman, conceived that besides bringing the war to a quick end, it would improve the chances of arranging a satisfactory peace both in Europe and in the Far East. Stimson and Byrnes certainly had that thought in mind. For would not the same dramatic proof of western power that shocked Japan into surrender impress the Russians also? . . . In short, the bomb, it may have been thought or hoped, would not only subdue the Japanese aggressors, but perhaps also monitor Russian behavior.[119]

The bomb seemed to yield benefits: Japan surrendered, and the Americans moved quickly to build a "sympathetic Japan . . . in case there should be any aggression by Russia in Manchuria."[120] The attempt to contain Soviet influence in Asia was furthered by the order to the Japanese in Korea, the Philippines, Indochina, and East Asia to surrender only to forces that General Douglas MacArthur would designate. The order was calculated to minimize the possibility that the Japanese would surrender to partisan resistance forces under Mao Zedong, Ho Chi Minh, or others fighting in Indonesia, Korea, and the Philippines, and thereby strengthen the influence of left-led partisans who presumably would have been sympathetic to Russian power. The Russians protested, but they had not been able to establish much of a presence in Asia by dint of arms, and more important, their major concern was Central Europe. Thus, although the Russians largely respected the West's claims in Asia, the bomb probably had less to do with it than the balance of Soviet and American capability deployed in the Far East at the end of the war. This was, of course, a mirror image of the situation in Central Europe; but in Europe, Truman would concede nothing.

Potsdam and Beyond

In the meantime, at Potsdam, Truman proceeded to push claims against the Soviets that denied them the kind of exclusive arrangement the West had pursued in Greece, Italy, and North Africa. The discussion became increasingly sharp and Truman soon wearied of it, thinking it futile — and perhaps, believing that soon the great demonstration of American power over Hiroshima and Nagasaki would give the Soviets second thoughts. The issue of whether Eastern Europe was to be open or closed to Western influence remained, however, unaffected by the bomb. This issue turned instead on the disposition of forces during and immediately after the war. The question of postwar Germany's political and economic future became, therefore, the most frequently debated issue in the Potsdam conference.

Early in the war, Roosevelt had approved of the plan of his secretary of the treasury, Henry Morgenthau, to fragment Germany, "pastoralize it," and bring to Germany the forceful lessons of a Carthaginian peace. When the plan was originally proposed to him, the president endorsed it enthusiastically: "We have to castrate the German people or you have to treat them in such a manner so they can't go on reproducing people who want to go on the way they have in the past."[121] Roosevelt's advisers and Churchill, however, did not fully support this vision, fearing that it would bankrupt European reconstruction, encourage nationalist irredentism, and open the way for communism. By Yalta, the president was also becoming wary of some of the implications of this plan; Roosevelt did not want mass starvation to occur, nor did he want a repetition of the reparations experience after World War I that had contributed to the economic instability of

Germany in the 1920s and 1930s. Subsequently, therefore, Roosevelt rejected the harsh "planned chaos" of the initial Morgenthau proposal, while accepting other implications of the plan concerning some reduction of the German standard of living. Hence, at Yalta, Roosevelt became committed, as a basis of discussion, to the figure of $20 billion or 50 percent of German wealth drawn from all of Germany as the basic reparations payment. Thus, although divided politically into occupation zones, Germany was to be treated as a single economic unit.

At Potsdam, however, the Americans demanded that no specific figure be set for reparations. It was a harsh blow for the Soviets, who had been promised a $20 billion talking figure. The Russians knew that the action of cutting off lend–lease and of procrastination on Soviet loan requests left reparations drawn from Germany as the only reasonable recourse, in terms of outside assistance, for postwar reconstruction of Russia. In part, Truman's decision to withdraw reparations from the Russians was prompted by concern that, eventually, Americans would wind up subsidizing German reparations payments to the Russians. Second, Truman proposed that any reparations paid to the Allies should be drawn from their respective zones of occupation, rather than from Germany as a whole as envisioned at Yalta. A zonal approach to reparations, it was argued by the Americans, would minimize conflict about what the Germans could or could not afford. The Russians protested, however, that such an arrangement would deprive them of access to the industrialized Western zones, especially the Ruhr. Soviet-controlled East Germany was largely agricultural, and the Russians had removed in a draconian fashion almost all its rolling stock, cattle, a good deal of industrial plant, and even toilets before the Big Three convened in Berlin. It was, they declared, "war booty" and not part of the reparations calculation.

More important, would not this mean, Molotov asked, "that each country would have a free hand in their own zone and would act entirely independent of the other?"[122] In other words, the American proposal outlined a divided Germany in which Four Power control would be minimized if not eliminated in the respective zones. In view of the Soviet desire to maintain access to and influence on any and all facets of German political and economic reconstruction, this turn of events could not be viewed with optimism in Moscow. The Russians were aware of the need for a German economic reconstruction sufficient to maintain reparations. But they were concerned primarily with the security implications of a Germany, or any part of it, not open to their influence and, if possible, an administrative veto over German policies. At Yalta, Churchill had remarked to Stalin, "If you want a horse to pull a wagon, you have to give it fodder." The Soviet dictator replied, "But care should be taken to see that the horse did not turn around and kick you."[123]

At Potsdam, therefore, the contentious nature of the German question—the pivotal issue of the next crucial five years—was drawn. Germany was the key variable in opposing Soviet and American conceptions of a secure and stable Europe. On the other hand, the conference did seem to offer the Soviets a softening of the Western position on Poland. It was not inconceivable, therefore, that the German problem could be worked out by the foreign ministers in the fall of 1945.

Atomic Diplomacy Proves Inadequate

The mushroom clouds from the bombs exploding in the Orient reached silently over the shoulders of the statesmen who sat at the London foreign ministers' meeting, discussing Eastern Europe in the fall of 1945. It was not mentioned in the conference proceedings, but cartoonists drew pictures of it perched on the conference table. As *Time* magazine commented: "at the . . . conference, U.S. diplomats had been reluctant to talk about the bomb. When the subject came up in private conversation they would say something like 'of course, the world knows that the U.S. would never. . . .' Such sentences usually trailed off in inaudible mumbles."[124] But in the end, the bomb served only to exaggerate the reactions of both sides. Secretary Byrnes's whole negotiating strategy seemed infused with a sense of atomic omnipotence.[125] At London, the tenor of the coming cold war was in evidence as diplomacy turned vitriolic. The conference degenerated into a series of alternating press conferences in which the two sides explained their own positions and castigated each other concerning their respective policies in their European spheres of influence. The atomic threat was always present if unarticulated, but Molotov and the Russians were unmoved—the existing balance of forces in Europe, not the vague if ominous threats of atomic diplomacy, moved the Russians. The conference stalemated.

Byrnes decided to shift his tactics in the next foreign ministers' conference, to be held in Moscow in December 1945. Rather than pursue his London tack of public diplomacy, he undertook a more secretive style and approached Stalin and Molotov with offers of recognition for the Rumanian and Bulgarian regimes if the Russians would agree to a German peace treaty as well as a general set of agreements covering all of Eastern Europe. In Byrnes's scheme, all of these issues would be resolved in a large peace conference that would negotiate the political agreements as well as provide economic access to Central Europe.

The Soviets seemed satisfied,[126] but President Truman was not. He was more than a little miffed at Byrnes's secrecy and the latitude exercised by the secretary of state in his negotiations. From all appearances in Washington, Byrnes was free-lancing and making vague concessions to the Russians without presidential approval. Moreover, such diplomacy opened Truman to attacks from conservative Republicans who were labeling Roosevelt's actions at Yalta and Democratic party diplomacy in general a sellout. Senator Arthur Vandenberg, ranking member and then chair of the Senate Foreign Relations Committee, grumbled that the conciliatory language of the Moscow meeting and the lack of progress reminded him of "Chamberlain and his umbrella appeasement." House Leader Joe Martin called it a "betrayal of the small nations of the world in the making of peace."[127] Under such attack, an already tough Byrnes was pushed even further to the right and into a more inflexible policy line as the postwar conferences began again in 1946.

From the Soviet perspective, the American course in Germany was unacceptable. Indeed, it was potentially dangerous, for it implied a reconstituted Germany perhaps ruled by the very class of people who had directed the destruction of 20 million Russians during the preceding five years. All in all, it was not a prospect that would win Russian favor or evoke Russian confidence and trust. Western proposals in Germany — an area regarded by the Soviets as the very core of their security interests — were, predictably, rejected. Instead, the Soviets and the Americans turned to the imposition of greater control of their respective zones of occupation. The Allied Control Council for Germany became merely an administrative shell as the military commanders in each occupation zone assumed supreme political as well as military authority. The division of Germany seemed assured when, in May 1946, General Lucius Clay informed the Russians that no more reparations would be paid to them from the Western zones. Similarly, the Soviets, at about the same time, stopped removing machinery from East Germany and apparently decided to regenerate industrial production within the East German zone.

In a highly publicized speech in Stuttgart on September 4, 1946, Secretary of State Byrnes announced that Germany needed to develop a "self-sustaining" economy and a capacity to export. "Germany is a part of Europe, and European recovery . . . will be slowed with her great resources turned into a poor house," Byrnes explained.[128] Germans, he declared, should be given primary responsibility for running their own affairs. Moreover, the United States would never recognize the Oder-Neisse as the eastern boundary that separated Poland and East Germany. More than 3.5 million Germans expelled from Poland were living in Western zones. Byrnes's speech gave them hope that they would return and tied the future German government to that assumption for twenty-five years. Byrnes's speech also implied that the United States would keep its troops in Germany for "a long time to come," but a provisional government would be set up to manage German contributions to its own and general European recovery. Such a state of affairs, a reconstituted Germany administered by those who had lost the war, could be held up to the Eastern Europeans as a bogey of revenge — and tie the whole area to the Russians.

The East Germans made little pretense at being self-governing. They would be only a hypothetical security threat to Russia's satellites; they had no refugees and were "satisfied." Still, the specter of American troops guarding the Western sectors of a divided Germany with claims to the East promised no immediate reconciliation of the partitioned Germanies. The Americans did not recognize Soviet security interests in Central Europe and feared Soviet designs and Soviet power. Soviet actions were almost without exception interpreted as challenges to the West that had to be met with stern resolve. Unity became an imperative, and the recovery of Europe was only a part of the larger need for sustained resistance to the Soviet threat. In this way, a set of conditions were established that were to serve as a persistent flashpoint of East–West contention for the next twenty-five years.

NOTES

1. N. Gordon Levin, Jr., *Woodrow Wilson and World Politics: America's Response to War and Revolution* (New York: Oxford University Press, 1968).
2. Ray S. Baker and William E. Dodd, *The Public Papers of Woodrow Wilson, III* (New York: 1927), pp. 147–148, as cited by Robert E. Osgood, *Ideals and Self-Interest in American's Foreign Relation: The Great Transformation of the Twentieth Century* (Chicago: University of Chicago Press, 1953), p. 178.
3. Albert Shaw, ed., *President Wilson's State Papers and Addresses* (New York: George A. Doran Co., 1918), pp. 380–381.
4. A good summary of the literature of Woodrow Wilson's view of world order can be found in Lloyd E. Ambosius, "The Orthodoxy of Revisionism: Woodrow Wilson and the New Left," *Diplomatic History*, Vol. 1, No. 3 (Summer 1977), especially pp. 209–211.
5. Cited by Inis Claude, *Power and International Relations* (New York: Random House, 1962), p. 101.
6. G. H. Stern, "The Foreign Policy of the Soviet Union," in F. S. Northedge, ed., *The Foreign Policies of the Great Powers* (New York: Praeger Publishers, 1962), p. 77. An exhaustive review of the "Soviet diplomatic method" can be found in Joseph G. Whelan's *Soviet Diplomacy and Negotiating Behavior: Emerging New Context for U.S. Diplomacy*, Special Studies on Foreign Affairs Issues, Congres-

sional Research Service for the Senate Committee on Foreign Relations, July 11, 1979.

7. Woodrow Wilson, Speech at Kansas City, Mo., September 6, 1919, reprinted in Thomas G. Paterson, ed., *Major Problems in American Foreign Policy: Documents and Essays*, Vol. 2 (since 1914) (Lexington, Mass.: D.C. Heath, 1978), pp. 96–97.

8. The figure is from Betty Miller Unterberger, "President Wilson and the Decision to Send Troops to Siberia," *Pacific Historical Review*, Vol. 24 (February 1955), pp. 63–74. A good review of the documents and literature is Unterberger, ed., *American Intervention in the Russian Civil War* (Lexington, Mass.: D.C. Heath, 1969).

9. See Betty Miller Unterberger, "Woodrow Wilson and the Bolsheviks: The 'Acid Test' of Soviet–American Relations," *Diplomatic History*, Vol. II, No. 2 (Spring 1987), p. 83, fn59ff.

10. Levin, op. cit., p. 107.

11. One soldier penned a bit of doggerel that captured their misery: "It's the land of the infernal odor, the land of the national smell. The average United States soldier would rather be quartered in L." *Literary Digest*, Vol. 60 (February 8, 1919), p. 99, cited in Thomas A. Bailey, *America Faces Russia* (Ithaca, N.Y.: Cornell University Press, 1950), p. 242.

12. See Linda Killen, "The Search for a Democratic Russia," *Diplomatic History*, Vol. 2, No. 3 (Summer 1978), p. 241. Alongside the American military effort, Wilson directed American grains to be sent to the White controlled area since this was a "most effective means of limiting the spread of Bolshevism." The wheat never arrived, however, because its destination, Petrograd, fell to the communists before American ships could deliver the consigned grain.

13. Ibid., p. 251.

14. John G. Stoessinger, *Nations in Darkness* (New York: Random House, 1971), p. 116.

15. Walter Lippmann and Charles Merz, "A Test of the News," *New Republic*, Vol. 2 (August 4, 1920), pp. 1–42. For an excellent recent summary of the literature on the public's attitudes toward the Soviet Union as a function of official policy, see Ralph B. Levering, *The Public and American Foreign Policy 1918–1978* (New York: William Morrow, 1978).

16. Stoessinger, op. cit., p. 119, citing the *Saturday Evening Post*, July 6, 1918.

17. Ibid.

18. Ibid., p. 120.

19. Ibid., p. 133.

20. Ibid., p. 141.

21. Stephen Pichon, "Allied Policy in Russia," *Current History*, Vol. 10, No. 2 (May 1919), pp. 280–281.

22. George F. Kennan, *Russia and the West Under Lenin and Stalin* (Boston: Little, Brown, 1961), p. 117.

23. *Foreign Relations of the United States, 1920*, Vol. 3, pp. 466–468, cited in perhaps the best study of early Soviet diplomacy, Teddy Uldricks's *Diplomacy and Ideology: The Origins of Soviet Foreign Relations: 1917–1930* (London: Sage, 1978), p. 51.

24. Kennan, op. cit., p. 137.

25. Ibid., p. 138.

26. Bailey, *America Faces Russia*, p. 257.

27. Stoessinger, op. cit., p. 143.

28. Ibid., p. 143.

29. *Literary Digest*, Vol. 116 (December 2, 1933), p. 13.

30. Louis Fisher, *Russia's Road from Peace to War* (New York: Harper & Row, 1969), p. 261.

31. Indeed, some have suggested that the brutal purges in 1937 can be seen as as means of ridding the Soviet Union of potential opposition to a *modus vivendi* with Hitler. See Kennan, op. cit., pp. 315–316. Thomas Maddux suggests that Stalin "backed away" from active cooperation with the West in early 1936. See Maddux, "Watching Stalin Maneuver Between Hitler and the West: American Diplomats and Soviet Diplomacy, 1934–1939," *Diplomatic History*, Vol. 1, No. 2 (Spring 1977).

32. Kennan, op. cit., p. 317.

33. *The Times* (London), September 28, 1938, and John Wheeler-Bennett, *Munich: Prologue to Tragedy* (London: Macmillan, 1948), pp. 157–158.

34. The American role was minor but noteworthy for the sense of guilt that it caused. Roosevelt stated to Hitler, just before Munich, that Germany did not have to concern itself about American protest. "The Government of the United States has no political involvements in Europe," Roosevelt declared, "and will assume no obligations in the conduct of the present negotiations." Robert A. Divine, *Roosevelt and World War II* (Baltimore: Johns Hopkins University Press, 1969), p. 22.

35. Adam B. Ulam, *Expansion and Coexistence, History of Soviet Foreign Policy, 1917–1967* (New York: Praeger, 1968), p. 263 *passim*.

36. The British did not want to be responsible for defending the Baltic states but were requesting the Soviets to aid Holland and Belgium.

37. Winston S. Churchill, *The Grand Alliance*, Vol. III of *The Second World War* (Boston: Houghton Mifflin, 1950), p. 369.

38. George F. Kennan, *Memoirs, 1925–1950* (Boston: Little, Brown, 1967), pp. 133–134.

39. Divine, op. cit., pp. 81–82.

40. Ibid., p. 84

41. Kennan, *Russia and the West Under Lenin and Stalin*, pp. 350–351.

42. As the U.S. Chiefs of Staff reported in 1941, "It should be recognized as an almost invariable rule that wars cannot be finally won without the use of land armies." M. Watson, War Department, Chief of Staff; *Pre-War Plans and Preparations (United States Army in World War II)*. Washington, D.C.: U.S. Government Printing Office, 1950, pp. 400–410; cited in John Bagguley, "The World War and the Cold War," in David Horowitz, ed., *Containment and Revolution* (Boston: Beacon, 1967), p. 91.

43. Churchill, op. cit., pp. 645–651.

44. James MacGregor Burns, *Roosevelt: The Soldier of Freedom* (New York: Harcourt Brace Jovanovich, 1970), p. 231.

45. Churchill, op. cit., pp. 457–458.

46. Paul Carell, *Hitler Moves East: 1941–1943* (New York: Ballantine, 1963), p. 196 *passim*.

47. Ibid., p. 202.

48. Churchill, op. cit., pp. 469–470.

49. Churchill, *The Hinge of Fate*, Vol. IV of *The Second World War* (Boston: Houghton Mifflin, 1950), p. 201.

50.   Burns, op. cit., pp. 111–112.

51.   John L. Gaddis, *The United States and the Origins of the Cold War, 1941–1947* (New York: Columbia University Press, 1972), p. 7.

52.   Robert E. Sherwood, *Roosevelt and Hopkins* (New York: Harper & Brothers, 1948), p. 577.

53.   Churchill, *The Hinge of Fate*, p. 342.

54.   H. C. Butcher, *The Years with Eisenhower* (New York: Simon & Schuster, 1946), p. 12.

55.   Ibid., p. 29; and Stephen Ambrose, *Rise to Globalism: American Foreign Policy Since 1938* (Baltimore: Penguin Books, 1970), p. 53.

56.   Burns, op. cit., p. 236.

57.   Churchill, *The Hinge of Fate*, p. 475.

58.   Cited in Andre Fountaine, *History of the Cold War* (New York: Vintage Books, 1968), p. 160.

59.   Bagguley, "The World War and the Cold War," in David Horowitz, ed., *Containment and Revolution* (Boston: Beacon Press, 1967), p. 91; and Churchill, *The Hinge of Fate*, Vol. IV of *The Second World War* (New York: Bantam Books, 1962), Appendix A, Book 2, Memo: Prime Minister to Ismay, January, 1943, p. 806, and March 3 and 4, 1943, p. 816.

60.   Churchill, *The Hinge of Fate*, Bantam ed., pp. 663–679, and Memos: Prime Minister to Ismay, March 4, 1943, p. 816.

61.   Richard M. Leighton and Robert W. Corkley, *Global Logistics and Strategy: 1943–1945, The United States Army in World War II* (Washington, D.C.: Office of the Chief of Military History, 1968), p. 846.

62.   Gordan A. Harrison, *The European Theater of Operations: Cross-Channel Attack (The United States Army in World War II)* (Washington, D.C.: Office of the Chief of Military History, 1951), p. 141.

63.   Fontaine, op. cit., p. 160.

64.   Ibid., pp. 160–161.

65.   Indeed the Joint Chiefs of Staff had predicted as much. Burns, op. cit., pp. 312–316.

66.   Bagguley, op. cit., p. 95.

67.   Basil Liddell Hart, *History of the Second World War, Vol. II* (New York: Capricorn, 1972), p. 488; Vojtech Mastny, "Stalin and the Prospects of a Separate Peace in World War II," *The American Historical Review*, Vol. 77, No. 5 (December 1972), pp. 1365–1388; and Lynn Etheridge Davis, *The Cold War Begins: Soviet American Conflict over Eastern Europe* (Princeton, N.J.: Princeton University Press, 1974), pp. 51–52.

68.   Herbert Feis, *Churchill, Roosevelt and Stalin* (Princeton, N.J.: Princeton University Press, 1957), p. 584. The Germans, and especially Himmler, were apparently very interested in piquing the Western Allies' interest in a separate deal. Such a move would, at the least, cause disruption in the Allied cause, and might become serious. As Himmler explained to the Swedish diplomat Count Bernadotte, a deal with the Western Allies would save as great a part of Germany as possible from a Russian invasion. "I am willing to capitulate on the Western Front in order to enable the Western Allies to advance to the East." Gar Alperovitz, *Cold War Essays* (Cambridge, Mass.: Schenkman, 1970), p. 26.

69.   Allen Dulles, *Secret Surrender* (New York: Harper & Row, 1966), pp. 146–151.

70.   Joseph Stalin, *Correspondence Between the Chairman of the Council of Ministers*

of the U.S.S.R. with Churchill, Atlee, Roosevelt and Truman, 1941–1945, Vol. II (New York: Dutton, 1958).

71. Gaddis, op. cit., p. 93.
72. Michael A. Pezke, article in the *Journal of the American Aviation Historical Society*, cited in *The New York Times*, November 8, 1973.
73. Sherwood, op. cit., p. 899.
74. Ibid., pp. 899–900.
75. Churchill, *The Grand Alliance*, p. 391.
76. John A. Lukacs, *The Great Powers and Eastern Europe* (New York: American Book, 1953), p. 506.
77. Divine, op. cit., pp. 91–92.
78. Divine, *Foreign Policy and U.S. Presidential Elections 1940–1948* (New York: Franklin Watts, 1974), pp. 130–137.
79. Burns, op. cit., p. 572.
80. Gaddis, op. cit., p. 173.
81. W. Averell Harriman, *America and Russia in a Changing World: A Half Century of Personal Observation* (Garden City, N.Y.: Doubleday, 1971), pp. 35–36.
82. Milovan Djilas, *Conversations with Stalin* (New York: Harcourt, Brace & World, 1962), p. 114, and Ronald Steel, "Did Anybody Start the Cold War?" *New York Review*, Vol. 26 (September 2, 1971), p. 26.
83. See Arthur Schlesinger, "The Origins of the Cold War," *Foreign Affairs*, Vol. 46 (October 1967), pp. 22–52.
84. Ambrose, op. cit., pp. 58–59. Jews were still persecuted, still unable to practice professions, attend schools, or own property; Arabs continued to be beaten and exploited; the French generals who had cooperated with the Nazis and fought the Americans lived in splendor amid the squalor that surrounded them.
85. *Times* (London), April 17, 1945.
86. Churchill, *Triumph and Tragedy*, Vol. VI of *The Second World War* (New York: Bantam, 1962), p. 258.
87. Ibid., p. 247 *passim*.
88. Ibid., p. 610.
89. Perry McCoy Smith, *The Air Force Plans for Peace: 1943–1945* (Baltimore: Johns Hopkins University Press, 1970). American plans at sea were to put U.S. ships "everywhere" so, in the words of one planner, the U.S. fleet would outnumber the fleets of the world. Thomas G. Paterson, *On Every Front* (New York: Norton, 1979), p. 81, and unpublished monograph by James E. King.
90. Kennan, *Memoirs*, p. 57. For Harriman's views see Daniel Yergin, *Shattered Peace: The Origins of the Cold War and the National Security State* (Boston: Houghton Mifflin, 1977), pp. 81, 84, and 93.
91. Kennan, op. cit., p. 70.
92. Edward R. Stettinius, *Roosevelt and the Russians* (Garden City, N.Y.: Doubleday, 1949), p. 347.
93. Harry S. Truman, *Memoirs*, Vol. II, *Year of Decision* (Garden City, N.Y.: Doubleday, 1955), p. 71.
94. Ibid., p. 82. For a milder rendition of this conversation, see Robert J. Donovan, *Conflict and Crisis* (New York: Norton, 1977), p. 42, fn. 33, and p. 445.
95. Churchill, *Triumph and Tragedy*, Bantam ed., pp. 421–422. This quotation is partly a paraphrase of Stalin's words by Churchill and partly a direct quote of Stalin's message to Churchill.
96. William D. Leahy, *I Was There* (New York: Whittsley House, 1950), pp. 384–385.

97. Gabriel Kolko, *The Politics of War* (New York: Vintage Books, 1968), pp. 439–444; and Schlesinger, op. cit., p. 43.

98. Alperovitz, *Cold War Essays*, p. 98.

99. Sherwood, op. cit., p. 894.

100. And, in the view of some observers, it may have been a bureaucratic mistake: Gaddis, op. cit., p. 219.

101. Truman op. cit., p. 87.

102. Jonathon Daniels, *The Man of Independence* (Philadelphia: J. B. Lippincott, 1950), p. 266. Also see Martin J. Sherwin, *A World Destroyed: The Atomic Bomb and the Grand Alliance* (New York: Alfred A. Knopf, 1975), pp. 188 and 191 for a dispute about exactly when the bomb and Poland became bound together as issues.

103. Gar Alperovitz, *Atomic Diplomacy* (New York: Random House, 1965), p. 64. For a critique of Alperovitz's "delayed showdown" thesis, see Martin J. Sherwin "The Atomic Bomb, Scientists, and American Diplomacy During the Second World War" (unpublished doctoral dissertation, University of California, Los Angeles, 1971) pp. 252–269. On the other hand, see Yergin, op. cit., pp. 101 and 115, who apparently accepts part of Alperovitz's controversial thesis about a showdown with the Soviets until after a successful test of the atom bomb. His rather elliptical essay on this point can be found in his notes of p. 433, fn. 19, where he suggests Alperovitz "overinterprets" the data.

104. Gaddis, op. cit., p. 234.

105. Truman, op. cit., p. 314.

106. Churchill, *Triumph and Tragedy* (Houghton Mifflin ed.), p. 639.

107. William A. Williams, *Tragedy of American Diplomacy*, rev. ed. (New York: Delta, 1962), p. 249.

108. Ibid.

109. Churchill, *Triumph and Tragedy* (Houghton and Mifflin ed.), pp. 545ff.

110. Walter Millis, ed., *The Forrestal Diaries* (New York: Viking, 1951), p. 78.

111. Truman, op, cit., p. 412.

112. Gaddis, op. cit., p. 264.

113. Cited in Alperovitz, *Cold War Essays*, p. 70.

114. Harry S. Truman, *Public Papers of the President — 1945* (Washington, D.C.: U.S. Government Printing Office, 1961), p. 212.

115. Cited in Alperovitz, *Cold War Essays*, p. 54.

116. Herbert Feis, *The Atomic Bomb and the End of World War II* (Princeton. N.J.: Princeton University Press, 1966), pp. 111–116.

117. *The United States Strategic Bombing Survey*, "Japan's Stuggle to End the War," War Department, July 1, 1946, p. 13, and Alperovitz, *Cold War Essays*, pp. 62–63. The thesis that the bomb might not have been a military necessity is sharply challenged but not refuted by Professor Edward Shapiro, "The Military Options to Hiroshima: A Critical Examination of Gar Alperovitz," *Naval War College Review*, Vol. 30, No. 4 (Spring 1978), pp. 101–113, The thesis that the Japanese would not have surrendered until at least the first atomic bomb is argued by John Toland, *The Rising Sun: The Decline and Fall of the Japanese Empire, 1936–1945* (New York: Random House, 1970), pp. 809–866. See also the comments of former U.S. ambassador Edwin O. Reischauer in *Washington Post*, August 3, 1983, p. D1.

118. Discussions of these options may be found in Feis, op. cit., and Alperovitz, *Cold War Essays*. Also see the remarks of Isidor Rabi, a Nobel laureate conversant with both the physics and politics of the decision not to warn the Japanese

ahead of time, in Donovan, op. cit., p. 61, and p. 95 for Truman's thinking on this matter.

119.   Feis, op. cit., p. 194. The decision to use the bomb may have been reinforced by a certain momentum that was somewhat independent of diplomatic or strategic subtleties. Among the elements that could have been at work in this regard, one might note the following:

1. The expenditure of $2 billion, in secret, would presumably have to be justified.
2. Thousands had already been slaughtered in Europe and Japan in air raids against civilian targets. The raid against Japan did not seem all that extraordinary and was perhaps facilitated by popular racist beliefs about Japan.
3. As Ambrose points out, "The bomb was there . . . to use it seemed inevitable." To Truman, it appeared little else than an ace in the flush hand of military capability. It was only after their use, and some reflections, that atomic weapons created the respect they now command for themselves. See also Donovan, op. cit., chaps. 5, 7, and 10.

Still another argument drawing on the implicit momentum of the development process by emphasizing Truman's inexperience is advanced by Kenneth M. Glazier, Jr., "The Decision to Use Atomic Weapons Against Hiroshima and Nagasaki," *Public Policy*, Vol. 18 (Summer 1970), pp. 463–516. See also the important essay by Barton Bernstein, "Roosevelt, Truman and the Atomic Bomb," *Political Science Quarterly*, No. 90 (Spring 1975), pp. 23–29, for some of the uncertainties policy makers harbored regarding the efficacy of the bomb. On balance, however, their hopes for the weapon seem beyond question. See Yergin, op. cit., p. 120.

120.   Kolko, op. cit., p. 599.
121.   Gaddis, op. cit., p. 119.
122.   Gaddis, op. cit., p. 241.
123.   Charles Boheln, Minutes of Second Meeting, February 5. 1944, *Foreign Relations of the United States, Diplomatic Papers: The Conferences of Malta and Yalta, 1945* (Washington, D.C.: U.S. Government Printing Office, 1955), pp. 620–621.
124.   Lloyd C. Gardner, *Architects of Illusion: Men and Ideas in American Foreign Policy, 1941–1949* (Chicago: Quadrangle, 1970), p. 98.
125.   Atomic scientist Leo Szilard wrote of his conversations with Byrnes at this time, that his "sense of proportion" was appalling. Szilard recalls:

I shared Byrnes' concern about Russia's throwing around her weight in the post-war period, but I was completely flabbergasted by the assumption that rattling the bomb might make Russia more manageable.

I began to doubt that there was any way for me to communicate with Byrnes in this matter, and my doubt became certainty when he turned to me and said, "Well, you come from Hungary—you would not want to stay in Hungary indefinitely," but what Byrnes said offended my sense of proportion. I was concerned at this point that by demonstrating the bomb and using it in the war against Japan, we might start an atomic arms race between America and Russia which was not disposed at this point to worry about what would happen to Hungary.

Leo Szilard, "Reminiscences" in Donald Fleming and Bernard Bailyn, eds., *Perspectives In American History II* (Cambridge, Mass.: Harvard University Press, 1968), pp. 94–151.

126. Feis, *From Trust to Terror: The Onset of the Cold War 1945–1959* (New York: W.W. Norton, 1970), p. 54.

127. Gaddis, p. 291.

128. The Stuttgart Speech, Typescript, National Archives, Washington, D.C., Regional File of the Department of State 740-00119 (Germany), p. 8. For an important dissent on the meaning of the Stuttgart address and review of the literature see John Gimbel, "On the Implementation of the Potsdam Agreement: An Essay on U.S. Post War German Policy," *Political Science Quarterly*, Vol. 87 (June 1972), pp. 242–269.

Chapter 2
The Onset of the
Cold War

By late 1945 it was apparent that Soviet and American policies were no longer joined by even the most tenuous of the strands that had held the wartime alliance together. During the last months of 1945 and throughout 1946, a new and inexperienced American president sought to master American policy even as that policy collided with Soviet interests on a global scale. It was, as former Secretary of State Dean Acheson put it, a time of "learning."[1] Out of it emerged the political reflexes and some of the most fundamental policy principles of the next quarter century.

A WORLD VIEW TAKES SHAPE

As positions hardened in Germany, the Soviets and the West issued "appropriate declarations of the Cold War."[2] In a speech on February 9, 1946, Stalin took note of the relatively weak position of the Soviet Union and the need, in spite of the hardships of the war, to redouble its efforts to achieve economic recovery, for the power of the West did not allow the Soviet Union the luxury of returning to a peacetime footing.[3] Stalin asserted that communism and capitalism were incompatible and that true peace was impossible until the former supplanted the latter. Most people in the United States received the speech as a warlike call to confrontation between communism and the West.[4] Less than a month later, Winston Churchill replied with his famous "iron curtain" speech at Fulton, Missouri, in which he asserted that the Soviets did not want war but rather "the fruits of war and the indefinite expansion of their power and doctrines."[5] The proper response, in Churchill's view, was a show of military strength.[6]

The Soviet Threat Defined

Churchill's position seems to have been compatible with a fairly widespread but basically private mood of American policymakers, a mood that had been articulated in an 8-thousand-word telegram from the chargé d'affaires of the Moscow Embassy, George F. Kennan. A response to an exasperated Department of State request for some explanation of Soviet behavior, the "long telegram" of February 22, 1946, painted an extremely frightening picture of a Soviet Union that would expand inexorably unless opposed:

> Soviet power [is] . . . [i]mpervious to logic of reason, and it is highly sensitive to logic of force. For this reason it can easily withdraw — and usually does — when strong resistance is encountered at any point. Thus, if the adversary has sufficient force and makes clear his readiness to use it, he rarely has to do so.[7]

Although Kennan's recommendations concerning what American policy should be in the face of this threat were vague,[8] his description of the horrors and implied horrors of failing to confront communist power had tremendous impact and was a crucial element in subsequent American foreign policy. The conclusion seems to have been drawn that the United States was confronted with a multidimensional threat aimed at nothing less than Western civilization. The only apparent remedy to Soviet power was struggle and confrontation because all they understood was force. Negotiations were considered of limited utility if not impossible. Therefore, the manipulation of the threat of war had to become the most important facet of diplomacy in dealing with the Soviets.

A few officials within the government openly displayed their opposition to the emerging anti-Soviet consensus of the Truman administration.[9] But when Secretary of Commerce and former Vice President (under Roosevelt) Henry Wallace publicly disagreed with Truman in September 1946, he was fired.[10] The message was clear: The policy of getting tough with the Russians was now official orthodoxy, and those who challenged it did so at their peril. The hard line articulated in Churchill's public warning and Kennan's private epistle was matched by the events of 1946.

"Another War Is in the Making"

During late 1945 and throughout 1946, the Soviets pressured both Turkey and Iran to allow a greater Soviet presence in the region. In the latter case, Truman threatened to move American forces to Iran unless Soviet troops stationed in northern Iran during the war were removed. In January of 1946, as Soviet pressure on Turkey for increased access to the Mediterranean through the straits was building, Truman had written:

> There isn't a doubt in my mind that Russia intends an invasion of Turkey and the seizure of the Black Sea Straits to the Mediterranean. Unless Russia is faced with an iron fist and strong language, another war is in the making. Only one language do they understand — "How many divisions have you?"
>
> I do not think we should play compromise any longer. I'm tired of babying the Soviets.[11]

In August of 1946, an aircraft carrier was dispatched in support of Turkey. A month later the announcement was made that the United States would maintain a permanent naval presence in the Eastern Mediterranean.

In the meantime, deterioration began of the fragile cease fire in China negotiated by General George C. Marshall in 1945 between Mao Zedong's Communists and Chiang Kai-shek's Kuomintang. It was apparent by late 1946 and early 1947 that Chiang's military ineptitude was exceeded only by the corruption of his civil administration and his consequent loss of popular support. Mao was, of course, a Communist, but Mao and Stalin had profoundly disagreed over the course to political power in China since the 1920s. Indeed, evidence suggests that Stalin feared a postwar China united under the strong leadership of Mao. Washington's primary concern, however, was Europe. Chiang was, therefore, provided inspiration and limited material aid. He was not given the commitment of American troops probably necessary to save his regime. Nonetheless, as the situation worsened in Europe, the Russians became identified as agents of China's internal agony.

Yet another element in this mix of developments was the total breakdown of efforts to establish some form of international control over atomic energy. An American proposal gradually to transfer control of atomic weapons to a United Nations (UN) agency while other parties to the agreement would open themselves up for inspection was rejected by the Russians. They called instead for the immediate destruction of all atomic weapons followed by the gradual development of international controls while they maintained their veto over the process. Thus, at the very outset of the cold war, the problem of parity and perceived gaps in capability impinged on efforts to control arms. The Soviets, perceiving themselves behind in nuclear weapons technology and thus vulnerable, were not prepared to commit themselves to any arms control scheme that implied freezing the Soviet Union into a position of inferiority. They would seek a level of equality either through the destruction of existing atomic stockpiles and then discuss the possibilities of control or by building their own atomic weapons. The United States, on the other hand, viewed Soviet fears of the American atomic monopoly as evidence of neurotic stubbornness and as a smoke screen to camouflage their attempts to gain nuclear secrets.[12]

Retrospectively, these events of 1945 and 1946 might appear to form a pattern. At the time, however, events were imperfectly connected. Still, to conclude that no relationship existed among the events would be naive. President Truman's "iron fist" and "strong language" and the talk of "another war" strongly indicate that he and others in his administration were drawing parallels between the world of 1946 and the world of 1938 and 1939, when war had come about because the British did not draw the conceptual linkage between force and order now drawn by Truman. Truman, his advisers, and their British allies had only just brought to a close the horrible consequences of the failure to show an iron fist and strong language to Hitler. That mistake was not going to be repeated by the Truman administration.

The American Public
and the Onset of Cold War

Apart from the inevitable difficulties surrounding his assumption of the presidency, Truman was faced with an American public whose concerns ran to anything but foreign policy in 1946. The war was over, and most Americans were interested in returning their personal lives to a state of normalcy. What they found in 1946, however, was hardly normal.[13] Strikes, unemployment, inflation, two race riots in the North and lynchings in the South beset an America rapidly demobilizing in the wake of the pervasive economic and social mobilization necessary to fight World War II.

The presidency became, as it almost invariably does, the focus of these frustrations and jarring discontinuities. Much of the power of the president stems from his position at the center of the American people's image of their government. But this fact not only is a source of presidential power, it also can become a source of weakness. The man in the White House for the preceding fourteen years strode like a giant through the Depression and then World War II. Truman was inevitably the center of invidious comparisons and enormous expectations following the war; he was also the target of the frustrations that set in. All of it—the economic disruption, the social malaise, and the uneasiness concerning foreign affairs—culminated in the 1946 elections. The Republicans, who had not controlled either the Congress or the White House since the presidency of Herbert Hoover, asked the American people, in effect, "Had enough?", and the American electorate responded by sending fifty-six new Republicans to the House and thirteen new

Republicans to the Senate, thereby giving the GOP control of both houses of Congress.

The perceptions of and reactions to this domestic situation on the part of the Truman administration are perhaps as important as its reactions to external events. To many of the men around Truman, this unfolding spectacle seemed to confirm all of their preconceptions concerning the self-indulgent isolationism of the American people. Indeed, Undersecretary of State Dean Acheson was of the view that "focusing the will of 140,000,000 people on problems beyond our shores . . . [when] people are focusing on 140,000,000 other things" was perhaps the most important problem confronting American foreign policy.[14]

Public opinion polls taken during this period indicate that throughout 1946, less than 25 percent of the American people thought that foreign problems were the most vital ones confronting the country.[15] Such a finding is not surprising given the state of the economy and the understandable expectations of a nation only recently dragged through one of the most intense periods of involvement in foreign affairs in American history. Moreover, less than one year earlier, the American people and their representatives in Congress had been convinced of the necessity of accepting and participating in one of the greatest efforts at institutionalized multilateralism and internationalism undertaken up to that time, the founding of the United Nations.

Furthermore, the Truman administration, while circulating copies of Kennan's long telegram internally, was, at least prior to the summer of 1946, still taking a somewhat conciliatory *public* stance toward the Russians. Indeed, the increasingly bitter negotiations at Yalta, Potsdam, and subsequent meetings of foreign ministers were kept largely secret — thereby feeding public suspicion and lending credibility to Republican charges of appeasement, sell outs, and secret agreements. In short, public awareness and sensitivity was disoriented and distracted. But as subsequent events were to demonstrate, public opinion was also ultimately permissive and accepting of executive leadership when it was provided.[16]

To Truman and his closest advisors, however, there seemed little public awareness of the awesome threat they perceived and with which they had been dealing since early in 1945. The situation was little better in Congress. It was true that Senator Arthur Vandenberg had come around during and immediately after the war to an internationalism that tended to support the stance developing with the Truman administration. But the extent to which the senator's newly gained world view was shared by others in the Republican party was questionable. Indeed, what the Truman administration saw, as it confronted the 80th Congress, was a Republican majority that had bashed the Democrats the previous November for their "appeasement" of communism but now would cut the administration's defense budget.

WORLD VIEW BECOMES POLICY: THE TRUMAN DOCTRINE AND THE MARSHALL PLAN

From within the administration, it seemed that the direction of history was hanging in the balance. The post–World War II international system was perceived as on the verge of being overwhelmed by the onslaught of Soviet expansion. However, "the danger of these Soviet moves," despaired one inside chronicler, "was not generally realized by the American people";[17] without such a realization, the full power of the United States could not be mobilized to curb the impending disaster. Thus, when the British informed Washington in February 1947 that they were no longer economically able to deal with the volatile Greek domestic situation, which had once again flared into open civil war, the adminsitration viewed the situation as both a crisis and an opportunity. "[R]apidly, in an orderly manner, and [with] virtually no dissent, the executive branch of the government decided to act"[18] in the form of a spectacular special message to Congress requesting $400 million in economic assistance for Greece and Turkey. The lack of dissent indicates how well established the predisposition was toward U.S. intervention in the face of perceived Soviet expansion. American involvement in Greece and Turkey was never really in question in the Truman administration. If a crisis existed in the spring of 1947, it concerned whether Congress and the American people could be convinced to enlist in the crusade that had been taking shape within the administration for more than a year.

The congressional leadership was enlisted in a dramatic meeting on February 27 in which Undersecretary of State Acheson, believing that "we were met at Armageddon,"[19] presented the crisis in appropiately apocalyptic terms. A "highly likely Soviet breakthrough" in Greece, he said, could open up three continents to "Soviet penetration. . . . Like apples in a barrel infected by one rotten one, the corruption of Greece would infect Iran and all to the east." Africa, Asia Minor, Egypt, and then Europe — via the communist parties of France and Italy — would all succumb to the "infection." An "eager and ruthless opponent" — the Soviet Union — was prepared to seize the moment if the United States would not.[20]

The stunned congressional leadership agreed that they would support the president if he would go before Congress and the American people and state matters in Acheson's forceful manner.[21] Thus, from the onset, the Truman Doctrine had a dual purpose. First, it was a public statement of the foreign policy assumptions and positions that formed the basis for the emerging consensus within the Truman administration. Second, Truman's statement was aimed at the American public as it attempted to mobilize them in support of a world role for the United States.[22] Thus, Truman sought and in large measure succeeded in setting forth the idiom of the debate and the central questions of American foreign policy for the next twenty-five years. Truman's speech was to be, in Hans Morgenthau's words, the "intellectual capital" of the cold war.[23]

The Truman Doctrine

Truman's presentation to the Congress centered on what he termed the "broader implications" of U.S. assistance to Greece and Turkey. The postwar world, he asserted, was divided between two antithetical ways of life: one based on freedom, another on coercion.[24] More important:

> We shall not realize our objectives, however, unless we are willing to help free peoples to maintain their free institutions and their national integrity against aggressive movements that seek to impose upon them totalitarian regimes. This is no more than a frank recognition that totalitarian regimes imposed upon free peoples by direct or indirect aggression, undermine the foundations of international peace and hence the security of the United States.[25]

The security of the United States, the most basic of foreign policy values, was found only in "international peace," that is, in a system of international order. American security was, therefore, interdependent with the security of particular states such as Greece and Turkey. Moreover, the security of each state was vital to the security of the whole system.

> It would be an unspeakable tragedy if these countries which have struggled so long against overwhelming odds, should lose that victory for which they have sacrificed so much. Collapse of free institutions and loss of independence would be disastrous not only for them but for the world. Discouragement and possibly failure would quickly be the lot of neighboring peoples striving to maintain their freedom and independence.[26]

Acheson had spoken privately of "rotten apples . . . spreading corruption and infection"; the president was now speaking of "confusion and disorder," the "collapse of free institutions," and "discouragement"; and future American leaders would warn of falling dominoes. In each case, the underlying premise was the same: Peace and world order were now indivisible. Hence the loss of one country carried with it ominous implications for the entire structure of world order. (This, after all, was the lesson of Munich.) In essence, therefore, the security of the world and the security of the United States were entwined, perhaps synonymous. It was now imperative that the United States build and then maintain a world order congenial to its own way of life. In the analysis of Truman and his advisers, if aggression were allowed to proceed, the fabric of global security would unravel, and American security would inevitably be jeopardized.

Truman's statement implied, however, that U.S. policy involved a great deal more than a simple internationalism. The threat to international security was defined in terms of the regimes and domestic systems of other members of the international system.

> [I]t must be the policy of the United States to support free peoples who are resisting attempted subjugation by armed minorities or by outside pressures.
> I believe that we must assist free peoples to work out their own destinies in their own way.[27]

The internal affairs of other states were now an essential component of world order. Whether a country's political, economic, and social system was "totalitarian" or "democratic" — whether, in short, its way of life conformed to the American vision of what was best or to the Soviet vision — was now central to the question of world order. The internal political economies of states were fused with the quality of world order; and intervention in the former was now regarded as legitimate to preserve an American vision of the latter. The administration's reluctance to extend further aid or American combat support to Chiang Kai-shek and Acheson's refusal under questioning on Capitol Hill to equate the Chinese and Greek cases suggested that there were limitations on the scope of this argument.[28] But there remained an underlying activist and globalist impulse in the Truman Doctrine that was to transcend this initial caution and play itself out over the following decades in Korea, Lebanon, Berlin, the Bay of Pigs, the Dominican Republic, and Vietnam.

The president seemed unequivocal about the instruments to be employed in implementing his doctrine: "I believe that our help should be primarily through economic and financial aid which is essential to economic stability and orderly political processes."[29] Truman's concept of economic assistance involved much more than simple bilateral aid. Rather, the use of economic assistance must be placed in the context of a broad conception of world economic order. Both the Roosevelt and the Truman administrations tied economic recovery to the creation of an international economic order predicated on the reduction and eventual elimination of tariffs and other obstacles to free trade. A fundamental element in free and expanding international trading systems was stable international monetary affairs, the absence of which during the 1930s had abetted the general economic collapse of the Depression and thereby contributed directly to World War II. To prevent a recurrence of this situation and establish the basis for stable world economic order, a set of loosely related institutions had been set up during and after the war: the International Monetary Fund (IMF), the International Bank for Reconstruction and Development (World Bank), and the General Agreement on Tariffs and Trade (GATT).[30] Thus, a primary thrust of American economic policy prior to the Truman Doctrine can be seen as economic recovery, reconstruction, and ultimately the development of a strong and monetarily stable free-trading international economic system as an end in itself. Yet even then, the central role of the dollar and the solitary strength of the American economy ensured American well-being and domination of such a system.[31] Furthermore, given American hegemony in the world economy, one could certainly anticipate the intrusion of American political objectives into the nascent world economic order of 1945 and 1946 despite the efforts of the framers of this economic order to separate trade and other international economic questions from political and security issues.[32]

The Truman Doctrine suggested, however, that the imperatives of the security policy might transcend the desire or logic of treating international economics and other political questions as separate domains. Truman had asserted that "the seeds of totalitarian regimes are nurtured by misery and want. They spread and grow in the evil soil of poverty and strife."[33] Thus, Truman seemed to view the two tracks of economic and politico–military policy as interrelated. Indeed, his appeal for economic assistance assumed that the relationship of "totalitarian regimes" and the "evil soil of poverty" was reversible, and that the instrumentations and processes of economic policy could be employed to bring about international order in the realm of "high" or security diplomacy. In summary, the germ of a grand design was implied by the Truman Doctrine: the transformation of a heretofore piecemeal use of economic assistance for recovery into a comprehensive assault on the conditions that gave rise to totalitarian regimes.

The Marshall Plan and the Soviet Union:
The Truman Doctrine's Meaning Emerges

Against a backdrop of worsening economic conditions in western Europe and in the presence of intensifying Russian suspicion and hostility toward American initiatives,[34] Acheson indicated the fundamentals of the economic policy that had been developing within the administration. First, the United States was seen as having to absorb large quantities of imports to stimulate productivity abroad. Second, additional emergency U.S. financing would be necessary. Furthermore, he stated: "We must take whatever action is possible immediately, *even without full Four Power agreement, to effect a larger measure of European, including German*, recovery."[35] In calling for European recovery and including German recovery and participation, Soviet objections notwithstanding, the opportunity for avoiding a further deterioration of Soviet–American relations was reduced. Acheson's emphasis on using American assistance to promote and defend democratic institutions subjected to totalitarian pressure indicated an acceptance, even encouragement, of a bifurcated Europe, and by implication a divided Germany as well. International economic instrumentalities and processes were, therefore, absorbed into the national security equation of the Truman Doctrine.

The fully elaborated European Recovery Program was proclaimed by Secretary of State Marshall at the Harvard University commencement in early June 1947. The secretary's speech restated the nexus of political and economic order at the heart of the administration's policy: "It is logical that the United States should do whatever it is able to do to assist in the return of normal economic health in the world, without which there can be no political stability and no assured peace."[36] It followed that American policy "should be the revival of a working economy in the world so as to permit the emergence of political and social conditions in which free institutions can exist."[37] The substance of Marshall's speech was a proposal for European economic integration rather than a piecemeal aid program. It required that the Europeans assume the initiative in establishing the structure within which they would receive American aid. At the same time, the Europeans could hardly refuse the American offer — and preconditions. Thus, the United States might realize its postwar objective of an integrated economic system encompassing most of the market economies of the world. An unspoken dilemma remained: How were the Soviets to fit into this scheme?

Soviet participation in the Marshall Plan seemed inconsistent with the explicit linkage of economic instrumentalities and American national security drawn by Acheson. Furthermore, members of the Department of State feared that allowing Soviet participation in the planning and administration of the program would lead to Soviet disruption of European integration and political exploitation of the continuing economic stagnation. The additional concern was raised that Soviet and Eastern European participation could undercut congressional support for the billions of dollars that would have to be requested. Nevertheless, disadvantages were inherent in not at least inviting the Russians: The onus for precipitating the inevitable political and economic division of Europe would fall on the United States and the Western Europeans if the Russians were snubbed.

The resolution of the dilemma lay in a course of action proposed by Kennan: The Soviets would be invited to participate,[38] but only on the condition that they would contribute raw materials and abide by any arrangements for mutual planning and economic integration that emerged.[39] In other words, the Soviets were to be asked to open up their economic planning and control and the economies of Eastern Europe to the scrutiny and implied control of capitalistic Western Europeans and ultimately the United States. Furthermore, they were to contribute raw materials to the reconstruction of these same Western states, including Germany. The prospect was breathtaking. The Soviets were being asked, in effect, to accept absorption into the American vision of world economic and political order. "If they are unwilling to do this," Kennan said, "we would simply let them exclude themselves. But we would not ourselves draw a line of division through Europe."[40] Predictably, but not without some preliminary negotiations with the United States in Paris in June and July,[41] the Soviets rejected the Marshall Plan.

The Soviets had been maneuvered precisely as Kennan had projected; thus, post–Marshall Plan diplomacy may be viewed as a brilliant tactical victory for American diplomacy. However, in the long run it proved to be a decisive turn toward the depths of the cold war. The Soviets now seemed convinced that American policy was committed to European hegemony and ultimately the political and economic penetration of Eastern Europe.[42] The United States redoubled its efforts to bring about European economic integration, including deciding to go ahead with German redevelopment and the creation of an independent West German state. In Herbert Feis's words, "The rift over Germany became an irreparable rupture."[43] On December 19, 1947, a Marshall Plan request for $17 billion was submitted to Congress for approval, and at the end of the month, informal talks were begun on the formation of some kind of Western European defense arrangement.

THE SUMMING UP:
CONTAINMENT IS DEFINED

In the summer of 1947, George Kennan, writing under the pseudonym "X," published a public restatement of his earlier theses concerning Soviet behavior and added a somewhat more distilled set of policy prescriptions.[44] There is perhaps no better summary statement of official thinking at this time than Kennan's article, for it encompasses most of the prevailing American assumptions concerning Soviet behavior and the appropriate American response to the situation.

Kennan wrote of Soviet policy as "a fluid stream which moves constantly, wherever it is permitted to move, toward a given goal. Its main concern is to make sure that it has filled every nook and cranny available to it in the basin of world power."[45] The flexibility of Soviet policy suggested dangers, but the internal weaknesses of their system also provided opportunities. In the first place, Soviet pressure would be on-going and not easily discouraged; "if it finds unassailable barriers in its path, it accepts these philosophically and accommodates itself to them."[46] Kennan believed, however, that

> the United States has it in its power to increase enormously the strains under which Soviet policy must operate, to force upon the Kremlin a far greater degree of moderation and circumspection than it has had to observe in recent years, and in this way to promote tendencies which must eventually find their outlet in either the break-up or the gradual mellowing of Soviet power.[47]

The manner whereby these "frustrations" and "strains" were to be induced and "moderation" and "circumspection" brought about is the prescriptive core of Kennan's argument:

> In these circumstances it is clear that the main element of any United States policy toward the Soviet Union must be that of a long-term vigilant containment of Russian expansive tendencies. . . . The Soviet pressure against the free institutions of the Western world is something that can be contained by the adroit and vigilant application of counter-force at a series of constantly shifting geographical and political points, corresponding to the shifts and maneuvers of Soviet policy.[48]

Kennan's statement was, in some respects, a more subtle and moderate assessment of Soviet behavior and prescription for American behavior than the public statements of other members of the Truman administration. One suspects, for example, that Kennan's admonition "that such a policy has nothing to do with outward histrionics; with threats or blustering or superfluous gestures of outward 'toughness'"[49] was directed at no less a figure than the president himself, for Kennan and others (notably Secretary of State Marshall) were known to have reacted nega- tively to the ideologically belligerent tone of the Truman Doctrine.

Nevertheless, because the article was a reflection of a consensus about the roots of Soviet behavior and a suitable response, Kennan's statement also was characterized by much of the expansive optimism and vague rhetoric of officials in the Truman administration. Thus, his language about a "firm containment designed to confront the Russians with unalterable counter-force at every point where they show signs of encroaching upon the interests of a peaceful and stable world" was more than a faint echo of Truman's and Acheson's rhetoric. The interrelated motifs of containment, confrontation, and "unalterable counter-force at every point" were sufficiently open-ended as to allow more militant prose- cutors of American policy to recast Kennan's vision of political and eco- nomic containment of Soviet power in Europe to one of global military containment.[50]

THE COLD WAR

If the view of the world from Washington was grim in the winter of 1947–1948, it was no less so from Moscow. Under American leadership, the capitalist countries seemed to be consolidating their position. Stalin may have surmised that American political and economic hegemony of the West would be the first step in forming a strong base for bringing pressure to bear on the Soviet dominance of Eastern Europe. The ini- tial pressure on the Soviets may have been limited to economic entice- ments, but then again the Americans would in time perhaps become sufficiently bold to instigate and support unrest in Eastern Europe. In sum, Soviet security seemed to require the maintenance of a strong So- viet political, economic, and military presence in the Eastern European countries occupied after the war.[51]

The Red Army, though reduced in size,[52] was adequate to what- ever immediate external military threat may have existed. Internally, however, Stalin felt compelled to strengthen his hand. He purged Eastern European regimes of anticommunist elements as well as nationalist Com- munist parties that were unwilling to subordinate themselves to the Soviet vision of the future. Stalin's policy collided most spectacularly with that of Tito in Yugoslavia. Tito's nationalism undercut Stalin's drive for con- solidation of Eastern Europe. Consequently, tensions heightened, replete with veiled threats, and eventually, in mid-1948, Tito broke with Sta- lin (with some confidence in U.S. economic assistance).[53]

In the meantime, replication of this insolence and insubordination had to be anticipated. A quick crushing of the Yugoslavs might have served Stalin's ends, but the Soviet leader seems to have entertained some doubt that he could end the matter quickly. The possibility of resource-consuming guerrilla conflict with Yugoslav Communists led by the same Tito who had successfully prosecuted a largely partisan war against the Germans two and a half years earlier could not have been appealing to Stalin. Stalin is said to have boasted that he could "shake my little finger and there be no more Tito" — but he did not behave as if he believed it. The image of the Russian bear grappling perhaps ineffectually with the Yugoslav midget would not inspire awe on the part of other Eastern Europeans. The Yugoslav situation deteriorated slowly while more decisive moves were made elsewhere. In Hungary, Bulgaria, and the other communist countries, "potential Titos were tracked down, demoted, tried and often executed. In none of the other satellites was there in fact that combination of factors which had enabled Yugoslavia to launch her definace, but the Soviets were not taking chances."[54]

The Czechoslovakian Coup

Nowhere was this militancy more manifest and with greater consequence for the future of East–West relations than in Czechoslovakia. Prior to 1948, Czech opposition parties coexisted in a coalition government, with the Communists maintaining a slight popular plurality. By February of 1948, however, the Communists were instructed to consolidate control in a country whose borders touched western and eastern Germany, Poland, Hungary, and the Soviet Union. Czechoslovakia was perhaps the most industrialized of the Central European states, and unlike eastern Germany and Poland, its industrial base had come through the war more or less intact. In short, Czechoslovakia was the geographic and industrial heart of the Soviet Central European glacis. Furthermore, the avowed American intention to integrate Western Europe, including Germany, into the Marshall Plan (which was received favorably among noncommunist Czechs), the fears of the possible magnetic effect of Western European recovery and even future political and economic penetration, intimations of a Western European alliance, and now the intraempire Titoist threat were apparently seen by Stalin as dangerously cumulative. In such an environment, he believed that he could not tolerate a Czech government whose president, Eduard Beneš, had proclaimed in May 1946, "Culturally we are Europeans. We will never range ourselves with East alone, or with the West alone, but always with East and West simultaneously."[55] Accordingly, on February 25, 1948, with the Russian army arrayed on the border and local Communists poised in and around Prague, the Czech Communist party took control of the government.

The West Reacts

In the West, however, Stalin's actions were seen as anything but defensive. The elimination of a few Eastern European Communists with nationalist visions was one thing, but the sight of the Czechs' bullied into submission created "coursing emotion" and "gave an emotional tone to the Western reaction."[56] The immediate reaction was an intensification of tentative discussion among the Western Europeans and Americans concerning some form of defensive alliance. By the third week in March, Britain, France, the Netherlands, Belgium, and Luxembourg signed in Brussels a 50-year mutual assistance pact "clearly directed at the Soviet Union."[57] On March 17, 1948, President Truman informed Congress that the growing menace of the Soviet Union was threatening the reconstruction of Europe. He called on Congress to provide full support for Western Europe and especially those countries that were, as Truman spoke, linking themselves through the Brussels accord.

Still, Truman and his top advisers moved cautiously. Although there was agreement within the upper levels of the administration on the general direction of American policy, disagreement existed concerning the instrumentalities to be employed. Second, also broad and deep concern was manifested about support from a Republican-dominated Congress for the imminent departure in policy toward a peacetime military alliance. Finally, we should not overlook Truman's domestic political circumstances: The fall of 1948 was to be a national time of reckoning. And in view of the Republican majorities in both houses of Congress that had resulted from the 1946 election, and the generally held opinion that the Republicans were already ahead in the race for the White House, it is understandable that Truman was uncertain of his base for a bold foreign policy.

Thus, Truman instructed Undersecretary of State Robert Lovett during April and May 1948 to work with Senator Vandenberg to produce a declaration of senatorial support for an American–Western European alliance. Simultaneously, the State Department entered into preliminary talks with the British, Canadians, and other representatives of the Brussels Pact concerning the structure and obligations of signatories of such an arrangement.[58] On May 19, Vandenberg, well briefed by high State Department officials, introduced his resolution; three weeks later, on June 11, 1948, the Senate passed the Vandenberg Resolution by a margin of sixty-four to four. President Truman could now claim bipartisan support for whatever course he chose.

The successful steering of the Vandenberg Resolution through the Senate seemed to confirm the existence of some operational latitude for President Truman. But the president faced seemingly irreconcilable, conflicting demands. His sense of fiscal needs and his domestic political strategy compelled him to advance his domestic programs aggressively, yet within a framework of fiscal responsibility. On the other side, however, was the ominous drift of events in Europe, which seemed to confirm the need for some kind of unified Western response, presumably underwritten by the United States. Indeed, the president had encouraged this in his March speech supporting the Brussels Pact and in his subsequent effort to get a Senate resolution of support for his European policy. But now he was being warned that a significant increase or the mere consideration of new defense spending could so inflate the economy that extensive economic controls would be inevitable—an unpleasant prospect in an election year.[59]

Complicating matters further was that, as of early 1948, no clear-cut strategic policy had yet emerged. The air force and congressional airpower advocates were urging reliance on an atomic-armed, long-range air force as the basis for the American defense posture. However, a good deal of skepticism existed concerning the viability of this posture.[60] It is probable, therefore, that in the event President Truman had been predisposed to rely heavily on military instrumentalities, the means were not available. In fact, Truman's approach to postwar defense requests indicates that he was not so predisposed. His rhetoric was tough, even belligerent, but, in the aftermath of the Czech coup, it was Marshall's European Recovery Program that received Truman's support as the best means for filling out the American relationship with the Europeans. He would support some increase in the defense budget, but not the $9 billion requested. In contrast to the Marshall Plan, which received complete and intensive support when it went before Congress, Truman cut the Defense Department's supplemental request by two thirds.

An identifiable structure of policy and programmatic assumptions seemed to be crystallizing. The most fundamental assumption set forth by Marshall, and apparently accepted by Truman, was that there was not going to be a war with the Soviet Union in the foreseeable future. The recent behavior of Stalin suggested that the Soviets would seek an oppressive politico–economic control of Eastern Europe, undergirded by Soviet conventional military strength. But also assumed was that the Soviets did not then have atomic weapons and were unlikely to possess them within the next five years. American strategic superiority was not in question. Prudence and the need for bureaucratic compromise might dictate that the new Department of Defense be allowed to develop and maintain the ability to deal with a theoretical Soviet strategic threat.

However, Marshall and the president did not perceive the threat as imminent. Far more important to the American posture envisioned by Truman and Marshall at this time was the economic reconstruction of Europe.

THE DEATH OF DIPLOMACY

The idea of European recovery as the foundation of American policy had many appealing qualities. Not the least of these was the possibility that, through European recovery, the United States might simultaneously frustrate the Soviets, unify all of Europe, and reduce or even eliminate the future need for massive U.S. economic assistance appropriations.[61] There were collateral benefits. A productive and economically integrated Western European economy might prove irresistible to Eastern Europeans and ultimately the Soviets themselves. Further, containment, and perhaps the eventual taming of communist excesses, could be implemented while avoiding the domestic dislocations brought on by the development and maintenance of a large military establishment. Thus, the response to Truman's call for international commitment and involvement could be both dynamic and economically finite. In the longer run, a growing capitalist Western Europe promised benefits for the postwar American economy. European recovery through the Marshall Plan held out the promise of an Atlantic community. This American–European relationship might become the basis of an even larger global economic system. In such a liberal, free-trading, and essentially capitalistic world, the United States, its economy unscathed by World War II, could not help but benefit, indeed, predominate.

In 1948, American efforts focused on the short-term dimensions of this Atlantic vision. In January 1948, German officials were urged to consider the formation of more centralized government structures that might assume some political functions.[62] And on January 22, 1948, the British called for a meeting the following month in London to discuss the future of Germany. Invitations were extended to the Americans, the French, and the Benelux countries. Pointedly, the Russians were not invited.

The London Conference urged the Western zones to move quickly toward the establishment of West German political institutions and processes that would allow the West Germans to assume control of their own political and, in large measure, economic affairs.[63] The means whereby this West German federal constitution was to be drawn up, ratified, and its relationship to the three occupation administrations defined were to remain points of contention until early 1949. Communists as well as some conservatives in the French parliament were especially reluctant to accept the degree of German autonomy implied by the conference recommendations and urged the greater control be reserved to the occupation powers.[64] Despite French ambivalence concerning reconstructed German economic power, the London conference summarized and institutionalized the developments of the preceding two years. The Western powers had now officially recognized "that German reconstruction is essential to the well-being of Europe."[65] Of equal importance, the commitment to the formation of a West German state and the exclusion of Soviet interests in that decision marks yet another intensification in the reciprocating dynamics of East–West distrust.

The thrust and specifics of the Marshall Plan proved discomforting to the French; to the Russians, they must have been appalling. As events unfolded in late 1947 and early 1948, Stalin's worst fears were materializing: Internal problems had developed in Eastern Europe. The Western powers were moving resolutely toward the reestablishment of the European political economy. Perhaps more distressing to Stalin, the seed of a new German state had finally sprouted with the completion of the London Conference. Prior to mid-1947, U.S. policy had been rhetorically tough, but there had been limited action to go with American posturing. Now, however, the United States had initiated a comprehensive and apparently long-run program of economic assistance designed to set in motion Western European economic integration and the creation of a new West German state that would eventually control the important Ruhr Valley industrial complex.[66] Moreover, the Soviets were isolated from and unable to influence these events directly. The Soviet Union's isolation was in part a product of its own actions beginning with Molotov's walk-out at the Paris conference in June 1947. But the United States was not entirely displeased with Soviet behavior, and, in the development of the Marshall Plan, had sought to structure the proposal, its promulgation, and its operation to make it unacceptable to the Soviets. The London Conference of early 1948 was the culmination of Western unilateralism[67] in that it expressly excluded Soviet participation and made clear that any future Four Power agreements would have to be consonant with the measures the West was initiating.[68]

In sum, both sides shared responsibility for the breakdown of diplomacy and for debasing the medium of diplomatic exchange. The early postwar period had been marked by tough negotiations and sometimes bitter diplomatic exchanges; nevertheless, there had been more than the semblance of diplomatic interaction as the two sides felt their respective ways through the ambiguities of the new postwar world. Now, however, things were taking an uglier turn, for East–West relations "had begun to assume the proportions of a struggle between two competing theologies. It has passed out of the realm of ambiguity into a period of moral clichés based on absolute definitions of good and evil that were to blight relations between the super powers for more than a decade."[69]

The increasing diminution of diplomacy left each side with the crudest and most dangerous of means for communicating with the other: threat, counterthreat, confrontation, and the escalation of confrontation. The actions and intentions of the adversary were to be evaluated in the worst light. The modalities of interaction were now to be played out within a syndrome of tests and demonstrations of will, a reciprocating and mutually reinforcing diplomacy of threat.

The Berlin Blockade

The norm of future East–West interaction emerged from Stalin's efforts to check what he now perceived to be a concerted Western effort to undermine Soviet security. First, he turned to the remaining point of institutionalized diplomatic contact in what may have been at best a half-hearted attempt to communicate his concerns about what was, to him, a deteriorating German situation. In February 1948, Stalin filed a formal protest in the Control Council before the London talks began and again in March when the conference ended. When, during the March meeting, the Russians were unable to get information on or a discussion of the London meeting, they broke off the talks. Stalin now turned to more direct means to communicate his position and influence Western behavior so that the German question could be reopened.

In April 1948, Stalin halted Western military supplies to West Berlin, located deep within the Russian zone. The Western reaction was to press on with the plans laid out at the London Conference. The Russians responded in turn with further interference with traffic into Berlin. Finally, in mid-June, at precisely the moment Tito's heresy broke into a total rupture with Stalin, culminating in Tito's formal expulsion from the Cominform (after a Russian-inspired coup directed at Tito had failed), the Western powers initiated a currency reform regarded by the Soviets as a precursor to economic chaos in their zone because they envisioned the old devalued German currency being dumped in the eastern zone. The Soviet reaction was to initiate on June 24, 1948, a full blockade of Berlin.

All surface movement in and out of Berlin was at a complete standstill, and both sides quickly defined the situation as a mutual testing of will. General Clay, in messages described as "pulsating," implored the president to resist and break the blockade with force; others advised conceding Berlin to the Russians. Truman never seriously contemplated the latter.[70] Nor, on the other hand, did he adopt the bold course of action proposed by Clay. Instead, he ordered an airlift of supplies into West Berlin. Two weeks later, he ordered two groups of atomic-capable B-29's to England, although it is not clear that nuclear weapons were in fact deployed outside the United States. Nevertheless, by the end of July, more than sixty B-29's were in Europe, and no effort was made to conceal the fact.[71]

In August 1948, Stalin granted an interview with the ambassadors of the Western Allies. The Allied ambassadors were interested in reasserting Western access routes to West Berlin, whereas Stalin sought to shift negotiations to the broader question of recent events in West Germany, most notably the outcome of the London Conference. He wanted nothing less than the cessation of efforts to form a West German government and the full restoration of Four Power control of Germany, in which case the Western powers were welcome back in Berlin. It seems, therefore, that Stalin was attempting to use the blockade as leverage to get at the far more salient issue of Germany's political future. The West, on the other hand, was now committed to a diametrically opposed course, because the West Germans were to begin drafting a constitution within weeks. Talks deadlocked, and the situation in Germany reached a perilous state as Truman asked his advisers in early September to "brief me on bases, bombs, Moscow, Leningrad, etc. I have a terrible feeling . . . that we are close to war. I hope not . . . Berlin is a mess."[72]

Border incidents or conflict in and around Berlin were available if either side had wanted to fight. The airlift itself provided ample opportunity. From June–July 1948 until February 1949, food and fuel deliveries increased to more than seven thousand tons daily. To accomplish this, the Western Allies were landing a plane in West Berlin every two minutes. The Soviets, therefore, had no lack of targets if they had sought an igniting incident. Harassment continued, but no provocative incident occurred.

The unwillingness or inability of the Soviets to provoke open conflict may be attributed to the ambiguous threat posed by the American B-29's. More likely is the fact that, by blockading Berlin, Stalin hoped to force the West to negotiate about the political and economic future of all Germany. Simple diplomacy had proved inadequate during the preceding months, as the Western Allies had gone ahead unilaterally with their plans for the integration of a West German state into the European Recovery Program. Stalin undertook, therefore, the slow strangulation of West Berlin as a means for dramatizing his own demands.

If this was Stalin's intent, he misread feelings in Washington, London, Paris, and Ottawa. Officials in these capitals responded to Stalin's actions by accelerating the very trends the Soviet dictator sought to deflect.[73] From July through early December 1948, European military and diplomatic representatives met with counterparts from the United States and Canada and began developing a concrete proposal for joining the North Atlantic countries in a defense pact. In January 1949, Truman made passing reference to the new defense treaty in his State of the Union message, and, by February 1949, negotiations on the final language of the treaty were underway. Paralleling these events, a West German parliamentary council was elected in August 1948 and began drafting a West German constitution in September 1948. Simultaneously, the Americans, British, and French began to develop terms for the international authority of the Ruhr and to draft a new occupation statute, which would define Allied authority once the new West German state was in place. These arrangements included German management and, in some instances, German ownership of the Ruhr industries. Agreement on the West German constitution moved more slowly, but, by the spring of 1949, a constitution or basic law was approved by the military governors in the three Western zones.

It must have been clear to Stalin by early 1949 that the blockade would fail and that its effect had been totally unproductive. Rather than split the Western Allies and hasten the resumption of negotiations on Germany's future, the blockade brought the Allies together and probably facilitated intra-Allied bargaining on such contentious questions as the Ruhr authority and occupation rights. In addition, the Western powers, when confronted with the blockade, had moved quickly to extend the Brussels Pact into a North Atlantic defense arrangement that now included the United States. All of this activity pointed to a divided Germany with the West German state increasingly a part of an economically integrated Western Europe operating under an as yet undefined American military commitment.

Faced with these cumulating reverses, Stalin sought a way back from the confrontation of the blockade while at the same time trying to hold off the formation of West Germany. The blockade had originally been used as a stick with which Stalin sought to prod the West into acceptance of his position. Now he would try unsuccessfully to use the removal of the blockade as a carrot.

The Blockade
Is Lifted — The West Ascendant

In January and February 1949, the Russians made public overtures through press conferences followed by secret contacts at the United Nations proposing that, if the formation of West Germany could be delayed until after a foreign ministers meeting, the Soviets would consider lifting the blockade. Acheson, who had taken over as secretary of state in the second Truman administration, was aware of the thrust of Stalin's diplomacy:

> We . . . saw the danger in allowing Stalin to edge his way into the incomplete and delicate negotiations among us regarding our relations among ourselves and with the Germans in our zones, which could lead to disunity among us and no progress in lifting the blockade. The greatest danger of disunity lay in any postponement of our tripartite preparations together and with the Germans.[74]

The Soviets continued the secret contacts throughout April 1949, seeking some form of commitment to postpone preparations for the formation of the West German government, but the West would not yield. On May 4 the Russians finally agreed to go ahead with the lifting of the blockade on May 12, 1949, because it was clear now that private negotiations could take them no further. Perhaps Stalin concluded that public negotiations would bring pressure to bear on the West to make concessions. At a minimum, Stalin could end the blockade and perhaps save face.[75]

In the meantime, Secretary of State Acheson was working almost feverishly to ensure the complete isolation of the Soviets. In April 1949, while negotiations on the lifting of the blockade were underway, the NATO pact was completed and the German constitution drafted. In addition, the Western Allies hammered out agreements on virtually all outstanding issues concerning Germany. Moreover, just prior to the foreign ministers' meeting, a common understanding concerning tactics and procedures at the conference was reached. The Western powers' consensus hinged on the idea that they would turn down any Soviet proposal concerning Germany's political and economic future if that proposal was based on any other than Western policy and procedure.[76] In summary, the only things the Soviets wanted to discuss were to be nonnegotiable; or, as at Paris in 1947, negotiable only on Western terms.

The West expected very little from the conference, and the prophecy became a reality. "Our requirements" were deemed "not impossible"[77] by Acheson, but the Russians found them so, and the Paris meeting quickly settled into mutual recrimination. By all accounts, President Truman was not unhappy with the results of the conference. He publicly applauded Acheson for the skill with which he had carried off the tasks of ending the blockade while simultaneously maintaining the thrust of American policy in Europe. For the Russians, however, the dismal end of the conference marked the collapse of their effort to counter the Marshall Plan, the formation of West Germany, and NATO. It was, as Professor Marshall Shulman has noted, the "low point of Soviet diplomacy."[78] Washington's attention was now free to focus on the problem of institutionalizing and providing resources for the alliance that had been struck in the heat of the Berlin crisis — and the deteriorating situation in Asia.

FORMATION OF THE NORTH ATLANTIC TREATY ORGANIZATION

Robert E. Osgood, in his study of the early years of the NATO alliance,[79] has suggested that two conflicting concepts of the NATO alliance emerged in late 1948 and persisted even after the signing in April and ratification of the treaty in July 1949. First, the view was held, for the most part by American and European military planners, that NATO should be a large and fully integrated "trans-Atlantic military coalition." In line with this view, the defense ministers of the Brussels Pact countries had agreed that the alliance should proceed with a common defense policy under some sort of integrated command buttressed by a permanent group concerned with logistical and supply problems. The American Joint Chiefs of Staff were already on record as supporting such a concept, including an American supreme commander if fighting actually occurred. Furthermore, this concept of the alliance carried with it the implication of a local and forward defense of Western Europe. This was necessary because it was assumed that the most basic threat to European security was the large standing army of the Soviet Union. Moreover, from a continental perspective, there was the concern that unless the alliance formally committed to the forward defense of the continent, the Americans, the British, or both might revert to the kind of peripheral strategy they had adopted in World War II. The continental powers and especially France did not look forward to another prolonged liberation struggle. The logic of this position, therefore, was to commit the alliance partners and especially the Americans and the British to an automatic response to external aggression.

Opposition to this view existed in the Department of State, the White House, and the Congress. Instead of viewing the alliance as an American military trip wire, the treaty was interpreted as "intending to provide political and psychological reinforcement in the continuing political warfare of the Cold War."[80] This view held that it was the political, economic, and social weakness of Western Europe itself that opened up subversive opportunities for Soviet communism. The purported propensity for the Soviets to use force, as displayed in Czechoslovakia and Berlin, was viewed as "defensive reactions on the Soviet side to the initial success of the Marshall Plan initiative and to the preparations . . . to set up a separate German government in West Germany."[81]

Many advocates of a more political concept of NATO believed that communist political and economic pressure in the shadow of Soviet conventional military strength might force the Western Europeans into a neutral stance between East and West (in the jargon of a later time, they might be "Finlandized"), thereby threatening the Marshall Plan. In this view, the response was the intensification and success of the Marshall Plan itself, not a comprehensive and expensive U.S. military commitment to Europe's defense. At most, NATO was to be a "modest military shield" behind which the primary task of economic construction would go forward and European self-confidence be reestablished. From the perspective of many in the U.S. Congress, such a political and economic commitment should not entail an automatic commitment of U.S. military involvement.

The procedural question of automatic commitment was to be the most contentious issue in the drafting of the final language of the treaty. The Senate, with Acheson serving as both advocate and mediator, and the Western ambassadors struggled over this point during February and March 1949 and produced a compromise. The United States was not automatically committed to war if the treaty[82] came into force, thereby satisfying American minimalists, particularly those in the Senate. Conversely, by signing the treaty, the United States was committed to its provisions, which implied certain obligations on the part of the United States, including mutual aid, but what those obligations were and how they were to be fulfilled were not yet clear. But then, precision was not required in the spring of 1949, for in the heat of the Berlin crisis, a show of unity and agreement in broadest principle was all that was deemed necessary; operational specifics could be resolved later.

In his memoirs, Acheson noted that the April 4, 1949, NATO treaty signing ceremony was "dignified and colorful." He added, "The Marine Band added a note of unexpected realism as we waited for the ceremony to begin by playing songs from the currently popular musical play *Porgy and Bess*, 'I've Got Plenty of Nothin' and 'It Ain't Necessarily So.'"[83] The debate on the $1.3 billion Mutual Defense Assistance Program (MDAP), which was conceived by the Truman administration as the first installment on the NATO agreement, in no way clarified the strategic thinking underlying U.S. policy.

The NATO treaty was described by Acheson to the Senate as limited in its commitment of assistance. Indeed, the administration presented the request for the MDAP only after the treaty was approved in July

1949, thereby separating the more explosive question of material support from the principle of the alliance. When asked whether the treaty would lead to the United States' sending large numbers of troops to Europe "as a more or less permanent contribution to the development of these countries' capacity to resist," Acheson replied, "The answer to that question, Senator, is a clear and absolute 'no.'"[84]

Acheson was to eat these words eighteen months later. In the meantime, the administration's gambit was to minimize the apparent costs of the commitments under the NATO agreement; but this was, in the final analysis, a tactical extension of their own belief in the primacy of the Marshall Plan and that the material cost and implications of NATO could be minimized. The best evidence of this lies in the less than $15 billion defense budget President Truman had recommended to Congress in January 1949, the midpoint of the Berlin crisis. Furthermore, the logic of the fiscal year 1950 budget was carried forward with even greater vigor in the planning for fiscal year 1951. Louis Johnson replaced Forrestal in the Defense Department in 1949,[85] and held the fiscal year 1951 budget to a $13.5 billion ceiling. The secretary of defense chose as the target of his reductions the Army and especially the Navy's desire for a piece of the strategic bombing mission then monopolized by the Air Force. Congressional sentiment tended to run with the air power advocates, and the thrust of Truman's policy remained intact.[86]

The MDAP was received less enthusiastically, however, for it implied that the alliance was based on a doctrine of large-scale land war in Europe and was, therefore, inconsistent with the strategic doctrine that supposedly underlay the budget request. Moreover, the armed services, especially the Army, did not show much enthusiasm for the proposal because the military assistance program had been and continued to be a competitor for funds. The MDAP stalled in Congress and was passed only after being reduced to $1 billion and only after the president announced in late September that the Soviets had exploded their own atomic bomb. Its passage in this manner, resulting in large measure from the perceived urgency of the moment, obscured and left unanswered the many questions raised in the preceding months. Nevertheless, alliance planning went forward in the months after MDAP's passage and the explosion of the Soviets' atomic bomb. The specifics of initial NATO planning were not published, but Osgood has speculated that they involved the assignment of strategic bombardment and protection of sea lines of supply and communication to the United States and foresaw Europe providing the basis of conventional land forces.

By 1950, therefore, the political and economic reconstruction of Europe encompassing that of West Germany was well underway. Furthermore, an alliance structure had been established with Western Europe and a modicum of defense integration achieved that anticipated the reconstruction of European conventional capability by means of U.S. assistance. In the meantime, U.S. strategic superiority, coupled with the accelerating success of the Marshall Plan, was deemed adequate to the task of containing Soviet power in Europe.

In the long run, however, if American strategic superiority could be eliminated, even as its monopoly on atomic power was now broken, the prospect of some form of mutual atomic deterrance arose in which a conventional balance of forces would assume more and perhaps decisive importance. Of course, an erosion of American atomic superiority was not going to occur overnight, given the paucity of Soviet intercontinental delivery aircraft. Furthermore, it is doubtful that Stalin contemplated strategic warfare five years after the appalling losses of World War II. Indeed, Stalin's primary concern at this time was his vulnerability to the West's nuclear advantage.[87] No one in the administration, in short, saw war with the Soviets as imminent.

Nevertheless, the explosion of the Soviet atomic bomb contributed to the cross-currents and implicit contradictions that underlay the compromises and apparent success of American European policy in late 1949. In addition, the Chinese civil war built to a climax in late 1949, and with the collapse of the Nationalist Chinese, a chain of events was set in motion that eventually consumed the Truman administration.

CRISIS AND COLLAPSE IN ASIA

The momentous events in China did not take the Truman administration unawares. In view of American involvement in China during and immediately after World War II, it cannot be said the administration lacked information or concern about events in China. It is true, however, that the evolution of events in China was a lower-priority item for the Truman administration. China, indeed Asia, was thought to be on the periphery of the "basin of world power" of which Kennan had written. If countries or continents were to be reconstructed by and in the likeness of America, better that they be at the epicenter of world politics. On the periphery, America would, in Acheson's words, "wait until the dust settles," and then concern itself with the emergent balance of forces. But this was not enough for those in America who thought they had heard a call for world ideological confrontation and crusade in the Truman Doctrine.

The Civil War in China—and in Congress

Marshall had spent a good deal of 1946 in China trying to bring about some kind of reconciliation between the Communists and Chiang Kaishek. By the end of the year, however, negotiations had collapsed and Marshall had been recalled to Washington to assume direction of the Department of State. In January 1947, Marshall's report on the Chinese situation was made public. In it, Marshall pronounced a plague on both the Communist and Nationalist Chinese houses for their mutual distrust and extremism. By the end of January, the United States terminated all efforts at mediating the struggle; and in February and March 1947, full-scale fighting was renewed.

American policy was characterized by ambivalence, incrementalism, and what must have appeared to both the Communist Chinese and the conservatives in Congress as disingenuousness. In June 1947, more than $6 million in ammunition was provided the Nationalists, while Marshall claimed that the sale did not signify U.S. support for Chiang's regime. Lieutenant General Albert Wedemeyer was sent to China on a fact-finding mission and to inform Chiang that future assistance would be under American supervision and predicated on internal reform. Wedemeyer's report was unfavorable to the Nationalists and suggested that the Nationalists could succeed only by undertaking far-reaching political and economic reforms to correct what Wedemeyer saw as widespread corruption and inefficiency. Nevertheless, the Truman administration found itself unable or unwilling to cut Chiang's regime completely adrift. Thus, in November 1947, Marshall announced a new $300 million economic assistance program for China to begin the following year, although he conceded that the United States was finding it difficult to develop a course of action in which American funds could be expended with expectations of "getting about a 70-percent return in effectiveness of use."[88]

The Truman administration seemed to have convinced itself that the best strategy in 1947 and early 1948 was to stay in the Chinese game by means of economic assistance. No one seems to have been terribly optimistic—but then maybe something would turn up. The alternatives seemed unpleasant: China would fall to the Communists and the administration would be open to a merciless attack—in an election year—by the Republicans that, even as Roosevelt had sold out Eastern Europe at Yalta, Truman and the Democrats had now lost China. Moreover, cutting the Nationalists loose might threaten the bipartisan support so carefully nurtured for the administration's policy in Europe. The important thing in the short run, therefore, was not to lose nerve—press on, commit the minimum resources necessary to keep in the game in

Asia and simultaneously hold domestic critics at arm's length until after the election in November. Once the election was over, the entire situation could be reassessed.

In the meantime, this incremental holding strategy could never satisfy the Republicans who were calling for an all-out commitment similar to that in Europe. More important in the long run, the provision of *any* aid to Chiang, no matter how symbolic, could only reinforce Mao's suspicion and distrust, thereby complicating any future effort at reconciliation. By Christmas of 1947, Mao was publicly calling the Nationalists "reactionary forces" and "running dogs of American imperialism." Simultaneously, Chiang's regime and the Republicans were blaming President Truman for increasing communist control in Manchuria. Throughout the first half of 1948, political pulling and pushing over the size and conditions to be attached to American aid to Chiang persisted in the Congress. The game was not unlike the one to be played out twenty years later in Southeast Asia by another Democratic president.

But nothing changed in China as the military reverses accumulated. While members of Congress were demanding a firm position, Secretary Marshall and the State Department remained ambivalent. In August, Secretary Marshall had advised the American embassy in China that the United States would not support a coalition government that included Communists. On the other hand, the United States would not try to mediate the civil war again. Beyond the provision of some economic and military assistance, Mr. Marshall advised the embassy that it was "not likely that the situation will make it possible for us at this juncture to formulate any rigid plans for our future policy in China."[89]

A Decision To "Let the Great Tree Fall"

President Truman's reelection in 1948 allowed the administration to resist a commitment of full support for Chiang. Thus, when two weeks after the election Chiang requested an increase in aid to save his regime, President Truman was noncommittal. Moreover, when Chiang's wife arrived in Washington in December with a request for $3 billion in aid, she was ignored by the administration. Just prior to her arrival, the administration had received the report of Major General David Barr, Director of the U.S. Military Advisory Group to the Government of China. General Barr's belief was that:

> The military situation has deteriorated to the point where only the active participation of United States troops could effect a remedy. . . . No battle has been lost since my arrival due to lack of ammunition or equipment. Their military debacles in my opinion can all be attributed to the world's worst leadership and many other morale destroying factors that

lead to a complete loss of will to fight. . . . The Generalissimo has lost much of his political and popular support.[90]

Secretary Marshall agreed that the only way to save Chiang's regime was to commit American troops, but he would not recommend such a course.

The inference was clear: The administration would now attempt to put even more distance between itself and the Nationalist Chinese without moving to a position of real neutrality. In early 1949, the White House instructed the State Department "that in order not to discourage Chinese resistance to communist aggression, military aid should not be suspended, but no effort should be made to expedite it." Throughout May, June, and much of July 1949, major cities in southern China continued to fall to the Communists, but the administration stood fast in its refusal to intervene. Earlier, in February 1949, Acheson had been asked by members of Congress to predict the course of events in China and had responded that "when a great tree falls in the forest one cannot see the extent of the damage until the dust settles."[92] Acheson insists that his "waiting until the dust settles" was not a description of American policy, but it was taken as such.[93] Certainly Acheson's willingness to watch mutely the chain of Nationalist disasters in China stood in marked contrast to his feverish activity during this same period concerning American European policy. He was clearly not prepared to let the great European tree fall.

With the NATO treaty ratified in mid-July 1949 and the MDAP submitted to Congress, Acheson prepared to go to the public with what had been American policy for months. On July 27, he announced that American policy in Asia would be subjected to a full review. Ten days later, the Department of State released a White Paper of more than a thousand pages that sought to absolve the United States of all responsibility for the impending collapse of the Nationalist Chinese. The White Paper emphasized that the only manner in which the Nationalists could be saved would be through American intervention but noted that such an intervention would have been "resented by the mass of the Chinese people, would have diametrically reversed our historic policy, and would have been condemned by the American people."[94]

The report was met with a firestorm of criticism from all sides but especially from the right, where the report was labeled "a 1,054-page whitewash of a wishful, do-nothing policy which has succeeded only in placing Asia in danger of Soviet conquest."[95] But the rage of Nationalist China's supporters in the Congress could not prevent what Acheson was prepared to accept when he took office. On September 21, 1949, the Nationalist Chinese tree crashed to the ground as the People's Republic of China was proclaimed. On October 1, Mao Zedong's new government was inaugurated in Beijing (Peking) with Zhou Enlai as premier and foreign minister. By the end of the year, Chiang Kai-shek had ensconced himself on Taiwan and was calling for American aid.

AMERICAN POLICY REAPPRAISED

The combined reverberations of the Nationalist Chinese collapse and the Soviets' atomic explosion gave impetus to a reassessment of American policy. The result in early 1950 was Policy Paper Number 68 of the National Security Council, "United States Objectives and Programs for National Security," or NSC-68, which became an overarching conceptual framework incorporating past American policy up to 1950 and establishing important parameters for future policy.[96] Before it was completed, however, one of the questions of late 1949 was resolved, for on January 31, 1950, the president decided to go forward with the development of the hydrogen bomb.

The Hydrogen Bomb Decision

One of the most immediate effects of the Soviet atomic bomb explosion was a debate within the American foreign and defense policy-making community over how the United States might maintain its pre-1949 nuclear superiority. The debate was intensified by the fact that moving up to the next level of nuclear weaponry, the hydrogen bomb, would involve a truly awesome increase in explosive capacity—a thousandfold increase over the atomic weapons used at Hiroshima and Nagasaki. The military advantages seemed more decisive than had been the case with atomic weapons, hence the military attractiveness of technological escalation. This very fact of a quantum leap in destructiveness made the weapon especially repugnant to many in the scientific community. With the government, all of the members of the General Advisory Committee to the Atomic Energy Commission (AEC), as well as a majority of the commission itself, opposed going forward.[97] The Defense Department favored development on a crash basis, but AEC Chairman David Lilienthal refused to move until all the foreign policy implications of the hydrogen bomb had been considered. This meant, of course, that the Department of State was brought into the debate, but disagreement existed also within the department.

George Kennan, who was leaving as director of the Policy Planing Staff, had prepared a memorandum on the question of the hydrogen bomb and, more broadly, U.S. nuclear policy as it related to international control.[98] Kennan underscored what he regarded as extreme ambiguity and confusion in American policy on nuclear weapons and their use. He urged, therefore, that there be a complete review of the entire question of the "first use" of these weapons by the United States, and he emphasized that he was opposed to any doctrine of "first use." He did not challenge the necessity of maintaining such weapons until some form of disarmament arrangements could be worked out. In the meantime, however, Kennan urged that "we remain prepared to go very far, to show considerable confidence in others, and to accept certain risks for ourselves, in order to achieve international agreement on their removal from international arsenals."[99] In opposition to this position were Paul Nitze, the new director of the State Department's Policy Planning Staff, and Dean Acheson, who believed that immediate research and development should begin, given the likelihood that Soviet research was proceeding.[100] President Truman concurred with Acheson's view that further delay would not be wise, and announced on January 31, 1950, that the United States would proceed with the development of the hydrogen bomb.

Thus, on the hydrogen bomb decision, the worst-case assumption concerning Soviet capabilities and behavior was made and assumed primary importance in the American decision. Kennan sensed a "growing tendency in Washington . . . to base our own plans and calculations solely on the *capabilities* of a potential adversary, assuming him to be desirous of doing anything he could to bring injury to us, and to exclude from consideration, as something unsusceptible to exact determination, the whole question of that adversary's real *intentions*."[101] Kennan's concerns were regarded by Acheson and Nitze as "obscure argument" based on a kind of intuitive approach to policy making. Such an approach, Acheson conceded, had great utility and applicability in foreign operations; however, in his view, "its value . . . was limited in Washington." In Acheson's opinion, "what [the president] needed was communicable wisdom, not mere conclusions, however soundly based in experience or intuition. . . ."[102] Acheson saw himself providing such "communicable wisdom" in the hydrogen bomb decision, and he sought to do the same in the drafting and promotion of NSC-68.

NSC-68

The drafting of NSC-68 was undertaken by a group of Department of State and Department of Defense planners working under the immediate direction of Paul Nitze and the Policy Planning Staff. Not unlike the authors of the Truman Doctrine, the authors of NSC-68 saw the world as essentially bipolar, only now the polarization of world politics was not a temporary one, but rather a "fundamentally altered" distribution of world power such that two nations, the United States and the Soviet Union, confronted each other with profoundly antithetical objectives and ideals in an international system in which "conflict has become endemic."[103] The Soviets' objectives were threefold, involving (1) consolidation of their hold on the Soviet Union as the ideological and political center of world communism; (2) consolidation of control over existing and extension of control to new satellites; and (3) the "complete abolition or forcible destruction" of power centers that opposed the Soviet aspiration for world hegemony. These Soviet objectives were "wholly irreconcilable" with the objectives of a free society. Moreover, "the assault on free institutions is worldwide now, and in the context of the present polarization of power a defeat of free institutions anywhere is a defeat everywhere. . . . In a shrinking world which now faces the threat of atomic warfare, it is not an adequate objective merely to seek to check the Kremlin design, for the absence of order among nations is becoming less and less tolerable. This fact imposes on us, in our own interest, the responsibility of world leadership," which would require "a much more rapid and concerted build-up of the actual strength of both the United States and the other nations of the free world. . . . [T]his will be costly and will involve significant domestic financial and economic adjustments."[104]

NSC-68 provided a generally bleak assessment of the respective capabilities of the United States and the Soviet Union in this total struggle between "free society" and the "implacable purpose of the slave state." First, the nuclear superiority of the United States was deemed to be of limited duration, with a stalemate of nuclear power anticipated in 1954, although the United States might extend its advantage if hydrogen weapons were perfected rapidly. The Joint Chiefs of Staff were cited as concluding that the Soviets would be able by 1950 to overrun most of Western Europe, drive into the Middle East, consolidate control of Asia, and initiate air and sea attacks in the Atlantic basin, including attacks on "selected targets with atomic weapons, now including targets in Alsaka, Canada, and the United States."[105]

Faced with this grim prospect, what should the West, and especially the United States, do? First, Western European recovery and the NATO alliance should be fully implemented, because only in this way could the purported Soviet conventional military advantage be countered. The prospect was long-run unrelieved tension and danger, and, under these circumstances, the framers of NSC-68 recommended "a rapid build-up of political, economic, and military strength in the free world" with the United States as the center of the effort. Furthermore, the reconstructed military capability of the United States and the West should be such that it surpassed that of the Soviet Union, and the West should be prepared to employ the capability in a clear-cut, unequivocal, and even "offensive" manner when challenged by communist power.[106]

The authors of NSC-68 were fully cognizant of the domestic implications of this proposal: a prolonged commitment of resources to military purposes and reduction of expenditures for other programs. More specifically, the paper argued that the national economy was sufficiently dynamic that "in an emergency the United States could devote upward of 50 percent of its gross national product" to national security if necessary. That is, rather than the $13 to 15 billion defense budgets of the postwar years, military budgets proportionate to those of World War II were acceptable—and perhaps essential in view of the threat confronting the United States and the free world.[107]

Summary

The picture painted by Nitze's group was, to say the least, a dark one. The inference was that the policies developed within the Marshall Plan framework were no longer adequate, because the fall of China and the acquisition of nuclear weapons by the Soviets suggested "a permanent and fundamental alteration in the shape of international relations. . . . The issues that face us are momentous, involving the fulfillment or destruction not only of this Republic but of civilization itself."[108] Under these circumstances, if the ideals and objectives of "American life" were to be protected and furthered, an equally permanent and fundamental change in American policy must occur. Significantly, NSC-68 concluded that in such a transformation of American policy, negotiations—especially negotiations concerned with nuclear weapons, mutual arms reduction, or the control of atomic energy—were not likely to be beneficial.

> Negotiation is not a possible separate course of action but rather a means of gaining support for a program of building strength, or recording, where necessary and desirable, progress in the cold war, and of facilitating further progress while helping to minimize the risk of war. Ultimately, our objective [is] to negotiate a settlement with the Soviet Union . . . on which the world can place reliance as an enforceable instrument of peace. But it is important to emphasize that such a settlement can only record the progress which the free world will have made in creating a political and economic system in the world so successful that the frustration of the Kremlin's design for world domination will be complete.[109]

Negotiations were conceived, therefore, not as viable good faith instruments of Soviet–American interaction, but rather as ratifications of "progress in the cold war." In view of this jaundiced and narrowly in-strumental conception of negotiations, it is not surprising that the thrust of the proposal was that the United States and the West must seek and maintain military superiority over the Soviet Union so as to confront and override the inevitability of Soviet aggression at each turn. Indeed, NSC-68 refused to rule out the first use of nuclear weapons by the United States.[110]

THE POLICY REAPPRAISAL APPRAISED

Thinking at the top of the Department of State had turned very nearly 180 degrees in less than two years. Whereas Marshall concerned him-self, to an extent, with how the Russians might perceive and react to an American action, Acheson seemed to care primarily about Russian capabilities. Attempts to evaluate Soviet intentions were deemed "in-teresting" but not really applicable to the task confronting the new secre-tary of state. The task, as Acheson saw it, was a redirecting of American policy away from the "soft" political and economic containment of the Marshall Plan. World politics was now cast in harsh relief—the grim remorseless struggle of nuclear-armed and ideologically driven comba-tants: "Our analysis of the threat combined the ideology of communist doctrine and the power of the Russian state into an aggressive expan-sionist drive, which found its chief opponent and, therefore, target in the antithetic ideas and power of our own country."[111]

In Secretary Acheson's view, however, the power of America was not yet realized because too many in the United States persisted in two outmoded beliefs. The first had been held by Marshall when he was secretary of state—that the primary threat to world peace was the so-cial and economic chaos of Western Europe, a threat that could be elimi-nated through American economic and moral assistance culminating in the economic unification of Europe. "This I did not believe," Acheson asserts.

> The threat to Western Europe seemed to me singularly like that which Islam had posed centuries before, with its combination of ideological zeal and fighting power. Then it had taken the same combination to meet it: Germanic power in the east and Frankish in Spain, both energized by a great outthrust of military power and social organization in Europe. This time it would need the added power and energy of America, for the drama was now played on a world stage.[112]

The crisis was not mere economic recovery; the barbarian was once again quite literally at the gates of Europe. And, once again, it would

require "a great outburst of military power and social organization" —
a reconstructed Europe but, most importantly, NATO (including "Germanic power") — to ensure that civilization might hold. Mobilizing Europe was necessary, but not sufficient, because the barbarian was at the gates everywhere, and in this global confrontation, American "energy and power" were also necessary. Acheson and his colleagues were convinced that this energy and power, if mobilized, would also be sufficient.

However, the mobilization of American power on the scale deemed necessary ran up against the second of the great misconceptions thought to be widely held in Washington — that domestic ruin would follow on the heels of the reallocation of resources proposed by Secretary Acheson. The problem was complicated by the fact that no less a figure than the president and his White House staff seemed sympathetic to this view: in early 1950, the president was sticking to his $13 billion ceiling for the Defense Department's fiscal 1951 budget, and "talk of even a $10 billion budget ceiling for fiscal 1952 was serious enough to have prompted preliminary soundings on it."[113]

Yet, the administration was obviously not of one mind. NSC-68 had been, after all, presidentially commissioned and signed, and Truman was certainly aware of his new secretary of state's predispositions concerning the Soviets and the threat they posed. Moreover, the rationale for his hydrogen bomb decision indicated Truman's receptivity to the views set forth in the document, even though his economic instincts may have forced him to recoil. Acheson did not suffer from any indecisiveness. He relates, "The purpose of NSC-68 was to so bludgeon the mass mind of 'top government' that not only could the President make a decision but that the decision could be carried out."[114] Indeed, much of the emphasis on and overstatement of the Soviet threat can and has been explained as a rhetorical tactic adopted by Nitze and Acheson as a means for stating the case for an increased American defense effort as persuasively as possible.[115]

> The task of a public officer seeking to explain and gain support for a major policy is not that of the writer of a doctoral thesis. Qualification must give way to simplicity of statement, nicety and nuance to bluntness, almost brutality, in carrying home a point. It is better to carry the hearer or reader into the quadrant of one's thought than merely to make a noise or to mislead him utterly.[116]

The perspective and policies to which the listeners were to be persuaded were not without their detractors. Within the Department of State, George Kennan and Charles Bohlen, the two foremost Soviet experts in the U.S. government, were skeptical of both the analysis of Soviet policy set forth in NSC-68 and the way in which the analysis was to be employed. Kennan persisted in a more subtle and complex view of Soviet behavior and viewed Nitze's statement of Soviet intent as simplistic. Both Bohlen and Kennan regarded Soviet behavior as too complex to encompass in such a planning document. Indeed, they expressed reservations concerning the entire exercise because it forced extremely complex and delicate considerations of policy into the sterile abstractions of a planning document. From such a statement, higher officials lacking perspective and a sense of nuance would be prone to draw even more simple-minded conclusions.[117] Acheson's perceived need for serving as militant missionary among the benighted of the Truman administration underscores and extends Kennan's point. For, having bludgeoned the top minds of government, can one realistically expect that same government to respond to the ambiguity and change of world politics with sophistication and conceptual elegance?

Let us reemphasize, however, that fundamental substantive differences existed between the positions represented by Kennan and Acheson. To Kennan, the real threat confronting the West was political and economic. He saw no real military threat either to Western Europe or Western ideals. Ironically, as we have traced in this chapter, the policies developed and pursued by Marshall, although he may have regarded them as limited and no real threat to Soviet security, were taken as such by Stalin. An economically strong Western Europe, including a new German state, when combined with his own difficulties in Eastern Europe and at home, were unacceptable pressures from Stalin's increasingly isolated standpoint. Moreover, the means adopted by the West for implementing their policies excluded Soviet participation, hence Stalin's trying, through the Berlin crisis, to force his way into the West's decisions on Germany. The Berlin crisis became in turn the opportunity for the emergence of the position represented by Acheson: The threat to Western Europe was essentially military, and Stalin's moves were not — as Kennan argued — desperate, but limited actions by an isolated Soviet dictator playing his last cards. The fall of China and the explosion of the atomic bomb by the Soviets seemed to confirm that Stalin represented a deeper and darker threat, a dislocation of history, to which NATO, the Mutual Defense Assistance Program, the hydrogen bomb, and a massive increase in U.S. military preparedness were the answers.

In summary, the president, the bureaucracy, Congress, and the country were suspended in mid-1950 between a past that was captured in Kennan's admonition that American policy must be one of a "long-term vigilant containment" of Soviet power that avoided "outward histrionics: without threats or blustering or superfluous gestures of outward toughness" and Acheson's Wagnerian vision of "the road to freedom and to peace," which was a "hard one." In Acheson's view:

> The times in which we live must be painted in the dark sombre values of Rembrandt. The background is dark, the shadows deep. Outlines are obscure. The central point, however, glows with light; and, though it often brings out the glint of steel, it touches colors of unimaginable beauty. For us, that central point is the growing unity of free men the world over. This is our shaft of light, our hope, and our promise.[118]

The main difference in the perspectives lay in their proposals for action. Kennan, like Acheson, saw a prolonged confrontation, but it was to be one of political and economic containment — like the Marshall Plan, a largely symbolic alliance — in which even risks were to be taken to bring about arms control and broader negotiations. Acheson feared world domination by Soviet ideology and military power, the containment of which would require a full-fledged military alliance with Europe abroad and a subordination of domestic priorities to national security needs, which were in fact indistinguishable from global security needs. Moreover, meaningful negotiations were deemed unlikely except when carried out in the presence of Western political, economic, and above all, military strength — in short, "the glint of steel."

President Truman apparently stood somewhere between those perspectives and prescriptions. Perhaps by mid-1950 he was somewhere closer to Acheson's view of the threat but unwilling to pursue vigorously Acheson's response.[118] The policy proposed in NSC-68 remained, therefore, tentative. But on June 24, 1950, the North Korean army crossed the 38th parallel into South Korea, and most of the remaining uncertainties vanished. Acheson's road would be taken.

NOTES

1. Dean Acheson, *Present at the Creation* (New York: W.W. Norton, 1969), p. 196.
2. Walter LaFeber, *America, Russia and the Cold War 1945–1971* (New York: John Wiley, 1972), p. 30.
3. Marshall Shulman, *Stalin's Foreign Policy Reappraised* (New York: Atheneum, 1963), pp. 13–21. See also Fraser J. Harbutt, *The Iron Curtain: Churchill, America, and the Origins of the Cold War* (New York: Oxford University Press, 1986), p. 28.
4. For examples of American reaction, see John L. Gaddis's discussion of the speech and its aftermath in *The United States and the Origins of the Cold War, 1941–1947* (New York: Columbia University Press, 1972), pp. 299–302.

5. Winston Churchill, "The Sinews of Peace," March 5, 1946, *Vital Speeches of the Day*, Vol. 12 (March 15, 1946), p. 332.

6. Ibid.

7. George F. Kennan, "Excerpts from Telegraphic Message from Moscow of February 22, 1946," *Memoirs, 1925–1950* (Boston: Little, Brown, 1967), pp. 557–558. Kennan has admitted that he now reads the long telegram with "horrified amusement" because "it reads like one of those primers put out by alarmed congressional committees or by the Daughters of the American Revolution, designed to arouse the citizenry to the dangers of the Communist conspiracy" (p. 294).

8. Kennan's recommendations in this regard are not unlike the proposals of Senator J. William Fulbright, two decades later, that America should become "an intelligent example to the world" [Fulbright, *The Arrogance of Power* (New York: Vintage, 1967), p. 257]. Kennan suggested, for example, that the United States should "apprehend, and recognize [the Soviet Union] for what it is," "see that our public is educated to the realities," take "courageous and incisive measure[s] to solve internal problems of our own society," "formulate and put forward for other nations a much more positive and constructive picture of the sort of world we would like to see," and "have courage and self-confidence to cling to our own methods and conceptions of human society" (Kennan, op. cit., pp. 558–559).

9. Kennan claims, in retrospect, to have been uncomfortable with the emphasis placed on the threat of force (Kennan, op. cit., p. 558). For recent scholarly debate about Kennan's view of military strength and its utility at this time, see John Lewis Gaddis, "Containment: A Reassessment," *Foreign Affairs*, Vol 55, No. 4 (July 1977), pp. 873–887; Eduard Mark, "The Question of Containment: A Reply to John Lewis Gaddis," *Foreign Affairs*, Vol. 56, No. 2 (January 1978), pp. 430–440; and Gaddis' response in ibid., pp. 440–441. A final minisalvo between these two is in the *Newsletter* of the Society for Historians of American Foreign Relations, Vol. 9, No. 3, (September 1978), pp. 28–31. See also Kennan's contribution to this debate in "George Kennan on Containment Reconsidered," (with a reply from Mark), *Foreign Affairs*, Vol. 56 (April 1978), pp. 641–647; and David Mayers, "Containment and the Primacy of Diplomacy: George Kennan's Views, 1947–1948," *International Security*, Vol. 11 (Summer 1986), pp. 124–162.

10. Harry S. Truman, *Memoirs I: Year of Decisions* (Garden City, N.Y.: Doubleday, 1955), p. 556. Interestingly enough, Wallace had personally cleared his speech with Truman before delivering it. Truman, either through oversight or incomprehension, did not glean its departure from the tougher line he wished to establish with the Soviets. Truman did not fire Wallace, however, until Byrnes, his secretary of state, in Paris at a foreign ministers' meeting, threatened to resign "immediately." Richard Walton, *Henry Wallace, Harry Truman and the Cold War* (New York: Viking, 1976); and Robert J. Donovan, *Conflict and Crisis: The Presidency of Harry S. Truman, 1945–1948* (New York: Norton, 1977), pp. 224–228.

11. Truman, *Year of Decisions*, p. 552; and Gaddis, op. cit., p. 289.

12. See Shulman, op. cit., pp. 21–24; and Thomas W. Wolfe, *Soviet Power and Europe, 1945–1970* (Baltimore: Johns Hopkins University Press, 1970), p. 37. See also David Holloway, "Entering the Nuclear Arms Race: The Soviet Decision to Build the Atomic Bomb, 1939–1945," *Working Papers, The Wilson Center* (Washington, D.C.: July 25, 1979), p. 47. An atomic spy ring was broken in Canada in 1946, although most of the supposed secrets delivered to Soviet agents were already known to Soviet physicists (Ibid., fn. 76, p. 58).

13. See Eric F. Goldman, *The Crucial Decade — And After: America, 1945–1946* (New York: Vintage, 1960), pp. 25–41.

14. *Department of State Bulletin*, Vol. 14, No. 363 (June 16, 1946), p. 1045.

15. Gabriel Almond, *The American People and Foreign Policy* (New York: Praeger, 1960), p. 73.

16. See Kenneth Waltz's comments on "Electoral Punishment and Foreign Policy Crises," in James Rosenau, ed., *Domestic Sources of Foreign Policy* (New York: Free Press, 1967), p. 293.

17. Joseph M. Jones, *The Fifteen Weeks* (New York: Harcourt, Brace & World, 1965), p. 47. For some idea of the world as viewed from within the Department of State at this time, see pp. 39–47.

18. Ibid. p. 11

19. *Present at the Creation* (New York: W.W. Norton, 1969), p. 219.

20. Ibid.

21. Some disagreement exists concerning exactly what Vandenberg, speaking for the group, said. Acheson recalls Vandenberg saying: "Mr. President, if you will say that to the Congress and the country, I will support you and I believe that most of its members will do the same" (Ibid., p. 219). Goldman, on the other hand, has Vandenberg saying: "Mr. President, if that's what you want, there's only one way to get it. That is to make a personal appearance before Congress and scare hell out of the country." (Goldman, op. cit., p. 59.)

22. For an extended discussion of the Truman Doctrine as essentially domestic propaganda, see Richard M. Freeland, *The Truman Doctrine and the Origins of McCarthyism: Foreign Policy, Domestic Policies, and Internal Security, 1946–1948* (New York: Schocken, 1974).

23. Hans J. Morgenthau, *A New Foreign Policy for the United States* (New York: Praeger, 1969), p. 1.

24. Truman, "The Truman Doctrine: Special Message to the Congress on Greece and Turkey, March 12, 1947," *Public Papers of the Presidents of the United States. Harry S. Truman. 1947.* (Washington: Government Printing Office, 1948), p. 178.

25. Ibid.

26. Ibid., p. 179.

27. Ibid., pp. 178–179.

28. See, for example, Acheson's testimony before the Senate Foreign Relations Committee on *S. 938 Assistance to Greece and Turkey*, 80th Cong., 1st Sess., March 24, 1947, esp. pp. 19–31.

29. "The Truman Doctrine," op. cit., p. 179.

30. For a straightforward introduction to international economic policy, see Joan Spero, *The Politics of International Economics*, 3rd ed. (New York: St. Martin's Press, 1985).

31. See Harry Magdoff, *The Age of Imperialism: The Economics of U.S. Foreign Policy* (New York: Monthly Review, 1968), esp. pp. 54–113, for a Marxist exposition of this thesis. William Diebold's *The United States and the Industrial World: American Foreign Economic Policy in the 1970s* (New York: Praeger, 1972) provides the conventional and more benign view of American policy. David P. Calleo and Benjamin Rowland's *America and the World Political Economy: Atlantic Dreams and National Realities* (Bloomington, Ind.: Indiana University Press, 1973) is a less conventional treatment.

32. On the separation of "low policy," i.e., economic policy, from the "high policy" of security issues, see Richard Cooper, "Trade Policy is Foreign Policy," *Foreign Policy*, No. 9 (Winter 1972–1973), pp. 18–21.

33. "The Truman Doctrine," p. 180.
34. Soviet hostility toward American economic plans were quite evident at the Foreign Ministers Conference held in the spring of 1947. See Feis, op. cit., pp. 208–220.
35. Dean Acheson, "The Requirements of Reconstruction," *Department of State Bulletin*, Vol. 16 (May 18, 1947), p. 994 (emphasis added).
36. George C. Marshall, "European Initiative Essential to Economic Recovery," *Department of State Bulletin*, Vol. 16 (June 15, 1947), p. 1160.
37. Ibid.
38. Ibid.
39. Accounts of Kennan's position are numerous but essentially alike. See Kennan, *Memoirs, 1925–1950*, p. 342; and Feis, op. cit., pp. 242–243. See also Jones, op. cit., p. 253.
40. Kennan, *Memoirs, 1925–1950*, p. 342.
41. Adam Ulam, *The Rivals* (New York: Praeger, 1973), pp. 128–129.
42. Shulman, op. cit., pp. 14–15; and Ulam, op. cit., p. 130.
43. Feis, op. cit., p. 281.
44. "X" (George F. Kennan), "The Sources of Soviet Conduct," *Foreign Affairs*, Vol. 25 (July 1947), pp. 566–582.
45. Ibid., p. 575.
46. Ibid.
47. Ibid., p. 582.
48. Ibid., p. 575–576.
49. Ibid., p. 575.
50. See Kennan, *Memoirs, 1925–1950*, pp. 364–365; and Ronald Steel, "Man Without a Country," in his *Imperialists and Other Heroes: A Chronicle of the American Empire* (New York: Vintage, 1973), pp. 53–55.
51. Ulam, op. cit.; and Shulman, op. cit., pp. 14–15, 258.
52. The actual size of the Soviet military at this time is a question of some dispute. For a review of the issue and the numerous estimates, see Wolfe, op. cit., pp. 9–11.
53. Ulam, op. cit., pp. 139–140. See also Robert M. Blum, "Surprised by Tito: The Anatomy of an Intelligence Failure," *Diplomatic History*, Vol. 12, No. 1 (Winter 1988), p. 57.
54. Ibid., pp. 140–141. Ulam notes that Stalin's boast concerning Tito's destruction is probably not a literal quotation, but Professor Ulam observes, "that is how he felt" (p. 140).
55. Quoted by Feis, op. cit., p. 292.
56. Ibid., p. 294.
57. Ibid., p. 296.
58. Truman's careful preparation was not always successful. The *sine qua non* of a meaningful alliance was seen by the Army as a sufficient standing army. The first time that universal conscription was suggested to Congress, it was voted down. There were reports, as the *Chicago Tribune* put it, that "in March, apparently in desperation, the Army handed President Truman a false intelligence report which 'pictured the Soviet Army as on the move,' when 'actually the Soviets were redistributing their troops to spring training stations'" (*Chicago Tribune*, June 19, 1948). Thus, when Truman called a joint emergency session of Congress to consider issues of defense, he had "evidence" that aided the passage of conscription as well as the Vandenberg Resolution.
59. For the most thorough analysis of the Truman administration's fiscal policy and its relationship to defense spending, see Warner R. Schilling, "The Politics of Na-

tional Defense: Fiscal 1950," in Warner R. Schilling, Paul Y. Hammond, and Glenn H. Snyder, *Strategy, Politics, and Defense Budgets* (New York: Columbia University Press, 1962). Most accounts of Truman's planning and budgeting eventually draw on this excellent set of essays; the following analysis is no exception.

60. For a full account, see George H. Quester, *Nuclear Diplomacy: The First Twenty-Five Years* (New York: Dunellen, 1970), p. 6 *passim;* the Report of the President's Air Policy Commission, *Survival in the Air Age* (Washington, D.C.: U.S. Government Printing Office, 1948); and David MacIsaac, "The Air Force and Strategic Thought 1945–1951," *Working Paper* No. 8, Wilson Center, International Security Studies Program, June 21, 1979, Washington, D.C., p. 27.

61. See the testimony of Undersecretary of State Robert Lovett before U.S. Congress, Senate Committee on Foreign Relations, *Interim Aid for Europe*, 80th Congress, 1st Session, 1947, esp. p. 99. See also Testimony of Secretary George C. Marshall before U.S. Congress, Senate Committee on Foreign Relations, *U.S. Assistance to European Economic Recovery*, 80th Congress, 2nd Session, 1948.

62. John Gimbel, *The American Occupation of Germany: Politics and the Military, 1945–1949* (Stanford, Calif.: Stanford University Press, 1968) pp. 195–196. Gimbel notes that relations within the Bizonal Economic Council had deteriorated through the latter half of 1947 as decision making was brought to a standstill by internal German political disagreements between the Social Democratic party and the Christian Democrats—Christian Socialists concerning the control of the council and struggles growing out of food shortages (pp. 186–194).

63. "London Conference Recommendations on Germany: Text of Communique," *Department of State Bulletin*, Vol. 18 (June 10, 1948), p. 808. This discussion is drawn, for the most part, from Gimbel, op. cit., and from Feis, op. cit., pp. 318–323.

64. "London Conference Recommendations on Germany: Explanation of the Conference," *Department of State Bulletin*, Vol 18 (June 20, 1948); p. 812. The "explanation" under its section on "security" noted French concern explicitly: "The French Government in particular has been acutely aware of the possible dangers inherent in the reconstruction of a German state and the substantial revival of German economy."

65. Ibid., p. 811.

66. Testimony of John Foster Dulles in Hearings before U.S. Congress, Senate Committee on Foreign Relations, *U.S. Assistance to European Economic Recovery*, 80th Congress, 2nd Session, 1948, p. 589.

67. Testimony of Secretary of State George C. Marshall before U.S. Congress, Senate Committee on Foreign Relations, *U.S. Assistance to European Economic Recovery*, p. 12.

68. "London Conference Recommendations on Germany: Text of Communique," p. 808; and Feis, op. cit., pp. 320–321.

69. John G. Stoessinger, *Nations in Darkness* (New York: Vintage, Random House, 1971), p. 148.

70. Walter Millis, ed., *The Forrestal Diaries* (New York: Viking, 1951), entry dated June 28, 1948, p. 454; quoted by Feis, op. cit., p. 342.

71. Quester, op. cit., pp. 48–49.

72. Quoted by Feis, op. cit., p. 352.

73. This historical review is reconstructed from ibid., pp. 366–383.

74. Reprinted from *Present at the Creation* by Dean Acheson. By permission of W. W. Norton, Inc., and Hamish Hamilton, Ltd. Copyright © 1969 by Dean Acheson, p. 272.

75. Shulman, op. cit., p. 73.
76. See Acheson, op. cit., 286–292.
77. Ibid, p. 292.
78. Shulman, op. cit., p. 77.
79. Robert E. Osgood, *NATO: The Entangling Alliance* (Chicago: University of Chicago Press, 1962). Unless otherwise noted, this account is drawn from Osgood, Feis, and Walter Millis, *Arms and the State* (New York: Twentieth Century Fund, 1958).
80. Osgood, op. cit., p. 30.
81. Kennan, op. cit., p. 401.
82. U.S. Congress, House Committee on Foreign Affairs, "North Atlantic Treaty Between the United States of America and Other Governments," *Collective Defense Treaties*, 91st Congress, 1st Session, 1969, p. 77.
83. Acheson, op. cit. p. 284.
84. U.S. Congress, Senate Committee on Foreign Relations, *Hearings on the North Atlantic Treaty*, 81st Congress, 1st Session, 1949, p. 47.
85. According to psychohistorian Arnold Rogow, James Forrestal, the first secretary of defense, "regarded the final outcome of the 1948 defense debate as both a personal defeat and conclusive evidence that the nation lacked the leadership and stamina necessary for victory in the Cold War. The personal defeat, he felt, had been administered less by Congress than by Truman, and [Secretary of the Air Force] Symington." On March 28, 1948, Forrestal resigned. On April 2, 1948, he was formally admitted to Bethesda Naval Hospital in Washington. On Sunday, May 22, despondent that what he regarded as a coalition of high administration dupes of Jews and Communists had chosen him "as their Number One target for liquidation as a consequence of his efforts to alert Americans to the Communist menace," Forrestal leapt to his death from his sixteenth-floor suite at the hospital. Arnold A. Rogow, *James Forrestal: A Study of Personality, Politics and Policy* (New York: Macmillan, 1963), pp. 6–7, 299.
86. See Paul Y. Hammond, "NSC-68: Prologue to Rearmament," in Schilling et al., op. cit., pp. 280–282.
87. Wolfe, op. cit., p. 32.
88. Committee on Foreign Affairs, U.S. Congress, *Hearings on Emergency Foreign Aid*, 80th Congress, 1st Session, 1947, p. 14.
89. Quoted in *China and U.S. Far East Policy, 1945–1967* (Washington, D.C.: Congressional Quarterly Service, 1967), p. 45.
90. U.S. Department of State, *United States Relations with China with Special Reference to the Period 1944–1949* (Washington, D.C.: U.S. Government Printing Office, 1949), pp. 358–359.
91. Acheson, op. cit., p. 306.
92. Ibid.
93. Mr. Acheson contends that the analogy was used to emphasize his inability to peer into the future. He continues: "Of course, any stick is good enough to beat a dog, but this was an example of my unhappy ability–if I may mix a metaphor–to coin a stick" (p. 306).
94. Letter of transmittal, *United States Relations with China*, p. xvi.
95. *China and U.S. Far East Policy*, p. 47.
96. NSC-68, described by Dean Acheson as one of the most important documents of American history, has now been declassified after more than twenty years of secrecy: NSC-68, A Report to the National Security Council: *United States Objectives and Programs for National Security* (Washington, D.C.: Photocopied, April

14, 1950). Hereafter cited as *NSC-68*. Previous analyses of it had to be drawn from secondary sources. Of these, there is wide agreement that the account of Paul Y. Hammond, "NSC-68: Prologue to Rearmament," in Schilling et al., op. cit., pp. 305–308, is the best review. Acheson's autobiography is also useful, especially pp. 344–349 and 373–381.

97. For a detailed discussion of the General Advisory Committee's view, see Richard Sylves, *The Nuclear Oracles* (Ames, Iowa: Iowa State University Press, 1987).

98. A full review of the memorandum, described by Kennan as "in its implications one of the most important, if not the most important, of all the documents I ever wrote in government," may be found in his *Memoirs, 1925–1950*, pp. 471–476.

99. Ibid., p. 474.

100. Acheson, op. cit., p. 349; and Robert J. Donovan, "The Devastating Times: The Hydrogen Bomb, China, and Korea," *Working Paper* No. 6, Wilson Center, International Security Studies Program, Washington, D.C., April 19, 1979, p. 23.

101. Kennan, op. cit., p. 475 (emphasis in original).

102. Acheson, op. cit., p. 347; and Samuel Wells, Jr., "Sounding the Tocsin: NSC-68 and the Soviet Threat," *Working Paper* No. 7, Wilson Center, International Security Studies Program, Washington, D.C., September 26, 1979, p. 11.

103. "NSC-68," p. 4.

104. Ibid., pp. 6–9.

105. Ibid., pp. 63–64.

106. Ibid., pp. 17–18.

107. Ibid., pp. 54–58.

108. Ibid., pp. 3–4.

109. Ibid., p. 48.

110. Ibid., pp. 39–40.

111. Acheson, op. cit., p. 375.

112. Ibid., p. 376.

113. Hammond, op. cit., p. 331.

114. Acheson, op. cit., p. 374.

115. Hammond, op. cit., pp. 309–318.

116. Acheson, op. cit., p. 375.

117. Hammond, op. cit.

118. Acheson, op. cit., p. 380.

119. Hammond, op. cit., pp. 340–341. As RAND Analyst Paul Hammond notes, some effort was made to incorporate NSC-68 guidelines into Defense Department budgeting in early 1950.

Chapter 3
Korea and the Militarization of Containment

More than anything else, two events, the Soviet Union's first successful atomic test in the fall of 1949 and the Korean War beginning in the late spring of 1950, confirmed the increasingly military definition of America's global role. Indeed, the Soviet test was seen privately as something of a blessing. Acheson relates, "Once again the Russians had come to the aid of an imperiled nonpartisan foreign policy, binding wounds and rallying the divided Congress."[1] Similarly, the crisis of communist military action in Asia pushed forward the rearmament advocated in NSC-68. One of Acheson's aides remembered the trepidation the administration felt when contemplating the "sale" of NSC-68 to the American people: "We were sweating over it, and then . . . thank God, Korea came along."[2]

THE ORIGINS
OF THE FIRST LIMITED WAR

The focus of containment in Asia was vague in NSC-68. As Acheson explained American interests on January 12, 1950, to the National Press Club, "this defensive perimeter runs along the Aleutians to Japan and then goes to the Ryukus [sic] . . . [then] . . . runs from the Ryukus to the Philippine Islands."[3] In defining American interests in this manner, Acheson's analysis seemed like an ambiguous call for local self-help from countries on the mainland. If military attacks were to come, "the initial reliance must be on the people attacked to resist it and then upon the commitments of the entire civilized world under the Charter of the United Nations."[4] The primary threat in these areas was not military aggression, but rather "subversion and penetration that cannot be stopped by military means."[5]

Conspicuous by its absence in this outline of American security interests in Asia was Taiwan. The week before Acheson's speech to the National Press Club, the president had made it clear that the United

States had no intention of providing more than economic assistance to Chiang Kai-shek's government.[6] Indeed, the eventual fall of Taiwan was assumed by the Department of State, which was so certain of Chiang's doom and the fall of Taiwan that" [it] had already prepared and distributed an information paper to be used as a guide for information officers on what they were to say after the Chinese Communists had overrun the islands."[7]

Korea seemed an even more remote concern than Taiwan. Under the postwar occupation agreements, the United States had been responsible for the administration of South Korea until reunification under UN auspices could take place. When the Soviets refused to submit the question of Korean reunification to the United Nations, separate administrations were established. As early as 1947, President Truman asked the Joint Chiefs to evaluate the military significance of Korea. In September 1947, they reported that "from the standpoint of military security, the United States has little strategic interests in maintaining the present troops and bases in Korea."[8]

Nevertheless, both Soviet and American assistance continued to their respective clients during 1948 and 1949. But by 1950, Syngman Rhee, the president of the South Korean regime, was becoming something of an embarrassment to the Americans. He severely restricted civil liberties, balked at holding elections, and did so only after withdrawal of American aid was threatened. Between September 1948 and April 1949, more than eighty thousand people were arrested in South Korea. Sporadic demonstrations took place in the capital, and, by October 1949, 7 percent of the national assembly had been jailed by Rhee. By spring of 1950, economic conditions had worsened dramatically. Although Rhee arrested more than two dozen of his opponents prior to the May 30, 1950, elections, he lost heavily, and more than half of the new assembly favored a move toward reunification with the North.[9]

To many observers in the Truman administration, Rhee was taking on all the attributes of a lesser Chiang Kai-shek. The most explicit public statement of growing ambivalence toward the South Koreans came from Democratic Senator Tom Connally of Texas, the chairman of the Senate Committee on Foreign Relations. Just after the elections, Senator Connally asserted in an interview that South Korea might have to be abandoned.[10] Secretary of State Acheson refused to comment on the Connally interview, thereby heightening the uncertainty or, at a minimum, the seeming indifference of American policy in early May of 1950.

Little or no evidence exists that Beijing was in any way involved in the North Korean attack on the South that came in late June. The

North Koreans were armed with Soviet weapons and had been trained by Soviet advisers, leading most observers to regard the North Koreans as a Soviet satellite.[11] A victory by the North Korean Communists might benefit the Chinese in that it would undercut the image of American power in Asia. Still, for Beijing, the main military problems remained the conquest of Taiwan and Tibet, the pacification of southern and central China, and the reduction of military expenditures to relieve inflationary pressures.[12]

Soviet interest in Korea was long-standing and focused in part on its proximity to Japan and the geopolitical centrality of the peninsula in East Asian politics. It was possible that a communist victory in Korea might lead the Japanese to reconsider their relationship with the Americans. Even if the Americans responded by intensifying their commitment to Japan, the Russians may have reckoned that this would require a drawing down of the American presence in Europe. Then, too, an increased American presence in Asia would contribute to increased Chinese dependence on the Soviets.[13] Thus, for the Soviets, the benefits to be gained from encouraging or allowing a North Korean attack on the South seemed significant, the costs acceptable.

The evidence that the Soviets *directed* the attack is inconclusive at best. Next to speculation in the West that Stalin instigated the Korean adventure (he may well have known about it) is Khrushchev's testimony: "I must stress that war wasn't Stalin's idea, but Kim Il-Sung's. Kim was the initiator."[14] Khrushchev's accusation can be supported. There had been, since 1948, a declining number of Russian advisers in North Korea who might have exercised an effective veto on Kim's action. In 1948, there were 150 Russians per North Korean army division; but, by spring 1950, a State Department historian estimates that there were only from three to eight Russians to advise each North Korean division,[15] perhaps a total of fewer than forty[16] at the moment of attack. As interpreted in Washington, Soviet intentions were, in the words of Assistant Secretary for Far Eastern Affairs Dean Rusk, "fuzzy."[17] And as Harvard Kremlinologist Adam Ulam speculates:

> The American reaction to the North Korean invasion on June 25 must have been one of the greatest surprises of Stalin's life. Having acquiesced in the loss of China, these unpredictable people now balked at the loss of a territory they themselves had characterized as unimportant. . . . Had there been any inkling . . . the Soviet delegate would not have boycotted the Security Council since January . . . and Moscow would have been ready with diplomatic notes and propaganda campaigns. . . . Between June 27 and July 3, the news from Korea was tucked in the back pages of the Soviet press.[18]

If Korea's place in the U.S. defense perimeter had been left ambiguous in January by Secretary of State Acheson and very nearly
disavowed by his silence in May,[19] why was it a security interest in
June? In part, Korea was seen as an overt communist military attack;
that is, the form of communist aggression had changed decisively.[20]
But also, the North Korean attack was deemed a Soviet probe by proxy,
aimed at Japan, and Japan was most definitely a well-marked American interest. If Korea was perceived by mainland Asians as a bridge
for Japanese aggression, the Japanese had historically conceived of
Korea as a dagger pointed at their heart. The combination of a weak
South Korean regime and a strong Soviet-backed North Korean government, in the analysis of President Truman and his advisers, provided
the means for extending communist control of the peninsula at minimal
cost.

But to President Truman and his advisers, that danger was more
than specific to any country. The menace was now aggression and its
attendant dangers to global order:

> Communism was acting in Korea just as Hitler, Mussolini, and the Japa-
> nese had acted ten, fifteen, and twenty years earlier. I felt certain that
> if South Korea was allowed to fall Communist leaders would be embold-
> ened to override nations closer to our own shores. If the communists were
> permitted to force their way into the Republic of Korea without opposi-
> tion from the free world, no small nation would have the courage to re-
> sist threats and aggression by stronger communist neighbors. If this was
> allowed to go unchallenged it would mean a third world war, just as simi-
> lar incidents had brought on the second world war.[21]

Thus, President Truman's decision to seek a UN mandate for military assistance to the South Koreans, the immediate positioning of the
Seventh Fleet between Taiwan and the mainland, and increases in assistance to the Philippines and the French in Indochina that grew out
of the Korean crisis were acts meant to demonstrate American will. In
so acting, "the safety and prospects for [the] peace of the free world
would be increased."[22] The rationale and the rhetoric should be familiar, for they are virtually synonymous with that of March 1947 . . . or
August 1964. Even if the substantive essence of the Truman Doctrine might remain European, its applicable limits had now become
global.

NSC-68 summarized this notion about the integrity of world order
and also predicted military probes and feints by the Soviets that had
to be answered. Otherwise, as Acheson explained, "To back away from
this challenge [in Korea] would be highly destructive of the power and
prestige of the United States. By prestige I mean the shadow cast by

power, which is of great deterrent importance." [23] Thus, the United States would escalate its commitment, for if the aggressor was not stopped on the frontiers of containment, the integrity of the entire concept would be compromised. If the commitment were debased, it would indicate a lack of will to defend the heart of the system — Europe. Korea was not, therefore, essential in the same sense as Germany or Britain. Nonetheless, President Truman and his advisers were convinced that "the Korean situation [was] vital as a *symbol of the strength and determination of the West.*"[24]

To President Truman and his advisers, intervention in Korea held great dangers. First, the danger of world war was apparent. Once the decision had been made to use force, the possibility existed that the violence might get out of hand and escalate into a Soviet–American confrontation. Consequently, an overriding consideration was keeping the Soviets out of the conflict. At the very outset, therefore, the Soviets were not accused of starting the war; they were simply asked to disavow any responsibility for the attack. Some observers have suggested that this approach by the United States, when combined with President Truman's reluctance to equate explicitly the Soviet Union with communism in his June 27 statement, indicates that the United States was not convinced that the Soviets had started the war.[25] In any event, the Soviets replied that the South Koreans had started the fight and that they (the Soviets) advocated a policy of noninterference by outside powers in Korea. Secretary Acheson and the State Department's Russian experts took this response, the lack of any further follow-up by the Soviets, and the cumulating string of North Korean victories as conclusive evidence that the Soviets would not intervene in the short run.[26]

Second, concern existed about Chinese intervention, although the immediate threat was perceived to be an attack on Taiwan. Ostensibly, this fear was the basis for moving the Seventh Fleet into the Taiwan Strait. President Truman recognized, however, that Communist Chinese intervention might be provoked by Chiang Kai-shek's actions. Consequently, he called on Chiang to cease all actions against the mainland and declined, on Secretary Acheson's advice, the offer by Chiang and General Douglas MacArthur of some thirty thousand Nationalist Chinese troops.

The delicacy of the Nationalist Chinese position in the crisis was compounded by the militancy of the China lobby in the United States, and also by the presence in Asia of General MacArthur, who had long disagreed with the European focus of American policy. Ironically, this European orientation of U.S. policymakers allowed General MacArthur to build for himself, in Asia after the war, a position of considerable personal power and a network of personal contacts and confidences among East Asian anticommunists, including a strong attachment to Chiang and his cause. A European-oriented White House, State Department, and Defense Department were prepared to leave the administration of American policy—primarily occupation policy—to the Supreme Commander of the Allied Powers in Tokyo. From his Pacific command in Tokyo, General MacArthur possessed power and authority comparable to that of a head of state, powers never before possessed by an American military man. Indeed, his staff compared him to Napoleon and Alexander.[27] As President Truman put it later, "There was never anybody around to keep him in line. . . . He just wouldn't let anybody near him who wouldn't kiss his ass . . . there were many times when he was . . . out of his head."[28]

From his position of virtual control of American military and political policy in Asia, General MacArthur was uniquely situated to assist Chiang and Rhee in their struggle for survival. In late 1949, Rhee had sought out General MacArthur's help in obtaining an increase in American arms. Almost simultaneously, the South Korean defense minister stated after a conference with General MacArthur "that he would gladly march on Pyongyang," the North Korean capital. Also, in early 1950, Rhee visited General MacArthur in Tokyo, outlined his increasingly desperate position, and reportedly called for an Asian anticommunist crusade under General MacArthur's leadership.[29]

The MacArthur problem would eventually dominate war and domestic policy; in the meantime, a buildup of military forces was culminating on both sides of the 38th parallel. From March 1949 until June 1950, Rhee expanded his military forces from 114,000 to more than 150,000 men. Rhee's American arms were light weapons, perhaps reflecting U.S. anxiety concerning his intentions.[30] In contrast, the North Koreans began a rapid buildup of their forces to a level of 135,000 men after January 1950, with large shipments of Soviet equipment, including armor, arriving as late as April and May. Despite the North Korean advantages in armor, American intelligence, aware of the mini–arms race then underway, reported that Rhee was fully capable of defending the South.[31]

Tensions between the two Korean governments grew steadily. Philip Jessup, a State Department official, declared in April 1950 that "the boundary at the 38th parallel . . . is a real front line. There is constant fighting. . . . There are very real battles, involving one or two thousand men."[32] One authority on Korea, Robert Simmons, summed up the situation thus: "Koreans were accustomed to the fighting and the possibility of war; each side believed that an early unification was worth a war."[33] As tensions and arms increased along the 38th parallel, John

Foster Dulles (then acting as Republican special consultant to the State Department) visited Asia. In a speech before the South Korean national assembly on June 18, 1950, Dulles struck a rather different note than indicated by Secretary of State Acheson in his January "defense perimeter" speech. Dulles denounced the North Koreans and then added, concerning South Korea, "You are not alone. You will never be alone as long as you continue to play worthily your part in the great design of human freedom."[34] Dulles did not promise any specific form of aid. But these statements before a national assembly controlled by Rhee's opponents must have encouraged Rhee — and frightened the North Koreans. After leaving Korea, Dulles traveled to Tokyo, and, after meeting with General MacArthur, made vague references to positive action by the United States in the future.

Thus, the circumstances surrounding the outbreak of fighting in Korea remain, after four decades, confusing. The American perception of the importance of the peninsula was deeply divided between MacArthur's desire for action and Washington's ambivalence, which was resolved only when the fighting began. The calculus of interests regarding the motives of the Soviet Union, China, and the two Koreas is no less controversial. But the hazy facts now surrounding the origins of the Korean War did not inhibit the crystallization of a policy consensus that allowed President Truman swiftly to insert an American military presence in Korea when the apparent North Korean attack came on June 25, 1950.[35] Stewart Alsop remembered that even George Kennan (now, in 1950, seen as an iconoclast in his views about how to manage Soviet power) did a "jig of delight" on hearing that the United States would now confront "Stalin's carefully calculated challenge in Korea."[36]

THE "FOG OF WAR"

On the morning of June 24, 1950 (June 25, Korean time), about ninety thousand men of the Korean People's Army of North Korea (KPA), supported by more than one hundred Russian-built T-34 tanks, crossed the 38th parallel, the border between North and South Korea.[37] Within hours, the North Koreans were claiming that their forces had pushed ten to fifteen miles into the Republic of Korea. Confusion as to what was happening was extensive. At least one official in General MacArthur's headquarters in Tokyo believed that the South Koreans had attacked the North Koreans. Some observers characterized events as a complete surprise followed by the fairly rapid collapse of South Korean resistance. Other more skeptical analysts have suggested that the Republic of Korea (ROK) Army recovered quickly from a North Korean surprise attack, launched a counterattack, and had established a more or less stable defensive line by June 26.[38]

In any case, news in Washington throughout June 27 and 28 was confused. General MacArthur and Syngman Rhee predicted imminent collapse. Other journalistic sources suggested that any report from the battlefield had to be viewed cautiously.[39] Hanson Baldwin, military correspondent of *The New York Times*, reported on June 29: "The normal fog of war—greatly accentuated in the Korean campaign by the paucity of communications—has left Washington with insufficient information to determine with precision our future course."[40]

The response in Washington to these perplexing reports was, nonetheless, decisive. Secretary of State Acheson had received the news from Korea, and, before contacting the president—who was in Independence, Missouri, on family business—requested that the UN Security Council be called into session. The council met on the afternoon of June 25. Absent was the Russian delegate, who was boycotting the council over the issue of its exclusion of the People's Republic of China as the legitimate representative of China to the United Nations. An American-drafted resolution that labeled the North Koreans the aggressors and demanded their withdrawal from the South was quickly passed.[41]

By June 26, President Truman had returned to Washington. There he received an alarming message from General MacArthur: "South Korean units unable to resist determined Northern offensive. . . . [O]ur estimate is that a complete collapse is imminent."[42] Mr. Truman has recorded his reaction to this message:

> There was now no doubt! The Republic of Korea needed help at once if it was not to be overrun. . . . I told my advisers that what was developing in Korea seemed to me like a repetition on a large scale of what had happened in Berlin. The Reds were probing for weaknesses in our armor; we had to meet their thrust without getting embroiled in a worldwide war.[43]

President Truman was prepared, in short, to assume the worst, draw what were becoming the conventional analogies of his administration, and move.

The president ordered American air and naval forces into action in support of what were assumed, in Washington, to be retreating South Korean units. The President then requested that the UN Security Council meet again the next day, June 27, and recommend that the member states provide assistance to South Korea. The council was thus put in the position of meeting to consider whether it should approve the sanctions against the North Koreans that the United States had already initiated. Inasmuch as the council had already declared the North Koreans aggressors on June 25, the decision was a foregone conclusion. The Security Council passed a resolution recommending that "members of the United Nations furnish such assistance to the Republic of Korea as may be necessary to repel the armed attack and to restore international peace and security in the area."[44] The command of UN forces was under General Douglas MacArthur. It was clear, therefore, that the UN effort in Korea would be United States conceived, administered, and implemented.

THE LIMITED WAR
AT HOME: DOMESTIC
POLITICS AND REARMAMENT

The Korean War cannot be understood as merely a military operation, a case study in the problems of limited war,[45] or primarily a problem of civil–military relations.[46] It was seen by the Truman administration also as a crucial part of the complex and interrelated domestic and foreign milieu of 1950.

Domestic Politics

The concept of a limited war was never completely understood by the American people. This was due in some measure to the combination of President Truman's actions and his hyperbolic rhetoric. As the war progressed, the public grew uneasy with the notion that the United States was circumscribing its military activities both geographically and in terms of the means employed. Discontent was perhaps increased by the fact that many of the men called on to carry the brunt of this limited war had brought to a successful close a massive total war effort only five years earlier. Moreover, World War II had been conducted so as to crush the same forces of aggression that now were said to be loose again.

Exacerbating the domestic situation immeasurably was a second factor: an executive–legislative struggle with conservative Republicans pitted against President Truman and Secretary of State Acheson. The battle was engaged by men with mixed motives, who had not held the presidency and had held a congressional majority only once in twenty years. Conservatives such as Senators Knowland, Bridges, Jenner, Wherry, Taft, and McCarthy are frequently identified as isolationists in that they attacked the Truman administration's deepening involvement in Europe. Curiously, however, these same men assailed Truman, Marshall, and Acheson for not doing enough in Asia to stop the spread of communism. The inconsistency is striking and confusing unless one admits the possibility that the majority of congressional Republicans, as well as a significant portion of congressional Democrats, were simply ideological conservatives opposed to every facet of Truman's public policy as crypto–New Dealism. The backdrop of conservative suspicion was what they saw as Roosevelt's "treasonous maneuvering" over Eastern Europe. The only remedy suggested by Republicans to amend Roosevelt's perfidy was liberation, not containment. Containment was seen as involving coexistence with and, thus, the continuation of communism — not its destruction. To many conservatives, the final proof that containment would not work could now be found in Asia: first in Mao Zedong's success in China and now in the attack on South Korea.

Under these circumstances, Truman administration policy in Asia became a target of criticism from the right. Republicans reproached Truman not for any love they may have had for Asia (although this was undoubtedly the case for a few of Truman's critics such as Congressman Walter Judd, who had a long personal attachment as a missionary doctor in China prior to Mao's victory), but simply because containment in Asia was beset by difficulties in contrast with the apparent success of containment in Europe.

The expediency of the conservative position is apparent: Republicans could support Truman's decision to intervene in Korea while simultaneously criticizing the administration's policy for having brought on the attack in the first place. They charged that all of this could have been avoided if the Truman administration had been willing to commit U.S. troops and greater aid to save China and support Asian anticommunists such as Syngman Rhee. Ironically, these were the same conservatives who supported Truman's reduction of U.S. conventional military strength and advocated a greater reliance on air power.

The Senator from Wisconsin: "A Pig in a Minefield"[47]

Perhaps the best example of the political opportunism underlying much of the attack from the right is to be found in the rise of Senator Joseph McCarthy to national prominence. Beginning in February 1950 and continuing until December 1954, Senator McCarthy maintained that the U.S. government was and had been for a decade infiltrated with Communists, former Communists, communist sympathizers, and unknowing instruments of communism. Their presence throughout the government, but especially in the Department of State, was the explanation for all the failures of American foreign policy during the preceding decade. Their influence explained the willingness of the Roosevelt administration to accept the Soviets in Central Europe, and, above all, communist influence among the Department of State's Asian experts explained the loss of China.[48]

On February 9, 1950, Senator McCarthy unveiled his blunderbuss: "While I cannot take the time to name all the men in the State Department who had been named as members of the Communist Party and members of a spy ring, I have here in my hand a list of two hundred and five that were known to the Secretary of State as being members of the Communist Party and who, nevertheless, are still working and shaping policy in the State Department."[49] On other occasions Senator McCarthy referred to 207, 57, 10, 116, 121, 106, and 81 Communists in "foggy bottom"; sometimes he spoke merely of "a lot" of subversives. In July, a Senate committee and then a full vote of Congress attested that Senator McCarthy's charges were without foundation. But Republicans, as journalist David Halberstam writes, "welcomed him; the more they assaulted the Democrats the better for the Republicans." "Joe," said John Bricker, one of the more traditional conservatives and a candidate for vice president in 1944, "You're a real SOB. But sometimes it is useful to have SOB's around to do the dirty work."[50]

The assault on Democratic and State Department integrity and patriotism was a clever strategy. It explained how it was that Americans were now fighting a curious war in Asia without confronting the complexities and ambiguities of world politics and American policies: There were traitors in high places. Moreover, it appealed to America's alienated, and it preyed on the endemic fear deeply rooted in American society that America might not be equal to the task of global involvement.[51] Senator McCarthy's answer was reassuring: America's difficulties were not the product of inexperience and naivete, but rather treason.

Senator McCarthy was a much-sought speaker. He coveted the publicity that rapidly came to him. His simplistic views articulated the fears and confusion of many Americans. In time, it would be demonstrated that he was, in Richard Rovere's words, "in many ways the most gifted demagogue that ever lived on these shores. No bolder seditionist ever moved among us—nor any politician with a surer, swifter access to the dark places of the American mind."[52] But even in early 1954, as he neared censure in the U.S. Senate, 50 percent of the American people held a favorable opinion of him; only 29 percent reacted negatively.

"It was a melancholy time," Rovere has observed, "and the Chief Justice of the United States was probably right when he said at the time that if the 'Bill of Rights were put to a vote, it would lose.'"[53]

McCarthy's meteoric rise made him the rallying point for the rather large number of Americans who found American foriegn policy under Harry Truman confusing and burdensome. This characteristic made Senator McCarthy attractive to the Republican leadership in the Senate, including "Mr. Republican," Senator Robert A. Taft.

Senator Taft's association with McCarthy is striking in view of Taft's reputation for conservative probity and sensitivity to civil liberties, all of which was in contrast with McCarthy's insensitivity and demagogic excesses. However, Senator Taft wanted the Republican presidential nomination in 1952, and he was going to do nothing that would cost him the support of conservative Senate Republicans. When it became clear that the center of Republican opinion, searching for any means to strike at Truman, had begun to move with or was at least willing to tolerate McCarthy, Taft abandoned his early uneasiness with the senator from Wisconsin and began to support him. Senator Taft began castigating "the procommunist group in the State Department who surrendered to every demand of Russia at Yalta and Potsdam, and promoted at every opportunity the communist cause in China."[54] Taft's biographer, William W. White, has said of the senator at this time, "it seemed to some of his friends and admirers that he began, if unconsciously, to adopt the notion that almost *any* way to defeat or discredit the Truman plans was acceptable. There was . . . a blood in the nostrils approach."[55]

On June 2, 1950, Senator Margaret Chase Smith, Republican of Maine, issued what she termed a "Declaration of Conscience" in which she attacked the Republican leadership. She noted, "The nation sorely needs a Republican victory. But I do not want to see the Republican Party ride to political victory on the Four Horsemen of Calumny — fear, ignorance, bigotry, and smear."[56] It is a mark of the effects of Truman's stunning 1948 victory on Robert Taft and the Republican party, Taft's personal ambition, and the fear and the polarization brought about by McCarthy that Senator Taft could not or would not associate himself with Senator Smith's declaration.[57]

Rearmament

Against this backdrop of increasing vitriolic conservative opposition, President Truman sought to use the emergency of Korea and, subsequently, Chinese intervention in the war, to flesh out the framework of

NSC-68. As Paul Nitze, chairman of the committee that drafted NSC-68, recalled:

> The dilemma involved in choosing between an unbalanced budget, higher taxes, and more stringent economic controls on the one hand, and an adequate military posture on the other was not resolved at the policy decision level until some three months prior to the outbreak of the North Korean agression. Those decisions were translated into specific action *only after* the aggression into South Korea had given *concrete and bloody confirmation to the conclusions already produced by analysis.*[58]

By the end of 1951, total requests for defense spending had reached $74 billion. NSC-68 had argued that American defense spending expand from $13.5 billion to $50 billion. The added difference of some $24 billion represented the cost of Korea *per se* and a sudden inflationary surge to the economy under the impact of war. The sheer magnitude of this defense spending is awesome given the defense budgets and philosophy that had existed for the past several years. Even more important, however, was the programmatic content of the requests, for what was being funded carried implications far beyond Korea.

The fiscal year 1952 budget request reflected the administration's decision to go over to a basically conscript army. The president asked that draft authority be extended to 1955 and a permanent military obligation of eight years total and two years active duty be imposed on all males between the ages of eighteen and twenty-six. Expansion of the American overseas military base system was proposed to Congress. More than seventy new bases and support facilities were to be constructed in the United States, North Africa, and the Middle East. The Air Force was to be placed within striking range of the Soviet Union, expanded, and its strike capability augmented by the decision to deploy a new bomber, the B-47. The construction of atomic weapons forged ahead to the point that the secretary of the air force could claim in November 1951 that the United States had entered the age of atomic plenty. At the same time, the last technical problems standing in the way of a thermonuclear device or hydrogen bomb were surmounted in the spring of 1951. The Navy was in no sense left out of this quantum jump in American global capability. With virtually no opposition, the Congress approved $2.4 billion in fleet construction and modernization. Included in this program was the first super-carrier, the fifty-seven-thousand-ton *Forrestal*, and the first nuclear submarine, the *Nautilus*. If, as envisaged in NSC-68, a "year of maximum peril" was closing on the United States in 1953 or 1954, the Truman administration would be ready.

In 1951, the foundations were also established for a permanent U.S.

defense presence in Asia. Most important was the Japanese Peace Treaty, signed in September 1951. The treaty simultaneously excluded any Russian involvement in the future of Japan and ensured future American basing. The Japanese treaty was supplemented by a similar arrangement with the Philippines and a third mutual security treaty with Australia and New Zealand. An increase in aid to the French in Indochina was also extended. Finally, the administration moved toward permanent support of Chiang Kai-shek's regime on Taiwan as U.S. military assistance increased.

In short, the fiscal year 1952 budget that went before and was approved by Congress in 1951 provided the basis for the expanded military capability envisaged by NSC-68. But there was more to Truman's budget than a request for increased spending; he also proposed increasing the number of American troops stationed in Europe. In so doing, Truman sparked a great debate on both sides of the Atlantic: with Senator Taft, on the one hand, attacking the premises of the president's policy, and with the Europeans, on the other hand, concerned with the future of NATO.

The Great Debate

Truman's announcement on December 19, 1950, that now U.S. troops would be needed in Europe prompted Senator Taft to argue for a "re-examination" of the entire course of postwar foreign policy. Taft charged that Truman, "without authority . . . involved us in the Korean War. Without authority he is now attempting a similar policy in Europe. This matter must be debated."[59] Taft did not wish to return to the old isolationism of one-hemisphere hegemony, but the senator was bothered by the financial and constitutional costs involved in securing and maintaining a global role. Thus, he implored the Truman administration to "not assume obligations by treaty or otherwise which require an extensive use of American land forces."[60] The defense of Japan and an unequivocal commitment of Chiang Kai-shek were exceptions, Taft argued, but the American obligation to Europe was fulfilled with the mere existence of NATO — nothing else was mandated.[61] Otherwise, the country's economy would be seriously distorted through a disastrously inflated economy, deficit spending, and hence a mortgaged future. To control the effects on the U.S. economy of a spiraling arms budget would require, according to Senator Taft, wage and price controls — controls that would eventually extend to other dimensions of American life. In short, the very antithesis of the free-market capitalist domestic system that comprised the ideological bedrock for conservatives such as himself.[62]

The only recourse, to Senator Taft and his followers, was a defense policy predicated on air and naval superiority. Taft also called for an aggressive effort to sell the American system abroad by means of propaganda and, where necessary, clandestine infiltration and support of "those millions who yearn for liberty in satellite countries. . . ."[63] Sympathetic elements of Soviet-bloc nations would be cultivated, for Taft hoped that they "may be organized to seize power wherever they have support of their fellow citizens."[64] Senator Taft recognized the irony implicit in this policy: It would rely on the very methods of those he would fight.[65] But it was essential, he believed, to pursue a course of subversion and propaganda if a limited military posture was to succeed.

Three days after Senator Taft spoke, a resolution was introduced into the Senate by the conservatives that would require congressional action before any troops could be moved to Europe. During February and March of 1951, the administration sent a parade of witnesses before the Senate Foreign Relations Committee to counter Senator Taft's position, including his proposition that the president did not, in fact, already have the authority to move the troops to Europe. Similarly, military leaders including General Dwight Eisenhower testified in favor of European deployment. Administration officials led by Acheson and Marshall emphasized that the United States was thinking in terms of four to six divisions. By April 1951, conservative opposition began to diminish,[66] and the Senate acted on President Truman's request, passing a retroactive endorsement of the president's decision and approving the appointment of General Eisenhower as NATO commander.

CONVENTIONAL FORCES
FOR NATO: PLANS AND STALEMATE

Parallelling the great debate in the United States was another within NATO. The outbreak of fighting in Korea provided the Truman administration with some leverage on the stalemated situation within the NATO alliance. Prior to the Soviet acquisition of atomic weapons, American planning for the defense of Europe was based solely on the deterrent capacity of American atomic superiority. The Soviets' test explosion in 1949 brought American deterrence into question. Sharing the American nuclear umbrella with others was potentially a risk now. First, the umbrella could be swept away if the Soviets ever attained the ability to launch a disarming blow. Second, sharing the American umbrella implied that an ally was not only a target but also, perhaps, a negotiable asset. After all, the French, Germans, and British would muse, why would America want to risk Chicago for Dusseldorf or Lyons? Could not European targets become chips in a great-power poker game unless the Europeans became equipped to play the game too and obtained nuclear weapons for themselves?

The questions were still hypothetical. Most Europeans continued to believe, and correctly, that American military predominance would not be effectively undercut for some time to come. The problem was viewed with greater urgency in the United States and especially by Secretary of State Acheson. The conclusion of NSC-68 — that rearmament should begin immediately in both the United States and NATO — was in anticipation of a nuclear stalemate predicted to materialize in the mid-1950s. It was estimated that by then the balance of conventional forces would assume overriding importance.

Consequently, the American position at the foreign ministers' meeting of the North Atlantic Council in May 1950 was that planning for increased European conventional forces was essential. For their part, the Europeans were reluctant to move rapidly toward reinvigorating their military establishments. They feared that an emphasis on rearmament would divert scarce resources away from the continuing economic reconstruction of Europe, including a proposal for integrating the coal and steel industries of Europe as "the setting-up of common foundations for economic development as a first step in the federation of Europe."[67]

From the very outset, the concept on which NATO conventional force planning was based was weakened by what proved to be an irresolvable tension between the needs of imperial powers — such as the French, Dutch, Belgian and Portuguese — to retain control of crumbling empires and the requirements of a collective ground force. In the end, the NATO allies settled for a vague statement of principle and an equally vague concession from the Americans and the British that they would increase their levels of participation in the defense of the continent. Obviously, another source of manpower existed — Germany. But the idea of German rearmament was still nearly unmentionable given French sensitivity to a new *Wehrmacht*.[68] Hence, on the eve of the Korean War, the NATO allies were forced to admit that grave differences existed between their rhetoric and the resources they were willing to commit to any collective effort.

The outbreak of the Korean War caused some movement on these problems. American assistance was now predicated on an increased effort on the part of the Europeans.[69] Truman skillfully forced the issue by linking his announcement of the increased American contribution to NATO with an insistence that the question of a German contribution be confronted at the September 1950 NATO conference, where a forward strategy for the defense of Europe was adopted. A conventional defense of Western Europe as far east as possible clearly required troop levels above those that the Europeans were prepared to raise. Thus, the NATO council also accepted, as a matter of great urgency, the consideration of how the Germans might best be integrated into the common effort and formally approved the idea of an integrated military force under a centralized command structure. Still, the precise nature of German participation in all of this was not resolved. Nor could the issue be forced by the Americans in view of European uneasiness with the entire notion of German rearmament. However, it was clear that the Germans would be integrated in some way into the European army concept that now seemed to be emerging.

Yet, as one authority, Robert Osgood, has noted, great uncertainty existed as to just what kind of aggression would be deterred by the NATO structure, whether skeletal or fully muscled. Acheson does not appear to have believed that the Russians could be matched along every military dimension, but he and the Joint Chiefs clearly sought to avoid Europe's being overrun. However, this seemed to require a NATO force of almost one hundred divisions. As Osgood observes, "Yet in 1951 it was already obvious that only the fear of imminent invasion . . . could conceivably inspire the Europeans to make sufficient contribution of men, money, and equipment to support a strategic objective which the United States herself expected to support primarily with airpower."[70]

By 1951, however, the Korean emergency lost its catalytic force as negotiations for a cease fire began. Moreover, throughout Europe, rearmament cut into the social welfare efforts of European governments and brought on the defeat of the Labor government in Britain and the reassumption of power by Winston Churchill in 1951. Churchill immediately emphasized his belief that nuclear deterrence was still quite valid. Although he agreed that NATO's conventional forces were a problem, he stated that the British would have to stretch out their general armament plan; similar problems and sentiments emerged throughout Western Europe. When the Truman administration announced that its fiscal year 1953 budget would show some cuts in defense spending, it was a clear signal to Europeans that military imperatives could be compromised in the face of domestic political and economic realities.[71]

UP AND DOWN
THE KOREAN PENINSULA

In the meantime, the military events that had given rise to the great debate and the parallel intra-alliance negotiations were approaching a turning point. General MacArthur had consolidated the UN position at the tip of the South Korean peninsula around Pusan and was preparing to take the offensive — an offensive that would crush the North Korean army, pull the Chinese into the war, and bring the general and the president into hand-to-hand conflict.

MacArthur Takes the Offensive

By September 1950, four American divisions had been committed to Korea — twice what General MacArthur had first requested — and they had been driven with their backs to the sea in the Pusan perimeter. Nevertheless, UN troop strength began to mount until it surpassed that of the North Koreans. Total UN air superiority complicated the North Koreans' position, for their lines of supply now stretched the length of the peninsula and were, therefore, vulnerable to air interdiction. Even as the North Koreans pushed deep into the South, General MacArthur had begun planning for an amphibious landing far in their rear at the port city of Inchon on the west coast of the Korean peninsula just west of Seoul below the 38th parallel. Simultaneously, UN forces would break out of the Pusan perimeter, push up the peninsula, and link up with General MacArthur's forces at the 38th parallel. The landing at Inchon would be extremely dangerous; one military planner said, "We drew up a list of every conceivable natural and geographic handicap and Inchon had 'em all."[72] But General MacArthur did not heed nearly unanimous advice. Instead, in his own words, he heard "the voice of his father telling him years before 'Doug, councils of war breed timidity. . . .' " And General MacArthur was nothing if he was not bold.[73]

The Joint Chiefs came to Korea to counsel against the adventure and refused General MacArthur what he considered an adequate number of Marines for the assault. Rear Admiral James Doyle, his amphibious commander, said, "I have not been asked . . . my opinion about this landing. If I were asked however, the best I can say is that Inchon is not possible."[74] Inchon had incredible tides. Water would rise and then fall some thirty feet each day. As the tide came wooshing out, vast banks of mud reaching some three miles from shore were exposed. Some landing assault and troop vehicles drew twenty-nine feet of water; there were only two days each year when high tide would be up enough to allow the vessels to port at the harbor of Inchon. Even then, the LSTs would have only two or three hours to debark their Marines—not on the beach, for none existed, but on a concrete seawall—before they would be pounded into the murky slime of Inchon. Not only were the logistics difficult, the purported advantage of surprise, the key to the operation, had been lost for some time. In Japan, plans for the assault had become a topic of barroom conversation, where it was termed "operation common knowledge." Indeed, the landing preceded a Korean mine-laying effort by a hairsbreadth. Yet, it was undeniable that if the two phases of the operation, the assault from the sea and the drive from the south, could be carried out, the North Korean army would be trapped between the pincers of General MacArthur's UN force. If it worked, the original objectives of the UN action would be attained.

On September 15, 1950, the Inchon landing was effected with remarkably low casualties. Within two days, the port was secured and the push toward Seoul began as UN troops began to rush up from their enclave in the South. By September 23, North Korean resistance was collapsing. And by September 26, virtually the entire North Korean army had been cut off and destroyed, with only thirty thousand North Koreans able to retreat across the 38th parallel. On September 27, 1950, Seoul was retaken after terrible destruction, described by one historian as "apocalyptic"—the result of massive U.S. firepower turned on the city.[75] By the end of September UN forces were back on the 38th parallel.

After Inchon, the military momentum grew infectiously. General MacArthur apparently assumed from the outset that his mandate extended to the military reunification of Korea.[76] However, after the collapse of the North Korean army resistance, his ambitious designs for Korea became the Western norm. Louis Halle remembers:

> The political leaders in Washington, in London, and elsewhere were themselves in a state of *hubris* brought on by success after long failure. They were themselves swept along by the momentum of victory, and they allowed themselves to be swept along the more readily because anything else was politically impossible for them.[77]

With victory, Washington now believed that American power could control events beyond the 38th parallel. President Truman was preparing to go beyond containment into the uncharted terrain of liberation.

Certain domestic political considerations undoubtedly influenced Truman's decision. The Republican leadership had already announced that it would regard failure of the administration to go north of the 38th parallel as evidence of appeasement. In addition, midterm elections were coming up in November. Total victory in Korea on the eve of the elections would, perhaps, undercut the McCarthyites. Domestic realities, therefore, limited Truman's ability or willingness to respond to Chinese hints of a desire for a political settlement or to take seriously similar Soviet proposals in early October 1950. The forward dynamic of policy was gathering, and, on September 30, 1950, UN Ambassador Warren Austin submitted a U.S.-drafted resolution calling on UN forces to take measures "to ensure conditions of stability throughout Korea."[78] The UN General Assembly approved overwhelmingly the motion, which sanctified destroying North Korean military forces and unifying the country under a UN command led by General MacArthur. There is some evidence that George Kennan and others at the Department of State did have reservations about the American advance toward China.[79] These men, however, were precisely those toward whom McCarthy was then directing his withering fire. It was a time, as one inside observer could remember, when "a noble boldness, rather than a craven timidity, became the order of the day—and everyone wanted to be identified with it."[80]

Sinologist and former intelligence official Harold Hinton described how the Chinese must have felt about events in Korea:

> [O]ne need only imagine American reaction if a large Soviet army, under an especially anti-American commander, were to move up the Lower California peninsula toward the California frontier. The analogy is improved if one further imagines that Southern California is the main heavy industrial region in the United States, as Manchuria was (and is) in the CPR.[81]

The Chinese were not coy or hesitant in airing their view of the imminent collapse of North Korea. In late September, the chief of staff of the Chinese People's Liberation Army informed the Indian ambassador to China that the People's Republic would not "sit back with folded hands and let the Americans come to the border." Again, on September 30, Zhou Enlai gave a public warning: "The Chinese people . . . will not supinely tolerate seeing their neighbors being savagely invaded by the imperialists." Chinese warnings were accompanied by a redeployment of their best troops into the Yalu frontier area. American intelligence was aware of the troops, although their exact disposition and intentions remained unclear.[82] Finally, on October 1, when ROK units entered North Korea, the Indian ambassador was called. In a midnight meeting, he was informed by Zhou that although the Chinese were not concerned about the South Koreans, the movement of U.S. troops north of the 38th parallel would be regarded by the Chinese as a reason for Chinese entry into the war. Professor Allen S. Whiting, a former State

Department official, notes, "In the next few days Washington received additional reports of [Zhou's] warning through allied and neutral channels and through American embassies in Moscow, Stockholm, London and New Delhi."[83] Evidently, President Truman brushed aside Zhou Enlai's warnings by discounting the credibility of the Indian ambassador who served as the channel of communication.[84] Secretary of State Acheson, astonishingly, asserted that Zhou was not an authoritative spokesman.[85]

Mao Zedong, General MacArthur, and Harry Truman: Three's a Crowd

The political *hubris* that attended General MacArthur's punch toward the north on October 7 seemed to sweep away doubts about Chinese ability or interest in Korea. The peninsula would be unified by the victorious UN juggernaut. On October 9, President Truman informed General MacArthur:

> Hereafter in the event of the open or covert employment anywhere in Korea of major Chinese Communist units, without prior announcement, you should continue the action as long as, in your judgment, action by forces now under your control offers a reasonable chance of success.[86]

Moreover, Truman also seemed ready at least to consider actions against China itself. In place of the earlier absolute prohibition on operations against China, the commander-in-chief closed his October 9 dispatch to General MacArthur with the cryptic statement, "In any case you will obtain authorization from Washington prior to taking any military action against objectives in Chinese Territory."[87]

Since the North Koreans had been beaten, China made repeated attempts to explain that they were concerned about their own security more than they fretted over the future of a fraternal communist state. The Chinese even hinted that they might be able to live with the conquest of North Korea, providing that North Korea were occupied by South Koreans and the Americans stayed below the 38th parallel. Even after U.S. troops crossed the 38th parallel, the Chinese indicated that they could live with a rump North Korean state that would buffer China's Manchurian boundary.[88] Mao Zedong, it has been reported, was up seventy-two hours before making his decision, which took effect October 16, when Chinese General Lin Biao's Fourth Field Army began crossing the Yalu at night and in secret.

On October 19, the North Korean capital of Pyongyang fell to American forces, and General MacArthur prepared to press on for his

much-heralded quick victory. North Korean Premier Kim fled to the
Yalu, leaving behind vast supplies of military equipment. Soon the North
Korean defeat turned into a rout. U.S. soldiers parachuted in front of
the retreating Koreans, and Kim's forces began to surrender *en masse.*
By the end of October, more than 135,000 North Koreans had been
captured.

General MacArthur's plan called for the Eighth Army to move up
the west coast of Korea to the Yalu River and the Tenth Corps to move
toward the Yalu somewhat farther east. But the spine of mountains running down the middle of the peninsula separated the two elements of
General MacArthur's force by more than fifty guerrilla-filled miles. The
Chinese would exploit this tactical blunder within weeks. In mid-
October, General MacArthur and his commanding general were eye-
ing an early and easy victory. Lt. General Walton H. Walker, the commander of the Eighth Army, for instance, thought the entire advance
was not unlike a quail shoot in his native Texas.[89] On October 24, 1950,
General MacArthur ordered his commanders to move all units, Korean
and non-Korean, forward to the Yalu, thus violating Joint Chiefs directives of late September. When reminded of this by Washington, General
MacArthur cited a personal message of Marshall's giving MacArthur tactical and strategic discretion. The matter was dropped. Was it reasonable, Washington pondered, to countermand the man who had
masterminded the amazing Inchon landing? By October 26, elements
of a South Korean division on the American Eighth Army's eastern flank
reached the Yalu; that night they were surrounded by Chinese Communist troops, ambushed, and sent fleeing south, encountering Chinese
ambushes throughout the withdrawal.

By November 1, U.S. forces were heavily engaged by Chinese
troops. Yet, on November 7, almost as swiftly as the Chinese had attacked, they curiously broke off contact. During this two-week period,
MacArthur's analysis of what was taking place along the front swung
from optimism to deep pessimism. He urgently requested and received
permission to bomb the Yalu River bridges, and then, once his request
was satisfied, he manifested a kind of befuddled optimism. General
MacArthur was still not prepared to view those initial, sharp contacts
with the Chinese as conclusive proof of Chinese intervention.

On November 15, he proposed to the Joint Chiefs that he press
forward with his advance. But November 15 was the date the Communist Chinese had been invited to the United Nations to discuss the
Taiwan situation and perhaps Korea as well. Nevertheless, Washington approved MacArthur's advance. In the meantime, the Chinese announced that their arrival at the United Nations would be delayed until

November 24. Inexplicably, MacArthur delayed his attack until then, when he pressed forward again announcing that the "boys would be home by Christmas." Needless to say, the Chinese diplomats refused to proceed with negotiations as the UN offensive churned ahead.

General MacArthur's final blow had only a day's momentum when the Eighth Army was hit by a strong Chinese attack. By November 26, it was clear that a full-scale counterattack was underway by six Chinese armies. In two days, the entire right flank of the UN forces was collapsing. During the next eight days, the UN forces fought heroically for their lives as they retreated south. Pyongyang was evacuated in early December; by Christmas, the boys were back on the 38th parallel.[90]

As the military defeat began to unfold, the tenuous politico–military consensus that had marked the onset of the campaign disintegrated. While victorious armies had marched north, all parties sought identification with General MacArthur's successes. Now, however, politicians and generals alike sought to disassociate themselves from one another and, of course, the deepening disaster on the Korean peninsula. This self-serving and confused scramble revealed the deep disagreements between Washington and UN military headquarters in Tokyo, brought into the open Europe's unease, and exacerbated the profound domestic frustration with the war and President Truman's foreign policy.

THE MACARTHUR PROBLEM

If there were any worries within the highest levels of the Truman administration about expanding the war, they centered on General MacArthur and not his mission. These misgivings were reflected in the hedged, frequently contradictory language of the directives sent to the general. Both the White House and the Pentagon were sensitive to General MacArthur's domestic following and his personal vanity. Indeed, during World War II, the general's independence came to be thought of as the "MacArthur problem."[91] Consequently, it was deemed necessary to qualify most of his orders heavily to ensure control of his military activities.

With the outbreak of the Korean War, the MacArthur problem resurfaced. One example occurred on July 31, 1950, when General MacArthur paid a visit to Chiang Kai-shek on Taiwan, ostensibly to inform him of the progress of the fighting in Korea and explain the decision not to use his troops. However, General MacArthur pointedly refused to invite a State Department representative to the talks, claiming that only military matters were to be discussed. Nevertheless, both

MacArthur and Chiang issued statements after the conference was over in which they praised one another's great leadership and called for closer Sino–American cooperation. Washington was upset, given the implications of these statements, that is, that the United States should support Chiang's desire to return to the mainland.

MacArthur's position was that the United States remove its prohibition against Taiwan's attacks on the mainland. To clarify Washington's position, Averell Harriman was immediately sent to Tokyo to discuss matters with General MacArthur. MacArthur told Harriman: "We should fight the communists every place — fight them like hell!"[92] After Harriman left, MacArthur issued a public statement defending his talks with Chiang and charged that his purpose was being "maliciously misrepresented to the public by those who invariably in the past have propagandized a policy of defeatism and appeasement in the Pacific."[93]

Again on August 17, 1950, MacArthur lashed out at the Truman administration. In a letter to the Veterans of Foreign Wars to be read at their annual meeting on August 28 and also printed in *U.S. News & World Report*, General MacArthur stated that it was merely his intent to evaluate the strategic position of the United States in Asia. However, the letter, which was never cleared in Washington, went on to emphasize the vital position of Taiwan in America's strategic posture. General MacArthur asserted, "Nothing could be more fallacious than the threadbare argument by those who advocate appeasement and defeatism in the Pacific that if we defend [Taiwan] we alienate Continental Asia."[94] President Truman and his advisers reacted, in Truman's words, with "surprise and shock," and Truman apparently considered relieving MacArthur of his command.[95] In the end, however, Truman merely ordered MacArthur on August 26 to withdraw the statement, although the action came too late to prevent its public appearance in *U.S. News & World Report*. By late August, the plans for the Inchon landing were well advanced, as was the decision to invade North Korea. To have fired MacArthur at the end of August 1950 would have destroyed the building momentum. Moreover, Truman's decision to invade the North brought him into line with MacArthur's aggressive spirit. Given the sense of forward movement after months of retreat, forcing the issue of MacArthur's independence could be politically disastrous. An ultimate confrontation was, therefore, avoided. By October, however, Truman felt compelled once again to discuss the relationship of his political objectives to the general's military activities. On October 9, two U.S. Air Force aircraft had attacked a Soviet airfield near Vladivostok, some sixty-two miles inside the Soviet Union. This was hardly a routine cold war border incident, and it was precisely the kind of event that could provoke the larger conflict Truman hoped to avoid. The incident was certainly the sort of thing that might heighten Truman's distrust of MacArthur and trigger any latent desire of the president to communicate face to face with the general.[96]

On October 10, 1950, three days after American troops had crossed the 38th parallel, President Truman announced that he would be flying to Wake Island in the Pacific to discuss the military effort with General MacArthur. However, the hasty manner in which the conference was arranged and its brevity once undertaken—the talks lasted only five hours—have puzzled observers. Truman has stated that he went to Wake simply because he had never met MacArthur personally and thought that the general should have a better appreciation of the "situation at home."[97] It would seem, however, that such matters and the establishment of personal contacts would have been more appropriate prior to the launching of the northern invasion. What now seems likely is that some emergency had arisen, perhaps caused by MacArthur or members of his command—such as the Vladivostok incident—that precipitated a meeting Truman may indeed have wanted for some time.

Although the meeting was brief and, on the surface, somewhat *pro forma*, it nevertheless betrayed some of the tension between the men. When, for example, the president stepped from the plane, General MacArthur greeted him cordially. But the general was dressed in a casual manner and did not salute the president, his commander-in chief. Truman, on the other hand, planted an eavesdropping secretary behind a partially opened door adjacent to private conversations between the president and the general, who, supplied with legal pad and pen, automatically took down everything she overheard. Later, when relations between Truman and MacArthur collapsed over the crisis brought on by the Chinese intervention, MacArthur's assurances that the Chinese would face the "greatest slaughter" if they intervened were released.

Truman seemed, said the *New York Times* reporter who covered the conference, "like an insurance salesman who has signed up an important prospect." MacArthur, in contrast, was said to seem "dubious." His mood was not improved, notes a biographer, when Truman left the general's entourage without transportation from the spot from where the president's plane took off. He tried to hail a passing jeep but was unsuccessful. Finally, he thumbed a ride in a pickup truck.[98]

In less than a month, of course, Truman would have reason to question the success of his Pacific journey on grounds far more consequential than the general's lack of attention to protocol. At Wake Island, General MacArthur had been confident that Chinese intervention would not occur, and, if it did take place, he expected no more than fifty to sixty thousand Chinese troops.[99] But almost as MacArthur spoke the Chinese began moving tens of thousands of troops into North Korea. Between mid-October and the first of November 1950, the Chinese had deployed between 180,000 and 228,000 members of the Fourth Field Army across the Yalu. The disaster of late November followed in due course.

MacArthur's Last Stand

Even as UN forces began their retreat back to the 38th parallel, General MacArthur released self-serving public explanations of his military strategy and the defeat he now confronted. His difficulties, General MacArthur explained, could be traced to the limitations imposed on him by Washington. This most serious burden, MacArthur complained, was his inability to do anything about the Manchurian sanctuary beyond the Yalu. This was, he said, "[a]n enormous handicap, without precedent in military history."[100] The implication was clear: he could have avoided the present disaster if he had been free of Washington's constraints.

What MacArthur presented as an unnecessary tactical inhibition was, of course, the very heart of Truman's attempt to keep the war limited, and MacArthur knew this. In short, MacArthur was attempting to use the crisis presented by the Chinese intervention to force the issue that had divided him and his congressional supporters from the administration. Truman recognized from the very outset of the fighting what MacArthur was attempting to do. Truman's reasons for not firing the general at this juncture are, one suspects, not entirely candid. Truman's explanation was that "I did not wish to have it appear as if he were being relieved because the offensive failed. I have never believed in going back on people when luck is against them, and I did not intend to do it now."[101] Truman's humanity and compassion notwithstanding, much public and certainly conservative congressional opinion still supported the general.

Thus, Truman's only real response to MacArthur's challenge was a presidential directive, issued on December 5 to all "officials overseas, including military commanders, and diplomatic representatives," that all public statements on foreign and defense policy be cleared in Washington. The president's domestic situation was sufficiently delicate that he had to camouflage a direct order to MacArthur to stop engaging in behavior for which Truman was confident MacArthur would have justifiably court-martialed a second lieutenant.[102] In the meantime, confusion, bordering at times on despair, settled over Washington. On

November 30, President Truman caused great consternation as he stated in a press conference that the United States was and always has been actively considering the use of the atomic bomb in Korea. The British were almost panicked, and Prime Minister Clement Attlee urgently requested an immediate conference with Truman, which took place between December 4 and 8. Truman's loose talk about using nuclear weapons had given rise to a British desire to participate in some manner in any future decision on the use of nuclear weapons. Most important, however, was what the British perceived to be a dangerous incipient reversal of American security priorities. Unlike congressional conservatives and MacArthur—who were pressuring Truman to do more in Asia—Attlee wanted the Americans to do much less, thereby returning containment to its original dimensions. The best way to accomplish this, in the opinion of the British, would be to begin negotiations with the Chinese Communists concerning an end of the war as well as recognition of the Beijing regime. Little was resolved, however, because alliance concerns were overtaken by the more demanding crisis represented by General MacArthur.

During December, General MacArthur's reports underscoring the threats to his small command deepended the gloom and near despondency in Washington. MacArthur restated his public position that the fight should be taken to China itself, emphasizing the "great potential" of guerrilla war in China and attacks from Taiwan. The White House and the Pentagon were besieged by a series of hysterical cables from MacArthur, requesting "permission to take whatever measures necessary to save his command. His plans . . . [include] the use of 20–30 atomic bombs against China, the laying down of a radioactive belt across North Korea to seal it off from China and the use of half a million Chinese Nationalist troops."[103]

The Joint Chiefs flatly rejected MacArthur's proposed retaliatory measures on China, and on January 13, 1951, the administration opened a counteroffensive as President Truman sent a personal letter to MacArthur urging him to hold his position or, at a minimum, only withdraw to islands off the coast of Korea. For emphasis, Truman sent generals J. Lawton Collins and Hoyt Vandenberg of the Joint Chiefs of Staff to Korea; they confirmed what the Truman administration had come to suspect: General MacArthur was consciously overestimating the threat to his command in an effort to gain approval for an attack on the Chinese mainland. Truman responded by sacking General Emmett O'Donnell of the Far East Air Force Bomber Command, a well-known advocate of bombing China. It was a clear signal to MacArthur to keep his own advocacy of attacks on China to himself and support the counteroffensive soon to be launched by General Matthew Ridgeway. Ridgeway's willingness to stand and fight *in* Korea marked him as more responsive to Washington's concept of how the war should be fought. Moreover, as military historian David Rees noted, "Henceforward, MacArthur [located in Tokyo], who had now ceased to exercise close supervision over the Eighth Army, was increasingly bypassed by Truman and the JCS in dealing with Ridgeway."[104]

In mid-February, the general went public again. MacArthur branded Ridgeway and Washington's strategy "wholly unrealistic and illusory."[105] On March 7 in a press statement, General MacArthur called the prevailing limited approach to the war as "Die for [a] Tie"[106] and pointed to Washington as being responsible for the "savage slaughter that the current strategy would bring about."

By March 12, Ridgeway reached the 38th parallel and Seoul was retaken. President Truman now prepared a diplomatic initiative that anticipated the beginnings of cease-fire negotiations and a settlement of the entire Korean question. Moreover, this was to be followed, in turn, by consideration of other problems in Asia. Presumably, this referred to the entire China question, including recognition and UN representation.[107] When the news of this overture to China was sent to General MacArthur, he was requested not to initiate any major advance north of the parallel while negotiations were in the offing. MacArthur sullenly agreed.

Suddenly, without any warning, General MacArthur thundered his own public ultimatum to the Chinese before the president had taken his planned initiative. The general arrogantly threatened the Chinese with an expansion of the war and then set out his own terms for negotiations:

> [T]here should be no insuperable difficulty in arriving at decisions on the Korean problem if the issues are resolved on their own merits, without being burdened by extraneous matters not directly related to Korea, such as [Taiwan], or China's seat in the United Nations.[108]

The legendary warrior then, magnanimously, offered his services as a negotiating partner to end the war — on Western terms.[109]

President Truman's pending offer would have signaled that he was tacitly offering the Chinese the opportunity to discuss their broader concerns in Asia if they would begin negotiations on a cease fire. General MacArthur's ultimatum explicitly precluded Truman's offer and indicated to the Chinese instead that they could expect a general war if they would not come to the negotiating table. He must have known that his ultimatum would so complicate matters for the administration that it would be unable to proceed with its diplomatic effort. Finally, it has been suggested that he was also aware that his action would jeopardize his career; for, in making this public statement, he was clearly in violation of Truman's December 6, 1950, directive that all public statements by theater commanders be cleared by Washington.

The man in the White House was infuriated.[110] Still, Truman did not relieve MacArthur. Instead, the president reminded MacArthur of the December order concerning public statements and awaited the general's response. His response came in a letter to Congressman Joseph Martin, the House Minority Leader, who had said earlier that he had "good reason" to believe that MacArthur and the Pentagon had favored using "800,000" Chinese Nationalist troops in Taiwan to fight with the United States in Korea. "If we are not in Korea to win," Martin concluded, "then Truman's administration should be indicted for the murder of thousands of American boys." Martin sent a copy of the speech to MacArthur and asked for the general's comments. On March 20, MacArthur congratulated the Republican leader for having "lost none of your old time punch" and ended by writing:

> It seems strangely difficult for some to realize that here in Asia is where the communist conspirators have elected to make their play for global conquest, and that we have joined the issue thus raised on the battlefield; that here we fight Europe's war with arms while the diplomats there still fight it with words; that if we lose this war to communism in Asia the fall of Europe is inevitable; win it and Europe most probably would avoid war and yet preserve freedom. As you have pointed out, we must win. There is no substitute for victory.[111]

The breaking point had now been reached. Truman initiated a week-long round of discussions with his top advisers concerning his next step. All agreed the president had but one course of action open to him: the removal of MacArthur and his replacement by Ridgeway. The announcement was made on April 11, and the nation was immediately caught up in one of the great spectacles of U.S. history as the general came home.

Truman was vilified throughout the country. He and Acheson were burned in effigy, and his public approval ratings dropped to less than 30 percent according to the Gallup poll. In Congress, calls for impeachment of Truman, Acheson, and Marshall were commonplace. Senator Richard Nixon characterized Truman's action as "appeasement of communism" and demanded that Truman be censured if the general were not reinstated. Others were less discreet. Senator McCarthy declared that the president was a "son-of-a-bitch,"[112] and Senator William Jenner of Indiana spoke for many when he charged on the floor of the Senate:

This country today is in the hands of a secret inner coterie which is directed by agents of the Soviet Union. We must cut this whole cancerous conspiracy out of our government at once. [Applause from the public gallery.] Our only course is to impeach President Truman and find out who is the secret invisible government which has so cleverly led our country down the road to destruction.[113]

The general and his wife arrived in San Francisco on April 17, 1951, and paraded fourteen miles in two hours to their hotel. The next day, the general told a crowd that "he was not running for President. . . . The only politics I have is contained in a single phrase well known to you — God Save America."[114] On April 19, he appeared in the House of Representatives for his farewell address. He described the global communist menace and reviewed his proposals for ending the war in Korea. Next, MacArthur hammered away at his conception of war — a conception shared by millions of Americans — and its relationship to events in Asia:

[O]nce war is forced upon us, there is no other alternative than to apply every available means to bring it to a swift end. . . . War's very object is victory, not prolonged indecision.

He concluded, choked with tears:

I am closing my 52 years of millitary service. When I joined the Army even before the turn of the century, it was the fulfillment of all by boyish hopes and dreams. The world has turned over many times since I took the oath on the Plains at West Point, and the hopes and dreams have long since vanished. But I still remember the refrain of one of the most popular barracks ballads of that day which proclaimed most proudly that, "Old Soldiers never die; they just fade away." And like the old soldier of that ballad, I now close my military career and just fade away — an old soldier who has tried to do his duty as God gave him the light to see that duty.
    Good-by.[115]

The scene in the House of Representatives was pandemonium. Senators, members of Congress, and spectators leaped to their feet, many with tears streaming down their faces. Afterwards, Harvard-educated Congressman Dewey Short proclaimed, "We saw a great hunk of God in the flesh, and we heard the voice of God."[116] Former President Herbert Hoover saw only a "reincarnation of St. Paul into a great General of the Army."[117] A distinguished senator was overheard to remark after the speech, "I have never feared more for the institutions of the country. I honestly felt . . . that if [the General's] speech had gone on much longer there might have been a march on the White House."[118] If the senator had been outside, he would have been concerned that the march had in fact begun; for as David Rees has noted;

> In the afternoon MacArthur drove down Pennsylvania Avenue to be given the freedom of the City of Washington. It was a public holiday and, as hundreds of thousands watched, bombers and jet fighters flew overhead and artillery boomed out over the capital.[119]

The next step for the legendary American general, who had led American troops into one of the greatest military disasters since the first battle of Bull Run and openly flouted his oath of office with his insubordination of his commander-in-chief, was New York. The city gave him a six-hour-and-five-minute parade, longer and larger than any in its history, including that given for Lindbergh in 1927, and twice as large as Eisenhower's victorious return in 1945. The New York Police Department estimated that more than seven million people lined the parade route. Signs along the way read, "God Save Us from Acheson," and the city hired sky-writing fliers who spelled in two-mile-long heavenly script, "Welcome Home" and "Well Done."[120]

The MacArthur Hearings:
Denouement of Domestic Confrontation

Clearly, the general was not just fading away. There followed a series of speeches throughout the country. MacArthur extolled the simple virtues of a pastoral America he hadn't seen for more than fifteen years. Yet, the years of his absence, especially the five years since the war, were among the most crucial in America's history.[121] Truman, Marshall, and Acheson had argued that containment was a commitment to world involvement and expensive military strength, but power had to be employed in a limited and controlled manner lest events elude them and war ensue. By the time of Korea, Americans had begun to accommodate themselves to this new situation. But Korea ripped at the emerging consensus, and MacArthur represented, for many Americans, a needed point of reference and seeming stability. It was reassuring for the general to state, "Though without authority or responsibility, I am the possessor of the proudest of titles. I am an American."[122] In city after city, MacArthur appeared with one arm around Mrs. MacArthur, another around his son. The general seemed the unabashed symbol of home and patriotism and what he delighted in calling the simple eternal truths of the American way.[123]

For tens of millions of other Americans, the Depression, World War

II, and the onset of the cold war had proved that there were no more simple eternal truths. Truman recognized this and counterattacked effectively by using the forum presented in the Joint Senate Foreign Relations and Armed Services Committee hearings on MacArthur's dismissal and the conduct of the war. MacArthur led off the hearings and stated once again his objection to any concept of a limited war under the close control of political leadership.[124]

The Truman administration responded as it had in meeting Taft's challenge. A solid phalanx of administration officials — Marshall, all of the Joint Chiefs, and Acheson — carefully detailed MacArthur's insubordination and attacked his notion of all political control shifting to a theater commander once war began as beyond the pale of the American civil–military tradition and the Constitution. Moreover, MacArthur's broader strategic vision was deemed dangerously in error in that his proposals would not result in an end to the war, but a wider war that would divert American resources from the truly fundamental confrontation with the Soviet Union. Finally, the administration witnesses instructed the Congress that a commitment to a full-scale Asian conflict was opposed by our European allies. Therefore, pursuing the course advocated by the general might drive a wedge between us and the Europeans. The specter of a weakened or collapsed NATO was outlined, and the fulfillment of Soviet objectives in Europe was detailed.

The result of Truman's effort was to deflect MacArthur's simplistic appeal to patriotism, which masked a notion of civil–military relations subversive of the American Constitution. The Joint Chiefs supported Truman's conception of American priorities and would not allow wedges to be driven between them and the civilian leadership of the administration. Most important, however, was the united front maintained on the issue of civilian supremacy and agreement on MacArthur's violation of this precept. Because the administration was generally successful in framing the debate in these terms, it was successful in shifting the focus of confrontation. Questions of grand strategy could and did provoke disagreement, but the principle of civilian supremacy was broadly accepted. Once the issue was set in these terms, the emotion of the general's return began to settle, and public opinion shifted away from MacArthur.

Moreover, as the hearings ended, negotiations finally got underway in Korea. The Chinese advance south stalled under the combined weight of appalling casualties inflicted by American firepower and overextended lines of supply, vulnerable to UN air superiority. The burst of optimism that greeted the opening of talks and military success would turn to growing cynicism in the fall and winter of 1951 as the talks deadlocked and stalemated fighting resumed. In the summer of 1951, the news of negotiations in a domestic context of a booming, if inflated, economy produced an atmosphere little conducive to MacArthur's case.

THE OLD COLD WARRIOR
FADES AWAY: THE END OF
THE TRUMAN ADMINISTRATION

In the longer view, however, President Truman's success in exploiting the MacArthur hearings was but a holding action because he was never able to translate his victory into increased support for himself. He may have been able to convince most of the American people that Douglas MacArthur and the conservative Republicans did not possess a prudent and constitutionally acceptable way out of the cold war and Korea, but he could not convince the same group that Harry Truman knew where the exit lay.

Further diminishing Truman's domestic support was a series of revelations, beginning in 1950 and running throughout 1951, of deficient and even corrupt administration within many agencies of the government.[125] The succession of scandals and Truman's announcement in March of 1952 that he would not seek reelection reduced the Truman administration to virtual caretaker status unable to conclude the war through negotiations or force. Senator McCarthy unleashed a renewed attack on the members of the Truman administration, starting with Marshall, whom he characterized as being a member of "a conspiracy so immense, an infamy so black, as to dwarf any in the history of man."[126] The vilification of Acheson grew, and one commentator noted that "many people burst into profanity at the mere mention of Truman's name."[127]

In July 1952, the parties nominated their candidates and went to the American people. Adlai Stevenson and the Democrats told the nation for the next three months that they "never had it so good" and raised the specter of another depression if the Republicans were elected. The Republicans behind Eisenhower, who had defeated Taft for the nomination, systematically attacked the Democrats concerning Korea, communism, and corruption. The Democrats, it was charged, had given the American people a corrupt administration at home, compounded by subversion by Communists and communist sympathizers. The endless war in Korea was proof that containment as a foreign policy was, in the words of the Republican platform (drafted largely by John Foster Dulles, who was assumed to be the next secretary of state if Eisenhower was elected), "negative, futile and immoral."

As the campaign seemed to be gaining momentum for the Republicans, it was revealed that Richard Nixon, the Republicans' vice presidential nominee, had been the beneficiary of an $18,000 special fund established for him by some wealthy California businessmen. General Eisenhower was furious and demanded that Nixon explain matters to the American people if he was going to remain on the ticket. Senator Nixon then went before the nation through a televised address on September 23, 1952, and delivered his now famous "Checkers" speech, in which he denied that he had ever used any of the money for his personal use; it had all been used to clean out the Communists and crooks in Washington. He emphasized that he, like many Americans, had found it difficult to meet payments on his car and his mortgage, and that he and his wife were struggling financially. He did admit to one gift, however:

> Do you know what it was? It was a little cocker spaniel dog in a crate . . . sent all the way from Texas. Black and white spotted. And our little girl—Trisha, the six year old—named it Checkers. And you know the kids love the dog, and I just want to say this right now, that regardless of what they say about it, we're going to keep it.[128]

The public response was overwhelmingly positive, for Nixon succeeded in aligning himself and the Republican party with the little man struggling with inflation, the war, the corruption, and the desire for a better life.[129] It may have been corny, tear-jerking stuff, but in the domestic malaise of 1952, it was devastating electoral politics.

A month later, General Eisenhower, whose attacks on Truman had become more and more pointed and slashing, announced that the first thing he would do, if elected, was make a trip to Korea for a personal assessment of the situation. This promise and a stunningly effective nationally televised speech by General MacArthur on October 27 brought the campaign to an end. A week later, twenty years of Democratic party rule came to an end in the landslide election of Dwight Eisenhower.

CONCLUSION

The Korean experience was critical in a number of ways. As Professor Robert Tucker has noted:

> In the decade following the initiation of containment, Korea stands out as the decisive event in the evolution of American policy. The Korean experience largely determined the form and course that the great transformation in American foreign policy eventually took. . . . In Europe, the

Korean conflict led to the reestablishment of American forces, the establishment of an integrated command structure, the decision to rearm Germany, and the agreement on a common defense strategy. In Asia, the Korean War led to American intervention in the Chinese civil conflict and prompted the conclusion of a series of bilateral and multilateral alliances that continue today roughly to define the extent of the American commitment in that area.[130]

In the end, this effort was widely adjudged by American academics and policymakers to be a success. Robert Osgood, for instance, observes that "one can hardly overestimate the importance of the United States achievement in containing the Communist attack on South Korea without precipitating total war. By this achievement the nation went a long way toward demonstrating that it could successfully resist direct military aggression locally by limited war in the secondary strategic areas. . . ."[131] Yet, if the war was limited, it was only so in some rather specific aspects. It was limited geographically, and nuclear weapons were not used on the peninsula. Beyond this, however, Korea was one of the most destructive wars ever fought. An estimated four million Koreans were killed out of a population of about thirty million.

General O'Donnell, head of the U.S. Bomber Command in the Far East, testified: "I would say that the entire, almost the entire Korean peninsula, is just a terrible mess. Everything is destroyed. There is nothing standing worthy of the name." Just before the Chinese came in, he elaborated, "We were grounded. There were no more targets in Korea." General MacArthur testified on May 3, 1951, "The war in Korea already almost destroyed that nation. . . . I have never seen such devastation. I have seen, I guess, as much blood and disaster as any living man, and it just curdled my stomach, the last time I was there. After I looked at that wreckage and those thousands of women and children and everything, I vomited."[132] The authoritative military publication, *The Armed Forces Yearbook*, said in its 1951 edition:

> The war was fought without regard for the South Koreans, and their unfortunate country was regarded as an arena rather than a country to be liberated. As a consequence, fighting was quite ruthless, and it is no exaggeration to state that South Korea no longer exists . . . its towns have been destroyed . . . its people reduced to a sullen mass dependent on charity. . . . Few attempts were made to explain to the American soldier why they were fighting. . . . The South Korean . . . was regarded as a "gook" like his cousins North.[133]

The war also introduced the notion of relating force to political objectives prior to achieving a thorough military victory. Negotiating while fighting was obviously not congruent with the "unconditional" military posture employed by U.S. forces just six years earlier. As Professor Thomas Schelling elaborates, "The war in Korea [was] a 'negotiation' over the political status of the country. But, as in most bargaining processes, there was also implicit bargaining about the rules of behavior, about what one would do, or stop doing, according to how the other side behaved."[134] Or as Dean Rusk has observed, "In the Korean war there came a point when the other side was ready to negotiate. . . . [I]n the Korean war . . . we . . . tried to use the amount of force that [was] required to achieve the essential objectives without letting it escalate."[135] Thus, "diplomacy of violence"[136] received its conceptual baptism in Korea. The Truman administration's response in Korea consummated a trend toward primary reliance on military instrumentalities and the use of the threat of war as the basis of containment. The economic tools of the Marshall Plan and global economic cooperation were now subordinated to military assistance and the use of force.

The war reversed an emerging policy of differentiating between the new Communist Chinese regime and the Soviet Union. After American troops were committed to Korea and the Seventh Fleet blocked Mao from storming the Nationalist redoubt on Taiwan, and especially after Chinese and American forces began to bloody each other, normal relations became almost impossible to contemplate. Indeed, the domestic distortions and convulsions of the Korean experience—epitomized by the antics of Senator McCarthy—scarred the American consciousness. Communism, not just Soviet power, but a sinister conspiracy, became the whipping boy of ruthless men and the fear of Americans great and small.

The war also had the effect of being something of a self-fulfilling prophecy. Earlier, Dean Acheson in his January 12, 1950, "defense perimeter" remarks to the National Press Club, had tried to distinguish between historic Chinese and Russian aspirations by asserting that eventually Chinese nationalism would turn against Soviet imperialism. After the Korean conflict had begun, Assistant Secretary of State Dean Rusk would say of China in 1951, "It is not the government of China. It does not pass the first test. It is not Chinese."[137]

But early relations between Mao's new China and the Soviet Union were not those of partners. The initial formal state instrument between Communist China and Soviet Russia was negotiated by Mao in Moscow in February 1950. It took Mao three months to secure the treaty, and he was gone so long "that rumors arose about Mao being detained against his will."[138] Stalin, according to Adam Ulam, was "incredibly stingy," negotiating an "embarrassingly small loan," a "pittance." Even the European satellites had "received . . . credits greater than now extended to the most populous country in the world."[139]

After the Korean War had begun, however, China became increasingly dependent on the Soviet Union. The Chinese were forced to borrow at least $2 billion to finance the Korean War, and the Soviets charged interest. The Soviets became a deterrent force on which the Chinese were forced to rely, and it was the Soviet Union that now was the voice of the Chinese position in international councils. Occasionally, the Soviets did not always inform the Chinese as to how they were proceeding in the Chinese interest, but the Chinese, in a period of profound isolation, had little choice but to use Moscow as their intermediary.[140]

The Korean War served ultimately to debase the United Nations by employing expedient stratagems to avoid the processes elaborated in the charter. Using the Soviet absence from the Security Council to vote UN sanctions against a Soviet client, though of questionable legality, would not likely be precedent if the Soviets remained alert in the future. However, using the General Assembly to obtain a warrant to move into North Korea would come to haunt the United States when the character of the General Assembly was to change dramatically in the early 1960s. The Uniting for Peace Resolution, proposed by Acheson, "provid[ed] for an emergency session of the General Assembly upon twenty-four hours' notice if the Security Council should be prevented from acting."[141] Under the charter, the assembly can only "recommend," not authorize action. But the Uniting for Peace Resolution blurred the distinction between recommendation and authorization.* By the mid-1960s, when the number of members of the UN Assembly had expanded enormously and proved unresponsive to U.S. pressure, the United States tried to move important decisions back to the Security Council. Bit by bit, however, the General Assembly slipped from U.S. control and influence.

The decision to go into Korea was predicated on the perception that American will was being tested. Although the arena was peripheral, the United States, it was believed, had to respond to establish a reputation for action that would deter probes at the center. The perception may have been in error given the murky origins of the Korean civil war. Yet, having committed American reputation or honor on the

---

*The assembly recommended that "all appropriate steps be taken to ensure conditions of stability throughout the whole of Korea." This was taken as a legal justification by the United States for crossing the 38th parallel.

periphery, the principle of containment was instantly extended to that periphery and, in theory at least, virtually everything within it.

In February of 1950, Secretary of State Acheson observed:

> The only way to deal with the Soviet Union, we have found from hard experience, is to create situations of strength. Wherever the Soviet detects weakness or disunity — and it is quick to detect them — it exploits them to the full. . . . [W]hen we have eliminated all of the areas of weakness that we can — we will be able to evolve working agreements with the Russians.[142]

During the Korean War, the Truman administration set about creating situations of strength on a global scale. Thus, the Japanese Peace Treaty, encompassing military basing rights as well as similar arrangements in Australia, New Zealand, the Philippines, the Middle East, and North Africa, began the process of institutionalizing global containment. Likewise, support of the French in Indochina or the Dutch in Indonesia, or extension of aid to Chiang Kai-shek could be rationalized as essential to this process of establishing a global network of situations of strength.

However, as Coral Bell has emphasized in her analysis of the 1950s, negotiating from strength is elusive at best and probably a contradiction in terms, especially if strength is conceived of as superiority — as seems to have been the case in NSC-68.

> The idea of negotiation from strength has had . . . the true mirage-like quality of some of the most effective political myths: shimmering promisingly, always a little farther off, across a stony waste of effort, keeping its distance at each apparent advance.[143]

If the United States found superiority and strength to be the only prudent posture from which to negotiate, why should the Soviet Union settle for less? Why should it be prudent for the Soviets to negotiate from relative weakness?

The Korean War caused profound distortions at home. Arms expenditures reached 67 percent of the budget by 1952. There were dramatic price rises and shortages, and wage and price controls were imposed as wholesale prices began to rise at the rate of 25 percent a year. In September 1950, Congress passed the McCarran Act, banning aliens who had belonged to "totalitarian organizations." In June 1951, in the case of *Dennis v. United States*, the Supreme Court held that, given the state of tension in the world, advocating or teaching revolutionary philosophy constituted a crime. The State Department began to lose some of its best people — especially in Asian affairs — as experienced diplomats were asked if they had ever dealt with Communists. After all, communism was killing American sons in Korea; why should those who truck with it at home or on the job abroad be given the benefit of the doubt?

Finally, the United States became tied to a client regime with a reputation for terror that gnawed the conscience of jurists and journalists who witnessed the political conditions of South Korea. The American effort to liberate both North and South Korea had contributed to the maintenance of highly militarized, authoritarian regimes: North Korea, according to Amnesty International, is the most closed society in the world, and in South Korea, documentation about the abuse of human rights is abundant.[144] Thomas Schelling is, no doubt, correct when he points out: "We lost thirty thousand dead in Korea to save face for the United States and the United Nations, not to save South Korea for the South Koreans." Schelling's conclusion is, however, debatable: "It was," he writes, "undoubtedly worth it."[145]

NOTES

1. Reprinted from *Present at the Creation* by Dean Acheson. By permission of W. W. Norton and Hamish Hamilton, Ltd. Copyright © 1969 by Dean Acheson.

2. Edward W. Barrett in a debriefing seminar for Acheson and his close associates, Princeton University, October 10–11, 1953. Box 65, Acheson Papers, cited by Thomas G. Paterson, *On Every Front* (New York: W. W. Norton, 1979), p. 171.

3. Dean Acheson, "Crisis in Asia — An Examination of U.S. Policy," *Department of State Bulletin*, Vol. 22 (January 23, 1950), p. 116. Acheson was paraphrasing MacArthur's observation of the preceding year: "Our defensive dispositions against Asiatic aggression . . . starts from the Philippines and continues through the Ryuku Archipelago, which includes its main bastion, Okinawa. Then it bends back through Japan and the Aleutian chain to Alaska." *The New York Times*, 2 March 1949, quoted in Acheson, *Present at the Creation*, p. 357.

4. Acheson, "Crisis in Asia," p. 116.

5. Ibid.

6. "Statement: United States Policy Towards Formosa," *Department of State Bulletin*, Vol. 22 (January 16, 1950), p. 79.

7. John Spanier, *The Truman-MacArthur Controversy and the Korean War* (New York: W. W. Norton, 1965), p. 56. For an exegesis of recently declassified documents confirming that the U.S. fully expected Taiwan to fall, see Robert R. Simmons, "Contradictions in 'Fraternal Relationships': Moscow, Peking, P'yongyang and the Korean War," *Conference on Security Arrangements in Northeast Asia from 1945 to Present*, Harvard University, June 19–23, 1978. pp. 7–8.

8. Quoted in Merle Miller, *Plain Speaking: An Oral Biography of Harry Truman* (New York: Berkeley, Medallion, 1974), pp. 286–287. See also the testimony of

General L. Bolte, Director of Plans and Operations in testimony for the Korean Assistance Act, June 16, 1950, *United States Policy in the Far East*, Vol. VIII, Historical Series of the Committee on Foreign Relations, United States Senate, 1976, p. 46. A good review of Acheson's view of the significance of Korea is in David S. McLellan, *Dean Acheson: The State Department Years* (New York: Dodd, Mead, 1977), pp. 209–211.

9. Robert R. Simmons, "The Korean Civil War," in Frank Baldwin, ed., *Without Parallel* (New York: Pantheon, 1974), p. 149.

10. "World Policy and Bipartisanship: An Interview with Senator Tom Connally," *U.S. News & World Report*, Vol. 28 (May 5, 1950), p. 30.

11. Allen S. Whiting, *China Crosses the Yalu: The Decision to Enter the Korean War* (Stanford, Calif.: Stanford University Press, 1960), pp. 42–43.

12. Ibid., p. 45.

13. Harrison E. Salisbury, "Image and Reality in Indochina," *Foreign Affairs*, Vol. 49 (No. 3, April 1971), p. 388. Mr. Salisbury has speculated that the real target of the North Korean offense, "instigated" by Stalin, was Communist China. He writes: "I think it reasonable to assume that Stalin felt he could take Washington's word—that we did not feel obligated to rise to the defense of South Korea. . . . [I]f he could overrun all of Korea he would be able to dominate Peking from positions in Mongolia, Manchuria and Korea. He would possess the power to deal with Mao as he once said he would deal with Tito. . . ."

14. Strobe Talbott, tr. and ed., *Khrushchev Remembers* (Boston: Little, Brown, 1970), p. 378. See also Robert M. Slusser, "Soviet Far Eastern Policy, 1945–1950; Stalin's Goals in Korea," in *The Origins of the Cold War in Asia* edited by Yonosuke Nagai and Akira Iriye (Tokyo and New York: University of Tokyo Press, 1977), pp. 141–142, 146.

15. U.S. Department of State, *North Korea: A Case Study in the Technique of Takeover* (Washington, D.C.: U.S. Department of State, 1961), p. 114.

16. According to a purported defector, Lt. Col. Kyril Kalinov, "How Russia Built the North Korean People's Army," *Reporter Magazine* (September 26, 1950), pp. 4–8. Also see Robert R. Simmons, *The Strained Alliance: Peking, P'yongyang, Moscow and the Politics of the Korean War* (New York: Free Press, 1975), p. 120 *passim*.

17. Glenn D. Paige, *The Korean Decision, June 24–30, 1950* (New York: Free Press, 1968), p. 97. (Paige is citing an interview he had with Rusk in 1955.)

18. Adam B. Ulam, *The Rivals: America and Russia Since World War II* (New York: Random House, Vintage, 1971), p. 171.

19. Moreover, the year before, Truman was extraordinarily cautious when arguing for a $150 million military aid bill. "It is a question of defense by the Southern Korean government . . . against Koreans from the North. I do not think our forces should be mixed up in that. The Russians would love to see that. . . . They would sit back and laugh their heads off if we got our forces engaged at all . . . and the one thing that causes me some surprise is that the Russians have not realized how much damage they could do if they really did begin to let military events start in Southern Korea. I will feel relieved when we get these [American troops] out of there" (*United States Policy in the Far East, Part II, Korean Assistance Act*, Vol. VIII, U.S. House, Committee on International Relations, Historical Series, 1976, pp. 33, 46).

20. Statement by President Truman, "U.S. Air and Sea Forces Ordered into Supporting Action," *Department of State Bulletin*, Vol. 23 (July 3, 1950), p. 5.

21. Harry S Truman, *Memoirs: Years of Trial and Hope* (Garden City, N.Y.: Double-day, 1956), p. 333.
22. Ibid., p. 340.
23. Acheson, *Present at the Creation*, p. 405.
24. Truman, op. cit., p. 339 (emphasis added).
25. Joyce and Gabriel Kolko, *The Limits of Power: The World and United States Foreign Policy* (New York: Harper & Row, 1972), pp. 579–582. In any event, even if they did not initiate the conflict, there is good reason to believe the following points: (1) They probably knew about it in advance and did not attempt to prevent the conflict. (2) They probably could have had the North Koreans withdrawn early and with honor if they were willing to exercise sufficient influence. In this sense, the Soviets' relation to the North Koreans may have been similar to Russian-Syrian and Egyptian relations in 1973. The Soviets may not have provoked the Arab attack *per se*, but the Arab attack was preceded by large arms delivery and Soviet advisers were at Arab command headquarters and with Arab field units. (3) No matter what the initial Soviet reason for acquiescence in the North Korean adventure, some evidence exists that the Soviets made it clear that they would not become involved in what they called a "Korean *civil* war" (emphasis added) but that the Chinese had more direct interests. The Chinese, in turn, tried to implicate the Soviets without success. See Simmons, "Contradictions in 'Fraternal Friendships,'" pp. 11–13.
26. Ulam, *Expansion and Coexistence* (New York: Praeger, 1968), pp. 523–525, and Acheson, *Present at the Creation*, pp. 408–412.
27. David Rees, *Korea: The Limited War* (Baltimore: Penguin Books, 1964), pp. 67–69.
28. Quoted in Miller, op. cit., p. 313.
29. Kolko and Kolko, op. cit., p. 572.
30. Ibid., and *The New York Times*, February 17, 1950.
31. Kolko and Kolko, op. cit., pp. 573–574.
32. Philip Jessup, in *Department of State Bulletin*, Vol. 22, No. 564 (April 24, 1950), p. 627.
33. Simmons, op. cit., p. 152.
34. John Foster Dulles, "The Korean Experiment in Representative Government," *Department of State Bulletin*, Vol. 23 (July 23, 1950), esp. p. 13.
35. Some observers, notably journalist I.F. Stone and historian Gabriel Kolko, have drawn from these events in Seoul and Tokyo an interesting hypothesis combining the circumstances in the months before the war with the confusion and curiously contradictory reports emanating from the battlefield during the week of June 25. Specifically, the U.S. command in Tokyo is viewed as being quite aware of the North Korean buildup and seeking to provoke a fight or perhaps maneuver the North Koreans into attacking. Thus, Dulles, as a representative of Republican conservatism, along with General MacArthur, publicly supported an increasingly belligerent Rhee. Such support, it is argued, could only have increased tensions and fears in the North, perhaps raising the fear that American military assistance was about to increase dramatically. If there was a new rapid buildup in the South, then the North Koreans would lose their recently acquired arms advantage. Once the attack occurred, whether started by South Korean incursions (as Stone suggests) or as the result of a preemptive strike (Kolko), General MacArthur and Syngman Rhee, the revisionists suggest, allowed the situation to deteriorate so as to ensure a significant U.S. intervention. Washington was, in this analysis, rather ignorant of this maneuvering. President Truman and his advisers were more or

less dependent on General MacArthur for information as to what was going on in Asia. Having been misled by General MacArthur, they were pulled into the involvement and consequent redirection of American policy in Asia desired by General MacArthur, Syngman Rhee, and Chiang Kai-shek. See I.F. Stone, *The Hidden History of the Korean War*, Second Modern Reader Edition (New York: Monthly Review, 1952), esp. pp. 1–107.

36. Cited by George F. Will, "Right Out of the '30s," *Washington Post*, January 17, 1980, p. A27.

37. Numerous accounts of the Korean War are available. Among the more concise yet comprehensive are David Rees, op. cit., and John Spanier, op. cit. Also important and provocative is the revisionist I.F. Stone, op. cit. Shorter but useful accounts and analyses are provided by Bernard Brodie, *War and Politics* (New York: Macmillan, 1973), pp. 57–112; and Martin Licterman, "Korea: Problems in Limited Wars," in Gordon B. Turner and Richard D. Challener (eds.), *National Security in the Nuclear Age* (New York: Praeger, 1960), pp. 31–58. The major documentary source on the war is U.S. Congress, Senate Committee on Armed Services and Committee on Foreign Relations, *Military Situation in the Far East*, 82nd Congress, 1st Session, 1951. Finally the civilian–military implications are dealt with in Spanier, op. cit.; and also in Walter Millis, *Arms and the State* (New York: Twentieth Century Fund, 1958), pp. 259–332.

38. Rees, op. cit., pp. 3–7, 21–26; and Kolko and Kolko, op. cit., pp. 579–582. Recently, debate concerning the origins of the war resurfaced in the pages of *China Quarterly*. Karwnakar Gupta argues that South Korean forces attacked first at the North Korean border city of Haeju on June 25, 1950, and that the North Korean onslaught was a response. See Gupta's "How Did the Korean War Begin," *China Quarterly* (October–December 1972), pp. 699–716. This article prompted a refutation and a rejoinder by Gupta. See Chang-sik Lee, W. E. Skilend, and Robert Simmons, "Comment," *China Quarterly* (April–June 1973), pp. 354–368.

39. *The Times* (London), June 29, 1950, quoted in Kolko and Kolko, op. cit., p. 583.

40. Hanson Baldwin, "Ground Aid in Korea," *The New York Times*, June 29, 1950, p. 4.

41. *Department of State Bulletin*, Vol. 23 (July 3, 1950), pp. 4–5.

42. Quoted in Truman, op. cit., p. 337.

43. Ibid., p. 337.

44. "Text of Security Council Resolution," *Department of State Bulletin* (July 3, 1950), p. 7.

45. See Brodie, op. cit., or Licterman, op. cit.

46. See Spanier, op. cit.

47. David Halberstam, *The Best and the Brightest* (New York: Random House, 1972), p. 119.

48. Perhaps the best short analysis of McCarthy is Richard H. Rovere's *Senator Joe McCarthy* (New York: Harper & Row, 1959).

49. Halberstam, op. cit., p. 118.

50. Ibid., p. 119.

51. Hans J. Morgenthau, *The Purpose of American Politics* (New York: Random House, Vintage Books, 1960), p. 146.

52. Rovere, op. cit., p. 3.

53. Ibid., p. 23. McCarthy's influence had a half-life of more than a generation. Even after his name had become an oath, in 1968 when *Eugene* McCarthy challenged Lyndon Johnson in the snows of a New Hampshire primary as an anti-Vietnam

War peace candidate, many of his supporting votes were cast in the belief that he was *Joe* McCarthy.

54. Richard P. Stebbins, *The United States in World Affairs, 1950* (New York: Harper & Row, 1951), p. 57.

55. William S. White, *The Taft Story* (New York, Harper & Row, 1954), pp. 84–85.

56. Margaret Chase Smith, "Declaration of Conscience," *Congressional Record*, Vol. 96, Part 6 (June 1, 1950), p. 7894.

57. Indeed, only six other Republicans did: Tobey of New Hampshire, Aiken of Vermont, Morse of Oregon, Ives of New York, Thye of Minnesota, and Hendrickson of New Jersey.

58. Paul H. Nitze, "The United States in the Face of the Communist Challenge," in C. Grove Haines, ed., *The Threat of Soviet Imperialism* (Baltimore: Johns Hopkins University Press, 1954), p. 374 (emphasis added).

59. Senator Robert A. Taft, *Congressional Record*, January 5, 1951, 82nd Congress, 1st Session, p. 59.

60. Ibid.

61. Ibid., p. 58.

62. Ibid., p. 60.

63. Ibid., p. 61.

64. Ibid.

65. Ibid.

66. See Acheson, *Present at the Creation*, pp. 494–495, on this point. However, Acheson quoted Taft as saying "[I] would not object to a few more divisions simply to show the Europeans that we are interested and will participate in the more difficult job of land warfare while we carry out also our larger obligations" (p. 495).

67. Announcement of the French government, May 9, 1950, quoted in Acheson, *Present at the Creation*, p. 384. The Schumann Plan envisaged that the integration of German heavy industrial capacity would make more difficult the development of independent military power. The French and any other Europeans who chose to join would sacrifice some of their sovereignty, but in return they would gain an unprecedented margin of control over German productive capability.

    A split immediately developed between the British and the French. The British perceived problems with the Schumann Plan apart from their ancient ambivalence concerning the continent and the more recent notion that the British possessed a special relationship with the Americans that would be diminished as the result of close political and economic ties with the continent. Specifically, the Labor government in power in the spring of 1950 feared that entering into any such supranational arrangement would diminish their capacity to exercises socialist principles of domestic economic planning. All this was sufficient to keep the British out of the new European economic integration for almost two decades.

68. Ibid., p. 399.

69. See Robert E. Osgood, *NATO, The Entangling Alliance* (Chicago: University of Chicago Press, 1962) for further elaboration.

70. Ibid., pp. 80–81.

71. Ibid., *passim*.

72. Malcolm W. Cagle and Frank Manson, *The Sea War in Korea* (Annapolis: U.S. Naval Institute, 1957), p. 81.

73. Robert Leckie, *The Wars of America*, Vol. II: *San Juan Hill to Tonkin* (New York: Bantam, 1969), pp. 357–358.

74. Capt. Walter Karig, Comdr. Malcolm Cagle, and Lt. Cmdr. Frank A. Manson,

The War in Korea Battle Report, Vol. VI (New York: Holt, Rinehart & Winston, 1952), p. 5.

75. This description is drawn from Rees, op. cit., pp. 77–97; see esp. pp. 90–92 for an account of the fighting in and around Seoul.
76. Millis, op. cit., p. 274.
77. Louis J. Halle, *The Cold War as History* (New York: Harper & Row, 1967), p. 220.
78. *Department of State Bulletin*, Vol. 23 (October 9, 1950), p. 580.
79. Halle, op. cit., p. 220.
80. Ibid.
81. Harold C. Hinton, *Communist China in World Politics* (Boston: Houghton Mifflin, 1966), p. 213.
82. Rees, op. cit., p. 109.
83. Whiting, op. cit., pp. 108–109.
84. Truman, op. cit., p. 362.
85. Acheson, *Present at the Creation*, p. 452.
86. Truman, op. cit., p. 362.
87. Ibid.
88. This offer was conditional on a withdrawal of diplomatic recognition, protection, and aid to the Nationalists on Taiwan. *Manchester Guardian*, November 18, 1950, cited by Harold Hinton, op. cit., p. 213.
89. Rees, op. cit., p. 128.
90. The best short account of the military action from October 19 through the Chinese intervention is Rees, op. cit., pp. 123–177. The classic study of the Chinese offensive is S. L. A. Marshall, *The River and the Gauntlet* (New York: William Morrow, 1953). There has been some speculation that MacArthur's battle plan had been betrayed by the now notorious British spy "Kim" Philby and his associates. Philby was a Soviet mole in the British Embassy in Washington and a liaison between the British and the Central Intelligence Agency. The British had a commonwealth brigade under MacArthur's command; much information regarding common concerns was channeled through the British Embassy. See William Manchester, *American Caesar: Douglas MacArthur, 1880–1964* (New York: Dell, 1979), pp. 711–713.
91. Millis, op. cit., p. 267, although Truman was fairly successful in his relationship with the general while MacArthur was Supreme Commander for the Allies Pacific.
92. Quoted by Harriman in Truman, op. cit., p. 353.
93. Quoted by Spanier, op. cit., p. 73.
94. Douglas MacArthur, "Formosa Must Be Defended," *U.S. News & World Report*, Vol. 29 (No. 9, September 1, 1950), p. 34.
95. Truman, op. cit., pp. 355–356.
96. Stone, op. cit., pp. 145–150.
97. Truman, op. cit., pp. 362–363.
98. Manchester, op. cit., pp. 706–709.
99. Richard H. Rovere and Arthur M. Schlesinger, Jr., *The General and the President* (New York: Farrar, Straus & Young, 1951), p. 258.
100. "MacArthur's Own Story," *U.S. News & World Report*, Vol. 29 (December 8, 1950), p. 17.
101. Ibid., p. 384.
102. Ibid.
103. Douglas MacArthur, "Reply to the Joint Chiefs of Staff, December 30, 1950," in U.S. Congress, Senate Committee on Armed Services and Committee on Foreign

Relations, *Hearings on the Military Situation in the Far East*, 82nd Congress, 1st Session, 1951, p. 2180; and Gaddis Smith, "After 25 Years — The Parallel," *The New York Times Magazine*, June 22, 1975, p. 20.

104. Rees, op. cit., p. 183.
105. Quoted in ibid., p. 206.
106. Ibid., p. 207.
107. Truman, op. cit., pp. 439–440.
108. Ibid., p. 441.
109. Ibid.
110. Ibid., p. 442.
111. Manchester, op. cit., p. 736; and Rees, op. cit., p. 213.
112. Spanier, op. cit., p. 212.
113. Rees, op. cit., p. 222.
114. Quoted in ibid., p. 224.
115. Quoted in ibid., p. 226.
116. Spanier, op. cit., p. 220.
117. Ibid.
118. Quoted in William S. White, *Citadel: The Story of the U.S. Senate* (New York: Harper & Row, 1957), p. 244.
119. Rees, op. cit., p. 227.
120. Spanier, op. cit., p. 217.
121. See Eric Goldman, *The Crucial Decade and After: America 1945–1960* (New York: Vintage, 1960).
122. Ibid., p. 208.
123. Ibid., pp. 208–209.
124. MacArthur, *Hearings*, p. 45.
125. For a review of the details, see Cabell Phillips, *The Truman Presidency: The History of a Triumphant Succession* (Baltimore: Penguin Books, 1969), pp. 402–414.
126. Senator Joseph McCarthy, *Congressional Record*, June 14, 1951, Vol. 97, Part 5, p. 6556.
127. Quoted by Rees, op. cit., p. 386.
128. Richard M. Nixon, "My Side of the Story," *Vital Speeches of the Day*, October 15, 1952, pp. 11–15.
129. Goldman, op. cit., p. 232.
130. Robert W. Tucker, *Nation or Empire? The Debate over American Foreign Policy* (Baltimore: Johns Hopkins University Press, 1968), p. 28.
131. Robert E. Osgood, *Limited War: A Challenge to American Strategy* (Chicago: University of Chicago Press, 1957), p. 178.
132. U.S. Congress, Senate Committee on Armed Services and Committee on Foreign Relations, *Hearings on the Military Situation in the Far East*, 82nd Congress, 1st Session, 1951, pp. 3075, 3082.
133. Cited in Stone, op. cit., p. 313.
134. Thomas G. Schelling, *Arms and Influence* (New Haven: Yale University Press, 1966), p. 136.
135. Dean Rusk, "The Revisionist Historians," *Firing Line* (Transcript), PBS broadcast, January 27, 1974 (Columbia, S.C.: Southern Educational Communications Associations, 1974), pp. 7–8.
136. See James A. Nathan and James K. Oliver, "The Diplomacy of Violence," *Society*, Vol. 11 (September/October 1974), pp. 32–40.

137. Marvin Kalb and Elie Abel, *Roots of Involvement: The U.S. in Asia, 1784–1971* (New York: W. W. Norton), p. 65.
138. Ulam, *Expansion and Co-Existence*, p. 493.
139. Ibid., p. 495; see also Salisbury, op. cit.
140. Allen S. Whiting, "'Contradictions' in the Moscow-Peking Axis," *Journal of Politics*, Vol. 20, No. 1 (February 1958), p. 120. Apparently, for instance, when Soviet Ambassador Malik made his speech of June 23, 1951, calling for negotiations to bring the war to a close, the Chinese were surprised, not having been informed prior to Jacob Malik's proposal (Simmons, op. cit., p. 165).
141. Acheson, *Present at the Creation*, p. 450.
142. Dean Acheson, *Department of State Bulletin*, Vol. 22, No. 559 (March 20, 1959), pp. 427, 429.
143. Coral Bell, *Negotiations from Strength* (New York: Knopf, 1963), p. 5.
144. Amnesty International, *Report on Torture* (London: Duckworth, 1973), pp. 143–145; see also Gregory Henderson, "The 'Other Boot' in Seoul," *New York Times*, January 16, 1980.
145. Schelling, op. cit., p. 124.

Chapter 4
Conserving
Containment

The two dominant figures in the formulation of American foreign policy during the Eisenhower years were the president and his secretary of state. The two men had come to power as the result of deep national and partisan disaffection. Most of the animus was directed toward the Democratic architects of containment. Both Eisenhower and Dulles had served that policy with considerable distinction during and after World War II: Eisenhower as supreme commander of NATO and Dulles as a diplomat.[1] The fact that they had helped build and then served that policy explains much of the continuity underlying the campaign rhetoric announcing the new administration.

The Republican party, however, was under the thrall of Joseph McCarthy, the man who had viciously attacked Eisenhower's mentor and commander-in-arms, General George Marshall, a man of enormous prestige.[2] Concessions to the McCarthy wing of the Republican Party were, therefore, inevitable. For the first two years of the Eisenhower administration, the Republicans controlled the House and Senate, and the leadership of the congressional Republicans was in the hands of the right. Eisenhower repeatedly displayed ambivalence toward this ideological bloc within his own party. The result was a tendency to yield before what he feared would be disruptive attacks from the right.[3] Nevertheless, Eisenhower was personally committed to the global structure of containment and the commitments that were implied by this doctrine. Indeed, he was to enlarge the scope of these commitments vastly before his presidency ended. In the meantime, however, he and Dulles were lined up in a mutual effort to contain the Republican right.

CONTAINING THE
REPUBLICAN RIGHT

During the first two years of his administration, President Eisenhower refused to rebut Senator McCarthy's brutalizing of the foreign service and State Department. Instead, the president adopted a strategy of waiting for McCarthy's excesses to double back on the senator and destroy him.[4] In the meantime, John Foster Dulles would proclaim the rhetoric of rolling back communist power and liberating so-called captive peoples, while appeasing Senator McCarthy by allowing him and his cohorts virtual freedom to investigate and vilify the foreign service.[5]

President Eisenhower probably did not feel these pressures as intensely. However, he, too, was not prepared to take on McCarthy publicly.[6] This reluctance on President Eisenhower's part according to many, including his vice president, was due to Eisenhower's naïveté and inexperience in political warfare.[7] But this analysis is now undergoing a revision.[8] He was above all a realist and pragmatist who was conserving and deliberate in the use of his resources, not a man to come out swinging against a McCarthy. In 1953, he assumed the presidency of a country that was torn by suspicion and hysteria. He would in later life assert that his greatest domestic accomplishment as president was the calming of this mood.[8] As Eisenhower remembered it, he "got the job done, without trumpets."[9]

This temperate attitude and approach was institutionalized in his staff system.[10] Especially in the areas of foreign and defense policy, President Eisenhower replicated the elaborate staff system to which he had become accustomed and employed so successfully in the army. The National Security Council (NSC) expanded dramatically as committees and subcommittees proliferated. Undoubtedly this slowed the decision process, but it was Eisenhower's view that the frantic effort to build the wall of containment in the preceding administration had led to the overextension of American power, and the accompanying charged domestic atmosphere contributed to the destruction of Truman's authority and threatened containment itself. Perhaps Gary Wills is correct: "Eisenhower had the true professional's instinct for making things look easy. He appeared to be performing less work than he actually did. And he wanted it that way. An air of ease inspires confidence." Furthermore, Eisenhower's style "allowed him to evade responsibilities, in the sense that if any head had to roll, it would not be his."[11]

Dulles, on the other hand, appeared to dominate American foreign policy.[12] Dulles vigorously proselytized his moralistic message of a new "political offensive" within "a policy of boldness."[13] The front page of the morning papers seemed at times permanently highlighted with pictures of the secretary of state grimly boarding or deplaning either in Washington or some other world capital. President Eisenhower, in contrast, was affable, relaxed, always smiling. His speeches on foreign policy frequently emphasized the positive, the opportunities for relaxing East–West tensions. Eisenhower articulated a deep and seemingly genuine desire to end the confrontation of Soviet and American power that, by now, was the key to world politics. And if Dulles's photographs seemed to come from the travel section, Eisenhower's came from the sports pages, for the president seemed to be perpetually teeing-off at Burning Tree or Augusta. In retrospect, however, Eisenhower's style and especially his relationship with Dulles were admirably suited to dealing with his priorities of Korea and conserving containment within the politically dangerous domestic environment confronting his administration.

Regarding Korea, Eisenhower had reached some very definite conclusions. He had carried out his campaign pledge of visiting Korea during the first week of December 1952. He came away with the conviction that further offensive military action would be enormously costly and ultimately fruitless given the strong defensive positions established by the Chinese and North Koreans during the year of stalemated negotiations.[14] To go for anything less than total victory,[15] however, risked bringing the wrath of the Republican party right down on the administration. Yet Eisenhower, by allowing Dulles to take the public initiative with his tough and belligerent rhetoric and, in some instances, adopting the same stance publicly and privately himself, put forth an image that many in Congress and America wanted to see. Though morally repugnant and ultimately destructive of the State Department Dulles's and Eisenhower's willingness to sacrifice the careers of many in the foreign service also contributed to the functional equivalent of a smoke screen. In the meantime, Eisenhower moved to end the war in Korea in a manner for which President Truman might well have been impeached.

A Korean Truce: Continuing Containment along the 38th Parallel

On returning to the United States from Korea, Eisenhower noted that America was dealing with an enemy that could not be impressed by words "however eloquent, but only deeds — executed under circumstances of our own choosing."[16] The deeds came very quickly, a pattern of escalating military pressure that would be replicated in another Asian war almost two decades later. In his State of the Union Address in February 1953, Eisenhower announced that the Seventh Fleet would be removed from the Taiwan Strait — a clear threat to the mainland Chinese, for Eisenhower was indicating a willingness to allow the Nationalists to step up their guerrilla activities against the mainland and perhaps go even further. Eisenhower was also prepared to use threats and words as well as deeds, and the threat that followed was blunt and awesome, if quietly communicated.[17] "In February, at his orders," Peter Lyons reports, "word had been discreetly passed that if the truce negotiations did not begin to show results, a few atomic weapons might, to use the jargon of the military, be 'wasted.'"[18]

Eisenhower and others in his administration believed that these threats were responsible for subsequent movement in the peace talks in March. This is arguable. At the end of March, Stalin died. It was an event of monumental importance. Suddenly, the symbol of Soviet and communist power and intransigence was gone. An extended period of transition followed in the communist world during which long-standing policies underwent important change. Among these changes was some increase in the policy latitude available to Beijing. Within weeks of Stalin's death, the Chinese decided to move to end the Korean War. In April 1953, an exchange of sick and wounded took place, but negotiations bogged down concerning prisoners in the hands of the South Koreans who might choose to stay in the South after an armistice.

Eisenhower again privately threatened the use of nuclear weapons and simultaneously bombed the only remaining strategic targets in North Korea: hydroelectric dams on the Yalu River and irrigation dams in North Korea. The latter attacks were directed at civilian populations. Such raids had been undertaken by the Nazis in Holland in 1944 and 1945 and "as all military leaders everywhere well knew, [had] been stigmatized as a war crime by the Nuremberg Tribunal."[19] A dozen or more dams remained, but the message was clear—the United States was prepared to do virtually anything, including the starvation and/or incineration of North Korea (and China?), to end the war.[20] On June 8, 1953, the Communists signed an agreement that seemed to meet most of the objectives of the Americans.

For Syngman Rhee, however, the specter of a settlement left him little better off than in 1950. Rhee denounced the negotiations, called instead for yet another march to the Yalu, said he would withdraw his troops from the UN force if the Chinese remained in the North, boycotted the talks at Panmunjom, and, when it was announced that the repatriation obstacle had been surmounted, organized street demonstrations against the impending settlement. Finally, on June 18, 1953, Rhee started releasing more than twenty-five thousand prisoners in the hope that North Koreans would be sufficiently embarrassed by the reality of thousands of their former soldiers choosing to stay in the South that the Chinese would break off the talks and resume fighting. In Congress, Senator McCarthy commented that "freedom-loving people throughout the world should applaud" Rhee's actions.[21]

Eisenhower did not applaud. In fact, an air of crisis settled on the White House as the president feared that the Chinese would refuse to participate in any further talks given the Americans' apparent inability to control their ally. But the Chinese, having made a firm decision to end the war, waited for the Americans to bring Rhee in line. By July 12, 1953, the Americans had succeeded, but only after promising Rhee a mutual security treaty, hundreds of millions of dollars in military assistance and economic aid, a voice in any postwar conferences concerning Korea, and thinly veiled threats to remove Rhee from power.[22]

On July 13 and 14, the Chinese struck at South Korean units, pushing them back several miles and inflicting thousands of casualties while the American Eighth Army stood by. As Eisenhower notes: "One possibly useful result was to remind President Rhee of the vulnerability of his forces if deprived of United Nations support."[23] On July 19, the chief UN negotiator informed the Chinese that the UN command would honor any armistice reached no matter what the ROK did.[24] Final arrangements were quickly worked out for the repatriation of remaining prisoners, and the truce was signed on July 27.

A year earlier, the secretary of state had written into the Republican platform strong words concerning "hampering orders" on the part of the Truman administration leading to "stalemate and ignominious bartering with our enemies . . . [with] no hope of victory" in Korea.[25] The Eisenhower administration had countermanded some of the hampering orders and allowed the bombing of irrigation dams and threatened the use of nuclear weapons, thereby providing the appearance of having decisively forced the end of the war. In the end, however, there had been no victory. Moreover, some of the most "ignominious bartering" of the war was of necessity carried out between America and its South Korean allies. Finally, when the war ended, the Eisenhower administration found itself agreeing, through the truce and promise of massive aid to South Korea, to accept a militarily stalemated line not unlike the one that had existed in June 1950.[26] In summary, the use of escalating force and the threat of nuclear weapons, combined with even more important changes in the communist world, had the net effect of formalizing the preexisting balance of political and military power on the Korean peninsula.

Reassessment and Continuity

Under the urging of Senator Taft and his own economic advisers, President Eisenhower reduced the outgoing Truman administration budget by more than $6 billion. At the same time, Eisenhower announced what he termed a radical departure in his first defense budget, which would be sent to Congress in January 1954: rejection of the year of crisis concept that had appeared in NSC-68 and other planning documents of the Truman administration. In its place, Eisenhower would substitute "a strong military position which can be maintained over the extended period of uneasy peace."[27] The implication was that the older planning concepts were unsound because they introduced into military budgets and planning a feast or famine cycle rather than sustained effort.[28] The Eisenhower administration believed that it could stretch out the build-up in military capability called for in NSC-68, achieving its target levels in 1957 rather than the end of 1955. Eisenhower gave to his defense planning, however, the image of a new departure. It was after all essential — as in Korea — that the appearance of change be maintained.

In fact, the Eisenhower administration's assumptions and expectations concerning a period of extended Soviet–American confrontation were very similar to those held by the Truman administration. However, the Eisenhower administration held that the rearmament effort, already well under way as a result of the Korean War, could be completed and sustained at a lower rate of expenditure than planned by Truman. This contention was the fundamental principle of Eisenhower's planning: National security was a function of a balanced budget, and economic principles must be incorporated into all military planning. The new Joint Chiefs of Staff had been selected by Eisenhower to ensure that they would be totally responsive to the new administration's defense priorities and concepts. Nonetheless, the broad foreign policy concepts on which the defense posture rested were increasingly similar to those held by Truman's administration.

As in the case of defense policy, Eisenhower had set in motion a parallel reassessment of foreign policy out of which three alternative politico–military strategies emerged:

1. *Containment:* a continuation of the basic structure of policy during the Truman years.
2. *Global deterrence:* American commitments would be actually extended and communist transgressions met with severe punishment.
3. *Liberation:* political, psychological, economic, and even paramilitary warfare designed to penetrate the communist empire, "roll it back," and liberate the captive peoples.

Global deterrence was a defensive military posture; but if aggression occurred, the response of the West would not be confined to a limited conventional response à la Korea. If American interests were global and indistinguishable and the threat to those interests monolithic, undifferentiated Soviet Communist aggression, then the United States and the free world now felt free to direct a response directly against the Soviets (or any other communist aggressor such as China). Moreover, Dulles claimed that having thus resolved the problem of military defense, the free world "can undertake what has been too long delayed—a political offensive"[30]—liberation.

Eisenhower, however, was skeptical about the notion of liberation. He did not understand how Dulles could ever effectively implement his political offensive. In fact, the first opportunity for liberation occurred in June 1953, when East Berlin workers rioted. The United States did nothing beyond an offer of free food and the establishment of soup kitchens in West Berlin. The uprising was crushed. The detonation in August 1953 of the Soviets' first hydrogen bomb made explicit what Eisenhower knew all along: Given the Soviets' growing military capacity and the importance of Eastern Europe to their security designs, liberation was at best an incredibly dangerous policy. The option was "firmly rejected."[31] In contrast, the deterrence option, with its emphasis on air and sea power, was clearly looked on favorably by Eisenhower. The appointment of Arthur William Radford ("whose maxim as a carrier Admiral in the war against Japan had been 'kill the bastards scientifically'"[32]) as chairman of the Joints Chiefs and the economic constraints issued him with his initial planning directives led almost inevitably to support for a less manpower-intensive defense posture.

In October 1953, the task of integrating foreign policy assumptions and defense planning into the first Eisenhower budget was begun. The president approved an NSC paper that allowed the services to "plan on using nuclear weapons, tactical as well as strategic, whenever their use would be desirable from a military standpoint."[33] Apart from small brush fire conflicts, all wars were now assumed to be, at a minimum, tactical nuclear wars. Moreover, massive retaliatory capability rather than ground troops was now regarded as the major deterrent to Soviet aggression. It was agreed that some American ground forces should be available to deter local aggression, but vagueness surrounded the assumption that local indigenous forces would be employed. These decisions, especially cuts in the size of the Army, opened the way for a reduction in the military budget through 1957, when the administration intended to complete the implementation of the new look.[34]

On January 12, 1954, Dulles, in a speech before the Council on Foreign Relations, explained the outcome of the new administration's policy deliberations and planning. The speech included criticism of the purported defensive, reactive, and expensive character of Truman's containment.[35] The Eisenhower administration was advancing a new conception of American policy—"a maximum deterrent at a bearable cost,"[36] in which

> local defenses must be reinforced by the further deterrent of massive retaliatory power. . . . The way to deter aggression is for the free community to be willing and able to respond vigorously at places and with means of its own choosing.[37]

Dulles succeeded through the massive retaliation speech in projecting an American policy with a tough and rigid image that obscured the administration's decision to continue American policy within the framework of containment developed by the Truman administration.[38] If anything, the options were now fewer. In the event of local aggression, the United States would rely on local forces, perhaps backed by American air and sea support; if that was not sufficient or if the aggression was major, there remained only nuclear war.

CONTAINMENT IN
A CHANGING WORLD

The rapid contraction of British power in the Middle East and the French in Southeast Asia accelerated the struggle for national independence in the non-Western world. To Eisenhower and Dulles, these momentous changes were understood in terms of the quasi-theological dogma of confrontation between communism and the free world. The Middle East, Latin America, and Vietnam were, therefore, "vacuums" into which Soviet and Chinese communism would move unless anticipated by a free world—that is, American—presence. The remnants of the Chinese civil war in and around the Taiwan Strait were formalized as the eastern frontier of the cold war and the testing ground for the notion of deterrence.

There was also a continuation of economic motives in U.S. policy in these years. The Truman Doctrine and the development of the Marshall Plan underscored the interdependence of economic, political, and military considerations in American policy in Europe. Eisenhower and his secretary of state generally framed their policies in the lofty rhetoric of ideological confrontation. But, as was the case in the Truman administration, the freedom that American power was to protect usually encompassed a notion of a particular way of life. Moreover, that way of life—its political forms and, inseparably, its economic essence—was deemed appropriate to the rest of the world.

During the Eisenhower administration, a primary objective was to protect world economic and ideological order in the emerging third world of the 1950s. However, this effort reflected a profound misunderstanding of the forces at work in the Middle East, Southeast Asia, East Asia, and Latin America. To Eisenhower and his advisers, the revolutionary changes that seemed to be activated all over the globe by the collapse of European colonial empires were not viewed as the result of complex and fragile societies being thrust into the crucible of rapid decolonization and modernization. Instead, the often violent unrest was regarded as merely the newest form of world communist aggression, requiring an American response not unlike that undertaken in Europe.

The effort to restructure emerging societies in the American image had three consequences. First, the frequently brusque shouldering aside of America's European allies as they proved unable to deal with what was perceived as communist penetration of the non-Western world introduced near irreconcilable strains in the NATO alliance. Second, this assumption of the postcolonial Western presence in the non-Western world meant that the Americans would now be confronted with forces they could not understand until the United States was itself tragically and irretrievably enmeshed in a colonial war in Asia. Finally, the preoccupation with formalizing containment outside of Europe contributed to the inability of Eisenhower and Dulles to explore developments in Soviet–American relations that might have allowed movement into a postcontainment phase of world politics.

Vietnam

By the early 1950s, after seven years of bloody counterrevolutionary warfare in Indochina, it was inescapably apparent that French colonial control could not be reestablished. American assistance was substantial but could not offset the material and psychological costs of the war the French had been waging against the Viet Minh, a Communist-led coalition of Vietnamese revolutionaries under the direction of Ho Chi Minh. The Viet Minh, with the active support of the American Office of Strategic Studies (the forerunner of the CIA), had fought the Japanese effort to impose their political and economic order on Indochina during World War II. When the French attempted to reimpose colonial rule after the war, the Viet Minh continued to fight for national independence. By 1954, the price the French were paying to deny self-government to the Viet Minh had become inordinate. The French suffered 92,000 dead and 114,000 wounded.[39] In early 1954 the French, with a garrison of fifteen thousand surrounded at Dien Bien Phu,

accepted a Russian proposal for a five-power foreign ministers conference — to include the Soviet Union, United States, Britain, France,
and Communist China — that would discuss both the Korean and Indo-
chinese situations.

Dulles and the president were concerned that an important and
vital front in the cold war was about to be compromised. Both worried that the outcome of negotiated withdrawal of France would lead
to "shift[s] in the power relations throughout Asia and the Pacific [that]
could be disastrous. . . ."[40] Neither man viewed what was going on in
Vietnam as the continuation of a struggle for independence. The Eisenhower administration came to see the imminent collapse of French power
as the breaching of the dike holding back the tide of Chinese Communist–promoted aggression throughout southeast Asia. As the president
explained in April 1954:

> First of all, you have the specific value of a locality in its production of
> materials that the world needs.
>   Then you have the possibility that many human beings pass under
> a dictatorship that is inimical to the free world.
>   Finally, you have . . . what you would call the "falling domino" prin-
> ciple. You have a row of dominoes set up, you knock over the first one,
> and what will happen to the last one is the certainty that it will go over
> very quickly.[41]

With the Geneva Conference beginning at the end of April 1954,
an air of crisis developed in Washington. The immediate reaction, especially on the part of the head of the Joint Chiefs of Staff, Admiral
Radford, was for military intervention by means of an air strike, with
nuclear weapons if necessary, on the Viet Minh positions around Dien
Bien Phu. Dulles was no less prone to intervention, although he announced publicly that any U.S. action should be within the context of
"united action." This ambiguous notion reflected Eisenhower's view that
any U.S. intervention would have to meet certain preconditions. First,
American intervention would have to have the support of Congress, and,
second, any intervention would have to be undertaken in concert with
the Southeast Asians and the British.[42]

Eisenhower wanted a victory as intensely as anyone in Washington. But Eisenhower, perhaps more than most, was aware of the domestic limits in the situation. Korea had ended less than a year earlier, and
the military situation in Vietnam seemed to require a commitment of
American manpower similar to Truman's effort at military containment
in Asia. Aside from the fact that the manpower necessary for such an
engagement would not be available under the new look, Eisenhower

sensed that there was no national stomach for another fight and probably knew that Congress, the Republican right wing notwithstanding, would not support another engagement in Asia. In fact, the congressional leadership, when consulted, further strengthened the president's hand against immediate military intervention by echoing his precondition of British approval and support for military involvement.

To meet Eisenhower's and Congress's preconditions would require a considerable diplomatic effort that precluded a quick intervention. In the meantime, the Indochina phase of the conference began on May 7, the day after the commander of Dien Bien Phu surrendered all his remaining men to the Vietnamese after fifty-seven days of seige. The United States, however, refused to participate formally in the talks. Rather, it sought to impede progress toward a settlement by dangling before the French the possibility of U.S. intervention including, it was later claimed by the French, the offer of nuclear weapons. By late May 1954, the conference had stalemated, the French government fell, and the talks were suspended pending French elections.

By the end of June 1954, the French had elected as premier Pierre Mendès-France, who assumed direct responsibility for the negotiations and promised to have a settlement within thirty days. The Geneva Conference now moved quickly to a conclusion. The substance of the agreement was to provide for a resolution of the military conflict by means of a temporary partition of the country at the 17th parallel. The final declaration of the conference explicitly stated that "the military demarcation line is provisional and should not in any way be interpreted as constituting a political or territorial boundary."[43] The political future of the country was to be resolved in 1956 in national elections. Subsequent South Vietnamese and U.S. justifications for refusing to carry out the election provisions of the Geneva Accords rested on the assertion that "conditions in North Vietnam during that period were such as to make impossible any free and meaningful expression of popular will."[44] In fact, the participants in the talks agreed that the establishment of democratic institutions or the free and meaningful expression of popular will was not something to be guaranteed by the Geneva Accords. Rather, democratic institutions and processes would be a product of elections. The elections were not dependent on any specified political conditions in the provisional regroupment zones, and the zones were clearly not viewed as political units or nascent nation-states.[45]

On the understanding and misunderstanding of these agreements rest the respective claims concerning subsequent American intervention in Vietnam. If one construes the Geneva Accords to have established two Vietnamese states, American involvement appears legally unexceptional. If, on the other hand, the language of the final declaration is interpreted as above, subsequent development of the Vietnam War is clearly a civil war and not a case of aggression as insisted by the Eisenhower, Kennedy, Johnson, Nixon, and Ford administrations.

Dulles and Eisenhower moved immediately to undo the results of the Geneva agreement on Indochina. Within six weeks Dulles convened a meeting in Manila of representatives of the United States, Britain, France, Australia, New Zealand, Pakistan, Thailand, and the Philippines for the purpose of establishing a Southeast Asia Treaty Organization (SEATO) to prevent the extension of communism.[46] Dulles sought but could not get, either from the participants in the conference or from the Congress, the kind of precommitments to the defense of the area embodied in the NATO agreement.

Dulles also sought to include the French Associated States of Laos and Cambodia, and the state of Vietnam, in SEATO. This effort was resisted vigorously by the French. The French pointed out that such an act would violate the Geneva Accords proscription against Vietnam or the other associated states from entering into alliances. However, Dulles persisted and got everyone to agree to at least a protocol to the SEATO agreement that extended the protection of the treaty to Laos, Cambodia, and the "free territory under the jurisdiction of the state of Vietnam."[47] What had been left by the signatories as a nonpolitical provisional separation of the parties in Vietnam pending elections, Dulles and Eisenhower set out to make politically permanent. The SEATO agreement and the reference in its protocol to the "free territory" in Vietnam was a clear indication of Eisenhower and Dulles's intent to transform the 17th parallel into a permanent political boundary with American support going to a separate state of South Vietnam. Indeed, the SEATO protocol extended protection to South Vietnam even before it existed.

During and immediately after the Geneva Conference, a confused struggle for power developed in the southern part of Vietnam. The government of the Vietnamese chief of state, Emperor Bao Dai, had served as a front for French colonial control since 1948. With the impending collapse of French power, Bao Dai had left Vietnam seeking refuge in France, and, in 1954, Ngo Dinh Diem became prime minister. Diem, a Catholic, had spent much of the preceding four years in the United States and gained the support of the American Friends of Vietnam, an analogue of the China lobby. He was also supported by a collection of American politicians including such senators as Mike Mansfield, Hubert Humphrey, and John F. Kennedy; a spectrum of academics; and Catholic religious leaders, most notably Francis, Cardinal Spellman.

In November of 1954, full U.S. support for Diem was announced. To ensure Diem's control, more than $325 million in economic and military assistance was pumped in the South. Included in this aid were, by some accounts, more than $12 million that Diem employed in early 1955 to bribe the leadership of the remaining domestic political opposition.[48] In October 1955, Diem organized a referendum in which the South Vietnamese had to choose between Diem and Bao Dai. Diem won more than 98 percent of the vote, and, on October 26, 1955, the prime minister proclaimed the founding of the Republic of Vietnam and himself the first president.

Meanwhile, Diem had refused to begin negotiations with the Viet Minh concerning elections. In July 1955, Diem asserted that he had not signed the Geneva agreements and that he could not, therefore, be bound by them. In this, Diem was merely reflecting the position of Dulles, who had claimed, in June 1955, that the preconditions for free elections did not exist in the North. Hence, Diem had no obligation to proceed. Instead, Diem continued his consolidation of control and, with the establishment of the Republic of Vietnam, provided the United States with a political entity in name as well as fact.

Iran

As in Southeast Asia, American intervention in the Middle East was related to the collapse of colonial control on the part of an American ally, in this case Great Britain. In 1951, the Iranians had nationalized the Anglo-Iranian Oil Company. Fearing Soviet involvement if the Iranian economic structure collapsed, Truman had maintained a low-level economic assistance program even as he refused to prevent the oil companies from trying to bring Iran and the nationalist government of Premier Mohammed Mossadegh to their knees. Eisenhower and Dulles decided very early in their administration that Mossadegh would have to go. Significantly, however, it was not Eisenhower's intention merely to retrieve British interests and influence in the area. Rather, the president sought to replace the British in Iran even as he replaced the French in Indochina and would try to replace the British throughout the Middle East during 1956 and 1957. The conviction existed that British power was forever broken, thereby leaving a politico–strategic vacuum in the area. Underlying these balance-of-power abstractions were the realities of oil.

Eisenhower's election had been heavily financed by the American oil industry; and numerous oil men, investment bankers, and other titans of the corporate world constituted a clear majority of the men Eisenhower counted as his closest friends. He was, therefore, intuitively responsive to their interests and concerns, and his entire conception of the national economy and America's role in the global economy was pervaded with their views concerning free enterprise, access to raw materials, and world markets.[49] It is unlikely, therefore, that the dangerous implications of a nationalist success in Iran for American oil interests throughout the Middle East escaped him. And finally, the situation in Iran, if carefully orchestrated, provided an opportunity for replacing British power and its economic presence.

In March 1953, Eisenhower, Dulles, and Undersecretary of State Walter Bedell Smith had agreed with Eden to seek "alternatives to Mossadegh."[50] This understanding was reached after the United States had tried and failed in the first weeks of the Eisenhower administration to bring Mossadegh in line with a threatened cut-off in U.S. economic assistance. Mossadegh had responded that he would turn to the Soviet Union if need be, although he would prefer to work with the Americans. The Americans urged the Iranian premier to settle with the British, then the United States would consider further aid. Mossadegh refused, and, in early August 1953, Kermit Roosevelt, Theodore Roosevelt's grandson and the Central Intelligence Agency's primary operative in the Middle East, was dispatched to Iran for the purpose of bringing down Mossadegh's government and turning U.S. support to the Shah.

By this time, the situation in Iran was seething and amenable to Roosevelt's efforts. On August 19, Roosevelt, using a Tehran basement as a command post, engineered a coup.[51] Within three days, Mossadegh had been arrested and the Shah returned from Rome, where he had been consulting with Allen Dulles, the head of the CIA. Earlier, on August 21, Eisenhower received a note, probably from Roosevelt, that read in part: "The Shah is a new man. For the first time, he believes in himself because he feels that he is king of his people's choice and not by arbitrary decision of a foreign power."[52] The new government of Iran was immediately extended $45 million in economic assistance, and, a month later, Kermit Roosevelt was awarded the National Security Medal by Eisenhower.[53]

Next, the United States undertook the negotiation of a new oil arrangement that reduced substantially the British position while increasing the American share. American antitrust laws were adjusted to permit the formation of the American portion of the cartel, and Iranian oil production was carefully controlled by the consortium to avoid a reduction of world oil prices.[54]

Guatemala

The situation in Guatemala a year later was somewhat different than the Iranian case in that the regime of Jacobo Arbenz Guzmán accepted and depended on domestic Communists for support.[55] The existence of leftist and Marxist politics in Guatemala is not surprising in view of the country's postwar history. Prior to 1944, a series of dictators had served as a governmental front for a vast concentration of private American political and economic power, the United Fruit Company. Since the late nineteenth century, it had bought hundreds of square miles of banana-producing and nonproducing acreage, employed forced labor, and controlled the only railroad in the country. In 1944, however, the last dictator, General Jorge Ubico, who admired and compared himself favorably to Hitler, was overthrown and replaced by a military junta that included Arbenz.

Arbenz was subsequently elected president in 1951, and Marxist activity increased as Communists were taken into the government. Moreover, during 1952 and 1953, heavy-handed suppression of anticommunist labor and political leaders became commonplace, although this activity cannot be dissociated from the ongoing antigovernment and anticommunist activities of United Fruit, which included the end of tourism promotion by American companies and, more important, the reduction of both international and bilateral economic assistance from the United States. In March 1953, matters came to a head as Arbenz expropriated more than 230 thousand acres of uncultivated land for which United Fruit was compensated $600,000 in long-term interest-bearing bonds — the low valuation previously placed on the land by United Fruit to escape Guatemalan taxes. The president of United Fruit reportedly remarked at this time: "From here on out it's not a matter of the people of Guatemala against the United Fruit Company; the question is going to be communism against the right of property, the life and security of the Western Hemisphere."[56]

Washington saw matters in a similar light. U.S. Ambassador to Guatemala John E. Peurifoy described his first impression of Arbenz in 1953:

It seemed to me that the man thought like a Communist and talked like a Communist, and if not actually one, would do until one came along.

I so reported to Secretary Dulles, who informed the President; and I expressed to them the view that unless the Communist influences in Guatemala were counteracted, Guatemala would within six months fall completely under Communist control.[57]

This was hardly news to Eisenhower and Dulles. They had, in fact, sent Peurifoy to Guatemala to coordinate the activities of the CIA and other U.S. ambassadors in Central America — activities explicitly directed at the overthrow of the Arbenz regime.[58]

The coup itself did not come until June 1954, for the liberation army had to be prepared. The CIA employed Carlos Castillo Armas, a graduate of the U.S. Army Command and General Staff School, to lead a band of mercenaries from their base camp in Honduras with air support flown by American CIA pilots out of Managua International Airport in Nicaragua. Eisenhower closed a personal review of the coup d'etat plans on June 16, 1954, with the observation, "I want all of you to be damn good and sure you succeed. I'm prepared to take any steps that are necessary to see that it succeeds. When you commit the flag, you commit it to win."[59]

Within four days, Castillo Armas had led his rebel army across the border, and a handful of CIA piloted aircraft were bombing the capital. On June 20, Peurifoy, with a .45 pistol strapped to his hip and with marine guard accompaniment, negotiated the final exchange of power, as American pilots bombed the radio station and army headquarters. Within a week, Castillo Armas arrived in Peurifoy's private plane and assumed power.

The first act of Castillo Armas in the aftermath of the coup was disenfranchisement of about 70 percent of the population. Next, an election was held in which Castillo Armas received 99.9 percent of the votes cast. There was no opposition. Eisenhower noted in his memoirs:

> Castillo Armas was . . . confirmed . . . by a thundering majority, as President. He proved to be far more than a mere rebel; he was a farseeing and able statesman . . . he enjoyed the devotion of his people.[60]

This "farseeing and able statesman" proceeded to suspend congress and all constitutional rights, end agrarian reform, thereby returning all land to United Fruit, and end all rights and privileges of labor organizations. Finally, Castillo Armas established a committee for defense that could secretly name anyone, without appeal, a Communist who was in turn subject to arrest and death; 72,000 people were so named within four months.[61] For this display of leadership, the Castillo Armas regime received $90 million in American aid over the next two years. In contrast, from 1944 through 1953, the leftist regimes received — apart from road-building subsidies — less than $1 million in economic assistance.[62]

Intervention and Containment

In April 1953, the President had proclaimed that among the "few clear precepts, which govern its conduct in world affairs, the United States counted: . . . Any nation's right to form a government and an economic system of its own choosing is *inalienable*. . . . Any nation's attempt to dictate to other nations their form of government is *indefensible*."[63] In view of the preliminary planning then underway for both the Iranian and Guatemalan coups, how are we to explain the gross inconsistency of this statement with contrary policies already in motion?

One answer might be simply to discuss the Iranian and Guatemalan coups as sordid but nonetheless deviant cases designed to protect the particular interests of political benefactors, past business associates, present investments, or future employment opportunities. Eisenhower's connection with American oil interests has been noted. As a lawyer, John Foster Dulles had drawn up the contracts between United Fruit and the Guatemalan government by which whole provinces were turned over to the company; the assistant secretary of state for inter-American affairs at the time of the coup held a significant block of United Fruit stock; Allen Dulles, the head of the CIA, had been president of the company; and Walter Bedell Smith, the undersecretary of state, would join the board of directors of United Fruit on leaving the State Department.

Although this line of analysis is straightforward and on its face powerful, the Guatemalan and Iranian coups must be placed in a broader context of policy development during the early Eisenhower administration. Viewed in relation to parallel events in Vietnam, a systematic set of attitudes and pattern of policy with respect to change in the non-Western world is apparent. In all these instances, anti-Western nationalism or revolutionary leftist political activity was viewed by Washington as externally derived, the product of international communist penetration. Men such as Eisenhower and Dulles found it impossible to accept that revolutionary change in the non-Western world could result solely or even primarily from indigenous conditions. And if they did accept the possibility, such change was nevertheless a threat to their conception of acceptable political and economic order. Moreover, even if they had regarded such revolutionary change as legitimate — and there is no evidence whatsoever that they did — perceived domestic political constraints were such that they could not admit it.

In summary, the Eisenhower administration had begun, during its first years in office, to develop and elaborate a conception of containment in those non-Western areas regarded as peripheral by Kennan, Acheson, and the other framers of the containment policy. The modalities of containment in the non-Western world were as yet crude — these coups were frenetic affairs conducted by romantic types straight out of contemporary fiction. Kermit Roosevelt directing a nation's destiny from a basement or an American ambassador personally conducting a coup d'état with a gun appended to his hip is almost comical until we reflect on the consequences of their actions for the people of the countries in question. Nevertheless, their activities were consistent with Eisenhower's view that containment must be carried out at lower cost than in the Truman years if it was to be domestically acceptable. From this standpoint, the immediate ends achieved, the salaries, the bribe funds, the limited equipment required by a Roosevelt or Peurifoy, and, subsequently, the few hundred million dollars in military and economic assistance compared favorably to the tens of thousands of casualties and billions of dollars consumed by containment in Korea.

CONTAINMENT
THROUGH BRINKMANSHIP

The crisis of the Taiwan Strait during 1954 and 1955 is another example of the Eisenhower view of global containment. Because the crisis involved the Chinese civil war, the situation was perhaps as dangerous domestically as it was internationally. On no other issue was the Republican right more vocal; indeed, it had emerged as an important political force because of the China issue. Consequently, the contours of the crisis were shaped by Eisenhower's concern for this domestic right flank. At the same time, the Eisenhower administration confirmed its willingness to threaten nuclear war. By the end of the crisis, Dulles would formalize nuclear threats as the preeminent component of an American-constructed peace.

The Onset of the Crisis

The tensions of 1954 were the ongoing essence of the relationship between Chiang's regime in Taipei and Mao's in Beijing. During 1953 and early 1954, the Eisenhower administration announced that it was removing the Seventh Fleet from the Taiwan Strait and, in response to strong lobbying, increasing American economic and military assistance to Chiang. The Chinese Communists, anticipating increased military pressure from Taiwan, felt compelled to signal their disfavor. By midyear 1954, the Communists and Chiang were exchanging threats of invasion. Air and naval incidents gradually intensified and increased in number. In August 1954, Syngman Rhee, speaking in the U.S. House of Representatives, called for the United States to join him and Chiang Kai-shek in a full-scale invasion of the mainland. In September 1954, the Communists began shelling the Nationalist island of Quemoy two miles off the mainland, and the confrontation was joined.

Perhaps the most difficult aspect of this early phase of the escalating confrontation was in Washington, where Senate hawks demanded a decisive response to the Communists' use of force. The initial American response was a proposal to submit the issue to the United Nations, but Chiang refused, fearing that the United Nations might resolve the broader question of the civil war against him. The only apparent remaining course, therefore, was the defense treaty with Chiang that was negotiated and eventually signed on December 2, 1954.

The Communists may have begun their escalation as an essentially "preemptive or spoiling attack."[64] By the end of the year, however, they were confronted with a U.S. guarantee of mutual assistance to Chiang. Moreover, the public agreement was ambiguous concerning the American commitment to the defense of the offshore islands and the use of force by Chiang. It is probable that this ambiguity was inevitable and consciously contrived. Eisenhower and Dulles sought simultaneously to balance the pressures of the congressional hawks who would have been infuriated by any withdrawal of U.S. support, Chiang's desire to extend U.S. commitment and involvement, and the administration's private wish to avoid precisely such involvement and commitment.[65] Mao, however, continued to probe, bombing the strategically insignificant Tachen Island and assaulting amphibiously the island of Ichiang near Tachen. The administration now had to deal with an escalation of the crisis. The mutual security treaty may have contained the home front, but it clearly had not stabilized the situation in East Asia.

The Crisis Goes to the Brink

Eisenhower resolved that the most appropriate response would be an embellishment of the treaty — a precommitment on the part of Congress to give the president discretion in the implementation of the treaty and in meeting the renewed crisis. The resulting "Formosa [i.e., Taiwan] Resolution" found the Congress affirming Eisenhower's "inherent powers" to deal with the situation as he saw fit.[66]

The specifics were left vague and ominous. Ambiguity and its manipulation were, however, the essence of the American position. Thus, after a trip through Southeast and East Asia, Dulles returned to Washington in March 1955 and informed President Eisenhower that the odds were even that the crisis could not be resolved without war and that war would require the use of nuclear weapons. Vice President Nixon publicly noted that "tactical atomic explosives [are] now conventional,"[67] and Eisenhower agreed: "I see no reason why they shouldn't be used just exactly as you would use a bullet."[68] The president's statement was qualified with disclaimers as to the difficulties of using these weapons on a battlefield; however, this orchestration of ambiguity and threat brought the crisis to a peak. The Joint Chiefs, through a public statement by Admiral Robert Carney, chief of naval operations, recommended a preemptive strike, but American allies such as Britain and Canada stated flatly that they would not join in any fight to protect the offshore islands.

Eisenhower now found himself caught between his administration's rhetoric, domestic hawks urging escalation, and America's allies, who were quickly placing distance between themselves and the United States. Eisenhower reacted by leaking a statement denying dire predictions of imminent aggression from the mainland. Moreover, in April 1955, Eisenhower moved diplomatically by urging Chiang to withdraw his troops from Quemoy and Matsu in exchange for an increase in the American military presence on Taiwan and a blockade of the mainland. Chiang demurred, but there was no further escalation, and the crisis petered out in late April 1955. The Communists, like the United States, were under pressure from third parties — in this case, third world countries urging a reduction in tension. Desiring greater influence with these countries and perhaps concerned about American threats, the Communists relaxed the pressure on the offshore islands.[69] In addition, Soviet support for Mao weakened as the crisis intensified and the possibility of war, including the use of nuclear weapons, increased.[70]

Dulles would, in subsequent months, take this turn of events as evidence that the threat of massive retaliation was a viable foundation for American policy. Creating an atmosphere of risk and ambiguity was by definition dangerous, the secretary of state would argue, but it could be managed to deter your opponent:

> You have to take chances for peace just as you must take chances in war. Some say that we were brought to the verge of war. Of course we were brought to the verge of war. The ability to get to the verge without getting into the war is the necessary art. If you cannot master it, you inevitably get into war. If you try to run away from it, if you are scared to go the brink, you are lost.[71]

Eisenhower and Dulles' brinkmanship in the Taiwan crisis seems to have been directed as much toward America and world opinion as toward China.[72] They tried to force a cease fire with this nuclear brinkmanship, but they also attempted to demonstrate the administration's willingness to work at the outer limits of the diplomacy of violence. A reputation for recklessness was a weapon with many surfaces. Its psychological purpose was not meant to be limited to just Quemoy and Matsu.

The payoff in East Asia was limited. More important, perhaps, Eisenhower and Dulles were able to put on display in early 1955 the operational crux of the new look—deterrence by threatening massive nuclear retaliation. The dramatic display of will, the bold walking to the brink, assumed added importance. In the early spring of 1955, the pressures on the United States to meet the Soviets at the summit were becoming irresistible. Eisenhower and Dulles agreed with the general assessment of Truman and Acheson that if there were to be negotiations, they should be conducted from positions of strength.

NEGOTIATING FROM STRENGTH AND CONTAINING DETENTE

In mid-1955, the Eisenhower administration seemed to be making considerable headway in its effort to consolidate global containment. Paradoxically, the presumed source of America's and the free world's danger was undergoing significant changes. Stalin's death released great anxiety and confusion within the Soviet ruling elite. Fears of a coup prompted the dispersal of security troops throughout Moscow, and the members of the Presidium sought to avoid disintegration of the government by agreeing to form a fragile collective dictatorship with Georgi M. Malenkov as prime minister. By July 1953, an uneasy equilibrium of ambition and power seemed to have developed.[73] In the meantime, Malenkov and the Presidium started to de-Stalinize Soviet life and Soviet foreign policy. Ten days after Stalin's death, Malenkov proclaimed that there were no disagreements or disputes between the Soviet Union and other states, especially the United States, that could not be resolved by peaceful means.

The View from Washington

Washington's reaction to the death of Stalin was, at the outset, as confusing as the events in Moscow. By the end of March 1953, Eisenhower had decided that a speech acknowledging and reviewing the changed

circumstances was in order.[74] In contrast to Eisenhower's instinct to respond positively, Secretary Dulles was prepared to stand Eisenhower's
argument on its head. Yes, an opportunity was available to the United
States in Stalin's demise — an opportunity to take advantage of what was
seen as the fatal weakness of the Soviet or any totalitarian society — the
problem of leadership transition. Dulles argued that any apparent concessions on the Soviets' part resulted "because of outside pressures, and
I don't know anything better we can do than to keep up these pressures right now."[75] For months after the news of Stalin's death, Dulles
seemed preoccupied and enthusiastic about the possibility that the new
leadership would devour itself as its members struggled for power.[76]

Accordingly, Dulles fought a vigorous rearguard action against the
speech. When it was clear that the president intended to give it anyway, Dulles worked to make its tone as tough and uncompromising as
possible or to qualify it so as to render it meaningless. When the speech
was finally delivered on April 16, 1953, it emerged as a mix of new
hope and cold war gamesmanship. Eisenhower, while proclaiming that
"this is one of [the] times in the affairs of nations when the gravest
choices must be made, if there is to be a turning toward a just and
lasting peace,"[77] required of the Soviets nothing less than a renunciation and reversal of their entire foreign policy since the end of the war.
Eisenhower saw a "chance for peace" only if the Soviets would
concede — as "genuine evidence of peaceful purpose" — every point at issue
in the cold war.

Significantly, the Soviets published the Eisenhower speech in its entirety and publicly responded to it on April 25, 1953, using the front
page of *Pravda* to do so.[78] But nothing else followed; perhaps it was
too much to expect a breakthrough. Both governments were caught up
in their respective periods of governmental transition, with the Soviets
perhaps facing the more difficult task.[79] In any event, Eisenhower seems
not to have expected an immediate response and suggests that the speech
was as much for the record as it was a serious effort to indicate negotiations.[80] The Soviets, in their response, indicated a willingness to proceed to "serious businesslike discussions," but, as Peter Lyon notes, "in
the White House nobody picked up the telephone."[81]

An Opportunity Missed?

Some students of American and Soviet foreign policy have suggested that
this period was one of those rare moments when serious Soviet–American negotiations on the future of Europe could have been undertaken.[82]
In 1952 prior to Stalin's death, the Soviet Union had proposed Four

Power talks on a German peace treaty and agreed to the rearmament of a reunified Germany if it accepted strict neutrality and nonalignment with any bloc or coalition.[83] A neutralized Germany, even rearmed, was clearly more appealing to the Russians than a rearmed West Germany integrated into an avowedly anti-Soviet military alliance.[84]

Of no less importance in evaluating this period of Soviet–American relations was the nature of the strategic balance between the two countries. Perhaps at no other time than between 1952 and late 1953 did the United States possess greater strategic superiority over the Soviet Union. The Soviets possessed a very limited supply of atomic weapons and no intercontinental bombers with which to deliver them. Moreover, even the Soviet explosion of a thermonuclear device in August 1953 did not transform this situation; it would be still another year or more before the Russians would acquire credible intercontinental delivery capability.[85] Thus, if ever a situation existed in which the United States could negotiate from strength, it was during the last year of the Truman administration and the first one to two years of the Eisenhower administration.

Churchill clearly thought the time was auspicious and, in May 1953, called for a summit conference to seize the moment. "The Great Khan is dead," he exclaimed. He cautioned that "it would be a mistake to assume that nothing could be settled with Soviet Russia unless or until everything was settled."[86] Churchill thought he saw "a profound movement of Russian feeling" and hoped that the West would move to encourage the positive development of this situation. During both 1953 and 1954, Soviet budget allocations for defense declined.[87] In Washington, however, detente would have to contend with Dulles and a reluctant Eisenhower. The whole thing, Dulles grumbled, was a "phony peace campaign."[88]

By early 1954, however, the opportunity, had it ever existed, began to slip away. The Russians removed their offer of a unified but neutralized Germany and advocated a settlement that would maintain the two Germanies.[89] The stiffening Soviet posture may have been a reflection of an evolving debate within the Presidium. Malenkov's priorities had their opponents in the military, and there were those within the Presidium, notably Nikita Khrushchev, the leader of the Soviet Communist Party, who were prepared to use these disagreements to their own personal ends. The debate in the Kremlin leadership centered on Malenkov's downgrading of the traditional Soviet emphasis on heavy industry and his denigrating of nuclear weapons as realistic war-fighting implements. Khrushchev sided with those in the collective leadership who remained skeptical of Malenkov's contention that the use of nuclear weapons had become unthinkable. As the debate gained momentum in the Soviet Union, it was fed by Dulles' statement concerning "massive retaliation," and the rumblings of nuclear intervention in Vietnam and, later, in the Quemoy-Matsu crisis.

Moreover, developments in NATO confirmed the central role of nuclear weapons in American strategy. In the view of the "new look," it was clear that the United States would not be providing increased manpower. The only recourse, therefore, was the implementation in Europe of "a strategy based upon a tactical nuclear response to conventional aggression in order to support this objective [the defense of Western Europe] at a level of economic and manpower contributions that the allies were willing to pay"[90] — and the rearmament of Germany.

In the Soviet Union, the new look, the evolving strategy of brinksmanship, a nuclear strategy for NATO, and the prospect of German rearmament could not help but reinforce the arguments of those within the Presidium who spoke against Malenkov. Notwithstanding Ambassador Bohlen's warning from Moscow,[91] West German rearmament was announced in December 1954. The Soviets responded by forming the Warsaw Pact — a more tightly integrated structure than NATO.[92] Furthermore, the debate within the Presidium came to an end, with Khrushchev supplanting Malenkov as the primary spokesman for the collective leadership. With the shift of control in early 1955, the odds in favor of serious negotiations about Germany, arms control, or any other issues probably decreased. Whereas Malenkov seemed willing, for the foreseeable future, to accept the implications of Soviet strategic inferiority, Khrushchev was not. In time, Khrushchev would come to display ambivalence over the costs of achieving parity with the United States. But in 1955 one of his first acts was to increase the defense budget by 12 percent.

By not vigorously exploiting the opportunities presented after Stalin's death, Eisenhower and Dulles may have undercut forces working for detente. In the place of Malenkov, they got Khrushchev, a man who was prepared to use anything to gain for the Soviet Union a position of strength from which to negotiate. This is not to say that Khrushchev was never serious in his off-and-on pursuit of detente over the next decade. He was clearly, however, a tough adversary because he, like Dulles and Eisenhower, did not believe in negotiating from a position of apparent weakness. Consequently, after February 1955, the United States and the Soviet Union were once again led by men whose behavior would, as in the late 1940s, reinforce their respective suspicions about one another.[93]

The "Spirit of Geneva"

Following the 1954 elections, in which the Democrats recaptured the House and Senate, the new Democratic leadership in Congress was urging Eisenhower toward the summit. Because Eisenhower was now dependent on the Democrats for support of his programs, he found it difficult to resist their urgings for a Soviet–American meeting. Furthermore, Khrushchev began to maneuver in early 1955 to cut away some of the preconditions thrown up by Dulles and Eisenhower; there were two simultaneous and dramatic Soviet actions. In April 1955, the Soviets requested that the foreign ministers of the four major powers meet in Vienna to work out a treaty to end the occupation of Austria, thereby neatly removing one of Dulles's preconditions to negotiations. Dulles held, however, that the neutralization treaty was one more piece of evidence that the hard line worked, for he took the treaty as evidence of the liberation of Austria.[94]

The second major Soviet overture concerned disarmament and involved the Soviets' accepting positions of the disarmament position previously adopted by the United States. The Soviets dramatically reversed their previous policy: dropping their demand for the abolition of nuclear weapons at the outset and accepting Western European (but not U.S.) proposals on manpower level reduction formulas. Finally, they accepted the notion of international control, including some form of inspection and access to internal military budgetary processes and defense installations.[95] The Soviet proposal included "jokers": a ban on nuclear testing at the outset (unacceptable to the West); the use of nuclear weapons would have to be approved by the UN Security Council (thereby subject to Soviet veto); force levels would be conditional on the end of all overseas bases (thus the end of U.S. bases in NATO, SEATO, North Africa, and Japan); and uncertainties concerning inspection.[96] Nevertheless, they caught the United States absolutely unprepared.

A good deal of embarrassed obfuscation followed as the administration scrambled to prepare a fallback position. The outcome was the administration's "open skies" inspection proposal. It called for the exchange of detailed information about the respective defense establishments and open aerial inspection of each other's territory; however, such information about the American defense establishment was relatively available and information about the Soviets' was not. Thus, the Soviet Union had little to gain by accepting the American proposal. Indeed, open aerial inspection might reveal the magnitude of Soviet weakness.[97] The plan was unacceptable to the Russians, and Eisenhower and Dulles apparently anticipated that it would be. Eisenhower recalled: "We knew the Soviets wouldn't accept, we were sure of that."[98]

Both the United States and the Soviet Union approached a summit conference that had been gestating for years with limited expectations and skepticism: the Soviets in the hope that they could gain time to close the strategic gap with the United States[99] and the United States because they could not gracefully avoid going and because of their difficult propaganda position.

Under the circumstances, the conference — at least as a public relations exercise — would have to be counted something of a success. Eisenhower's open skies proposal, dropped extemporaneously and unannounced into a formal discussion on disarmament, had the desired effect: maximum press coverage, minimum Soviet response apart from momentary confusion, and a vague commitment to study the proposal. No movement was made on other agenda items, as virtually all substantive items were deferred to a foreign ministers' conference to follow in the fall. Nonetheless, in the formal and the few informal contacts that occurred, the president, to the chagrin of Dulles, succeeded in "project[ing] an earnest and pacific intent, a serious yearning for conciliation, a readiness to grant the other side a rectitude no less than his own." The Soviets responded with what Eden termed a "new found . . . enthusiasm for free and easy methods."[100] Virtually all observers agree that at a minimum it was a refreshing change in style for all concerned and that there was indeed a new spirit of discourse among the heads of state. On the issues, however, no movement was made either at the Geneva conference or later at the foreign ministers' conference in October 1955.

The notion of a *spirit* of Geneva is therefore appropriate because it conveys the idea of something ethereal and lacking in substance. Opportunities for serious negotiations at the Geneva Conference may have existed. However, given the attitude with which the United States and the Soviet Union approached the conference, such opportunities were extremely narrow. The period of opportunity passed when the Soviets achieved thermonuclear status and began moving toward building their own positions of strength in 1954. Earlier, during the period of leadership transition in both countries, the United States seemed to possess the strength, even superiority, that it had deemed the necessary prerequisite for negotiations since the end of the war.[101] Kennan, in his long telegram, had argued that it was incumbent on the United States to be able to respond to what he thought would be the inevitable domestic changes in the Soviet Union. In the early 1950s, the United States possessed the military superiority to have risked a testing of the Soviets' responsiveness. However, the signal that the United States was willing to move into a postcontainment era was at best ambiguous and perhaps unwillingly sent. Once Khrushchev began consolidating his power, it was no longer clear that anyone was listening. By then, Khrushchev sought to anticipate and contain the pressures in Soviet foreign and domestic policy foreseen by Kennan.

THE SUEZ CRISIS

If the vision and spirit was perhaps emerging at Geneva, the body of one of the participants soon failed. On returning from Geneva, Eisenhower, now sixty-five years of age, took a long vacation in Colorado that included strenuous and extended rounds of golf. On September 23, 1955, the president suffered a heart attack; he lay near death in Fitzsimmons General Hospital in Denver. For almost a year, the effects of the heart attack and an intervening attack of ileitis were to be apparent. In the meantime, perhaps the greatest crisis of his administration was set in motion in the Middle East.

The Suez crisis had its origins in Dulles's and Eisenhower's obsession with international communism and their inability to grasp fully non-Western nationalism. In early 1955, the British, sensing that their hold on their base at Suez was increasingly tenuous, sought to shore up their Middle East military presence and isolate the nationalist views of Egyptian President Gamal Abdel Nasser. American interests paralleled those of the British. Dulles wanted to replicate the SEATO arrangement in the Middle East to prevent communist penetration of the area. At length, in February and April 1955, an alliance—"The Baghdad Pact"—was completed that linked the so-called northern tier of states in the region—Turkey, Iraq, Iran, and Pakistan—with Britain. The United States declined formal association in deference to the Israelis. Nasser was deeply disturbed by this intrusion of what he took to be neocolonialist meddling directed at him personally and launched a vigorous propaganda campaign against the alliance. Nassar calculated that British influence might best be offset by going to the Soviets for military assistance. After long negotiation, a Soviet–Egyptian arms deal was consummated in September 1955—almost the very day Eisenhower had his heart attack. The Russians now had leapfrogged the Baghdad Pact defensive alliance.

Nasser attempted to maintain his image of neutrality by approaching the World Bank and the United States to gain financing for the construction of a high dam across the Nile River at Aswan. The Soviets had also offered to provide aid, but Nasser preferred to work with the West. The dam was to be the centerpiece of Nasser's plans to modernize Egypt; and, at least at the outset, the fact that he turned to the West for financing impressed the usually skeptical Dulles. On December 19, 1955, a tentative American decision to loan the Egyptians the money was made and negotiations were opened. Yet Nasser, suspicious of losing control of the Aswan project to his creditors, bargained slowly, a delay that was reciprocated on the American side.

Nasser now grew anxious about his loan and hedged his bet. He turned East. Nasser extended recognition to the Chinese Communists as a possible alternative source of arms. Dulles, grumbling that Nasser was playing both sides,[102] informed the Egyptians on July 19, 1956, that the United States would withdraw its support from the Aswan project.[103] Dulles reportedly handled the matter with insensitivity to Egyptian pride, accusing them of blackmail and making gratuitous comments on the state of the Egyptian economy.[104] A week later, a furious Nasser, in an impassioned speech, announced that he was nationalizing the Suez Canal and would operate it himself.

A crisis was now all but inevitable. Both the British and the French protested that Nasser's foot was on their necks. For Anthony Eden, his health and domestic political base deteriorating,[105] the canal seizure seemed more than adequate justification for the use of force to eliminate a menace he compared to Mussolini. But Eden's bellicosity ran counter to Eisenhower's political needs of the moment, for the last thing Eisenhower needed going into a presidential campaign was a war in the Middle East in which two NATO allies were acting in clear violation of international law. Eden, however, had lost control of his own emotions and was determined to push the issue through to a definitive conclusion. Throughout August, September, and most of October 1956, diplomatic activity was frantic. The Americans sought to prevent Anglo–French intervention, and Eden, in a near frenzy of persistence, pushed the crisis forward.[106] Dulles's role was that of ambivalent middleman between a president who absolutely refused to countenance Anglo–French military intervention (but seemed to acquiesce in other forms) and the British and French, who sought to pull the United States into the intervention in some form or, if they could not gain American support, ensure noninterference. Dulles's ambivalence stemmed from his sympathy for the Anglo–French position, for he shared their antipathy toward Nasser's action and ideology. Moreover, he tended to view Nasser's Arab nationalism as being, if not communistic, then vulnerable to communist penetration. At the same time, Dulles was secretary of state and, therefore, an advocate of Eisenhower's interest, which was, quite simply, no war. By the time Eisenhower suffered his heart attack, the alliance was strained to the point that the British and French felt free to go their own way.

In late September 1956, the French, who had been supplying the Israelis with arms in anticipation of a major Israeli attack in the Sinai, decided to use the Israeli attack as a pretext for their own involvement. By mid-October, the Franco–Israeli plans had neared completion, and the British were brought into the conspiracy. Between October 16 and 24, the three countries agreed on a plan that would have the Israelis attack Egypt's Sinai positions and push toward the canal to provide the pretext for Anglo–French intervention. On October 16, the British and French cut off the flow of normal communications with Washington, and the president was forced to employ high-altitude U-2 aerial surveillance flights over the Middle East to gain generally inconclusive information as to what was going on.

On October 23, the confusion of Anglo–French silence, a brewing crisis, and a presidential election was compounded by the eruption of an uprising in Hungary against Soviet power. For a week, Dulles and Eisenhower watched what Dulles hoped would be the fulfillment of his wish for liberation, but little else could be done because events were surging to a climax in the Middle East. The Israelis launched the attack against Egypt on October 29. The British and French vetoed a U.S. and Soviet cease-fire resolution in the Security Council and joined the assault on October 31. The fighting continued for another five days as the Israelis routed the Egyptians and the insertion of British and French troops was carried out. While the assault on Egypt was underway, the Russians crushed the Hungarian revolt.

At the height of the crisis, Eisenhower employed diplomatic and economic instruments against both the Israelis and the Anglo–French effort. French and British sensibilities were important, for Eisenhower was concerned about the impact of the crisis on the alliance. However, the delicacy of the situation did not prevent extreme anger and toughness on Eisenhower's part when he learned that the British and French were using force on a mere pretext without consulting their major NATO benefactor.

Eisenhower delivered a trans-Atlantic telephonic tongue lashing to Eden[107] and hit the British at their most vulnerable point — their economy. As October turned to November, it became apparent that the pound sterling was under immense pressure with much of the selling of sterling taking place in New York. There was speculation that it was being initiated by the Treasury Department at Eisenhower's direction. Foreign Secretary Macmillan now warned Prime Minister Eden of British economic collapse. Macmillan knew that there was no help in Washington[108] unless an immediate cease fire was called. It came on November 6.

As the crisis waned, American diplomacy turned to the task of patching up the damage. The damage within the alliance was a complex mix of personal bitterness and the inevitable sensitivity of those who had once possessed great imperial power now being confronted with the reality of their impotence. Nevertheless, during February and March 1957, talks were held with the French and British in which much of the personal rancor was dispelled. It was clear, however, that the French and, especially, the British were rethinking the nature and magnitude of their NATO commitment. The French had withdrawn most of their conventional combat units from NATO to deal with a new colonial struggle in Algeria, and the British, for economic reasons, were moving toward similar reductions in their conventional forces.

The other area in which the pre-Suez crisis status quo was threatened was the Middle East itself, because British power and credibility had collapsed in the area. Eisenhower concluded that an American presence was urgently required even as the lingering problem of Israeli withdrawal was being dealt with. Thus, the president went before Congress and urged the adoption of a special program of economic and military assistance in the Middle East. He asked for a congressional prior commitment "to use armed forces to assist any nation or group of such nations requesting assistance against armed aggression from any nation controlled by international Communism." The presidential discretion to use force was essential, Eisenhower argued, because the Middle Eastern vacuum had to be "filled by the United States before it is filled by Russia."[109] However, a Democrat-controlled Congress refused to move quickly on what was now referred to as the Eisenhower Doctrine.

Dulles's alarmism about an imminent penetration of the area by international communism no longer startled a Congress that had been asked to prepare for the coming of the wolf almost daily for four years. In fact, Dulles was forced to concede that there were no nations in the Middle East controlled by communism. Moreover, Congress, under intense pressure from American Jewish groups, refused to legitimize any effort to force the Israelis out of the Sinai. The onus fell, therefore, on Eisenhower, who publicly avowed his intention of cutting off U.S. assistance to Israel as well as eliminating tax loopholes for private American contributors to Israel's welfare. On March 1, 1957, the Israelis gave way and withdrew. Only after the Israelis moved out of Sinai did Congress pass the Middle East Resolution.

THE NEW LOOK CHALLENGED

It had been a desperate fall and winter. The NATO alliance had gone through a traumatic and wrenching experience, and Dulles had earned the everlasting enmity of many Europeans, but the 1957 springtime NATO conferences provided some reason to believe that relations were on the mend. Even more impressive was the way Eisenhower had moved to expand the American presence in the Middle East. With the Eisenhower Doctrine, the United States had succeeded in closing a ring of American power, alliances, and commitments around the communist world: NATO in Europe; the Eisenhower Doctrine and Baghdad pact in the Middle East; SEATO; the Korean and Taiwan mutual security agreements; the treaties Dulles had negotiated in the late Truman years—ANZUS and the Japanese arrangements; and finally, of course, the revised Rio Pact with its heightened defenses against communist subversion.[110] In sum, Eisenhower and Dulles, by early 1957, seemed to have succeeded in institutionalizing containment on a global scale.

However, beneath the image of a carefully nurtured and now stable system of containment were signs that all was not well. There was, of course, the distressing inability to grasp the magnitude and nature of revolutionary change in the non-Western world so evident in the Suez crisis. Militant anti-Western and anti-American nationalism was consistently equated with international communism and therefore subject to unilateral American policing under such abstract rationales as the Eisenhower Doctrine.[111] In addition, however, there were intimations of major problems at the strategic core of the Eisenhower approach to the world.

In August 1957, the Soviet Union announced that it had successfully tested a long-range intercontinental ballistic rocket. In October, the Soviets orbited the first artificial earth satellite, Sputnik I; in November 1957 and May 1958, the second and third Soviet satellites went into orbit. In the meantime, Khrushchev made sure, through a seemingly endless stream of interviews and public statements, that the strategic implications of this feat would not be lost on the West.[112] Soviet rocket development threatened to compromise the entire structure of the new look. By all appearances, the Soviets would soon equal the American threat of massive retaliation. If this were the case, was the nuclear threat that constituted the underpinning of Eisenhower and Dulles's foreign policy credible any longer? Was it not necessary to reexamine the entire question of force in the nuclear age? Sputnik provided, therefore, the immediate fillip to a reexamination of American defense posture.

As early as 1956, Maxwell Taylor, the sophisticated army chief of staff, had been lobbying diligently for an army role and capability to deal with the changed strategic environment.[113] Taylor was concerned that the army was being dangerously shortchanged by overreliance on an air-borne deterrent. Strategic weapons might prevent a massive general war, but they could not be used believably—especially with the advent of potential Soviet retaliation—as an instrument of policy for controlling local pressures.[114] Coups d'état in the Middle East, insurgencies in Asia and Soviet pressure on Berlin could not be credibly countered by brandishing atomic weapons.

Among the leaders of concerned scholars in this area was Harvard instructor Henry Kissinger. In 1956, Kissinger maintained that the use of nuclear weapons was inevitable if war were to break out between the Soviet Union and the United States. The question, therefore, was how to limit the scope of the war.[115] In *Nuclear Weapons and Foreign Policy*, Kissinger argued for a spectrum of military capability available to American policymakers: "a twentieth century equivalent of 'showing the flag,' an ability and readiness to make our power felt quickly and decisively, not only to deter Soviet aggression but also to impress the uncommitted without capacity for decisive action." In short, a willingness to meet any level of force with at least an equivalent response,[116] including a strategy of limited war, using tactical nuclear weapons that promised "the best chance to bring about strategic changes favorable to our side" from Indochina and Korea to Eastern Europe and Berlin.[117]

By the end of 1958, most strategists in the scholarly community had written off massive retaliation as a viable strategic concept. They agreed that the United States needed the capacity and will to fight limited wars.[118] The only contention left centered on the point at which nuclear weapons should be introduced into a "local war."[119]

Concerns also existed about the adequacy of the strategic arsenal. A report prepared in 1958 by the head of the Ford Foundation, H. Rowan Gaither, pronounced America's defense capability to be in desperate condition.[120] The report argued that the Soviet Union's economic strength was growing at a pace twice as fast as the American economy and that Soviet expenditures for arms were currently at least equal to American expenditures. By 1959, the report forecast, the Soviet Union would have one hundred ICBMs in position to attack preemptively the vulnerable U.S. strategic bomber force, docked on crowded airfields.[121] The Gaither Committee called for defense spending increases for a fallout shelter program, missile forces, strategic air command dispersion, and ground forces to more than $60 billion, an increase of some $25 billion over what the Eisenhower administration had expected to spend.[122]

Many of those who were pushing for a reenergized defense posture were Democrats associated with the Truman administration. No doubt this fact, plus the deep suspicion Eisenhower harbored of an unbalanced budget and what he later termed the military–industrial complex, contributed to his resisting the burgeoning pressure for an increased American military capability. In addition, Eisenhower was now the beneficiary of strategic intelligence being gathered by the secret U-2 reconnaissance aircraft that had been overflying the Soviet Union since mid-1956. The information thus gathered suggested a far less alarming balance than advanced by the Gaither Committee. Eisenhower did, however, initiate a long-term process of transforming the American strategic posture by authorizing the development of a new sea-based nuclear deterrent on nuclear submarines and the new, solid-fueled Minuteman missile. Also, at the November 1957 NATO conference, the United States urged an increase in the number of tactical nuclear weapons and intermediate-range ballistic missiles in Europe.

POLICY IMMOBILITY

The last year of the Eisenhower–Dulles partnership was marked by a predictable sameness. The observer of the event in the Middle East and Asia in 1958 experienced déjà vu. In May, pro-Nasser Lebanese nationalists rebelled against a conservative government that announced that it would remain in power beyond its constitutional term. The Lebanese and Jordanian governments were in a state of panic, fearing an imminent intervention from Iraq, Syria, or both. They urged immediate Anglo-American intervention. Eisenhower decided to go in, and, on July 15, the United States landed the first of 14,300 troops in Lebanon, and the British put more than 3,000 troops in Jordan. The Lebanese government stepped down and was replaced by another acceptable to all parties. In the meantime, hatred of the United States was increased, and the Arab left was driven closer to the Russians.

During the summer and fall of 1958, the Taiwan Strait crisis was rerun as the Communists resumed the shelling of Quemoy, and Chiang Kai-shek dispatched a frenzied call for help to Washington. As in the earlier crisis, Dulles marched to the brink, claiming that the American commitment to the defense of the offshore islands was unequivocal and total. And once again, Eisenhower let matters ride at the outset as Dulles and the Joint Chiefs of Staff began talking privately of "no more than small air bursts without fallout. That is of course an unpleasant prospect, but one I think we must face up to."[123] Khrushchev added his ambiguous threats, naval and air incidents increased. At the same time, Khrushchev refused to provide Mao Zedong with a guarantee of support up to and including the use of nuclear weapons. Mao's capacity to escalate the crisis was truncated, as was, in fact, the entire Sino–Soviet relationship. However, the fundamental structure and assumptions of U.S. foreign policy remained unchanged.[124]

In Europe, Khrushchev had grown anxious to resolve what was for him the dangerously ambiguous question of Germany. Khrushchev's concern by late 1958 was that the West Germans, as they were integrated into NATO, would gain access to nuclear weapons. To counter this, Khrushchev had backed the proposal made in late 1957 by the Polish foreign minister, Adam Rapacki, that Central Europe be transformed into a nuclear-free area. In January 1958, Rapacki had issued, through Soviet Premier Bulganin, a call for a summit to discuss this and other issues. The Soviet call for a summit conference was viewed favorably by many in Europe, especially the British. Khrushchev took dead aim at this soft spot by declaring on November 27, 1958, that he would turn over all remaining Soviet occupation functions in Berlin to the East Germans within six months unless there was a summit conference to create a normal situation in Germany. The fear of a renewed Berlin blockade ran through Europe, only now the confrontation would be even more dangerous. Demands for a conference rose throughout Western Europe.

Dulles and Eisenhower, once more on the defensive, sought to hold the alliance in line. Dulles was now only six months away from death. All who saw him were struck by his declining physical appearance.[125] Yet, in December 1958 and February 1959, Dulles made two trips to Europe in an effort to hold things together. Those who met with him were awed by his courage, but they, and one suspects Dulles as well, knew that he would no longer captain containment. The initiative was now in the hands of the more pliant and pragmatic Macmillan, who had succeeded Eden after the Suez fiasco. The British prime minister, in an eleven-day visit to Moscow in February and March 1959,[126] found Khrushchev willing to defer the crisis deadline as long as diplomatic movement was in evidence.

THE OPENING TOWARD DETENTE

When John Foster Dulles died, Eisenhower assumed personal control of American foreign policy and sought, through the force of his personality, to redirect American policy in the time left to his administration. Eisenhower's attempt to exploit personal diplomacy was paralleled by his Soviet counterpart. Khrushchev, although prone to mercurial theatricality and even boorishness, was also attempting to impose his own personal stamp on a Soviet foreign and defense bureaucracy that was, in many respects, the mirror image of that in the United States. Khrushchev's own domestic needs, his interest in expanding economic contact with the West, the bitter fight with the Chinese, and perhaps his own personal instincts as well moved him toward a positive response to Eisenhower's new departure.

The Confluence of Personal Diplomacies

The 1958 election had not been successful for the Republicans, the economy was in the third and and deepest recession of the administration, and Eisenhower's personal prestige among independent voters and the press had been eroded by his ambivalence toward the civil rights movement in the South. Sometimes reporters laughed at his circumlocutions at press conferences. References to the "program of the President" drew laughter from members of Congress and staffers.[127] Jokes were aired on television about the Eisenhower doll: You would wind it up and it wouldn't do anything. Then, too, there was the contrast of the Russians and the Chinese, both actively on the offensive in the Third World, pursuing nonaligned nations with aid offered at nominal interest and with no visible strings attached. Khrushchev became the first Soviet leader to make diplomatic travels abroad, leaving in his wake major loans for projects with high visibility.[128] Similarly, China had broken its diplomatic isolation and had begun a small, but increasingly effective effort to convince neutralist nations of Chinese good intentions.

Given the seeming loss of élan in America and a declining prestige abroad, Eisenhower prepared to undertake a series of global tours of good will. Eisenhower's itinerary took him to Europe, Asia, and, less successfully, to Latin America. It was clear to Eisenhower that the ultimate extension of personal diplomacy would have to be talks with the Soviets themselves. Khrushchev was prepared to stake much prestige and a good deal of his reputation on his ability to deal with Eisenhower. By January 1960, for example, Khrushchev would use his relationship with Eisenhower to convince the Soviet military to accept a cutback of about one third of Soviet forces.[129] But Khrushchev had significant domestic opposition to a detente with the United States. Molotov, ideologically not unlike a Soviet Dulles, writing from exile as ambassador to Mongolia, sent an article to *Kommunist* that recounted the older themes of the inevitable incompatibility of communism and capitalism and the need for vigilance. The Chinese proclaimed that they were "able to see no substantial change in the imperialist war policy, the policy of the United States Government and of Eisenhower himself." The Western press began to report the Soviet Union's internal disagreements, and Khrushchev indicated that there was considerable truth in them. He complained bitterly about the "libelous tales" that "other socialist countries [China and Albania] are demanding that the Soviet Union abandon its policy of detente." Khrushchev objected that it was "the silliest inventions . . . that officers and generals who lost their jobs owing to a cut back in the armed forces are opposed to [peaceful coexistence]."[130]

The Spirit of Camp David

Clearly, therefore, Khrushchev was taking a chance in his pursuit of detente through personal diplomacy. His hugely successful trip through the United States in September 1959 seemed to justify the risks. Indeed, the talks at the presidential retreat at Camp David, Maryland, may have led Khrushchev, and perhaps the president as well, to believe that detente was possible after all.[131] For a time, it seemed that the crucial territorial issues of the cold war might be arranged by a series of summit conferences. First, there was the remarkable meeting of Khrushchev and Eisenhower at Camp David, then a series of consultations among the allies of both camps, followed by a meeting of the Big Four scheduled to take place in Paris in the spring of 1960. The planned capstone of all this activity was to be Eisenhower's visit to Moscow, scheduled to take place in the summer of 1960. It was, in short, a harbinger of the manner in which detente would unfold some fourteen years later.

Nikita Khrushchev's 1959 visit had startled Americans. On his arrival, Khrushchev behaved as if he were running for office. He lunched with Hollywood stars Bob Hope, Marilyn Monroe, and Frank Sinatra, and had his picture taken laughing and joking with corn farmers in Iowa. Then, at the end of his journey, Khrushchev visited the Eisenhower farm at Gettysburg and played with the Eisenhower grandchildren. Both the press and the public had the impression that these two benign men, both grandfathers, had become partners for peace.

About to leave, Khrushchev delivered an amazing farewell to the American people over national television. The speech was almost completely devoid of what the Soviet premier termed the "old boring arguments of the Cold War period." "Goodevening, American friends," he began. After complimenting America's "beautiful cities and kind-hearted people," the nominal leader of the world communist movement referred to scripture and Christ to explain to the American people Soviet socialism. Then, in English, Khrushchev concluded his farewell speech, "Goodbye, good luck, friends." Historian and former State Department official Louis Halle commented: "All this is not a dream. The record of the visit is there."[132]

It was a remarkable break with the past. Senator Stuart Symington, then a potential presidential candidate, in contrasting the domestic change that accompanied the Soviet premier's visit, averred that if Harry Truman had invited Stalin to dinner at the White House, he would have been impeached.[133] To Halle, the Khrushchev trip signified no less than the end of the cold war. "All that remained," Halle wrote, "was to put it into practice."[134]

THE OLD REFLEXES REEMERGE

Yet, almost as soon as Khrushchev departed, the spirit of Camp David appeared steadily less substantial. To be sure, there was some initial appearance of forward movement at the disarmament meeting in Geneva. On February 16, 1960, the Soviets proposed that Western inspection teams be allowed to visit "the site of virtually any earth tremor in the Soviet Union in order to see if this was due to natural causes or an atomic test." To the British prime minister, Harold Macmillan, this offer seemed to be a "complete reversal of the previous Soviet position." But Macmillan sensed an inexplicable lack of interest by the United States.[135]

In part, the hardening of the American position was a response to pressure from America's allies. French President Charles de Gaulle wanted to negotiate only after there had been a successful test of France's new atomic bomb. De Gaulle's principal purpose was to undercut the beginnings of a great power condominium — a situation in which France would not be relevant as a negotiating partner. De Gaulle calculated that if the summit could be delayed and placed in the shadow of a presidential election, it would be less likely that a lame duck president could undertake any startling innovation with the Russians.

In the meantime, Khrushchev let the timing of his deadline on Berlin become ambiguous.[136] Instead of seizing on this element of apparent retreat, the State Department, concerned about fissures in the alliance and worried about long-range Soviet intentions, chose to respond as if a final treaty with the East Germans might still be signed by Khrushchev. A treaty meant that Germany would be permanently divided and that Soviet claims in Eastern Europe would gather some additional legitimacy. To meet these fears, real and imagined, Undersecretary of

State C. Douglas Dillon delivered a speech in which he warned Khrushchev that by threatening a separate peace with the German Democratic Republic, he was "skating on very thin ice." "Germany," he said "represents a critical test of Soviet good faith. . . . The problem of Germany and Berlin can only be solved through German reunification."[137] In addition, Dillon insisted that all the remaining issues of East–West relations had to be resolved before meaningful agreements could be negotiated. Similar statements by the secretary of state and the vice president suggested that the United States was not prepared to move from its previous position on Berlin, Germany, or the cold war in general. The Soviets, through a variety of channels, expressed dismay at this toughening of the American position in the wake of Camp David and on the eve of the Paris summit.[138]

The Curious Death
of Detente: The U-2 Incident

On the morning of May 1, fourteen days before the scheduled conference in Paris, over Sverdlovsk, a large industrial area in the Urals twelve hundred miles deep in the Soviet Union, an American U-2 spy plane was brought to earth. Uncertainty still surrounds how the plane descended,[139] but the identity of the pilot and his employer were never in doubt. The pilot, Francis Gary Powers, carried two military identification cards; a U.S. and an international driving license; a Selective Service card; a Social Security card; a PX ration card; a medical certificate; two flying licenses; American, French, Turkish, Italian, German, and Soviet currencies; two gold watches; gold coins; and seven gold rings, as Khrushchev put it sarcastically, "for the ladies." Indeed, Powers was a multilingual billboard for American espionage. Along with his pistol with a silencer, morphine, a needle dipped in lethal curare poison, and flares, he also carried a "large silk American flag poster" reading in fourteen languages, "I am an American and do not speak your language. I need food, shelter and assistance. I will not harm you. I bear no malice toward your people. If you help me, you will be rewarded."[140]

On May 5, Khrushchev announced to the Supreme Soviet that an aircraft had penetrated Soviet airspace but neglected to mention that Powers or much of his plane and equipment were intact and in Soviet hands. Khrushchev asked, "Who sent this aircraft across the Soviet frontier? Was it the . . . President? Or was this token aggressive act carried out by Pentagon militants?"[141] Lincoln White, the Department of State spokesman, responded to Khrushchev emphatically, "There was absolutely no — n-o — no deliberate attempt to violate Soviet airspace.

There never has been." But on May 7, Powers was shockingly produced, alive. Khrushchev claimed, however, that he was prepared to grant that the president had no knowledge of a plane being dispatched to the Soviet Union and failing to return.[142]

The American response was hardly a disavowal.[143] On May 11, just four days before the conference was scheduled to open and six days after Khrushchev had asked the president to abjure responsibility, Eisenhower spoke to the American people saying the U-2 flight and flights like it were a "vital necessity" because the Russians "make a fetish of secrecy and concealment." And, echoing a statement by Secretary of State Christian Herter on May 9, he indicated that the flights would continue.[144] Nonetheless, Khrushchev still insisted that he would come to Paris.

On May 16, Khrushchev, pale and with shaking hands, appeared in front of world television at a Paris news conference side by side with his splendidly decorated defense minister, Marshall Rodin Malinovsky, and proceeded to roast Eisenhower. "The President," Khrushchev demanded heatedly, "must apologize for his wrong and punish his responsible confederates, if a meeting would proceed."[145] According to Bohlen, who was at Paris, "Khrushchev had come to Paris determined to get an apology." And if he could not elicit Eisenhower's regrets, then Khrushchev, speculated Bohlen, "was not authorized to participate in the conference."[146] Eisenhower did edge away from his position of May 11, but it was too late. No apology was forthcoming. After a thirty-six–hour delay, perhaps waiting for Eisenhower to change his position, Khrushchev departed, saying that he hoped he would be able to deal with the new administration more successfully than he had with Eisenhower.[147]

Adlai Stevenson summarized the Paris Conference: "We handed Khrushchev that crowbar and sledge-hammer to wreck the meeting."[148] Khrushchev recalls that he was "haunted by the fact that just prior to this meeting the United States had dared to send its U-2 reconnaissance plane against us. It was as though the Americans had deliberately tried to place a time bomb under the meeting, set to go off just as we were about to sit down with them at the negotiation table."[149] Recent American scholarship on the incident concludes that the past success of the program (the flights had been conducted since 1956 with the most recent in April) and CIA assurances that, in the unlikely event a plane were brought down, the craft and its pilot would be deniable, led the President to become overconfident and careless.[150] Moreover, the President had assumed sole responsibility for assessing the political damage that might follow from a failed flight. Thus, when the secretaries of state and defense, the director of the CIA, and the chairman of the

Joint Chiefs of Staff—notwithstanding that each of them was far more skeptical of the likely success or desirability of detente than the President—all advocated the May flight, Eisenhower approved.[151]

Denouement

Whatever the explanation for the flight and the confused American response when it failed, with the collapse of the Paris summit conference, Eisenhower's ability to deal with the Russians on any basis other than through traditional cold war modalities had ended. The opening of lines of communication by means of personal diplomacy required, above all else, the credibility of the instrument. However, Eisenhower's personal credibility with Khrushchev had been shattered by the U-2 incident. Indeed, continued positive interaction with Eisenhower was a liability for Khrushchev: The U-2 and the aborted summit conference made Khrushchev's personal diplomatic efforts suspect to Soviet hardliners and to the Chinese, who were now prepared to bring their feud with Moscow into the open.

Moreover, the Twenty-second Amendment, with its prohibition on presidential succession after two terms, now decisively entered into the picture. The Eisenhower administration would, of necessity, pass from the scene within a matter of months. In the meantime, Khrushchev could simultaneously refuse to deal with Eisenhower and attack him, thereby underscoring the president's impotence. Khrushchev's ebullient and sometimes belligerent personality, had, therefore, a clear field during the election and transition period. And he exploited the situation to its fullest by berating Eisenhower but also trying to replace detente on the agenda of the incoming administration. For its part, "the Eisenhower administration ran steadily down like a tired clock, its energies spent, its coherence blurred."[152] Under the circumstances, it fell back reflexively on the cold war stance of the Dulles years.

To preserve containment, Eisenhower and Dulles constructed a ring of commitments around the perimeter of a communist world that, by the end of the 1950s, was fractious and preoccupied with its internal problems but perceived the United States as being monolithic and expansive. The circle of treaties, guarantees, and bases were predicated on clear American strategic superiority. The United States seemed to possess, especially at the outset of the Eisenhower and Dulles years, the requisite strength to negotiate the issues of the cold war, but the second phase of containment foreseen by Kennan never took place:

> The failure consisted in the fact that our government, finding it difficult to understand a political threat as such and to deal with it in other than

military terms, and grievously misled, in particular, by its own faulty interpretations of the significance of the Korean War, failed to take advantage of the opportunities for useful political discussion when, in later years, such opportunities began to open up, and exerted itself, in its military preoccupations, to seal and to perpetuate the very division of Europe which it should have been concerned to remove. It was not "containment" that failed; it was the intended follow-up that never occurred.[153]

But in relying on the maintenance of a policy implemented through the threat of war, Eisenhower institutionalized the very thing against which he would warn the nation in his farewell address:

We have been compelled to create a permanent armaments industry of vast proportions. . . .

We recognize the imperative need for this development. Yet we must not fail to comprehend its grave implications. Our toil, resources, and livelihood are all involved; so is the very structure of our society.

In the councils of government we must guard against the acquisition of unwarranted influence, whether sought or unsought, by the military-industrial complex. The potential for the disastrous use of misplaced power exists and will persist.[154]

An irony of the Eisenhower–Dulles era, therefore, is that although there was no war during their stewardship, their most significant legacy to America was an institutionalized cold war. Not the least of its manifestations and consequences was the massive and potent union of U.S. government and private politico–economic power necessary to wage that cold war and man the defenses of containment—a joining of public and private power that would, as Eisenhower, Dulles, and Taft feared, come to dominate the institutions and spirit of America during the next decade.

An additional, external legacy existed in Eisenhower and Dulles's policy of institutionalized and globalized containment. By failing to distinguish international communism and nationalist or anticolonial revolution, by seeing the latter as indistinguishable from the former. Eisenhower and Dulles set American policy against the nationalist revolutions of the non-Western world. There was much of real and imagined economic necessity in this: the presumed need for raw materials, export markets, and the implied integrated world economy built on low tariffs and the free flow of U.S. private investment.[155] But this was very quickly subordinated to the incompatible imperatives of what was thought to be a more immediate threat: the penetration of the global political economy by international communism *through* these anti-Western nationalist revolutions. Thus, Ho, Nasser, Mossadegh, Arbenz, and the mobs that attacked Richard Nixon in Venezuela in 1958 were not viewed as primarily products of a collapsing colonial and traditional milieu, they were instead the political and even military instruments of communism.

The threat of massive or tactical nuclear retaliation based on U.S. strategic superiority could check communist expansion in Europe or the Taiwan Strait, but, in the Third World, something else was required if Korea was not to be replicated. The answer was intervention in a counterrevolutionary mode. The form of intervention was often crude, as in Lebanon, Iran, or Guatemala. Such intervention, although it did not always work, was nevertheless relatively cheap. By the end of the Eisenhower–Dulles era, a somewhat more sophisticated range of instrumentalities was being employed, including the use between 1952 and 1959 of $37.3 billion in foreign aid, of which almost $21 billion was military assistance in support of essentially counterrevolutionary regimes on the periphery of the communist world and incorporated into Dulles's alliance system. Moreover, the economic aid was usually structured, as in South Vietnam after 1956, to benefit those most likely to resist revolutionary activity.[156]

Nevertheless, the thrust of the Dulles–Eisenhower effort was the containment and suppression of non-Western political, social, and economic revolution. Economic instruments were simply not, in the emerging view of the 1950s, sufficient in themselves to this great task. As in Europe and Japan, American power supplemented by economic and military aid would establish the political preconditions for world economic order, integration, and stability. In this respect, what Eisenhower and Dulles tried to do in the non-Western world was merely an extension of what Truman, Marshall, and Acheson saw themselves doing in Europe after World War II. The legacy for the 1960s was that insofar as Eisenhower and Dulles succeeded, they set their faces and the face of American power against history. They were, at least superficially, successful in the short run of their eight years. In the meantime, revolutionary forces were growing, and the 1960s would demonstrate that American political and military power was ultimately and tragically limited in its ability to contain them.

TRANSITION

Khrushchev next took his attack on the lame duck Eisenhower administration to the United Nations when he announced that he would return to the United States to head the Soviet delegation to the General Assembly on September 20, 1960. The visit would also place him precisely in the middle of the American presidential election campaign. While at the United Nations, Khrushchev conspicuously conferred with leaders of the Third World, notably Fidel Castro, the new leader of the increasingly anti-American Cuban regime. During debate in the General Assembly, Khrushchev pressed his attack on the West and on Secretary General Dag Hammarskjold's purportedly pro-Western UN leadership. This performance reached its peak during a speech by Macmillan as Khrushchev's rather startling and discourteous interruptions were climaxed by his removing his shoes and alternately banging on his desk and waving it at the imperturbable British leader.[157] The shocking and frightening spectacle suggested that the Kremlin was headed by a man so reminiscent of earlier totalitarians that the world of negotiation seemed barely applicable.

In marked contrast with this behavior, however, was Khrushchev's attitude toward the American election and the new president-elect. During the campaign, Khrushchev made references to the unacceptability of Richard Nixon as the next president — an oblique endorsement of Kennedy that nonetheless contributed to much discomfort in the young senator's camp.[158] Following Kennedy's victory, Khrushchev's persistent overtures to the president-elect during the interregnal period between November 1960 and the inauguration in January 1961 sounded the refrain of harmony and new opportunities for detente.

The incoming Kennedy administration, however, was no less an advocate of negotiating from strength than its predecessors. On October 8, 1960, during the second of the famous televised debates between Kennedy and Nixon, Kennedy had agreed completely with Nixon concerning the preconditions of negotiation with the Soviets:

> Before we go into the summit, before we ever meet again, I think it's important that the United States build its strength — that it build its military strength, as well as its own economic strength.
>
> If we negotiate from a position where the power balance or wave is moving away from us, it's extremely difficult to reach a successful decision on Berlin, as well as the other questions.[159]

This statement was more than mere campaign puffery designed to demonstrate that the Massachusetts Democratic senator was as tough as his experienced Republican opponent. One would be hard-pressed to find a more straightforward statement of this most fundamental conception of world politics and Soviet–American relations during the cold war. John Kennedy, along with the "best and the brightest" he brought to the presidency, would continue the vigorous pursuit of military superiority before any serious effort would be made to negotiate the outstanding issues of the cold war. Thus, Kennedy's conception of America's world role and the hostile nature of the international system within which that role would have to be played out, was consistent with the principles that had guided American foreign and national security policy during the preceding fifteen years.

NOTES

1. Dulles came from a family long associated with the formulation and administration of American foreign policy. His grandfather had served briefly as secretary of state during 1892 and 1893. In 1907, he accompanied his grandfather, then an adviser to the Chinese government, to the Second Hague Peace Conference of 1907. In 1917, he performed diplomatic service in Latin America for his uncle, Robert Lansing, President Wilson's secretary of state, and served with distinction as a legal adviser to the American delegation to the Versailles Peace Conference following World War I. For a complete review of Dulles' early life see Townsend Hoopes, *The Devil and John Foster Dulles* (Boston: Little, Brown, 1973), pp. 9–61. See also Hans J. Morgenthau, "John Foster Dulles: 1953–1959," in Norman A. Graebner, ed., *An Uncertain Tradition: American Secretaries of State in the Twentieth Century* (New York: McGraw-Hill, 1961), p. 293.

2. Eisenhower's concern for his domestic flank, and specifically Joseph McCarthy, was apparent during the campaign. While speaking in Wisconsin, Eisenhower had carefully deleted an intended tribute to General Marshall. Some accounts have it that Eisenhower did this only under the most intense pressure from Republican politicians who trembled before the junior senator from Wisconsin. Nevertheless, Eisenhower would not risk McCarthy's ire, even though the man for whom the tribute was intended had fostered Eisenhower's military career throughout the war. See the account of this incident in Peter Lyon, *Eisenhower: Portrait of the Hero* (Boston: Little, Brown, 1974), p. 522.

3. Perhaps this interpretation of President Eisenhower's early administration is most thoroughly and eloquently developed by Emmet John Hughes, *The Ordeal of Power* (New York: Dell, 1964), especially chaps. 3 and 4.

4. Hughes, op. cit., pp. 81–83.

5. See Gary May, *China Scapegoat: The Diplomatic Ordeal of John Carter Vincent* (Washington, D.C.: New Republic, 1978).

6. Lyon, op. cit., p. 524.

7. See Richard M. Nixon, *Six Crises* (Garden City, N.Y.: Doubleday, 1962), p. 97.

8. Gary Wills, *Nixon Agonistes: The Crisis of the Self-Made Man* (Boston: Houghton Mifflin, 1970), p. 119. Wills's essay on Eisenhower is a brilliant and perceptive piece. For a similar analysis focused on Eisenhower's administrative style, see Fred Greenstein, *The Hidden Hand Presidency* (Washington, D.C.: New Republic, 1979); and Lyon quoting "CBS Reports, Eisenhower on the Presidency," Part I, October 12, 1961, p. 851.

9. Wills, op. cit., p. 133.

10. See James A. Nathan and James K. Oliver, *Foreign Policy Making and the American Political System* (Boston: Little, Brown, 1983), chap. 2.

11. Wills, op. cit., pp. 131–132.
12. See Morgenthau, op. cit.
13. See John Foster Dulles, "A Policy of Boldness," *Life*, Vol. 32, No. 20 (May 10, 1952), pp. 146–160.
14. Dwight D. Eisenhower, *Mandate For Change* (Garden City, N.Y.: Doubleday, 1963), p. 95.
15. General Mark Clark, *From the Danube to the Yalu* (London: Harrap, 1954), p. 221; quoted in David Rees, *Korea: The Limited War* (Baltimore: Penguin Books, 1964), p. 402.
16. Lyon, op. cit., p. 472.
17. Eisenhower, op. cit., p. 181.
18. Lyon, op. cit., p. 534. See also the newly released documents on Eisenhower's inclination to use nuclear weapons: Bernard Gwertzman, "U.S. Papers Tell of '53 Policy to Use A-Bomb in Korea," *The New York Times*, June 8, 1984, p. A8.
19. Ibid., p. 536.
20. See ibid., and Joyce Kolko and Gabriel Kolko, *The Limits of Power: The World and United States Foreign Policy, 1945–1954* (New York: Harper & Row, 1972), p. 681. Kolko adds that, in view of these attacks, the communist charges of bacteriological warfare assumed added credibility (ibid., fn. 10, p. 794).
21. Quoted in Lyon, op. cit. p. 541.
22. Eisenhower, op. cit., p. 185, *The New York Times*, August 4, 1975; and "Eisenhower Considered A-Bomb in Korea," *Washington Post*, June 9, 1984, p. A8.
23. Eisenhower, op. cit., p. 189.
24. At the same time, however, the South Koreans were informed that the United Nations would not use force to stop them from breaking an armistice. What really emerged in the unspoken agreement between the two sides on July 19 was that if Rhee's army was foolish enough to attack the Communists, the war need not be expanded if the Chinese merely pulverized the South Korean forces without involving the United Nations' Command's western divisions.
25. Republican Platform in *National Party Platforms, 1840–1968*, compiled by Kirk H. Porter and Donald Bruce Johnson (Urbana, Ill.: University of Illinois Press, 1970), pp. 497–498.
26. Some adjustment of the border between North and South Korea was made as the result of the fighting. The ROK had gained some 2,350 square miles on the eastern end of the main line of resistance but lost 850 square miles to the west. Military historian David Rees is of the view that the newer line was more defensible than the old boundary (Rees, op. cit., p. 431).
27. "Message of the President: National Security," *The Budget of the United States Government for the Fiscal Year Ending June 30, 1955* (Washington, D.C.: U.S. Government Printing Office, 1954), p. M-38.
28. Ibid., p. M-39.
29. This analysis is drawn from Glenn H. Snyder, "The New Look of 1953," in Warner Schilling, Paul G. Hammond, and Glenn H. Snyder, *Strategy, Politics, and Defense Budgets* (New York: Columbia University Press, 1962), pp. 401–406.
30. Dulles, op. cit., p. 152.
31. Hoopes, op. cit., p. 195; and Snyder, op. cit., pp. 408–409.
32. Quoted by Hoopes, op. cit., p. 194.
33. Snyder, op. cit., p. 436. The top secret internal study NSC-162/2 seriously considered nuclear weapons in a wide range of circumstances. At one point, Eisenhower even suggested to Dulles that preventive war might have to be considered.

John Lewis Gaddis, *Strategies of Containment* (New York: Oxford University Press, 1982), pp. 149–150.

34. A complete account of the struggle of the army against these cuts can be found in Snyder, op. cit., pp. 443–455. See also Hanson W. Baldwin, "'New Look' of the U.S. Armed Forces Is Emerging at the Pentagon," *The New York Times*, December 13, 1953, p. 5E; the *Budget of FY 1955*, op. cit., p. M–45; and Snyder, op. cit., pp. 457–460. See also the testimony of Secretary of Defense Charles E. Wilson and Admiral Arthur William Radford before U.S. Congress, Senate Committee on Appropriations, *Department of Defense Appropriations, 1955*, 83rd Congress, 2nd Session, 1954, pp. 2–15, 79–91.

35. John Foster Dulles, "The Evolution of Foreign Policy," speech made to Council on Foreign Relations, January 12, 1954, *Department of State Bulletin*, Vol. 30, No. 761 (January 25, 1954), p. 107.

36. Ibid., p. 108.

37. Ibid.

38. Robert R. Bowie interview, Oral History Research Office, Columbia University, quoted in Lyon, op. cit., footnote on p. 520.

39. Joseph Buttinger, *Vietnam: A Dragon Embattled*, Vol II: *Vietnam at War* (New York: Praeger, 1967), pp. 797–798, and Lauran Paine, *Viet Nam* (London: Robert Hale, 1965).

40. Eisenhower, op. cit., p. 346.

41. News Conference, April 7, 1954, *Public Papers of the Presidents, Dwight D. Eisenhower, 1954* (Washington, D.C.: U.S. Government Printing Office, 1960), pp. 382–383.

42. Eisenhower, op. cit., pp. 340–341.

43. "United States Declaration on Indochina," July 21, 1954, in Richard A. Falk (ed.), *The Vietnam War and International Law* (Princeton, N.J.: Princeton University Press, sponsored by the American Society of International Law, 1968), p. 558. Although refusing to sign the agreement, the United States did make a "unilateral declaration in which Under Secretary of State Walter B. Smith stated that the United States will refrain from the threat or the use of force to disturb" the agreements. Smith made no reference to a North or South Vietnam, and, although he refused to sign any documents, the American declaration could certainly be taken as American acceptance of the politically provisional nature of the agreement. The U.S. offer of atom bombs is recounted in John Prados, *The Sky Would Fall: Operation Vulture, The Secret U.S. Bombing Mission to Vietnam, 1954* (New York: Dial, 1983), p. 152.

44. "The Legality of United States Participation in the Defense of Viet Nam, March 4, 1966," in ibid., p. 596.

45. See the excellent discussion of this point in George M. T. Kahin and John W. Lewis, *The United States in Vietnam*, rev. ed. (New York: Dell, 1969), pp. 48–57.

46. Marvin Kalb and Elie Abel, *Roots of Involvement: The U.S. in Asia, 1784–1971* (New York: W. W. Norton, 1971), p. 89.

47. Protocol to the Southeast Asia Collective Defense Treaty, in Falk, op. cit., p. 564.

48. Kahin and Lewis, op. cit., p. 70.

49. Lyon, op. cit., pp. 497–499, 513–514.

50. Eden, op. cit., p. 236.

51. Lyon, op. cit. p. 551.

52. Quoted in ibid., p. 552; and drawn from *Mandate for Change*, p. 165.

Eisenhower claims in the latter that he did not know who had written the memorandum, p. 164.

53. Ibid., and see also Richard Barnet, *Intervention and Revolution*, rev. ed. (New York: Mentor, 1972), pp. 264–268.

54. See Leonard Mosely, *Power Play: Oil in the Middle East* (New York: Random House, 1973), pp. 219–222; and Lyon, op. cit., pp. 553–554.

55. Throughout the Iranian crisis, Eisenhower and Dulles had tried to tie Mossadegh's activities to the influence of the Iranian Communist party, the Tudeh. The effort was transparent. Mossadegh's National Front coalition had repeatedly refused to include the Communists. In fact, in 1951, the premier turned the army on a Tudeh demonstration against the oil companies, killing one hundred and injuring another five hundred Communists. Once again, during the American-inspired coup attempts of mid-August 1953, Mossadegh unleashed the army against Tudeh demonstrators. Manfred Halprin, "The Middle East and North Africa, in *Communism and Revolution: Uses of Politcal Violence* (Princeton, N.J.: Princeton University Press, 1964), pp. 316–319; and Barnet, op. cit.

56. Quoted by Lyon, op. cit., p. 590.

57. Testimony before U.S. Congress, House Select Committee on Communist Aggression, Hearings Before the Subcommittee on Latin America, 83rd Congress, 2nd Session, 1954, pp. 24–26.

58. See the testimony of Ambassador Whiting Willauer before the Senate Internal Security Subcommittee, 87th Congress, 1st Session, 1961, as quoted by Lyon, op. cit., pp. 590ff.

59. Quoted in Lyon, op. cit., p. 611.

60. Eisenhower, op. cit., p. 426.

61. Lyon, op. cit., p. 614; and Barnet, op. cit., pp. 275–276.

62. Barnet, op. cit., p.. 275.

63. Dwight D. Eisenhower, "The Chance for Peace," an address delivered before the American Society for Newspaper Editors, April 16, 1953, in *Public Papers of the Presidents, Dwight D. Eisenhower, 1953* (Washington, D.C.: U.S. Government Printing Office, 1960), p. 180; and Barnet, op. cit.

64. Harold C. Hinton, *China's Turbulent Quest* (Bloomington, Ind.: Indiana University Press, 1972), p. 67.

65. See Hoopes's discussion of these factors, op. cit., pp. 268–272. The latter position was confirmed in an exchange of private understandings between Dulles and the Nationalist foreign minister that the use of force from territory controlled by the Nationalists would have to be approved by the United States.

66. "The Formosa Resolution," 69 Stat. 5, January 29, 1955.

67. *The New York Times*, March 18, 1954.

68. Eisenhower press conference, March 16, 1955. *Public Papers of the Presidents, Dwight D. Eisenhower, 1955* (Washington, D.C.: U.S. Government Printing Office, 1959), p. 332. For an analysis—based on newly available documents—that emphasizes the intensity of Eisenhower's belligerence and willingness to use nuclear weapons, see Gordon H. Chang, "To the Nuclear Brink: Eisenhower, Dulles, and the Quemoy-Matsu Crisis," *International Security*, Vol. 12, No. 4 (Spring 1988), pp. 96–123.

69. See Hinton, op. cit., pp. 68–69; and Hoopes, op. cit., pp. 282–283.

70. Chang, op. cit., pp. 117–118.

71. James Shepley, "How Dulles Averted War," *Life*, Vol. 40, No. 3 (January 19, 1956), p. 78.

72. Hoopes, op. cit., p. 277. See also H. W. Brands, "Credibility and Crisis Management in the Taiwan Strait," *International Security*, Vol. 12, No. 4 (Spring 1988), pp. 124–151.

73. Adam Ulam, *Expansion and Coexistence: Soviet Foreign Policy 1917–1973*, rev. ed. (New York: Praeger, 1974), pp. 539–540; and Bohlen, op. cit., pp. 354–355.

74. Hughes, op. cit., p. 90.

75. Ibid., p. 96.

76. Bohlen, op. cit., p. 356.

77. Eisenhower, "The Chance for Peace," p. 183.

78. Lyon, op. cit., pp. 533–534.

79. Ulam, op. cit., pp. 540–541.

80. Eisenhower, *Mandate for Change*, p. 148.

81. Lyon, op. cit., p. 534.

82. See especially Coral Bell, *Negotiation from Strength: A Study in the Politics of Power* (New York: Knopf, 1963), pp. 100–136, for perhaps the best treatment of this subject and also Ulam, op. cit., pp. 534–571. The following discussion is drawn primarily from these analyses and that of Bohlen, who was the American ambassador to the Soviet Union during this crucial period.

83. See Ulam's analysis, op. cit., pp. 535–536; and the text of the Soviet proposal in *Documents on International Affairs, 1952* (London: Royal Institute for International Affairs, 1955), p. 88.

84. Ulam, op. cit., p. 537.

85. Arnold L. Horelick and Myron Rush, *Strategic Power and Soviet Foreign Policy* (Chicago: University of Chicago Press, 1966), p. 17.

86. Winston Churchill, House of Commons debate, 5th Series, Vol. 515, cols. 896–897, quoted in Bell, op. cit., p. 106.

87. Raymond L. Garthoff, *Soviet Strategy in the Nuclear Age* (New York: Praeger, 1958), p. 23; and Horelick and Rush, op. cit., pp. 18–20.

88. Private memorandum, late April 1953, Dulles Papers. Quoted by Hoopes, op. cit., p. 173. See also Bohlen, op. cit., p. 371.

89. Ulam, op. cit., pp. 551–552.

90. This strategy was formally ratified in December 1954. It promptly generated turmoil within NATO over control of the nuclear trigger, an issue that would plague the alliance for the next two decades. See Robert Osgood, *NATO: The Entangling Alliance* (Chicago: University of Chicago Press, 1962), p. 116.

91. Bohlen, op. cit.

92. See Malcolm Mackintosh, *The Evolution of the Warsaw Pact*, Adelphi Paper No. 58, June 1969 (London: International Institute for Strategic Studies). For Bohlen's reporting during this period, see Bohlen, op. cit., pp. 366–367.

93. Bohlen, op. cit., p. 371.

94. Dulles maintained that it was "just one of these breaks that comes if you steadily, steadily [keep] the pressure on." Cited by Vojtech Mastny, "Kremlin Politics and the Austrian Settlement," *Problems of Communism* (July/August, 1983), p. 37.

95. One of the best detailed reviews of these proposals is in John W. Spanier and Joseph L. Nogee, *The Politics of Disarmament: A Study in Soviet–American Gamesmanship* (New York: Praeger, 1962), pp. 86–92.

96. Ibid, pp. 88–89.

97. Ibid., for a review of "open skies," esp. p. 92.

98. Lyon, op. cit. p. 653 fn.

99. A strong statement of this view can be found in Malcolm Mackintosh, "Three Detentes: 1955–1964," in Eleanor Lansing Dulles and Robert Dickson Crane (eds.), *Detente: Cold War Strategies in Transition* (New York: Praeger, 1965), pp. 103–120.

100. Eden, op. cit., p. 341.

101. Ibid., p. 215. See also Mastny, op. cit., passim., who argues that NATO "mesmerized" the Soviets and gave the U.S. an opening for negotiations, but they let it pass.

102. Hoopes, op. cit., p. 337.

103. Eisenhower's role in this decision seems to have been minimal. In early June he suffered a recurrence of the ileitis. His intestinal problem required major surgery, and, during the crucial five-week period that the Suez Crisis was set in motion, Dulles had near-total control of policy.

104. Hoopes, op. cit., pp. 341–342.

105. Anthony Nutting, *No End of a Lesson: The Story of Suez* (New York: Clarkson Potter, 1967), pp. 32–33.

106. Among the accounts of the crisis, perhaps the standard analysis has been that of Herman Finer, *Dulles' Own Suez: The Theory and Practice of His Diplomacy* (Chicago: Quadrangle, 1964). However, Finer's book was, of necessity, written without benefit of access to Dulles's papers. For an account that does have benefit of this primary source, see Hoopes, op. cit., pp. 318–414. The following analysis draws most heavily on the latter.

107. Finer, op. cit., p. 386.

108. His request that a portion of British capitalization in the International Monetary Fund be rebased to support the pound had been referred to the I.M.F. in Washington and rejected.

109. Eisenhower, *Waging Peace*, p. 178.

110. Notes for testimony before the Senate Foreign Relations Committee, February 1957, in the Dulles Papers, quoted by Hoopes, op. cit., p. 408.

111. Earlier, U.S. interventionism had been in evidence in Syria, where a coup had been planned. The operation was aborted by the Israeli attack. See Wilker Crane Eveland, *Ropes of Sand: America's Failure in the Middle East* (New York: W.W. Norton, 1980); and Donald Neff, *Warriors at Suez: Eisenhower Takes America into the Middle East* (New York: Linden, 1981), pp. 383ff.

112. For a review of Khrushchev's claims, see Arnold L. Horelick and Myron Rush. *Strategic Power and Soviet Foreign Policy* (Chicago: University of Chicago Press, 1966), pp. 42–50.

113. His efforts are recounted in Maxwell D. Taylor, *The Uncertain Trumpet* (New York: Harper & Row, 1960).

114. Ibid., p. 185.

115. Henry Kissinger, "Force and Diplomacy in the Nuclear Age," *Foreign Affairs*, Vol. 34 (April 1956), pp. 349–366.

116. Henry Kissinger, *Nuclear Weapons and Foreign Policy* (New York: W. W. Norton, 1957), p. 265.

117. Ibid., p. 147.

118. Morton Halperin, *Limited War in the Nuclear Age* (New York: John Wiley, 1963), p. 62.

119. Henry Kissinger, "Limited War: Conventional or Nuclear? A Reappraisal," in Donald G. Brennan (ed.), *Arms Control, Disarmament and National Security* (New York: Braziller, 1961), p. 146.

120.　This report was declassified in February 1973. It is entitled "Deterrence and Survival in the Nuclear Age," Security Resources Panel of the Science Advisory Committee, NSC Cover Sheet 5724, November 7, 1957, Office of Presidential Libraries, Reference Copy No. 43.

121.　Ibid., p. 6; and Morton L. Halperin, "The Gaither Committee and the Policy Process," *World Politics*, Vol. 13 (April 1961), pp. 360–384.

122.　See the Gaither Report, op. cit., table "C." For Eisenhower reaction see *Waging Peace*, pp. 220–221.

123.　Harold Macmillan, *Riding the Storm* (London: Macmillan, 1971), pp. 547–548. The Joint Chiefs' inclination to use atomic weapons became almost a fixation according to Morton Halperin, a Defense Department official in the Johnson administration.

124.　Hoopes, op. cit., pp. 442–457.

125.　Macmillan, op. cit., p. 587.

126.　Ibid., pp. 592–632.

127.　Richard Neustadt, *Presidential Power* (New York: Signet, 1964), p. 83.

128.　Marshall Goldman, *Soviet Foreign Aid* (New York: Praeger, 1967), p. 116.

129.　Michael Tatu, *Power in the Kremlin: From Khrushchev to Kosygin*, translated by Helen Katel (New York: Viking, 1969), p. 50.

130.　Ibid., pp. 49–52.

131.　Hoopes, op. cit., p. 496.

132.　Louis Halle, *The Cold War as History* (New York: Harper & Row, 1967), p. 366.

133.　*The New York Times*, September 28, 1959.

134.　Louis Halle, op. cit., p. 367.

135.　Harold Macmillan, *Pointing the Way* (London: Macmillan, 1972), p. 179. Macmillan wrote that he was "concerned at the slow American reaction to these undoubted advances."

136.　Adam Ulam, *Expansion and Coexistence: Soviet Foreign Policy, 1917–1967* (New York: Praeger, 1968), pp. 626–627.

137.　C. Douglas Dillon, "American Foreign Policy Today," *Department of State Bulletin*, Vol. 42, Speech of April 20, 1960, pp. 724–725, 727.

138.　See Charles E. Bohlen, *Witness to History, 1929–1969* (New York: W. W. Norton, 1973), p. 451; David Wise and Thomas B. Ross, *The U-2 Affair* (New York: Random House, 1962), p. 141; and *Current Digest of the Soviet Press*, Vol 12 (May 25, 1960), p. 7.

139.　See James A. Nathan, "A Fragile Detente: The U-2 Incident Reexamined," *Military Affairs*, (October 1975), pp. 97–104; and Michael R. Bechloss, *Mayday: Eisenhower, Khrushchev, and the U-2 Affair* (New York: Harper and Row, 1986).

140.　Francis Gary Powers and Curt Gentry, *Operation Overflight* (New York: Holt, Rinehart, and Winston, 1970), p. 45.

141.　*The New York Times*, May 6, 1960.

142.　*The New York Times*, May 8, 1960. Speech of May 7, 1960.

143.　Wise and Ross, *The U-2 Affair*, p. 100; Jack Shick, *The Berlin Crisis, 1958–1962* (Philadelphia: University of Pennsylvania Press, 1971), p. 114; and *The New York Times*, May 8, 1960.

144.　*The New York Times*, May 12, 1960.

145.　*The New York Times*, May 30, 1960.

146.　Bohlen, op. cit., p. 470.

147.　*Events*, pp. 238–248.

148.　*The New York Times*, May 30, 1960.

149. Nikita Khrushchev, *Khrushchev Remembers: The Last Testament*, translated and edited by Strobe Talbott (Boston: Little, Brown, 1974), pp. 450–451.

150. See Michael Bechloss, *MayDay: Eisenhower, Khrushchev and the U-2* (New York: Harper and Row, 1986), and James A Nathan, "A Fragile Detente: The U-2 Incident Reexamined."

Nathan's article notes the still unexplained anomalies in this event that Bechloss, by far the most competent and thorough effort to date, did not address. They are:

1. The plane was claimed by virtually all official Washington to have been "shot down" at its "assigned ceiling." Yet the U-2 operated at over 110,000 feet. No Soviet surface-to-air missile could reach higher than 60,000 feet.

2. Given that the plane was allegedly "hit" by an airburst at high altitude, the pilot and downed plane, when they appeared on display, were in phenomenal condition. U.S. authorities maintained in private that the plane had suffered a "flameout." But Powers, in a personal communication (in 1976) to Nathan, vigorously denied that anything other than his original assertion was the case.

3. The "spy kit" Powers was issued was unusual in the extreme. For instance, the curare-tipped needle in a coin would cause a slow and terrible strangulation. The classic spy suicide drug was cyanide. No retired intelligence official could ever recall ever seeing such a flashy and really worthless bit of flight baggage and most contended that it was "for show."

4. Powers' mission was failure by any standard, yet heroic measures and enormous diplomatic energies were expended to retrieve him. In short, a simple "air-jockey," by all accounts, was exchanged for the highest ranking Soviet espionage agent ever collared in the United States (Colonel Rudolph Able—a resident, in the argot of the profession), as well as two other lower-ranking individuals. Powers—who did not keep his silence at his trial—on his return was awarded an Intelligence Star, the highest award given by the CIA.

151. See Bechloss, op. cit., pp. 370–374.

152. Hoopes, op. cit., p. 504.

153. George F. Kennan, *Memoirs: 1925–1950* (Boston: Little, Brown, 1967), p. 365.

154. Eisenhower, op. cit., p. 616.

155. See Joyce and Gabriel Kolko, *The Limits of Power, 1945–1954* (New York: Harper & Row, 1972), esp. the introduction and conclusion.

156. U.S. Congress, Senate Committee on Foreign Relations, *Some Important Issues in Foreign Aid*, 89th Congress, 2nd Session, 1966, pp. 6–7 and table 1.

157. *The New York Times*, September 30, 1960.

158. Arthur M. Schlesinger, Jr., *A Thousand Days: John F. Kennedy in the White House* (Boston: Houghton Mifflin, 1965), p. 50.

159. "Transcript of the Second Nixon–Kennedy Debate on Nation-Wide Television," *The New York Times*, October 8, 1960, p. 11

Chapter 5
Containment on
the New Frontier

John F. Kennedy and his administration had a flair and style that set them apart from the generation that had shaped American policy during the late 1940s and then institutionalized the cold war during the mid-1950s. As he eloquently proclaimed in his inaugural address, "The torch has been passed to a new generation of Americans." Nevertheless, it was a generation "tempered by war, disciplined by a hard and bitter peace, proud of our ancient heritage." Not the least of the elements retained from that heritage were the old objectives and reflexes of the "hard and bitter peace."

When the Democratic nominee, John Kennedy, rose to give his acceptance speech, his central theme was the interrelationship between world affairs and the American mission. It seemed an almost cosmic challenge, "a new frontier" where we would be asked "more sacrifice instead of more security." "Can a nation organized and governed such as ours endure?" asked Kennedy. "Have we the nerve and the will? . . . Can we carry through in . . . a race . . . for mastery of the sky and the oceans and the tides the far side of space and the inside of men's minds?"[1] The American people, declared Kennedy, stood "at a turning point in history," and had to choose "between the public interest and private comfort, between national greatness and national decline . . .; all mankind awaits upon our decision."[2]

The Kennedy victory in the 1960 election was razor thin; but the sense of power and vitality that the young president brought to the tasks thus won was almost contagious. On Inauguration Day, Kennedy stood before the American people and called them to their destiny: "Let every nation know, whether it wishes us well or ill, that we shall pay any price, bear any burden, meet any hardship, support any friend, oppose any foe to assure the survival and success of liberty. We will do all this and more." Thus, the first message of the new administration was an eloquent reaffirmation of the Truman Doctrine. It was containment with vigor. The problem, as Kennedy saw it, was not the objectives of the Eisenhower administration but its reluctance to develop and exploit a full range of American instrumentalities to implement containment. "Eisenhower," Kennedy complained, "had escaped" the burden of making good on the far-flung commitments rendered during his administration. Kennedy, however, had premonitions that "all the pigeons are coming home on the next President."[3]

THE THREATENED NEW FRONTIER

The view from the new frontier was frightening. The domestic preoccupations of the Communists during the mid-1950s had provided the Eisenhower administration a respite. However, during that time, deep forces had been at work throughout the international system. By the end of the decade, the members of the Kennedy administration thought they could discern the shape of these forces. Indeed, they believed that the Eisenhower administration had seen them as well, especially those in the Third World, but had chosen to ignore them or confront them with the inapplicable rigidities of the new look and massive retaliation. The years since 1957 were viewed as an unrelieved succession of cumulating disasters. Soviet missile strength seemed to grow, and the pressure on Berlin became very nearly unbearable. Simultaneously, the Soviets and the Chinese expanded their activities in the Middle East, South and Southeast Asia, and Africa. Castro's victory in the Cuban civil war marked the penetration of the western hemisphere.

In the face of this burgeoning assault on fifteen years of American order, America seemed no longer able to respond either spiritually or materially. Thus, the Kennedy administration moved immediately to reinvigorate American will through the bedazzling rhetoric and energy of the New Frontier. It was, however, but an eloquent reaffirmation of the absolutism of John Foster Dulles and the sense of mission of Dean Acheson. As for the instruments of containment on the new frontier, they would have to be commensurate with the scope of the purported challenge. Because the challenges were apparent at every level of potential conflict, it seemed imperative that the United States be able to respond at all levels and arenas of potential conflict. "We are moving," Kennedy told Americans, "into a period of uncertain risk and great commitment . . . ; thus we must be able to respond with discrimination and speed, to any problem at any spot on the globe at any moment's notice."[4]

This search for a wide-spectrum response to the far-ranging demands of containment prompted the development of interrelated instrumentalities and doctrine ranging from general nuclear war to the problems of public health in the Third World. Military forces were conceived and designed for a flexible response: to fight total thermonuclear war, limited nuclear war, conventional war in Europe or Asia, or unconventional warfare anywhere in the world. At the same time, the Kennedy administration sought to expand American military and economic assistance programs in an effort to anticipate and defeat communist efforts in the Third World. The problem of building nations that reflected American political and economic values was but a natural extension of the effort to maintain an international strategic environment conducive to historic American purposes and principles. Indeed, American involvement in nation-building, whether by means of military or politico–economic intervention, constituted a demonstration of the will and commitment deemed crucial to the maintenance of the strategic balance.

The Kennedy administration's concern with the problem of nation-building resulted in part from the circumstances existing in the Third World when Kennedy assumed office. The situation in the Congo, insurgencies in Laos and Vietnam, and Castro's success in Cuba meant that, in virtually every corner of the Third World, the Kennedy administration was compelled to deal with revolutionary developments. This concern was given even more urgency by the prevailing view of the nature of the Soviet and Chinese relationship to these events. The American perception of these events was complicated by the Sino–Soviet schism. Disputes within the communist world notwithstanding, the conclusion was drawn that the Third World was to be a major, if not the primary, testing ground of communist and American will. Consequently, nation-building within the Third World revolutionary context became much more than an end in itself. It was to become a major element in the overarching global struggle.

The Sino–Soviet Dispute, Revolutionary War, and American Policy

By the early 1960s, American officials knew that communism was no monolith. The Sino–Soviet dispute was apparent to all but the most insensitive observer even by the late 1950s. In the wake of Khrushchev's refusal to back the Chinese during the last Taiwan crisis in 1958, what had been latent Sino–Soviet tension broke into open conflict. Khrushchev withdrew all technical advisers. Unfinished cement factories were abandoned as Russian engineers returned to the Soviet Union, taking their architectural drawings with them. China was militarily deprived of the Soviet nuclear shield and, at supposedly fraternal international conclaves, was denounced as "irresponsible" by the Soviets. The Chinese were bitter in the extreme. They had expected that the appearance of a Soviet retaliatory capability as evidenced by large thermonuclear explosions and the launching of Sputniks and working model

ICBMs could be used to contain American pressure on China. When their hopes did not materialize, the Chinese rhetorically reverted to a kind of exorcism of the danger. The Americans with their atomic bombs, they declared, as much to Russia as to the United States, were paper tigers. War with the capitalists, they pointed out, was inevitable, and, although other societies might perish, "victorious peoples would create very swiftly a civilization thousands of times higher than the capitalist system and a truly beautiful future for themselves."[5] To believe otherwise was proof of declining ideological purity, revolutionary will, and capacity for leadership of the communist world.

Official Washington, as well as alert readers of *The New York Times*, were aware, therefore, that the one-time "Sino–Soviet monolith" was cracking.[6] But the Kennedy administration, ever sensitive to the memory of Truman's difficulties in trying to differentiate between Moscow and Beijing, though perhaps accepting that the two powers were now analytically distinct, nevertheless dealt with them as functional equivalents. In the young president's first State of the Union message, only ten days after his inauguration, Kennedy told the nation that "each day we draw near the hour of maximum danger" in foreign affairs. The "great obstacle," proclaimed Kennedy, was the Soviet Union and Communist China. "We must never be lulled into believing that either power had yielded its ambitions for world domination. . . . On the contrary, our task is to convince them that aggression and subversion will not be profitable routes to pursue these ends."[7] Secretary of State Dean Rusk made the same point some six months later when he told the National Press Club: "The central issue . . . is the announced determination to impose a world of coercion upon those not already subject to it . . . it is posed between the Sino–Soviet empire and the rest, whether allied or neutral; and it is posed on every continent."[8]

Sino–Soviet
Enthusiasm for Emerging Nations

The consequence of this image of the Sino–Soviet relationship held by the new administration and the Sino–Soviet perception of revolutionary war is critical to the history of this period. The military doctrine of the Soviet Union traditionally had shown little attention to the Third World.[9] However, in 1955, as part of the new effort at world activism assumed by the Khrushchev regime, Moscow made new overtures to the developing nations. Yet, rather than working to promote revolution, Soviet strategy, after the Bandung Conference of 1955, strove toward detaching former colonial areas from the imperialist bloc by working with the national bourgeoisie. Indeed, the nonaligned nations might jail local Communists and still count on Soviet moral and material development assistance.[10]

By the end of 1960, however, the ebullient and chimerical Khrushchev began to propound a theory of "wars of national liberation" which neatly mirrored the analysis of American defense intellectuals who were arguing for a capacity to wage limited war. The Soviets announced that they were prepared to sponsor and promote insurgencies. Although they had refrained from military activity previous to 1960 in the Third World, support would now be forthcoming: first, in the form of doctrinal approval and, second, with economic assistance. This policy was articulated on January 6, 1961, two weeks before Kennedy's inauguration, in which Khrushchev reviewed the full range and dangers of modern war and declared:

> The armed struggle by the Vietnamese people or the war of the Algerian people, which is already in its seventh year, serve as the latest examples of national liberation wars. These wars began as an uprising by the colonial peoples against their oppressors and changed into guerrilla warfare. Liberation wars will continue to exist as long as imperialism exists, as long as colonialism exists. These are revolutionary wars. Such wars are not only admissible but inevitable, since the colonialists do not grant independence voluntarily. Therefore, the peoples can attain their freedom and independence only by struggle, including armed struggle. . . .
> What is the attitude of the Marxists toward such uprisings? A most positive one.[11]

But Khrushchev's analysis of the need to support wars of national liberation was tempered by his awareness of the need for caution in the face of the potential price.[12] Thus, Khrushchev's redefinition of Soviet strategy was part of his rejection of the traditional historical inevitability of communism's triumph in any circumstance, even war. But Khrushchev's call to support wars of national liberation also helped him counter Chinese charges that Russia had grown too soft to challenge capitalism. Nevertheless, he remained essentially cautious; he circumspectly chastened the Chinese:

> We must be realistic in our thinking and understand the contemporary situation. Of course, this does not in any way mean that if we are so strong, we should test the stability of the capitalist system by force. This would be wrong. The peoples would not understand and would never support those who took it into their heads to act in such a way. We have always been against predatory wars. Marxists have recognized and still

do recognize only wars of liberation, wars that are just, and have condemned and still do condemn wars that are predatory and imperialistic.[13]

China, it was widely purported, held markedly more activist and militant doctrines,[14] but it is debatable that Mao Zedong's notion of "people's war" was a grand design for world conquest. However, Mao's writings on guerrilla warfare, penned from the perspective of his defensive war against the Japanese and civil war against Chiang Kai-shek, were not taken as a description of a defensive effort carried out by indigenous nationalist revolutionaries. Rather, Dean Rusk and others in the policy-making community believed that the resurrection of Mao's writings on people's war was an advocacy of a formula for aggressive Chinese Communist expansion. However, beginning in 1949, there was a seventeen-year hiatus in which Chinese officials made almost no statements that could be interpreted as actively encouraging wars of national liberations, and later, the 1965 statement of Lin Biao concerning revolutionary war (called a Chinese *Mein Kampf* by Secretary of State Rusk) had ambiguous support at best. As Arthur Huck, an Australian scholar working at London's International Institute for Strategic Studies, wrote: "Far from being a blue print for the direct expansion of Chinese influence [Lin Biao's] 'Long Live the Victory of People's War'[15] argues that revolution cannot be exported and that the people's forces must be almost entirely self-reliant."[16]

The American Misperception

American policymakers chose to believe that China's militant rhetoric of the late 1950s and early 1960s, although directed at Moscow and primarily the product of the Sino–Soviet ideological and political dispute, indicated an intensely aggressive nature, especially with respect to South and Southeast Asia. The threat of insurgent communist war as articulated by Khrushchev was therefore interpreted to be as much a Chinese menace to world order as were the purported designs of Stalin and his successors.

The trumpet of worldwide testing, then, had been sounded over the issue of the expansion of power from *either* the Soviets or the Chinese. The issue was, as it had been since the days of Woodrow Wilson, whether aggression was tolerable in an orderly world environment where American ideals and institutions would prosper. In this way, it made no difference what its source or instruments, disorder had to be contained. It was this conviction that could lead Dean Rusk to explain to the Senate Foreign Relations Committee that the differences among the great communist rivals did not erase their fundamental similarities.

> *Secretary Rusk:* It was said here the other day that Hitler was a unique phenomenon. Well, there were some unique aspects. An airedale and a great dane are different but they are both dogs.
> Now, we have this phenomenon of aggression.
> *Senator Aiken:* They bite you in different places.
> *Secretary Rusk:* That is right. We have the phenomenon of aggression. Hitler could see that the Japanese militarists in Manchuria were not stopped. He saw that Mussolini was not stopped in Ethiopia. This encouraged him.
> Now, what happens here in Southeast Asia, if Peiping [Beijing] discovers that Hanoi can move without risk or can move with success? What further decisions are they going to make? What difference will that make in Moscow about what would happen to our commitments elsewhere, whether they should make choices as between peaceful coexistence and a more militant policy of world revolution?[17]

Secretary Rusk's response to an assumed communist challenge was one in which Sino–Soviet differences did not really matter.[18] Intellectually, therefore, Americans had by 1960 changed very little from the view expressed by Truman that global war was a seamless web, which, if threatened by aggression anywhere, was liable to collapse into Armageddon. As President Truman stated the notion of American policy matters in a radio talk April 11, 1951:

> If history has taught us anything, it is that aggression anywhere in the world is a threat to peace everywhere in the world. When that aggression is supported by the cruel and selfish rulers of a powerful nation who are bent on conquest, it becomes a clear and present danger to the security and independence of every free nation.[19]

The instruments of aggression were different, for now as Robert McNamara observed:

> The faces of *world communism* operate in the twilight zone. Their military tactics are those of the sniper, the ambush and the raid, their political tactics are terror and assassination. We must help the people of threatened nations to resist these tactics.[20]

Moreover, a new and in some ways more perplexing arena of conflict had been opened up in the emergence of revolutionary political and economic dynamics in the Third World. But if the slightest doubt existed as to the necessity of a multifaceted response, it was dispelled by events in Cuba and the failure of Kennedy's first crude attempt at counterrevolution in the style of the 1950s.

The Bay of Pigs

In Cuba, a handful of men under the leadership of Fidel Castro had arrived by boat in 1956 to begin a successful three-year struggle to topple a dictator who was an American client. After seizing power on New Year's Day in 1959, Castro had begun to restructure Cuban institutions while professing a socialist-revolutionary ideology profoundly disturbing to Americans. Almost at a stroke, one of the most advanced nations in Latin America had been converted to socialism. If only a few dozen men or so could manage such a feat in a traditional zone of American preeminence, then what, American policymakers despaired, would be the fate of countries in areas that were in dispute among the superpowers? The Kennedy administration saw the Third World symbolically interlaced in a structure of political and economic order in want of an American guarantee to maintain order.

It is not surprising, therefore, that Kennedy did not stop the preparations set in motion by the CIA with Eisenhower's approval for an invasion of the island by Cuban exiles to overthrow Castro's regime. Arthur Schlesinger, Jr., and Theodore Sorensen have tried to portray Kennedy as being misled about the operation by the Eisenhower holdovers in the CIA and Defense Department.[21] It may well be that Kennedy was unclear concerning the details of the intervention, but he did approve it. That is to say, he accepted the underlying premise of Eisenhower's policy—the Castro regime should be destroyed.

The operation itself was an absolute disaster. Slightly fewer than fifteen hundred Cuban exiles hit the beaches at the Bay of Pigs, and some five hundred men were promptly and efficiently cut to pieces by Castro's well-disciplined forces. The remaining one thousand men were ignominiously captured. Contrary to what the CIA had confidently predicted, no uprising of the Cuban people greeted the invaders to provide the necessary assistance.[22] The full dimensions of the disaster were apparent, and Kennedy accepted complete responsibility for the failure. Kennedy's candor and remarkable rapport with the press and the willingness of the American people to rally around the presidency at moments of crisis eased the administration's handling of the failure at home. Covertly, however, the Kennedy administration established an extensive clandestine operation against the Castro regime using the Cuban exile community in south Florida as as source of manpower under CIA direction. This harassment and several attempts to assassinate Castro would continue until Kennedy's assassination more than two years later.

The Bay of Pigs fiasco is important for what it tells us of the Kennedy administration's attitude toward revolution and intervention.

In a speech only hours after it was clear that the invasion had failed, Kennedy warned of the dangers posed by the "menace of external communist intervention and domination in Cuba."[23] Kennedy reemphasized the intention of his administration to reorient American force structure to be able to counter the revolutionary challenge to American power. "We dare not fail," he asserted, "to see the insidious nature of this new and deeper struggle. We dare not fail to grasp the new concepts, the new tools, and new sense of urgency we will need to combat it—whether in Cuba or South Vietnam."[24] This was essential if "the United States was to win in a struggle in many ways more difficult than war, where disappointment will often accompany us."[25] Kennedy concluded with reaffirmation of the grim vision of the inaugural address:

> I am convinced . . . that history will record the fact that the bitter struggle reached its climax in the late 1950s and the early 1960s. Let me then make it clear as the President of the United States that I am determined upon our system's survival and success, regardless of the cost and regardless of the peril![26]

Activism and American involvement were absolutely essential, and, as in Europe after World War II, the United States was prepared to act with or without the assistance of others.

> Let the record show that our restraint is not inexhaustible. Should it ever appear that the inter-American doctrine of noninterference merely conceals or excuses a policy of nonaction—if the nations of this hemisphere should fail to meet their commitments against outside communist penetration—then I want it clearly understood that his government will not hesitate in meeting its primary obligations which are to the security of our nation![27]

The possibility of American intervention remained; indeed, Kennedy had proclaimed that the national security of the United States required that the "right" of intervention be retained by the United States. In the meantime, "any free nation under outside attack of any kind can be assured that all of our resources stand ready to respond to any request for assistance."[28]

NATION BUILDING
AND COUNTERREVOLUTION

The preoccupation of the Kennedy administration with the role of communism in the Third World led to a search for economic, cultural, and social instrumentalities that could parallel military counterinsurgent tactics and lead to a stabilizing of revolutionary situations in the underdeveloped world. Communism would not be allowed a foothold or would be stifled while it was little more than an idea. Revolution was perhaps inevitable, but the Kennedy administration sought a way to redirect revolution away from a communist conclusion.

Nation Building

Khrushchev's January speech about "sacred wars of national liberation" prompted Kennedy in February 1961 to reconvene one of his transition task forces under the leadership of Adolph Berle and Thomas Mann with a mandate "to develop politics and programs which channel the revolution . . . in Latin America . . . and prevent it being taken over by the Sino–Soviet bloc."[29] Earlier, the task force had reported to the new president that the social revolutionaries were targets for "capture by Communist power politics."[30] According to the report, the Communists intended "to convert the Latin American social revolutionaries into a Marxist attack on the United States itself." This threat, the report warned, "is more dangerous than . . . the Nazi Fascist threat."[31] The report held that the primary threat was of armed revolutionaries and the essential remedy was a combination of military action and development aid.

The report, stimulated by the relationship Castro had established with Moscow, was the foundation of Kennedy's March proposal for "a vast new ten-year plan for the Americas." The Alliance for Progress was envisioned as a $20 billion development assistance program whereby the nations of Latin America would establish a new legitimacy through reforms of archaic tax and land systems and through expanded assistance to the public sector: education, housing, and health. But there was more to the proposal than an economic assistance program having as its objective simply the economic development of Latin America or the Third World. The entire national security establishment was coordinated by a special interdepartmental task force chaired by the attorney general, Robert Kennedy, who, in turn, reported to his brother after each meeting. The resources detailed to the Special Counterinsurgency Group constituted a massive undertaking "blazing new and uncharted paths in the tradition of such recent triumphs as the Marshall Plan."[32]

There evolved with the Alliance for Progress and the revitalized aid program an infusion of governmental funds to universities and think tanks designed to foster a body of scholarship that was to support the policy objectives of the Kennedy administration in the Third World. Political development or political modernization was to emerge in the early 1960s as a distinct subfield of social science, bridging such diverse disciplines as psychology, sociology, political science, and economics. The purpose of this study was to describe, predict, and ultimately assist in the management of the process of development.

Nation building was a heady undertaking. Yet few government officials or academics hesitated before the exhilarating prospect of social architecture.

> As a house can be built from timber, bricks, and mortar, in different patterns . . . according to the choice, will and power of its builders, so a nation can be built according to different plans, from various materials, rapidly or gradually, by different sequences of steps, and in partial independence from its environment.[33]

The prescriptive elements and the tools of the study of nation building are a bit chaotic to summarize easily. Essentially, they shared a belief that the poor nations of the world would achieve a modest prosperity without succumbing to what Walt Rostow called "the scavengers of modernization," communism.[34] As a society modernized, became more Western, urbanized, and literate in its attitudes, there was an assumption that liberal governmental and capitalist economic forms would take hold. In short, in winning the battle of modernization in the developing societies the developing countries would expunge communism and, perforce, attune themselves to a process of building a stable, orderly community where American ideals would be vindicated and would flourish. As one academic put it to a War College audience in 1963:

> Here is one place where "winning over communism" has clear and specific meaning. When we look ahead over the next ten years our aim should be to have laid the foundation for good relations with those countries *after* they have passed through the first rude stages of transition from colony to nation, from asleep to awake, from medieval to twentieth century. Our investment today in these countries is in many ways a great gamble, with very real costs of which the financial is only one.
>
> The only meaningful payoff to this great investment is in the establishment of societies in the new countries that will be friendly to us, democratic in political complexion, and preferably capitalist rather than socialist in their economic structure.[35]

The search for the secret of making developing societies compatible with the historic American purpose was the essential endeavor of the theorists and practitioners of modernization. To many of the academic devotees of nation building, a developed society was cohesive. Tribalism, multiethnicity, or autonomous regions were not believed to be congruent with development. The growth of a city-dwelling population was deemed especially important. Urbanization was seen as related to integration and the beginning of differentiation where urban dwellers begin to have specialized services, market facilities, access to societal agents of socialization, and political learning. Further, urban environments bring security from the unpredictable, overpopulated, and perhaps insecure countryside. Moreover, urbanization provides the setting for the building of strong central institutions. After all, what could be more useful than a recognizable capital with some ambit of control and the possibility of diffusing its control outward from a central policy. To development theorist Samuel Huntington, "modernization is, in large part, measured by the growth of the city."[36] Professor Huntington praises the great serendipity that

> in an absent-minded way the United States in Vietnam may well have stumbled upon the answers to "wars of national liberation." The effective response lies neither in the quest for conventional military victory nor in the esoteric doctrines and gimmicks of counterinsurgency warfare. It is instead forced-draft urbanization and modernization which rapidly brings the country in question out of the phase in which a rural revolutionary movement can hope to generate sufficient strength to come to power.[37]

Paralleling integration — purportedly the by-product of urbanization — was the need for strong institutions: "A society with weak institutions lacks the ability to curb the excesses of personal and parochial desires."[38] Almost by definition, weak institutions lack authority and cannot do their job. They are "immoral in the same sense in which a corrupt judge, a cowardly soldier or an ignorant teacher is immoral."[39] But also by definition, few strong institutions exist in developing societies — with one exception: In developing societies, one almost universally strong institution is the military. The purpose, therefore, of American military and economic assistance was to strengthen the most logical central institution that has been widely conceived of as providing the *sine qua non* of development — security and order.

> All nation-building efforts will encounter resistances requiring a combination of persuasion and coercion. In the earliest stages, coercion must be a primary instrument and nation-builders must give prime attention to improving organizational capability (e.g., army, police, foreign assistance) in this area. The degree of coercion will vary with the degree of heterogeneity (e.g., class, religion, ideology, economic development) a would-be national territory manifests.[40]

The support of military regimes seemed an almost inexorable conclusion of the nation builders because contemporary coups in Asia and Africa may be regarded as providing necessary and tolerable periods of transition. The coup is a necessary link in the process of modernization. For the new nations, it seems far better to accept a military government that preserves law and order than to face radical subversives or guerrilla warfare.[41]

Thus, to rival the appeals of communism in the Third World, the prescription of many American development theorists and practitioners was to search for strong leadership in command of well-functioning institutions that could form alternatives to communism.[42] This, then, was the struggle that development theorists saw between revolution and collectivist doctrines on the one hand and "liberal development" on the other.[43] It was the same Manichean struggle of the Truman doctrine given new terms: WHAM — Winning Hearts and Minds.

Counterrevolution

The ultimately counterrevolutionary thrust of nation building was apparent in the Alliance for Progress, the ten-year, $20-billion economic assistance program established to counter the influence of Castro throughout Latin America. Schlesinger has written that Kennedy was quite sensitive to the need to remain responsive to revolutionary demands if reform and development were to take place.[44] But the court historian of Camelot also recounts that Kennedy employed revealing criteria to test whether a regime could be supported:

> There are three possibilities in a descending order of preference: a decent democratic regime, a continuation of the Trujillo regime [a right-wing dictatorship], or a Castro regime. We ought to aim at the first, but we really can't renounce the second until we are sure that we can avoid the third.[45]

Decent democratic regimes were clearly desirable, but it is clear from this arraying of preferences that Kennedy would settle for a good deal less if there was a chance he might get a replication of Castro.

Kennedy sought through the alliance to bring about a 5.5 percent annual economic growth rate in Latin America, but the conditions under which the program was implemented included the provision that American aid had to be spent on American goods and services, which were more expensive than could be obtained elsewhere. The real infusion of resources was, therefore, correspondingly reduced. The alliance was, however, successful in encouraging private American corporations to expand their holdings in Latin America during the period.[46] Finally, and most indicative of the purpose of the Alliance, was that even as the economic assistance programs were receiving special attention, the Department of Defense was emphasizing the training of Latin American units in counterinsurgency and counterguerrilla activity at Fort Bragg, North Carolina, home of the Green Berets, and in the Jungle Warfare School in the American-controlled Panama Canal Zone. In addition, hundreds of Latin American policemen were given special instruction in pacification and civic action at an Agency for International Development school also based in the Canal Zone.

Kennedy, in effect, simultaneously supported economic and (presumably) democratic political development but would not risk Latin America's extant social structure and pattern of privilege if the cost might include revolution from the left. The former was, of course, the declaratory policy of the Alliance. However, if development took an unfavorable turn to the left, the Kennedy administration wanted to be able to draw on those indigenous forces that would be able to stem or channel the revolutionary tide. Furthermore, if U.S. intervention was necessary, material would be available to construct a pro-American regime.

The Dominican case is illustrative. Following Trujillo's ouster by assassination, Juan Bosch, a leftist but noncommunist writer who had been in exile for twenty years, was elected president. Bosch appeared weak, however. He was described by Schlesinger as a "literary figure, better as short story writer than as statesman."[47] Consequently, Kennedy maintained support of the Dominican military, which subsequently overthrew Bosch in 1963 just before Kennedy's death. Theodore Draper summarizes Kennedy's policy and problems succinctly: "When the latter decided to stage the coup, this double bookkeeping proved to be the undoing both of Bosch's regime and Kennedy's Dominican policy."[48]

Beset by such anomalies and contradictions, the Alliance did not prosper. The hoped-for 5.5 percent growth projections could not be achieved until the fifth year of the program, and then it required a good deal of prodding and juggling of indicators. It was apparent that the countries of the Alliance would not respond to the simplistic notion that growth would come about primarily as the result of the infusion of American capital. Social and political transformation were essential to the development effort. But transformation implied a disruption of class structures and patterns of privilege. How could those who had the most to lose be expected to lead a campaign that would enervate their power? In countries where personalist rule prevailed, a civic culture was but a transplanted social science fantasy, and the whole notion of a ruling elite's becoming the agent of its own enfeeblement was absurd. Forceful removal of these elites would have placed Kennedy in the quadrant of the collectivists and revolutionary elements he opposed. Thus, Kennedy was forced to fall back on the contradictory notion that

> the men of wealth and power in poor nations "must lead the fight for those basic reforms which alone can preserve the fabric of their own societies. Those who make peaceful revolution impossible will make violent revolution inevitable. These social reforms are at the heart of the Alliance for Progress."[49]

It might be said that Kennedy's developmental programs saw three possibilities in descending order of preference: Development in all its dimensions was desirable, stability was the minimum that was acceptable, and leftist revolution was simply unacceptable. The Kennedy administration would aim for development, but under no circumstances would the second be surrendered in the face of the third possibility. Kennedy's warning to the elites of Latin America and the Third World that they might well be crushed by violent revolution if they stood in the way of reform reflects an important ambivalence in Kennedy and his administration. He was, on the one hand, sensitive and perhaps emotionally responsive to the revolutionary ferment of the Third World. On the other, however, he saw America locked in mortal struggle with world communism, and from this higher strategic vantage point, revolutionary ferment was conceived as more of a threat than an opportunity. Accordingly, revolution was to be anticipated by means of development.

But the effect of such an approach was the subordination of development as an end in itself. Development assistance became an instrument in the larger strategic struggle and was justified to Congress primarily as an instrument in the cold war. Indeed, a report prepared for the Senate Foreign Relations Committee in 1966 concluded that among the numerous rationales advanced by all administrations since 1950, the most common were, first, the enhancement of American national security; second, containment of communist aggression; and third, "to assist economic development in the less-developed countries." Moreover, American foreign assistance has been concentrated — more than 75 percent in most years — in a handful of forward or confrontation countries on the periphery of the Soviet Union and China.[50] Contrary to the charge that American aid has been distributed indiscriminately in pursuit of unrealistic altruistic ends, it had in fact very much served as the instrument of American national security policy.

The American attitude toward development in the Third World was marked by a perhaps irreconcilable ambivalence. Decent democratic development could be, was, and continues to be thought of by many Americans as an end in itself—the ultimate long-run preemption of communism in the Third World. At the same time, however, Kennedy and his successors saw an immediate problem of revolutionary unrest that had to be stabilized through support of strong institutions if the perceived Sino–Soviet threat was to be contained.

One cannot be sure that the elimination of this ambivalence would have ensured the success of American aid as an instrument of nation building and development. Indeed, it is now increasingly apparent that the development of so-called decent regimes in the Third World is an immensely more complex task than envisioned by the proponents of nation building. In any event, development was at best one, and probably not the primary, objective of nation building. As an objective, it has always competed with another generally overriding objective—containment of communism's advance in the Third World. Thought of in this way, nation building is understood as a major addition to the spectrum of political, economic, unconventional and conventional military, and strategic capability—otherwise known as flexible response—that the Kennedy administration sought to develop and employ during the decade of the 1960s.

FLEXIBLE RESPONSE

At the other end of this spectrum of capability was the realm of conventional and strategic military power. As with nation building, Kennedy called for a reappraisal and augmentation of American potential. In his first State of the Union message, the new president noted:

> *We must strengthen our military tools. . . .* In the past, lack of consistent, coherent military strategy . . . [has] made it difficult to assess accurately how adequate—or inadequate—our defenses really are. I have, therefore, instructed the Secretary of Defense to reappraise our entire defense strategy.[51]

The signal that a massive infusion of funds would be available to the various defense agencies set off an internal wrangle over the allotment of funds among the various services. The Air Force asked for three thousand new solid-fuel Minuteman missiles to replace the huge, liquid fueled Titan. The Air Force had more than fifty Titan missiles. They were comparatively vulnerable, and were enormously expensive. A squadron of nine Titan IIs cost hundreds of millions of dollars.[52] Some requests for new missiles apparently went as high as ten thousand missiles. McNamara "compromised" and submitted a request for appropriation to build 950 new Minutemen.[53]

The Air Force insistence on massive superiority illuminates a remarkable coincidence of manipulation of information for bureaucratic reasons and the Kennedy administration's sense that the way to deal with the Russians was to outdistance them at every level of armaments. Indeed, the notion of a missile gap originated with inspired leaks from the Air Force. *The New York Times,* on January 17, 1959, based an article on interviews with "numerous persons having intimate knowledge of the defense effort" and estimated that by 1962 Soviet ICBMs would outnumber American missiles by 1,000 to 130 and would increase in 1964 to 2,000 to 130.

In his farewell speech, President Eisenhower had told Congress that the missile gap showed every sign of being a fiction.[54] Eisenhower's evidence was fairly conclusive. The U-2 flight of May 1, 1960, was the last of a series that had revealed, according to Eisenhower, "information of the greatest importance to the nation's security. In fact, their success has been nothing short of remarkable."[55] What the U-2 flights (and other intelligence means) had demonstrated was that the Soviets had only a handful of missiles, perhaps 30 to 35. More important, no massive build-up was underway.

By the end of 1960, Khrushchev knew that the United States probably was aware that no missile gap existed, and he made several attempts to signal the incoming administration of the possibility of limiting deployment on both sides. In the December 1960 "Pugwash" conference on disarmament, W. W. Kuznetsov worriedly approached the American representatives, Walt Rostow and Jerome Wisner, about the campaign rhetoric concerning the missile gap. Kuznetsov suggested that if the new administration went in for massive rearmament, it could not expect the Russians to sit still. Rostow told the Soviet official "that any Kennedy rearmament would be designed to improve the stability of the deterrent, and the Soviet Union should recognize this as in the interests of peace."[56]

Schlesinger despairs that Kuznetsov, "innocent of the higher calculus of deterrence recently developed in the United States, brusquely dismissed [Rostow's] explanation."[57] Apparently, the higher calculus was one of overwhelming American superiority. As the International Institute for Strategic Studies (IISS) noted, the acceleration of United States ICBM and submarine-launched ballistic missile (SLBM) production

TABLE 5-1. Growth of ICBM/SLBM Strength, 1960–1964 (Mid Years)

		1960	1961	1962	1963	1964
USA	ICBM	18	63	294	424	834
	SLBM	32	96	144	224	416
USSR	ICBM	35	50	75	100	200
	SLBM	—	some	some	100	120

Source: The Military Balance 1970–1971 (London: International Institute for Strategic Studies, 1971), p. 106. Reprinted by permission.

during the first two years of the Kennedy administration created a missile gap—but a gap clearly advantageous to the United States. The IISS comparisons of American and Soviet strategic missile deployment at the end of the Eisenhower years and during the Kennedy administration are shown in Table 5-1.

As the Kennedy administration assumed office in early 1961, it found already in place a two- or three-to-one American advantage in strategic weapons. Moreover, the Eisenhower administration had provided the basis for maintaining such an advantage for the immediate future. It will be recalled that the response of Eisenhower to the ferment of the late 1950s following the launch of Sputnik and the reappraisal of massive retaliation was a modest increase in American strategic weapons programs, especially the Polaris and Minuteman systems. By 1960 to 1961, these strategic systems had been moved from the research, development, and testing phase to actual procurement. Therefore, at least at the strategic level, Eisenhower had provided Kennedy with more than ample resources to deal with whatever threat might have existed.

Indeed, it was argued by McNamara that the Eisenhower-approved strategic bomber, the B-70, was unnecessary and perhaps of obsolete strategic capability. Professor Schlesinger suggests that McNamara accepted the arguments for massive ICBM superiority because the new defense secretary

> was already engaged in a bitter fight with the Air Force over his effort to disengage from the B-70, a costly, high-altitude manned bomber rendered obsolescent by the improvement in the Soviet ground-to-air missiles. After cutting down the original Air Force missile demands considerably, he perhaps felt that he could not do more without risking public conflict with the Joint Chiefs and the vociferous B-70 lobby in Congress. As a result, the President went along with the policy of multiplying Polaris and Minuteman missiles.[58]

Even if one grants this bureaucratic political necessity, one should not lose sight of the fact that Kennedy and McNamara sought to maintain overwhelming strategic superiority over the Soviets. Thus, in spite of some administration doubts and perhaps abetted by some administration logrolling, the first ten months of the Kennedy administration witnessed a $6 billion increase in the military budget, from $43,685,000 to $49,878,000. The capacity to produce Minuteman missiles was increased 100 percent, and the number of Polaris subs to be produced by 1964 was increased by 50 percent. Moreover, about one quarter of the Strategic Air Command bomber force was put on 50 percent alert, thus increasing by 50 percent the number of long-range bombers on alert status. This buildup was undertaken although, as Schlesinger has pointed out, Kennedy and the White House staff "wondered whether the new budget was not providing more missiles than national security required" and thereby threatened the Soviets' retaliatory capability. But the "President," reports Schlesinger, "was not prepared to overrule" the recommendation of Secretary of Defense McNamara.[59]

Considering the level of strategic superiority when Kennedy took office, these increases were awesome. Congressman Melvin Laird entered into the *Congressional Record* some estimates of the considerable baseline from which the Kennedy team advanced:

two Polaris submarines with a combined total of 32 missiles, each missile capable of much more destruction than was rained upon Hiroshima;

about 16 Atlas ICBM's;

over 600 long-range B-52 jet bombers, each carrying more destructive explosive power than that used by all the combatants in World War II;

nearly 1400 B-47 medium-range jet bombers based abroad and at home with a 4500-mile range and distances beyond with air-to-air refueling;

B-58 Hustlers, the first U.S. supersonic medium-range jet bombers;

fourteen aircraft carriers able to launch more aircraft than the entire Soviet heavy bomber force;

eighteen wings of tactical aircraft, each wing with a substantial nuclear attack capability deployed globally;

sixty Thor IRBM's (intermediate-range ballistic missiles) deployed in England, capable of raining nuclear destruction on Russia, and thirty Jupiter IRBM's being installed at bases in Italy, from which Russia can be hit.

or "well over 2000 nuclear carrying vehicles capable of reaching Russia."[60]

Kennedy was also willing to move toward expansion of American military capability at the subnuclear level. "Flexible response," as Henry Kissinger had indicated in the late 1950s, required superiority not only at the strategic level but at all levels of potential conflict. Thus, at the same time as American strategic forces were being augmented, Kennedy and McNamara moved to build up the conventional capability that Eisenhower had cut back. During the first eighteen months of the Kennedy administration, McNamara strove to increase the size of the Army, the Navy, and the Air Force. By mid-1962, after a year of intense and escalating crises (to be described below), McNamara would have available sixteen combat-ready divisions (up from eleven), along with twenty-one tactical air wings (up from eighteen), and three marine divisions and their air wings, or the equivalent of a ten-division strategic reserve. William Kaufmann notes:

> With it, he could handle a Korean size engagement and still have several divisions left over for another emergency. Alternatively, he could triple the size of the American forces in Europe, and do so in fairly short order, since he had prepositioned in Europe the equipment for two divisions and was continuing to expand the airlift and sealift to move the strategic reserve. . . . His conventional options were expanding steadily.[61]

The interfaces between strategic nuclear and conventional war on the one hand and conventional war and nation building on the other were not ignored. The basis for a graduated response between conventional war and strategic nuclear war was already present in the Eisenhower administration's tactical nuclear capability. Apart from improving existing systems, therefore, all that remained to be done was the development of a doctrine of controlled use or graduated escalation from convention war up to and through limited or tactical nuclear war to, finally, general war. Throughout this spectrum of force McNamara sought options:

> Our new policy gives us the flexibility to choose among several operational plans, but does not require that we make any advance commitment with respect to doctrine or targets. We shall be committed only to a system that gives us the ability to use our forces in a controlled and deliberate way.[62]

Finally, McNamara developed an American potential for dealing with what he termed the "gray areas" of the Third World. Nation building was conceived as an anticipation of unconventional military conflict.

But if conflict or what Khrushchev had called wars of national liberation broke out, the United States was to be prepared to respond in kind.
Specifically, McNamara called for a more than $1.5 billion increase in
military assistance and soon noted proudly that the ability to fight guerrilla wars had been augmented by a 150 percent increase in antiguerrilla forces in all services but especially the Army's Special Forces or
Green Berets.[63]

In time, McNamara would come to question elements of this doctrine, especially the notion of the controlled and limited use of nuclear
weapons. By the late 1960s, McNamara would be warning publicly that
neither the United States nor the Soviet Union possessed or could at-
tain the capacity for a nuclear first strike against the other without inviting the certainty of unacceptable nuclear destruction in retaliation.[64]
He would also shift to an advocacy of deterrence grounded in "assured
destruction capability" as the basis of American strategic planning and
forces. However, in 1961 and 1962, nuclear weapons were viewed as
but one of several instrumentalities to be employed — a "complement"
to nonnuclear antiguerrilla forces that, taken together, "aimed at achieving the best balance of military capabilities — over the entire range of
potential conflict, in the various areas of the globe where the Free World
has vital interests, and over the years, as far ahead as we can reasonably plan."[65]

In summary, the Kennedy administration prepared feverishly for
confrontation with communist aggression at whatever level of conflict
or wherever it appeared. In the meantime, however, Khrushchev continued to pursue the more moderate diplomacy that had marked his
overtures to Kennedy during the interregnal period.

AMERICAN AIMS IN THE
FIRST ROUND: THE BERLIN CRISIS

Immediately following Kennedy's inauguration, Khrushchev moved dramatically to demonstrate his desire to improve communications between
the United States and the Soviet Union. On January 21, 1961, Khrushchev met for two hours with U.S. ambassador Llewellyn E. Thompson
and informed him that he earnestly desired an improvement in communications between the United States and the Soviets. To demonstrate
this, Khrushchev announced to Thompson that he would release the two
survivors of the RB-47 shot down in July 1960. Khrushchev noted that
he had deliberately waited until now to benefit Kennedy rather than
the Republicans.[66] Finally, Khrushchev made it clear to Thompson that

he was very interested in a meeting with Kennedy as soon as possible.[67] This Russian overture, announced by Kennedy in his first news conference on January 25, was taken by the new administration as an indication that the Russians wanted a reduction in tensions, but Khrushchev's "Wars of National Liberation" speech of January 6 was not overlooked. Khrushchev's gesture was, therefore, accepted, but with a note of caution.[68]

Kennedy's cautious receipt of Khrushchev's overture indicated a basic need of the new administration at this stage in the transition—time. Kennedy had been in office less than a week. He was confronted with a crunch of demands, including the preparation of numerous messages for the new Congress and the completion of his legislative program. Furthermore, Kennedy had not yet had an opportunity to confer with his Soviet experts as to a future course of action. An immediate and dramatic response to Khrushchev at this point was, therefore, not forthcoming, although Kennedy did announce during his January 25 news conference that during his administration, the U-2 flights would not be resumed. The door was not, however, closed on a meeting between Kennedy and Khrushchev; at this point, Kennedy did want more time before moving to the summit level of negotiations. This point was communicated to Khrushchev by Ambassador Thompson in his meeting with the Russian premier on January 21, and apparently Khrushchev did not challenge Kennedy's request. Rather, he restricted himself to an expression of his wish that lines of communication might be reopened.[69]

Russian reaction to Kennedy's February announcement of a stepped-up strategic armaments program was noticeably restrained. *Pravda*, for example, confined itself to a bland denunciation of the defense passages in the address and urged that the new administration follow a course of peaceful coexistence.[70] Beyond this, there was little official reaction on the part of the Kremlin. The Russians seemed content to exercise a degree of restraint until Kennedy's position would be more clearly spelled out.

In the meantime, events were transpiring that endangered the still-developing contacts between the Soviet Union and the United States. The civil strife in Laos was an explosive situation given the presence of Russian aid and a commitment of American prestige. Kennedy moved to demonstrate to Khrushchev that he was willing to commit U.S. troops to ensure in Laos what he called in his first press conference a "peaceful country—an independent country not dominated by either side."[71] The Communist-backed Pathet Lao forces launched an offensive against Vientiane in early March, and on March 23, Kennedy gravely warned that there could be no peace unless the external support of the Pathet

Lao was halted.[72] Kennedy followed up his warning by moving American troops into neighboring Thailand across the Mekong River from Vientiane. Apparently the show of force had its desired effect, for, by April, Khrushchev had agreed to discuss proposals for the neutralization of the country.

An earlier event in February that also implied difficulties for Soviet–American relations was the very peculiar murder of Patrice Lumumba in the Congo.[73] The Russian reaction to the event indicated, however, that they would confine their attacks to charges against Secretary-General Dag Hammarskjold and the United Nations, while avoiding direct attacks against the United States. Indeed, on the day of the incident, February 13, Khrushchev, in a reply to a congratulatory telegram from Kennedy (on the occasion of the launching of a Soviet Venus probe), indicated that he was interested in exploring joint Soviet–United States space efforts.

The event that evoked the greatest concern for Soviet–American relations, however, was the abortive Bay of Pigs invasion. If the Russian actions with respect to Laos and the Lumumba murder provided some hope that Soviet–American relations might be improving, the sharp diplomatic exchange between Kennedy and Khrushchev over Cuba seemingly returned those relations to their preinauguration status.[74] Within three weeks following the U.S. Caribbean failure, however, events were to take a dramatic turn as Khrushchev renewed his request for a summit meeting and Kennedy replied positively, agreeing to meet with Khrushchev in Vienna on June 3 and 4, 1961.

Kennedy's decision to go to Vienna can be attributed to the deterioration of the position of the United States resulting from the Bay of Pigs disaster. Kennedy feared that Khrushchev might miscalculate the strength and position of the United States and thereby dangerously overestimate his position; thus, the opportunity for talks was seized by Kennedy as a means for making the U.S. position clear. Khrushchev's motivations were, however, somewhat problematic. One might surmise that Khrushchev was as anxious as Kennedy to take the measure of his counterpart and may also have believed that the American president's position had been sufficiently weakened by the Cuban affair to make him prone to bullying—a tactic that Khrushchev had shown some propensity to use in the past.[75] There is also evidence that Khrushchev's specific intent was to attempt to force the German question to a solution.[76] Khrushchev reportedly informed the American ambassador, Llewellyn Thompson, that he had waited long enough on the Berlin question, and noted that the matter of his own prestige was involved. Thompson reported in turn that Khrushchev was faced with a Communist party congress in the fall and needed some action on the Berlin question to protect himself.[77]

Kennedy's desire that he enter into negotiations from a position of apparent strength manifested itself in a disconcertingly tough speech to Congress on May 25, less than two weeks before the Vienna summit. The title of his message was "On Urgent National Needs." The president explained his appearance by declaring: "These are extraordinary times . . . and . . . I am here to promote the doctrine of freedom." The Soviets, he declared, "possess a powerful intercontinental striking force, large forces for executing war, a well trained underground in nearly every country . . . the capacity for quick decision, a . . . society without dissent . . . and long experience in the techniques of violence and subversion."[78] The challenge was formidable, but the young president proceeded to describe a wide range of strategies to meet it. Along with his request for increased conventional and unconventional war capability, Kennedy also announced a new national fallout shelter program. Every federal, state, and local building, and even private homes, were to be subsidized by an immediate tripling of the then-pending budget request. A great civil defense effort had been advocated by civilian strategists, notably Harvard's Henry Kissinger and Herman Kahn, then at RAND.

This school of strategists believed that a massive fallout shelter program and new methods for quick evacuation of cities and for dealing with the results of thermonuclear destruction by improved communication capabilities would prepare for the worst and could well save millions of lives. More important, it would demonstrate the United States' willingness to take the worst the Soviets had to offer, if the stakes were high enough. In short, fallout shelters were a concrete, burlap, and sandbag symbol of national will to uphold commitments at any level of violence necessary. Critics, however, pointed out that shelters could also be interpreted by the Soviets as a preparation for an American first strike. Given the number of missiles and planes that the Soviets could send to the United States after they had been hit by a disarming blow, fallout shelters would minimize damage to an extent where an American victory could be contemplated without the thought of a mountain of American corpses. To that extent, critics held, the program was provocative. Political scientist J. David Singer wrote worriedly in the *Bulletin of Atomic Scientists:*

> The Kremlin strategists might well want to ask how useful a shelter program would be to the nation whose doctrine is a purely retaliatory one. More specifically, how many lives would be saved by such a program if we were the victims of a surprise attack?

> If the [surprise] attack were against our cities, it is evident that very few people would be able to get to their shelters in time, and those that did would not find them particularly protective. . . . [Therefore,] the Soviets might begin to wonder whether the shelters are for protection against [a] surprise attack, or whether they may not reflect a first-strike strategy.[79]

Kennedy and McNamara were later to yield to these arguments. In the meantime, so near to the summit, the announcement of vastly enlarged civil defense programs had a clear and immediate diplomatic purpose. "Our greatest asset," Kennedy concluded "in this struggle [for freedom] is the American people['s] willingness to pay any price. . . . It is heartening to know, as I journey abroad, that our country . . . is ready to do its duty."[80]

The Vienna Conference

The Vienna Conference, described as "useful" in the joint communique issued at the conclusion of the meetings on June 4, produced substantive agreement on only one point, Laos. Agreement was reached on the second day of the talks with the conclusion that a cease fire should be a "priority matter."[81] The remainder of the conference produced frank, well-defined, but courteous disagreement.

The first day of the conference was devoted to a thorough airing of the world views of both leaders. By becoming involved in such an ideological debate, Kennedy was forced to talk on Khrushchev's grounds; hence, Khrushchev apparently held the initiative throughout this initial day of talks. Such ideological debate was, as Schlesinger has pointed out, inevitably fruitless.[82] Kennedy sought, therefore, in the second day of the talks, to turn the discussion to more concrete matters. On disarmament, a complete stalemate was reached. The discussion then turned to Berlin and the German question, and, in so doing, the first great confrontation on the new frontier was initiated.

Khrushchev repeated the oft-stated position of the Soviet Union that a peace treaty had to be signed so as to eradicate the threat of the West German militarists starting a third world war. He wanted agreement with the West, but, if none were forthcoming, he would sign a separate treaty with East Germany. A free city of West Berlin would be established, with control of all access in the hands of the German Democratic Republic. Kennedy replied that, unlike Laos, Berlin was considered by the United States to be a point of vital interest. The position of the United States vis-à-vis Berlin and Germany was the result of legal contractual rights as decided by World War II. If the United States withdrew from Berlin, it would ultimately mean the abandonment of the rest of Europe. In summary, Kennedy made it clear to Khrushchev that he would not accept an ultimatum from the Soviet Union. He would not "acquiesce in the isolation of his country."[83]

Khrushchev now became considerably more harsh. He repeated that he wanted only to ensure that the "most dangerous spot in the world" would not cause war. He in effect closed the question as he noted that nothing could possibly prevent him from signing a peace treaty with East Germany by the end of the year;[84] and, from that time on, any infringement on the sovereignty of the German Democratic Republic would be considered an act of aggression.[85]

The Berlin Crisis:
Emergence from Transition

Khrushchev had given to Kennedy at Vienna two *aide-mémoires* that restated in more formal diplomatic language the position advanced by Khrushchev during his conversations with Kennedy.[86] The memoranda did not include Khrushchev's pledge that he would sign a peace treaty by the end of the year, but his television and radio talk to the Russian people on June 15, 1961, did state the pledge clearly.[87] Kennedy made the following statement a week earlier:

> I made it clear to Mr. Khrushchev that the security of Western Europe and therefore our own security are deeply involved in our presence and our access rights to West Berlin, that those rights are based on law and not on sufferance, and that we are determined to maintain those rights at any risk.[88]

When joined with Khrushchev's pronouncement, this announced to the world that another Berlin crisis was full blown.

Throughout the summer, the crisis was gradually escalated. On June 21, Khrushchev noted that the United States was increasing its appropriations for military expenditures. The Soviet leader indicated that such a move might necessitate a similar increase on the part of the Soviet Union. Khrushchev went further and threatened to resume nuclear testing if the United States did so.[89]

On the following day, Secretary of State Rusk reaffirmed the intention of the United States to stay in Berlin, and refused to consider the Russian peace treaty as valid.[90] The president, in his news conference of June 28, solemnly restated the position of the United States to honor its commitments and warned the Russians not to "underestimate the will and unity of democratic societies where vital interests are concerned."[91] Khrushchev reciprocated these sentiments and stepped up the pressure. On July 8, he announced that, in response to increased U.S. defense expenditures, the Soviet Union would be forced to increase its own defense preparations by suspending all proposed reductions in the size of the Soviet armed forces until the German question was resolved and by increasing defense spending by 3,144,000,000 rubles.[92]

The initial reaction of the United States to this new Soviet move came in the form of a note given to the Soviet Union on July 17. This note was, in fact, a reply to the Soviet *aide-mémoires* of June 4, and was composed of a legalistic point-by-point refutation of that document.[93] The White House seems to have been disappointed by the document, particularly with the "maddening" slowness with which it had been produced by the State Department.[94] Kennedy was reportedly dismayed that the document was only a "compilation of stale, tedious, and negative phrases, none of them very new."[95] Kennedy believed that a new and more dynamic statement of the United States was needed; a clear delineation of the overall response of the United States to the German question had to be presented to the American people and the world.

Kennedy's new response was televised to the American people on July 25, 1961. At the outset, the president repeated the intention and right of the United States to be in Berlin. Again he restated that the U.S. position was considered vital to the national interest:

> We cannot and will not permit the Communists to drive us out of Berlin, either gradually or by force. For the fulfillment of our pledge to that city is essential to the morale and security of Western Germany, to the unity of Western Europe, and to the faith of the entire Free World.[96]

Kennedy next set forth his specific proposals, which were to constitute his response to Khrushchev's escalation of the crisis. The president called for an additional $3,247,000,000 in defense appropriations. He asked for an increase in the size of the Army from 875,000 men to approximately 1,000,000; and an increase in the Navy and Air Force of, respectively, 29,000 and 63,000 men. The draft was to be doubled and then tripled within the near future, and Kennedy announced that he was requesting authority to call on reserve units. The numbers required were unstated, but soon more than 150,000 men, veterans of Korea and World War II, and National Guardsmen, were called from their jobs to active service. Also, the planned deactivation of ships and aircraft such as the B-47 was to be delayed. Fifty percent of "our missile power . . . and of our B-52 and B-47 bombers" were on "ground alert which would send them on their way with 15 minutes warning." Moreover, Kennedy announced that $1.8 billion of the funds he had requested would be spent for the procurement of nonnuclear war materials.[97] Defense programs were to be enlarged yet another $205 million. The year's appropriation of $3.5 billion for civilian defense was to be applied toward procuring adequate food, water, first aid kits, household warning kits to detect dangerous levels of home radiation, and a national air raid warning system ranging from sirens to telecommunications.

The Berlin crisis did not, of course, end with Kennedy's speech. In the tension-filled weeks following Kennedy's talk, the exodus of refugees from East Berlin increased, thereby prompting Khrushchev to seal off East Berlin on the night of August 12 and, in the days that followed, to construct the Berlin wall. Possibly this cessation of the flow of refugees to the West was seen by Khrushchev as his only obtainable goal (other than using the circumstances as a pretext for renewing atmospheric testing). After inconclusive negotiations had been initiated, Khrushchev announced, in a six-hour report to the 22nd Congress of the Communist Party, that he would no longer insist on a peace treaty.[98]

Just before Khrushchev rose to make his speech, the probability of a Soviet–American showdown seemed unusually high. The calling up of 150,000 American reservists, the increase in the American arms budget, the inauguration of a nationwide fallout shelter system that indicated Americans would be prepared to accept the worst from the Soviets and still, in the words of the Pentagon's second in command, "not be defeated," all indicated an assurance that America's full might could well be called into play in Berlin. Reports of the wall — the sordid details of land mines, barbed wire, and watchtowers — reached the morning papers in Washington on an especially inauspicious Friday, October 13, 1961. General Lucius Clay, the U.S. military governor general of Berlin, who was largely responsible for the Berlin airlift, returned to the city. As he arrived, White House spokesmen announced that a battle group of fifteen hundred men was heading down the Autobahn to reinforce the American garrison in Berlin.

While the 22nd Congress was being held in Moscow, the East German authorities began to slow Western traffic, including American armored columns, headed for Berlin. On October 26, Soviet tanks moved in the East Berlin sector so as to be separated by a strip less than seventy-five yards from the position of American tanks. Reports stated that American bulldozers had joined the American tank columns and infantry positions. In his memoirs, Khrushchev claims that Marshal Ivan Konev reported to him that the Americans were preparing to cross the frontier and destroy the wall.[99] However, on October 27, Khrushchev spoke to the 22nd Congress: "What counts most," he declared, "is not the particular date" of the settlement of the German problem, "but a businesslike and honest settlement of the question."[100] Soviet tanks withdrew as Khrushchev finished speaking.

The apparent successful manipulation of threats and signals again seemed to indicate Soviet susceptibility to the diplomacy of threat. After the Cuban missile crisis, this lesson seemed to displace almost all other approaches for dealing with America's most powerful adversary. Soviet power was depreciated. For a while, Americans believed that an American-constructed international system would endure without challenge for the foreseeable future. Yet, the Berlin crisis and the successful installation of the Berlin wall had further significance. Khrushchev was probably correct in pointing out that Western acquiescence to the implied permanent division of Germany that the wall portended also prepared the ground for future German leaders to live with the results of World War II. Khrushchev claimed that he "forced Kennedy and the Western Allies to swallow a bitter pill."[101] In the long run, the medicine did not seem pernicious. In the short run, both the patient and the good Soviet doctor almost died as the cold war moved to a climax in the waters off Cuba.

CONCLUSION

Nation building and a flexible response provided the Kennedy administration with a policy construct predisposed toward activism. Flexible response, of course, was in part rooted in the concepts of the past; however, the thrust of the Kennedy administration was to free itself of the "reactive elements" that to them characterized the massive retaliation of the Eisenhower years. That is to say, Kennedy, through Robert McNamara and his collection of defense intellectuals, sought to develop a spectrum of usable force in addition to an expanded and embellished strategic retaliatory capacity at the upper end of the scale of possible violence. Indeed, with the incorporation into the Kennedy Department of Defense of many of the men who had criticized the massive retaliation doctrines of the 1950s, American nuclear forces began to reflect a limited nuclear war potential as well as an expansion of conventional capability. Nowhere is the propensity toward an activist interventionist posture more apparent than in the area of unconventional warfare. In fact, the doctrines of insurgency and counterinsurgency stand as a kind of conceptual and practical bridge between the coercive diplomacy embodied in the doctrines of flexible response and the ostensibly peaceful activism of nation building.

Nation building as a concept and policy was clearly activist and interventionist. Whether the intervention was to be by means of a Peace Corps volunteer or a massive aid grant, the objective was the same. Forces of economic, social, and cultural development were to be set in motion and then monitored to allow the country to take off toward self-sustaining economic growth. At the same time, however, this economic growth "should aim at the strategic goals of a stronger national independence, an increased concentration on domestic affairs, greater democracy and a *long-run association with the West.*"[102] President Kennedy concerned himself with the development of a world marked by "diversity and independence," but "above all, 'this emerging world is incompatible with the communist world order.'"[103] The direction of history, Kennedy asserted, "represent[ed] the very essence of our view of the future of the world."[104]

Like the Truman administration, the Kennedy administration could not leave the historical process alone. America was now thought to be benefactor and monitor of the development process. This was the corollary of the mission set forth in the Truman Doctrine: to build and maintain a global order among great powers such that American values of political economy might flourish. Moreover, the burden was now doubly great, for had not Khrushchev proclaimed support of national wars of liberation a primary thrust of Soviet policy? Previously, external aggression was clear warrant for American intervention. Now the presence of armed insurgents was *ipso facto* grounds for intervention. The Kennedy administration accepted wholeheartedly, therefore, the somewhat enigmatic charge of the Truman Doctrine that we must help others "work out their own destiny in their own way."

Yet, this was a slippery slope; for intervention pulled the United States into a process inevitably marked by enormous social, cultural, and economic discontinuity. Traditional structures were, of necessity, cracked open, often violently. But the mechanistic concepts and policies of nation building were marked by a naïve belief that somehow violence could be avoided. Indeed, if violence persisted, it was not unreasonable to assume that it was related in some way to Khrushchev's January 2, 1961, pledge, in which case reliance on military force either indigenous or external was perfectly appropriate to the development process. The paradox was that in turning to the military and others of a conservative bent in the developing world, the United States was aligning itself with those least predisposed to a world of diversity and social justice. Moreover, it is notable that despite his protestation of willingness to allow pluralistic forces to work, Kennedy adopted and maintained intense personal interest in the Green Berets, the elite group of men responsible for insurgency and counterinsurgency—the gray nether world that joined nation building to flexible response.

The doctrinal basis of the Kennedy administration foreign and defense policy was, therefore, a return of the activism of the late Truman administration. By adopting many of the modalities implied by NSC-68, the Kennedy administration worked to build and maintain an international system not unlike that envisioned in the 1950s as well as the 1940s. Indeed, what is commonly regarded as the finest hour of the Kennedy administration, the Cuban missile crisis, was in some ways a classic example of the brinkmanship of the 1950s.

NOTES

1. Theodore H. White, *The Making of the President: 1960* (New York: New American Library, Signet Edition, 1967), pp. 204–205.
2. Theodore C. Sorensen, *Kennedy* (New York: Bantam, 1966), p. 189.
3. Ibid., p. 256.
4. John F. Kennedy, "Annual Message to the Congress on the State of the Union, January 30, 1961," *Public Papers of the President, 1961* (Washington, D.C.: U.S. Government Printing Office, 1962), pp. 23–24.
5. "Long Live Leninism!" *Red Flag*, April 16, 1960, translated in *Peking Review*, No. 17 (1960).
6. Bernard S. Morris, *International Communism and American Policy* (New York: Atheneum, 1968), pp. 133–148.
7. Kennedy, op. cit., p. 23.
8. Cited by John Kenneth Galbraith, "The Moderate Solution," in John R. Boettiger, ed., *Vietnam and American Foreign Policy* (Lexington, Mass.: D.C. Heath, 1968), p. 130.
9. For a good review, see Herbert Dinerstein's classic *War and the Soviet Union*, rev. ed. (New York: Praeger, 1962). There had been some writing on partisan warfare and some attention by Trotsky and Lenin to the revolutionary potential in the Third World, but the dominant part of Soviet intellectual energy had been to diagnose the nature of capitalist ambitions and capacities and prepare a deep defense. Soviet diplomatic and revolutionary activity in Asia were especially muted as Stalin's campaign began in the late 1920s to build "socialism in one country" after disastrous attempts to bestir communist revolution in the colonial world.
10. John A. Armstrong, "Soviet Policy in the Middle East," in Kurt London, ed., *The Soviet Union: A Half-Century of Communism* (Baltimore: Johns Hopkins University Press, 1968), pp. 423–454, esp. pp. 440–450.
11. Reprinted in "Selected Readings: Counter Insurgency" (U.S. Army War College, Carlisle Barracks, Pa., 1962), and in *Selected Readings in Guerrilla and Counter*

Guerrilla Operations (U.S. Infantry School, Fort Benning, Ga., July 1967), pp. 54–62. Also see his speech reprinted in *World Marxist Review*, January 1961, and Robert McNamara's exegesis of it in his speech given to the Fellows of the American Bar Association, February 17, 1962, reprinted in *Selected Readings in Guerrilla and Counter Guerrilla Operations*, pp. 9–17.

12. Khrushchev in January 6, 1961, "Za Novye Pobedy Mirovogo Kommunisticheskogo Dvizheniia Kommunist" (January 1961), p. 20; cited by Michel P. Gehlen, *The Politics of Coexistence: Soviet Methods and Motives* (Bloomington, Ind.: Indiana University Press, 1967), p. 105.

13. Cited in Gehlen, op. cit., pp. 105–106.

14. Especially important in perpetuating this understanding was the influential translation of Mao Zedong, *On Guerrilla Warfare* by Samuel Griffith (New York: Praeger, 1961), especially p. 4, where Griffith equates a statement made in November 1949 by Liu Shaoqi to the effect that other Asian revolutions "would follow the Chinese pattern," to Khrushchev's remarks in December 1960 and January 1961 on national liberation wars. Griffith's translation was considered "classic," and the Praeger distribution was the first major dissemination of Mao's thought in English by an American publishing firm.

15. *Peking Review,* No. 36 (September 3, 1965) for the full text.

16. Arthur Huck, *The Security of China: Chinese Approaches to Problems of War and Strategy* (New York: Columbia University Press, 1970), p. 50.

17. Dean Rusk, in U.S. Congress, Hearings before the Senate Committee on Foreign Relations, *Supplemental Foreign Assistance, Fiscal Year 1966, Vietnam*, U.S. 89th Congress, 2nd Session, p. 596.

18. This view was not confined to policymakers. The perception was widely shared by academics. As Professor Frank Trager of New York University wrote, "To support this view of the communist challenge in Southeast Asia, one does not have to argue for a supposed total identity of Sino–Soviet objectives, strategies and tactics in the area: that is, for world monolithicism . . . variations help make it possible for Moscow and Peking to advance their overriding communist objectives. Separately or together, they acquire more strings to their respective bows for the greater success of the communist symphony . . . there should be no doubt that basic purpose of the exercise in both Moscow and Peking is to overwhelm, that is to communize Southeast Asia." Frank N. Trager, in William Henderson, ed., *Southeast Asia: Problems of United States Policy* (Cambridge, Mass.: The M.I.T. Press, 1963), pp. 163–164.

19. *Public Papers of the President of the United States: Harry S. Truman — 1951* (Washington, D.C.: U.S. Government Printing Office, 1965), p. 224.

20. Secretary Robert McNamara, February 17, 1962, speech to the American Bar Association in Chicago, p. 11 (emphasis ours), cited in *Selected Readings in Guerrilla and Counter Guerrilla Operations*.

21. Arthur Schlesinger, Jr., *A Thousand Days* (Boston: Houghton Mifflin, 1965), pp. 296–297; and Sorensen, op. cit., pp. 332–333.

22. Richard J. Walton, *Cold War and the Counterrevolution: The Foreign Policy of John F. Kennedy* (New York: Viking, 1972), pp. 44–45. In a press conference five days before the invasion on April 17, Kennedy skillfully dissembled when asked about American support for any such invasion, rumors of which had been in the press for weeks. Castro had obviously learned from the Guatemalan experience. The Cubans made more far-reaching land reforms, dismantled the prerevolutionary military, and organized the peasantry to fight off invasion. See Richard H.

Immerman, *The CIA in Guatemala: The Foreign Policy of Intervention* (Austin, Tex.: University of Texas Press, 1982), p. 196.

23. "Speech to American Society of Newspaper Editors," in *Public Papers of the President of the United States: John F. Kennedy — 1961* (Washington, D.C.: U.S. Government Printing Office, 1962), p. 305.

24. Ibid., p. 306.

25. Ibid.

26. Ibid.

27. Ibid., p. 304.

28. Ibid., p. 305.

29. Schlesinger, op. cit., p. 202.

30. Ibid., p. 195.

31. Ibid.

32. Douglas A. Blaufarb, *The Counter-Insurgency Era: U.S. Doctrine and Performance, 1950 to Present* (New York: Free Press, 1977), p. 88.

33. Karl W. Deutsch and William J. Foltz, *Nation-Building* (New York: Atherton, 1966), p. 3.

34. "Guerrilla Warfare in the Underdeveloped Areas," address made at graduation ceremonies at the U.S. Army Special Warfare School, Ft. Bragg, N.C., June 28, 1961, *Department of State Bulletin*, Vol. 45, No. 1154 (August 7, 1961), p. 234.

35. Lincoln S. Bloomfield, "Vital Interests and Objectives of the United States," paper delivered to the Naval War College on August 26, 1963, reprinted in Wesley Posvar et. al., eds., *American Defense Policy* (Baltimore: Johns Hopkins University Press, 1965), pp. 18–19 (emphasis in the original).

36. Samuel Huntington, *Political Order in Changing Societies* (New Haven, Conn.: Yale University Press, 1968), p. 72.

37. Samuel P. Huntington, "The Bases of Accommodation," *Foreign Affairs*, Vol. 46 (July 1968), p. 652.

38. Huntington, *Political Order in Changing Societies*, p. 24.

39. Ibid., p. 28.

40. Joseph La Palombara, "Political Science and the Engineering of National Development," in Monte Polner and Larry Stern, eds., *Political Development in Changing Societies: An Analysis of Modernization* (Lexington, Mass.: D.C. Heath, 1971), p. 52.

41. David W. Chang, "The Military and Nation Building in Korea, Burma and Pakistan," *Asian Survey*, Vol. 9, No. 11 (November 1969), p. 830.

42. See especially Charles Wolf, Jr., *The United States Policy and the Third World: Problems and Analysis* (Boston: Little, Brown, 1967), for an elaborate panegyric to the military contribution to development.

43. See Gabriel Almond and J.S. Coleman, eds., *The Politics of the Developing Areas* (Princeton, N.J.: Princeton University Press, 1960); or Edward C. Banfield, *American Foreign Aid Doctrines* (Washington, D.C.: American Enterprise Institute, 1963).

44. Schlesinger, op. cit., p. 201. Professor Schlesinger writes:

> But the revolutionary point remained primary. For Kennedy fully understood — this was, indeed, the mainspring of all his thinking about Latin America — that, with all its pretensions to realism, the militant anti-revolutionary line represented the policy most likely to strengthen the communists and lose the hemisphere. He believed that, to maintain contact with

a continent seized by the course of revolutionary change, a policy of social idealism was the only true realism for the United States.

45. Ibid., p. 769.
46. See, for example, U.S. Department of Commerce, Statistical Abstract of the United States, 1971 (Washington, D.C.: U.S. Government Printing Office, 1972), p. 755.
47. Schlesinger, op. cit., p. 773.
48. Theodore Draper, "The Dominican Crisis: A Case Study in American Policy," Commentary, Vol. 40, No. 6 (December 1965), p. 34.
49. Schlesinger, op. cit., quoting Kennedy, p. 789.
50. Legislative Reference Service, Library of Congress, Some Important Issues in Foreign Aid, A Report Prepared for the Senate Committee on Foreign Relations (Washington, D.C.: U.S. Government Printing Office, 1966), pp. 10-13; and Agency for International Development, U.S. Overseas Loans and Grants and Assistance from International Organizations: Obligations and Loan Authorizations, July 1, 1945–June 30, 1972 (Washington, D.C.: U.S. Government Printing Office, 1973), passim.
51. Annual Message to the Congress on the State of the Union, January 30, 1961, in Public Papers of the Presidents, John F. Kennedy, 1961 (Washington, D.C.: U.S. Government Printing Office, 1962), p. 24 (emphasis added).
52. Louis Fitzsimmons, The Kennedy Doctrine (New York: Random House, 1972), p. 233, citing an oral history interview with Doctor Herbert York.
53. Ibid., pp. 233–234.
54. The New York Times, January 12, 1961.
55. Television and Radio Address of May 25, 1960, Department of State Bulletin, Vol. 42, No. 1093 (June 6, 1960), p. 900.
56. Schlesinger, op. cit., p. 301.
57. Ibid.; I. F. Stone, in New York Review of Books, April 23, 1970, p. 21.
58. Schlesinger, op. cit., p. 500.
59. Ibid., pp. 499–500.
60. Melvin Laird, Congressional Record, January 25, 1961, House p. 1228; also cited by I. F. Stone, New York Review of Books, April 23, 1970, p. 22. In addition, Stone notes that Republicans pointed out that under the final Eisenhower budgets, there would be "600" Minuteman missiles by the end of 1964; 129 Atlas and 126 Titan ICBM's by the end of 1962; 4 more Polarises in service by the end of 1961, with 64 more missiles; and . . . 15 Jupiter IRBMs."
61. William W. Kaufmann, The McNamara Strategy (New York: Harper & Row, 1964), pp. 79–80.
62. Robert S. McNamara's Address in Atlanta, Ga., November 11, 1961, quoted in ibid., p. 75.
63. Ibid., pp. 69–72.
64. See, for example, McNamara's speech before the annual convention of United Press International editors and publishers at San Francisco, Calif., on September 18, 1967, printed in Department of State Bulletin, Vol. 57, No. 1476 (October 9, 1967), pp. 433–451.
65. Quoted in Kaufmann, op. cit., p. 76.
66. Schlesinger, op. cit., pp. 301–302. See also Seymour Topping, "Kremlin Initiation Step," The New York Times, January 22, 1961, pp. 1–3.
67. Sorensen, op. cit., p. 541.

68. See "Secretary Rusk's News Conference of February 6," *Department of State Bulletin*, Vol. 44, No. 1131 (February 27, 1961), p. 302.
69. There does exist some disagreement on the question of whether Khrushchev forcefully pushed for an immediate meeting with Kennedy. Sorensen, as we have noted, merely states that Khrushchev expressed a desire for such a meeting. Others, notably Dana Schmidt—"Kennedy to Seek Delay in Parley and Atom Test Ban," *The New York Times*, January 25, 1961, p. 1—and William Jorden—"U.S.-Soviet Approaches Studied," *The New York Times*, January 25, 1961, p. 2—report that Khrushchev was not forceful in his expression of a desire for talks. Apparently, the wish was expressed but not pushed.
70. "Only Sane Course Is Peaceful Coexistence," *Current Digest of the Soviet Press*, Vol. 13 (March 1, 1961), pp. 29–31.
71. "The President's News Conference of January 25, 1961," *Public Papers of the President, 1961*, p. 16.
72. "The President's News Conference on March 23, 1961," *Public Papers of the President, 1961*, pp. 213–214.
73. The authors of a Senate investigation some fifteen years later wrote: "The chain of events revealed by the documents and testimony is strong enough to permit a reasonable inference that [a] plot to assassinate Lumumba was authorized by President Eisenhower." But even though "the Congo station [of the CIA] had advanced knowledge of the Central Government's plans to transport Lumumba into the hands of his bitterest enemies, where he was likely to be killed, . . . there is no evidentiary basis for concluding that the CIA conspired in *this* plan. . . ." U.S. Congress, Select Committee on Governmental Operations with Respect to Intelligence Activities, *Alleged Assassination Plots Involving Foreign Leaders*, Report No. 94–463, November 20, 1975, pp. 48 and 51.
74. "Message from N. S. Khrushchev, Chairman of the U.S.S.R. Council of Ministers, to U.S. President John F. Kennedy," *Current Digest of the Soviet Press*, Vol. 13 (May 17, 1961), pp. 4–5; and "Message to Chairman Khrushchev Concerning the Meaning of Events in Cuba, April 18, 1961," *Public Papers of the President, 1961*, pp. 286–287. Also in "United States and Soviet Union Exchange Messages in Regard to Events in Cuba," *Department of State Bulletin*, Vol. 44, No. 1141 (May 8, 1961), pp. 661–667.
75. Schlesinger, op. cit., p. 344. Schlesinger is the only person who has spoken of the exact contents of Khrushchev's letter; see also Louis J. Halle, "The Job to Be Done at the Summit," *The New York Times Magazine*, May 28, 1961, p. 48.
76. "For New Victories of the World Communist Movement," *Current Digest of the Soviet Press*, Vol. 13 (February 22, 1961), p. 10.
77. Schlesinger, op. cit., p. 347.
78. "Special Message to the Congress on Urgent National Needs, May 25, 1961," *Public Papers of the President, 1961*, pp. 396–397.
79. Ibid., pp. 402–403; and J. David Singer, "Deterrence and Shelters," *Bulletin of the Atomic Scientists*, Vol. 17, No. 8 (October 1961), p. 313.
80. "Special Message, May 25, 1961," p. 406.
81. Schlesinger, op. cit., pp. 367–368; and Sorensen, op. cit., pp. 548–549.
82. Schlesinger, op. cit., p. 367.
83. Ibid., p. 371.
84. Sorensen, op. cit., p. 585. Sorensen and Schlesinger disagree on chronology here. Schlesinger does not mention Khrushchev's pledge of an end-of-the-year treaty until

after lunch of the second day. Sorensen records the pledge as being made during the morning talks.

85. Schlesinger, op. cit., pp. 370–374; and Sorensen, op. cit., pp. 584–586.

86. "On the Memorandum Handed by N. S. Khrushchev to U.S. President Kennedy," *Current Digest of the Soviet Press*, Vol. 13 (July 5, 1961), pp. 4–7.

87. "Radio and Television Address by N. S. Khrushchev on June 15, 1961," *Current Digest of the Soviet Press*, Vol. 13 (July 12, 1961), pp. 3–8. The East German leader Walter Ulbricht added emphasis to Khrushchev's statement by noting that he intended to maintain absolute control of access when the treaty was signed. "Ulbricht Warns on Berlin Access," *The New York Times*, June 16, 1961, pp. 1–2.

88. "Radio and Television Report to the American People on Returning from Europe, June 6, 1961," *Public Papers of the President, 1961*, p. 444.

89. "Speech by Comrade N. S. Khrushchev at Meeting of the Representatives of Moscow Public Park to Mark 20th Anniversary of Beginning of Great Patriotic War, June 21, 1961," *Current Digest of the Soviet Press*, Vol. 13 (July 19, 1961), p. 20.

90. "Secretary Rusk's News Conference of June 22," *Department of State Bulletin*, Vol. 45, No. 1150 (July 10, 1961), p. 51.

91. "The President's News Conference of June 28, 1961," *Public Papers of the President, 1961*, p. 477.

92. "Speech by Comrade N. S. Khrushchev at Reception for Graduates of Military Academies of U.S.S.R. Armed Forces, July 18, 1961," *Current Digest of the Soviet Press*, Vol. 13 (August 2, 1961), p. 5.

93. "Note from the United States to the Soviet Union, Replying to the Soviet Aide-Memoire Handed to President Kennedy at Vienna, July 17, 1961," *Department of State Bulletin*, Vol. 45 (August 7, 1961), p. 224.

94. Schlesinger, op. cit., p. 406.

95. Sorensen, op. cit., p. 587. Schlesinger describes the reply as "a tired and turgid rehash of documents left over from the Berlin crisis of 1958–1959," p. 384.

96. "Radio and Television Report to the American People on the Berlin Crisis, July 25, 1961," *Public Papers of the President, 1961*, p. 534.

97. Ibid., pp. 535–536.

98. "Report of the Central Committee of the Communist Party of the Soviet Union to the 22nd Congress — II," *Current Digest of the Soviet Press*, Vol. 13 (November 3, 1961), p. 5.

99. Nikita Khrushchev, *Khrushchev Remembers: The Last Testament*, Strobe Talbott, ed. (Boston: Little, Brown, 1974), pp. 506–507.

100. "Concluding Remarks by Comrade N. S. Khrushchev at the 22nd Party Congress, October 27, 1961," *Current Digest of the Soviet Press*, Vol. 13, No. 46 (December 13, 1961), p. 24.

101. Khrushchev, *Khrushchev Remembers*, p. 509.

102. Schlesinger, op. cit., p. 588 (emphasis added).

103. Schlesinger noting Kennedy, op. cit., p. 617.

104. "Address in Berkeley at the University of California, March 23, 1962," *Public Papers of the President, 1962*, p. 265.

Chapter 6
The Apotheosis
of Containment

Historians know there is a rhythm to their craft. Events are examined, and orthodoxies are established. Then comes a chipping away of previously held convictions. New understandings emerge and stand—for a while—and then comes another tide of reevaluation. Similarly, the Kennedy administration's shimmering hour—the Cuban crisis—is now subject to review in terms of the assumptions, policy processes, and relationships of the cold war. Our contention is that the crisis became something of a misleading model for the foreign policy process and diverted attention from profound changes under way in the world political economy.[1]

The model has seven central tenets, each of which was confirmed by the lessons of the Cuban crisis:

1. Crisis is typical of international relations. The international environment is a constant collision of wills that is, at once, both a surrogate of war and taking place at the doorstep of war. Crises are objective elements of the international system—but they also have a profoundly psychological element of will and resolve.
2. Crises are assumed to be manageable. Those skills of personality, training, and organizational expertise that had developed in the national security machinery during the previous twenty-five years could be orchestrated by a vast bureaucracy in controlled and responsive movements.
3. Although crises are a characteristic of the international system, the domestic system is one of order and consensus and is insulated from the necessities of international politics. Public opinion, in this view, can be controlled to lend support for a particular foreign policy.
4. Diplomacy is a mixture of force and bargaining. An essential element of crisis management is the ability to reconcile the inherent forward dynamic of violence, threats of violence, and the instruments of violence with negotiation.
5. Americans can control the process of crisis negotiation to win.
6. The Soviets seldom negotiate serious matters except under extreme duress.

7. Military questions are too critical to be left in the hands of military men and organizations that are not in step with the needs of crisis management. Crisis management can and must be a civilian enterprise.

After the Cuban missile crisis was resolved, there were beginnings of detente with the Soviet Union. The test ban treaty, the hot line, and a more civil exchange between the two powers are widely believed to stem from the favorable resolution of the missile crisis. Yet, the model and its inherent assumptions on the meaning of Cuba can be challenged. Cuba does indeed stand as a watershed in the cold war and the history of the international system. However, it is properly understood as a part and product of the cold war; indeed, the Cuban crisis was in many ways the climax of the cold war.

Even as the crisis occurred, evidence was emerging that the structure of the world's political economy was changing irrevocably and in a manner that would constrain the future exercise of American political and military power. More than a decade of American foreign military spending could no longer be dismissed as temporary or nonrecurring. The surfeit of American dollars in foreign hands — formerly the necessary liquidity for a rebuilding Western economy — was, by the early 1960s, regarded by Europeans as a threat to their new prosperity. But the Americans, now reinvigorated by the successful management of the Cuban crisis, saw such concerns as secondary. Granted that communism had been faced down at the brink of nuclear Armageddon, now a new crisis brewed in the rice paddies of Southeast Asia.

MASTERY OR LUCK?

By far the most intense experience in East–West relations began on October 14, 1962, when the Russians were discovered to have placed forty-two medium range missiles in Cuba. For the next week, an ad hoc committee of top officials met in secret to consider the American response. This executive committee, or ExCom as they called themselves, arrived at two options: (1) an air strike on the missile sites or (2) a blockade of the island coupled with a demand that the missiles be removed. In a dramatic, nationally televised speech on October 22, President Kennedy announced that the United States was imposing a blockade around Cuba that would be removed only if the missiles were taken out by the Soviets. If they were not, and Soviet ships carrying new missiles encountered the Navy's warships, a Soviet–American military conflict seemed likely.

During the next four days, some ships carrying Russian goods were stopped and searched and some Soviet vessels carrying missiles turned back, but the crisis intensified. On October 26, Khrushchev sent an emotional private message to Kennedy indicating a willingness to remove the missiles if the United States would guarantee that it would not invade Cuba. The next day, however, a more formal and much tougher message was delivered to Kennedy that demanded that the United States remove its missiles in Turkey (missiles Kennedy had earlier ordered removed because they were deemed obsolete) in exchange for the removal of the Soviet missiles from Cuba. On October 27, in private talks between Robert Kennedy and Soviet Ambassador Anatoly Dobrynin, the Soviets agreed to remove the missiles in return for the U.S. noninvasion pledge and ambiguous assurances that the missiles in Turkey would be removed if the NATO countries agreed. The next day, October 28, the Soviets announced that the missiles would be removed; the world exhaled.

In Khrushchev's apt description, it was a time when "a smell of burning hung heavy" in the air.[2] Kennedy's apparently controlled and masterful way of forcing Khrushchev to withdraw the missiles in the thirteen-day crisis has become a paradigmatic example of the way force can be harnessed to a policy by an elaborate manipulation of threats and gambits, negotiation and intimidation. Academic and government analysts have viewed Kennedy's response as a highly calibrated dissection of alternatives instead of seeing his actions as largely an intuitive response to a threat to his administration's electoral future, pride, and strategic posture. As Hans J. Morgenthau, the eminent scholar and a critic of the Kennedy administration, concluded: "The Cuban Crisis of 1962 . . . was the distillation of a collective intellectual effort of a high order, the like of which must be rare in history."[3] Much of this analysis — so drenched in the cool light of hindsight — bears a suspicious resemblance to the logical and psychological fallacy of reasoning *post hoc ergo propter hoc*.[4] Nevertheless, the dominant lesson Americans have drawn from the Cuban experience has been a joyous sense of the United States regaining mastery over history.

For many years Americans had felt threatened by the Soviet challenge to world order — especially since that challenge had been reinforced by growing Russian strategic capability. But after Cuba, the fears of precipitate expansion of a Soviet–American dispute into a final paroxysm of nuclear dust were dissipated. After Cuba, escalation became the *idée fixe* of academics and policy makers — a vision of a ladder of force with rungs separated by equivalent spaces of destruction, each with its own "value," running out toward darkness. Escalation became the dominant metaphor of American officialdom. Each rung could be ascended or descended with the proper increment of will and control. Events and military machines could be mastered for diplomatic ends. As Robert McNamara exalted after the exciting and frightening Cuban climax: "There is no longer any such thing as strategy, only crisis management."[5] Dennis Healy, the British Labor party "shadow" defense minister, called the Kennedy administration's performance a "model in any textbook on diplomacy."[6] Journalist Henry Pachter described Kennedy's execution of crisis management as "a feat whose technical elegance compelled the professionals' admiration."[7] Similarly, Albert and Roberta Wohlstetter made Cuba into a general historical principle about the use of force in times of great stress: "Where the alternative is to be ruled by events with such enormous consequences, the head of a great state is likely to examine his acts of choice in crisis and during it to subdivide these possible acts in ways that make it feasible to continue exercising choice."[8]

The decisions as to what steps should be taken to deal with the implantation of the missiles were hammered out in the ExCom meetings. Although court chroniclers of the Kennedy administration have pored over each detail, the impression now is not one of all choices having been carefully weighed and considered. Rather, in retrospect, there appears to have been a gripping feeling of uncertainty and pressure. Robert Kennedy, for instance, at the height of the crisis, looked across at his brother and almost fainted at the horror contemplated: "Inexplicably, I thought of when he was ill and almost died; when he lost his child, when we learned that our oldest brother had been killed; or personal times of strain and hurt. The voices droned on, but I didn't seem to hear anything."[9]

There were reports that one assistant secretary was so disconcerted and fatigued that he drove into a tree at 4 A.M. Robert Kennedy recalled, "The strain and the hours without sleep were beginning to take their toll. . . . That kind of pressure does strange things to a human being, even to brilliant, self-confident, mature, experienced men." Robert Kennedy suspected that Dean Rusk, the secretary of state, "had a virtually complete breakdown mentally and physically."[10] And President Kennedy, although deliberately pacing himself, wondered how many of his principal advisers might suffer mental collapse from the long hours and pressure. Tense, fearful, and exhausted men planned and held together the American policy response to the Russian missiles.

Strain and fatigue commonly produce actions that are "caricatures of day-to-day behavior."[11] Although the stress of crisis decision making concentrates and focuses the collective mind, it does not necessarily allow for the kind of elegant dissection of events that is now read into the Cuban affair. Events can take charge of decision makers; on October 25, 1962, Robert Kennedy reported that he believed, as Soviet ships drew near the edge of the American quarantine, that "We were on the edge of a precipice with no way off. . . . President Kennedy had initiated the course of events, but he no longer had control over them."[12] John F. Kennedy's calm public face, discipline, and cool control gave a sense of intellectual engagement in the crisis that yielded no hint of the mute wasteland he was contemplating. Nevertheless, his private anxiety is well recorded, and a case can be made that dispassionate analysis was interlaced with cold war reflexes and constrained by bureaucratic politics.

It was very close. The military and the "hawks" — a term coined by journalistic descriptions of the ExCom deliberations — were pushing for actions ranging from a "surgical strike" to an all-out invasion of Cuba. Such options would have demanded the stark choice of an even greater Soviet humiliation or a Soviet response in kind. Ironically, a surgical strike was not really practical, for there was no guarantee that more than 90 percent of the missiles could be extirpated. Even after an American air attack, some of the missiles could have survived and been launched. And "surgical" always was a misnomer to describe an estimated twenty-five thousand Cuban fatalities, not to speak of the five hundred sorties that American planes would have had to run to destroy the Soviet missiles and bombers. Nevertheless, if six of fourteen members of the ExCom group had had their way, the blockade of Cuba would have been an attack, which Robert Kennedy called a "Pearl Harbor in reverse." It is no wonder that President Kennedy estimated the world's chance of avoiding war at between one of three and even.[13]

The illusion of control derived from the crisis was perniciously misleading. Although many Americans shared the belief of historian Arthur Schlesinger that the Cuban crisis displayed to the "whole world . . . the ripening of an American leadership unsurpassed in the responsible management of power . . . [a] combination of toughness . . . nerve and wisdom, so brilliantly controlled, so matchlessly calibrated that [it] dazzled the world,"[14] President Kennedy's control was in fact far from complete.

McNamara had sensed the Navy's lack of responsiveness to civilian commands and had gone to the "Flag Plot," or Naval Operations Center, where he could talk to ship commanders directly by voice-scrambled radio. McNamara pointed to a map symbol indicating that a ship was in a spot where he had not wanted it. "What's that ship doing there?" he asked. Chief of Naval Operations Admiral William R. Anderson confessed, "I don't know, but I have faith in my officers."[15] McNamara's unease with the apparent lack of responsiveness of the Navy to civilian command prompted him to inquire what would happen if a Soviet captain refused to divulge his cargo to a boarding American officer. Anderson picked up a Manual of Naval Regulations and rose to defend the Navy against any implied slight about Navy procedure. "It's all in there," Anderson asserted. McNamara retorted, "I don't give a damn what John Paul Jones would have done. I want to know what you are going to do, now!" The last word—again—however, was the Navy's: Admiral Anderson patronizingly soothed the fuming defense secretary, "Now, Mr. Secretary, if you and your deputy will go to your offices, the Navy will run the blockade."[16] As McNamara and his entourage turned to leave, Anderson called to him, "Don't worry, Mr. Secretary, we know what we are doing here."[17]

Just when the first Soviet–American encounter at sea seemed imminent, William Knox, the president of Westinghouse International, who happened to be in Moscow, was surprised by an abrupt summons from Premier Khrushchev. The voluble Soviet leader, perhaps half-convinced that Wall Street really manipulated American policy, gave a frightening summary of the strategic situation in the Caribbean. The Soviet Mission in New York, the FBI discovered, had begun to burn its files. He warned that if the U.S. Navy began stopping Soviet ships, Soviet subs would start sinking American ships. That, Khrushchev explained, would lead to World War III.[18]

Only a little later, the Navy began to force Soviet subs to the surface to defend its blockade—well before Kennedy had authorized contact with surface vessels. Kennedy was appalled when he learned that military imperatives are distinct from diplomatic necessities and can, all too often, conflict. When he found out that the Navy was intent on surfacing Soviet submarines, he was horrified: "Isn't there some way we can avoid having our first exchange with a Russian submarine—almost anything but that?" McNamara replied flintily, "No, there's too much danger to our ships. There is no alternative." Robert Kennedy wrote that "all six Russian submarines then in the area or moving toward Cuba from the Atlantic were followed and harassed and, at one time or another, forced to surface in the presence of U.S. military ships."[19] One can only wonder what would have happened if one of the Russian subs had refused to surface and had instead turned on its pursuers.

Events were only barely under control when, at the height of the crisis, on October 26, an American U-2 plane fixed on the wrong star and headed back from the North Pole to Alaska via Siberia. To compound matters, the Alaskan Air Command sent fighter-bombers to escort the plane home, and the U.S. fighters and the spy plane met over

Soviet territory before proceeding back.[20] To survive a Dr. Strangelove series of incidents like these, even given the assumptions of the day, can hardly be characterized as exquisite management. It would not seem to be the mastery that Schlesinger and other court scribes delight in recalling and extolling.

THE DOMESTIC FACTOR

Why was there a crisis in the first place? The answer was found in part, in one of the unacknowledged necessities in the conduct of American international affairs — domestic political considerations.[21] The Kennedy administration's sense of its own precarious electoral position, the coming of the November midterm elections, and the place Cuba had occupied in public debate, all argued for an immediate and forceful response, no matter what the strategic reality was of having Russian missiles near American borders. The imperatives of American domestic politics during an election year had been building for some time. On August 27, 1962, for example, Republican Senator Homer E. Capehart of Indiana declared, "It is high time that the American people demand that President Kennedy quit 'examining the situation' and start protecting the interests of the United States."[22] Former Vice President Nixon, on the gubernatorial campaign stump in California, proposed that Cuban communism be "quarantined" by a naval blockade.[23] Republicans in both houses had warned the administration that Cuba would be "the dominant issue of the 1962 campaign."[24] The chairman of the Republican national committee jabbed at Kennedy's most sensitive spot — his concern for foreign policy resolve: "If we are asked to state the issue in one word, that word would be Cuba — symbol of tragic irresolution of the administration."[25]

The pressure mounted. As the political campaign began, one observer spotted a sign at a Kennedy rally in Chicago that read, "Less Profile — More Courage."[26] The widely respected and conservative London *Economist* reported that America had become "obsessed" by the "problem" of Cuba[27]; and I. F. Stone despaired in his *Weekly* that Cuba was a bogey that shook Americans, in the autumn of 1962, even more than the thought of war.[28] The domestic pressure on the American president was so intense that one member of Camelot, former Ambassador John Kenneth Galbraith, wrote: "Once they [the missiles] were there, the political needs of the Kennedy administration urged it to take almost any risk to get them out."[29] This skeptical view was shared by none other than former President Eisenhower, who suspected "that

Kennedy might be playing politics with Cuba on the eve of Congressional elections."[30]

Nor, as Ronald Steel pointed out, were the principals — the ExCom — insulated from domestic considerations in their deliberations.[31] One Republican member of the crisis planners sent Theodore Sorensen — Kennedy's alter ego — a note that read: "Ted — have you considered the very real possibility that if we allow Cuba to complete installation and operational readiness of missile bases, the next House of Representatives is likely to have a Republican majority?"[32] Similarly, McGeorge Bundy, chief adviser to two presidents, wondered, when the missiles were first reported, whether action could be deferred until after the election.[33] If the missile installations were completed earlier, there would be, arguably, both a strategic and an electoral problem facing the administration.

What was the worrisome substance of change in the strategic balance represented by the placement of forty-two missiles? To Robert McNamara, the secretary of defense, it seemed that "a missile is a missile. It makes no great difference whether you are killed by a missile from the Soviet Union or from Cuba."[34] About two weeks later, on television, Deputy Secretary of Defense Roswell Gilpatric confirmed the debatable meaning of the missiles: "I don't believe that we were under any greater threat from the Soviet Union's power, taken in totality, after this than before."[35] Indeed, Theodore Sorensen wrote in a memorandum to the president on October 17, 1962 — five days before the blockade was ordered — that the presence of missiles in Cuba did not "significantly alter the balance of power." Sorensen explained, "They do not significantly increase the potential megatonnage capable of being unleashed on American soil, even after a surprise American nuclear strike." Sorensen confessed, in conclusion, that "Soviet motives were not understood."[36]

JUST A DIRTY TRICK?

To Khrushchev, the missiles offered the appearance of what former State Department analyst Roger Hilsman called a "quick fix" to the Soviet problem of strategic inferiority. Khrushchev was under enormous pressure from the Russian military, who rejected his promise of "goulash communism" and who were pushing for a vast increase in the Soviet arms budget.[37] The Cuban missile ploy was probably Khrushchev's response to the prospect of Russian strategic inferiority, which was reported by the Kennedy administration as it admitted that the Democratic preelection charge of a missile gap had not been based on fact. The American announcement that the gap had been closed was accompanied by a Defense Department plan, dated October 19, 1961, for production of more than one thousand missiles by 1964.[38]

One purpose of the Soviet moves in Cuba was, therefore, to gain the *appearance* of parity with the Americans. The employment of twenty-four MRBMs and eighteen IRBMs *seemed* to be a dramatic movement in that direction. But such an increase posed no real threat to American retaliatory strength, or to increasing American superiority. As Henry Kissinger noted at the time: "The bases were of only marginal use in a defensive war. In an offensive war their effectiveness was reduced by the enormous difficulty—if not impossibility—of coordination of a first strike from the Soviet Union and Cuba."[39]

The Kennedy administration knew that the Soviets were not striving for more than an appearance of strategic equality. As Kennedy later reflected, they were not "intending to fire them, because if they were going to get into a nuclear struggle, they have their own missiles in the Soviet Union. But it would have politically changed the balance of power. It would have appeared to, and appearances contribute to reality."[40] In the 1970s, by contrast, appearances were less important while the Americans were arranging a complex international order that verged on duopoly. Indeed, beginning in 1970, Soviet missile-firing submarines and tenders began to visit Cuban ports.[41] What protest there was by the Nixon administration seemed so muted as to be almost inaudible.[42]

Why was Kennedy so concerned about appearances? Perhaps he thought that the American people demanded an energetic response, given their purported frustration over Cuba. The administration's evaluation of the public mood supported the notion that firmness was a requisite of policy. Although repeated Gallup polls before the crisis showed 90 percent of Americans opposing actual armed intervention in Cuba,[43] Kennedy's own sense was, as his brother pointed out, that if he did not act, he would be impeached.[44]

Another explanation for Kennedy's concern that he would not appear credible to Khrushchev dates from the time, less than two years earlier, when he decided not to use air support for the Bay of Pigs invasion. According to James Reston's impression on seeing Kennedy ten minutes after the two leaders had met in Vienna, "Khrushchev had studied the events of the Bay of Pigs; he would have understood if Kennedy had left Castro alone or destroyed him; but when Kennedy was rash enough to strike at Cuba but not bold enough to finish the job, Khrushchev decided he was dealing with an inexperienced young leader who could be intimidated and blackmailed."[45] Similarly, George F. Kennan,

then the U.S. ambassador to Yugoslavia, met the president after the
Vienna summit session and reported that he found Kennedy "strangely
tongue-tied" during these talks. Later, he recalled for a Harvard oral
history interviewer:

> I felt that he had not acquitted himself well on this occasion and that
> he had permitted Khrushchev to say many things which should have been
> challenged right there on the spot.
>
> I think this was definitely a mistake. I think it definitely misled
> Khrushchev; I think Khrushchev failed to realize on the occasion what
> a man he was up against and also that he'd gotten away with many of
> these talking points; that he had placed President Kennedy in a state of
> confusion where he had nothing to say in return.[46]

Kennedy expressed concern to Reston and others that Khrushchev
considered him a callow, inexperienced youth and that he soon expected
a test. "It will be a cold winter," he was heard to mutter as he left
the Vienna meeting. As Khrushchev's advisor, Fyodor Burlatsky put it
recently: "Yes, I know this; Khrushchev thought Kennedy too young,
intellectual, not prepared well for decision-making in crisis situations.
Maybe John Kennedy had a wrong feeling about Khrushchev, too."[46a]
Khrushchev may indeed have been surprised at the forceful reaction of
Kennedy, particularly after the young president had accepted the Berlin wall in August 1961 with no military response and had temporized
in Laos in 1961 and 1962.

Perhaps, as Hilsman has argued, the Soviets assumed that the fine
American distinctions between "offensive and defensive" missiles were
really a *de facto* acknowledgment of the Soviet effort in Cuba. One could
conjecture that this was what led Khrushchev to promise, and to believe that Kennedy understood, that no initiatives would be taken before the elections. In any case, Kennedy's concern about his appearance
and the national appearance of strength kept him from searching very
far for Soviet motivation. His interpretation was that it was a personal
injury to him and his credibility, as well as to American power. He
explained this sentiment to *New York Post* reporter James Wechsler:

> What worried him was that Khrushchev might interpret his reluctance
> to wage nuclear war as a symptom of an American loss of nerve. Some
> day, he said, the time might come when he would have to run the su-
> preme risk to convince Khrushchev that conciliation did not mean hu-
> miliation. "If Khrushchev wants to rub my nose in the dirt," he told
> Wechsler, "it's all over." But how to convince Khrushchev short of a show-
> down? "That son of a bitch won't pay any attention to words," the Presi-
> dent said bitterly on another occasion. "He has to see you move."[47]

TRUE GRIT AND CRISIS DIPLOMACY

The missile crisis illuminates what came to be considered a requisite personality trait of the cold war: being tough. Gritty American determination had become the respected and expected stance of American leaders under stress in confrontations with the Soviets from the earliest days of the cold war. When Truman, for example, dispatched an aircraft carrier, four cruisers, a destroyer flotilla, and the battleship *Missouri* to counter Soviet pressure on the Turkish Straits, he told Acheson, "We might as well find out whether the Russians [are] bent on world conquest now as in five or ten years."[48] Clark Clifford gave more formal expression to this sentiment when he advised Harry Truman, in a memo, in late 1946:

> The language of military power is the only language which disciples of power politics understand. The United States must use that language in order that Soviet leaders will realize that our government is determined to uphold the interest of its citizens and the rights of small nations. Compromise and concessions are considered, by the Soviets, to be evidence of weakness and they are encouraged by our 'retreats' to make new and greater demands.[49]

The American concern with its appearance of strength was a mark of the Kennedy administration. One White House aide recalled that, especially after the failure of the Bay of Pigs, "nobody in the White House wanted to be soft. . . . Everybody wanted to show they were just as daring and bold as everybody else."[50]

In the Cuban crisis, the cold war ethic of toughness exacerbated the discrepancies between the necessities of force and the necessities of diplomacy and negotiation. As a result, diplomacy was almost entirely eclipsed. In fact, it was hardly tried. According to Adam Yarmolinsky, an inside observer of the executive committee of the National Security Council, "90 percent of its time" was spent studying alternative uses of troops, bombers and warships. Although the possibility of seeking withdrawal of the missiles by straightforward diplomatic negotiation received some attention within the State Department, it seems hardly to have been aired in the ExCom. "Yarmolinsky confesses that it is curious that no negotiations were considered. Nor were economic pressures ever suggested by the foreign affairs bureaucracy. Only a series of military plans emerged, and they varied from a blockade to a preemptive strike."[51]

Kennedy knew the Russians had deployed missiles on October 16. But, instead of facing Soviet Foreign Secretary Gromyko with the evidence while the Russian was giving the president false assurances that missiles were not being installed, the president blandly listened without comment. Whether or not the Russians believed that Kennedy must have known, the effect of the charade was an absence of serious negotiations. Instead of using private channels to warn the Russians that he knew and intended to act, Kennedy chose to give notice to the Russians in a nationwide TV address. After that, a Soviet withdrawal had to be in public, and it almost had to be a humiliation. When the Soviets attempted nonetheless to bargain for a graceful retreat, their path was blocked. Kennedy refused Khrushchev's offer of a summit meeting "until Khrushchev first accepted, as a result *of our deeds* as well as our statements, the U.S. determination in the matter."[52] A summit meeting, Kennedy concluded, had to be rejected; for he was intent on offering the Russians "nothing that would tie our hands." We would negotiate only with that which would "strengthen our stand."[53] If there were to be any deals, Kennedy wanted them to seem a part of American munificence. He did not want a compromise to be tied to the central issue of what he conceived to be a test of American will and resolve. "We must stand absolutely firm now. Concessions must come at the end of negotiation, not at the beginning," Robert Kennedy cautioned.[54]

In other words, the Soviets had to submit to American strength before any real concessions could take place. When Khrushchev offered to exchange the Cuban missiles for the Jupiter missiles stationed in Turkey, Kennedy demurred, even though he had ordered the missiles out months earlier; in fact, he had thought they were out when Khrushchev brought them to his attention. (The Jupiters were all but worthless; a marksman with a high-powered rifle could knock them out. They took a day to ready for firing, and the Turks did not want them.[55]) Kennedy, however, did not want to appear to yield to Soviet pressure even when he might give little and receive a great deal. An agreement would have confounded the issue of will. As Kennedy's Boswell put it, the president wanted to "concentrate on a single issue — the enormity of the introduction of the missiles and the absolute necessity of their removal."[56]

In the final act of the crisis, Kennedy accepted one of two letters sent almost simultaneously by Khrushchev. One contained the demand for removal of the Turkish missiles; the other did not. Kennedy accepted the latter. Khrushchev's second letter began with a long, heartfelt, personal communication and made no mention of a quid pro quo. Kennedy's response was a public letter to Khrushchev, temperate in tone, in which he accepted the more favorable terms he preferred and further detailed American conditions. It is said that Kennedy published his response "in the interests of both speed and psychology."[57] Kennedy, not even wanting the ExCom group to know that he had authorized both his brother and Dean Rusk to seek something of a quid pro quo (with the U.S. Jupiter missiles based in Turkey), played a subtle hand. Kennedy replied to Krushchev's first private message, accepting its conditions, and ignored the second, more pugnaciously phrased message from the Soviet General Secretary.

But this procedure of publishing the private terms of an interchange with another head of state was a considerable departure from diplomacy. It was not negotiation; it was, in this context, a public demand. Public statements during a crisis lack flexibility. Compromise is almost foreclosed by such a device, because any bargaining after the terms have been stated seems to be a retreat that would diminish a statesman's reputation.

McGeorge Bundy, Kennedy's national security adviser, recalled:

> The basic problem for us was that we had repeatedly taken the public position that the presence of offensive missiles in Cuba was unacceptable. This was a powerful fact of our political consciousness, *regardless of the international legal question.* Soviet nuclear missiles in Cuba posed a particularly difficult problem, because our public simply would not tolerate them so close to us. So the first premise of our discussion was that a policy must be found which leads to the removal of those missiles. This was a premise.
>
> Now, that leads to [the] question: what happens if we go quietly to Khrushchev and tell him we know what he's doing, and that we cannot tolerate it? Why didn't we try that first? *We* believed that if we did that, he would be tempted to go public *first*, and make the international legal case . . . thereby digging himself in and making it all the harder to find a way to get those missiles out.[58]

Because reputation was the stake in Cuba as much as anything else, Kennedy's response was hardly more than a polite ultimatum. In private, Kennedy was even more forceful. Robert Kennedy told Soviet Ambassador Dobrynin: "We had to have a commitment by tomorrow that those bases would be removed. . . . If they did not remove those bases, we would remove them. . . . Time was running out. We had only a few more hours—we needed an answer immediately from the Soviet Union. . . . We must have it the next day."[59]

As result of the crisis, force and toughness became enshrined as instruments of policy. George Kennan observed, as he left forty years of diplomatic service: "There is no presumption more terrifying than that of those who would blow up the world on the basis of their personal judgment of a transient situation. I do not propose to let the future of mankind be settled, or ended, by a group of men operating on the basis of limited perspectives and short-run calculations."[60] In spite of occasional epistles from the older diplomatist, the new managers who proliferated after Cuba routed those who most favored negotiations. In an article in the *Saturday Evening Post*, one of the last moderates of the Kennedy administration, Adlai Stevenson, was attacked for advocating "a Munich." The source of the story, it was widely rumored, was President Kennedy himself.[61]

The policy of toughness became dogma to such an extent that nonmilitary solutions to political problems were excluded. A moderate in this circumstance was restricted to suggesting limited violence. Former Undersecretary of State George Ball explained his later "devil's advocacy" in Vietnam, in which he suggested that there be a troop ceiling of seventy thousand men and that bombing be restricted to the South: "What I was proposing was something which I thought had a fair chance of being persuasive . . . if I had said let's pull out overnight or do something of this kind, I obviously wouldn't have been persuasive at all. They'd have said 'the man's mad.'"[62]

This peculiar search for the middle ground of a policy defined in terms of force was abetted by the sudden sense on the part of Kennedy's national security managers that the military was filled with Dr. Strangeloves. There was some warrant for this fear. Time and time again, during the crisis, the military seemed obsessed by the opportunity to demonstrate its potential. When asked what the Soviet reaction would be to a surgical raid on their missiles and men, General Curtis Le May snapped, "There will be no reaction."

McNamara recalled:

> The alternatives were an air strike and invasion, or some other kind of action. By Saturday, the tension had really increased and there was a tremendous sense of urgency. . . . Maxwell Taylor . . . he always displayed terrific judgment and professionalism to me—but Taylor was *absolutely convinced* we had to attack Cuba. The pressure was on.
>
> Some of you recall that story that I left the White House that evening through the Rose Garden, and it was reported that I said I thought I might never see another Saturday. Last night I was asked why. It was because there was so much pressure for action, . . . that night the preponderance of opinion was in favor of an air strike and invasion that week.
>
> Of course, recently the revelation that the President had set up a channel through Dean Rusk and Andrew Cordier to the UN by means of which, if he wanted to, he could accept the Soviet offer of a public deal on the Jupiter missiles, coupled with the instructions to Robert to communicate to Dobrynin our intention to withdraw those missiles unilaterally, clearly indicates that at that time, President Kennedy had

not finally decided to invade. But there was great uncertainty — a *tremendous* amount of uncertainty.[62a]

When the crisis ended on Sunday, October 25, one of the Joint Chiefs suggested that they go ahead with a massive bombing the following Monday in any case. "The military are mad," concluded President Kennedy.[63] Robert Kennedy recalled acidly that "many times . . . I heard the military take positions which, if wrong, had the advantage that no one would be around at the end to know."[64]

In part, it was a result of the Cuban crisis that the civilians of the American defense and foreign policy bureaucracy grew to despise the military. Hilsman reports that, later in the Kennedy administration, an official prepared a mock account of a high-level meeting on Vietnam in which Averell Harriman "stated that he had disagreed for twenty years with General [Brute] Krulak [commandant of the Marines] and disagreed today, reluctantly, more than ever; he was sorry to say that he felt General Krulak was a fool and had always thought so." It is reported that President Kennedy roared with laughter on reading this fictitious account.[65] Hilsman also delighted in telling a story about General Lyman Lemnitzer, chairman of the Joint Chiefs of Staff, who once briefed President Kennedy on Vietnam: "This is the Mekong Valley. Pointer tip hit the map. Hilsman, watching, noticed something, the pointer tip was not on the Mekong Valley, it was on the Yangtze Valley."[66] Hilsman's recollection of the general's error became a common office story.

Ironically, while the military was increasingly thought to be rather loutish and ill-prepared, civilians were starting to rely more and more on military instrumentalities in the application of which, with few exceptions, they were not trained, and whose command structure they depised as being second-rate at best. Civilian crisis managers believed, after Cuba, that they should have control and that the military could not be trusted and had to be made more responsive to the political and civilian considerations of policy. To many observers, as well as to these managers, the failures of the Cuban missile crisis were not failures of civilian judgment but of organizational responsiveness. The intelligence establishment, for instance, had not discovered the missiles until the last minute. McNamara never really secured control over the navy. U-2 flights were sent near the Soviet Union to excite Soviet radar at the height of the crisis. U.S. alert messages were sent "In the clear"; and until Kennedy ordered their dispersal, American fighters and bombers were wing to wing on the ground, almost inviting a preemptive Soviet blow. Moreover, American tactical nuclear weapons and nuclear-tipped IRBMs in Turkey and Italy were discovered to be unlocked and lightly guarded.[67] All this led observers and policy makers to believe that crisis management demanded the president's organizational dominance and control, because the military and intelligence organizations were inept, and their judgment was not reliable or, at times, even sane.

CUBA AND THE AMERICAN CENTURY

After Cuba, confidence in the ability of U.S. armed superiority to command solutions to crises in a way that would favor American interests expanded in such a way that Americans again began to speak of the American century. For a period before the crisis, there had been a national reexamination. People feared national decline in the face of startling Soviet economic growth. Advances in Russian rocketry had led Americans to believe that not only were they in a mortal competition with the Soviets but that the outcome was uncertain. Now, however, most of these doubts seemed to have dissipated.

The Cuban missile crisis revived the sense of the American mission. Henry R. Luce once rhapsodized in a widely circulated *Life* editorial that Americans must "accept wholeheartedly our duty and opportunity as the most powerful and vital nation in the world and in consequence to exert upon the world the full impact of our influence for such purposes as we see fit, and by such means as we see fit."[68] After the crisis, Arthur Schlesinger could lyrically resurrect this tradition: "But the ultimate impact of the missile crisis was wider than Cuba, wider than even the western hemisphere. . . . Before the missile crisis people might have feared that we would use our power extravagantly or not use it at all. But the thirteen days gave the world—even the Soviet Union—a sense of American determination and responsibility in the use of power which, if sustained, might indeed become a turning point in the history of the relations between east and west."[69]

Similarly, Zbigniew Brzezinski, then a member of the planning council of the Department of State, proclaimed that American paramountcy was the lesson of Cuba. Brzezinski explained, "The U.S. is today the only effective global military power in the world."[70] In contrast to the United States, Brzezinski declared, the Soviets were not a global power. Although Khrushchev may at one time have believed otherwise, the Cuban crisis demonstrated the limits of Soviet capabilities. "The Soviet leaders were forced, because of the energetic response by the United States, to the conclusion that their apocalyptic power [nuclear deterrent power] was insufficient to make the Soviet Union a global power. Faced with a showdown, the Soviet Union didn't dare to respond even in an area of its regional predominance — in Berlin. . . . It had no military capacity to fight in Cuba, or in Vietnam, or to protect its interests in the Congo." No doubt the historic American sense of divine purpose and the almost Jungian need to be the guarantor of global order received a strong fillip from the Cuban crisis. Brzezinski concluded: "What should be the role of the United States in this period? To use our power responsibly and constructively so that when the American paramountcy ends, the world will have been launched on a constructive pattern of development towards international stability. . . . The ultimate objective ought to be the shaping of a world of cooperative communities."[71]

The overwhelming belief of policy makers in American superiority seriously eroded deterrence. The Soviet Union reached the same conclusion as the United States — that a preponderance of military power, ranging across the spectrum of force from PT craft to advanced nuclear delivery systems, was the *sine qua non* of the successful exercise of political will. Before the fall of 1962, Khrushchev's strategic policy, in the words of a RAND Kremlinologist, "amounted to settling for a second-best strategic posture."[72] The missile crisis, however, manifestly demonstrated Soviet strategic weakness and exposed every Soviet debility that Khrushchev's verbal proclamation of superiority had previously covered.

CUBA AND DETERRENCE

After Cuba, the Soviet military, responding to the humiliating American stimulus, demanded a higher priority to strategic arms and a cutback on the agricultural and consumer sectors of the Soviet economy. Although Khrushchev and Kennedy were by then moving toward a detente — best symbolized by the signing of the test-ban accords of mid-1963 — many in the Kremlin saw this as but a breathing spell in which the Chinese might be isolated and Soviet arms could catch up. Naval preparations, especially the building of Polaris-type submarines, were intensified.[73] Soviet amphibious landing capability — something in which the Soviets had shown little interest before — was revitalized and expanded. As Thomas W. Wolfe noted: "From the time of the first test-launching . . . of 1957 to mid-1961 only a handful of ICBM's had been deployed. . . . After Cuba, the pace of deployment picked up, bringing the total number of operational ICBM launchers to around 200 by by the time of Khrushchev's ouster."[74] Although the West still outnumbered the Russians by four to one in number of launchers at the time, the Russians worked furiously and, by September 1968, they commanded a larger force than the United States.[75] Worldwide "blue water" Soviet submarine patrols were initiated; and a decision was made under Brezhnev and Kosygin to extend the Soviet navy to "remote areas of the world's oceans previously considered a zone of supremacy of the fleets of the imperialist powers."[76]

After the missile crisis, the cold war establishmentarian John McCloy, representing President Kennedy, was host to Soviet Deputy Foreign Minister V. V. Kuznetzov. McCloy secured an affirmation from Kuznetzov that the Soviets would indeed observe their part of the agreement to remove the missiles and bombers from Cuba. But the Soviet leader warned, "Never will we be caught like this again."[77]

The Soviets were to yield again to U.S. strength in Vietnam and the Middle East. Each time, however, the usable strategic leverage of the United States grew weaker. Thus, the structure of the international system and international stability was shaken in three ways. First, the United States became confident that its power would prevail because global politics had become "unifocal."[78] In truth, American military primacy began to erode as soon as it was proclaimed, when the Soviets fought to gain at least a rough strategic parity.

Second, nations, once cowed, are likely to be less timid in the next confrontation. As Kennedy admitted some time later, referring to the Cuban missile crisis, "You can't have too many of those."[79] Just as Kennedy feared that he had appeared callow and faint-hearted in successive Berlin crises and thus had to be tough over Cuba, the Soviets were likely to calculate that they must appear as the more rigid party in future confrontations or risk a reputation of capitulationism. For weeks after the missile crisis, the Chinese broadcast their charges of Russian stupidity and weakness to the four corners of the globe. The Chinese labeled Khrushchev an "adventurist" as well as a "capitulationist," and therefore not fit for world communist leadership. The Russian answer was to accuse the Chinese of being even "softer" than they for tolerating the Western enclaves of Macao and Hong Kong.[80] The charge of who was the most capitulationist, the Chinese or the Russians, grew almost silly; but these puerile exchanges had their own dangers in terms of deterrence.

Third, once a threat is not carried out — even after an appearance of a willingness to carry it out has been demonstrated — the ante is upped just a bit more. Morgenthau described a two-step process in nuclear gamesmanship: "diminishing credibility of the threat and ever bolder challenges to make good on it. . . . [T]he psychological capital of deterrence has been nearly expended and the policy of deterrence will be close to bankruptcy. When they reach that point, the nations concerned can choose one of three alternatives: resort to nuclear war, retreat, or resort to conventional war."[81]

Morgenthau's observation captured the dilemma of American policy makers after Cuba. The problem was that nuclear superiority had been useful, but each succeeding threat (because no nuclear threat has ever been carried out) would necessarily be weaker than the last. Yet how could security managers translate military power into political objectives without such threats? Daniel Ellsberg recalled the quandary of U.S. security managers:

> McNamara's tireless and shrewd efforts in the early sixties, largely hidden from the public to this day, [were to] gradually control the forces within the military bureaucracy that pressed for the threat and use of nuclear weapons. [He had] a creditable motive for proposing alternatives to nuclear threats. . . . [I]n this hidden debate, there was strong incentive — indeed it seemed necessary — for the civilian leaders to demonstrate that success was possible in Indochina without the need either to compromise Cold War objectives or to threaten or use nuclear weapons.
>
> Such concerns remained semi-covert: for it was seen as dangerous to lend substance to the active suspicions of military staffs and their Congressional allies that there were high Administration officials who didn't love the Bomb.[82]

But after a Cuban crisis, the option of low-level violence became more and more attractive. Conventional and limited deployments of force became increasingly necessary as conventional force was considered less forbidding than the nuclear abyss. After all, the symbolic or psychological capital of deterrence rested on the notion of resolve. And one way to demonstrate political will was through the resurrection of conventional force as an instrument of demonstrating commitment — a commitment whose alternative form was a threat of nuclear holocaust. The latter was bound to deteriorate with the advent of a viable Soviet retaliatory capability and the knowledge that the Soviets had collapsed once under a nuclear threat and might not be willing to be quite so passive again. Many national security managers found they could navigate between the Scylla of nuclear war and the Charybdis of surrender with the serendipitous discovery of the lifeboat of the 1960s — limited war. It would not prove to be a sturdy craft.

Of course, the assumptions of the planners of limited war — as they emerged victorious from the Cuban crisis — were as old as the cold war. They dated from the Truman Doctrine's Manichean presentation of a bipolar global confrontation where a gain to one party necessarily would be a loss to the other. A world order of diverse centers of power, with elements of superpower cooperation, where gains and losses would be less easily demonstrable, was not so demanding of military remedy. A multipolar world would be less congenial to the belief that the only options available to policy makers were either military force or retreat. Maneuver and negotiation, in such a world, would again become part of diplomacy. But such a development was to come about only after the tragic failure of the military remedy had been demonstrated in Vietnam.

THE BY-PRODUCTS OF SUCCESS

Other effects were related to the exuberant reaction to the Cuban crisis. As the United States began to feel that power and force were successful solvents to the more sticky problems of the cold war, the role of international law declined precipitously.[83] Hypocrisy, in the words of H. L. Mencken, "runs, like a hair in a hotdog, through the otherwise beautiful fabric of American life."[84] Moral pontifications appeared increasingly hypocritical after Cuba. The participants in the crisis knew the blockade was an act of war that had little basis in international law. After the crisis was over, even lawyers began to see law as but another instrumentality of American policy. The conclusion reached by American academics was that "international law is . . . a tool, not a guide to action. . . . It does not have a valid life of its own; it is a mere instrument available to political leaders for their own ends, be they good or evil, peaceful or aggressive. . . . [The Cuban missile crisis] merely reconfirms the irrelevance of international law in major political disputes."[85]

Dean Acheson summarized the code of the cold war as it was confirmed by the Cuban experience: "The power, prestige and position of the United States had been challenged. . . . Law simply does not deal with such questions of ultimate power. . . . The survival of states is not a matter of law."[86] George Ball, former undersecretary of state, wrote: "No one can seriously contend that we now live under a universal system or, in any realistic sense, under the 'rule of law.' We maintain the peace by preserving a precarious balance of power between ourselves and the Soviet Union — a process we used to call 'containment' before the word went out of style. It is the preservation of that balance which, regardless of how we express it, is the central guiding principle of American foreign policy."[87] The United Nations was used in the Cuban crisis, not as Kennedy had told the General Assembly the year before, as "the only true alternative to war,"[88] but as a platform where Adlai Stevenson, the eloquent American representative, could deal "a final blow to the Soviet case before world opinion."[89]

Epitomized by Cuba, crisis after crisis pointed out the stark irony: Americans, who had so long stroked the talisman of international law, now seemed to do so only when their interests were not jeopardized. Otherwise, law became merely a rhetorical flourish of U.S. policy. International law was still a part of the admonition that armed aggression and breaches of the peace cease and desist. Behind these legalistic and moralistic injunctions, the armed cop became more and more apparent. As Charles de Gaulle had observed earlier, the conclusion that American idealism was but a reflection of the American will to power became almost inescapable after the Cuban crisis.[90] Few obeisances about the need for law in international society disguised the sense that America had abandoned its ancient, liberal inheritance in the zesty pursuit of world order.

Another effect of the crisis was to differentiate the great powers — the United States and the Soviet Union — from other states, which were literally frozen out of a major role in structuring global politics. After all, the major chips of big-power poker were simply not accessible to other governments — even those with modest and nominally independent nuclear forces. No other nations had the capability of making even plausible calculations of either preemptive or second-strike blows against a great power, much less basing national strategies on such possibilities. As a result, Europeans were offered the appearance of some control in their nuclear lot with the ill-fated multilateral force, although the nuclear trigger was still in the hands of the United States, as was the final squeeze. Not only were the weapons of great-power diplomacy increasingly inaccessible to other states, but the other tools of statecraft also receded from the grasp of those with modest resources. The spy, for instance, was largely replaced by satellite reconnaissance. Intellectual musings on great-power conflicts became differentiated from other strategic thinking. Gradually, the Soviets and the Americans created a shared private idiom of force, and a curious dialogue began between the congressional budget messages of the secretary of defense and the periodic revisions of *Military Strategy* by Marshal Sokolovsky.[91]

Allies became mere appurtenances of power whose purpose, in the duopolistic structure of international society, was increasingly symbolic. Thus, for example, the Organization of American States was asked to validate the U.S. blockade at the same time the American quarantine was announced. Similarly, Dean Acheson flew to Paris and other European capitals to confer with American allies about the coming confrontation over Cuba.

"Your President does me great honor," de Gaulle said, "to send me so distinguished an emissary. I assume the occasion to be of appropriate importance." Acheson delivered President Kennedy's letter, with the text of the speech to be delivered at P-hour, 7 P.M. Washington time. He offered to summarize it. De Gaulle raised his hand in a delaying gesture that the long-departed Kings of France might have envied. "May we be clear before you start," he said. "Are you consulting or informing me?" Acheson confessed that he was there to inform, not to consult. "I am in favor of independent decisions," de Gaulle acknowledged.[92]

For the Europeans, Gaullists and leftists alike, there appeared a high likelihood of nuclear annihilation without representation.[93] In spite of European gestures of support, the alliance received a shock from which it did not recover. The British, in the midst of a vicious internal debate about whether to abandon nuclear weapons, decided they were necessary to buy even minimum consideration from their American allies. The French did not debate; they accelerated their nuclear programs while withdrawing from a military role in the alliance in 1964. Henceforth, NATO would be, in Henry Kissinger's words, a "troubled partnership."[94]

On the Soviet side, it was equally apparent that Russian interests would not be sacrificed to fellow socialist states. Castro was plainly sold out. The weak promise tendered by the Kennedy administration not to invade the island was probably cold comfort as Castro saw his military benefactors beat a hasty retreat from American power. Embarrassingly, Castro began to echo the capitulationist theme of Chinese broadcasts. Privately, Castro said that if he could, he would have beaten Khrushchev to within an inch of his life for what he did. Soviet Foreign Minister Mikoyan was dispatched to Cuba and stayed there for weeks, not even returning to the bedside of his dying wife, but Castro's fury was unabated. Whatever the motive for Khrushchev's moves in Cuba, the Chinese were also enraged.[95] Any attempts the Soviets had made to dissuade the Chinese from assuming a nuclear role prior to October 1962 lost their validity when it became obvious that the Russians would not risk their own destruction for an associate.

By 1963, a new era of East–West relations was unfolding. The Americans still cultivated the asymmetrical assumptions of the cold war, but the Soviet Union was at least admitted as a junior partner in a duopolistic international system that was now increasingly characterized as one marked by detente.

Indications of this new spirit appeared in the administration's desire for improved economic relations with the Soviet Union. This effort extended into the early years of the Johnson administration, as Lyndon Johnson spoke enthusiastically of improved East–West economic relations as a bridge-building exercise and Zbigniew Brzezinski wrote early in 1965 in his book *Alternative to Partition*, sponsored by the prestigious Council on Foreign Relations, "The Cold War in Europe has lost its old meaning. There was a vitality and a passion to it as long as either side had reason to believe that it could prevail and as long as either side felt genuinely threatened by the other. Neither condition truly exists today."[96] The relaxation was favorable to Kennedy, who wanted to explore diplomacy with the Soviets without the ideological rancor that had poisoned previous relations and who had a vision of Soviet responsibility that would be enlarged by succeeding administrations. The Soviets too sought a detente. Another series of confrontations, given their acknowledged strategic inferiority, could hardly be successful. Moreover, the Chinese began to present formidable ideological and political difficulties for the Soviets. The Soviets' new interest in improved relations with the Americans brought intense fears from China of American–Soviet collusion. At the same time, the Soviets began to fear a Sino–American agreement that would be detrimental to their interest. As the chief ideologue of the Soviet Union, Michael Suslov explained, in early 1964:

> With a stubbornness worthy of a better cause the Chinese leaders attempt to prevent the improvement of Soviet–American relations, representing this as "plotting with the imperialists." At the same time the Chinese government makes feverish attempts to improve relations with Britain, France, Japan, West Germany, and Italy. It is quite clear that they would not refuse to improve relations with the United States but as yet do not see favorable circumstances for such an endeavor.[97]

THE ECONOMICS OF CONTAINMENT

The events of October 1962 and the euphoria and renewed sense of American power that followed this great climax of the cold war also had as a by-product the obscuring of economic elements of the new era of world politics that seemed to be opening up. By 1961 and 1962, the international position of the American dollar had begun to weaken markedly. A favorable balance of payments situation in the years after World War II had turned to a small but nagging deficit of around $1.4 billion a year by 1956. Between 1958 and 1960, this average annual deficit had jumped to more than $3.5 billion and, during the early 1960s, persisted at just over $2.5 billion annually.[98]

Making this situation especially perplexing was the fact that this deteriorating U.S. balance of payments position could not be readily explained in a conventional manner. Normally, a persistent deficit in a nation's balance of payments situation can be attributed to domestic circumstances, usually inflation, leading to its goods' and services' being too expensive to maintain a competitive position in world markets. Under these circumstances (and assuming relatively low barriers to trade), a nation imports more than it exports, leading to a net outflow of wealth and a deficit in its balance of payments. Another source of such a deficit might be an export of currency to finance foreign investment, but, in this case, the return of profits, fees, and royalties should in the long run equal or even exceed outflow, leading ultimately to a net gain for balance of payments.

Recent analysis of the American international economic position during the cold war years suggests that the growing balance of payments problem cannot be explained in these traditional terms. Indeed, for the fifteen years following World War II, U.S. private sector transactions showed an annual average surplus. Between 1960 and 1964, these private transactions slipped slightly into deficit (less than $400 million a year on the average), then recovered to a surplus of more than $1.2 billion in 1965 and 1966, before sliding into deficit again between 1967 and 1970. However, even in the troubled decade of 1960 to 1970, the more than $2 billion annual average deficit cannot be explained easily by conventional economic factors. Throughout the late 1950s and well into 1963 and 1964, the American domestic economy was actually in recession, the recovery from which during late 1963, 1964, and 1965 was marked by sustained economic growth without significant inflation. Thus, it would not seem that American goods were priced out of the world market, leading to an excess of imports. Moreover, American export strength has never rested with low-priced goods, but rather with relatively high-priced but technologically sophisticated goods and agricultural commodities.

International conditions facilitating the movement of private capital developed after 1958 and led to an outflow of American private investment in the late 1950s and early 1960s, especially to Europe. But it is not clear that these seemingly negative short-run transactions were detrimental to the American balance of payments situation in the long run. Thus, Raymond Vernon, a foremost student of American multinational corporations and their investment behavior has noted that one outcome of this investment activity in the late 1950s and early 1960s had been the development of substantial American claims on the assets of other countries.[99] Moreover, by the end of the 1960s, much of what the United States was exporting to the world was in the form of services:[100] "The rewards to the U.S. economy from these activities are to be found not in the merchandise balance, but in sales of business services, in interest and dividends, and in the build-up of the earnings left abroad in subsidiaries and branches. When these are taken into account, the U.S. performance appears a good deal less bleak."[101] Thus, it would seem that the balance of payments problems of the 1950s and early 1960s cannot be easily explained by focusing on private foreign economic transactions. Instead, we must turn our attention to the foreign expenditures of the U.S. government, and, in so doing, we are drawn to the economic dimension coercive diplomacy.

America's International Economic Position in the 1960s

The underlying causes of the balance of payments crisis that confronted the Kennedy administration in the early 1960s seem best understood in terms of the long-term and accumulating costs of containment increasingly dependent on the instrumentalities of military threat and capability. Containment relied originally on the Marshall Plan and then, in time, came to rest on NATO, military intervention in Korea, and subsequently large economic and military assistance to Europe and the Third World — in short, foreign expenditures by the U.S. government that in most instances did not have a financial return as private foreign investment might have yielded. The upshot was, logically and in practice, a net deficit in American balance of payments. It is, of course, accurate to respond that these expenditures purchased something of great value for the United States — national security. However, this is a form of transaction that cannot be factored into a balance of payments statement.

These large public expenditures contributed decisively to a negative balance and accumulating quantities of American dollars in the hands of foreigners. Moreover, during the 1950s and 1960s, as this quantity of dollars grew steadily, the amount of gold backing them remained relatively unchanged. As long as those governments and traders holding dollars maintained their confidence in the capacity and willingness of the U.S. government to back these dollars, they might be content to hold and use the currency. By 1960, however, foreign confidence in the recession-ridden American economy's ability to sustain growth (while the Eisenhower administration continued to expand military assistance and other forms of foreign expenditure) dwindled. By October 1960, the American deficit had become sufficiently large that many of those holding dollars were willing to gamble that the United States would have to devalue the dollar. Accordingly, dollars were exchanged for gold on the London free gold market, forcing up the price of gold from $35 to $41 an ounce. This speculative surge was fueled in some measure by expressions of official concern about the balance of payments situation.

The roots of this situation go back to the Marshall Plan. During the late 1940s, the reconstruction of Western Europe—the bedrock of containment—required a large infusion of American foreign assistance to the West Europeans so that they might finance the purchase of American goods and services necessary to European recovery. Similarly, between 1949 and the early 1950s, the United States provided large amounts of assistance to fund the establishment of NATO through the MDAP and, subsequently, spent billions extending containment to Asia. This combination of economic and military assistance meant that the United States was running slight deficits in its balance of payments by 1956, although net private transactions were in the black by more than $3 billion annually. Nevertheless, these government expenditures were not regarded in the early years of the cold war as normal transactions, and they were not, therefore, viewed with alarm. By and large, they were seen as temporary and, over the long run, nonrecurring.[102] In any event, they were thought essential to the national security and acceptable as long as the annual deficit remained, as it did, around $1.5 billion a year.

Between 1958 and 1960, however, the deficits increased dramatically—up to an average of $3.7 billion per year. A combination of factors contributed to some deterioration (although not a net deficit) in private transactions. For the most part, these events marked the culmination of trends set in motion by the Marshall Plan. Thus, between 1958 and 1960, the industrialized economies of Western Europe had recovered sufficiently to be able to enter into export competition with the United States. At the same time and with the encouragement of the United States, Europeans moved forward with the creation in 1958 of the European Economic Community (EEC) or the Common Market. A key element of the Common Market included some tariff protection to encourage even more rapid development of a truly European economy. At the same time, all European currencies became convertible with one another to facilitate the movement of capital for investment purposes. Finally, this combination of economic growth and internationalization of capital *behind* the Common Market tariff wall served as incentives for American investment to move behind these tariff barriers. Trade through these tariffs proved difficult, but, on the other hand, the internationalization of capital within Europe and growing European economies led to American business "discovering" Europe, and a tripling of American investment occurred there in the late 1950s and early 1960s.[103]

In the short run, therefore, the positive private transactions balance was reduced. Far more important, however, was the fact that American foreign and military expenditures could no longer be regarded as temporary. Indeed, if anything, increased Soviet activism implied an indefinite and perhaps growing level of such expenditures. As this fact began to sink in during the late 1950s, concern with the constantly growing deficit began to increase in official American circles and, inevitably, abroad. This concern was high in Western Europe and especially in France, where this seemingly unending stream of U.S. government spending came to be viewed as a potential threat to new-found prosperity.

The European position was paradoxical in that in the past they had encouraged U.S. foreign assistance to stimulate their own growth. Similarly, during the late 1940s and early 1950s and even at the start of the 1960s, the Europeans benefited from the American military presence. At the same time, however, the European economy was now being forced to absorb large quantities of public as well as private investment dollars—dollars that seemed to have less and less gold to back them. The problems posed for the Europeans were twofold. First, of course, was the growing doubt that the Americans would be able to exchange gold for their dollars, and, as the number of dollars increased, the doubts could only increase. Nevertheless, if governments and international traders were willing to continue using the dollars as if they had backing (i.e., as the international money rather than the gold to which the dollar was theoretically pegged in value under the postwar Bretton Woods system of monetary agreements), there need not be an international monetary crisis. However, for this forebearance, the Europeans had to pay an increasing price in terms of their own domestic economies.

If the Europeans remained faithful to the postwar International Monetary Fund rules, devaluations or revaluations upward were not permitted. Thus, for example, the German, French, or British governments were obligated to exchange their currencies for dollars at a fixed rate whenever the holders of dollars (e.g., a French, British, or German merchant engaged in export—import trade) wanted to convert them into francs, pounds, or marks. As long as the holders of dollars were willing to use them, there was little consequence for European domestic economies. But as confidence in the dollar began to slip, the demand for gold or other, seemingly stronger currencies would increase. The governments responsible for the currencies in demand were obligated to supply the marks, francs, pounds, or whatever.

The net effect of this process was an increasing supply of the Europeans' currencies in their own economies as they sought to sop up the steady stream of dollars and maintain the fixed exchange rate system. To the extent that their own economies grew faster than this supply of money, inflation might be controllable. But it was apparent to European national bankers and economic planners that the expanding presence of American dollars constituted a virtually uncontrollable inflationary pressure both in the short and, especially, in the long term. As long as the fixed exchange rate system remained in place, the European domestic money supply would have to increase, not necessarily because of real growth in the production of their own goods and services (although this was taking place as well), but in response to diminishing confidence in the bloated quantity of dollars sloshing about in the European and world economy.

Thus, by the end of the 1950s, American economic policy had finally succeeded in fostering the rebirth of the European economy but, paradoxically, the decline of European confidence in the dollar. At the same time, the American foreign and defense policy-making community was not prepared to forego what it regarded as an essential instrument of containment — U.S. foreign and military assistance — at the very moment the cold war seemed to be reaching a point of tolerable adjustment.

Sound and Fury . . .
and More of the Same

The American response did not attempt to remove the source of the balance of payments problem — American economic assistance and military spending abroad. Instead, during the last two years of the Eisenhower administration, conditions were attached to these programs that were designed to increase American exports and otherwise reverse or restrain the flow of dollars abroad. First, in the case of economic assistance, recipient countries were required to use their American economic assistance dollars to purchase American goods and services. Second, military expenditure regulations were restructured to emphasize a "Buy America" approach. By the 1960s, these latter provisions required that government agencies purchase American goods, although this meant frequently paying as much as 50 percent more for goods and services than would have been the case if purchased from foreign suppliers. By the late 1960s, more than 90 percent of U.S. economic assistance funds were being spent in the United States. In many instances, however, this meant that the cost of aid projects increased by as much as 30 percent to recipient countries.[104]

In summary, the cost of the Buy America measures led to the cost of government overseas programs increasing for the American taxpayer. At the same time, American economic assistance recipients, forced to spend their receipts on more expensive American goods and services, actually were receiving less for their aid dollars. Moreover, aid recipients were subsidizing frequently noncompetitive American exporters. In terms of balance of payments, however, these measures combined with loan repayments from previous years allowed the United States actually to make money on much of its economic program in the 1960s. Nevertheless, military assistance spending remained high, and the net flow of U.S. government-generated dollars was, therefore, slowed but not stopped.

The Kennedy administration maintained the "tied aid" concept and undertook a number of scattered measures including minor adjustments in the tax laws and interest rates in an effort to repatriate more U.S. private dollars. When these actions did little to change the rate of private investment by the mid-1960s, President Johnson introduced a program of voluntary constraints that were subsequently made mandatory. Moreover, presidents Kennedy and Johnson initiated vigorous arms sales programs abroad in an effort to improve the American export picture.

In the area of export expansion, Kennedy sought and received new trade legislation from Congress, the Trade Expansion Act of 1962. The negotiating authority under the Trade Expansion Act (TEA) was to be used by the administration to bring about significant mutual reduction in tariffs between the United States and Europe so as to allow for the expansion of U.S. exports. However, other motives were involved. Specifically, the TEA gave the president the authority to negotiate tariff reductions of 50 percent across the board and to eliminate tariffs altogether on those product groups where U.S. and EEC exports equaled 80 percent or more of world exports.[105] In the latter case, however, this "dominant supplier" provision was meaningful only if the British were in the Common Market, because otherwise there were very few EEC-U.S. traded product groups that could meet the 80 percent requirement.

Thus, the TEA of 1962 was oriented toward export expansion, but the United States was also trying to use the TEA's dominant supplier provision as an inducement to the EEC countries to admit the British into the EEC. The Kennedy administration's hope was that British entry would offset the economically and politically troublesome French and transform the EEC into an outward-looking Europe more open to U.S. exports. De Gaulle saw through the American effort, however, and, fearing that Britain would serve as an American Trojan horse in Europe, vetoed British entry into the EEC in 1962.[106] Kennedy's "grand design" for export expansion, British entry in the Common Market, and the diminution of De Gaulle's political and economic influence in Europe was never consummated. Some tariff reductions were brought about over the extended "Kennedy round" of negotiations, but, generally the EEC turned increasingly inward and fostered expansion of its internal trade.[107] American exports did increase, but only rapidly enough to very nearly balance American imports—and certainly not enough to offset the continued export of American dollars associated with U.S. military spending.

Indecision and Marginal Measures

By the mid-1960s, therefore, the various American efforts to check or reverse the U.S. balance of payments deficits could claim only the most marginal success. Indeed, after 1965 and 1966, the deficit began to creep back up toward $2 billion plus, despite a booming U.S. economy in which U.S. exports were increasing. American military spending continued to expand at a rate far in excess of the surplus generated by private trade and investment income. And, of course, a major source of this growing hemorrhage of dollars was the escalating conflict in Southeast Asia. Moreover, once the war became thoroughly Americanized after 1966, the costs of military spending cut even deeper. Not only did the export of dollars directly attributable to military spending increase to more than $3.2 billion annually, the domestic inflation set in motion by the war undercut the American competitive position abroad as the prices of American exports increased.

Choosing 1967 as a typical year for the international economic position of the United States during the 1960s, economist Robert Stevens summarizes the conditions underlying the American balance of payments situation:

> When we compare the gross and net impacts on the figures of these three major types of outflow, we find that in 1967 Pentagon-inspired arms exports offset only 29 percent of gross foreign military spending, whereas 86 percent of U.S. foreign aid was offset by purchases made in the United States and 133 percent of private investment outflows were offset by return flows of foreign investment income. Thus, viewed in this context, the government's net foreign military spending has had a much more deleterious effect on the balance of payments than foreign aid or private foreign investment.[108]

This situation could always be rationalized domestically, however, because the outflow of dollars was presumably buying security, and, until very late in the 1960s, the American economy felt no negative effects of this spending.

The situation abroad, especially in Europe, was, of course, quite different, for Europeans were more or less compelled to absorb the exported American dollars. Insofar as the dollar was the basis of the industrialized world's economy, serving as the key currency (and the United States as a kind of banker for the system), the United States could, unlike other countries, escape until very late the need to settle its deficits. As the banker, the United States possessed seemingly unlimited credit symbolized by an unending series of deficits, which the rest of the world and primarily Europe were asked to assume by holding rather than converting American dollars. In time, however, the feared inflation of European economies began, and pressure for international action increased.

During the 1960s a series of short-run measures were developed to deal with speculative pressures as currency swaps, short-term credit arrangements, and an international gold pool were established. In addition, the United States created a new form of credit with issuance of medium-term securities (Roosa bonds) designed to repatriate some of the excess dollar assets in European and other central banks. For a while, these arrangements stemmed somewhat the short-term flow of dollars and diminishing American gold into Europe. Nonetheless, these measures did not get at the fundamental weakness of the dollar's position — a currency that was serving as the key international currency even as it was being used to finance global containment. This patched-up system stumbled through most of the 1960s, then staggered under the added burden of even more military spending in the late 1960s and, along with the foreign policy it was to finance, collapsed in the swamp of Vietnam.

By the end of the 1960s, it was increasingly clear, therefore, that the American dollar could no longer be viewed as an instrument simultaneously serving American foreign policy and the international economic system. The actors composing this system now had economic and political interests of their own. It mattered not that American balance of payments deficits had, in large measure, financed the development of those interests, for they were no longer congruent with an American foreign policy that seemed to require that industrialized countries of the world passively and indefinitely absorb American dollars as their own economies inflated.

CONCLUSION

Thus, by the mid 1960s, the beginning of the end of the cold war had precipitated a change in the global structure of power even as it deflected attention from another growing crisis. American paramountcy had been self-proclaimed, the seeds of detente were sown by a shared vision of nuclear oblivion, and the ingredients for a great power condominium were becoming clear. Tragically and ironically, however, the lessons of the Cuban missile crisis—that success in international crisis was largely a matter of national guts; that the opponent would yield to superior force; that presidential control of force can be suitable, selective, swift, effective, and responsive to civilian authority; and that crisis management and execution is too dangerous and events move too rapidly for anything but the tightest secrecy—all these inferences contributed to the Johnson decision to use American air power against Hanoi in 1965. Even the language of the Gulf of Tonkin Resolution was almost identical to that which Kennedy's legal advisers had drawn up for the OAS in October 1962.[109]

The Cuban crisis changed the international environment but riveted American expectations to the necessities of the diplomacy of violence. Although the Cuban crisis created substantial changes in distinguishing superpowers from other states, the realization both of the parity of the superpowers and the indications that they could join in a relationship that had some elements of condominium and other elements of the classic balance of power was suppressed until the end of the Vietnam War.

Finally, the shimmering image of the "American century" blinded American policy makers to the magnitude of an emerging crisis in the industrialized world's political economy. The construction of containment and the surmounting of the apparent strategic crisis of 1961 and 1962 were all immensely costly, requiring a steady flow of American capital into the reconstruction of the industrialized world's political economy. Just as the Soviet–American political–military confrontation at the center of the cold war climaxed in Berlin and in the waters off Cuba, the political economic dynamics that the Marshall Plan and the flow of American government dollars had sought to set in motion finally took hold in Europe. The eventual result would be the establishment of an international political economy of interdependence that no single government could control. But reflection, modesty, and humility were not characteristic traits of the activists who had just managed one of the great turning points of history. Thus, the importance of the opportunities and risks attendant to these new transnational economic forces seems to have been misunderstood or, if comprehended, deemed manageable as the missile crisis had been managed.

In retrospect, therefore, the great cold war strategic crisis of 1961 and 1962 and the economic crisis of the early and mid-1960s seem to mark the beginning of a major transformation of the international system and American foreign policy. The realization of this profound fact was obscured in some measure by the management of the crises themselves. In any event, the full implications of this transformation could not be dealt with until the American agony in Vietnam drew to a close.

NOTES

1. Revisionist critiques of the Cuban crisis are becoming more frequent. But most are rather polemical and thin. For a sample of some of the better ones, see Richard J. Walton, "The Cuban Missile Crisis" in *Cold War and Counter Revolution* (Baltimore: Penguin Books, 1972), pp. 103–143; Leslie Dewart, "The Cuban Crisis Revisited," *Studies on the Left*, Vol. 5 (Spring 1965), pp. 15–40; John Kenneth Galbraith, "Storm over Havana: Who Were the Real Heroes?" (review of *Thirteen Days* by Robert F. Kennedy), *Book World*, January 19, 1969, p. 16; Ronald Steel, "Endgame," (review of *The Missile Crisis* by Elie Abel), *New York Review of Books*, March 13, 1969, reprinted in Ronald Steel, *Imperialists and Other Heroes* (New York: Vintage, 1971), p. 115; Louise FitzSimmons, *The Kennedy Doctrine* (New York: Random House, 1972), pp. 126–173; and R. Ned Lebow, "The Cuban Missile Crisis: Reading the Lessons Correctly," *Political Science Quarterly*, Vol. 98 (Fall 1983), pp. 431–458. For a criticism of the interpretation developed here, see Irving Janis, *Group-think*, 2nd ed. (Boston: Houghton Mifflin, 1982), p. 291.
2. Roger Hilsman, *To Move a Nation* (New York: Dell, 1967), pp. 48, 157; also cited in Steel, op. cit., p. 115.
3. Hans J. Morgenthau, *Truth and Power, Essays of a Decade, 1960–1970* (New York: Praeger, 1970), p. 158.
4. A current review of this enormous literature is contained in Charles F. Hermann, ed., *International Crises: Insights from Behavioral Research* (New York: Free Press, 1972).
5. Cited by Coral Bell, *The Conventions of Crisis: A Study in Diplomatic Management* (London: Oxford University Press, 1971), p. 2.
6. Alexander George et al., *The Limits of Coercive Diplomacy* (Boston: Little, Brown, 1971), p. 132.
7. Henry Pachter, "J. F. K. as an Equestrian Statue: On Myths and Myth Makers," *Salmagundi* (Spring 1966); cited in George, op. cit.
8. Albert and Roberta Wohlstetter, "Controlling the Risks in Cuba," *Adelphi Paper No. 17* (London: Institute for Strategic Studies, April 1965), p. 19.
9. Robert F. Kennedy, *Thirteen Days: A Memoir of the Cuban Missile Crisis* (with afterword by Richard Neustadt and Graham T. Allison) (New York: W. W. Norton, 1971), p. 48.
10. Ibid., p. 22; Theodore C. Sorensen, *Kennedy* (New York: Bantam, 1969), p. 705. Hermann, op. cit., p. 33; and Arthur M. Schlesinger, Jr., *Robert Kennedy and His Times* (New York: Ballantine, 1979), pp. 546–547.
11. See Thomas W. Milburn, "The Management of Crisis," in Hermann, op. cit., esp. pp. 263–266. Also see Janis, op. cit.
12. Kennedy, op. cit., pp. 48–49.

13. Sorensen, op. cit., p. 705.
14. Arthur M. Schlesinger, Jr., *A Thousand Days* (Boston: Houghton Mifflin, 1965), pp. 840–841.
15. Jack Raymond, *Power at the Pentagon* (New York: Harper & Row, 1964), pp. 285–286.
16. Elie Abel, *The Missile Crisis* (Philadelphia: J. P. Lippincott, 1969). Abel interviewed the witnesses to this episode, some of whom did not agree as to Anderson's exact words. Anderson, Abel reports, could not recall ever having said this.
17. William A. Hamilton, III, "The Decline and Fall of the Joint Chiefs of Staff," *The Naval War College Review*, Vol. 24 (April 1972), p. 47.
18. Abel, op. cit., p. 151–152; Hilsman, op. cit., p. 214; W. E. Knox, "Close-up of Khrushchev During a Crisis," *The New York Times Magazine*, November 18, 1962, p. 128. Blight, et al., *Foreign Affairs*.
19. Kennedy, op. cit., p. 55.
20. Irving Janis, *Victims of Group Think* (Boston: Houghton Mifflin, 1972), p. 163; Henry Pachter, *Collision Course* (New York: Praeger, 1963), p. 58.
21. Leslie Gelb and Morton Halperin, "The Ten Commandments of the Foreign Affairs Bureaucracy," *Harpers*, Vol. 244 (June 1972), pp. 28–37; Leslie Gelb, "The Essential Domino: American Politics and Vietnam," *Foreign Affairs*, Vol. 50 (April 1972), pp. 459–476.
22. Homer E. Capehart: "U.S. Should Act, Stop 'Examining Cuba,'" *U.S. News & World Report*, September 10, 1962, p. 45.
23. *The New York Times*, September 19, 1962.
24. "Cuban Crisis," *Data Digest* (New York: Keynote Publications, 1963), p. 35; cited by Thomas Halper, *Foreign Policy Crisis: Appearance and Reality in Decision Making* (Columbus, Ohio: Merrill, 1971), p. 132.
25. "Notes of the Month: Cuba: A U.S. Election Issue," *World Today*, Vol. 18, (November 1962), p. 543; Halper, op. cit., p. 132.
26. Quincy Wright, "The Cuban Quarantine of 1962," in John G. Stoessinger and Alan Westin (eds.), *Power and Order* (New York: Harcourt, Brace and World, 1964), p. 186.
27. *Economist*, October 6, 1962, p. 15.
28. "Afraid of Everything but War," *I. F. Stone's Weekly*, September 17, 1962, p. 1.
29. Quoted in Steel, op. cit., p. 119.
30. Abel, op. cit., p. 78.
31. Steel, op. cit., p. 121.
32. Sorensen, op. cit., p. 688.
33. George, et al., op. cit., p. 89.
34. Hilsman, op. cit., p. 195.
35. *The New York Times*, November 12, 1962.
36. *Wilmington Morning News*, January 25, 1974.
37. Walter W. Layson, "The Political and Strategic Aspects of the 1962 Cuban Missile Crisis," unpub. Ph.D. Diss. (University of Virginia, 1969), pp. 18–87; Thomas W. Wolfe, *Soviet Power and Europe, 1945–1970* (Baltimore: Johns Hopkins University Press, 1970), pp. 73–99, 100–194.
38. The political adviser to Khrushchev at the time, Burlatsky, was adamant that the real motivation in placing Soviet missiles was to achieve security parity, and the second reason guarantee the security of Cuba. Burlatsky was emphatic that the strategic equation drove Khrushchev's decisions.

Perhaps the richest and most significant addition to the mountain of material that has emerged about the Cuban missile crisis, from the Soviet side, especially, is the transcript of a conversation between the son of Soviet Prime Minister Mikoyan, Khrushchev's personal political advisor to Khrushchev and Excom participants: McGeorge Bundy, Robert MacNamara as well as several academic experts on this event. The meetings occurred on October 11–12, 1987. They were sponsored by the Ford Foundation and Harvard University. David Welch was the reporter. *Proceedings of the Cambridge Conference on the Cuban Missile Crisis,* Oct. 11–12, 1987 (Cambridge, Mass.: The Ford Foundation and Harvard University, 1987); hereinafter cited as *Proceedings.* According to Mikoyan,

> The idea to send missiles to Cuba was first expressed at the end of April by Khrushchev to Mikoyan. The main idea was the defense of Fidel's regime. Khrushchev had some reasons to think the United States would repeat the Bay of Pigs, but not make mistakes anymore. He also thought Kennedy was not a strong politician and would submit to CIA preference, led by Allen Dulles. In 1962, at Punta del Este, Cuba was excluded from the Organization of American States. Khrushchev regarded this exclusion as a diplomatic isolation and a preparation for an invasion.
>
> So, the main reason for sending missiles to Cuba was the defense of Cuba, though, of course, Malinovsky and others talked of the strategic balance. But this was the second idea. I agree with Fyodor, by the way, that Khrushchev did not think through the U.S. reaction. He thought that after they were informed of the missiles, U.S.-Soviet relations would improve. *Proceedings,* pp. 37 and 40.

39. Henry Kissinger, "Reflections on Cuba," *The Reporter,* Vol. 27 (November 22, 1962), p. 22.
40. Interview, December 17, 1962, *Public Papers of the Presidents, John F. Kennedy* (Washington, D.C.: U.S. Government Printing Office, 1963), p. 898.
41. *The New York Times,* December 6, 1970. According to the authoritative *Aviation Week,* the Russians also began to schedule regular stops of long-range aircraft at about the same time. December 21, 1970, pp. 16–17.
42. For a description and forceful but private insistence that the building of the Soviet submarine base at Cienfuegos, Cuba, be halted, see Henry Kissinger, *The White House Years* (Boston: Little, Brown, 1979), pp. 636–651. Nevertheless, sporadic press reports indicate that missile-firing Soviet submarines were putting into Cuba long afterwards; see Barry Blechman and Stephanie Levinson, "U.S. Policy and Soviet Subs," *New York Times,* October 22, 1974; *Washington Post,* October 12, 1979, p. A15. Pincus reports that in 1972 a nuclear armed "Golf II" submarine anchored off Cuba and was serviced by a Soviet tender. Another visit was made in May of 1974, by another "Golf II"—a submarine that usually carries three missiles. Neither time were the visits protested.
43. "How U.S. Voters Feel about Cuba," *Newsweek,* October 13, 1962, p. 138; Halper, op. cit., p. 133.
44. Kennedy, op. cit., p. 45, and Afterword, p. 114.
45. Reston, "What Was Killed Was Not Only the President but the Promise," *The New York Times Magazine,* November 15, 1964, p. 126.
46. *The New York Times,* September 1, 1970; *New York Daily News,* August 31, 1970.
46a. *Proceedings,* p. 30.
47. Schlesinger, *A Thousand Days; op. cit.,* p. 391.
48. Walter Millis (ed.), *The Forrestal Diaries* (New York: Viking, 1951), p. 192.

49. Arthur Krock, *Memoirs* (London: Cassel, 1968), pp. 228–229.

50. Hugh Sidey, *John F. Kennedy, President* (New York: Atheneum, 1964), p. 127.

51. Adam Yarmolinsky, *The Military Establishment* (New York: Harper & Row, 1971), p. 127.

52. Kennedy, op. cit., pp. 44–45 (emphasis added).

53. Sorensen, op. cit., p. 699.

54. Schlesinger, op. cit., p. 811.

55. Hilsman, op. cit., p. 202. Donald F. Hafner, a State Department officer, in an article—"Bureaucratic Politics and those 'Frigging Missiles': JFK, Cuba and U.S. Missiles in Turkey," *Orbis*, Vol 21 (Summer 1977), p. 313—claims that Kennedy was not surprised that the missiles were in place and that the assertion that Kennedy refused to negotiate is a "myth." More recently, however, Arthur Schlesinger, in *Robert Kennedy and His times*, supports the idea that Kennedy was surprised (p. 559) and engaged in "no *quid pro quos*" but thought that, in four or five months, "matters would be resolved" (p. 563).

56. Schlesinger, *A Thousand Days*, op. cit., p. 810.

57. Sorensen, op. cit., p. 714.

58. *Proceedings*, p. 30.

59. Kennedy, op. cit., p. 87.

60. Schlesinger, op. cit., p. 397; also cited by I. F. Stone, *In a Time of Torment* (New York: Random House, 1968), p. 23.

61. Walton, op. cit., p. 119. The article was by Stewart Alsop and Charles Bartlett, "In Time of Crisis," *Saturday Evening Post*, December 8, 1962.

62. Gelb and Halperin, op. cit., p. 36.

62a. *Proceedings*, pp. 86–87.

63. Schlesinger, op. cit., p. 831; Neustadt and Allison, in Afterword, in Kennedy, op. cit., p. 126.

64. Ibid., p. 26.

65. Hilsman, op. cit., pp. 512–513; John McDermott, "Crisis Manager," *New York Review of Books*, Vol. 9 (September 14, 1967), pp. 4–10. The fictitious paper, written by James Thompson, also took on the whole Vietnam decision-making team.

66. David Halberstam, *The Best and the Brightest* (New York: Random House, 1971), p. 255.

67. *Washington Post*, May 26, 1974.

68. Luce, *The American Century* (New York: Farrar and Rinehart, 1941), p. 23; and *Life*, February 17, 1941, p. 63. Actually, Luce had been on record with this message from the age of twenty. See W. A. Swanberg, *Luce and His Empire* (New York: Dell, 1972).

69. Schlesinger, op. cit., pp. 840–841.

70. "Background" remarks to a conference for editors and broadcasters, May 22, 1967, cited in Hans J. Morgenthau, *A New Foreign Policy for the United States* (New York: Praeger, 1969), p. 19. For Brzezinski's edited remarks, see "The Implications of Change for United States Foreign Policy," *Department of State Bulletin*, Vol. 57 (July 3, 1967), pp. 19–23.

71. Ibid.

72. Wolfe, op. cit., p. 134.

73. David Woodward, *The Russians at Sea: A History of the Russian Navy* (New York: Praeger, 1964), pp. 229–230.

74. Wolfe, op. cit., pp. 182–183.

75. Statement by Secretary of Defense Clark M. Clifford, *The Fiscal Year 1970–1974 Defense Program and Defense Budget*, Department of Defense, January 15, 1969, p. 35.

76. Fleet Admiral V. Kasatonov, "On Battle Watch," *Krasnaia Zvezda*, July 30, 1967; cited in Wolfe, op cit., p. 446.

77. John Newshouse, *Cold Dawn: The Story of SALT* (New York: Holt, Rinehart and Winston, 1973), p. 68.

78. George Liska, *Imperial America: The International Politics of Primacy* (Baltimore: Johns Hopkins University Press, 1967), pp. 36ff.

79. K. J. Holsti, *International Politics*, 2nd ed. (Englewood Cliffs, N.J.: Prentice-Hall, 1972), p. 325.

80. Michel Tatu, *Power in the Kremlin: From Khrushchev to Kosygin* (New York: Viking, 1968), p. 319–320.

81. Hans J. Morgenthau, *A New Foreign Policy for the United States*, pp. 212–213.

82. Daniel Ellsberg, *Papers on the War* (New York: Simon and Schuster, 1972), pp. 292–293.

83. Dean Rusk reflected earlier obligatory American statements about international legal order and American foreign policy when he declared:

> Our foreign policy has been reflected in our willingness to submit atomic weapons to international law, in feeding and clothing those stricken by war, in supporting free elections and government by consent, in building factories and dams, power plants and railways, schools and hospitals, in improving seed and stock and fertilizer, in stimulating markets and improving the skills and techniques of others in a hundred different ways. Let these things stand in contrast to a foreign policy directed towards the extension of tyranny and using the big lie, sabotage, suspicion, riot and assassination as its tools. The great strength of the United States is devoted to the peaceful pursuits of our people and to the decent opinions of mankind. But it is not healthy for any regime or group of regimes to incur, by their lawless and aggressive conduct, the implacable opposition of the American people. The lawbreaker, unfortunately in the nature of things, always has the initiative, but the peacemaking peoples of the world can and will make themselves strong enough to insist upon peace. [Cited in Halberstam, op. cit., p. 327.]

84. H. L. Mencken, "Editorial," *American Mercury*, Vol. 9 (November 1926), p. 287. Cited in Halper, op. cit., p. 157.

85. William P. Gerberding, "International Law and the Cuban Crisis," in Lawrence Scheinman and David Wilkinson, eds., *International Law and Political Crisis: An Analytic Casebook* (Boston: Little, Brown, 1968), pp. 209–210.

86. Richard J. Barnet and Marcus Raskin, *After Twenty Years* (New York: Random House, 1965), p. 229n.

87. George Ball, "Slogans and Realities," *Foreign Affairs*, Vol. 47 (July 1969), p. 624.

88. John F. Kennedy, "Let Us Call a Truce to Terror," address to the General Assembly of the United Nations, September 23, 1961, *Department of State Bulletin*, October 16, 1961, p. 619.

89. Schlesinger, op. cit., p. 824.

90. For General De Gaulle's analysis, see his *Mémoires de Guerre*, Vol. 2, *L'Unité* (Paris: Librairie Plon, 1956), pp. 97–98.

91. Marshal Z. D. Sokolovsky, *Military Strategy: Soviet Doctrine and Concepts* (In-

troduction by Raymond Garthoff) (New York: Praeger, 1963). (Subsequent editions were translated by RAND for internal use by government officials.)

92. Abel, op. cit., p. 112.

93. Amitai Etzioni, *Winning Without War* (Garden City, N.Y.: Doubleday, 1965), p. 46.

94. Henry Kissinger, *The Troubled Partnership: A Reappraisal of the Atlantic Alliance* (Garden City, N.Y.: Doubleday, 1966).

95. Adam Ulam, *Expansion and Coexistence* (New York: Praeger, 1968), p. 675. Ulam (pp. 668–670) suggested that Khrushchev aimed at precluding both Chinese and German acquisition of nuclear weapons.

96. Zbigniew Brzezinski, *Alternative to Partition: For a Broader Conception of America's Role in Europe* (New York: McGraw-Hill, for the Council on Foreign Relations, 1965), p. vii.

97. Cited by Ulam, op. cit., p. 691.

98. These figures and much of the following review of the deteriorating American international economic situation are based on the refreshingly clear analysis of Robert Warren Stevens in *A Primer on the Dollar in the World Economy: United States Balance of Payments and International Monetary Reform* (New York: Random House, 1972), esp. pp. 108–174. See also Lawrence Krause, *Sequel to Bretton Woods: A Proposal to Reform the World Monetary System* (Washington, D.C.: Brookings, 1971).

99. Raymond Vernon, "A Skeptic Looks at the Balance of Payments," *Foreign Policy*, No. 5 (Winter 1971–1972), pp. 52–65.

100. See Lawrence Krause, "Why Exports Are Becoming Irrelevant," *Foreign Policy*, No. 3 (Summer 1971), pp. 62–70.

101. Vernon, op. cit., p. 60.

102. On this point, see Stevens, op. cit., pp. 119–121.

103. Ibid.; and David P. Calleo and Benjamin M. Rowland, *America and the World Political Economy: Atlantic Dreams and National Realities* (Bloomington, Ind.: Indiana University Press, 1973), pp. 118–192.

104. Stevens, op. cit., p. 130.

105. For a detailed analysis of the TEA of 1962, see Ernest H. Prieg, *Traders and Diplomats* (Washington, D.C.: Brookings, 1970).

106. See Nora Beloff, *The General Says No: Britain's Exclusion from Europe* (Baltimore: Penguin Books, 1963), *passim*.

107. See Calleo and Rowland, op. cit., pp. 123ff.

108. Stevens, op. cit., p. 138.

109. Remarks by William P. Bundy, October 16, 1973, University of Delaware, Newark.

Chapter 7
Containment
"Turns the
Corner" . . . into
the Swamp

The running sore of the Vietnam War has become a scar. Vietnam, no longer a subject of sometimes violent public debate and confrontation, has become the object of cinematic art, the novel, the memoir, and the historian. But foreign policy analysts of the period who still survey the smoke and ruin of Vietnam and the concomitant domestic turmoil and near disintegration, like the ancient Mediterranean oracles who opened the bellies of oxen and burned their entrails to understand the past and predict the future,[1] ask: How did it happen and what did it mean?

CONTAINMENT ON THE MEKONG

To write of American combat involvement in the Indochina war in the past tense strikes the authors as somewhat odd. Both came to university during the truncated Kennedy years. We then lived through what seemed an interminable succession of presidential statements and news conferences: corners were turned and light was seen at the end of the tunnel. One fought to maintain some sense of the human implications of the argot of the decade: "gooks" and "slopes," "search and destroy," "free-fire zones," "pacification," and that omnipresent obscenity of the late 1960s, the daily "body count." And yet, in retrospect, what appeared to be an endless torrent of indistinguishable days, weeks, months, and years can be seen to have fallen into more or less definable periods or phases containing specific and crucial decision points. In this way, the war seems to have had an identifiable structure and, more important for our purposes, was an intellectual and historical culmination of the fundamental elements of American foreign policy mapped out in previous chapters.

The Period of Limited
but Escalating Commitment

John Kennedy's investment in the problem of Vietnam was unusual. He was one of the founding members of the American Friends of Vietnam. The Friends were established in the fall of 1955, as then–Senator Kennedy explained at one of their meetings, to offer an alternative to "revolution — a political and social revolution far superior to anything the Communists can offer."[2] Senator Kennedy's explanation to the assembly of Friends summarized the rationale for American involvement in Indochina as it was to stand for the next sixteen years:

> Vietnam represents the cornerstone of the Free World in Southeast Asia, the keystone to the arch, the finger in the dike. Burma, Thailand, India, Japan, the Philippines, obviously Laos and Cambodia are among those whose security would be threatened if the red tide of communism overflowed into Vietnam. . . . Her economy is essential to the economy of all of Southeast Asia; and her political liberty is an inspiration to those seeking to obtain or maintain their liberty in all parts of Asia — and indeed the world. . . .[3]

When President Kennedy came to the Vietnam question, therefore, his beliefs were already well defined, and, in general, they conformed to the prevailing concept of America's interests in the non-Western world and Southeast Asia. President Kennedy was aware, however, that the Diem regime had not conformed to the image one expects in a supposed proving ground for democracy. Between 1955 and 1961, Diem's control of the South had become more and more repressive. In late 1956, a Western observer described South Vietnam as a "quasi-police state characterized by arbitrary arrests and imprisonment, strict censorship of the press and the absence of an effective political opposition."[4] By 1959, Diem had abolished most local government at the village level and carried out a program of land reform that did little or nothing to break the hold of large and absentee land owners. Finally, in 1959, ordinances were passed that gave Diem's military courts very nearly complete latitude and the people no right to appeal the courts' decisions.[5]

Diem was soon confronted with a thriving indigenous insurgency. Organized opposition to Diem emerged in 1957 and 1958 but did not have the support of the communists in the North. Indeed, Radio Hanoi repeatedly attacked this new South Vietnam Liberation Front composed of Viet Cong, southern Viet Minh from the struggle against the French, and the newly disaffected. The communists in the North apparently feared, throughout 1958 and 1959, that this new political force in the South, while articulating an avowedly communist program of action, nevertheless constituted a threat to any subsequent reunification effort. Furthermore, the primary concern of the North at this time seems to have been its own internal economic reconstruction and development, not fomenting revolution in the South. By 1960, however, the South's opposition to Diem was threatening to move beyond the control of Hanoi. Thus, in September 1960, the Northern leaders moved to endorse the activities of the Southern insurgents. Nevertheless, the "socialist revolution in the North was to be regarded as the 'most decisive task for the development of the whole Vietnamese revolution for the cause of national reunification,' but the Southerners were now encouraged to take direct and militant action."[6] By the end of 1960 and into early 1961, the insurgency had escalated. Political assassinations, terrorism, and large battalion-sized battles were frequent. Contrary to what the American government would claim subsequently, observers at the time noted that "the insurrection is Southern rooted; it arose at Southern initiative in response to Southern demands."[7]

On assuming office, Kennedy sent, in succession, Vice President Lyndon Johnson, Chairman of the Joint Chiefs of Staff Maxwell Taylor, White House adviser Walt Rostow, and the secretaries of state and defense to Southeast Asia to evaluate the situation and recommend a course of action. All reported to Kennedy in essential agreement with Rusk and McNamara:

> The loss of South Vietnam would make pointless any further discussion about the importance of Southeast Asia to the free world; we would have to face the near certainty that the remainder of Southeast Asia and Indonesia would move to a complete accommodation with Communism, if not formal incorporation with the Communist bloc.
>
> The loss of South Vietnam to Communism would not only destroy SEATO but would undermine the credibility of American commitments elsewhere.[8]

Like Korea a decade earlier, a loss of a country on the periphery would not only undercut regional security and "involve the transfer of a nation of 20 million people from the free world to the communist bloc,"[9] it would also undermine the entire structure of global containment. Moreover, warned McNamara and Rusk, yet another Korean ghost was abroad in Southeast Asia: The "loss of South Vietnam would stimulate bitter domestic controversies in the United States and would be seized upon by extreme elements to divide the country and harass the Administration."[10] In sum, Kennedy's year-long review of the situation confirmed Eisenhower and Dulles's domino theory of aggression in Southeast Asia. Furthermore, Kennedy's advisers emphasized that at the end of the row of international dominoes was what Leslie Gelb, one of the authors of the *Pentagon Papers*, would term the "essential domino," American public opinion.[11] It seemed to Kennedy — a man who had been elected by less than one percentage point, stained by the disaster at the Bay of Pigs, again tarnished by the construction of the Berlin wall following the difficult Vienna Conference, and confronted with an even more rapidly deteriorating situation in Laos than in Vietnam — that there was really no choice; he would have to stay.

The next year and a half provided some basis for optimism. A strategic hamlet program that removed South Vietnamese peasants from insecure areas was initiated, and American troop strength went from five hundred Green Berets and other advisers in May of 1961 to more than ten thousand. Secretary of Defense McNamara reported that "Every quantitative measurement we have shows that we're winning this war."[12] Taylor had called in the previous year for both a troop increase and the bombing of the North. Kennedy had given him some of the personnel but had refused to initiate the bombing; it seemed by early 1963 that Kennedy's limited response was working well. Indeed, by 1963, McNamara had initiated planning for U.S. troop withdrawals and, on paper at least, was able to show a one-thousand-man reduction in force in December 1963. In the meantime, however, apparent success turned decidedly sour.

The Collapse of the Diem Regime

The sense of movement associated with the American buildup in 1962 had provided a deceptive image of progress. The strategic hamlets proved a disaster, as Diem used the program to disrupt traditional Vietnamese society in an effort to extend his authority. A program designed to increase security became, ironically, a contribution to the potential pool of insurgents. Within the South Vietnamese army, the situation was actually worsening. Government weapons losses increased as did Viet Cong terrorism. In May 1962, the resentment among the nation's Buddhist majority toward the Catholic minority symbolized by Diem and his brother, Ngo Dinh Nhu, broke into the open. During a demonstration in Hue, on May 8, government troops fired into a crowd of demonstrating Buddhists. Demonstrations escalated and, during the fall of 1962 and the summer of 1963, took a grisly turn as seven Buddhist monks committed suicide by public self-immolation, an act of protest sarcastically characterized by Nhu's wife as a "barbecue show."[13] Finally, in August, Nhu ordered government troops to raid major Buddhist pagodas throughout the country and arrest the Buddhist leadership; schools were closed, and the public suicides continued.

By September 1963, things were clearly out of control. Kennedy sent McNamara to South Vietnam with instructions to Diem that reforms must be forthcoming or U.S. assistance would be reduced. In the meantime, the U.S. embassy learned of a conspiracy within the army to overthrow Diem. Orders went out from Washington that the coup should be encouraged and supported if the plan showed likelihood of success. By November, after one false start, the planning for the coup was completed with assistance from the CIA and the American embassy, notably Ambassador Henry Cabot Lodge, and was carried out on November 1, 1963. Diem and his brother were assassinated, and an unstable Military Revolutionary Council took over.[14]

Kennedy was now increasingly ambivalent:

> In the final analysis, it is their war. They are the ones who have to win it or lose it. We can help them, we can give them equipment, we can send our men out there as advisers, but they have to win it — the people of Vietnam — against the Communists. . . . [A]ll we can do is help, and we are making it very clear.

"But," cautioned Kennedy, "I don't agree with those who say we should withdraw. That would be a great mistake."[15] As evidence of this conviction, American personnel reached fifteen thousand in November. At the same time, however, Kennedy intimates have reported that the president, fearing that the war was becoming an American war, was moving toward a decision in 1963 to end American involvement in 1965. The immediate restraining factor was, of course, the presidential election of 1964, the last time Kennedy would have to face the electorate. In the spring of 1963, Kennedy informed Senator Mike Mansfield, who, though an early supporter of Diem, now called for a complete American withdrawal, that he (Kennedy) now agreed, "But I can't do it until 1965 — after I'm reelected."[16] Kenneth O'Donnell, a confidant of the president, recalled:

> After Mansfield left the office, the President told me that he had made up his mind that after his reelection he would take the risk of unpopularity and make a complete withdrawal of American forces from Vietnam. "In 1965, I'll be damned everywhere as a Communist appeaser. But I don't care. If I tried to pull out completely now, we would have another Joe McCarthy red scare on our hands, but I can do it after I'm reelected. So we had better make damned sure that I *am* reelected."[17]

The country would never learn whether Kennedy's decision was a firm one, because he was himself assassinated three weeks after Diem. Lyndon Johnson came into office with the knowledge that the situation in the South was rapidly disintegrating. As McNamara would report in December 1963:

> Vietcong progress has been great during the period since the coup, with my best guess being that the situation has in fact been deteriorating in the countryside . . . to a far greater extent than we realized because of our undue dependence on distorted Vietnamese reporting. . . . We should watch the situation very carefully, running scared, hoping for the best, but preparing for more forceful moves if the situation does not show early signs of improvement.[18]

McNamara's closing recommendation would prove to be a prophetic description of American policy for the next four years. The situation would never show more than illusory signs of improvement, especially during 1964, when seven South Vietnamese governments moved in and out of Saigon, and Lyndon Johnson became increasingly fearful of a resurgent Republican right wing in the November 1964 elections.

Transforming the War
into an American War

Throughout early 1964, the United States steadily escalated the scale of American involvement in a covert war against North Vietnam in the hope that collapse of the South Vietnamese government could be staved off. The authors of the *Pentagon Papers* characterize Johnson's decision making at this time as being one of pursuing "noncommitting" actions, however, the covert war involved clandestine raids and attacks inside North Vietnam, air strikes in Laos, and destroyer patrols in the Gulf of Tonkin. Most important in the view of the authors of the *Pentagon Papers*, this covert war "carried with it an implicit symbolic and psychological intensification of the U.S. commitment. . . . A firebreak had been crossed."[19]

Significantly, almost no one in the Johnson administration believed that these covert actions would be sufficient to prevent the loss of the South. In May of 1964, after the Joint Chiefs of Staff had developed their proposals,[20] William P. Bundy prepared a scenario for the escalation of American involvement culminating in an all-out bombing campaign against the North. Included in the proposal was a draft congressional resolution that would give to the president the authority "to use all measures, including the commitment of armed forces" to ensure the survival of South Vietnam.[21] Thus, by midyear 1964, Johnson had secretly developed a plan for the escalation of American involvement in Southeast Asia even as he was executing a clandestine low-level war against the North and in Laos.

Despite a steadily deterioriating situation in South Vietnam, Johnson shelved the proposed escalation temporarily. The president had already moved into the 1964 campaign against Senator Barry Goldwater and was portraying himself to the American people as a man who would not pursue a rash escalation of the war because it would undercut his pursuit of the Great Society at home. Goldwater, in contrast, was calling for an escalation of force in Southeast Asia including the bombing of the North, with nuclear weapons if necessary. Johnson retorted that such a step would dangerously widen the war, perhaps bringing the Chinese or Russians into the conflict; it might also require the commitment of American ground troops to the war, a step that Johnson had scorned during the campaign: "We are not going to send American boys nine or ten thousand miles away from home to do what Asian boys ought to be doing for themselves."

Privately, however, Johnson was approving the very steps that he was publicly attacking Goldwater for recommending. As in the previous decisions to initiate covert actions against the North, the bombing was rationalized as a limited means to prevent collapse of the political situation in the South. The president could not begin the bombing immediately in view of the position he was taking in the presidential campaign. In the meantime, however, he was able to get the Southeast Asia Resolution passed in August as the result of extremely confusing and uncertain August naval engagements in the Gulf of Tonkin. The purported North Vietnamese attacks came in the wake of a provocative covert naval action against the North approved earlier in the year by the president. Moreover, Assistant Secretary of Defense John McNaughton suggested — after the Tonkin "attacks," President Johnson's air strikes in retaliation, and the hurried congressional passage of the open-ended Tonkin Gulf Resolution — that yet another incident might be staged later as a part of a "provocation strategy" to provide a pretext for the initiation of additional bombing of the North.[22]

The impression of deceit surrounding the Tonkin Gulf Resolution has, of course, been intensified by revelations subsequent to the events of August 1964. It is now apparent that considerable confusion and uncertainty surrounded the purported attacks on the *Maddox* and *C. Turner Joy*.[23] The *casus belli* for sending fighter bombers to bomb and strafe North Vietnam was said to be a second North Vietnamese attack on American warships in forty-eight hours. The administration maintained the ships were on "routine" patrol on the high seas and that the "attacks" were "piracy." In actuality, the vessels, as Anthony Austin points out in his account, "were not engaged in 'routine' sea patrol . . . but in a special espionage mission that took the ships well within North

Vietnamese waters. . . . The *Maddox* [was] running in and out of territorial waters" before the purported attack by North Vietnam, and after the night of August 3 and August 4, the *Maddox* again attempted to "excite" North Vietnamese radar. There was, in Austin's words, "considerable evidence that one objective of the patrol was to provoke the North Vietnamese and bloody them if they responded." Only hours after the radar operators on the two ships "confirmed" the second attack by Vietnamese torpedo boats, the Pentagon war room, with the personal approval of President Johnson and Secretary McNamara, dispatched US F-4s from a carrier battle group to bomb the North. When the planes were still away from the target, the two ships, the *Maddox* and *C. Turner Joy* tried to inform the carrier and Washington that the sightings were unconfirmed (and indeed, were probably "ghost" blips picked up from atmospheric changes and the ships' own wake). But it was too late.[24]

A White House official in a "position to know" confided to the *New York Times* columnist Tom Wicker "that the President had been carrying around the text of the resolution 'in his pocket' long before the Tonkin episode gave him the right opportunity to lay it before Congress."[25] When opportunity knocked, the secretary of defense hurriedly sent American fighter bombers over North Vietnam, bombing oil storage and port facilities. Secretary McNamara could report to the president that the "retaliatory" air strikes were a huge success. "Smoke was observed rising to 14,000 feet," he declared. Johnson was elated. One reporter heard him gloat, "I didn't just screw Ho Chi Minh; I cut his pecker off."[26] The Tonkin resolution was then brought out of Johnson's pocket to be used as the basis for legitimizing the planned expansion of the war — all that had been needed was an event to set things in motion. Publication of the *Pentagon Papers* makes the claims put forward in support of the resolution patently transparent. The *Papers* themselves and the documents published with them make it clear that, from February to August 1964, the United States was consciously pursuing a policy of escalating the conflict in Southeast Asia by overt and covert means. With the election safely behind him, President Johnson moved to the crucial decisions on the escalation and transformation of the war. Detailed plans for initiating a bombing campaign against the North were tentatively approved in early December. For the time being, however, the president gave final approval only to increased, but secret, bombing of the infiltration routes in Laos.

By the end of 1964, American aircraft had been shot down over South Vietnam, domestic political chaos had increased in Saigon, and the South Vietnamese army seemed on the verge of collapse.

Furthermore, much of the intelligence community was now warning the president that the increased U.S. military action envisioned in the bombing proposal could not save the situation on the ground in South Vietnam. Early 1965 was, therefore, a critical decision point, perhaps the most crucial period in the evolution of American policy in Southeast Asia. The administration was confronted with the undeniable fact that previous efforts had not halted the decline in the South. When the Viet Cong struck an American installation at Pleiku in February, Johnson ordered the initiation of Operation Rolling Thunder, the sustained bombing of strategic targets in the North that would continue for the next three years. This was probably not the only option available to the United States at this time, for Hanoi had initiated peace feelers during December and January. At a time when circumstances in the South were so obviously bad, the appearance of negotiating from weakness was a concern in Washington; therefore, talks were to be avoided until more military pressure could be brought to bear on the North.

The bombing of the North, including areas surrounding Hanoi, came as Soviet Premier Aleksei Kosygin arrived in North Vietnam. The Soviet Premier was widely reported as a moderate, and many Western intelligence analysts saw his visit as a means of dampening the war and reasserting Russian influence in the area against Chinese ambitions. While Kosygin was in Hanoi, the bombs fell. The Soviet Premier bitterly told Kissinger and Nixon some eight years later, "I shall never forget it."[27] David Halberstam relates a story that indicated it was not the attack on Pleiku that prompted American reprisal but rather that it was an opportune moment to head off negotiation and increase the pace of the war:

> A few days after the bombing campaign had begun, a White House reporter came across Bundy in the White House barbershop. Bundy was sitting there being lathered, and since he could not easily escape, the reporter thought it was a good time to ask Bundy something that had been bothering him since the incident. "Mac," he said. "what was the difference between Pleiku and the other indicents?"
>
> Bundy paused and then answered, "Pleikus are like streetcars" (i.e., there's one along every ten minutes).[28]

Nevertheless, the bombing could not prevent the next decision facing Johnson. The South Vietnamese army was collapsing, and bombing the North was not going to reverse this trend any more than covert raids and incremental increases of U.S. advisers had stopped the growth of the Viet Cong during the preceding two or three years. The authors of the *Pentagon Papers* underscore the dilemma:

Once set in motion, however, the bombing effort seemed to stiffen rather than soften Hanoi's backbone, as well as the willingness of Hanoi's allies, particularly that Soviet Union, to work toward compromise. . . .

The U.S. was presented essentially two options: (1) to withdraw unilaterally from Vietnam leaving the South Vietnamese to fend for themselves, or (2) to commit ground forces in pursuit of its objectives.[29]

On April 1, 1965, President Johnson ordered that American troops be used in offensive action in South Vietnam. In a National Security Action Memorandum issued on April 6, 1965, the president approved an eighteen- to twenty-thousand-man increase in U.S. forces, the deployment of two marine battalions in northern South Vietnam; and a change of mission for all marine battalions in South Vietnam "to permit their more active use." The memorandum also cautioned, "The President desires that with respect to the actions . . . premature publicity be avoided by all possible precautions."[30]

"I Want to Leave the Footprints of America There"[31]

On April 7, 1965, in a speech at Johns Hopkins University, the president sought to explain why the war must be fought. The reasons given were familiar ones:

> We are . . . there because there are great stakes in the balance. Let no one think for a moment that retreat from Vietnam would bring an end to conflict. The battle would be renewed in one country and then another. The central lesson of our time is that the appetite of aggression is never satisfied. To withdraw from one battlefield means only to prepare for the next. We must say in Southeast Asia — as we did in Europe — in the words of the Bible: "Hitherto shalt thou come, but no further."[32]

Vietnam was, in fact, no different from Europe before World War II, Johnson implied. Furthermore, Hanoi was analogous to Nazi Germany, because "the first reality is that North Vietnam has attacked the independent nation of South Vietnam. Its object is total conquest." This was no civil war; indeed, "over this war — and all Asia — is another reality: the deepening shadow of Communist China. The contest in Vietnam is part of a wider pattern of aggressive purposes."[33] The rationale for action put before the American people was, therefore, the same that had been advanced for almost two decades. There was a hint of the decision already secretly taken and of what was to come: "We know that air attacks alone will not accomplish all of these purposes."[34] By the end of the year, 184,314 American troops would be in South Vietnam.

In June and July 1965, those opposed to further escalation of the war marshalled their arguments, which had been passed over at the time the April decisions to commit American ground troops had been made. Central Intelligence Agency Director John McCone had argued for an increased air effort to avoid ground combat in this jungle quagmire.[35] By mid-1965, the "doves" insisted that, even with an increase in the air war, McCone's prophecy would be fulfilled. But on July 28, 1965, President Johnson announced that

> we did not choose to be the guardians at the gate, but there is no one else. . . . [W]e learned from Hitler at Munich that success only feeds the appetite of aggression. . . . I have asked the commanding general, General [William] Westmoreland, what more he needs to meet this mounting aggression. He has told me. We will meet his needs. . . . Additional forces will be needed later, and they will be sent as requested.[36]

This was clearly not a decision made in the absence of any debate or indication of what might come. The administration was fully aware that it was now embarked on a new course. The Pentagon analysts who prepared the three thousand page analysis of the Vietnam War provide the best summation of these private mid-1965 decisions.

> The major participants in the decision knew the choices and understood the consequences. . . . [The mid-July decision to approve forty-four maneuver battalions] was perceived as a threshold — entrance into an Asian land war. The conflict was seen to be long, with further U.S. deployments to follow. The choice at that time was not whether or not to negotiate, it was not whether to hold on for a while or let go — the choice was viewed as winning or losing South Vietnam. . . . This was sanctioned implicitly as the only way to achieve the U.S. objective of a noncommunist South Vietnam.
>
> The acceptance of the search and destroy strategy . . . left the United States commitment to Vietnam open-ended. The implications in terms of manpower and money are inescapable.
>
> Final acceptance of the desirability of inflicting defeat on the enemy rather than merely denying him victory opened the door to an indeterminate amount of additional force.[37]

American policymaking now assumed a kind of tragic predictability. On July 2, 1965, the Joint Chiefs were requested to estimate "the forces required to win in South Vietnam."[38] But it was soon apparent that no one knew, and Washington deferred to Westmoreland's estimate of what he said he needed. By August 1966 Westmoreland requested 542,588 men by the end of 1967. The war would be over, he said, by the end of 1967; 1968 was, of course, an election year.[39]

As American escalation of the ground war continued throughout 1966, the air war followed a similar pattern as previously untouched petroleum, oil, and lubricant supplies were hit and destroyed. Nevertheless, the North continued to match each American escalation, and, by the fall of 1966, a special report of the Institute for Defense Analysis commissioned by the Department of Defense concluded that

> as of July 1966 the U.S. bombing of North Vietnam . . . had had no measurable direct effect on Hanoi's ability to mount and support military operations in the South at the current level. . . .
>
> The available evidence clearly indicates that Hanoi has been infiltrating military forces and supplies into South Vietnam at an accelerated rate during the current year. Intelligence estimates have concluded that North Vietnam is capable of substantially increasing its support.

Finally, the report concluded with the observation:

> There is currently no adequate basis for predicting the levels of U.S. military effort that would be required to achieve the stated objectives — indeed, there is no firm basis for determining if there is *any* feasible level of effort that would achieve these objectives.[40]

In October, McNamara went to Vietnam for another evaluation of the war and, on returning to Washington, reported to Johnson that he was in substantial agreement with the institute's conclusions. This report by McNamara in October was accompanied by his recommendation that the United States set a limit to its troop levels and shift the pattern of American bombing away from the Hanoi–Haiphong area to infiltration routes in preparation for a negotiated settlement of the conflict. This recommendation sparked an intense debate within the administration, with the Joint Chiefs standing in opposition to McNamara. The Johnson administration was now split as to the future course of the war. The president compromised by allowing McNamara to cut the military's requested troop level to 469,000 by the end of 1968, but approving yet another step-up in the air war despite CIA findings that 80 percent of the casualties in North Vietnam during 1965 and 1966 were civilians. In February 1967, Johnson approved an increase in B-52 sorties from sixty to eight hundred monthly.[41]

Midway into 1967, the debate within the administration was at its peak and was intensified by General Westmoreland's request for 200,000 troops, or an ultimate troop strength of more than 670,000 troops by mid-July 1968. Moreover, pressure from within the military began to rise for unlimited bombing; an invasion of Cambodia, Laos, or even North Vietnam; and attacks on the port of Haiphong.[42] Johnson continued to resist the pressure for an expansion of the war on land. At the same time, the preconditions he attached to any peace overtures offered the North Vietnamese were such as to preclude real negotiations. These prior conditions were little changed from those Johnson offered in 1965 and 1966, when the president ordered bombing pauses while offering that, if the North Vietnamese and the Viet Cong would concede that they were the aggressors in the war and stop their infiltration of the South, the United States would end its bombing and begin negotiations. The entire position was rooted in the contention that the war was not a civil war, a position that was unacceptable and hence nonnegotiable to the North. The fighting continued.

By late 1967, disaffection with the war had begun to swell in the United States. Draft resistance increased during 1966 and 1967, and, during these same years, the War on Poverty turned into a skirmish because of the budgetary demands of the war; widespread rioting became almost commonplace in black ghettoes. Radical politics seemed to be the norm on many college campuses. And, within Congress, the bipartisan consensus of foreign policy disintegrated as congressional doves led by Senator J. William Fulbright and other liberal members of the Foreign Relations Committee openly challenged the administration's policies in Southeast Asia. Indeed, by the end of 1967, there was virtually no communication between the Foreign Relations Committee and the administration. Public opinion remained uneasily behind the president. As the nation approached the 1968 elections, polls found growing opposition to American policy in Indochina, especially the bombing of the North and the refusal of the Johnson administration to facilitate negotiations.

In the face of this disintegrating domestic base, Johnson reiterated the now worn justifications for the war, increased secret domestic surveillance on American antiwar dissidents, and brought General Westmoreland before the Congress to extol progress and eminent success in the war. It would all be over in two years, the general said, if, of course, he got the necessary forces. But Johnson would not go this far; instead, there would be more bombing and greater use of indiscriminate firepower as ever-larger areas of South Vietnam were declared "free fire zones." By one estimate, one third to one half of the people of Southeast Asia had become refugees.[43] Vast areas of land had been defoliated by American herbicides and weed killers. Between 1961 and 1971, the United States dropped more than one hundred million pounds of herbicide on South Vietnam (six pounds of herbicide for every man, woman, and child in South Vietnam). Dioxin, one of the ingredients of the defoliant Agent Orange, is now known to cause genetic mutation, liver damage, and cancer, according to a National Academy of Science study completed in February 1975. About one seventh of the territory of South Vietnam was sprayed to destroy crops and the jungle canopy that supposedly sheltered the Viet Cong. The 1925 Geneva treaty on chemical and biological warfare prohibits the deployment of gases and toxins. Just the same, some 36 percent of the mangrove swampland—the breeding ground of the staples of fish and rice of the Vietnamese diet—had been destroyed by 1974. The seventeen scientists commissioned to study the effect of these toxins estimated that it could take over one hundred years for the swamps to recover.[44] Moreover, by the late 1970s and early 1980s, this campaign would produce a grim irony as American veterans of the war began experiencing abnormally high rates of cancer.

Between 1965 and 1971, the enormous quantity of ordnance expended in Indochina as a whole represented some 142 pounds of explosives per acre of land and 584 pounds per person. "The average rate of detonation was 118 pounds per second," which equaled, in terms of explosive power, the equivalent of 450 Hiroshima-type atomic bombs.[45] Craters filled with water, causing mosquito populations to intensify and malaria to spread. Unexploded shells killed and maimed those who dared remain to work the land. The timber industry was wiped out. Workers attempting to cut wood with power saws risked being hit by shrapnel buried in the wood. The rubber industry was ruined, and the landscape of the once rich Mekong Delta became, according to observers, "gray porridge . . . torn as if by an angry giant." Senator Gaylord Nelson noted that "there is nothing in the history of warfare to compare with [it]. A 'scorched earth' policy has been a tactic . . . throughout history, but never has a land been so massively altered and mutilated."[46]

In a recent court case, McNamara testified that he had concluded, by the fall of 1965(!), when U.S. casualties stood at less than 10,000, that the war could *not be won* militarily.[46a] Yet by the end of 1967, more bombs had been dropped on Vietnam than in the entirety of Europe during World War II. McNamara now began to testify openly that the air war had failed to stop the infiltration of men and supplies into the South and that the destruction inflicted on the North could not be said to have broken Hanoi's will to go on. The secretary of defense was willing to contradict publicly and powerfully the Joint Chiefs. But by then U.S. casualties had exceeded 100,000. But McNamara had changed. Previously, students at Harvard had nearly overturned his car when he made one of his last public addresses in defense of what was once known as McNamara's War. Then, he had shouted, "I'm tougher than you. I was tougher in World War II and I'm tougher now!" But his doubts grew. He commissioned the Pentagon Papers. When the papers were handed to him, he confessed to a friend, "You know they could hang people for what's in there."[47] McNamara's son began turning up at peace demonstrations, and McNamara's behavior—once so controlled, determined, and calculating—became "erratic."[48] In the end, he was given to public weeping. He was the third secretary of defense in less than twenty-five years to break in office.

On January 31, 1968, the start of the Buddhist Tet holiday, the Communists launched large-scale attacks throughout South Vietnam. Communist forces penetrated to the heart of every major city in the South, including Saigon. Hue was captured, and it was only after weeks of fighting and the literal destruction of most of the ancient and culturally important city that it was retaken. Parts of Saigon and other cities could be saved only by calling destructive and indiscriminate air strikes down on them. The Communists took enormous casualties, and the Pentagon claimed a major battlefield victory, but, in fact, Tet marked the end of the open-ended American war in South Vietnam. If, after almost three years of steady escalation and expansion of the effort, the Communists could launch an attack of the magnitude of the Tet offensive, it was clear to almost everyone that a change in policy was necessary.

The crucial decision was made by Clark Clifford, who had replaced McNamara as secretary of defense in February 1968. Faced with a new Westmoreland request for 206,000 additional troops, Clifford recommended that it be denied. Moreover, the new secretary of defense asked on March 5, 1968, that the chairman of the Joint Chiefs of Staff evaluate a proposal from the Department of State that the bombing in the North be curtailed or halted, implying that he (Clifford) favored such a move. The domestic domino began wobbling as an avowed peace candidate, Senator Eugene McCarthy, claimed a moral victory in the New Hampshire primary with 40 percent of the Democratic vote. Then the American casualty figures were released. They numbered 139,801—exceeding the overall Korean War losses. At the same moment, an emergency meeting of European and American bankers was held in Washington to stem a rush on gold as the price soared. And, on March 13, Senator Robert Kennedy announced that he would seek the Democratic party nomination for president in 1968. The day Senator Kennedy announced he would run, Johnson rejected Westmoreland's troop request.

Within a week, the president recalled the general to become Army chief of staff.[49]

The Tet offensive simply could not be ignored, for it ran completely against the years of deceptively optimistic official reporting.[50] The president was forced to reconsider the entire course of the war. On March 25, Johnson convened a Senior Informal Advisory Group, which consisted of former members of the foreign and defense policy community and was informally headed by Dean Acheson. Almost without exception, these were men who had been hawks for years; many of them, such as Acheson and Omar Bradley, traced their service back to the immediate postwar period.[51] After a two-day review of the situation, this group, informally known as the "wise men," dramatically recommended that the president reverse course and deescalate the war. The president, according to the authors of the *Pentagon Papers*, was stunned by the position now taken by this group, which in previous years had recommended escalation. On March 31, 1968, the president announced that he was cutting back on the bombing. Moreover, he announced that, to facilitate the search for peace, he would not seek the presidential nomination in 1968. The domestic domino had fallen.

In his 1965 Johns Hopkins speech, Johnson had stated a desire to bring a $1 billion economic assistance program to Vietnam. "The vast Mekong River," he said, "can provide food and water and power on a scale to dwarf even our own TVA." He also noted that "we often say how impressive power is. But I do not find it impressive at all. The guns and bombs, the rockets and the warships, are all symbols of human failure . . . they are witness to human folly."[52]

UNDERSTANDING
THE QUAGMIRE AND
THE STALEMATE MACHINE

A combination of a misperception of the nature of the revolutionary conflict in Vietnam, the relationship of that conflict to America's broader world role, and presidential politics set a framework within which we might understand America's (and Vietnam's) Vietnamese tragedy. At the confluence of these streams lies the swamp into which American foreign policy was knowingly carried during the 1960s. John Kennedy was murdered even as he seemed to recognize the peril confronting his administration. Lyndon Johnson's administration died in the swamps as he tried to extricate himself from the quagmire first through violence and then through negotiations.

The International Costs of "Losing"

Those who have tried to grasp and explain America's deadly fascination with and involvement in Vietnam have frequently employed the image of a man floundering helplessly in a quagmire into which he had inadvertently slipped.[53] Other students of American policy have argued that American presidents in no way stumbled into the Vietnamese swamp. Rather, they entered knowingly into the bog. There may have been times, such as early and mid-1965, that the intense desire for victory made the wish seem a real possibility. But for the most part, American policy makers were aware that the actions they were taking at a particular moment at best would allow them to hold their position on what seemed eternally shifting and treacherous grounds and at worst would probably require subsequent additional commitment.[54]

If, in their frantic effort to press on or extricate themselves from the swamp, Kennedy, Johnson, and the "best and the brightest" who made up their administrations maimed and killed other creatures who lived in the swamp, the Americans should not be blamed, guilt should not be apportioned, for American intentions were good. It was necessary, or so it seemed, to Truman, Eisenhower, Kennedy, and Johnson, that we be in Vietnam, not because Vietnam itself was so vital to American security, but because if we were not willing to go in and stay there, "our word" and reputation would suffer. "We are there," said Johnson, "because we have a promise to keep. . . . We are also there to strengthen the world order. Around the globe from Berlin to Thailand are people whose well-being rests . . . on the belief that they can count on us."[55]

Assistant Secretary of Defense John McNaughton put matters in perspective in a memo he wrote laying out American war objectives as the Johnson administration approached the fateful escalation decision in late 1964 and early 1965. American aims should be:

70 pct. — To avoid a humiliating U.S. defeat (to our reputation as a guarantor).

20 pct. — To keep SVN (and then adjacent) territory from Chinese hands.

10 pct. — To permit the people of SVN to enjoy a better, freer way of life.

Also — To emerge from crisis without unacceptable taint from methods used.

[American aims should] not [be] — To "help a friend," although it would be hard to stay in if asked out.

McNaughton went further: even if the Viet Cong were not defeated, American involvement "would demonstrate that the U.S. was a 'good doctor' willing to keep promises, be tough, take risks, get bloodied and hurt the enemy badly."[56]

The McNaughton ranking of American priorities does suggest a plausible set of benchmarks against which the employment of American means were evaluated, otherwise one would have to argue that the Kennedy and Johnson administrations were filled with willful sadistic monsters. If the well-being of one's ally is evaluated on the order of magnitude of 10 percent out of a 100, whereas the avoidance of a "humiliating defeat" stands at or near 70 percent, then clearly the figurative and quite literal destruction of one's ally is a small price to pay if "humiliation" is avoided. If, as a doctor, you believe that your worth to society will be evaluated primarily in terms of your cool willingness to enter a potentially bloody operating room, then it does not matter much that the patient be disabled, disfigured, or die a horrible and lingering death.

Johnson's desire that the United States leave behind in Vietnam that which he regarded as truly "impressive" — schools, dams, a better life — is more understandable in this light. There is no reason to doubt that the president set forth in all honesty and with deep conviction this image of what Indochina could be. What is more important, however, was his belief that first "we must deal with the world as it is, if it is ever to be as we wish." The building of the world that we wish must be deferred as we deal with and contain the perceived threats and disorder of the contemporary system. In this vision, if the road be painful, so be it: "This nation [must] hazard its ease, its interest, and its power." Ultimately, however, we must do so not primarily, as Johnson implied, "for the sake of a people so far away," but rather because the American vision of the political and economic order of the world demands it. The difficulty and danger for those people "so far away" is, however, that the pursuit of that vision, as in Vietnam, frequently requires that *they* hazard *their* ease, *their* interest, and *their* power so that the American vision might be realized.

In one sense only, therefore, the quagmire metaphor is useful. Kennedy and Johnson, but especially Johnson, did behave as if they were men in a swamp. That part of the swamp in which they found themselves, Vietnam, was but a part of a much larger morass — a quagmire created and sustained, it was believed, by the flow of Chinese and Soviet communism. If that source of aggression threatened to turn the entire international system into a swamp, it was essential that the United States try to dam up Asian and Soviet communism. If that meant, in turn, that the United States must stay in the swamp indefinitely, it was, nevertheless, essential.

The persistence of Kennedy, Johnson, and subsequently Richard Nixon, once in the swamp, is understandable in terms of their fears of the international consequences of losing Vietnam. Given the perceived all-encompassing nature of the threat, to lose once is to lose everything. It does not follow, as Dulles used to insist, that one must win finally and definitely. But one must certainly not lose. All American presidents faced with the problem of Vietnam desired the final defeat of the Viet Cong and North Vietnamese. Yet, the larger international imperatives demanded at a minimum that the American client not be defeated. Thus, when Johnson found that, to avoid such a defeat, the commitment of American troops was necessary, he proceeded with the escalation of the war. Once in, of course, it was not only the American client who was at stake; rather, it was the United States itself. Indeed, the client was only a symbol of the higher stakes of battle. As Kissinger readily confessed in January 1969, Vietnam may not have been important intrinsically, but "the commitment of five hundred thousand Americans . . . settled the issue of the importance of Vietnam." Kissinger continued:

> For what is involved now is confidence in American promises. However fashionable it is to ridicule the terms "credibility" or "prestige," they are not empty phrases; other nations can gear their actions to ours only if they can count on our steadiness. . . . In many parts of the world — the Middle East, Europe, Latin America, even Japan — stability depends on confidence in American promises.[57]

In 1965, 1966, and early 1967, Johnson believed that the United States could have final victory. Certainly, events in the Dominican Republic in 1965, even as he was escalating the Vietnam War, might have suggested as much to him. In that case, when an American-backed regime was "deserted by everyone"[58] and subsequently attacked by leftists and conservatives, Johnson landed the Marines and imposed order. The original pretense was the protection of Americans in Santo Domingo, but, subsequently, the United States published a hastily drawn and largely inaccurate list of Communists and "Castroite leaders who were purportedly active in the revolution." A stable conservative government was installed.

The thrust of this policy was repeated throughout Latin America as Lyndon Johnson's new assistant secretary of state for inter-American affairs, Thomas Mann, redirected much of what was left of the Alliance for Progress to military governments, such as that established in

Brazil in 1964 following a coup that overthrew a liberal–leftist regime. The apparent success of these efforts may have reinforced Johnson's propensities to escalate the scale of military involvement in Vietnam. Arthur Schlesinger speculates that Johnson also "found it viscerally inconceivable that what Walt Rostow kept telling him was 'the greatest power in the world' could not dispose of a collection of nightriders in black pajamas."[59] Further, insofar as the Dominican intervention was carried out without much negative public outcry in the United States, it is conceivable that Johnson concluded that his domestic base was supportive.

Presidential Politics and the Cost of Losing

In contrast to Johnson's bold escalation of the fighting and American participation in it after 1965, there was the covert war, secret preparation for the escalation, and the outright public deception of 1964. These facts suggest that more was at work than the fear of the international consequences of a loss or overconfidence concerning U.S. power. Presidents have indeed been afraid of losing in Vietnam because of the international implications of such a loss, but they have also been preoccupied with its domestic consequences. Moreover, this concern and preoccupation with losing to Communists or looking "soft" when confronted with a communist challenge has extended to more than Vietnam. We have noted the import of containing the right at home on the Truman and Eisenhower administrations previously. John Kennedy's emotional and bellicose reaction to the Bay of Pigs disaster was due in some part to his fear that he would suffer during the next election or because he perceived the American people chastising him not for the blatant illegality of the act but for his failure. Similarly, the Cuban missile crisis over a year later seems to have been fed by this same anticipation of a popular backlash to a posture more conducive to a negotiated resolution of the conflict.

These fears were clearly at work throughout the Vietnam escalation. For Kennedy and Johnson, the war could not be lost if they and their administrations were to survive. Kennedy may have decided by late 1963 that he would have to reverse course, but he did not see his way clear to do so until after the 1964 election. The choice for Lyndon Johnson was even more complex. Johnson could no more "lose" the war before the 1964 election than the murdered Kennedy, but Johnson could not lose the war after the election either, because he hoped to face the electorate again in 1968. At the same time, Johnson sought to maintain an image of a calm moderate to set himself apart from Goldwater's bellicose proposals. To save the situation on the ground in Vietnam was difficult, because Johnson and his advisers knew that matters were disintegrating rapidly. Thus, the covert war, actually conceived in the Kennedy administration, was employed to hold the situation until November 1964. In the meantime, Johnson was planning secretly to do what Goldwater was proclaiming publicly that the United States should be doing.

Underlying this balancing act by Johnson was a perception of the American people with which Kennedy could have agreed:

> I knew our people well enough to realize that if we walked away from Vietnam and let Southeast Asia fall, there would follow a divisive and destructive debate in our country. . . . A divisive debate about "who lost Vietnam" would be, in my judgment, even more destructive to our national life than the argument over China had been.[60]

In Johnson's view, this debate would, in turn, undercut the capacity of the United States to play its global role.[61] Thus, the two streams converged precisely where the president of the United States stood. For Lyndon Johnson as well as his predecessors and his successor, the only way to survive in the midst of the crosscurrents was to avoid a loss in Vietnam. Or, as Daniel Ellsberg has argued, the end of policy became the production and maintenance of a stalemate.[62]

The problem after the 1964 election was no less complex, because by then the situation in Vietnam had become desperate as governments came and went and the South Vietnamese army fought indifferently. If the situation was to be held for another four years, it was clear that the Americans would have to do it. Now, however, Johnson sought a middle way along the escalatory path he had chosen. On one side were the doves who demanded withdrawal. The latter could be placated, at least in the short run, with breathless bombing pauses and peace initiatives. The hawks could be bought off by dribbling out the troop escalations that everybody knew were coming and inching up the bombing campaign while warning of the dangers of Chinese or Soviet intervention if the escalation went too fast or too violently. Finally, to maintain the support of that large number of confused and disoriented people in the middle, Johnson carefully avoided for as long as possible taking those steps that would significantly disrupt the lives of the average American. Thus, he resisted tax increases and a call-up of the reserves until 1967 and maintained draft deferments for college-age males as long as possible.[63]

At the same time, however, the incremental escalation necessitated by this approach simplified the problem of matching the escalation on the part of the North Vietnamese. There can be little doubt that Hanoi was quite aware of the nature of Johnson's domestic circumstance and sought to exploit it:

> American public opinion was the essential domino. Our leaders knew it. Hanoi's leaders knew it. Each geared its strategy — both the rhetoric and the conduct of the war — to this fact.
>
> Hanoi adopted what seems to have been a . . . strategy to cause U.S. withdrawal from Vietnam by playing on American domestic politics. The . . . aim was to try to convince Americans that unless U.S. forces withdrew, the killing of Americans would never end.[64]

The *Pentagon Papers* seemed to confirm that Johnson and his advisers were quite aware of Hanoi's appeal to the American public. Moreover, Johnson also knew that the course he had chosen would be arduous and long: "Johnson . . . knew that the intelligence analysts offered little promise of victory ever, while no one (except, most of the time, Walt Rostow) promised it quickly."[65] But the president also knew (or thought he knew) what the American people would do if he caved in. Thus, he was compelled to hang on and hope that something would turn up. These judgments fated him to play out the scenario presented to him by Undersecretary of State George Ball, perhaps the leading dove in the Johnson administration, who argued for no further escalation and lost in mid-1965:

> The South Vietnamese are losing the war to the Viet Cong. No one can assure you that we can beat the Viet Cong or even force them to the conference table on our terms, no matter how many hundred thousand white, foreign (U.S.) troops we deploy. . . . The decision you face now, therefore, is crucial. Once large numbers of U.S. troops are committed to direct combat . . . [and] once we suffer large casualties, we will have started a well-nigh irreversible process. Our involvement will be so great that we cannot — without national humiliation — stop short of achieving our complete objectives. Of the two possibilities I think humiliation would be more likely than the achievement of our objectives — even after we have paid terrible costs.[66]

Negotiating in Quicksand

After the Tet offensive and the collapse of his political career, Johnson was more or less personally free of presidential politics. These pressures remained for his party and his vice president, Hubert Humphrey, who would become the Democratic party candidate. Nevertheless, after March 1968, the American public, which had been hawkish earlier, no longer had any stomach for the war. In short the opportunities for a negotiated settlement in Vietnam seemed better than at any time since the 1950s. The North Vietnamese, in responding to Johnson's limited bombing halt of March 1968, agreed to discuss only the full cessation of the bombing at the outset; if there was to be only a limited bomb suspension, they would engage in only limited talks. The central questions of the war, unification and the illegitimacy of the Saigon regime, remained non-negotiable issues. The North Vietnamese probably concluded that time was on their side, because as the elections drew closer, the Americans might become more forthcoming.

In the meantime, however, Johnson refused to take the minimum steps necessary to move the talks to the level of true negotiations. Throughout April, May, and most of June 1968, the United States insisted that the bombing could stop completely only if the North Vietnamese demonstrated some restraint on the battlefield. The North Vietnamese refused any concession to the American demand, for to do so would be an indirect admission that they were aggressors in South Vietnam. Since the North Vietnamese refused to concede that South Vietnam existed and insisted that the United States was in fact the aggressor against Vietnam, no *formal* and *public* concession of this most fundamental of points was possible.

During June, July, and August 1968, however, the Viet Cong and North Vietnamese drastically reduced their offensive action, and the North Vietnamese reportedly withdrew more than eighty thousand of their troops as a gesture to the Americans. Johnson refused to respond, however, apparently believing that further concessions could be gained by the continued application of force. Furthermore, he was now under pressure from Saigon to make no concession that in any way recognized the Viet Cong; they should not be given any recognition at formal negotiations. To do so, argued President Nguyen Van Thieu of South Vietnam, would be to concede the point of the entire war.

In late July and early August, the administration took the position that the informal signals from the North were no longer adequate. There would have to be formal statement or assurance of what the North Vietnamese would do in the way of a response if the United States stopped the bombing. In effect, the United States had not modified its original hard position. The United States would maintain its military presence and pressure, thereby protecting the Thieu regime, but the North would have to withdraw — then true negotiations could begin. From the perspective of the North, this U.S. demand was tantamount to saying that the North must surrender what the United States had not been able to win on the battlefield, then negotiations could begin.[67] The North refused and promptly reescalated the violence in the South, with rocket attacks against major cities and the partial overrunning of Tay Ninh City in the northern part of South Vietnam. By early autumn 1968, American casualties rose dramatically after the marked decline during the lull of the preceding months.

By mid-October, with the election deadline closing fast but Hubert Humphrey lagging seriously, Johnson finally made a major concession that went to the heart of the twenty-year war. In an effort to move the informal talks to the level of full negotiations, he offered to allow the National Liberation Front (the South Vietnamese Communists) full representation at the conference, thereby extending tacit recognition of the Communists. In return, the North Vietnamese would accept a representative of Saigon. Johnson got around the question of bombing by not requiring a formal concession from Hanoi. He merely stated that he would halt the bombing and not resume it unless the demilitarized zone was violated or the Communists attacked Southern cities. The president announced the proposal publicly on October 31, 1968, less than a week before the elections, and the North Vietnamese and the NLF accepted immediately.[68]

Now, however, the South Vietnamese exercised what amounted to a veto: They simply refused to sit down with the United States, the North Vietnamese, and the NLF. For two months, they argued over any arrangements that implied recognition of the NLF, with the shape of the conference table becoming the symbolic issue over which the procedural wrangling continued. In the meantime, a surge of Humphrey support in the wake of the announcement that formal negotiations might be getting under way petered out just before election day as the delays by the Saigon regime created confusion. Only after president-elect Richard Nixon urged the Saigon regime to begin negotiations did the South Vietnamese reluctantly go along. Formal negotiations began on January 24, 1969, four days after Nixon had become president.[69]

Conclusion

The Nixon administration entered office intimating it had a secret plan to end the war. The plan consisted of a largely secret effort in 1971 and 1972 to negotiate a cease-fire, the return of American prisoners of war, and the conditions of postwar political processes in the South. In the meantime, however, the fighting continued for four more years. There was secret bombing and subsequent invasions of Cambodia and Laos by American and South Vietnamese troops,[70] massive bombing of Hanoi, and the mining of Haiphong harbor, and the Nixon administration initiated and carried out a program of Vietnamization in which American troops were withdrawn incrementally as the South Vietnamese army received the latest American equipment and training neglected for the most part during the Americanized portion of the war.

In at least one narrow respect, the Johnson administration's policy of stalemate was successful.[71] The Johnson administration never formally recognized communist claims in South Vietnam, and the Viet Cong flag was not run up over Saigon during Johnson's years in office. With respect to the broader and more important aspects of that policy, however, the outcomes are more problematic. First, Johnson's pursuit of stalemate cost him his administration, with respect to not only his foreign policy but his domestic policy as well, in that the important programs of the Great Society had to be sacrificed to support the war effort. Second, it is not clear that Johnson succeeded ultimately in demonstrating America's will to resist leftist revolution in the Third World. The enormous American effort in Southeast Asia never touched the core of the revolution underway for twenty years in Vietnam. The entire effort employed modalities of conflict designed to stop international and conventionally militarized aggression. So, while the Johnson administration succeeded in that mode of combat, it failed in countering and even exacerbated the social and economic revolution that was always the crux of the issue in Southeast Asia.

There is a paradox in this; for, as we have seen, the Kennedy and Johnson administrations began with a prodigious intellectual effort to anticipate unconventional war. What was lacking, however, was the full acceptance of the implications of Bernard Fall's observations even as the Johnson administration was undertaking the conventional militarized Americanization of the war in 1965:

> The "kill" aspect, the military aspect, definitely always remain[s] the minor aspect. The political, administrative, ideological aspect is the primary aspect. . . . by its very nature, the insurgency problem is military only in a secondary sense, and political, ideological, and administrative in a primary sense. Once we understand this we will understand more of what is actually going on in Vietnam or in some other places affected by [revolutionary war].[72]

Kennedy may have approached an understanding of this point, but no American president who believed in the necessity of containment and stalemating international communism's advance could act on such a realization, because it would involve concessions to and acceptance of much of the revolutionary's position. That is to say, one would have to recognize the corruption and repression of a Diem, which was the source and sustenance of much non-Western revolutionary activity.

Failing such a realization or willingness to act on it, the Johnson administration was committed to the course of escalation and frustration. The upshot was the maiming of Vietnam as well as of the spirit of the American people. Insofar as America's conception of world order is maintained by the willingness of the United States, its people, and its leaders to commit its resources to a global effort, the Vietnam War during the Kennedy and Johnson administrations undercut that willingness. Thus, the implementation of stalemate in Vietnam undermined the very will that the commitment was ostensibly to demonstrate.

SAVING THE STALEMATE MACHINE

The Nixon administration entered office with a dual problem. First, the Tet offensive had demonstrated to many, perhaps most, Americans the futility of incremental escalation of and continued American involvement in the war. The beginnings of talks with the North Vietnamese had raised expectations that meaningful negotiations might be possible that could bring to an end the years of frustrating carnage. Moreover, Nixon had, during his campaign, exploited the cumulating frustrations of the American people to help fashion his marginal victory over Hubert Humphrey. Thus, Nixon was confronted with a nebulous, rather inarticulate desire, encouraged by him during the campaign, that the war be ended. If he did not do this or show considerable progress in this direction, his own reelection in 1972 might be endangered.

On the other hand, Nixon maintained the belief that the American right wing remained a potent force. If the ending of the war took on the appearance of what he termed a "bug out," the country and his administration might be ravaged by that McCarthyite segment of public opinion that, of course, he, as much if not more than any American, had nourished and exploited throughout his public career. Therefore, the domestic domino was no less important to the Nixon administration than to those of his predecessors. Indeed, Henry Kissinger saw the domestic danger as not unlike the unraveling of Weimar Germany he had experienced as a boy.[73]

The new president's problem in dealing with this fact of political life was complicated by the second dimension of the overall problem confronting his administration. Although Nixon had attacked Johnson's policies in Vietnam, he nevertheless accepted the broad premises on which they rested. That is to say, he accepted the general notion that the United States must maintain its "special place in the world."[74] Or, as Henry Kissinger would argue a decade later:

> As the leader of democratic alliances we had to remember that scores of countries and millions of people relied for their security on our willingness to stand by allies, indeed in our confidence in ourselves. No serious policymaker could allow himself to succumb to the fashionable debunking of "prestige" or "honor" or "credibility." For a great power to abandon a small country to tyranny simply to obtain a respite from our own travail seemed to me—and still seems to me—profoundly immoral and destructive of our efforts to build a new and ultimately more peaceful pattern of international relations.[75]

On the other hand, Nixon and Kissinger were prepared to accept the proposition that "the postwar period in international relations has ended,"[76] and there were new opportunities for "negotiations" especially with the Chinese and the Soviets, who were no longer viewed as functionally monolithic. The new situation implied the possibility of reducing somewhat the American global presence. In sum, retrenchment was now a possibility, although retreat was out of the question.

Nixon sought, therefore, to maintain America's global role but to do it in such a manner that what appeared to be opportunities for a stable order could be maximized. At the same time, this process of fashioning what he termed a "new strategy for peace" had to be done on the debris of the Vietnam-shattered domestic foreign policy consensus. This constraint dictated the minimalist rhetoric of the Nixon Doctrine. Nixon and Kissinger knew that rhetoric would not, in itself, save the essential domino—the Nixon presidency. The two dimensions of his foreign policy problem were, therefore, joined in Vietnam: Nixon's own perception of the risks and opportunities in the international system required that he pursue the old objectives of a salient, even dominant, American world role, which seemed to imply, in turn, that Vietnam not appear to be "lost." Simultaneously, however, Americans had to be withdrawn from the swamp in such a manner that Nixon was not cut with either edge of domestic political opinion. The direction of the movement was to be different from that of the Kennedy and Johnson years, but the dangers were the same.[77]

Buying Time

The Nixon administration's effort involved a multitracked process of talking and fighting that the president characterized as the pursuit of "peace with honor." The fighting dominated most of the two and a half years after Nixon's election. There was, however, an important difference from the 1960s. In early June 1969, Nixon met with President Thieu on Midway Island and announced that the United States would begin withdrawing American troops from the South. The withdrawal would continue over the next four years in irregular increments. In the meantime, the scale of violence, especially in the air war, was increased as virtually all target restrictions were removed and reports of American air attacks on civilian targets proliferated. Moreover, a secret air war was opened against North Vietnamese supply areas in Cambodia, the reporting of which by the White House and Defense Department to the Congress and the American people was systematically distorted and covered up to hide its existence.

The land war was also expanded before American troop levels were reduced to levels that would be prohibitive of offensive ground action. Most spectacular was the invasion of Cambodia by American and South Vietnamese in the spring of 1970. This was followed by an invasion of southern Laos by South Vietnamese troops with American air support in February 1971. The Cambodian invasion could claim some success in that significant North Vietnamese and Viet Cong supplies were captured. On the other hand, the much-heralded command headquarters for the communist military effort in the South was not found, and large concentrations of communist troops were neither located nor destroyed.

North Vietnamese and Viet Cong capacity for waging offensive war in the South appeared to have been weakened somewhat by the Communists' Tet casualties and Nixon's actions, but their capacity to continue the war was by no means broken by these efforts. The Communists' reaction during this period of expanded American military activity was like that which they had exercised in the past. When the military pressure increased, they would simply avoid contact as much as possible. It was clear that it was only a matter of time before an active American ground effort would be precluded by reduced American troop levels. It was also apparent that the antiwar sentiment in the United States was undiminished. In fact, the antiwar movement was at its height during the first two years of the Nixon administration, with massive demonstrations in Washington and sometimes violent protest throughout the United States. These protests culminated in the tragic and cathartic events following the Cambodian invasion as four Kent State University students were shot to death by the Ohio National Guard, followed by an assault on a dormitory at Jackson State University in Mississippi in which two students were killed. Following these events, militant antiwar activity did drop off, although there was a notable increase in general antiwar sentiment nationwide. By early and mid-1971, sizeable portions of the American people — in excess of 60 percent — could be found consistently opposed to the war, now believing that it had been a mistake in the first place, and not believing that the Nixon administration was being truthful concerning plans for ending the fighting.[78]

Conversely, Nixon's expansion of the war did accomplish the end of neutralizing criticism of him from the right insofar as he had taken actions that they had advocated throughout the middle and late 1960s. Furthermore, Nixon allowed ongoing "protective reaction" air strikes against the North and approved the undertaking of a dramatic but fruitless raid on the Son Tay POW camp in North Vietnam. This kind of escapade had marginal impact on the military situation, but, as the White House saw it, it was great "theater" and held a feared segment of public opinion at bay.[79]

By roughly the middle of his first term, therefore, Nixon had mollified the right with his willingness to employ and even escalate the level of violence in Vietnam. The costs were enormous as American battle deaths continued to rise, though at a slower rate, toward the fifty-thousand mark. Vietnamese casualties and refugees increased by hundreds of thousands, and yet another Southeast Asian society and political system — Cambodia — disintegrated under the impact of an expanded war. By 1975, some 700,000 Cambodians had died and more than 250,000 tons of bombs had been dropped. From 1970 to 1975, nearly half the Cambodian population, some 3,389,000 people, had been made homeless by the war; which, to use Nixon's words of July 1, 1970, was waged to secure "Cambodia's chances of surviving as a neutral country."[80] Nixon was able, however, to defuse pressure from the left by changing and eventually ending the Selective Service System while initiating aggressive disruptive action against the antiwar left including surveillance, infiltration, and the use of the Justice Department under Attorney General John Mitchell to initiate numerous conspiracy cases against the leadership of the antiwar movement. None of these cases were ever won by the Justice Department. Nevertheless, as long as the antiwar left was tied up in litigation, it was not in the streets. Antiwar sentiment was rising in Congress, but the slow and incremental nature of congressional action directed against the war gave Nixon room and time for maneuver. Finally, Nixon's "middle America" seemed numb and willing to wait. They would not wait forever, however, and 1972 was approaching.

"Peace with Honor"

By the end of 1970, it was not inconceivable that the fighting could remain indefinitely stalemated. American ground forces were approaching a level one half of that of January 1969, or about 270,000 to 300,000 men. This reduction in American offensive military capability had been offset somewhat by increased air power. Nixon, however, had set in motion a process of withdrawal that would be virtually impossible to stop or reverse in terms of his domestic support. Moreover, continued escalation of American air power was not an indefinitely viable posture, for the North Vietnamese air defense system guaranteed that the number of American prisoners of war would increase.

But there was no certainty as to whether the South Vietnamese could stand without American support. Vietnamization was receiving optimistic evaluations, but vast uncertainty remained. The problem, then, was to extricate the remaining American forces yet leave behind a politico–military framework that would allow the South Vietnamese an opportunity to survive. At a minimum, Nixon would need a "decent interval" between United States withdrawal and a communist takeover in the South. That is, assuming the worst, the "loss" of the Saigon regime, it was essential that it not appear that the United States was responsible. If it could be argued that the good doctor had done all that he could and the patient died anyway, the expected international losses could be minimized. If the death could be delayed until after the 1972 elections, it would not matter domestically. If the patient lived, this would be a bonus from the standpoint of American policy, but it was not essential. All that was essential was that America's international interests and the Nixon administration remain alive.

The obvious way to go about building a real or at least an apparent continuation of stalemate by proxy or, at a minimum, a decent interval was through the Paris negotiations. The talks, however, had been deadlocked since 1969. The United States was calling for a cease-fire in place, a timetable for withdrawal of all foreign forces from the South, and the release of American POWs. Hanoi, on the other hand, refused to acknowledge that it had forces in the South and demanded as a precondition the removal of the Thieu regime in Saigon.[81] In other words, little had changed since Nixon entered office.

In May 1971, Kissinger sought to initiate movement on the diplomatic track in elaborately arranged and protracted secret talks with the North Vietnamese. The American position, in private, was agreement to a deadline for U.S withdrawal in exchange for the release of American POWs. In public, Nixon was dramatically refusing to set any deadline until all POWs had been released and emphasized "mutual withdrawals." But in private, Kissinger was ambiguous on this issue. The North Vietnamese did not reject the Kissinger proposal out of hand and continued the secret contacts throughout the summer of 1971. In September, however, they rejected the proposal. The United States responded with further secret proposals, which included having Thieu step down just before new elections were held in the South. The elections were to be supervised by an independent body. Finally, the NLF would be represented in overseeing the elections.

Nixon was now entering the election year with American forces significantly reduced but no peace agreement. To counter anticipated pressure from the left concerning his lack of peace efforts, he made a dramatic television revelation in January 1972 of the secret talks and the American proposals. The Nixon speech opened a round of public and private invective between the United States and the North Vietnamese. Nevertheless, the secret contacts were reestablished even as the North launched an Easter offensive, which succeeded in capturing the northernmost province of South Vietnam and seriously threatening Hue. During the battles that broke out all over South Vietnam, it became clear that the South Vietnamese army was not yet fully able to stand before the North Vietnamese without massive U.S. air support.

Nixon and Kissinger now turned to the use of other secret channels to the North, specifically the Russians. In a secret meeting with Brezhnev in April, Kissinger "produced what probably was the first major turning point in the history of Vietnam negotiations."[82] Kissinger informed Brezhnev that the United States was willing to allow the North Vietnamese to keep in South Vietnam those forces that were there prior to the Easter offensive. At the same time, however, Kissinger linked the offer to a North Vietnamese agreement not to demand the removal of Thieu prior to any agreement. During these negotiations, Nixon's public stance on these questions remained ambiguous. Moreover, the United States throughout all these negotiations had not consulted the South Vietnamese.

In the meantime, Nixon decided — despite the upcoming summit meeting with the Russians concerning strategic arms limitations — to punish the North Vietnamese for their spring offensive by resuming massive bombing of the North and, on May 8, 1972, by mining Haiphong harbor. It was a serious gamble, for it was conceivable that the Russians would cancel the summit and the excruciating process of negotiating the SALT agreement would be lost. The decision split the administration, but the Russians did not break off their negotiations with the United States. It was clear that their own interests came before those of their socialist brothers in Hanoi, and, in fact, they might be willing to help their common capitalist adversary out of the Vietnam swamp if the United States could provide needed trade and technology.

During the summit of late May 1972, Kissinger made more concessions to the North Vietnamese concerning political power sharing in the South. The United States was simultaneously pounding the North Vietnamese with the stick of American air power and offering them concessions that very nearly brought the American position in line with that of the North Vietnamese. Only the problem of the survival of the Thieu regime remained, and Kissinger took this up with Zhou Enlai during his secret visit to Beijing in mid-June. Zhou was reluctant to press Hanoi, but, according to one report, there were indications that the Chinese passed the word to the North Vietnamese that they should not be so adamant about the removal of Thieu prior to an agreement.[83]

Kissinger was now confronted with the problem of informing Thieu that he had been bargaining over his destiny for the preceeding year without consulting him. The meeting was held in mid-August. Kissinger insists that he provided Thieu with a full disclosure of the negotiations and that he "played with the idea" of a diversionary invasion of the North but asserts that both he and Thieu recognized that this was "a gimmick not a strategy."[84] Other analysts claim that these talks were a throwback to the end of the Korean War twenty years earlier, with Kissinger making extravagant but gossamer promises to Thieu that after Richard Nixon had been reelected it would be a different story. Any concessions that the United States might be making were, he implied, necessary because of the domestic political situation. The United States, he said, "would not hesitate to apply all its power to bring North Vietnam down to its knees,"[85] including the suggestion that Thieu begin preparations for an invasion of the North.

Perhaps Thieu was not "nonplussed" and baffled[86] by all this as some have reported, but even Kissinger concedes that very little was clarified by the negotiations. Confusion, he insists, was the result of diametrically different domestic positions now occupied by Thieu and Nixon: the former needing a continued and open-ended American presence; the latter committed to ending such a commitment. Kissinger now believes that unbridgeable cultural gaps existed between the allies and has tried to shift responsibility for subsequent misunderstanding onto Thieu.[87] Kissinger, for his part, probably intended leaving Thieu in as strong a military position as possible, but he was prepared to go forward with negotiations with Hanoi whether Thieu agreed or not. On the return flight to Washington, Kissinger reportedly remarked to his staff: "One thing is for sure: we cannot stand another four years of this. . . . So let's finish it brutally once and for all."[88]

Negotiations proceeded secretly with the North Vietnamese, and it was clear that agreement was within reach as Hanoi accepted the ideas advanced by Kissinger and Nixon through Moscow and Beijing, including acceptance of a continuation, in some form, of the Thieu government.[89] The news now had to be broken to Saigon, and General Alexander Haig was dispatched to tell Thieu, who adamantly opposed any arrangement that might lead to a coalition government that might undermine his position. Kissinger, desiring to maintain momentum, decided to press on without Thieu's concurrence, and, in October, achieved a breakthrough with the North Vietnamese, who nevertheless insisted that the agreements be initialed before the American election. The North Vietnamese, undoubtedly remembering the events of 1954 and 1955, sought to ensure the American commitment, fearing that after the election the Americans might renege. Kissinger agreed, but insisted that he would have to get Saigon's approval first.

Kissinger now flew to Saigon and met with Thieu between October 19 and 23. Thieu's fury was on this occasion unrestrained,[90] and he refused to agree to the arrangements worked out by Kissinger. Kissinger was compelled, therefore, to cancel his planned trip to Hanoi for the signing of the agreement and return to the United States. However, presidential politics remained paramount. Therefore, Kissinger announced, on October 26, that "peace is at hand," although he knew that this was simply not the case. If anything, it seemed farther away than ever. In the meantime, Hanoi, fearing that it was being used by the Nixon administration for domestic political purposes, announced publicly the terms of the agreement.

Kissinger returned to Paris with a list of South Vietnamese objections, which he read into the record. Kissinger insists that this was done primarily for appearance's sake, but he probably underestimated the North Vietnamese sensitivity to the delay even as he had underestimated Thieu's recalcitrance. By December 1972, the North Vietnamese began to display reluctance to proceed. They suggested changes in the agreement in mid-December, and Kissinger publicly denounced their action as "perfidy." Two days later, Nixon ordered "Operation Linebacker II," which included massive bombing of Hanoi and the rest of North Vietnam. William Saxbe, Republican Senator from Ohio and soon to become Nixon's fourth attorney general, guessed, along with many others, that Nixon had "lost his senses."[91] Reports of civilian casualties occupied the front pages of the world's newspapers,[92] but the attacks continued. Marvin and Bernard Kalb report one of their sources who reviewed the situation later as saying:

> Look, we were in an embarrassing situation. Could we suddenly say we'll sign in January what we wouldn't in October? We had to do something. So the bombing began . . . [it] creat[ed] the image of a defeated enemy crawling back to the peace table to accept terms demanded by the U.S. Maybe the bombing had some effect . . . but the B-52's weren't critical.[93]

On January 13, 1973, the North Vietnamese agreed to sign the agreements reached in principle months earlier. Thieu, now satisfied that the North had been seriously weakened and mollified by the American show of force, finally went along, and the negotiations were concluded on January 27, 1973.

Concluding Observations
on Leaving Swamps

In reviewing this final phase and termination of direct American combat involvement in Vietnam, one is taken back to 1953 when the United States sought to extricate itself from another Asian war fought to preserve the concept of containment. In both instances, the final agreement confirmed an existing stalemate. In both instances, the final agreement was delayed and very nearly precluded because of the actions of America's client. And in both instances, American firepower brutally savaged the negotiating adversary partner during the denouement of the bargaining process. In the Vietnamese case, this fact is especially tragic, for the Christmas 1972 bombings of Hanoi resulted only in part from anything the North Vietnamese had done. In no small measure, Hanoi was attacked because Henry Kissinger misjudged Thieu's willingness to accept cavalier treatment at Kissinger's hands.[94]

The question of whether the 1972 Christmas bombings could have been avoided raises the question of whether, for that matter, the violence of the preceding four years was necessary. It must have been known that the North Vietnamese would never leave the South. Why should they surrender in negotiations that which they had not been forced to surrender on the battlefield? The negotiation of peace treaties and postwar settlements seldom do more than ratify what has been wrought by the course of battle. If this is the case, it would follow that Nixon continued fighting for many of the reasons the United States entered the conflict in the first place.

The Nixon administration knew that North Vietnam and the NLF could not be defeated, that they could only be stalemated. But Nixon and Kissinger also believed that if an approximation of the Paris agreements of 1973 had been signed in 1969, the Saigon regime would have fallen quickly, thereby threatening the Nixon administration, the security of which we have since learned was an ultimately all-consuming obsession. The Nixon administration felt it could no more afford to "lose" Vietnam than could its predecessors. The survival of the Nixon administration is properly emphasized, we think, because, by their own perception and prescription concerning the international system, many if not most of the conditions of international politics that required a display of will and commitment in 1961 through 1965 and 1966 were no longer relevant in 1969. The Nixon administration heralded the advent of a new era of negotiations in 1969; why, then, not negotiate in 1969? The answer would seem to lie in Nixon's fear of the domestic consequences of the Viet Cong flag going up over Saigon while he was running for reelection in 1972. For this reason, then, the land and people of Vietnam were pulverized for four more years.

The style of the diplomacy leading to the Paris agreements is revealing. Throughout the process, Nixon maintained a public position that was at best ambiguous and frequently contrary to the position adopted in private by Kissinger.[95] To have revealed the positions being set forth by Kissinger not only would have enraged Saigon, which, like the American people, was kept in the dark, it also would have enraged those McCarthyites whom Nixon was so responsible for and yet so afraid of. Nixon was, after all, bargaining away many of the points over which the war had been stalemated for years. In the end, Thieu was enraged anyway, but his anger could be assuaged with the Christmas bombing of the North and the promise of increased military and economic assistance. The remnants of the McCarthyite segment of American public opinion could not, it was thought, be so easily bought off.

In fairness to the Nixon administration, it should be emphasized that they also feared that the appearance of a "loss" in Vietnam could severly limit their freedom of action in pursuing the other dimensions of the Nixon Doctrine. The opening of relations with China and the negotiation of significant arms control agreements with the Soviets was undoubtedly seen as requiring a good deal of support from the American people. If the potential for a right-wing backlash was as great as the Nixon administration seemed to fear, a bitter national debate over who "lost" Vietnam had to be avoided if the other pressing business of building Nixon's vision of world order was to go forward. Thus the larger vision of world order could be used to justify the further destruction of Vietnam, and gave the insurance, if brutally purchased, that Nixon thought he needed.

There may be one additional tragic irony in all of this. In view of the large body of opinion against the war by the middle of the Nixon administration, one wonders whether the potential for the backlash was real or, if real, as substantial as Nixon seemed to imagine. If, as Gelb suggests, domestic opinion had turned decisively against the war, the much-feared backlash was a figment of the imagination of an administration that, as the Watergate affair demonstrates, was almost paranoid about its public image. To the extent that the four years of war under Richard Nixon were conceived and prosecuted to anticipate a public opinion threat that existed primarily in the mind of Richard Nixon, these were the cruelest years of the war.

Thus, as it began, the direct involvement of the United States in Vietnam ended with Vietnam and the Vietnamese people being used as pawns in a much larger game. There was a new international system to be ordered and maintained. The dynamics of strategic weapons development set in motion by the Cuban missile crisis culminated in the early 1970s in rough strategic parity between the United States and the Soviet Union. The SALT agreements were by and large an effort to institutionalize this parity and make predictable the future growth of strategic arms. The Sino–Soviet split seemed irremediable and opened up possibilities for a new kind of balance of power diplomacy. Finally, the emergence of new and barely understood transnational economic forces could not be ignored. Tad Szulc reports that, during the Paris negotiations, "a senior White House official remarked . . . [that] Vietnam was a 'cruel side show' in the Administration's new world wide policies."[96]

For a short while, the war in Southeast Asia receded from the American consciousness, replaced by the drama of Nixon trying desperately to save his presidency from the spreading stain of Watergate. (Ironically, many of the Watergate horrors came about as a result of Nixon's efforts to protect his policy in Southeast Asia from domestic dissent.) The military situation remained stalemated throughout 1974. By early 1975, however, the new Ford administration was calling for emergency assistance from Congress as signs of increasing North Vietnamese pressure began to appear. In mid-March, the South Vietnamese undertook a poorly planned and poorly executed withdrawal from the strategic central highlands and thereby initiated massive panic and refugee flights into the Saigon area and the loss of hundreds of millions of dollars' worth of equipment. In the meantime in Cambodia, Communist-led Khmer Rouge forces completely surrounded and cut off the Cambodian capital of Phnom Penh; on April 17, 1975, the American-backed government surrendered. Four days later, President Thieu resigned in Saigon and angrily denounced the United States for reneging on secret promises made by the Nixon administration at the time of the Paris agreements. Thieu (with a sizeable sum of American dollars reportedly on deposit) went into exile in Taiwan.

A week later, the surrender of Saigon was negotiated between South Vietnamese officials and the Communists. For the United States, however, the last week of the American presence was marked by the tense withdrawal, often under North Vietnamese fire, of thousands of Americans from Tan Son Nhut Air Base, as South Vietnamese who had associated themselves with and, in some cases, profited from the American war effort desperately sought a way out of the country. By April 29, 1975, the air base had been closed, and a thousand remaining Americans and 5,500 South Vietnamese whose lives were assumed to be in danger had to be evacuated by helicopter from the grounds of the U.S. embassy to aircraft carriers in the South China Sea. In the process, yet another four American Marines lost their lives, the body of one being left behind in the frantic last moments of the evacuation.

At home, the long-feared wave of recrimination did not occur. The American people met the final unravelling of South Vietnam with an almost fatalistic detachment and some skepticism concerning the arrival of thousands of South Vietnamese refugees in the United States. Indeed, if there were signs of recrimination, they came from the Ford administration, as it tried to shift responsibility for the final collapse of Vietnam to Congress.[96] But even though one additional Southeast Asian domino — Laos — fell and Thailand and the Philippines seemed to wobble noticeably as they announced a reassessment of their relationship with the Asian communist powers in mid-1975, there was no hysteria or, for that matter, outward concern on the part of the American people. After all, the Nixon Doctrine itself was based on a similar reassessment, and, even more important, as public opinion analyses during the early 1970s revealed, the American citizenry was not the fickle, belligerent, and vengeful monster prophesied in the conventional wisdom of the foreign policy elite that had managed the cold war. Rather, the American people were in many ways more open to change than the foreign policy community.[97]

NOTES

1. We are indebted for this metaphor to Carl Oglesby, "The Vietnamese Crucible," in Carl Oglesby and Richard Schaull, *Containment and Change* (New York: Macmillan, 1967), p. 3.
2. From John Galloway, ed., *The Kennedys and Vietnam* (New York: Facts on File, 1971), citing speech of June 1, 1956, p. 13. Reprinted by permission.
3. Ibid., pp. 14–15.

4. William Henderson, "South Vietnam Finds Itself," *Foreign Affairs*, Vol 35 (January 1957), p. 285.

5. George M. Kahin and John W. Lewis, *The United States in Vietnam*, rev. ed. (New York: Delta, 1969), pp. 100–102. An excellent recent history of U.S. involvement in Vietnam is Stanley Karnow's *Vietnam: A History* (New York: Viking, 1983).

6. "Resolution of the Third National Congress of the Vietnam Workers' Party on the Tasks and Line of the Party in the New Stage," quoted in ibid., p. 115.

7. Ibid., p. 119.

8. "1961 Rusk-McNamara Report to Kennedy on South Vietnam," *The Pentagon Papers* (New York: Bantam Books for *The New York Times*, 1971), p. 150. Hereafter cited as *Pentagon Papers*.

9. Ibid.

10. Ibid.

11. Leslie H. Gelb, "The Essential Domino: American Politics and Vietnam," *Foreign Affairs*, Vol. 50 (April 1972), pp. 459–475.

12. Arthur Schlesinger, Jr., *A Thousand Days* (Boston: Houghton Mifflin, 1965), p. 549.

13. Cited in Walter LaFeber, *America, Russia, and the Cold War, 1945–1971*, 2nd ed. (New York: Wiley, 1972), p. 244.

14. See Kahin and Lewis, op. cit., pp. 143–146 and *The Pentagon Papers*, pp. 158–233.

15. CBS Interview of September 2, 1963, *Department of State Bulletin*, Vol. 49, No. 1266 (September 30, 1963), pp. 498–499.

16. Quoted by Kenneth O'Donnell in "LBJ and the Kennedys," *Life*, Vol. 69, No. 6 (August 7, 1970), p. 51.

17. Ibid. (emphasis in the original), p. 51–52.

18. "McNamara Report to Johnson on the Situation in Saigon in '63," *Pentagon Papers*, pp. 271, 272, 274.

19. Neil Sheehan, "The Covert War and Tonkin Gulf: February–August, 1964," quoting the authors of the *Pentagon Papers*, p. 240.

20. " '64 Memo by Joint Chiefs of Staff Discussing Widening of the War," in *Pentagon Papers*, pp. 274–277, esp. p. 277.

21. "Draft Resolution for Congress on Actions in Southeast Asia," in *Pentagon Papers*, pp. 286–288, esp. p. 287.

22. Neil Sheehan, citing authors of the *Pentagon Papers*, p. 240.

23. Anthony Austin, *The President's War* (Philadelphia: Lippincott, 1971), pp. 182–183. See U.S. Congress, Senate Committee on Foreign Relations, *Hearings: The Gulf of Tonkin, the 1964 Incidents*, 90th Congress, 2nd Session, 1968.

24. Austin, op. cit., pp. 182–183. See also Captain Herrick's suggestion that a complete evaluation of the available information be undertaken before the U.S. responded, pp. 205, 292–293. See Admiral James Stockwell, "Another Gulf, Other Blips on a Screen," *Washington Post*, August 7, 1988, p. B7.

25. Tom Wicker, *J.F.K. and L.B.J.: The Influence of Personality upon Politics* (Baltimore: Penguin Books, 1972), pp. 224–225.

26. David Halberstam, *The Best and the Brightest* (New York: Random House, 1972), p. 414.

27. Tad Szulc, "Behind the Vietnam Cease-Fire Agreement," *Foreign Policy*, No. 15, (Summer 1974), p. 42.

28. Halberstam, op. cit., pp. 533–534.

29. Neil Sheehan, "The Launching of the Ground War: March–July 1965," quoting *Pentagon Papers*, p. 383.

30. "National Security Action Memorandum 328, April 6, 1965," in *Pentagon Papers*, pp. 442–443.

31. *The New York Times*, August 27, 1966, p. 10.

32. Lyndon B. Johnson, "Pattern for Peace in Southeast Asia," *Department of State Bulletin*, Vol. 41, No. 1348 (April 26, 1965), p. 607.

33. Ibid., p. 607.

34. Ibid., p. 608.

35. "McCone Memo to Top Officials on Effectiveness of the Air War," in *Pentagon Papers*, p. 441.

36. Press Conference of July 28, 1965, in *Public Papers of the Presidents, Lyndon B. Johnson, 1965*, Vol. 2 (Washington, D.C.: U.S. Government Printing Office, 1966), pp. 796–797.

37. Sheehan, "Launching of the Ground War," quoting the *Pentagon Papers*, pp. 416–417.

38. McNaughton Memo to Andrew Goodpaster on "Forces Required to Win," in *Pentagon Papers*, pp. 455–456.

39. See Fox Butterfield, "The Buildup: July 1965–September 1966," in *Pentagon Papers*, pp. 455–456.

40. "The Effects of U.S. Bombing on North Vietnam's Ability to Support Military Operations in South Vietnam: Retrospect and Prospect," August 29, 1966, quoted in *Pentagon Papers*, pp. 502–504, 506–507.

41. Hedrick Smith, "Secretary McNamara's Disenchantment: October 1966–May 1967," in *Pentagon Papers*, pp. 510–541.

42. Ibid., pp. 524–535.

43. U.S. Congress, Senate Committee on the Judiciary, Hearings Before the Subcommittee to Investigate Problems Connected with Refugees and Escapees, *War-Related Problems in Indochina, Part 1, Vietnam*, 92nd Congress, 1st Session, 1971, pp. 1–3.

44. *The New York Times*, February 22, 1974.

45. Arthur Westin and E. W. Pfeiffer, "The Cratering of Indochina," in Herbert F. York, *Arms Control: Readings from Scientific American* (New York: Freeman, 1973), p. 329.

46. Ibid., p. 338.

46a. See Bob Brewen, *Vietnam on Trial: Westmoreland v. CBS* (New York: Atheneum, 1987). McNamara's testimony was presaged by his pretrial deposition reported in the *New York Times*. See footnote 48 infra.

47. Halberstam, op. cit., p. 633.

48. Ibid., pp. 632–634. McNamara has recently and reluctantly began to break with his past practice of silence on the war. In a subpoenaed deposition in early 1984, Mr. McNamara described his growing skepticism concerning American policy: "I did not believe the war could be won militarily," he asserted. By 1965, he claims to have begun doubting the veracity of data on infiltration, casualties, and the utility of further escalation. See Charles Mohr, "McNamara on the Record, Reluctantly, on Vietnam," *New York Times*, May 16, 1984, p. A22.

49. E.W. Kenworthy, "The Tet Offensive and the Turnaround," in *Pentagon Papers*, pp. 589–612.

50. See Henry Kissinger, "The Vietnam Negotiations," in *American Foreign Policy: Three Essays* (New York: W. W. Norton, 1969), p. 107.

51. The list of "wise men" comprised a "Who's Who" of U.S. foreign policy. They included General Omar Bradley, McGeorge Bundy, Arthur Dean (Eisenhower's negotiator in Korea), Douglas Dillon, Associate Justice Abe Fortas, former Justice

Arthur Goldberg, Henry Cabot Lodge, John J. McCloy, former diplomat Robert Murphy, General Matthew Ridgeway, Maxwell Taylor, former Deputy Defense Secretary Cyrus Vance, and George Ball. The best accounts of the "great reversal" are in *The New York Times,* March 6, 1969, and March 7, 1969, in stories filed by Hedrick Smith and William Beecher.

52. Johnson, op. cit. p. 609.
53. See Arthur Schlesinger, Jr., *The Bitter Heritage: Vietnam and American Democracy, 1941–1966* (Boston: Houghton Mifflin, 1968).
54. Daniel Ellsberg, *Papers on the War* (New York: Simon & Schuster, 1972), pp. 42–135; and Leslie Gelb, "Vietnam: The System Worked," *Foreign Policy,* No. 3 (Summer 1971), pp. 140–167. Gelb's analysis of the war has been expanded in his 1979 book written with the assistance of Richard K. Betts, *The Irony of Vietnam: The System Worked* (Washington, D.C.: Brookings, 1979).
55. Johnson, op. cit., p. 607.
56. Quoted in *Pentagon Papers,* p. 255.
57. Kissinger, op. cit., p. 112.
58. LaFeber, op. cit., p. 255.
59. Arthur Schlesinger, Jr., "The Quagmire Papers (Continued)," *New York Review of Books,* December 16, 1971, p. 41; also cited by Ellsberg, op. cit., p. 124.
60. Lyndon B. Johnson, *Vantage Point* (New York: Holt, Rinehart and Winston, 1971), pp. 151–152.
61. Ibid.
62. Ellsberg, op. cit., pp. 100–127.
63. See Gelb's discussion of this point in "The Essential Domino," pp. 463–466.
64. Ibid., pp. 459–460. See also the assessment of this factor by an important American military historian of the war in Col. Harry Summers, *On Strategy: A Critical Analysis of the Vietnam War* (Novato, CA: Presidio, 1982), esp. pp. 9–80.
65. Ellsberg, op. cit., p. 124.
66. *Pentagon Papers* (original), Vol IV, pp. 615–616, quoted by Ellsberg, op. cit., p. 124.
67. See the editorial in *The New York Times,* May 15, 1968; and Kahin and Lewis, op. cit., pp. 379–390.
68. Kahin and Lewis, op. cit., pp. 386–388.
69. After the election, there were reports that Nixon had communicated through Mrs. Anna Chenault to the South Vietnamese that they should delay their participation until after the election. This could achieve what in fact happened during the last week of the campaign, confusion in the minds of those undecided voters who might have been moving toward Humphrey because of apparent movement toward peace. Presumably, the quid pro quo from Nixon would have been a promise from Nixon to Saigon that they would get a better "deal" from his administration than from Humphrey's. Theodore H. White, *The Making of the President, 1968* (New York: Atheneum, 1969), pp. 380–381, 383. Much of this speculation was subsequently confirmed by Mrs. Chenault in her memoirs, *The Education of Anna* (New York: Times Books, 1980). See also the review by Robert Shaplan, "A Somewhat Naive Dragon Lady," *The New York Times Book Review,* February 3, 1980, p. 12.
70. A bitterly critical account and analysis of the bombing and all of American policy toward Cambodia is in William Shawcross, *Sideshow: Kissinger, Nixon and the Destruction of Cambodia* (New York: Pocket Books, 1979). Kissinger defends himself in *White House Years* (Boston: Little, Brown, 1979), chaps. 7 and 12. An

account of the extent to which Kissinger wrote portions of his memoirs in response to Shawcross's attack can be found in Wolfgang Saxon, "Kissinger Revised His Book More Than He Reported," *New York Times*, October 31, 1979.

71. There is important new literature on this period that sustains this interpretation. See Larry Berman, George McT. Kahin, *Intervention: How America Became Involved in Vietnam* (Ithaca, N.Y.: Cornell University Press, 1986) and Kathleen J. Turner, *Lyndon Johnson and War* (Chicago: University of Chicago Press, 1985).

72. Bernard Fall, "The Theory and Practice of Insurgency and Counterinsurgency," *Naval War College Review*, April 1965, reprinted in Mark E. Smith, III, and Claude J. Johns, Jr., *American Defense Policy*, 2nd ed. (Baltimore: Johns Hopkins University Press, 1968), p. 272.

73. Kissinger, *White House Years*, pp. 229–230. For other indications of the administration's concern about domestic opinion as well as the constraints imposed by the bureaucracy, see pp. 260–261, 282.

74. Richard Nixon, *U.S. Foreign Policy for the 1970's: A New Strategy for Peace* (Washington, D.C.: U.S. Government Printing Office, 1970), p. 2.

75. Kissinger, *White House Years*, pp. 226–235. Kissinger's initial appraisal of the problem before the Nixon administration as it entered office.

76. Nixon, *U.S. Foreign Policy for the 1970's: A New Strategy for Peace*, p. 4.

77. Gelb, "The Essential Domino," pp. 471–472.

78. See Gallup Polls for February through August 1971, and Gelb, "The Essential Domino," p. 473.

79. Szulc, op. cit., p. 33. Szulc uses the term "theater" with respect to the peace talks during 1971 and 1972, but the concept clearly applies here as well.

80. Statistics and Nixon quote cited by Anthony Lewis, "A Successful Operation," *The New York Times*, February 6, 1975. See also Shawcross, *passim*.

81. Szulc, op. cit., p. 25; and Kahin and Lewis, op. cit., pp. 392–405. The following analysis is based primarily on Szulc's essential analysis of the development of the 1973 Vietnam peace agreement, Kissinger's *White House Years* and the highly critical study of Kissinger by Seymour Hersh, *The Price of Power: Kissinger in the White House* (New York: Summit, 1983).

82. Szulc, op. cit., p. 36.

83. Ibid., p. 45.

84. Kissinger, pp. 1321–1324, esp. 1324.

85. Szulc, op. cit., p. 46.

86. Ibid.

87. Kissinger, pp. 1325–1326. For a less flattering account of these meetings, see Hersh, op. cit., pp. 570–572.

88. Szulc, op. cit., p. 47. Kissinger's memoirs are silent on this point.

89. Hersh, op. cit., p. 583.

90. See Hersh's account, op. cit., pp. 593–595.

91. For a summary of some domestic and foreign press comment, see Marvin Kalb and Bernard Kalb, *Kissinger* (Boston: Little, Brown, 1974), pp. 416–417. But it is important to note that the bombing policy was Kissinger's as much as Nixon's. It was a version of the good cop–bad cop routine, wherein a criminal gets brutally harassed by one man and then his partner comes into the interrogation room and offers the dazed man a cigarette and says, "If you cooperate I'll see to it that the despicable first interrogator doesn't return."

92. A less damning account of the bombing—and one favorably cited by Kissinger—

is Guenter Lewy, *America in Vietnam* (New York: Oxford University Press, 1978), pp. 413–414.

93. Kalb and Kalb, op. cit., p. 422.

94. See Hersh, op. cit., pp. 583–585.

95. It is evident that there *were* serious disagreements between Kissinger and Nixon — largely the result of Nixon's envy of Kissinger's popularity and fears that Kissinger was exercising too much latitude in the negotiating process. Indeed, as election day approached, Nixon — secure in his lead over George McGovern — may have tried to delay the peace treaty until after the election to deny to Kissinger the satisfaction of having delivered the peace *and* the election. He seems also to have been concerned about the appearance of getting an agreement literally hours before the election. For an account of Nixon's ambivalence toward Kissinger and the bizarre, cynical court politics of the Nixon White House, see Hersh, op. cit., *passim*, but especially pp. 561–635.

96. Szulc, op. cit., p. 35.

97. See, for example, "CBS News Excerpts," in *Congressional Quarterly Weekly Report*, Vol. 33, No. 17 (April 26, 1975), esp. pp. 853–854, Murrey Marder, "Public Called Wary on Foreign Policy," *Washington Post*, September 11, 1975, p. A2; and Leslie H. Gelb, "Poll-Takers Say Most Americans Oppose Isolationism," *The New York Times*, September 11, 1975, p. 18.

Chapter 8
The Nixon
Doctrine
and Beyond

The Nixon–Kissinger stewardship of foreign policy liquidated the major source of domestic criticism for American foreign policy—Vietnam—but did not relinquish American global commitments, and Vietnam was the logical result of extended commitments. The Nixon Doctrine did not repudiate the premise of American policy since World War II; rather, it sought to avoid the logical implication of those premises—intervention on a grand scale. Maintaining the means and rebuilding the will to uphold commitments and sustain order while not succumbing to sustained conventional combat intervention was the preoccupation of the Nixon administration. In short, the Nixon Doctrine was not unlike the new look which sought to conserve containment but at a lower cost.

THE NIXON–KISSINGER DOCTRINE:
CONTAINMENT AND MANAGEMENT

The paradoxical nature of the Nixon Doctrine is heightened by the fact that Nixon heralded its promulgation with the assertion that the "post-war period in international relations had ended."[1] Purportedly, new opportunities had opened for negotiation and for the movement of Soviet-American relations to a basis other than the bitter and frequently awesome confrontations that marked the cold war. Yet, the president insisted that the United States would not abandon its commitments—commitments incurred during the period of confrontation. A new era of international politics had dawned. Nevertheless, threats to American interests persisted, although the nature of these threats was never clearly delineated.

Nixon saw the continued need for the "defense and development of allies and friends."[2] Now, however, the effort would be part of a system of shared responsibilities:

The United States will participate in the defense and development of allies and friends, but . . . America cannot—and will not—conceive *all* the
plans, design *all* the programs, execute *all* the decisions and undertake
all the defense of the free nations of the world. We will help where it
makes a real difference and is considered in our interest.[3]

Indeed, the concept of "interests" moved to the center of American policy
during the Nixon years: "We are not involved in the world because we
have commitments; we have commitments because we are involved. Our
interests must shape our commitments, rather than the other way
around."[4]

But what were American interests? None of Nixon's four major statements on U.S. foreign policy defined them in terms other than in Wilsonian rhetoric concerning a "generation of peace." Reference was made
to the "creative possibilities of a pluralistic world," but are we to assume that this meant the free play of American and communist ideology with their fundamentally antithetical views of the human condition
and potentiality?[5] "We seek a new and stable framework of international relationships," Nixon said.[6]

The framework that emerged was far more traditional than its Wilsonian rhetoric implied. Nixon foreswore mere balance of power politics as the ultimate form and substance of U.S. foreign policy.[7] In the
absence of the more stable order that his rhetoric referred to and the
persistence of perceived threats to American interests, it remained the
only prudent course. The policy framework that emerged was designed
to balance and constrain Soviet strategic power as well as to pull the
Soviets into a detente or easing of tensions within which the Soviets might
be schooled in the behavior, expectations, and obligations of great
powers.

At least three major elements of the policy framework developed
by Nixon and his special assistant for national security affairs and later
secretary of state, Henry Kissinger, require close analysis. First, they
negotiated directly with the Soviets to salvage and institutionalize the
balance of strategic power between themselves and the Soviet Union
that they found when they entered office. Second, there was a historic
opening of relations with the People's Republic of China, which, when
combined with the extraction of the United States from Vietnam, eased
the military demands on the United States in Asia. More important,
however, Sino–Soviet animosities could be used by the United States
to apply diplomatic pressure to the Soviets. Finally, there was the notion of detente itself. The Soviets were to be offered recognition of their
status as a great power as well as access to American capital, technology, and agricultural assistance if they would, in turn, relax their

revolutionary impulses and support for those in the Third World who pursued revolutionary change. At a minimum, it was hoped that a relaxation of tensions would allow for minimal strategic arms control.

Strategic Arms Control

The Nixon administration's approach to strategic arms control negotiations with the Soviets was conditioned by two concerns: (1) a perceived deterioration in the strategic balance and (2) the relationship between that balance and what was feared to be declining American political capability. Concern existed for stabilizing the arms race and perhaps ultimately even reducing the high levels of strategic arms possessed by the United States and the Soviet Union. The overriding concern of the Nixon administration, however, was that any arms control negotiations and agreements with the Soviets be consistent with and serve the broader strategic concept defined by Henry Kissinger:

> Throughout history the political influence of nations has been roughly correlative to their military power. While states might differ in the moral worth and prestige of their institutions, diplomatic skill could augment but never substitute for military strength. In the final reckoning weakness has invariably tempted aggression and impotence brings abdication of policy in its train. . . . The balance of power, a concept much maligned in American political writing — and rarely used without being preceded by the perjorative "outdated" — has in fact been the precondition of peace. A calculus of power, of course, is only the beginning of policy; it cannot be its sole purpose. The fact remains that without strength even the most elevated purpose risks becoming overwhelmed by the dictates of others.[8]

Thus, Kissinger's conception of the relationship between military power and diplomacy remained consistent with what he had set forth during the debate over Eisenhower's new look more than a decade earlier. Furthermore, as in the late 1950s, Kissinger was troubled by the seeming disjunction of military power and political influence in a nuclear age. Finally, the dilemma was seen as being made more complex because its resolution would have to be undertaken by the Nixon administration in a domestic context of intense upheaval and "at a moment when technology, combined with earlier deliberate decisions, was altering the nature of the strategic balance."[9]

The earlier decisions alluded to by Kissinger had been made during the Johnson administration in the mid-1960s. Specifically, then Secretary of Defense Robert McNamara had concluded that the buildup in strategic forces initiated by the Soviet Union in the wake of the Cuban missile crisis made it inevitable that they would achieve a degree of strategic parity with the United States. The Soviet Union, having begun to increase its numbers of land-based intercontinental ballistic missiles (ICBMs) and to expand its fleet of submarine-launched ballistic missile (SLBM)-carrying submarines, would achieve, perhaps within a decade, the capacity to devastate the United States in a nuclear war even if the United States struck the Soviet Union first. Similarly, if the Soviet Union attacked the United States first, the United States would be able to retaliate with devastating effects on Soviet society destroying perhaps one fourth to one third of the Soviet population and two thirds of Soviet industry.

McNamara decided that, in the face of this inevitable parity, it made little sense to keep expanding the number of ICBMs and SLBMs in the American force structure. McNamara reasoned that once the United States and the Soviet Union had achieved "mutual assured destruction" (MAD) capability, it was wasteful to continue expanding their respective strategic force structures.[10] Accordingly, the United States unilaterally stopped deploying ICBMs and SLBMs after 1967, thereby sustaining a strategic force structure of 1,054 ICBMs and 656 SLBMs as well as several hundred B-52 bombers. Presumably, such a step by the United States would offer the Soviets an incentive to halt their force structure expansion and provide a basis for a more stable strategic relationship.

At the same time, however, the Johnson administration, in response to bureaucratic pressures within the defense establishment and political pressures from Congress,[11] went forward with research, development, and testing of two new weapons technologies that could serve as hedges against an uncertain future. The first technology was an antiballistic missile (ABM) defense system designed to disable nuclear warheads launched against the United States. The Soviet Union had begun to deploy a limited and, according to American analysis, easily penetrated ABM system around Moscow in the mid-1960s. The pressure to emulate the Soviets grew into what one observer has described as "a wave of ABM hysteria."[12] The Johnson administration responded with a decision to deploy a limited system, although McNamara justified deployment primarily in terms of a defense against what was thought to be an emerging Chinese ICBM capability. The second technological development involved increasing the number of nuclear warheads that each American ICBM and SLBM could launch toward separate targets. These multiple independently targetable reentry vehicles (MIRVs) would, therefore, significantly increase the destructive capability of the American strategic forces, although the number of missiles or launch vehicles comprising those forces remained fixed at the number that existed in 1967. Thus, for example, a portion of the ICBM fleet — ultimately 550 — would carry three MIRVs, and some 496 of the SLBMs would be capable of carrying from ten to fourteen warheads.

Either of the new technologies, once incorporated into the Soviet or American force structures, would complicate the attainment and maintenance of the strategic stability to which McNamara aspired. ABMs were the more immediate problem, however, for, if an ABM system could be made to work, the side deploying the system would be able to remove the threat to its population posed by the other side's strategic forces. In the calculus of deterrence developed in the United States, this scenario could be destabilizing because the retaliatory threat of the non-ABM state would be neutralized, leaving it open to blackmail or attack by the side deploying ABM. Moreover, some deterrence theorists and planners feared that the side that saw itself falling behind in the race to develop and deploy an ABM might well decide to use its strategic capability *before* the other side deployed its ABM.

MIRVs were rationalized in the Defense Department in part as a counter to the Soviet ABMs. Thus, it was argued, the deployment of hundreds if not thousands of additional warheads by the United States would allow the United States to overwhelm any ABM system that the Soviets might deploy. On the other hand, if the United States began testing and ultimately deployed MIRVs, was it reasonable to assume that the Soviets could accept a strategic relationship in which they did not also have their own MIRVs? Perhaps, therefore, MIRVs — and thus a further escalation of offensive arms development — could be headed off by an agreement to ban the deployment of ABMs. In fact, the Johnson administration initiated negotiations with the Soviet Union on precisely this point in early 1967 and again at the meeting between President Johnson and Premier Kosygin at Glassboro, New Jersey. The Soviet invasion of Czechoslovakia in early 1968 led to the termination of these initial attempts at strategic arms limitation talks (SALT) and to the development of the American ABM system. Meanwhile, the testing of MIRVs went forward, leaving to the Nixon administration the decisions concerning their deployment and the future of SALT.

For the Nixon administration, however, the primary question to be addressed was the appearance of a deteriorating strategic balance of forces between the Soviet Union and the United States resulting from the decision by the Johnson administration not to expand the number of American ICBMs and SLBMs even as the Soviet buildup continued. By 1969, the quantitative parity projected by McNamara was fast becoming a reality (see table 8-1). Notwithstanding the successful flight-

TABLE 8-1. Historical Changes in Strategic Forces, 1962–1970

		1962	1963	1964	1965	1966	1967	1968	1969	1970
USA	ICBMs	294	424	834	854	904	1054	1054	1054	1054
	SLBMs	144	224	416	496	592	656	656	656	656
	Bombers	600	630	630	630	630	600	545	560	400
USSR	ICBMs	75	90	190	224	292	570	858	1028	1513
	SLBMs	some	107	107	107	107	107	121	196	304
	Bombers	190	190	175	160	155	160	155	145	140

Source: The Military Balance 1975–1976; 1977–1978; 1979–1980; 1980–1981 (London: International Institute for Strategic Studies, 1975, 1977, 1978, 1979, and 1980). Reprinted by permission.

test of MIRVs in 1968 — which, when deployed, would expand significantly the capability of American launch vehicles — the fixed number of American launchers standing in contrast to a rapidly expanding Soviet force was a concern of Nixon and Kissinger. Moreover, if the numbers of larger Soviet launch vehicles continued to grow significantly beyond the parity point of 1968 and 1969, and those launchers were subsequently augmented by Soviet MIRVs, then some portion of the American retaliatory capacity might conceivably become vulnerable. Finally, apart from MIRVs, the United States could do little to redress the image of a deteriorating quantitative balance except to build more of the smaller (though technologically superior) Minuteman missiles, given the fact that a new American ICBM would take years to develop, test, and deploy.

By early 1969, the Nixon administration was confronted by growing pressure, especially in the Senate, for a unilateral American decision against the deployment of ABMs. Popular opinion in the cities picked in 1967 to be deployment sites for ABMs was opposed to deployment, and scientific opinion on the feasibility of the system was deeply divided. But Nixon and Kissinger did not want to give up the ABM without some concession from the Russians in return. Thus, the Nixon administration, while shifting the deployment of the ABM to defense of ICBM sites (generally located in the less populated areas of the Midwest), announced that the United States would go forward with the system — a decision sustained by a one-vote margin in the Senate in August of 1969. The administration had begun, therefore, to regard ABMs and MIRVs as bargaining chips to be used in the upcoming SALT negotiations, which the Russians had agreed to resume in November of 1969.

The Nixon administration's concept of SALT was grounded, therefore, in the view that a strategic arms control agreement with the Soviets might accomplish a slowing of the momentum of Soviet strategic force expansion and perhaps establish a more predictable and stable strategic relationship with the Soviet Union. Kissinger's negotiating strategy was to offer to limit ABM deployment in exchange for a freeze on further strategic force expansion during the life of the agreement, which was to run for five years. By the time the agreement was completed in 1972, the Soviets had achieved higher force levels than the United States in both ICBMs and SLBMs. But the superior quality of American strategic forces and the very large number of long-range bombers in the American arsenal were viewed as off-setting the quantitative advantages of the Soviet Union. The American advantage with respect to MIRVs was crucial in this accounting, because the ability of the United States to place accurate multiple warheads on its missiles meant that despite the greater number of Soviet missiles allowed under the agreement, the United States retained a significant advantage in the number of more effective warheads.

No less important than the force levels negotiated in the agreement, however, the Nixon administration was able to guarantee that the Soviets would not deploy any more strategic weapons than they had been planning to deploy as of 1972.[13] At the same time, the United States was not required to sacrifice any of its programs directed at offensive force expansion. The Soviets, for their part, retained the option to develop MIRVs in the future and achieved formal recognition by the United States that they had indeed reached a degree of parity with the United States.

Critics of SALT in the United States insisted that the Soviets had achieved a great deal more as well. Senator Henry Jackson (D., Wash.) quickly became the leader of a large group of Senate critics of SALT who insisted that the agreement confirmed in its freeze on the force structures in place in mid-1972, a substantial Soviet superiority, especially in a class of a very large Soviet ICBMs known as the SS-9. Although the agreement on limiting offensive weapons froze the number of SS-9s allowed the Soviets at approximately three hundred, Senator Jackson argued that if and when these large ICBMs were eventually married to accurate MIRVs, they might well make vulnerable the smaller number of American ICBMs. Thus, the quantitative advantages in large ICBMs and SLBMs conceded to the Soviets merely institutionalized the appearance of greater Soviet dynamism — a condition that, in the view of Jackson and a growing number of critics in the Congress and among conservative defense analysts, would ultimately be used by the Soviets for their political advantage. Accordingly, Jackson demanded during the Senate debate on the agreements that the administration negotiate equal ceilings on strategic systems as well as pursuing limitations on qualitative developments. The latter objective was already a primary element on the administration's agenda and, together with Jackson's demands, became the core of the next round of negotiations.

A second comprehensive agreement proved impossible to complete as Watergate plagued and truncated the second Nixon term. Gerald Ford was able, however, to initial an agreement with the Russians at Vladivostok in November 1974 that incorporated the principle of equal ceilings on strategic delivery vehicles (2,400) and the number of those vehicles that could be MIRVed (1,320). By that time, however, newer technologies developed by the two sides, and Ronald Reagan's conservative challenge to Ford, impinged on the negotiations, leading to a stalemate during the waning months of the Ford administration. SALT II, as it was now being called, became, therefore, the first item on the agenda of Soviet–American relations during the Carter administration.

In the meantime, the SALT process became the most tangible evidence of the Nixon administration's approach to preserving America's preeminent global role in the face of expanding Soviet strategic power and an American public grown ambivalent about an activist global role. SALT became, therefore, a process pursued not because it promised an end to or reversal of the dynamic of strategic arms development and certainly not because it promised any diminution of the American global role. Rather, the process promised a modicum of order and predictability in the ongoing interaction of Soviet and American strategic power.

The Opening to China

The restructuring of political and military order from American hegemony to a kind of duopolistic Soviet–American–managed global balance was a continuing process. It required the muting of strident ideological themes so that Soviet–American power and interest could face each other in a context uncluttered by emotionalism. Moreover, to the extent that a Soviet threat persisted, it was to be contained by drawing the Soviets' other rival, China, into a diplomatic and even strategic tripolar relationship. The administration's complex effort assumed that, once the American presence on the Asian mainland was reduced, America would be less of an anathema to Beijing than the Soviets were. During the late 1960s, the Soviets became the main enemy to the Chinese. The Soviets, in turn, found the Chinese to be a formidable ideological and diplomatic rival within the communist and Third worlds, with enormous territorial claims against the Soviet Union. Indeed, during the spring and summer of 1969, these territorial claims became a pretext for a series of Sino–Soviet border clashes along the Xinjiang province border and in the Amur River valley. A buildup of Soviet forces along these areas of the Chinese border undoubtedly deepened the Chinese sense of fear but also strengthened the hand of those within China who desired an opening toward the United States. The Nixon administration's response was an attempt to enlist the Chinese in its structure of world balance.

At the same time, however, improving Soviet–American relations could not help but concern the Chinese. For example, Soviet–American agreement on troop reductions in Europe could release Soviet military forces for the Sino–Soviet border. But insofar as the Chinese became more preoccupied with their northern borders, they would be less likely to fish in troubled waters beyond their southern and eastern boundaries. The American burden in Asia then might be transferred to others in the region. Brezhnev's summer 1973 journey to the United States was undoubtedly seen by the Chinese as a measure implicitly directed toward China. The Nixon policy, therefore, was in part to use the great Sino–Soviet dispute to retain American political, economic, and even military access to East, Southeast, and South Asia.[14]

The opening itself was developed over the course of the first two years of the Nixon administration, initially through indirect contacts.[15] On April 21, 1971, the Chinese extended a secret invitation to the United States asking that a personal envoy of the president be sent to Beijing to prepare the way for a formal reestablishment of contact between the United States and the People's Republic. Kissinger made the trip, and, within a year, President Nixon visited China for talks with Mao Zedong and Zhou Enlai. In a communique at the end of the visit, the United States affirmed that Taiwan was part of China and acknowledged that the peaceful resolution of the relationship between Taiwan and the People's Republic was a matter that they must decide for themselves. From the Chinese standpoint, however, these statements by the United States were not all that they might have hoped for. Substantively, the issue of American recognition of Taiwan remained, and this meant that, from Beijing's perspective, the crux of the problem of Sino–American relations also remained.

The Nixon administration, especially once the debilitating effects of Watergate set in, could never respond satisfactorily to this Chinese demand. The political support for full normalization was simply not available to a president fighting for his survival within eighteen months of the visit. Moreover, his successor, Gerald Ford, found himself locked in a bitter struggle for nomination with a representative of the right wing of the Republican party, Ronald Reagan, whose support for Taiwan was unqualified.

Apart from the significant psychological impact of the initiative, an air of unsubstantiality always existed about the China opening. It was, in a sense, all diplomatic nuance and no substance. From the administration's perspective, this was sufficient:

> Triangular diplomacy, to be effective, must rely on the natural incentives and propensities of the players. It must avoid the impression that one is "using" either of the contenders against the other; otherwise one becomes vulnerable to retaliation or blackmail. The hostility between China and the Soviet Union served our purposes best if we maintained closer relations with each side than they did with each other. The rest could be left to the dynamic of events.[16]

The Difficulties of Detente

The third element of the Nixon administration's foreign policy framework was ostensibly to complement the China opening. If the presidential visit to China was a stick to prod the Russians toward a more accommodating posture, detente was a carrot offered in reward for the move. Thus, as the SALT negotiations proceeded and were ultimately completed in 1972, the United States proffered agricultural sales (which proved disruptive to American food prices), credits, and the prospect of significantly increased trade. The latter inducements could not be delivered by the Nixon administration, however, for those in the congress suspicious of detente attached conditions to any trade liberalization that made the measures unacceptable to the Soviets. Specifically, Senator Jackson and others in the Senate and House were able to pass amendments to trade legislation that required the Soviets to liberalize Jewish emigration from the Soviet Union, before Moscow could benefit from more U.S. trade. Predictably, the Soviets regarded such conditions as interference in their internal affairs, and, consequently, the trade dimension of detente was never fully developed.

On the other hand, Soviet security concerns in Eastern Europe were given grudging recognition by the United States. In part, this was forced on the administration by West German acceptance in 1972 of the Central European status quo as the probable permanent outcome of World War II. All the same, this accommodation was granted reluctantly and incompletely. Something more than echoes of "liberation" and "rollback" lingered in Nixon's actions toward Eastern Europe. Thus, the Nixon visit to Rumania in 1969 left the Soviets furious for a year and probably stalled SALT negotiations.[17] And American diplomats continued saying that United States relations with Eastern European countries had nothing to do with the Soviet Union,[18] making it apparent that clear acknowledgment of the Soviet position in Eastern Europe was far form complete.

Similarly, funds for Radio Liberty and Radio Free Europe were sought at around $40 million a year. The existence of these organizations undoubtedly reflected bureaucratic politics, but they also suggested a less than complete acceptance of the internal structure of the Soviet empire. More direct evidence of this ongoing American reluctance finally to accept the outcome of World War II was to be found in the conditions the United States would impose on the comprehensive European security agreement sought by the Soviets during the 1970s and partially achieved in 1975, the Helsinki Accords. Specifically, the United States insisted that Eastern Europe be opened to Western cultural access. Such conditions were clearly unacceptable to a Soviet leadership that crushed the "Prague spring" and suffered Rumanian eccentricities only as long as Rumanian domestic life remained comfortably neo-Stalinist.

It was where spheres and interests overlapped outside Europe, however, the Soviet–American detente encountered its greatest difficulty. For its part, the Nixon administration used American power and diplomacy boldly to obviate any speculation that America was developing a "reputation for unsteadiness" or that the United States was becoming in Nixon's words, a "pitiful helpless giant." For example, North Vietnam was bombed and its harbors mined as part of a systematic escalation of violence to force American peace terms on a nominal ally of the Soviet Union and China. The boldness of the act was underscored by the fact that even as their ally was being pummelled, the Soviets and Chinese were being used as interlocutors between Washington and Hanoi.[19]

Again, in May 1975, as the American tragedy of Vietnam was ending, the Ford administration responded to the seizure of the American freighter *Mayaguez* by Cambodia with a dramatic show of force. Air attacks were initiated against Cambodia, and marines were landed on Koh Tang Island in the Gulf of Siam, where it was incorrectly assumed the American crew was being held. In contrast with the regular resort to diplomatic means when American fishing vessels had been seized, their crews beaten and even shot at off Ecuador, no diplomatic channels were used until after the show of force was completed. It mattered little, however, because the entire incident seemed a useful pretext to demonstrate that the United States would, in Henry Kissinger's words, maintain its "reputation for ferocity."[20]

Perhaps the most dramatic cases of colliding Soviet–American interests occurred in the Middle East. In that area, the Soviets were held responsible for disruptions of international order, while, at the same time, the U.S. tried to minimize Soviet influence. The schooling of the Soviet Union in the limitations of influence to be accorded to them by the United States was forceful and frequently undertaken without consultation with or the consent of America's allies, the Congress, and, in one instance, the Joint Chiefs of Staff.

In September 1970, American military might was displayed in an impressive effort to force the Russians to withdraw support from the Syrians when they moved tanks into Jordan to help the Palestinians against King Hussein. American troops were mobilized to intervene, but no congressional advice was sought, and objections of the Joint Chiefs of Staff, who opposed intervention on both political and military grounds, were overridden. No allies could be found to give American-based C-130's landing rights on their way to the Middle East. The Russians were warned of "the gravest consequences"[21] if the Syrian tanks did not desist. Kissinger told a tense, frightened Soviet diplomat, "The last time you told me that the Syrians would send no more troops."[22] The Russian minister councilor complained, "We didn't know the Syrians would cross the border, our own military advisers stopped at the border and went no further."[23] Kissinger retorted, "Your client started it, you have to end it."[24]

The episode has been described as another link in the chain of U.S.–Soviet confrontations, and the "management" of the "crisis" has been compared to Cuba.[25] The latter is overdrawn, inasmuch as Cuba involved a direct U.S.–Soviet confrontation. In contrast, the Nixon administration, in this instance, was instructing the Soviets in how to manage their clients and maintain stability.

> Nixon saw the situation in its broadest implications. Jordan to him was a microscopic spot on the map and yet he viewed it as having far-reaching implications on the world-wide stage and on American relations with the Soviet Union.
> The idea that Soviet–American relations must be viewed as a chain with each link representing a test of the validity of relations as a whole, was . . . uppermost in the President's mind.[26]

Once again in 1973, during the Yom Kippur War and two days after Egyptian and Syrian units moved on Israeli-occupied territory, Henry Kissinger pronounced that "we shall resist aggressive foreign policies. Detente cannot survive irresponsibility in the Middle East."[27] The news that the Soviet Union was actively encouraging other Arab states to join the conflict, the Soviet cargo planes were resupplying the Arab belligerents, and that Russian officers were leading Syrian tank columns again prompted the Nixon administration to point to the delicate linkages of detente. The expansion of trade and technological transfer crucial to the Soviets' pursuit of detente were pegged to their acting responsibly in restraining themselves from an urge to expand influence in the Middle East. American diplomats were given instructions that were unmistakable injunctions for the Soviets to realize the imperatives of detente. As one aide remembered, "We were told to tell the Soviets we hold them responsible for everything the Arabs do."[28]

American pressure was by no means confined to diplomatic remonstrances. As initial Arab military successes were checked by the Israelis in both the Sinai and on the Golan Heights between Syria and Israel, the Soviets proposed joint Soviet–American diplomatic and military intervention. The United States was prepared to undertake the former but not the latter because Kissinger feared that participation in the joint Soviet–American military force proposed by the Soviets would lead to a reestablishment of a strong Soviet presence in the region. When a United Nations cease-fire did not hold and the Soviet-backed Arab position began to deteriorate rapidly, the Soviets warned Washington that the Soviet Union was prepared unilaterally to prevent an Arab catastrophe. The United States reacted by placing American forces around the globe on alert and sternly warning the Soviets that the introduction of any troops into the area was unacceptable to the United States. The Soviets quickly backed away from the imminent confrontation with the United States, accepted a UN emergency force, and, more importantly, acceded to and ultimately lent some support to Kissinger's personal diplomatic effort to establish a cease-fire and develop a basis for some sort of permanent settlement of the Middle Eastern situation.

The Arab members of the Organization of Petroleum Exporting Countries (OPEC) introduced a new sense of urgency into the crisis by imposing an embargo on oil to Europe, Japan, and the United States, and demanding that Arab positions on the Arab–Israeli dispute be adopted in the West. The international oil distribution system ensured that the economic effects of the embargo did not affect any single importer inordinantly. Nonetheless, the Europeans and Japanese, being more dependent on Middle Eastern oil than the United States, shifted to a more accommodating position vis-à-vis the Arabs and, by and large, have remained so. By the late 1970s, this development would serve to introduce significant strains in the Atlantic alliance.

In the meantime, Kissinger not only succeeded in bringing about a cease-fire and disengagement of Arab and Israeli forces, but, through weeks of shuttling back and forth between Arab capitals and Israel in late 1973 and again in the spring of 1974, Kissinger firmly established the United States as the only mediator acceptable to the major parties to the Middle Eastern conflict. The Syrians remained dependent on the Soviets for military assistance but were nonetheless prepared to work with Kissinger in developing the cease-fire and disengagement agreements of June 1974. The Egyptians, having borne the brunt of four wars with Israel, became active and supportive participants in Kissinger's "shuttle" diplomacy. Kissinger's so-called step-by-step approach of dealing with immediate military problems and avoiding the deeper and more contentious issues of the establishment of a Palestinian state ultimately bogged down. In the interim, however, further recourse to military means was avoided; the United States was firmly positioned as inter-locutor between Egypt, the largest of the Arab states, and Israel; and, perhaps more important from the perspective of the Soviet–American relationship, the United States seized the diplomatic initiative and con-signed the Soviets to the sidelines.

By the same token, however, the Soviets were prepared to move in support of anti-American forces in Black Africa when the opportu-nity presented itself in southern Africa during the latter part of the Ford administration. From the outset of the Nixon administration, Ameri-can policy had been predicated on the assumption that the Portuguese colonial presence and the white regimes in Rhodesia and South Africa were likely to be permanent fixtures in the region. By 1974, however, the Portuguese presence had collapsed, a black nationalist regime had come to power in Mozambique, and civil war among competing na-tionalist groups raged in Angola. By 1975, a Soviet- and Cuban-backed group had emerged as the likely victor in the Angolan conflict. The Ford administration tried to extend U.S. assistance to competing insurgents but was blocked by overwhelming congressional votes against any fur-ther U.S. assistance to pro-Western Angolan insurgent groups. By early 1976, a Marxist regime was consolidating control of Angola. Meanwhile, Kissinger could only warn the Soviets that the structure of Soviet–Amer-ican relations was endangered by Soviet abuses of detente.

The Ambiguities of the Nixon–Kissinger Balance

The Nixon administration's effort to define a balance of power managed by means of Soviet–American condominial power, influence, and respon-sibility was asymmetrical at best, because it prohibited expansion of So-viet power and presence while demanding active Soviet cooperation. Indeed, in some instances, the Soviets were faced with the actual dimi-nution of their influence, as in the case of the Middle East, where Kis-singer's diplomacy was more or less successfully directed at undermining altogether what remained of Soviet influence in the area.

The Kissinger–Nixon policy in Asia was a variation on the theme of responsibility and order played in the Middle East. To no small extent, the Vietnam War was an effort to force the Chinese to control their purported clients, the NLF and Hanoi. The Chinese refusal to extend responsible authority south was a significant motivation for the American Vietnam adventure.[29] Under the Nixon administration, this ambition that the Chinese exert a conservative regional influence received some fulfillment. As a key member of the United States team that negotiated with the North Vietnamese, William H. Sullivan, pointed out:

> When President Nixon decided to put the mines into the harbors of North Vietnam on May 8, it produced a situation in which North Vietnam became one hundred per cent dependent upon China for the provision of its equipment. Everything coming from the Soviet Union had to transit Chinese territory. Nothing could go through the waters and come into Haiphong. . . . This means that China's preoccupation with Soviet encirclement came into play. This means that China's feeling that it would rather have four Balkanized States in Indochina rather than an Indochina that was dominated by Hanoi and possibly susceptible to Moscow, came into play.[30]

And, by early 1974, Chinese Premier Zhou was proclaiming publicly the end of Chinese assistance to insurgencies in Southeast Asia and was fretting publicly about Soviet influence in North Vietnam and among Thai insurgents.

A large part of the intellectual framework of this approach to foreign policy is found in the writings and thoughts of Nixon's and then Ford's principal adviser, Henry Kissinger. Professor Kissinger's major research was into the political prerequisites of international stability. To Special Assistant for National Security Affairs and Secretary of State Kissinger, it remained a universal principle that stability, not peace, is the hallmark of successful diplomacy.[31] In his view, the greatest contributors to international instability had been revolutionary powers: Napoleonic France in the nineteenth century, the Soviet Union in the twentieth. Revolutionary powers upset the established norms of governance because they refuse to accept the "legitimacy" of the international order, based on familiar, essentially conservative approaches to both international and domestic political life: order, stability, even hierarchy as the framework that "promotes social justice and human dignity." Yet now it appeared that, although the "Soviet Union is the greatest menace to peace," it could also be drawn into the international order. In short, revolutionary Russia could be instructed to become a status quo power as Britain was in the nineteenth century and as America has claimed itself to be in the cold war. As Kissinger explained:

> We are at a point where we can redefine the American position with re-
> spect to the world, where, for whatever reasons, it may be that even the
> Soviet Union has come to a realization of . . . the limits of . . . its ideo-
> logical fervor.[32]

A status quo power can be counted on to respond to the limited, rational demands of the balance of power. A status quo power can be
enlisted in the worldwide maintenance of order. In either condominium
or balance, the emphasis is to enlist the Soviets in achieving American
ambitions, which, it is argued in good Wilsonian fashion, are, in fact,
the "interests" of all.

But was all of this an accurate reading of Soviet interests and policy?
Skeptics argued that the Soviets could never accept such a vision. In
this dour view, the Soviets regarded the American pursuit of SALT as
but a demonstration that the historical "correlation of forces" was moving
against the West and that the West's pursuit of detente was only an
admission of the fact. From a Soviet standpoint, detente had the advantage of allowing them to consolidate these gains; but, in time, they
could be expected to continue exploiting the advantages conceded them
under SALT I and to redouble their support for revolutionary forces
in the Third World.[33]

However the Soviets perceived the historical dynamic, they did indeed take advantage of the latitude allowed them under SALT (as did
the United States). Moreover, when the opportunity presented itself,
through a combination of internal developments in southern Africa and
an American government distracted by Watergate and an anti-
interventionist reaction to Vietnam, the Soviets supported anti-Western
forces with military assistance or through their Cuban proxies. In this,
however, their behavior was consistent with American action in the Middle East.

Detente was characterized by this fundamental ambiguity: It was
heralded by Nixon as a relaxation of tensions tantamount to a new era
of international politics. Rhetoric aside, relations with the Soviet Union remained essentially competitive, and when, in time, the competitive essence of the relationship reemerged in the Middle East and in
Africa, public disillusionment invariably followed. Moreover, at that
juncture, those who had been arguing all along that the SALT process
was itself pernicious gained new credibility. Finally, when Ford was
confronted with a political challenge from the right wing of his own
party as he sought nomination in 1976, he felt compelled to move toward the policy positions of his adversaries. In the process, Ford pointedly forbade the use of even the word detente by members of his
administration.

THE LIMITS OF
TRIANGULAR BALANCE

The long-run vision of the international system that might emerge from the application of the Nixon–Kissinger and then Ford diplomacy was framed in the classic metaphors of diplomatic equilibrium and balance of power. As President Nixon remarked in early 1972, echoing Dr. Kissinger's doctoral thesis:

> We must remember that the only time in the history of the world that we have had any extended periods of peace is when there has been a balance of power. It is when one nation becomes infinitely more powerful in relation to its potential competitor that the danger of war arises. So I believe in a world in which the United States is powerful. I think it would be a safer world and a better world if we have a strong, healthy United States, Europe, Soviet Union, China and Japan, each balancing the other, an even balance.[34]

The U.S.–Soviet–Chinese dimensions of this vision were, as we have seen, assiduously developed by the president and Kissinger. Europe and Japan, on the other hand, never achieved comparable status in the "triangular diplomacy" of the Nixon Doctrine. Other problems existed as well. The developing world was also conspicuous by its absence in the framework of policy that developed, although — as was evident in Chile and Iran — the United States was prepared to intervene to destroy its ideological adversaries and support those who were prospective surrogates for American power. Moreover, the instruments of force encompassed by this concept of world order were and are increasingly problematic in their applicability. And, finally, domestic limits were inherent to the entire process.

Europe and Japan

There could be a Europe in the future that could control nuclear weapons and serve as a meaningful balance between the Soviets and America. There may be a nuclear Japan that could do the same. In the meantime, American policy did not push for the independence of Europe; the NATO alliance structure, its commitments, and obligations stood. The American–European relationship remained essentially one in which the Europeans were dependent on America for their security and open to U.S. economic access. How this political, military, and economic dependence could inspire a separate and credible European pole in the global balance was not explained.

Furthermore, not all Europeans seemed overly anxious to shed their military dependence for more strategic autonomy. Weapons technology is expensive, and Americans had always been willing, even aggressive merchants. The economies of Europe would be seriously distorted if they had to pay for large standing armies and significant production of military equipment. Indeed, to try to maintain the level of social services provided by most European governments as well as shoulder the added burden of a full defense budget would contribute to already painful European tax levels.

A credible European nuclear deterrent was at least conceivable, because both the French and English possess minimal nuclear systems, but they are somewhat incompatible technologically. More important, such a common defense policy would require that Europe's national forces first be merged and then managed by a political organization representing a "Europe" that does not yet exist. Finally, the thought of Germany with nuclear weapons or strong, more autonomous conventional forces, which would be a highly likely consequence of a military independent Europe, would be enough to give Europeans — East and West — considerable pause.

Even if a nascent Europe with marginal political and strategic independence is emerging, its interests will probably remain narrow and inner directed, too much so for the foreseeable future for Europe to serve as much more than a regional power. The task of political and economic integration is an immensely complex task. To be sure, many of the prerequisites of a European political economy were already in place, but others — a banking system, a European system of taxation, control of corporations, a European system of social welfare services, and above all, a strong, common political vision — are not present. Moreover, the global economic crisis brought on by the Arab exercise of their "petropower" in late 1973 and early 1974 demonstrated the vulnerability of European political and economic institutions dependent on external sources for more than 75 percent of their energy needs. In the Nixon-Kissinger years, Europe would not be concerned with Asia, or Latin America, or the Indian subcontinent, at least not in the sense that a fully dimensionalized balance of power anticipates. The global powers with global interest would still be the Soviet Union and the United States.

Neither could Japan then function as an independent and autonomous global power with global interests. Japan's increasingly global economic presence proved even more vulnerable than that of the Europeans; more than 90 percent of Japan's oil needs must be met with imports of petroleum from the Persian Gulf. By the mid-1970s, therefore, it was apparent that previous forecasts of an emerging political and economic East Asian "superstate"[35] required reevaluation. Japan's global military capacity is, to say the least, problematic. A nation that is constitutionally prohibited from using force as an instrument of policy is ill-suited to be a point of countervailing powers to the Soviets, Americans, Europeans, or Chinese. However, the Nixonian vision of a new balance of power sought to alter this situation. Even though Japan's geographical insularity gives it relative security from "conventional" aggression, Japan was increasingly encouraged to expand the definitions of its interest under pressure from the Nixon administration.

The Japanese had relied on the American nuclear umbrella and conformed to the rigid American policy toward mainland China despite much internal opposition and historic interest. When Nixon reversed American policy on China with no prior consultation with the Japanese, it was not only taken as an insult but also read as a humiliating incentive for Japan to elaborate an independent course toward China. A similar shock occurred when the Nixon administration sought unilaterally to force the Japanese to reverse their trading position with America by realigning the value of their currency. The heavy-handed import tariffs, quotas, and embargoes — combined with the decline of the dollar as a medium of international liquidity — were seen as another indication to the Japanese that they should start to make their own way. American policy under Nixon undermined the paternalistic relationship that had evolved from Japan's wartime defeat. The rather brusque treatment of Japan — a country where "face" is a national priority — served, however, to vitiate the surety of the American "nuclear umbrella." As Osgood relates: "Official statements suggest that Japan's nuclear abstention was contingent upon a confidence in the credibility of America's nuclear deterrence, which it no longer automatically takes for granted."[36]

The American effort to draw out the Japanese political and economic presence was designed to present both China and Russia with countervailing power in the Pacific — power that would not be directed against American interest in Asia. The extrusion of Japan could make it considerably less friendly toward the United States, but Japan's refusal to be so drawn could involve the Americans more than ever in guaranteeing stability in Asia and the Pacific. The consequence of commitments in Asia, pursued by the encouragement of expanding Japanese power and a new relationship with China, was and remains a problematic strategy undertaken in response to the costs of hegemonial power. The alternative of reexamining commitments and responsibilities in Asia seems to have been considered unwillingly if at all.

The Third World

The uncertainties surrounding the position of the Third World in the world balance were no less than those relating to Europe and Japan. If, for example, the Third World was to be stabilized by American management, the evidence of the Nixon–Kissinger–Ford years is mixed at best.

In the case of the Indo–Pakistani War of 1971, for example, the policy of great power management under American direction failed in almost every respect. In 1971, India had reversed its policy of nonalignment and signed a mutual assistance treaty with Russia aimed at the Chinese. In response, the Pakistanis and the Chinese became increasingly close, because both now feared the implied expansion of Indian power. It was also a time when the Americans were wooing China into a tripolar relationship. In this context, Pakistan, India's old rival, experienced a massive upheaval in her eastern wing, which was one thousand miles from dominant West Pakistan. East Pakistan exploded. An election that voted independence for the East was rescinded, and West Pakistani troops started to slaughter East Pakistani civilians in a barely concealed ethnic war. Despite an attempt to appear neutral, America sent arms to Pakistan, which was a member of the now defunct SEATO. A unified Pakistan was supported by the United States. The rebellion was not considered by the United States as merely an internal affair of Pakistan, but rather in terms of the regional and global balance of power. Although India was inundated with millions of refugees, American aid for refugee relief was little and late. Kissinger, on his way to China, stopped in Delhi and told the Indians that if they moved into Pakistan, China would move on India and the Americans would not help defend the Indians against the Chinese as they did in the Sino–Indian War of 1962.

Faced with the burden of supporting ten million refugees and tales of horror about the fate of the ethnically kindred people of Bangladesh, the Indians marched against Pakistan. It was India's opportunity to see that this old antagonist would be permanently weakened by a separation of its eastern province. Washington counted on the Soviets to restrain their new Indian clients. However, in spite of America's calculations, the Pakistani–Chinese and Indian–Russian balance served not to inhibit the conflict but to free India to move against Pakistan. The Nixon administration then proceeded to condemn the Indians in the UN for aggression and sent the nuclear carrier *Enterprise* in a barely disguised "Tilt" against India. The move failed. India achieved a spectacular military victory, capturing seventy thousand West Pakistani troops, and secured the independence of Bangladesh and the reduction of Pakistani power on its frontiers.[37]

Protestations by Nixon and Kissinger of their acceptance of "uncertainty or even turmoil . . . in the political flux which is likely to accompany growth"[38] in Africa proved no less problematic. The catalyst for greater American involvement in Africa[39] was the collapse of the Portuguese colonial presence and increasing pressure on the white regimes in Rhodesia and South Africa all within the context of increasing Russian activism in the area. During 1976, internal security within Rhodesia became increasingly tenuous as guerrilla activity expanded markedly. The South Africans, becoming alarmed at the growing threat to their north, proved supportive of an American–British diplomatic initiative late in the summer of 1976. Kissinger sought to replicate his Middle Eastern shuttle diplomacy successes by establishing himself as a mediator between the white regimes and the black governments in the region who were supporting black liberation efforts in Rhodesia. Kissinger tried to develop a framework for a gradual transfer of power from the white Rhodesian regime of Prime Minister Ian Smith to a black majority government. Despite some initial success, the initiative eventually died as the Ford administration was defeated for reelection and black resistance to the scope of white control during the proposed transitional period overwhelmed the negotiations in early 1977.

We cannot know, of course, whether a second Ford administration with Henry Kissinger as secretary of state would have proved more successful in resolving the fundamental political and racial issues that rent southern Africa than had Kissinger's diplomacy earlier in the Middle East. What is clear is that Kissinger's activism and diplomatic virtuosity were brought to bear only after the Soviet–American competition had become salient in the region. Moreover, Kissinger's declaration that American policy was designed to "achieve the great goals of national independence, economic development and racial justice" and that "white South Africa must recognize that the world will continue to insist that the institutionalized separation of the races must end" came only as a previous policy of support for European colonial rule and indifference or, at most, extreme gradualism toward ending white rule in South Africa, which was collapsing under the pressures of the black African liberation struggles.

In Chile, the administration was confronted with a constitutionally elected Marxist–socialist government under President Salvador Allende. Because Allende had not received an absolute majority of the presidential vote in September of 1970 (he received a plurality of 36 percent) his election by the Chilean congress was dismissed by Kissinger as a "fluke."[40] It was assumed that because he was a Marxist, he would set about the irreversible dismemberment of the Chilean democracy and become a base for communist subversion of the region.[41] Exactly what the United States did about this situation has been a matter of intense debate.[42] Kissinger concedes that the United States attempted to influence votes in the Chilean congress to prevent Allende's election, but he justifies the action as merely the continuation of the policies of past administrations at the time of the 1964 Chilean elections. More controversial is the extent to which the administration supported the attempts of International Telephone and Telegraph to bring down the government or whether the United States, after Allende's election, encouraged an invisible blockade of Chile through a tightening on Export–Import Bank loans and other forms of economic assistance. Money already authorized before Allende's election continued to flow to Chile, but new support from the United States, private bankers, and international agencies was restricted. On the other hand, the Allende regime's administrative capacity has been called into question as the basis for the development of internal conditions that made the country a poor credit risk for both governmental and nongovernmental financial institutions. It is worth noting, however, that poor administrative performance did not prove a sufficient basis for U.S. support to be withdrawn in other cases where the regimes in question were pro-American, such as the Mobutu regime in Zaire or the succession of American-sponsored regimes in South Vietnam.

In any event, economic conditions deteriorated within Chile throughout 1971 and 1972, and in a violent coup in September 1973, Allende was overthrown to be replaced by a military junta. Allende was killed — the junta has claimed by his own hand — and Chilean democracy was aborted. Subsequently, the junta's leadership undertook an international campaign of assassination of former officials of the Allende regime, including the car-bomb murder of Orlando Letelier, Allende's foreign minister, as Letelier drove along the streets of Washington, D.C. in 1976.

The character of American involvement in the descent of Chile into right-wing dictatorship remains somewhat obscure. Nonetheless, Kissinger has observed that "presidents of both parties have felt the need for covert operations in the gray area between formal diplomacy and military intervention throughout the postwar period."[43] Presumably, therefore, whatever the role of the United States in Chile, activity in this gray area remained an essential element of the Nixon administration's new framework for international order.[44]

The involvement of the Nixon–Kissinger–Ford administrations with the regime of Shah Mohammed Reza Pahlavi was a continuation of what had developed over the preceding three administrations. The Shah was regarded, in Kissinger's words, as "a friend of our country and a pillar of stability in a turbulent and vital region."[45] In sum, his regime was viewed as a surrogate for American power in the region, and it became the policy of the Nixon administration to provide the Shah with all the military assistance he thought he required for the pursuance of that role. Thus, by 1973, the Shah had placed orders, primarily with the United States, that would provide him with almost four hundred modern fighter-bombers including the F-14 fighter, over six hundred helicopters, more than fifty long-range transport aircraft, as well as maritime patrol air-craft. By 1974 to 1975, the Shah was placing orders for the most mod-ern United States Navy destroyers, hundreds of armored fighting vehicles, and still more fighter aircraft from the United States. By 1975, the Shah had spent in excess of $15 billion on arms purchases and had proclaimed a security mission for Iran that implied dominance of the region as well as responsibility for maintaining order in the northwestern Indian Ocean.[46]

Internally, the United States provided technical assistance and sup-port for the Shah's secret police, Savak. In return, the United States received permission to establish intelligence sites along the Iran–Soviet border, which provided significant access to Soviet missile testing as well as tactical weapons test ranges. But these benefits were not without their costs, for when OPEC began escalating the price of oil dramatically in 1975, the American dependency on its surrogate proved decisive. In-deed, by the late 1970s, allegations had become common that Kissinger had either tacitly accepted or had been blackmailed into accepting the price increases being proposed by America's ostensible ally, the Shah. The oil revenues were clearly necessary to pay for the massive arms im-ports. Moreover, the threat of closing down American assets in Iran was also available to Tehran. In any event, it is reported that Kissinger re-fused to support Saudi Arabian attempts to restrain the 1975 price increases.[47]

The pattern of American involvement in the Third World and its place in the larger framework developed during the Nixon–Ford years was uneven but still closely related to the larger concern with So-viet–American relations. That is, the countries of the Third World re-mained what they had traditionally been in American postwar policy: objects in a larger game, episodically important, but only insofar as they impinged on the traditional focus of the Nixon Doctrine. Yet, as has so often been the case since World War II, events on the periphery proved crucial to the development of American policy: Korea in the 1950s, Vietnam in the 1960s, and the Middle East in the 1970s.

The Limits of Force and Diplomacy

A further difficulty of the Nixon approach to a balanced world order was the problem of adapting force as an instrument of that policy. The difficulty with the use of force to maintain a balanced world order in the 1970s was that the consequences of large-scale intervention using conscript personnel had been shown to be unsuccessful and politically intolerable, especially in conflict situations requiring long-term, open-ended, and escalating commitment, such as counterrevolutionary war. Projecting force by symbolic means—the use of nuclear blackmail— has become increasingly unpalatable and problematic, especially with respect to countering revolutionary activity in the Third World. Hanoi knew that the United States possessed nuclear weapons but continued to fight. As Bernard Fall noted some time ago, revolutionary war is essentially a political, not a military, phenomenon and must be dealt with accordingly.[48]

How, then, can the end of stability based on military power be attained? If policy is based on power whose persuasive potential is equated with the implied threat of force, how and at what levels is the force to be employed? The answer of the Nixon administration was that each state has a responsibility for order. Within each region that is not a sphere of influence, balance of power would exist. The Nixonian vision held that access to each region should be open to American power in case stability or balances break down. Such breakdowns, although possibly unimportant in themselves, could affect the overall global equilibrium and, most important, the Soviet–American relationship. The employment of force was recognized to be difficult, so it was deemed best that local powers, such as Iran—with American military assistance that reached perhaps its highest levels during the Nixon–Kissinger years—fend for themselves to enforce stability.

However, the problem remains of what to do in the event that this approach proves inadequate. The issue was posed succinctly by Earl Ravenal: "The basic question is whether the Nixon Doctrine is an honest policy that will fully fund the worldwide and Asian commitments it proposed to maintain, or whether it coneals a drift toward nuclear defense or an acceptance of greater risk of local defeat."[49] The Nixon administration's effort to incorporate the Chinese into its system of global order suggests that the problem in Asia was mitigated somewhat, at least to the extent that the Nixon administration abjured the close-in containment of the People's Republic. Nevertheless, the dilemma remained, and one cannot escape the inference that the gap between conventional force and the use of nuclear weapons was compressed. Indeed, the nuclear threat seemed the only solution to the quandary of how to keep commitments and keep American ground forces out of ground combat. If forces were to be committed to combat, they would have to be professionals, and not draftees. But would there be enough of them for *global* commitments?

The Nixon Doctrine was marked by almost impenetrable ambiguity. On the one hand, we have the rhetoric of retrenchment and a "reduced profile," but the implementation of American strategy and diplomacy during the early 1970s suggests that there was no fundamental reduction of American objectives. The Nixon policy seems to have been one of keeping a high degree of policy latitude, especially with respect to the use of nuclear weapons: "Having a full range of options does not mean that we will necessarily limit our response to the level or intensity chosen by an enemy. Potential enemies must know that we will respond to whatever degree is required to protect our interests."[50]

The Nixon–Kissinger variation on John Foster Dulles's theme of nuclear retaliation was fraught with all the problems and dangers of the original doctrine. That the new version could achieve the kind of flexibility appropriate to the world of the 1970s, especially in the face of Soviet–American parity, was nowhere clearly demonstrated. Kissinger himself acknowledged the difficulties of the notion of limited or flexible application of strategic and tactical nuclear weapons.[51] Other experts have commented on the illusory nature of this approach:

> The trouble with this concept is that it rests on faulty assumptions (for example, that civilian casualties and collateral damage can be kept to low levels); it ignores a basic lesson that the leaders of the U.S. Government in all cold war crises have learned—that when faced with a decision to start a nuclear war, almost any other alternative looks better; and it is too risky to serve as the foundation for a preferred strategy.[52]

Domestic Constraints

Finally, some important domestic implications of the Nixon–Kissinger policies warrant at least passing mention. First, there was the problem of control. Balance of power politics with shifting alignments was possible in previous centuries when a few men were stewards of foreign policy. Modern states, however, are complex organizations no matter how centralized the foreign policy apparatus might be. As Graham

Allison and Morton Halperin have noted, the military and other foreign policy bureaucracies have inherent bureaucratic interests that can be reconciled only by compromises.[53] If control were to be achieved by a single will, as in the Kissinger management of the National Security Council, there is little assurance that these practices could continue or be institutionalized by succeeding administrations. Indeed, insofar as Kissinger succeeded in personalizing the formulation and conduct of American diplomacy, he completed the task of enfeebling the State Department begun by Senator Joseph McCarthy more than twenty years earlier. The Kissinger control of foreign policy has proved to be a hard act to follow.

Second, the old diplomacy, on which much of the Nixon–Kissinger approach was based, was secret and insulated from domestic politics. Foreign policy was a game of sovereigns, not nations. The representative of the state achieved glory for his prince, and the people were left, until the Napoleonic revolution and the rise of popular sovereignty, to the role of disinterested spectator. Arms were borne by mercenaries. Wars were financed with booty or the spoils of colonial exploration. Military adventure was expensive but had real compensation. Yet, in the twentieth century, little possibility exists of insulating foreign and domestic politics. As Stanley Hoffmann observed:

> In balance of power diplomacy, national interests were defined in terms that took only small account of domestic politics: secrecy, continuity and the primacy of foreign affairs were prerequisites. Today . . . [a]ny statesman, however shrewd a negotiator or profound a philosopher of history, who miscalculates the domestic effects of his moves here or abroad, will be in trouble.[54]

Nixon and Kissinger sought insulation of themselves and their diplomacy from domestic political constraints. Nixon was quite willing to use the flash and swirl of foreign affairs to buttress his eroding domestic position. Nevertheless, both he and Kissinger protested efforts to limit their freedom of maneuver. But, if freedom of maneuver requires illegal surveillance (wire tapping), deceit, and the other distortions of democratic values that were the essence of the Watergate crisis, one is entitled to ask whether a democracy could ever afford a new balance based on the old rules.[55]

Summary

Clearly, problems are inherent in this vision of a newly balanced world political and military order. Nevertheless, Kissinger's virtuosity in extricating the United States from Vietnam, his persistence in negotiating SALT, his development and manipulation of the Soviet–American and Sino–American dimensions of the balance, and his short-term success with "step-by-step" diplomacy in the Middle East were significant achievements. At the same time, however, as Kissinger assumed the sole stewardship of American foreign policy after Nixon's resignation, it was apparent that new forces were at work in world politics.[56] The massive transfer of wealth to the Arabs and a handful of other Third World countries resulting from the oil embargo and escalating prices in 1975 was perhaps the most salient of these challenges to the prevailing conception of world political reality. But other anomalies existed: the enormous growth and expansion of transnationally mobile private economic power — the multinational corporations — based in the industrialized world, the deep and simultaneous crises of the domestic and international economic systems of the industrialized world, and the rapid onset of widespread malnutrition and famine in much of the Third World.

Kissinger is reported to have once remarked, "I am not interested in, nor do I know anything about, the southern portion of the world from the Pyrenees down."[57] Whether or not the words were actually uttered, the sentiment expressed the practical effect of Kissinger's world view; indeed, it is a fair characterization of the outlook of much of U.S. statecraft from the onset of the cold war. But new political, military, and economic realities were increasingly apparent. It is difficult, for instance, to think of foreign politics as merely a matter of armed force meeting force. Rather, foreign policy is a mix of domestic and international factors — a close-knit interaction of economies, societies, organizations, and statesmen. And unlike the late 1940s, the 1950s, and the early 1960s, American foreign economic policy was, by the 1970s, something more than an instrument to be used in an overarching political and military confrontation. The American economy, in an interdependent world, had become subject to a gossamer international confidence, and the United States was no longer completely master of its economic and, hence, political destiny. The Nixon administration's policy of balance to maintain global commitments was shaken by the international effects of domestic politics and international economics in a way that Bismarck or Castlereagh could never have imagined.

THE LIMITS OF POWER AND POLICY IN AN INTERDEPENDENT WORLD

In the 1970s, the politico–military and strategic issues so long the preoccupation of American and other statesmen became increasingly diffused.

Instruments of policy such as alliances, threats of military action, and military force have been found uncertain in their effect and costly in use. Moreover, the formerly dominant sphere of foreign and national security policy is now penetrated by international and transnational economic issues.[58] The breakdown in the international hierarchy of the late 1940s through the early 1960s, the emergent salience of nonsecurity issues, and the problematic applicability of force are the result of this interpretation of security and nonsecurity issues. Understanding the linkage of politics and economics is critical to comprehending how these new phenomena impinged on the traditional notions of force, power, and influence that were central to the Nixon conception of order.

The Collapse of the Bretton Woods System

Economic considerations have occupied a dual position in American foreign policy.[59] At the end of World War II and under the strong influence of the United States, a particular conception of the international economic order was developed and institutionalized at the Bretton Woods Conference in 1944. It was a system that looked to the reconstruction of the world's economy and an institutionalization of conditions amenable to orderly growth and prosperity. Free enterprise, free trade, and the free movement of private capital in accordance with a capitalist conception of economic rationality were to be the basic structural elements of this system. Moreover, it was widely assumed that such an international economic order was absolutely necessary to the establishment and preservation of a stable political and military order commensurate with American national interests.

The building and maintenance of world economic order, conceived at Bretton Woods, was a primary objective of American foreign policy. At the same time, American foreign economic policy was frequently conceived of in an instrumental manner. American trade and foreign assistance programs (and in the case of East–West relations, their denial) became major instruments of American policy during the 1940s, 1950s, and 1960s. The persistent and growing American balance of payments deficits of these years were not thought of, within the context of the Bretton Woods system, as deficits that ultimately would have to be adjusted. Rather, they were seen as simply the price the United States was paying to establish the political and military preconditions of international order. Moreover, it was argued that the American deficits were a kind of international resource in that they provided an international money for a system that was desperately short of liquidity necessary for recovery and growth.

By the mid-1960s, however, this flow of American dollars under changed international conditions, especially in Europe, was no longer viewed as an unalloyed blessing. By the early 1970s, European economies were experiencing inflation in excess of 15 to 20 percent, American corporations were expanding their presence in Europe, and European currencies came under heavy speculative pressure. It was apparent to all that the international supply of dollars ($60 to $100 billion in Europe alone) far exceeded the capacity of the United States to back them with gold.

The Nixon administration's response was initially a policy of benign neglect. During 1969, 1970, and much of 1971, the Nixon administration refused to concede that a problem existed. The Nixon administration's political need as 1972 approached was for a booming domestic economy that required, in turn, an inflating of the economy.[60] If the Europeans did not want to hold the dollars, they were instructed to spend them on American goods (thereby helping the U.S. balance of payments) or revalue of their own currencies upward against the dollar (which would also help the American balance of payments because American goods would then become cheaper vis-à-vis European goods). In short, the Nixon administration told European governments that whether they liked it or not, the dollar and not gold was the basis of the international monetary system. The United States would not change the foreign policy that had made it so; nor would the U.S. government significantly restrain American multinational corporations that were taking advantage of the fact; nor, finally, would the United States significantly deflate its domestic economy (with attendant unemployment in an election year) to soothe European concerns.

In the short run at least, European governments were faced with having to accept the American position. Private holders of dollars were not, however, and began selling dollars for stronger currencies such as the German mark. The upshot was, of course, the threat of more inflation in already inflated economies and, additionally, a further drawdown of American gold reserves. By mid-1971, the dwindling stock of American gold had become intolerable, and Nixon acted by suddenly and without warning ending the convertability of dollars into gold and imposing an import surcharge of 10 percent on foreign goods. Months of speculation followed as the dollar sank on world currency markets, generally to the competitive detriment of other currencies. Finally, in December 1971, at a conference held in Washington at the Smithsonian Institution, the United States officially devalued the dollar but refused to restore convertability. International economic order was not restored, however, and yet another devaluation occurred in 1972 along with initial European efforts to construct some kind of monetary bloc to protect their own currencies.

By March 1973, the remnants of the Smithsonian Agreement had vanished. Worldwide inflation and currency speculation continued, and, by early spring, all governments had retreated from fixed exchange rates — the core of the Bretton Woods system — and were allowing market forces to determine the value of their currencies. Some central bank and private bank intervention was employed to avoid total collapse of the financial structure negotiated at the Smithsonian, but it was increasingly clear that governments, especially that of the United States, were surrendering leadership. Some encouragement could be taken from the fact that there was no return to the nationalistic protectionism of the 1930s. Indeed, steps were taken toward comprehensive reform of the international monetary system. But, before the work could be completed, the system was overwhelmed by the international oil crisis growing out of the Yom Kippur War in October of 1973.

The Exercise of "Petropower"

On October 16, 1973, as military events were beginning to turn against the Arabs, the Arab members of the Organization of Petroleum Exporting Countries (OPEC) imposed an embargo on shipments of oil to the United States and other industrialized countries. Simultaneously, OPEC increased the per barrel price of oil such that, when added to increases earlier in the year, the price of oil increased $2.50 per barrel to $11.65 per barrel by early 1974. Thus, an already disorganized industrialized world economy was confronted with an even more complex challenge. Apart from the immediate problem of how the vast sums of money implied in the price increase were going to be recycled from the industrialized countries to the oil exporters, there were the inflationary implications of the price increases.

The price of virtually everything produced in the industrialized world surged dramatically, but oil-dependent industrialized economies were now confronted with enormous debt stemming from oil import bills that were now four times higher than they had been a year earlier. Italy, France, and Britain faced economic chaos; Japan, importing virtually all of its oil from the Middle East, was faced with a payments deficit. The United States, because it was less dependent on OPEC oil imports, fared somewhat better and, along with the Germans and the Swiss, benefited from the fact that much of the oil wealth surplus now accumulating in the Middle East was deposited in their banks. The Germans were also able to handle their oil debts better than their European neighbors because of the strong surplus position they had developed before the crisis. In fact, the Germans loaned the Italians $2 billion to deal with their short-term deficit and assumed a more activist role in Common Market attempts to negotiate with the United States some form of industrialized world financial response to the crisis. By early 1975, a $6 billion loan facility had been established within the International Monetary Fund to aid countries in dealing with their oil debts. However, the immediate financial crisis was managed primarily by the private banking system of the industrialized world, which accepted deposits from the oil-producing nations and reloaned the money to the oil-importing countries in the industrialized and Third World.

The governments of the West, on the other hand, continued their desultory pursuit of monetary reform. Apart from ad hoc consultations among central bankers and marginal interventions in the floating exchange markets, the system had no real management. By late 1975, the West Europeans, under French and German leadership, had convinced the United States that the prevailing drift in national policies and lack of international coordination was sufficiently dangerous that a more systematic effort had to be made to reconstitute international monetary order. The talks culminated in a conference in Jamaica in 1976, which focused on the issues of international economic management and monetary reform. That the summit conferences would be so focused is testament to the new priorities imposed on Western leadership by interdependence.

In the final analysis, however, the Jamaica Conference could not produce reform of the system. Rather, the participants agreed that floating exchange rates were to remain the central feature of the international monetary system, although a return to fixed exchange rates by all countries, or the Europeans regionally, was not precluded. At the same time, multilateral management of the system was furthered insofar as finance ministers and central bankers agreed to consult closely concerning exchange rate developments and interventions in the currency markets. Nonetheless, by the end of the Nixon and Ford administrations, all that remained of the old international economic order was a weak consensus that some form of management was a necessity, although leadership toward that goal remained uncertain. The Bretton Woods system had been obliterated,[61] and those who beheld this new and extraordinary set of circumstances could discern no self-evident course for the future. Indeed, the very nature of power and order or the relationship between the two seemed even more problematic than in the past. In something less than a year during 1973 and 1974, the foreign ministries of the developed countries and the politico–military superpowers had to grant new status to a group of "petropowers." The concessions were not always made willingly as some, notably the United States, made threatening noises concerning the use of military force in response to the exercise of economic coercion in the Middle East.[62] In the end, however, the industrialized world turned to the uncertain international financial implications of the dramatic shift in economic power represented by the 1973–1974 oil crisis.

Despite short-term fears that the transfer of wealth to the oil exporting countries from the industrialized and non-oil-exporting developing countries would prove unmanageable, the mid-1970s saw a reasonably orderly adjustment to the problems of recycling and oil debt management throughout the international monetary system.[63] The amounts of money accumulating in the oil-exporting countries were indeed impressive. From 1973 to 1974, the current account surpluses of the major oil exporters (Algeria, Indonesia, Iran, Iraq, Kuwait, Libya, Nigeria, Oman, Qatar, Saudi Arabia, the United Arab Emirates, and Venezuela) surged from $6.2 billion to $67.4 billion, with some estimates of projected OPEC financial accumulations in excess of $400 billion by the early 1980s. In contrast, the industrial countries experienced a swing in their current account balances from an $11.1 billion surplus in 1973 to an $11.1 billion deficit in 1974,[64] with no less impressive deficits emerging in the less developed world.

The management of the financial difficulties posed by transfers of this magnitude was facilitated by a number of factors. First, the dramatic increase in the price of oil, in addition to stimulating additional international inflation, pushed the international economy into recession, including the first calendar-year decline in the volume of the world trade since 1968.[65] The recession led, in turn, to a reduction in demand for oil in the industrialized world, thereby slowing the growth of exporting countries' surpluses. In fact, between 1974 and 1975, the aggregate surpluses on current account of the oil-exporting countries dropped from $67.4 billion to $34.7 billion. Simultaneously, the oil-exporting countries were initiating substantial development programs that required imports from the industrialized world.[66] In a few instances, notably Iran, these imports included billions of dollars in arms from the United States and Western Europe.

At the same time, more than 90 percent of the oil-exporting countries' surplus in 1975 was concentrated in Saudi Arabia, Kuwait, the United Arab Emirates, and Qatar, none of which had the capacity or given their small size and considerable wealth, the need for massive imports from the industrialized world. During 1974, most of the surplus accruing to these countries was placed in Eurocurrency bank deposits and other short-term government securities where the money was then loaned back out to industrialized and less developed countries to finance their oil deficits. By 1976, however, these same oil-exporting countries were diversifying their holdings rapidly, with more than half of their investments now being placed in long-term and less liquid investments such as real property and long-term government securities in the industrialized world, especially the United States, Britain, and Germany.[67]

Finally, the immediate financial consequences of the oil crisis were found manageable because the vast network of essentially private international financial institutions proved able to serve as intermediaries in the recycling process. Private banks in the United States, Britain, and elsewhere in Europe became essential brokers in the transfer process by serving as willing receptors of oil-exporting countries' investments for relending to the oil-importing countries or managers of long-term investment by the oil exporters. Perhaps the most remarkable loan operations had to do with the non–oil-exporting Third World countries that borrowed heavily in 1974 and 1975 to finance their oil payment deficits. As the world economic recession deepened and industrial activity in the industrialized world slackened, it was this group of primary raw material–exporting countries that suffered under the greatest burden of the contraction of world trade. With their earnings thus reduced, they were compelled to engage in unprecedented borrowing from private sources in the industrialized world. Indeed, during 1974 and 1975 the non–oil-producing, developing countries borrowed more from private sources than they had borrowed from all other sources in any other year prior to 1974.[68]

The worst fears concerning the political and economic consequences of the oil crisis and the emergence of the petropowers were not, therefore, realized. On the other hand, it was clear that the distribution of world political and economic capability had changed significantly as the result of the crisis. By the end of the Nixon–Ford administration, this fact was reflected in the increasing status and institutional role accorded the OPEC states, especially Saudi Arabia, in the International Monetary Fund and other international financial institutions. Moreover, OPEC's biannual meetings in which the member states negotiated oil prices assumed importance and attracted Western media attention previously reserved for Soviet–American summit meetings.

The crisis and its aftermath also underscored the importance that large concentrations of private economic power now played in the world's political economy. Multinational corporations (MNCs) had been a fixture in the international economy since the early 1960s, when American corporations began moving in considerable numbers and with significant economic and political effect into Western Europe. Furthermore, for decades, the most common and pervasive form of the American presence of the political economies and even the cultures of the developing world, especially in Latin America, had been the American corporation. And, of course, American interests in the Middle East had always been tied to the fortunes of the international oil cartel, most of which was American. The oil crisis demonstrated that, in many instances, the MNCs are by no means as autonomous as some had argued and feared. When faced with OPEC and other forms of petropower action, the international oil companies were revealed to be essentially "tax collectors" (who nevertheless took their cut) for the oil-producing countries.[69] Finally, some evidence existed that, by the mid-1970s, many Third World countries had begun to approach more systematically — either individually or, in some instances, multilaterally — the problem of balancing, if not actually controlling, the MNCs in their midst.

Nonetheless, an international political economy in which MNCs control tens of billions of dollars and hundreds of subsidiaries throughout the world, and in which much of the world's trade flows among the MNCs, is a rather different world political economy than that envisaged at Bretton Woods. Furthermore, when this vast private activity is undergirded and facilitated by an essentially private international financial system through which hundreds of billions of dollars and other currencies can move for the most part beyond the immediate control of governments, the very concept of international economic management developed in the postwar period becomes questionable. Not only does such activity challenge the international financial instruments of governments, but as the rapidly transmitted inflation of the early 1970s suggests, the management of domestic economies is affected decisively by international economic activity. Indeed, by the end of the Nixon–Ford years, the increasing sensitivity and vulnerability of major sectors of American industry to the combination of increasing foreign competition, MNC exploitation of Third World labor markets, and raw materials price inflation were giving rise to demands for protection that threatened the internationalist economic orthodoxy of the post–World War II era.

Finally, a survey of the contemporary political economic system requires a refinement of our conception of the less developed world. In the first place, the onset of worldwide food shortages in the mid-1970s points up the existence of a "Fourth World" — a group of nations almost totally dependent on others for their survival. The combination of low productivity, short-term crop failures due to climate change, and over-population raises the specter of tens of millions starving within the next decade. Indeed, international food and relief experts began to take seriously the prospect of a kind of international system of *triage* in which those peoples who are beyond saving are simply allowed to perish, while limited international resources are directed to those for whom survival seems more likely.[70]

A second group at the bottom of any measure of world power and development are those traditionally thought of as "developing." These are nations able to achieve some growth as measured by traditional economic indices such as GNP. What is less clear, however, is whether this constitutes development in any holistic sense of social, economic, and political development. The answer is not obvious; for, despite positive changes in aggregate economic indicators, some observers argue that these changes mask the persistence of enormous social and political inequalities. The latter are frequently viewed as the necessary price that must be paid for economic development. But these inequities can also be seen as the by-product of the "development of underdevelopment" necessary to the preservation of an essentially exploitive relationship between the developed and underdeveloped world, a relationship within which the MNC serves as a kind of autonomous middle man.[71]

The success of the petropowers in exploiting their control of petroleum gave rise to much speculation that other less developed countries could replicate the petropowers' leap to instant economic and political power.[72] In fact, however, the unique combination of dependence of the industrialized world on petroleum and a mutually perceived threat that could mobilize joint action (in the Middle Eastern case, Israeli military power and the Palestinian question) simply did not exist elsewhere. Moreover, and ironically, the very success of OPEC may have made less likely its replication simply because the greatest burden of debt generated by its action fell on the Third World and drove the latter into even greater financial dependency on the private and intergovernmental financial institutions of the industrialized world. Nevertheless, the persistent and militant call during the mid-1970s by the Third World for a "new international economic order" embodying a radical redistribution of world wealth and the means whereby that wealth was distributed caused many to worry that the future of the international political economy was unlikely to include much order.[73]

BEYOND THE NIXON DOCTRINE

There were a number of advantages to the Nixon–Kissinger approach to establishing and maintaining world order. First, it represented a breach with fifty years of viewing the Soviet Union as an international leper, an abnormality with interests that were rational only in the context of a perverse dogma. The dogma was still viewed as perverse; the scabrous condition of communism and leftist revolution still existed, but the Russian pariah was seen as recovering if not cleansed. In this sense, therefore, these changes represented an abandonment of the vision of politics epitomized by Dulles, which held international politics as a contest between the forces of light and the forces of darkness. Second, the normalization of relations with China released the United States from a pathological illusion that the People's Republic had been an imperialist or expansionist power. China has been, if anything, the soul of caution, painfully aware of its backwardness and weakness. The rhetoric of "people's war," though interpreted in the West to be the framework for Asian aggression, was always an essentially defensive doctrine of warfare.[74] Third, the ability to deal with great powers as if they are normal and understandable, subject to logic and a calculus of interest and accommodation as well as force, allowed negotiations to proceed on both political and military issues.

Nixon, Kissinger, and Ford sought, with some success, to adjust American policy to what they saw as the new realities of the Soviet–American relationship, especially the conditions and implications of strategic parity. In this, Nixon and Kissinger were in fact confronting a reality over which they had little control. A Soviet strategic capacity that is essentially equivalent to the capacity of the United States was a condition that was bound to persist throughout the 1970s. SALT was aimed, therefore, at establishing an accommodation to this situation acceptable to both sides. There was, however, a price: institutionalizing the very bureaucracies, arms development, and deployment dynamic that they sought to restrain. In fashioning a new triangular balance of power incorporating China, Kissinger succeeded in finally suppressing American phobias that his two superiors (Nixon and Ford) had done so much to foster and take advantage of during their political careers. It remains to be seen, however, whether the trilateral balance that Kissinger tried to construct will truly aid the United States in containing Soviet power, or whether the United States will find itself drawn into conflict with the Soviet Union as the Chinese play their new American card in pursuit of their interests.

In the Middle East, Kissinger's tactical virtuosity was at its height as the United States succeeded in projecting itself into the position of mediator between the contending parties. The accomplishment was significant, because it also entailed a diminution of Soviet leverage. It should not be forgotten, however, that, in the end, this breakthrough could not be exploited beyond the fundamental issue of Israeli security concerns in the face of an Arab demand for recognition of Palestinian rights. Kissinger's shuttle and step-by-step diplomacy could get him no further than a necessary but ultimately insufficient disengagement of the combatants. And perhaps most important of all, American policy during the 1973 Yom Kippur War contributed directly to what may prove to be the most important event of the Nixon presidency, the 1973–1974 oil crisis and its consequences for the world political economy, which still reverberate through the international scene.

For one thing, the Arab oil boycott supplied the coup de grace to a Bretton Woods system then in its death throes. It is important to note that the oil boycott laid bare what many had come to suspect by 1973: American capacity and willingness to manage unilaterally the world's political economy was a thing of the past. In this respect, Nixon's economic policies of mid-1971 started what the Arabs finished in October of 1973. In the immediate wake of the boycott, the Europeans and the Japanese established a pattern of behavior that had emerged spasmodically during the 1960s and would become the norm during the latter 1970s: a decided tendency to pursue their own interests notwithstanding American appeals for unity and joint action, a posture rendered disingenuous if not absurd by American economic nationalism during the years leading up to the oil crisis. Thus, as Kissinger tried in the months after the embargo to establish an international energy agency and oil-sharing arrangement, the Europeans and the Japanese, much more dependent on Middle Eastern oil, also went their own way and developed separate arrangements with OPEC. Moreover, it was the Europeans, especially the French, who urged that the United States and the other industrialized powers engage in a formal dialog with the developing nations. The Europeans once again assumed the initiative in moving the United States and the Japanese toward the Jamaica Conference in early 1976.

In fairness, it must be said that, by the time the Nixon administration came to office, management of the international system solely by the United States may no longer have been possible. Parity was, by 1969, a virtual reality, and the Bretton Woods system was already burdened to the breaking point by the international costs associated with the last great but failing effort by the United States to manage and direct events in the Third World. The administration that confronted this situation, though expressing satisfaction with the onset of a new era of international relations — such as in President Nixon's initial State of the World message or Kissinger's conciliatory statement to the Third World before the United Nations in 1974[75] — nonetheless sought to preserve an international order antithetical in many respects to the change its rhetoric welcomed.

NOTES

1. Richard M. Nixon, *U.S. Foreign Policy for the 1970's: A New Strategy for Peace* (Washington, D.C.: U.S. Government Printing Office, 1970), p. 2.
2. Ibid., p. 6.
3. Ibid.
4. Ibid., p. 7.
5. See Richard M. Nixon, *U.S. Foreign Policy for the 1970's: Building for Peace* (Washington, D.C.: U.S. Government Printing Office, 1971), p. 6.
6. Ibid.
7. Richard M. Nixon, *U.S. Foreign Policy for the 1970's: Shaping a Durable Peace* (Washington, D.C.: U.S. Government Printing Office, 1973), p. 232.
8. Henry Kissinger, *White House Years* (Boston: Little, Brown, 1979), p. 195.
9. Ibid., p. 196.
10. See W. W. Kaufmann, *The McNamara Strategy* (New York: Harper and Row, 1964); and Robert McNamara, *The Essence of Security* (New York: Harper and Row, 1968).
11. Morton Halperin, "The Decision to Deploy the ABM," *World Politics*, Vol. 25 (October 1972).
12. John Newhouse, *Cold Dawn: The Story of SALT* (New York: Holt, Rinehart and Winston, 1973), p. 101.
13. For estimates of Soviet deployment rates at this time, see J. I. Coffey, "The Savor of SALT," *Science and Public Affairs* (May 1973), p. 11.
14. Kissinger, op. cit., pp. 191–192.
15. Ibid., pp. 684–712.
16. Ibid., p. 712.
17. Rowland Evans and Robert Novak, *Nixon in the White House: The Frustration of Power* (New York: Random House, Vintage, 1972), pp. 100–101.
18. See Deputy Secretary of State Kenneth Rush's statements, *The New York Times*, July 10 and 13, 1973.
19. See Tad Szulc, "Behind the Vietnam Cease-Fire Agreement," *Foreign Policy*, No. 15 (Summer 1974), pp. 21–69; and Seymour Hersh, *The Price of Power* (New York: Summit Books, 1983).
20. William Safire, "Puppet as Prince," *Harper's*, Vol. 250, No. 1498 (March 1975), p. 12.
21. Henry Brandon and David Schoenbrun, "Jordan: The Forgotten Crisis," *Foreign Policy*, No. 10 (Spring 1973), p. 172.
22. Ibid., p. 168.
23. Ibid.
24. Ibid.
25. Evans and Novak, op. cit., p. 265.
26. Brandon and Schoenbrun, op. cit., p. 170.

27. *The New York Times,* October 11, 1973.
28. *Newsweek,* October 22, 1973, p. 93.
29. See George Ball's statement in *The New York Times,* February 1, 1966.
30. "Meet the Press," Vol. 17, No. 3 (Sunday, January 28, 1973), Merkle Press, Inc., Washington, D.C.
31. Henry Kissinger, *A World Restored* (Boston: Houghton Mifflin, 1957), p. 1.
32. Text of a background briefing in New Orleans, August 14, 1970, p. 16; cited by David Landau, *Kissinger: The Uses of Power* (Boston: Houghton Mifflin, 1973), p. 128.
33. For an eleboration of this analysis based on an examination of Soviet writings, see R. Judson Mitchell, "A New Brezhnev Doctrine: The Restructuring of International Relations," *World Politics,* Vol. 30, No. 3 (April 1978).
34. *Time,* January 3, 1972.
35. Herman Kahn, *The Emerging Japanese Superstate: Challenge and Response* (Englewood Cliffs, N.J.: Prentice-Hall, 1970).
36. *The New York Times,* February 11, 1975, p. 15. See also his *The Weary and the Wary: U.S. and Japanese Security Policies in Transition* (Baltimore: Johns Hopkins University Press, 1972).
37. See U.S. Congress, Senate Committee on the Judiciary, Subcommittee to Investigate Problems Connected with Refugees and Escapees, *The Tilt: American Views of South Asia,* 93rd Congress, 2nd Session, 1973, p. 183.
38. Nixon, *A New Strategy for Peace,* p. 87.
39. For the background of Kissinger's policies in Africa, see Anthony Lake, *The "Tar Baby" Option: American Policy Toward Southern Rhodesia* (New York: Columbia University Press, 1976).
40. Kissinger, *White House Years,* p. 654.
41. Ibid.
42. See, for example, Paul E. Sigmund, "The 'Invisible Blockade' and the Overthrow of Allende," *Foreign Affairs,* Vol. 52, No. 2 (January 1974). See also Elizabeth Farnsworth, "More Than Admitted," and Paul Sigmund, "Less Than Charged," both in *Foreign Policy,* No. 16 (Fall 1974).
43. Kissinger, *White House Years,* p. 658.
44. Ibid., p. 677.
45. Ibid., p. 1258.
46. For a survey of the Shah's military purchases during this period, see *Strategic Survey 1973* and *Strategic Survey 1975* (London: International Institute for Strategic Studies, 1974 and 1976).
47. Among the more insistent advocates of this argument has been journalist Jack Anderson. See for example, "How the Oil Mess Got That Way," *Parade Magazine,* August 26, 1979, pp. 4–8. However, among Anderson's quoted sources are James Adkins, U.S. ambassador to Saudi Arabia at this time, and Secretary of the Treasury William Simon.
48. Bernard Fall, "The Theory and Practice of Insurgency and Counterinsurgency," *Naval War College Review,* April 1965.
49. Earl C. Ravenal, "The Nixon Doctrine and Our Asian Commitments," *Foreign Affairs,* Vol. 49 (January 1971), pp. 206–207.
50. Nixon, *Building for Peace,* p. 179. Moreover, as Nixon left office, the full logic of strategic sufficiency came to the fore as the "unthinkable" became thinkable again after more than a decade of suppression. In 1970 and again in 1973, Nixon's first two secretaries of defense could be found saying that "the President has made

it perfectly clear that we do not intend to develop counter-force capabilities which the Soviets could construe as having a first strike potential" [Secretary of Defense Melvin Laird, cited in *Congressional Record*, Vol. 116, Pt. 19 (July 29, 1970), 26386], and

> The President has also stated that the numbers, characteristics, and deployments of U.S. strategic forces should be such that the Soviet Union cannot reasonably interpret them as intended to threaten a disarming attack. Such a threat would be inconsistent with the U.S. desire to maintain a stable strategic balance and, thereby, reduce the likelihood of nuclear war. (U.S. Congress, Hearings before the Senate Committee on the Armed Services, *Fiscal Year 1974 Authorization for Military Procurement, Research and Development, Construction Authorization for the Safeguard ABM, and Active Duty and Selected Reserve Strengths*, 93rd Congress, 1st Session, 1973, p. 313.)

But in his "Posture Statement" on the Fiscal Year 1975 Defense Budget, Secretary of Defense James R. Schlesinger stated elliptically:

> Assured destruction must remain an essential ingredient in our overall deterrent strategy. However, under certain hypothetical circumstances, if the use of U.S. strategic capability were required in response to an act of aggression we might well reserve our assured destruction forces so as to deter attacks against the American and other free world cities into the wartime period — what we call intrawar deterrence.
>
> The emphasis in the new retargeting doctrine is to provide a number of options, selectivity, and flexibility, so that our response, regardless of the provocation, is appropriate rather than disproportionate to the provocation. I think that understanding of this will serve to shore up deterrence. (Secretary of Defense James R. Schlesinger, Hearings on *Military Posture and H.R. 12564, Department of Defense Authorization for Appropriations for Fiscal Year 1975*, before House Committee on Armed Services, 93rd Congress, 2nd Session, 1974, p. 14.)

In short, the secretary of defense sought to recoup some of the flexibilty lost at the lower end of the spectrum of force by building greater "flexibilty" and "options" into the strategic nuclear arsenal of the United States. However, some have suggested that such flexibility already existed because of improvements in American command and control capability, allowing for almost unlimited and immediate retargeting of American strategic forces [See John C. Baker, "Flexibility: The Imminent Debate," *Arms Control Today*, Vol. 4, No. 1 (January 1974), p. 2.] Also, it has been argued that the United States has possessed for some time the capacity to attack some Soviet missile silos; hence, any significant increase in U.S. capacity to attack the Soviet ICBM force would of necessity be viewed as provocative by them. [See the colloquy between Morton Halperin and Robert Ellsworth in "Should We Develop Highly Accurate Missiles and Emphasize Military Targets Rather than Cities?" *The Advocates* (Boston: WGBH, February 12, 1974), pp. 28–29; and Herbert Scoville, Jr., "Flexible MADness," *Foreign Policy*, No. 14 (Spring 1974), pp. 168–170.] The provocativeness of the step proposed by Schlesinger is undoubtedly heightened in the eyes of Soviet defense planners when viewed in conjunction with the accelerated U.S. ASW (antisubmarine warfare) program.

All in all, as Scoville demonstrated (see Scoville, pp. 171–174), it was extremely difficult to conceive of any *strategic* scenario in which increased hard-target killing capability on the part of the United States could, in the combat of the 1970s, contribute to strategic deterrence. Indeed, quite the opposite conclusion pushed to the fore: "No matter how often we disclaim it, the development of improved silo-killing missiles must inevitably look to the Russians like an attempt to acquire a firststrike counterforce capability against their ICBMs. Similar Soviet programs for getting high-yield MIRVs have been viewed here in exactly such alarming terms." (See Scoville, p. 170.)

51. Kissinger, *White House Years*, pp. 217–220.
52. Alain C. Enthoven and K. Wayne Smith, "What Forces for NATO? And From Whom?" *Foreign Affairs*, Vol. 48, No. 1 (October 1969), p. 82.
53. Graham Allison, *Essence of Decision* (Boston: Little, Brown, 1971); and Morton Halperin, *Bureaucratic Politics and Foreign Policy* (Washington, D.C.: Brookings, 1974).
54. Stanley Hoffmann, "A New Foreign Policy: Is It Possible? Do We Need It?" prepared statement before U.S. Congress, House Committee on Foreign Affairs, Hearings and Symposium Before the Subcommittee on National Security Policy and Scientific Development, *National Security Policy and the Changing World Power Alignment*, 92nd Congress, 2nd Session, 1972, p. 33.
55. For a more extended discussion of the analysis in this section, see James A. Nathan and James K. Oliver, *Foreign Policymaking and the American Political System* (Boston: Little, Brown, 1983).
56. Seyom Brown, *New Forces in World Politics* (Washington, D.C.: Brookings, 1974).
57. Gabriel García Márquez, "The Death of Salvador Allende," *Harper's*, Vol. 248, No. 1486 (January–June 1974), p. 46.
58. Richard N. Cooper, "Trade Policy Is Foreign Policy," *Foreign Policy*, No. 9 (Winter 1972–1973).
59. The information in this section is drawn from Robert Stevens, *A Primer on the Dollar in the World Economy* (New York: Random House, 1972), pp. 142–150; David P. Calleo and Benjamin M. Rowland, *America and the World Political Economy* (Bloomington, Ind.: University of Indiana Press, 1974), pp. 87–117; and Joan Spero, *The Politics of International Economic Relations* (New York: St. Martin's Press, 1977). Also useful is Robert Solomon, *The International Monetary System, 1945–1976: An Insider's View* (New York: Harper and Row, 1977).
60. See Edward R. Tufte, *Political Control of the Economy* (Princeton: Princeton University Press, 1978), for an analysis of presidential manipulation of the economy in election years.
61. See Robert Triffin, "Jamaica: 'Major Revision' or Fiasco?" in Edward M. Bernstein, et al., "Reflections on Jamaica," *Essays in International Finance*, No. 115 (Princeton: International Finance Section, Department of Economics, Princeton University, 1976).
62. "Kissinger on Oil, Food, and Trade," *Business Week*, (January 13, 1975), pp. 66–76.
63. The following discussion, unless otherwise noted, is drawn from: the *Annual Reports* of the International Monetary Fund for 1976 and 1977 (Washington, D.C.: International Monetary Fund, 1977 and 1978 respectively); Thomas D. Willet, "The Oil-Transfer Problem and International Economic Stability," *Essays in International Finance*, No. 113 (Princeton: International Finance Section, Department of Economics, Princeton University, 1975); Spero, op. cit.; and Raymond Vernon, ed., *The Oil Crisis* (New York: Norton, 1976).
64. *IMF Annual Report, 1977*, p. 14.

65. *IMF Annual Report, 1976,* pp. 9–12.
66. Ibid., pp. 14–15.
67. *IMF Annual Report, 1977,* p. 14; and Willet, *passim.*
68. *IMF Annual Report, 1976,* pp. 20–21.
69. See M. A. Adelman, "Is the Oil Shortage Real?" *Foreign Policy,* No. 9 (Winter 1972–1973), pp. 69–107.
70. Walter Sullivan, "Computer 'Model' of World Sought to Cope with Food Shortage," *The New York Times,* August 10, 1975, pp. 31–46.
71. For a succinct statement of this argument, see Osvaldo Sunkel, "Big Business and 'Dependencia': A Latin American View," *Foreign Affairs,* Vol. 50 (April 1972), pp. 517–531; and James D. Cockcroft, Andre Gunder Frank, and Dale L. Johnson, *Dependence and Underdevelopment: Latin America's Political Economy* (Garden City, N.Y.: Doubleday, Anchor, 1972). For a critique of this view, see Benjamin J. Cohen, *The Question of Imperialism: The Political Economy of Dominance and Dependence* (New York: Basic Books, 1973).
72. See the exchange of views, "One, Two, Many OPECs . . . ?" in *Foreign Policy,* No. 14 (Spring 1974), pp. 57–90.
73. Robert Tucker, *The Inequality of Nations* (New York: Basic Books, 1976), *passim.*
74. See Arthur Huck, *The Security of China: Chinese Approaches to Problems of War and Strategy* (New York: Columbia University Press, 1970).
75. "Challenges of Interdependence," address by Secretary of State Henry A. Kissinger before the Sixth Special Session of the United Nations General Assembly, New York, New York, April 15, 1974 (Washington, D.C.: Department of State, Bureau of Public Affairs, 1974).

Chapter 9
"Commitments in Search of a Roost"

By the late 1970s, American foreign policy had become suspended between its cold war past and an interdependent international future of which it had little vision. The new Carter administration avowed a unique sensitivity to this situation. Secretary of State Cyrus Vance and Secretary of Defense Harold Brown publicly acknowledged the inadequacies of the foreign policies of the Democratic administrations they had served during the 1960s. Andrew Young, a civil rights and anti–Vietnam War activist, a close associate of the slain Dr. Martin Luther King, Jr., and an eloquent proponent of a new—sometimes heretical—approach to the Third World, was appointed ambassador to the United Nations. The new security adviser, Zbigniew Brzezinski, had written of a new "technotronic age" in international relations that required a diplomacy quite different from the neoclassical approach of his predecessor, Henry Kissinger. Further, he expressed an intent to reduce the visibility of his office in policy formulation in deference to the secretary of state. Finally, the new president was inaugurated proclaiming a commitment to reduce the defense budget significantly, stop the proliferation of nuclear weapons and take steps to eliminate them from the earth, as well as place human rights at the very center of American foreign policy.

Within months, however, even supporters of the administration had begun calling for a clearer sense of direction and priorities among the many but sometimes conflicting objectives.[1] By midterm, "confusion," "incoherence," and "inconsistency" were terms being applied to the administration's actions. As his reelection campaign began, Carter had to go to the nation, not with an ambitious policy agenda completed, but with a strategic arms control agreement he could not get ratified in the United States Senate, Middle East peace negotiations that had deadlocked after a promising start, and fifty-three American hostages in Iran seemingly irretrievable after an embarrassingly failed rescue attempt and the refusal of America's European and Japanese allies to go through with strong economic and diplomatic sanctions against a revolutionary Iranian regime that had overthrown one of America's closest allies in the Middle East. No less important, relations with the Soviet Union had descended to perhaps their lowest point in more than a decade after the Soviets invaded Afghanistan in late 1979 and the United States called for—with mixed success—a boycott of the Olympic Games held in Moscow in the summer of 1980. The Afghanistan invasion contributed to the largest peacetime military buildup since the early Kennedy administration, with some projections of U.S. military expenditures during the first half of the 1980s running to a trillion dollars. The cold war—so fervently exorcised by part of the Carter foreign policy apparatus for nearly three years yet so feverishly conjured by others—had resurfaced.

INTERDEPENDENCE
AND CONTAINMENT

The Carter administration was forced to confront the implications of the two unifying ambitions of postwar U.S. foreign policy. Foremost, of course, has been the attempt to contain Soviet expansion. A necessarily more elusive but no less avidly pursued policy has been the attempt, as Carter's special assistant for national security affairs, Zbigniew Brzezinski, put it, "to make the world congenial to ourselves" and "to prevent America from being lonely."[2] To escape from solitude and to confine Soviet influence, few places have been immune from American concern. Throughout the cold war, formal guarantees were issued to more than forty countries. But it was clear, after the Korean War, that America's security perimeter was defined not merely by treaty but also by events. The Soviets' involvement in all this was viewed in more sophisticated terms than in the past. It was understood that they did not instigate every coup, insurrection, or international disturbance. Still, there has always been a central policy tenet that the Soviet Union gleaned profit from upheaval. The consistent positing of a cosmology— variously labeled "domino theory," "linkage," or the "spreading arc of crisis"—implied, at the least, the necessity for unfailing American vigilance lest there begin a changing rhythm of history. For in any retreat, there might be a gathering of miscalculations about American determination. Ultimately, then, the nuclear card itself might have to be played through inadvertence or as a desperate signal of American will.

The resort to an overtly threatening posture dependent on American strategic superiority was an option of limited credibility. In fact, strategic superiority was a thing of the past, and the Carter administration could initially find no alternative to the strategic arms limitations process initiated by the Nixon administration. Furthermore, the resort to lower levels of military capability as a response to revolutionary instability was deemed no less inappropriate in view of the Vietnam experience. It was little solace to the many members of the Carter administration who had criticized the Nixon and Ford administrations that they were now compelled to confront dilemmas that emerged and were, in some measure, exacerbated by those earlier administrations. The strategic arms limitations approach to the problems of strategic parity had been shaped by Carter's predecessors. The constraints—both political and material—on the use of force had been established in the preceding decade as had the decline of American economic hegemony. And American dependence on regional surrogates such as the Shah of Iran was the result of the Nixon–Kissinger–Ford pursuit of stability in the Third World without a substantial American military presence or capability. Nonetheless, it seemed that the worst fears of those who argued for the necessity of preserving some relationship between force and diplomacy (lest policy paralysis result from their divorce)[3] were met at the threshold of the Carter administration.

"Interdependence" as Policy

The response of the Carter administration to these problems was frequently ambivalent; at worst, it was almost inexplicably incoherent and unpredictable. Much of this inconsistency can be traced to contending and ultimately irreconcilable policy perspectives within the Carter foreign policy establishment.

One part of the administration sought to make a virtue of the dilemmas presented by the apparently limited utility of American military capability. Proponents of the position argued that the growing interdependence of the international system provided unique opportunities for the United States. These new conditions meant, for example, that economic transactions and issues within the industrialized world and between the West and the Third World now defined the crucial arenas of world politics. The cold war Soviet–American confrontation was, therefore, decreasingly relevant. If ideological questions remained important, they were not the old issues of Soviet communism versus American capitalism. The new issues concerned the Third World's aspirations for national dignity and a greater measure of autonomy in its relationship with the industrialized West. The Third World recognized that the relationship is necessary, because its aspirations for development required access to Western capital, technology, markets, and technical assistance.

It was argued by many in the departments of State and Treasury, and with particular force by Andrew Young, Carter's United Nations ambassador, that, in such a world, the United States possessed an enormously varied, appropriate, and readily applied set of economic and technical instrumentalities.[4]

In contrast, the Soviets had little to offer. Their influence on the development of an international economic order for the industrialized West was nonexistent. Moreover, Soviet influence on the more volatile conditions of the Third World was greatest where revolutionary conflict was underway. Young—who was appointed to the UN post because of his presumed sensitivity for and appeal to the non-West—and others argued that the United States should be less supportive of its traditional antirevolutionary clients and more responsive to the aspirations of those seeking change. Where violent change implied inordinate Soviet influence, such as in southern Africa, American policy should anticipate those circumstances through diplomatic efforts designed to facilitate the emergence of change-oriented, nationalistic, but pragmatic regimes. In some instances, this might require deferring to the United Nations or the diplomacy of other Western allies, such as the successful British mediation of the revolutionary situation in Zimbabwe in 1979 to 1980. In other cases, such as Nicaragua in 1978 and 1979, this approach would require at least a passive U.S. stance even though a former U.S. client, Anastasio Somoza, was threatened with ouster. In either case, it was argued, the United States would be well positioned to advance its interests in the postrevolutionary situation. Indeed, Young was prepared to assert publicly, to the administration's embarrassment, the heretical position that Soviet intervention in Africa or elsewhere via its Cuban surrogates need not be regarded as necessarily a bad thing if it contributed to the termination of revolutionary turmoil and the onset of circumstances in which the need for Western development assistance came to preoccupy a particular Third World country's foreign policy, as in Angola or in the Nicaraguan revolutionary government's initial turn to the United States rather than Cuba for assistance.

At the outset, therefore, some within the Carter administration seemed to accept the end of the cold war pronounced by Nixon in 1969 and baptized in Helsinki as the great given of contemporary history. The problem in formulating policy in a "post cold war environment," as Leslie Gelb, then at the State Department's Bureau of Politico–Military Affairs, explained in 1977, was that "fewer and fewer things had to do with the Soviet–American connection."[5] The question of how to proceed with Soviet–American relations since outstanding issues were seen as either settled or marginal to the larger course of history (a history that did not include an especially bright prospect for the Russians) was uncertain. Nonetheless, American capabilities in such an environment were far superior to those of the Soviet Union. Though the context of foreign policy would likely prove constraining for the old means and ends of American policy, there was considerable reason to believe that a new set of means and ends commensurate with these changed conditions could prosper.

Brzezinski Speaks to
Realpolitik . . . and Interdependence

At the same time, there was in the Carter administration another conception of the appropriate American response to these new conditions, a position forcefully articulated and advanced by Carter's special assistant for national security affairs, Zbigniew Brzezinski. Carter came to office with little background in foreign policy save his participation in the Trilateral Commission, a collection of political, economic, and academic notables from throughout the industrialized world (the United States, Canada, Western Europe, and Japan) under the leadership of David Rockefeller. The commission's executive director during Carter's association with it had been Brzezinski. Moreover, his secretary of state, Cyrus Vance, was usually heralded as more of a technician in negotiations than a conceptualizer. Thus, whatever coherent view of the world eventually emerged in the Carter administration would be heavily, even primarily, influenced by Brzezinski. He was, after all, as Carter explained, "the eyes through which I view the world."[6]

Brzezinski's views were not, at least superficially, totally inconsistent with the arguments advanced by those who saw an interdependent world potentially more responsive to American diplomacy than Soviet power. The world had entered a "technotronic age," according to Brzezinski, one in which "technology and electronics — particularly in the area of computers and communications" were now the dominant shapers of domestic and international society.[7] Simultaneously, "global politics are becoming egalitarian rather than libertarian, with demands from more politically activated masses focusing predominantly on material equality than on spiritual or legal liberty."[8]

There were in these conditions great dangers for the United States, especially if it adopted what Brzezinski called a "siege mentality," setting itself intransigently against these conditions, especially demands for greater equality. Preferable, said Brzezinski in an essay published during the bicentennial year, was an America that is cooperatively engaged in shaping new global relations, both despite and because of the rising global egalitarian passions. . . . America still provides to most people in the world the most attractive social *condition* (even if not the *model*) and that remains America's special strength. The Soviet Union is not even a rival in this respect. But that strength can only be applied if American foreign policy is sympathetically sensitive to the significant shift in global emphasis toward a value [egalitarianism] which has not been central to the American experience. This need not entail an embrace of egalitarianism as the supreme virtue. . . . But it does imply a policy that does not ignore (nor reciprocate with doctrinal hostility) the global pressures for reform of existing international arrangements.[9]

At the same time, however, Brzezinski departed from the interdependence perspective in that he persisted in the more traditional American preoccupation with the Soviet Union and especially its presence in Eastern Europe. He took great pains to distinguish his outlook and methods from those of the previous eight years. On the eve of the signing of the Helsinki accords, for example, when Carter was but a distant gleam in his eye, Brzezinski gave a remarkably candid assessment of his differences with the "Ford–Kissinger approach" to detente "which seeks to perpetuate the status quo" in Europe "with all that entails."[10] For Brzezinski, the whole purpose of Helsinki and the latter years of Kissinger's tenure was ill-conceived and ahistorical:

. . . the anachronistic division of Europe . . . is the source of instability. If we contribute to its legitimation in the form of some security declaration, we are not contributing to European security but to its opposite.[11]

Brzezinski's plan for the future of the Soviet Union was as fissiparous as it was for Eastern Europe. As he confessed to a Radio Free Europe interrogator:

. . . realistic encouragement of pluralism via nationalism and separatism may be our best answer to the Soviet challenge on the ideological front . . . [A]fter the disappearance of the communist state, a combination of residual socialism and internationalism would mitigate the power-oriented ambitions of extreme Russian nationalism. . . .[12]

For President Carter's soon-to-be-appointed national security adviser, the Soviets could be treated in a fundamentally different fashion from the status finally accorded to them by Kissinger and Ford. To Brzezinski, the Soviets' internal regime could be publicly questioned and loudly proclaimed illegitimate, irrelevant, and even pernicious to the tide of progress sweeping the globe. A "truly *comprehensive* [emphasis his] detente" would be "a challenge to [the Soviet Union's] legitimacy and thus . . . their very existence, and I must say their fears [would be] justified."[13] Carter echoed this theme when he told members of the Magazine Publishers Association:

> My own inclination . . . is to aggressively challenge . . . the Soviet Union and others for influence in areas of the world that we feel are crucial to us now or potentially crucial in 15 or 20 years from now.[14]

All this could not help but abrade the Soviets at their most irritable spots. When Carter visited Poland and Rumania early in his administration, Brzezinski was not unaware of the implications: "[I]t was," he explained, "a gesture which underlines our interests in pluralism in Eastern Europe."[15] Brzezinski elaborated Carter's reversal of American accession to Helsinki in his address to the Foreign Policy Association on December 20, 1978: "We do not believe that our relations with Eastern Europe should be subordinate to our relationship with Moscow. . . ."[16] It was widely noticed, but in his first budget request, Carter asked for a doubling of broadcast capability of Radio Free Europe and Radio Liberty. Voice of America broadcasts to the Soviet Union were increased by 25 percent.[17]

Brzezinski (as well as many of those he brought to the National Security Council) was not, therefore, insensitive to either the constrained condition of American military power or the complex interdependence that contributed to that condition. Furthermore, he seemed to accept that the emerging new age of world politics was potentially more amenable to a reformed American view of world order and new American instrumentalities (largely political and economic, but also American ideals in the form of an almost militant emphasis on human rights) than it was to Soviet power and policy. Brzezinski, however, was not prepared more or less to ignore Soviet power and international presence. Soviet strategic power had to be checked as a necessary condition of world order, but presumably this could be achieved by arms control agreements and the continued mobilization of American technological sophistication and superiority. Even more important, Brzezinski was prepared to engage — not merely coexist with — the Soviets within the context of the new interdependence, using American advantages and leverage to contribute to Soviet difficulties internally and especially within their East European empire.

Here, then, was a crucial difference, not only in Brzezinski's position with respect to many of his colleagues within the Carter administration, but compared with his Republican predecessors as well. A Soviet Union beset by internal weakness and dubious prospects for long-term successful participation in the new era of world politics was not merely to be accepted as a kind of struggling junior partner. Rather, wherever possible, its problems and difficulties were to be exacerbated. Its need for Western capital and technology was not to be approached as an opportunity to pull it gradually into a moderating web of detente but as a vulnerability to be exploited so as to hasten its decline. Soviet sensitivity to Chinese potential on its Asian border was not to be subtly and carefully manipulated through diplomatic maneuver but rather prodded and even inflamed through indirect and direct military assistance to the Chinese.

The ambivalence and indecision that many observers have attributed to the Carter years can be traced in considerable measure to these warring policy perspectives within the Carter administration. The media often explained things in terms of an intense personal and institutional clash between, on the one hand, Brzezinski and his National Security Council staff, and, on the other, Secretary of State Vance and his department, a clash culminating in Vance's resignation in early 1980. Although elements of such a struggle clearly permeated Carter administration policy, it is important to recognize that the two men represented subtly but consequentially different views of the world, American interests, the specific options available, and the means to be used.[18] Furthermore, to the extent that American policy in the late 1970s can be seen has having drifted toward the pole represented by Brzezinski, that outcome was made more likely by the president's desire to make human rights a centerpiece of his foreign policy.

Human Rights

In his inaugural address, Carter told the American people and the world: "Because we are free we can never be indifferent to the fate of human beings elsewhere . . . our commitment to human rights must be absolute." In March of 1977, he told the United Nations: "No member of the United Nations can claim that the mistreatment of its citizens is solely its own business."[19] Nonetheless, the specific meaning and application of the policy remained unclear and, upon examination, proves problematical.

The NSC spent innumerable hours in 1977 and 1978 attempting to assess what human rights means to Islamic, Latin, and Oriental societies. One participant at these meetings despaired: "It's a hard problem for a bureaucracy to come to grips with. It's a hard subject for people to discuss collectively."[20] Early on, the Carter administration discovered that, if it is difficult to discuss what constitutes human rights with people of the same cultural–political–ethnic backgrounds, it is downright confounding to discuss the matter of judicial torture and wholesale murder with representatives of other cultures that are often in revolutionary contexts.

The problem of cultural variability of human rights as an absolute principle of foreign policy stems from the necessarily indiscriminate nature of an absolute commitment to human rights. To most people educated in Judeo–Christian principles, humans have rights. If, then, their rights are violated and abused, how is one to express concern? If one manifests concern wherever there are abuses, one must be prepared to identify an enormous array of circumstances and activities that are, by most Americans' standards, obnoxious. But what, then, is one to *do*? Dealing with the problem implies a willingness to intervene in some fashion in the internal affairs of another society. Presumably, one should be prepared to chastise and even dispatch leadership if the abuses are gross enough. But also, if one's policy is to have significant moral force, its application would have to be consistent. But should moral opprobium and intervention be directed at the Saudis, South Koreans, or the Shah of Iran? Were the Chinese to be the object of moral condemnation even as the Carter administration sought to complete a *de facto* alliance with the Chinese to contain the Soviets?

One could, in theory at least, rank one's interests from the most important to the least important, trading lesser interests to safeguard the more serious. But how can one rank or differentiate the objects of great and absolute principles? Does sacrificing some segment of a principle weaken it altogether? One can compromise competing interests, but compromising with morality is a visible sin. The policy now seems to have been foredoomed, whether it was an "absolute principle" of foreign policy as Carter proclaimed, or "absolute in principle but flexible in application" as one of the president's NSC assistants explained to one of the present authors.[21]

The American public's sentiment that Carter perceived and sought to respond to with his pronouncements concerning human rights is, nonetheless, difficult to exaggerate and easy to underestimate. Among some Europeans and the Soviets, however, there was incomprehension and even hostility to Carter's concern for those who suffered abridgment of liberty or dignity. Among the Germans especially, fears existed that open letters to dissidents in the Soviet Union and the reception of Soviet exiles in the White House would jeopardize a decade of detente. Carter found it "surprising" that the Soviets would have an "adverse reaction." His policy had, he would in time confess, "provided a greater obstacle to . . . common goals, like SALT, than I had anticipated."[22]

If Carter had not suspected that the Soviets would be taken aback by his professions of sympathy for Soviet dissidents, his national security adviser might have pointed to the words that he and his associate, Samuel Huntington, authored as early as 1962. The main source of danger to the stability of the Soviet political system, wrote Brzezinski and Huntington, is

> any decline in the ideological and political monopoly of the ruling party. If tomorrow the Soviet Union were to open its frontiers to foreign books, newspapers and criticism of the system, the effect could be politically dramatic. . . .[23]

But, as we have seen, such a politically dramatic effect was, for Brzezinski, the most desirable of outcomes for American policy in the complex, interdependent world confronting the United States. Thus, Carter's emphasis on human rights vis-à-vis the Soviet Union was congruent with Brzezinski's conception of American policy. At the same time, however, this convergence of views merely underscored the traditional foci of American policy in the late 1970s. That is, notwithstanding much rhetoric and some policy initiatives that reflected awareness of interdependence, there was in the moralistic thrust of Carter's human rights emphasis a throwback to the globalism of Truman and, even beyond that, to Wilson. To the extent that this moralism came into focus with Brzezinski's approach to the new age through continued confrontation with the Soviet Union, this moralism was subject to becoming indistinguishable from NSC-68. In the short run, these irreconciled tensions between interdependence and containment complicated an already deteriorating Soviet–American relationship. In the longer run, they were reflected in most other aspects of the Carter administration's foreign policy as well.

CARTER AND THE WORLD

The context of Soviet–American relations for the Carter administration was considerably more complicated than that confronting the last Democratic president who assumed office after a Republican ascendancy. John Kennedy found the cold war oppressively in place in 1961. Indeed, he all but exulted in the challenge to American purpose presented by that stony prospect. Jimmy Carter, on the other hand, inherited a relationship still in the process of redefinition following the radical changes accompanying America's post-Vietnam retrenchment and the Soviet Union's achievement of strategic parity with the United States. SALT negotiations were moving forward, but Soviet–American consensus on relations beyond arms control was lacking. Furthermore, American domestic support for either SALT or, more importantly, detente was extremely fragile. In addition, there was the now chronic dependence on Middle Eastern oil and the nagging sense that that region was once again headed for war unless the diplomatic momentum of the period after the 1973 war could be regained. Notwithstanding the desire of many in the Carter administration to refocus American diplomacy on these and other interdependence issues, the Soviet–American nexus could not be displaced.

There seemed to be a general desire for better Soviet–American relations and especially an extension of the SALT process but also noticeable was an undercurrent of skepticism as to whether the detente atmosphere of the early 1970s could be regenerated or was even worth the effort. Continuing Soviet activism in Africa made it clear that they entertained a different conception of detente than the United States. Furthermore, concern was growing about the balance of Soviet–American military capability, as critics of SALT and the balance of forces in Central Europe warned ominously of Soviet superiority within a decade, a superiority that would surely be used to extract advantages from the United States. Such criticism was especially intense in the Senate, where, of course, any SALT II treaty would have to be ratified and could be blocked by a coalition of conservative Democrats and Republicans numbering only thirty-four — a number deemed well within the grasp of Senator Jackson, who was regarded as the leader of the anti-SALT and antidetente forces in the Senate. Apart from whatever uncertainties, ambivalence, or conflicting policy approaches existed in the Carter administration, these domestic political factors served as powerful and active constraints on the development of Carter's policies.

SALT

As we have seen, important differences in perspective coexisted within the new administration. On the question of strategic arms control, however, there was a degree of consensus — the Carter administration wanted to move rapidly to conclude a SALT II agreement. Such a step was consistent with the president's oft-repeated desire for arms reductions and defense expenditure cuts. Like Kissinger and Nixon before him, Carter viewed SALT as the only readily available means to limit Soviet force structure expansion. In addition, the SALT I agreement was due to expire in October of 1977. Finally, the Ford administration had left behind fifty pages of draft treaty text already agreed to by the

Soviets. In fact, it was widely believed that the only issues left to negotiate were problems associated with the Soviets' newly developed "Backfire" bomber — thought by some in the West to possess strategic capability — and the Americans' cruise missiles, which, because of technological developments since Vladivostok, could now be deployed in considerable numbers on virtually any air, land, or sea-based platform. They might also be easily deployed by the United States in Europe or transferred to the West Europeans for their own use. Finally, their small size presented significant verification problems given their easy concealment.

By late March, the administration was prepared to reopen negotiations on SALT II.[24] However, when Secretary of State Vance met with the Soviets in Moscow, the United States proposed a much more far-ranging agreement than had been negotiated within the Vladivostok guidelines. The Vladivostok guidelines placed equal ceilings on strategic delivery vehicles and MIRVed launchers at the relatively high levels already programmed by or acceptable to the Soviet and American military establishments. In contrast, the new Carter comprehensive package called for significant cuts in total forces and MIRVed launchers, but also proposed ceilings on MIRVed ICBM launchers that would have cut deeply into the muscle of Soviet forces. The Carter administration's proposal has been judged to have been a major departure in the strategic arms limitations process.[25] For the first time, a proposal was advanced that would have meant significantly reducing the capability of both sides as well as limiting the modernization of strategic arsenals. The Soviet Union, however, brusquely dismissed the plan, charging that, with its proposed deep cuts in ICBM numbers, the proposal was designed to extract unilateral advantage for the United States, because it was precisely by means of ICBM numbers and the size of Soviet warheads that the Soviet Union had achieved strategic parity with the United States. The Soviets insisted that negotiations return to the framework developed during the preceding five years.

In May, the United States brought forth another suggestion that sought to break the new impasse that had emerged. First, the United States would accept a treaty to run until 1985, based on the Vladivostok ceilings as a starting point, though the United States made it clear that it would pursue lower levels. Second, the two sides would develop a protocol to the treaty that would run for three years and cover all the systems and issues, such as cruise missiles, Backfire bombers, limits on new ICBMs such as mobile ICBMs, and qualitative restraints that the two sides could not negotiate into the treaty itself. Finally, a set of mutually agreed principles would be negotiated to apply to subsequent talks; in effect, agreeing in advance on the agenda for SALT III. It was recognized that the October deadline was not likely to be met, but the two sides agreed to observe the ceilings imposed under the 1972 agreement, and proceeded with what would prove to be a laborious 2½-year process of negotiations culminating in a treaty and protocol signed by presidents Carter and Brezhnev at Vienna on June 18, 1979.

The treaty signed at Vienna was in fact much closer to the American comprehensive package than might have been expected in March of 1977. The overall ceilings were higher than those desired by the United States: 2,250 strategic delivery vehicles, 1,320 of which could be MIRVed. However, subceilings on MIRVed ICBMs and SLBMs were agreed to, and many of the issues that had been thought likely to be included in the protocol for subsequent negotiations (such as modernization controls, new ICBM developments, and qualitative limits, e.g., limits on the number of warheads that could be deployed on MIRVed launch vehicles) were actually incorporated into the treaty. Only some of the issues involving the cruise missile and the Backfire bomber remained outside the treaty but within the protocol or other understandings incorporated under the Vienna package.

Yet, when the treaty and protocol were submitted to the Senate for ratification in the summer of 1979, it was clear that the treaty was in deep trouble. Notwithstanding an elaborate public relations campaign undertaken by the Carter administration, the hearings before the Senate Foreign Relations Committee revealed substantial opposition to the agreements. Objections included the familiar arguments that SALT II, like SALT I before it, did nothing to eliminate the Soviet lead in large ICBMs; doubts about whether the United States could verify key provisions of the treaty in view of the loss of intelligence facilities resulting from the fall of the Shah's regime in Iran in early 1979; and concern that acceptance of the treaty would lull the American people into complacency about what many senators saw as the growing threat of Soviet strategic superiority.

The administration responded to these questions on the treaty. But in the course of the hearings and debate, it was revealed by the administration that intelligence data suggested the presence in Cuba of about twenty-six-hundred Soviet combat troops with their equipment. Even staunch supporters of SALT II demanded that the president do something about the situation, although it was generally known that Soviet troops had been on the island for the preceding seventeen years, and it was not clear how a brigade of fewer than three thousand men with no amphibious transport constituted a threat to the United States. The fact that such an issue could command such attention, bring the treaty ratification process to a virtual halt, and require a presidential address to the nation was an indication that far more than a strategic arms control agreement was being debated in the United States in late 1979.

The Final Decline of Detente

Signs of trouble were apparent at the very outset of the Carter administration, as the Soviets complained privately and then publicly about the human rights policy of the administration. The president professed not to be concerned and wrote a sympathetic letter to the most well-known Soviet dissident, Andrei Sakharov. The week before the Moscow meeting in which the comprehensive SALT II package was to be presented, however, Brezhnev complained that the tone and thrust of the administration's policies constituted interference in Soviet internal affairs. The Soviet rejection of the administration's SALT package was undoubtedly based on objections to the proposal's contents, especially when they seemed to deviate so markedly from what had been negotiated previously. Nonetheless, the atmosphere surrounding a deteriorating detente had clearly not improved with the arrival of the new administration.

In the meantime, events in Africa continued as an irritant in Soviet–American relations. In February 1977, a Marxist regime seized control of Ethiopia and, while seeking assistance from the Russians, undertook full-scale war against Somalia over the latter's territorial claims in the Ogaden region of Ethiopia. The Soviets were initially in a difficult position, because they had previously supported the Somalis; however, by the fall of the year, the Soviets had aligned themselves with the Ethiopians and had begun providing military assistance, including the dispatch of thousands of Cuban troops. Earlier, in March, both Fidel Castro and then Soviet President Podgorny had visited the southern African "front-line states" and Castro visited Ethiopia and Somalia as well. Also in March, Zaire's resource-rich Shaba province was invaded by a rebel group operating out of Angola. The invasion was turned back after the insertion of some fifteen hundred Moroccan troops and additional U.S. military assistance.

By early 1978, however, relations had become even more strained, not only regarding Africa but also with respect to Carter's human rights policy. Early in the year, the United States and the Soviet Union exchanged warnings concerning each other's actions, with the Soviets asserting that the U.S. attitude on arms control and other issues was unhelpful, and the United States responding that Soviet actions in Africa threatened relations. In May, yet another invasion of Zaire was launched from Angola, with the president charging that Cubans were involved.

The United States responded with an airlift of French, Belgian, and Moroccan troops; by June, the situation was once again calm. Simultaneously, however, the Soviets had placed on trial a number of prominent dissidents, all of whom were convicted and sentenced to prison terms. Congress passed joint resolutions deploring the trials as Carter announced that Soviet–American exchange programs would be reevaluated and the sale of high technology to the Soviet Union would receive closer scrutiny and be subjected to tighter controls than in the past. In mid-July 1978, as two American newspapermen were being convicted of having libeled Soviet television and ordered to pay fines, the president canceled the sale of computer equipment to the Soviet Union.

Undoubtedly, even more alarming from a Soviet perspective, however, was the culmination of the American–Chinese rapprochement begun by Nixon. In late May, after Soviet attempts to improve relations with the Chinese had broken down, Brzezinski visited China to discuss SALT and normalization. On his return to Washington, the sale of technology (in this case infra-red scanning equipment) previously denied the Russians was approved for the Chinese. Throughout the remainder of the year, a parade of high U.S. officials went to China to discuss scientific exchanges and assistance, energy, and agriculture. Finally, in December 1978, after the Chinese had provided assurances to the United States concerning the future status of Taiwan, normal diplomatic relations were established and official ties with Taiwan broken, including the mutual defense treaty between the United States and Taiwan. By early spring of 1979, Deputy Prime Minister Deng Xiaoping visited Washington to sign scientific and cultural agreements but, more provocatively from a Soviet standpoint, issued stern lectures to American audiences concerning the threat posed by Soviet imperialism and "hegemonism."

Midway through Carter's term, therefore, little was left of the detente, save trade in grain, that the Nixon administration had sought to construct. The demise of detente was well underway by the time Carter came to the White House, and by mid-1978, he was warning the Soviets in language reminiscent of an earlier time: "The Soviet Union can choose either confrontation or cooperation. The United States is prepared to meet either choice."[26] In fact, very little remained except the common interest in a SALT agreement. Against a backdrop of increasingly cool relations along virtually every other dimension of contact, the last details of the treaty were worked out in early 1979 and the treaty submitted to the Senate at mid-year. By that time, however, SALT had become the last salient vestige and symbol of a policy of detente that was—in the minds of many, perhaps most, in the

Senate—a thoroughly discredited approach to dealing with Soviet power. Moreover, for many of these same skeptics and opponents of SALT and detente, the debate and ratification vote were nothing less than a vote on the Carter administration itself.

The domestic reaction against Carter's stewardship of American policy set in almost immediately on his assuming office. Carter had, of course, come to the presidency promising to reduce defense spending, and he immediately cut the Ford defense budget by about $2.8 billion. He also announced, however, that he wanted to reevaluate the need for procuring the new B-1 strategic bomber, which was nearing completion of its development. His appointment of Paul Warnke, a noted advocate of detente and arms control as his chief SALT negotiator, also provoked the more hard-line critics of American policy. But perhaps even more important was the president's apparent willingness to adopt a restrained posture toward Soviet policy in Africa, even as Ambassador Young articulated in forceful language his heretical views concerning the character of Third World revolutionary activity.

In addition, Carter's seeming inconsistencies lent support to the growing impression among those who wanted a harder and more uncompromising line toward the Soviet Union that this president was not the man for the job. Thus, in early 1978, after urging the West Europeans to accept deployment of the enhanced radiation or neutron bomb, Carter reversed course and deferred a production decision. For those Europeans, such as Chancellor Helmut Schmidt in West Germany, who had expended considerable political capital building support for the weapon, the reversal was a rude shock. For those in the United States who wanted to see a buildup of U.S. military capability, the decision was very nearly outrageous, especially when combined with what were deemed by them to be overly limited increases in defense spending by the United States. Moreover, Carter even took the unusual step in August of 1978 of vetoing a Defense Department appropriation and authorization bill when Congress included in it funds for a nuclear-powered aircraft carrier that the president had not requested.

The severing of relations with Taiwan necessary for the reestablishment of normal relations with the People's Republic and the playing of the China card against the Russians further incensed conservative critics of the administration. Conservatives and long-time supporters of Nationalist China refused to accept the president's rationale that the step was but the culmination of Richard Nixon's geopolitical balancing of Soviet power. No less galling to most conservatives was Carter's advocacy, signing, and active support in the Senate for treaties to return the Panama Canal Zone back to the sovereignty of Panama. The United

States retained operating rights over the canal and, as the result of un-derstandings and reservations to the agreements, increased its security access to the canal; but, to its opponents, the treaties were a giveaway of what Republican presidential hopeful Ronald Reagan insisted on call-ing "our canal." Here again, the president's view—that the treaty was the fulfillment of a diplomatic initiative originally undertaken in the Johnson administration and pursued by his Republican successors, and that it was, in any event, essential to establishing a more sensitive and responsive relationship with Latin America—was to no avail.

The Camp David Summit:
An Ambiguous Breakthrough

President Carter was able to deflect, for a time, this building resent-ment with his temporarily successful mediation of the Egyptian–Israeli peace-making process at Camp David in late 1978. But even here, the initiative was not the president's and the results proved far less certain than the president's rhetoric at the signing of the agreements suggested.

There was initially, in the Middle East, an attempt by the Carter administration to draw the Soviets into the negotiating process between Israel and its neighbors. The negotiating framework proposed was mul-tilateral negotiations in Geneva co-chaired by the United States and the Soviet Union. The Carter administration reasoned that no settlement would be lasting if the Soviets could always act the role of spoiler. The explicit tone of Kissinger's policy, which was designed to expel the Soviets from the Middle East, would, therefore, be reshaped. The melody that the Carter administration now whistled beckoned the Soviets back into the region in an effort to make their would-be proxies and clients in the Arab world—especially the Syrians, Libyans, and the Palestine Liber-ation Organization—more susceptible to an accord. But the lyrics of the song did not speak of any rewards to the Soviets apart from those of the psyche: mere acknowledgment of some residual Russian interests and influence by the Americans, who would continue to hold most of the cards. In sum, as in the early Nixon years, the Soviets were once again called to be of assistance in their own containment.

The astonishing announcement and subsequent trip of President An-war Sadat of Egypt to Jerusalem in November 1977 for the purpose of opening a direct dialogue between Egypt and Israel unhinged Ameri-can policy. Sadat, fearing precisely a superpower-designed and -imposed settlement, moved to establish a negotiating process in which he would have maximum control of the agenda, minimum Soviet involvement, and, by encouraging American intermediation, the benefit of whatever credits he had accumulated in Washington following his dramatic ouster of the Soviets in 1972 and his generally pro-American stance since the 1973 war and Kissinger's shuttle diplomacy. Sadat would thereby represent not only his own interests but, if successful, would seize leadership of the Arab camp. In the meantime, the rest of the Arab world reacted with dismay and hostility as the largest Arab state set out on its own, ostensibly in pursuit of common interests, but initially proposing a permanent end to Egyptian–Israeli hostilities and, though Sadat would deny it repeatedly, pursuing a separate peace with Israel.

The Soviets would be pushed not only away from center stage but almost out of the theater. Sadat was however, perilously poised, extending himself like some over-aged trapeze artist to an initially confused and even indifferent American assistant. The Carter administration, like much of the rest of the world, was knocked off stride by Sadat's initiative. Its planning had all reflected a great-power solution. But Sadat's initiative had its advantages — Soviet displacement — and its desired effect: The road toward a Middle East settlement via Geneva and Soviet participation was abandoned.

The American grip was breathtakingly late. But once in hand, a new "island of stability" — at a cost of up to $10 billion in economic and military assistance to Egypt — was to be established. There were other diplomatic costs, however, for in supporting what other Arab states regarded as treasonous behavior on Sadat's part, American diplomatic credibility in the region was diminished. Apparently, however, the Carter administration reasoned that if a settlement could be reached by using the opportunity presented by Sadat's boldness, the rest of the Arabs, the Palestinians, and even the Russians — confronted with a fait accompli — would in time accept.

After months of negotiations between Sadat and Israeli Prime Minister Menachem Begin produced no diplomatic breakthroughs, however, President Carter, in early September 1978, convened a tripartite summit at Camp David, Maryland.[27] For eight days between September 5 and 13, the president, with the assistance of Secretary of State Vance, served as a personal mediator trying to narrow differences for an Egyptian–Israeli peace treaty and what came to be known as a "Framework for Peace in the Middle East" within which detailed negotiations on the Palestinian issue might proceed. As always, the issue of Palestinian rights proved most difficult and very nearly led to the collapse of the talks. In the final analysis, however, President Carter's persistence won a compromise on the Palestinian issue with which Sadat and Begin could live: (1) provisions for the establishment of some form of elected self-governing Palestinian authority, (2) withdrawal of the Israeli occupation forces on the West Bank, and (3) negotiations concerning the final status of whatever Palestinian political entity was eventually formed out of the West Bank and Gaza.

Leaving aside the drama surrounding the negotiations and the fanfare with which the peace treaty and "framework for peace" were announced, it is important to underscore that nothing final concerning the Palestinian question was settled at Camp David. Rather, it was at most an attempt to get serious negotiations under way. Apart from whatever short-term domestic benefits accrued to President Carter, the ultimate success of the Camp David process would depend on the diplomatic follow-up to the summit.

Moreover, though the Camp David improvisation was masterful and courageous, it was also expensive and fraught with dangers. By excluding the Russians yet again in an area of traditional concern to them, it pinned the most radical Middle Eastern groups and states closer than ever to the Soviets. It is also likely that the Soviets' worst fears concerning the Carter administration's acceptance of the Soviet Union's new international status were confirmed by the diplomatic maneuvering in 1977 and 1978. The reaction was summarized by State Department Soviet expert Marshall Shulman in October of 1979:

> The action of President Sadat in going to Jerusalem and the development of a bilateral negotiations between Egypt and Israel has had the practical effect of excluding the Soviet Union from effective participation in the negotiating process. They bear this very resentfully and have spoken of it quite sharply many times. . . . It clearly is the situation that the Soviet position in the Middle East has deteriorated compared to what it was. That has been the outcome of diplomatic efforts on our part.[28]

But if the Soviets had been shoved aside once again, American diplomacy, as in 1973 and 1974, proved insufficient in itself to bring about a resolution of the Arab–Israeli dispute. Carter, like Kissinger before him, found it easier to get agreement and action by Israel and Egypt concerning territorial questions associated with their bilateral peace treaty, such as Israeli withdrawal from most of the Sinai still held by the Israelis after the 1973–1974 round of negotiations, return of oil producing facilities in the Sinai and the Red Sea to the Egyptians, return of the Gaza area with its large Palestinian refugee population to Egyptian sovereignty, and the reestablishment of normal diplomatic relations between Cairo and Tel Aviv. On the central question of a Palestinian homeland and its political status, little progress was made.

The framework for negotiating some measure of Palestinian autonomy developed at Camp David proved to be a point of diplomatic contention rather than an agreed agenda for action. Notwithstanding more or less constant American intermediation as well as direct Egyptian–Israeli talks throughout 1979 and early 1980, agreement proved elusive. Indeed, the Begin government – in the face of increasingly militant West Bank Palestinian reaction to the Camp David accords and continuous Jewish settlement in previously Arab areas – reaffirmed and expanded its support of Jewish settlement by groups of Jewish militants who denied any legitimate Arab rights on the West Bank. By mid-1980, open clashes between West Bank Arabs and these Jewish militants were becoming commonplace, and disagreements within the Begin government concerning settlement policy and the negotiations had broken into the open. Foreign Minister Moshe Dayan and Defense Minister Ezer Weizmann – both regarded as moderates on the Palestine question – resigned from the Begin government. Israeli–Egyptian talks stalemated; agreed deadlines for beginning the autonomy process passed; and, with the stalemate, the Carter administration was confronted with the possibility that the West Europeans were about to launch their own diplomatic initiative for a resolution of the Middle East situation. Such a move would further emphasize the disarray in the alliance and the lack of European confidence in Carter's leadership. It was also widely assumed that, given European dependence on Arab oil and the West European contention that no lasting settlement could be reached without Palestinian participation in negotiations, whatever proposals the Europeans might advance would likely be far more pro-Palestinian than could be acceptable to a Carter administration facing a difficult presidential election season.

As Carter's reelection effort began, what he had hoped could be advanced as decisive proof of his diplomatic skill – a genuine Middle East peace – seemed as far away as ever. He now found himself positioned between two weakening and, hence, inflexible partners within the region: the Begin government, torn internally by reaction to its West Bank settlement policy, and the raging Israeli inflation, fed in large measure by military spending; and Sadat, who found himself more and more isolated as he and his American benefactors proved unable to deliver the diplomatic breakthrough assumed to have been inherent in Sadat's courageous Jerusalem pilgrimage and the Camp David process. Furthermore, the entire structure of American policy was now being subjected to pressure from a new quarter: the West Europeans, concerned about their own economic interests in the region and the seeming inability of American diplomacy to protect those interests.

A return to Egyptian–Israeli belligerence seemed unlikely. The removal of Egyptian military capability from any potential Arab military coalition and the realignment of the Egyptians with the United States was an important, even fundamental, change in the Middle Eastern strategic situation. Moreover, war between Iraq and Iran and military confrontation between Syria and Jordan at the end of 1980 further underscored the Moslem world's inability to unite to meet the Israeli nemesis. Carter's rhetoric after Camp David seemed to promise much more than the continued isolation of the Soviets from the region and ambiguous geopolitical shifts in the Middle Eastern strategic equation. Furthermore, the uncertainties rather than accomplishments were underscored by the caveat that nearly everyone attached to analysis of the Camp David process: Consolidation of what had been achieved and progress within the Camp David process depended largely on Sadat's retention of power in Egypt—a condition that would prove increasingly problematic unless the Camp David process yielded both the international and internal developmental benefits foreseen and promised by Sadat when he undertook his momentous 1977 trip to Jerusalem.

One could not be sure that the Camp David framework was itself sufficient, for even if a major breakthrough in Egyptian–Israeli negotiations could be achieved, it was always unclear how the Palestinians and Arab states were to be incorporated into the agreement. In this respect, the initial position of the Carter administration in 1977 may have made more sense. In his diplomatic overtures to the Palestinians and his apparent commitment to multilateral negotiations that would have included Palestinian representation at Geneva in some form, Carter was developing a framework that might have been more readily perceived as legitimate by all parties in the region. The Camp David process, in addition to cutting the Soviets out of the action, seemed to preclude this necessary contact with the Palestinians and other Arabs—with the exception of King Hussein of Jordan, who refused to attend.

Finally, in addition to the Palestinian homeland/autonomy question, there remained the issue of Jerusalem's status. That Jerusalem should be again free of Israeli control seemed crucial to the Saudi Arabians and all other Arab states. However, the Saudis' aspirations seemed unlikely to be fulfilled as the Israeli Knesset passed legislation in mid-1980 to make Jerusalem the permanent capital of Israel. Moreover, as these and other issues (such as outstanding territorial issues regarding Jordan, Syria and even Lebanon) dragged on, no one in the Carter administration (or among his political adversaries) could offer ideas as to the next step. And, of course, the longer the impasse persisted, the more likely it became that Arab West Bank militancy would continue to develop in the direction of more of the violence that had emerged by the end of the 1970s. Indeed, by mid-1980, the specter of PLO *and* extremist Israeli nationalist terrorism appeared as Arab attacks on Israeli settlements elicited extremist Israeli retaliations in the form of attacks on West Bank Arab leaders. Such instability provided opportunities for increased Russian influence. The signing of a twenty-year friendship treaty by Syrian President Hafez Assad and the Russians in late 1980, for example, provided access for the Russians. The Soviet Union, it seemed, almost like some adolescent Romeo, was available to any client who would accept its advances.

Nicaragua and Iran

Whatever domestic political respite Carter received for undertaking this tactically impressive act of summit diplomacy was brief, for longstanding American clients on opposite sides of the world were toppling. In Nicaragua in 1978 and 1979, Anastasio Somoza's regime grudgingly and then violently gave way before a coalition of Marxist revolutionaries, the Sandinista National Liberation Front, in coalition with a broad-based collection of opposition groups within the country. The American posture was to push Somoza toward a mediated settlement. The effort failed, and, after another six months of fighting, the Somoza regime collapsed in mid-1979, with the Carter administration moving quickly to recognize the new revolutionary government and support with economic assistance its efforts to achieve economic viability.

The reluctance to support Somoza represented something of a departure in American policy in Latin America. Although it conformed to the policy approach preferred by interdependence advocates, it was disturbing to traditionalists. The collapse of the twenty-five–year American investment in Iran was even more dramatic evidence—for those longing for the more simple era of pre-Vietnam and pre-parity American hegemony—of the bankruptcy of the Carter administration's foreign policy.

Throughout 1978, what had been assumed to be the unshakeable regime of Shah Mohammed Reza Pahlavi and, hence, the surrogate for American interests in the Persian Gulf area, slowly disintegrated in the face of increasingly violent demonstrations and rioting. Beneath the religious rhetoric concerning the immorality of the modernization programs pursued by the Shah was deep and intense resentment of a regime that was perceived as illegitimate and only the extension and instrument of American control. By the fall, the religious leader, the Ayatollah

Ruhollah Khomeini, exiled from Iran for fifteen years, was calling from Paris for demonstrations to bring down the Shah and for the institution of an Islamic Republic that would expel the United States and its influence. Strikes shut down the oil industry in November, and by the end of the year, virtually all sectors of the economy were paralyzed in response to the Ayatollah's urging. By early January 1979, the Shah was expressing his willingness to take a "vacation" once a new government appointed by him was in power. Within a week, the United States government—after considering a coup d'état[29]—endorsed his leaving, and on January 16, the Shah departed on a desultory journey that would take him to Egypt, Morocco, the Bahamas, Mexico, Panama, and finally Egypt again, in search of a place of exile. In the meantime, the Ayatollah returned to Tehran and, despite the existence of a civilian government, he and his Revolutionary Council assumed power.

Within Iran, months of revolutionary turmoil ensued as the religious militants consolidated their control of the revolution and, in the face of rebellions among Kurds, Baluchis, and other ethnic minorities, prepared for parliamentary elections and the promulgation of an Islamic constitution. American policy at this juncture was ambivalent. There did seem to be a willingness on the part of the Carter administration to wait for a subsiding of the revolutionary disorder and, in the interim, to try to work with whatever government emerged while maintaining contact with presumably the most pro-American elements on the Iranian scene. Thus, for example, in early October, the Defense Department announced that it was resuming the shipment of spare parts for American aircraft previously sold to the Shah.

This American search for a moderate center proved to be a profound misunderstanding of what was occurring within Iran. The religious hierarchy, with its deep hatred and resentment of the Shah and his American benefactors, was in control of the revolution despite the presence of a government that seemed to give the impression of working toward more normal relations with the United States. The magnitude of this misunderstanding of the internal situation in Iran became dramatically apparent in late October when President Carter, reportedly yielding to pressure from former Secretary of State Henry Kissinger and David Rockefeller, admitted the Shah to the United States for cancer treatment.

The effect inside Iran was electric. On November 4, militant students seized the U.S. embassy in Tehran and made hostages of some sixty Americans in the embassy compound. They would be released— the militants told the world through the hundreds of media representatives that converged to cover the seizure and the massive demonstrations that accompanied it — only if the Shah and the wealth he had taken from Iran were returned. Subsequently, the militants released the women and black hostages but insisted that the remainder would be held until their demands were met or the Ayatollah ordered otherwise. The Ayatollah, however, gave full support to the militants and threatened to put the hostages on trial.

With the Ayatollah and his militant Revolutionary Council now in control, the Carter administration found it virtually impossible to carry out negotiations. A United Nations Security Council resolution and International Court of Justice ruling that the seizure was illegal, and demanding the immediate release of the hostages, were obtained. Moreover, a United Nations mediation attempt was undertaken under the secretary general's auspice even as some economic and diplomatic sanctions were being applied. None of the efforts gained anything, however, but the Islamic Republic's defiance and a reiteration of the demands for the Shah's return. Finally on April 24 and 25 (to the dismay of Secretary of State Cyrus Vance, who was trying to negotiate even more stringent economic sanctions with the Common Market countries and Japan against Iran — a condition of which was that the United States would not use force), Carter ordered a rescue attempt involving helicopters, C-130 aircraft, and commandoes from a special antiterrorist unit. The rescue attempt failed disastrously as equipment failures at the desert strike base led to a decision to abort the mission, followed by the collision of a helicopter and a C-130 aircraft. Eight crewmen died, and their bodies were then ghoulishly displayed by the Iranians. The United States government and people could only wonder in frustrated consternation, what, if any, instruments of power could now be brought to bear.

Apart from the collapse of the Pahlavi regime itself, what outraged conservatives in the United States was the seeming reluctance and then inept use of American military power by Carter in support of the Shah and afterward. Whether military capability was relevant to the crisis is an issue to which we turn below. However, Carter's performance during the crisis was noteworthy for its apparent indecisiveness. When the crisis broke, the president was not prepared to extend unequivocal support to a man he had earlier toasted as an "island of stability" and for the remarkable "respect and admiration and love which your people give to you." In fact, he mixed public statements of support with ambivalence concerning the positioning of a naval task force in the region. Later, Carter sent the task force, but when the Shah suggested his own withdrawal, the administration seemed to encourage him. Finally, of course, there was the embarrassing failure of the rescue mission itself. For those who had come to question the president's leadership, it was the quintessential example of what one proponent of using military force in the region called an "America in decline."[30] The president, however, as his poll ratings declined, asserted that matters were now under "better control" and returned to the campaign activities he had earlier forsworn until the hostages were returned.

Another Decade . . . Another Doctrine

By the end of the decade, therefore, policies that the president liked to characterize as involving "a combination of adequate American strength, of quiet self-restraint in the use of it, of a refusal to believe in the inevitability of war and of a patient and persistent development of all the peaceful alternatives"[31] were being rejected by a vocal and increasingly influential segment of the policy establishment. Indeed, that organ of the establishment, *Foreign Affairs*, gave the lead article of its retrospective evaluation of 1979 to a critic who judged Carter foreign policy to have been a "failure" burdened by its "self-inflicted wounds."[32] Moreover, as the decade turned into an election year, the president was confronted by poll after poll that showed diminishing popular confidence in his foreign policy leadership and the likelihood that, if the election had been held in mid-1980, he would have lost to his Republican adversary.

Confronted with these political facts, the president had already begun to move toward his critics' position. As it became apparent, for example, that the SALT treaty was in trouble, Mr. Carter expressed a willingness to increase defense spending at both the conventional and strategic levels. Furthermore, when, in November, the U.S. embassy in Tehran was seized, the president, while rejecting the immediate use of force, increased the American naval presence in the Indian Ocean and began planning a permanent military presence in the region. By early 1980, more than twenty naval vessels, including two aircraft carriers, were stationed in the Arabian Sea. However, it was not the hostage crisis or the travails of SALT alone that led to the crystallization of a new posture on the part of the Carter administration. Rather, on December 26, 1979, the Soviet Union launched an invasion by upwards of eighty thousand men into Afghanistan in support of a pro-Soviet coup directed against a Marxist regime whose leader, Hafizullah Amin, was proving unable to control an Islamic insurgency but also pursuing an increasingly independent line from that preferred by Moscow. By December 27, Amin was dead, and it was apparent within the next few weeks that the Soviets intended to stay in Afghanistan in force until a pro-Soviet regime was firmly in place. The reaction in Washington recalled the deep days of crisis in the five years after World War II.

The SALT treaty was withdrawn by the president, although ritual references were made to the need to pass the treaty, the administration's rhetoric was now predominantly that of confrontation. The last remnant of detente was to be consigned to the attic, its presence too embarrassing for a president who now asserted that the United States "must pay whatever price is required to remain the strongest nation in the world."[33] Just before the Afghanistan invasion, the secretary of defense had warned, "We must decide now whether we intend to remain the strongest nation in the world. Or we must accept now that we will let ourselves slip into inferiority, into a position of weakness in a harsh world where principles unsupported by power are victimized, and that we will become a nation with more of a past than a future."[34] Afterwards, in his State of the Union Address, Carter claimed that in "a world of major power confrontation . . . [W]e have a new will at home to do what is required to keep us the strongest nation on earth."[35] What was "required" in Carter's view was a defense budget some 5 percent larger than the previous year and proposed future spending on defense that would lead to about 5 percent per year through the middle of the decade.[36]

No less important, the security interests and commitments to which these resources were to be committed had now grown. There remained, of course, the traditional European and Asian commitments, which, in the president's words, "would be automatically triggered." Now, however, there was the Persian Gulf and its oil:

> The denial of these oil supplies—to us or to others—would threaten our security and provoke an economic crisis greater than that of the Great Depression 50 years ago, with a fundamental change in the way we live.
> Twin threats to the flow of oil—from regional instability and now potentially from the Soviet Union—require that we firmly defend our vital interests when threatened.[37]

Accordingly, the administration established a rapid deployment force to be capable, when fully developed at mid-decade, to move anywhere from a few ships to as many as a hundred thousand men anywhere in the world, but especially into the Persian Gulf region. Much of their equipment was to be prepositioned on storage ships permanently stationed in the Indian Ocean. The troops, if and when needed, would be rapidly deployed by air into bases, access to which was to be negotiated with countries in the region. Finally, in the fall of 1980, as war raged between Iraq and Iran at the head of the Persian Gulf, the

Carter administration responded to a Saudi Arabian request for aid by deploying an AWACS air defense aircraft and ground support personnel in Saudi Arabia. In addition, the American naval presence in the Persian Gulf itself was increased. A Carter Doctrine was born and baptized.

Nor was the buildup to be concentrated solely on the Persian Gulf. Modernization of NATO was to proceed, including the introduction of a new main battle tank for U.S. forces, a new fighter aircraft, the F-16, and an expansion of the ability of NATO to launch nuclear weapons against the Soviet Union in the form of a new Pershing II missile to be supplemented by ground-launched cruise missiles. Strategically, the MX missile, a mobile ICBM with three times the number of warheads and throwweight and twice the accuracy of the Minuteman III, and the new Trident SLBM and submarines would all be fully deployed by the end of the decade, giving the United States the capacity to threaten the Soviets' ICBMs, where some 70 percent of their deliverable warheads were deployed in 1980. Talk of "nuclear war fighting" and "victory" in a nuclear war became commonplace. Subsequently, a new American targeting doctrine was announced that officially confirmed the intention of the United States to attack hardened Soviet targets. Finally, and perhaps most ominously from a Soviet standpoint, observers of the evening news were treated to the extraordinary sight at midyear of a Chinese Communist defense official standing shoulder to shoulder with an American secretary of defense in the halls of the Pentagon and announcing that the United States would begin the sale of "nonlethal" military hardware to the Chinese. Combat equipment, the Chinese official noted, would not be made available "at this time."

FACING THE LIMITS

In its initial formulation, therefore, the Carter Doctrine had about it the kind of open-ended and globalist character contained in the first of the many cold war doctrines. In Southwest Asia, the pledge as well as the region to which it was directed were filled with uncertainties. "You are not alone," Brzezinski told refugees at the Khyber Pass in early 1980. Facing Soviet-occupied Afghanistan with an automatic weapon in hand, he exhorted, "You will go back to your villages and your mosques. Your cause is just. God is on your side."[38] The Almighty, the Americans, and the disaffected Afghan mountain people might form a league against atheistic Southwest Asian communism, but neither the petropowers nor the middle-range powers of Europe or even Pakistan were eager to be enlisted in the new crusade. All the more reason to be grimly steadfast. For as a stern Brzezinski lectured television audiences during the latter half of 1980, Southwest Asia was now regarded as of no less strategic importance than had been Europe and East Asia during the early cold war years:

> I think it is important to remember that since WWII there first emerged the central strategic zone of Western Europe. The second central strategic zone for us was the Far East. In both places we have permanently stationed American forces. The third central strategic zone is southwest Asia, the Persian Gulf. . . . Iran, Turkey, to some extent Pakistan, Afghanistan as a buffer were the protective shield. That shield is now being pierced. As a consequence, our friends in the region and our vital interest in the third central strategic zone are beginning to be threatened. This is why this is becoming a strategic problem.[39]

Although Brzezinski recognized the need for using a different mix of foreign policy instruments in this new central strategic zone than had been employed elsewhere, America's buildup of military capability was the primary evidence of its new commitment. Moreover, Brzezinski predicted that American involvement in the region would be prolonged, stretching for at least two or three decades into the future.[40] Thus, the hard ground of confrontation stretched toward a horizon beyond vision. And if Brzezinski's rhetoric on the Afghan border is translated into policy, then rollback and liberation may be conjoined with the newly invigorated nuclear threat. Carter and Brzezinski seemed to have found John Foster Dulles three hundred miles from the Indian Ocean.

The Limits of Military Instruments

One reason that the Carter administration turned toward a reemphasis of security policy was the fear that the visible presence of American firepower was fast becoming about as welcome and as valuable as a Susan B. Anthony dollar: A discounted coin of uncertain value would have to be either withdrawn from circulation or given special emphasis. This was clearly the case in the long Iranian ordeal, when American arms seemed irrelevant and when American-promoted reform seemed a proximate (but certainly, in fact, not the only) cause of the Shah's collapse. As the one who once warmed the Peacock Throne flew off to exile, a pivotal assumption of at least the Kissinger years was challenged: American clients, no matter how well stocked militarily, could not be counted to remain semiautonomous agents of American interests. They could even become a foreign policy nemesis.

A defining characteristic of the Iranian crisis was the hesitance of American policy makers to use force or even to broach the subject openly. The gestures of support that were offered seemed out of a comic opera. A carrier force was ordered to the Persian Gulf from Subic Bay in the Philippines and then, after barely reaching the Straits of Malacca, directed to steam around in a desultory fashion. Equally frustrating was the fact that some of the United States' most dependable European clients refused to allow their NATO air bases to be used as staging areas for even a rescue squadron for the evacuation of American personnel.

American reluctance to use force and the unwillingness of its allies even to contemplate abetting its efforts is not understandable merely in terms of military incapacity. It can neither be simply attributed to a frayed post-Vietnam consensus or explained by a fear of Soviet intervention. A comprehensive explanation for American restrained, albeit clumsy, behavior must also include the realization that, quite simply, nobody in or outside the Carter administration could see what bearing force had to the political, religious, and social tensions tearing at the Pahlavi regime. Even if a quick-strike team had entered Iran, no one could offer a reasonable scenario of what they might accomplish once they had arrived. In early 1978, as Iran sank into chaos, Secretary of Defense Brown despondently ruminated: "We are as yet unsure of the utility of U.S. military power in Persian Gulf contingencies."[41]

The Enlistment of Economic Interdependence

In part, in responses to the obvious uncertainty concerning the relevance of military responses and the unmanageable elements of Carter's human rights campaigns, the administration turned to economic coercion. Perhaps, it was felt, economic preponderance could do what armies and threats could not. Ironically, however, this use, or misuse, of economic power came at the nadir of America's relative economic strength in this century. That is to say, the Carter administration had been unsuccessful in leading the industrialized world to the establishment of a comprehensive new international economic order. Much had been made of the initial attempt of the Carter administration to promote a series of economic summit conferences among the industrialized powers to coordinate their domestic economic policies. This reflected acceptance of the fact that these economies were now inextricably linked but also vulnerable to one another. Within months, however, it had become apparent that none of the industrialized powers were prepared to accept readily the kind of political risks that such coordination implied.

In the United States, for example, the Carter administration was confronted with a number of powerful economic interests demanding protection from, not an increase in, interdependence. The automobile industry—both management and labor—the steel industry, and portions of the home appliance industry were all pressuring the Carter administration to impose new quotas or tariffs to protect them from Japanese and European competition. The Europeans and Japanese, in turn, were critical of the inability or unwillingness of the United States to move decisively against its domestic inflation and thereby restore confidence in the dollar. And, of course, suffusing all of this international economic anxiety was the persistent vulnerability of developed and developing economies alike to rising prices for their energy imports from OPEC.

In short, interdependence had served to emphasize the conflicting needs and vulnerabilities of those caught in its web. This suggested, in turn, the need for sensitive and systematic coordination of policies. For a Carter administration increasingly preoccupied with the Soviet–American and Iranian crises, a traditional emphasis on using economic relationships as instruments of coercion gradually assumed dominance. The irony of this was doubly intense because the administration had come to office rejecting such an approach to economic interdependence. Moreover, those officials responsible for the attempted enlistment of economic interdependence as an instrumentality of American confrontation with the Soviet Union and Iran, had been, in some instances, among the most forceful proponents of a new and more cooperative approach to managing interdependence before they assumed public office. Now, however, they were called on to design and administer a kind of economic cold war. In truth, as many of them understood, economic warfare was more a symbol of pique and a sop to domestic critics on the right than a realistic instrument to affect events.

In the case of the Soviet Union, it was argued that even if a cutoff of wheat, high technology, or phosphates hurt Americans as much as it did the Soviets, it was all for the better. Any step that involved a trivial cost to the United States would be treated unseriously by the Russians. Yet there were almost no specific commodities for which the United States was the most important supplier. In dollar terms, most American exports to the Soviet Union were agricultural. Even if the Russians could not find enough grain on the open market, there was little reason to believe they would not be able to survive the contretemps. In the end, they would obtain most of the grains they need from others or simply do without. And, there was no evidence that European, Japanese, and Latin American suppliers and creditors would treat the Soviets in any manner other than business-as-usual.

If a convincing argument could be made that the Soviet Union and Eastern Europe had reached a point of strategic vulnerability vis-à-vis technological imports from the West, it still remained unclear how or whether such a vulnerability could be manipulated. Restraining credits would, at best, reduce the subsidy Western governments give their business to export to the Soviet Union. Tighter controls—if obtainable—would only increase the cost to the Russians of their own modernization. It would neither prevent it nor signicantly retard it. Moreover, attempts to restrict exports of some oil and gas equipment and technology would, at best, reduce the energy-generating capacity of the Soviet Union and perhaps give a kind of ironic incentive to any Russian urge to increase their stake in the Middle East. Further, a cutback on United States or European oil-related technology might leave Eastern Europe without Russian oil supplies and would force Soviet bloc countries to import more oil from OPEC, thereby further undermining Eastern Europe's hard-currency credit reserves as well as drawing down scarce financial resources necessary to purchase Western technology.

In the Iranian case, as well, there were important questions concerning the American use of economic leverage unanswered by an administration attempting to substitute economic warfare for military coercion. Clearly, the boycott of Iranian oil was an effort to prevent Iran from blackmailing the United States over the hostages. But the application of financial pressure on Iran, begun with a freeze on Iranian financial assets in the West, could not be effective unless the rest of the industrialized world was enlisted in the American-designed and -led economic warfare. At the onset of the crisis with Iran, reports circulated that the Europeans might particpate in limited measures, including even a slowing of trade with the Iranians. But they were reluctant to go much further. The Japanese were accused by American officials of moving with "unseemingly haste" to buy on the spot market Iranian oil previously intended for the United States. The government of Masayoshi Ohira, having narrowly survived a parliamentary crisis during the fall of 1979, resisted having the almost totally import-dependent Japanese economy drafted into the American economic war against Iran. With about 15 percent of Japanese daily imports coming from Iran (in early 1980), Japanese sensitivity was or should have been predictable. Moreover, because the Japanese had been the primary target of the Ford and Carter administrations' attempts to get the rest of the industrialized world to relent in its export pressure on the American market, one suspects that not all that many American credits were left in Tokyo. Moreover, disruption of the overall United States–Japanese economic relations seems scarcely worth the gains of economic warfare. Indeed, one wonders whether, at some point, American pressures on the Japanese to act against their economic self-interests, presaged by the "Nixon shocks" of the early 1970s, do not risk setting off a syndrome of Japanese hostility similar to that of the interwar period.

The Europeans Resist Conscription

The Carter administration's almost frantic attempts to fashion a new doctrine incorporating some combination of military and economic instruments raised a final and disturbing set of questions concerning the traditional core of American policy—the Atlantic community. The cold war, after all, had begun because of the fate of Europe and had been centered there for the most part. Throughout the period of European economic reconstruction, American ends and means had been ultimately—though sometimes reluctantly—accepted by the Europeans. By the late 1970s, however, European leaders, especially in the largest countries of the European community, were often brutal in their rejection and defiance of American leadership. Only with respect to the military dimensions of the alliance was there acceptance of American conceptions. But as the SALT process moved through the 1970s, an undercurrent of European worry that the United States' strategic concerns were ultimately not their own became apparent. By the onset of the 1980s, the Europeans had insisted on and won from the Carter administration an American commitment to place in Europe a new generation of intermediate-range nuclear weapons that could threaten the Soviet Union from Europe. Presumably, this would counter the Soviets' new tactical theater nuclear weapons, especially the SS-20 missile. It was understood that this step would complicate subsequent strategic arms limitations talks and negotiations concerning force reductions in Central Europe. In the late 1970s, there seemed to be a diminishing prospect that such negotiations would lead to significant results in any event. In the larger sense, however, the nagging fear persisted that, at some point, American strategic concerns and policy would be decoupled from those of Europe.

On other matters, the decoupling seemed already to have occurred, largely at European initiative. Thus, the American attempt to conscript the Europeans into economic warfare against the Iranians and diplomatic isolation of the Russians was met with resistance and then outright defiance. Slowly and painfully throughout early 1980, the Common

Market countries and Japan negotiated a series of economic sanctions that they might bring to bear on Iran, perhaps in fear that unless they participated in some form of economic warfare, the Americans would attempt what, from a European perspective, would be a dangerously provocative use of military force in a region on which they were vitally dependent for oil. After the United States attempted precisely such an intervention, even this rationale for cooperation vanished. The Britsh government of Prime Minister Margaret Thatcher could not command the support of even its own Conservative party, and the common European–Japanese position disintegrated. An independent European initiative on the Midde East was discussed within the European Community. The French lectured the new American secretary of state, Edmund Muskie, about the lack of coordination of diplomacy within the alliance and then, with studied cynicism, undertook their own announced summit with the Russians.

Reports circulated that, throughout Europe, there was a mixture of condescension and despair concerning the Carter administration's leadership capacity and the prospect of submitting the leadership of the alliance to the winner of a Carter–Reagan presidential contest. An American reporter in Europe felt that the European mood was captured by a French satirical magazine that portrayed the differences between the likely American presidential contestants in terms of cross-sectional views of Reagan's and Carter's heads showing the former as empty and the latter containing only a small peanut.

European concern and skepticism about the wisdom and constancy of American diplomacy was not new. The 1970s, however, saw somewhat greater willingness and capacity to articulate policies often in conflict with those of the United States. Certainly, one would not view the institutional mechanisms of the European Community as being equal to the task of fashioning and sustaining a truly "European" diplomacy. At the same time, however, coordinated and coherent alliance policy on anything except perhaps elements of security policy seemed a thing of the past. Even here, difficulties seemed likely to multiply, especially if the major European states — France, Great Britain, and Germany — set out on some form of quasi-coordinated military cooperation involving the British and French nuclear forces coupled with cruise missile technology. Finally, if the decline of American economic and diplomatic preponderance and the arrested state of development of European-wide institutions could not be reversed, it was conceivable that the larger European political economies might well feel compelled to seek their independent resolution of the tensions of interdependence.

CONCLUSION

One by one, the means by which the Carter administration had, at first, wished to turn aside from the cold war proved vulnerable to the apparent immutability of the Soviet–American contest and the doctrines and commitments that have surrounded that conflict. By the beginning of 1980, the Soviet Union—once placed in an equivalent situation with other global issues—reemerged as the pivotal focus of the Carter administration. With the Afghan crisis, an even more expensive series of undertakings was contemplated and formal overtures were tendered to an embarrassingly coquettish constellation and would be satrapies in the Persian Gulf region. It could not be argued that Oman, Yemen, or Somalia were outposts of liberal values. But the cold war quandary of aligning with regimes of low repute and military advantage had, after all been customary to just about everyone but Carter and some of his younger State Department advisers. Perhaps, after Afghanistan, the reproduction of personal animus in Soviet–American relations made it easier to yield scruple to necessity. Moreover, tired critics of an undifferentiated definition of American interests seemed to have spent their energies as cold war policy routines, shaped in an era when American power had been little contested, reappeared. It seemed reasonably clear that early advocates of interdependence and world order policies no longer controlled much of the Carter administration's image of international reality. On the other hand, it was by no means clear whether the attempt to marry somehow the more traditional conception of American interests with the ambiguous conditions of contemporary interdependence could serve as a guide for policy either.

In the tenth century, foreign ambassadors would be called to Constantinople that they might be impressed with the military splendor of an enervated empire. There was, as Harold Nicholson once described,

> interminable reviews at which the same troops emerging from one of the gates and entering by another, came round and round again carrying different kinds of armour. In order to dazzle . . . [by] glamour and mystery, mechanical devices caused the lions on the steps of [the Emperor's] throne to roar terribly.[42]

By 1980, one had the feeling that the American empire, like that of Byzantium, was also largely held together with smoke and mirrors. Not that firepower was unavailable—rather, the real question was whether any volume or type of coercion could now service extended American commitments.

NOTES

1. See, for example, Stanley Hoffmann's two essays, "The Hell of Good Intentions," *Foreign Policy*, No. 29 (Winter 1977–78), pp. 3–26; and "A View from At Home: The Perils of Incoherence," *Foreign Affairs, America and the World 1978*, Vol. 57, No. 3, pp. 463–491.

2. See his interview with James Reston, *New York Times*, December 31, 1978, and again in the *New York Times*, March 30, 1980.

3. See, for example, Henry Kissinger, *White House Years* (Boston: Little, Brown, 1979), esp. pp. 54–70, 195–225; also Robert Tucker, "America in Decline: The Foreign Policy of Maturity," *Foreign Affairs, America and the World 1979*, Vol. 58, No. 3, pp. 449–484; and "A New International Order?" *Commentary*, Vol. 59 (February 1975).

4. Among the many analyses of the sort outlined here, see Robert O. Keohane and Joseph Nye, Jr., *Power and Interdependence: World Politics in Transition* (Boston: Little, Brown, 1977); C. Fred Bergsten and Lawrence Krause, eds., *World Politics and International Economics* (Washington, D.C.: Brookings, 1975); Seyom Brown, *New Forces in World Politics* (Washington, D.C.: Brookings, 1974), and "The Changing Essence of Power," *Foreign Affairs*, Vol. 51 (January 1973); Richard Cooper, *The Economics of Interdependence* (New York: McGraw-Hill, 1968); and Ed Morse, *Modernization and the Transformation of International Relations* (New York: Free Press, 1976). Nye, Bergsten, Cooper, and Morse all became part of the Carter administration.

5. Leslie Gelb, cited by *U.S. News and World Report*, January 20, 1980, p. 24.

6. Cited by James Wooten, "Here comes Zbig," *Esquire*, November 1979, p. 120.

7. Zbigniew Brzezinski, *Between Two Ages: America's Role in the Technotronic Era* (New York: Penguin Books, 1970), p. 9.

8. Brzezinski, "America in a Hostile World," *Foreign Policy*, No. 23 (Summer 1976), p. 65.

9. Ibid.

10. From a remarkably revealing interview in March of 1975, found in G. R. Urban, ed., *Detente* (New York: Universe Books, 1976), p. 263.

11. Ibid.

12. Ibid., pp. 278–279.

13. Ibid., p. 264.

14. Cited by Joseph Kraft, *Washington Post*, June 17, 1977.

15. Speech of November 21, 1977, Department of State, Bureau of Public Affairs, Washington, D.C., 1977.

16. Ibid.

17. *New York Times*, March 23, 1977.

18. See, for example, Vance's Harvard Commencement Address on June 5, 1980 in *New York Times*, June 6, 1980, p. A12.

19. "Human Rights: Selected Documents," No. 5 (Washington, D.C.: Department of State, Bureau of Public Affairs, n.d.).

20. Elizabeth Drew, "Reporter at Large: Human Rights," *The New Yorker*, July 18, 1977, p. 54.

21. For similar comments see ibid., *passim*.

22. Ibid., p. 56.

23. Zbigniew Brzezinski and Samuel Huntington, *Political Power: USA/USSR* (New York: Viking, 1964), p. 424.

24. Excellent surveys of the development of the Carter administration's SALT II positions and the negotiations themselves can be found in Strobe Talbot, *Endgame: The Inside Story of SALT II* (New York: Harper and Row, 1979); and Thomas W. Wolfe, *The SALT Experience* (Cambridge, Mass.: Ballinger, 1979). Useful documentary sources are Roger P. Labrie, ed., *SALT Handbook: Key Documents and Issues 1972–1979* (Washington, D.C.: American Enterprise Institute, 1979); and U.S. Department of State, *SALT II Agreement*, Selected Documents No. 12A (Washington, D.C.: Bureau of Public Affairs, June 1979).

25. Wolfe, op. cit., pp. 222–223.

26. Presidential address to the graduating class at the United States Naval Academy, June 7, 1978, *New York Times*, June 8, 1978.

27. For a review of the Camp David Summit and American policy during this period, see John C. Campbell, "The Middle East: The Burden of Empire," *Foreign Affairs, America and the World 1978*, pp. 613–632. Documentary materials may be found in U.S. Department of State, *The Camp David Summit, September 1978* (Washington, D.C.: Bureau of Public Affairs, 1978).

28. Testimony given at a hearing before the Subcommittee on Europe and the Middle East of the Committee on Foreign Affairs, House of Representatives, 96th Congress, 1st Session, October 16, 1979.

29. See the article by the former American ambassador William H. Sullivan, "Dateline Iran: The Road Not Taken," *Foreign Policy*, No. 40 (Fall 1980), pp. 175–186.

30. Tucker, op. cit.

31. Address at the United States Naval Academy, op. cit.

32. Tucker, op. cit., pp. 468ff.

33. State of the Union Message, *New York Times*, January 22, 1980.

34. *New York Times*, December 14, 1979.

35. State of the Union Message.

36. See U.S. Department of Defense, *FY 1981 DOD Report* (Washington, D.C.: Government Printing Office, 1980).

37. State of the Union Message.

38. CBS Sunday Night News, February 4, 1980. See also *Washington Post*, February 4, 1980. Brzezinski's more studied analysis of this event was revealed in an interview with television commentator Bill Moyers: "Bill Moyers' Journal: A Conversation with Zbigniew Brzezinski," Public Broadcasting System, November 16, 1980.

39. "National Security Adviser Brzezinski Interviewed on 'Issues and Answers,'" *Department of State Bulletin*, Vol. 80, No. 2039 (June 1980), p. 49.

40. *MacNeil/Lehrer Report*, Public Broadcasting System, October 15, 1980.

41. *Washington Post*, January 27, 1978.

42. Harold Nicholson, *The Evolution of Diplomacy* (New York: Collier Brooks, 1954), p. 41.

Chapter 10
The New
Cold War

Much of the Reagan administration seemed to reside in the realm of the demi-real. Reagan's formative experience seems to have been his small-town boyhood and his days in Hollywood. President Reagan's former speech writer and adviser, Patrick Buchanan, characterized the Reagan world view as the world of "legend and myth."[1]

"WHERE'S THE REST OF ME?"[2]

Reagan's old California friend, Ed Clark, when he was National Security Council assistant, used films and documentaries to brief the president. Serious observers believed that Reagan's attachment to his Strategic Defense Initiative, or "Star Wars," could be traced to his days in Hollywood and the 1940 role Reagan played in the film "Murder in the Air" in which the actor who would be president defeated enemy agents using a beam weapon.[3] Not suspecting that a microphone was left open and was picking up his comments, Henry Kissinger averred to a small group of scholars, "When you meet the president, you ask yourself how he should be governor much less the president?" Thomas P. O'Neil, the former Speaker of the House of Representatives, said, "He has a great tendency of going into space and star-gazing, but that's nothing new."[4] Associates would find him "out of touch," and his frequently employed anecdotes not infrequently simply missed the point. Seen on this level, the delegated presidency was a useful, even necessary, mask for Reagan's substantial ignorance across a myriad of issues.

Reagan forgot the names of trusted aides and cabinet officers. His cavalier treatment of facts in public statements were a matter of distress to his aides, who spent enormous energy amending the statements the next day. His aides were tormented before and after press conferences by the depth of the President's ignorance and his lack of attention to detail. "Each time," said Larry Speakes, his press aide and close

friend since Reagan had been Governor of California, "it was like rein-
venting the wheel." Matters were not helped much by the president's
lack of interest in current events. As Speakes put it, "He read the comic
pages first. And he did not read the rest of the newspaper with much
attention or thoroughness."[5] Lou Cannon wrote in 1982, seven years
before Reagan, at the age of 78, was to step down from his second term:

> . . . [H]e possessed only a rudimentary knowledge and was intellectually
> lazy. . . . Because of Reagan's knowledge gaps, his presidential news con-
> ferences became adventures into the uncharted waters of his mind. His
> advisors . . . crossed their fingers.[6]

Grave, but perhaps unfair, charges were levied by journalists,
critics, and academics who alleged that there was not a functioning President at all. Recollections of the presidency in the last days of Woodrow
Wilson were refreshed. There were reports that the Reagans believed
in ghosts,[7] and that both the president and his wife resorted to an as-
trologer for advice about auspicious dates for different presidential activities, including the signing of the Intermediate Nuclear Forces (INF)
treaty with the Soviet Union.[8] Academics expert in measuring "cognitive impairment" argued that Mr. Reagan's 1980 campaign promise that
if "he ever was thought to be senile, he'd submit to test," should be
enforced by Congress and that Reagan ought to have been subjected
to regular medical investigation of his declining mental faculties.[9] There
were even alarming assertions that, to the degree the president did have
"command," he was under the influence of dangerous notions. Thus,
he was accused of being a covert nuclear fatalist and a victim of "evan-
gelical determinists." To be sure, evidence existed. In October of 1983,
Reagan told Thomas Dine of the American–Israel Public Affairs
Committee,

> I turn back to your ancient prophets in the Old Testament, and the signs
> foretelling Armageddon, and I find myself wondering if we're the gener-
> ation that's going to see that come about . . . believe me, they certainly
> describe the time we're going through.

Another time, as his wife, Nancy, gasped "Oh, no!" the president told
journalists, "We must plan according to Armageddon."[10]

Reagan was aware of the charges and insinuations and resented
them. Indeed, Reagan felt compelled to protest, at the height of the
Iran–contra scandal, that he was "not a potted plant president."[11] The
president wrote many of his own speeches, especially the ones delivered each Saturday on noontime radio, and he redrafted the sometimes

confusing and contradictory bureaucratic messages "bucked up" to him by his aides.

The great unarticulated secret of Reagan's appeal and hold on the American mind was his charm and cordiality; the American people appreciated his grace. After the attempt on his life, and especially after his and his wife's battle with cancer, he faced every adversity with dignity, courage, modesty and humor. Of equal importance, he was courtly and generous to his opponents. Plain good manners and a pleasant disposition are, in most places — outside of the Boston–Washington corridor — the *sine qua non* of both collective and private life. Civility is the great glue of a fissiparous and disparate nation. Recent decades have seen the loss, at the highest levels of governance, of this core of what middle Americans expect from one another. If Reagan had a unique talent beyond luck and instincts, these attributes of amiability were it. Reagan made Air Force One available to the Kennedy family, unlike Nixon, Johnson, and, indeed, Carter, who resented the family as a clan of false pretenders. He flew family and friends to the funeral of his old liberal critic, Senator Jacob Javits. And when there was news of an illness or misfortune among those who he knew (and, not infrequently, among those he did not know), the president would often call to offer quiet comfort. He could tell spontaneous jokes and laugh at himself. Lew Cannon wrote: "Reagan spent a career being a 'Prospero' of American memories, a magician who carries a bright, ideal America like some holograph in his mind and projects its image into the air."[12]

One key to both Reagan's problems and successes was his passive nature.[13] He also did not like to be instrusive. Once, he did not report a fire in the Oval Office because he did not want to disturb his aides.[14] The penalty Reagan paid for this disengagement from policy substance was that the decision-making process was fragmented, ad hoc, and inconsistent. Donald T. Regan, the President's first-term treasury secretary, wrote: "I never saw the President alone and never discussed economic[s] . . . or policy with him one-on-one. From the first day to last . . . I was flying by the seat of my pants."[15] Former Secretary of State Alexander Haig confirms the accuracy of this picture of Reagan policy-making leadership:

> . . . [T]o me the White House was as mysterious as a ghost ship; you heard the creak of the rigging and the groan of the timbers and even glimpsed the crew on deck. But which one of the crew was at the helm? It was impossible to know for sure.[16]

The decision-making norm of the Reagan years was a kind of Brownian motion; contradictions marked the day-to-day stuff of policy. The seemingly nondirectional, almost random movement, to policies led some officials to act on what they believed to be the operating assumptions of "Reaganism." Reagan's press secretary, Larry Speakes, for instance, invented dialogue between Reagan and Gorbachev. If the testimony of Vice Admiral John Poindexter, National Security Assistant, can be believed, the NSC and the CIA Director William Casey calculated what Mr. Reagan really intended in Latin America and Iran, and then they acted without burdening the President with the liability of either knowledge or decision. Poindexter, two months into his job as national security adviser, claimed he made these decisions on his own,[17] without getting any formal authorization from anyone. Attorney General Edwin Meese explained on November 25, 1986, that Vice Admiral Poindexter's action was correct because "The President would approve if asked."[18]

This "decisional autonomy" led directly to the Iran–Contral scandal. A few presidential agents conducted a private foreign policy, selling, at a discount, arms to Iran, which was at war with Iraq. Iran was, however, proscribed by law as a recipient of U.S. weapons because of their contributions to a worldwide series of bombings, hijackings, and assassinations. At the same time the U.S. arms were showing up in Iran, the State Department was trying to coordinate a European arms embargo to isolate the radical Khomeini regime. Yet, in the midst of this "Operation Staunch," NSC staffers went off to make fresh overtures to Khomeini.[19] One of the aims of the operation was to secure sufficient profits from these arms sales to finance the antigovernment Nicaraguan guerrillas, the contras. The contras, however, were prohibited by congressional statute from receiving either material or nonmaterial U.S. combat assistance. The overture to Iran was also designed to help free U.S. hostages, but paying tribute to kidnappers was at odds with a U.S. policy dating back to Adams, Jefferson, and the Barbary pirates. The U.S. did not pay ransom, the administration told the French and Germans when they negotiated trades of their own to free their captives in Lebanon.

The peregrinations of NSC officials in this amazing exercise had been published in November of 1986 by a Lebanese magazine that had learned of these comings and goings via pro-Iranian broadsides that littered the streets of Beirut.[20] For several weeks after the revelations, the NSC initiative lurched along independently as Secretary of State George Shultz confessed to an obviously incredulous interviewer on Face the Nation that he could not speak with authority about U.S. policy toward Iran.[21] Later, the president explained variously that he forgot what U.S. policy was or that he did not know or that he did not understand what his administration was doing. The president's chief of staff, Donald T. Regan, blamed it on the NSC, who had told the president so many cover stories for press conferences that "this sort of confused the President's mind."[22] Whatever the president believed and "knew" at the time, the Iran–contra episode was a damning indictment of the perils of detachment and policy incoherence.

Reagan rarely determined specific policies or negotiated portentous issues with heads of state. This was delegated to his staff and the national security apparatus. The whole national security process had been distorted and misshapen by the hiccuping parade of staff changes within the White House and NSC. Facts were transcended. The question that each new set of advisers who coagulated on any given matter addressed was one of what would the president want if he were asked and if had been brought up to speed (apparently, no mean feat) on any given issue? As a result "ad hocism" was driven to a level of analytic supremacy. Policy became subject to two basic criteria: Would it "play well" on the evening news, and would the president "look all right"? It was almost as if the president was an old vaudeville hoofer who customarily asked his audience, "How am I doing?" and, not noticing the hook, jauntily proceeded with his act. The purpose was to entertain and satisfy. National goals still existed, husbanded by the permanent bureaucracy and a few officials with a sense of both institutional mission and historic policy. Later in the administration, when more pragmatic officials such as Howard Baker (chief of staff), George Shultz (secretary of state), Frank Carlucci (secretary of defense), James Baker (secretary of treasury), and Colin Powell (security adviser) assumed control after the Iran–contra scandal discredited and flushed from the administration many of the ideologues who had dominated affairs earlier, administration policy seemed more coherent, if not creative. In the long meanwhile, public debate suffered and not a few despaired. A fine historian, Barbara Tuchman wrote:

> A peculiar vacuum exists. . . . Where is the outrage? Where's the anger that ought to have met the death of 241 marines [blown up in poorly defended barracks while on service in Beirut in 1983] . . . and where's the anger over 37 deaths on the *Stark* [a ship hit by Iraqi missiles while patrolling the Persian Gulf in 1987]? And now, where is the outrage over the disclosures of misconduct and incompetence by public officials of the highest rank?[23]

REAGAN'S CONTAINMENT

At the end of his tenure, Reagan saw the assumptions that directed his term as president tattered and frayed. The radical conservatism that had been conjured by Reagan's victory was dispossessed, its religious fringe tainted by scandals befitting any Elmer Gantry. Many of the Reagan appointees to agencies, bureaus, and departments seemed to view public service with the gleaming eye of a Florida swamp developer. Two thirds of the White House "troika" of advisers that had been with Reagan from his days in California politics were under grand jury investigations, facing indictment, or had already received jail sentences. Reagan's economic policies succeeded in the sense that they corresponded with a revival of American industry and falling oil prices. But the seventy months of growth seemed to be buoyed by a gigantic scheme for "kiting" the national debt. Unscrupulous freebooters appended themselves to the National Security Council and U.S. covert activities.[24] Overseas, a sordid litany of officials who had been embraced by the Reagan administration were revealed as heinous dictators. The old "evil empire" of the first term, the Soviet Union, became manifestly more open and normal, and President Reagan turned to asserting that "a turning point in the history of East–West relations" had arrived and that he was willing to give Mikhail Gorbachev "the benefit of the doubt" that the Soviet leader was intent on meaningful economic and social reforms.[25] Howard Phillips, a conservative spokesperson, called Reagan a "useful idiot" for the communists because of his willingness to truck with the Soviets across the negotiating table. Allies sensing an increasing incoherence and even irrelevance to American power and purpose gradually began to move to independent arrangements. The Reagan Revolution, with its call for an invigorated containment, departed with Reagan. But there was less grace in the leave-taking than the advent. It seemed the end of a brief era.

Symbolic Defense Policy

The Reagan administration came to office with what is now often portrayed as a very different set of assumptions about arms control and the Soviet–American relationship. While, initially, any agreement with the Soviets was suspect to Reagan stalwarts of the first term, the overall position of the Reagan team toward an appropriate strategic posture differed from that of the Carter administration more in tone and style than in substance. The Reagan administration's steadfast belief, maintained for two terms, was that arms could make a difference. Under this premise, the Reagan administration worked furiously on an arms buildup designed in the last eighteen months of President Carter's term. Even the normally recondite Secretary of State Alexander Haig was able to give clear expression to this policy's operating premise:

Strategic nuclear arms do not exist in a world of their own. Fundamentally, they remain an expression of strength. Nations accumulate military power in order to give themselves freedom of action and deny it to their rivals. In seeking the protection of stronger nations, weaker ones tend to choose sides (or at least not offend) what they believe will be the winning side.[26]

Reagan's formal decision documents regarding nuclear war were rewritten in a language more startlingly confrontational, but virtually all the programs requested by the Reagan administration had been part of the Carter administration's last two budget requests. To be sure, new ships in abundance were added to the U.S. fleet — most conspicuously, two additional carrier battle groups. A healthy civil defense program received both more funds and more publicity. The B-1 bomber was rejuvenated despite evidence, later borne out by flight tests and engineer's reports, that the aircraft could not perform any plausible mission better than the thirty-year-old B-52s.[27]

In terms of performance, the Reagan funding spurt affected the margins of military effectiveness. Without tankers, oilers, ship replenishment vessels, and petty officers, for instance, the navy looked better but could not operate that many "ship days" longer. Strategic modernization cost a great deal, but most of the systems involved had been literally "in the ground" since the late 1960s. After eight Reagan years, there were no more land-based ballistic missiles than at the start of Reagan's tenure, although the number of warheads had been increased, and the fifty MX missiles had found a basing mode in old Titan missile silos of the early 1960s. The army had gained two more commands in the last of the Carter years and began a rolling, almost nonstop exercise in Central America. But, by 1989, the army was smaller. The army's lift capability — its ability to get from one point to another and, on arrival, to have enough prepositioned stocks to fight for any time — was given little attention. As Reagan left office, the army had shrunk considerably in numbers, and was insufficiently supplied and manned for most actions.[28]

Nonetheless, both Republicans and Democrats joined in creating an impression that, in the Reagan years, something vastly different had gone on beyond the vast sums that were delivered to the Pentagon for advanced research, more flight-time increases in military pay, and longer training tours. But even the space-based technologies that were at the heart of President Reagan's "dream," as he put it, of a new strategic defense system were well under way before Carter left office. Discussions in the NSC, in the last eighteen months of the Carter administration, had already led to the conclusion that the ABM treaty would have to be reviewed within the decade. All of Carter's departing national security team—Secretary of State Muskie, Defense Secretary Harold Brown, and National Security Adviser Zbigniew Brzezinski—in late 1980, were concerned that new Soviet suggestions to strengthen the ABM treaty would be inimical to U.S. plans to defend the MX.[29]

If the ABM treaty appeared problematical before Reagan assumed office, there was little disagreement among hard-line professionals in the defense department about the necessity for conserving the SALT II agreement. From the Joint Chiefs through the CIA, the NSC, and the Defense Department, the permanent bureaucracy was convinced the SALT II agreement worked in the United States' favor because at a minimum, it capped potential Soviet deployments and did little to limit U.S. programs. In private, the Reagan administration was aware of the SALT II treaty's advantages, even while publicly excoriating the treaty's shortcomings. As a result, for nearly seven years, until November 1986, Reagan's national security team stayed within the SALT II treaty's terms through the document's expiration date, even though the treaty had never reached the floor of the Senate. When the 131st cruise-missile-armed B-52 began flight testing, by all accounts, the "breach" was more symbolic than substantive.

Carter, however, was held by the Reagan team to have stood for almost everything wrong with U.S. foreign policy. But Carter's national security apparatus shared, in private, the Reagan team's concerns that the Soviets were not in "compliance" with significant arms control undertakings with the United States, specifically, the Threshold Nuclear Test Ban Treaty limiting Soviet atomic testing to 150 kilotons. Similarly, the Carter bureaucracy fretted about the "encryption" of Soviet missile tests and fragmentary reports of the use of poison gas in Afghanistan. Following the Soviet invasion of Afghanistan, apparently in the face of Brezhnev's personal assurances to President Carter that the Soviet military was about to do no such thing, the Carter administration was suffused by a sense that the Soviets were inveterate liars. When, therefore, there was an outbreak of what turned out to be naturally caused anthrax on the Soviet city of Sverdlovsk, Carter voiced a suspicion shared by many in the intelligence community that Soviet military experiments with lethal agents had gone terribly wrong, causing more than a thousand cases of a horrible, disfiguring disease deep in European Russia.[30]

President Carter and his national security bureaucracy submerged many of these concerns, not because they were irrelevant to U.S.–Soviet relations, but because Carter was running for another term, and there was hope that, later, SALT II could be returned to the Senate and ratified. The Carter administration calculated that raising these concerns before the election would merely further darken an atmosphere already little conducive to treaty signing. After SALT II had been brought forward and, presumably, approved, the belief existed, at least in some Carter administration quarters, that the U.S.–Soviet atmosphere would improve. Then, the pending agenda of Soviet treaty "compliance," and the funding of new U.S. weapons programs, could be addressed. But, of course, Jimmy Carter was resoundingly defeated.

In volume and in tone, it appeared to many observers that "something different" was going on in defense and foreign policy in the Reagan years. The out-of-office national security professionals from the Carter years cooperated with the Reaganites in generating this impression. Thus, to this extent, at least, if the 1980s were to be characterized by the ascendancy of symbols over substance, it was a bipartisan effort. The truth was that much of the ground work had been fully laid by regnant cold warriors of Carter's last days. To be sure, new wrinkles had developed. Not the least was the Reagan team's success in placing the Soviets in the worst possible light at almost every turn.

Germs and Bee Feces:
The Politics of Accusation —
and Defense Budgets

The Republican party platform "deplor[ed] the attempts of the Carter Administration to cover-up Soviet noncompliance with arms control agreements."[31] For Reagan's first four years—despite a number of newspaper stories on background and numerous speeches alleging Soviet perfidy—no specific, formal assertion was made that the Soviets had actually and assuredly broken treaties, save for the accusation that the Soviets had used a substance called trochothecone mycotoxins, in the form of a poisonous biological excrescence, labeled "yellow rain" by Lao and Cambodian refugees. The mycotoxin story promised proof of Soviet misdeeds on an epic scale. Deaths were said to number in the thousands as a result of biological proxy experimentation on hapless, noncombatant, and refugee peoples. The administration also asserted that credible evidence existed that mycotoxins had been deployed in Afghanistan as well. The evidence for all these hair-raising assertions rested on the single, uncorroborated, 1981 analysis of a leaf and a stem sample brought back to Washington from Cambodia.[32]

The use of mycotoxins would have been an important breach of the Geneva Protocols of 1925 and 1972 outlawing chemical and biological weapons. The formal U.S. charge against the Soviets was delivered in Berlin by Secretary of State Alexander Haig at the urging of Richard Burt, then the director of the State Department's Office of Political–Military Affairs. The "fact" that there was a report that mycotoxins had been used as weapons of terror normally would have been made known with a press conference. But the news was delayed for a while, so that European audiences might gain a fuller understanding of Soviet perfidy. The idea, Haig wrote to the president, was to gain "maximum impact from this issue."[33] The strategy of accusation was designed by Reagan's hardline stalwarts to allow time for the Reagan administration to position itself better in the context of massive European public unrest surrounding deployment of new U.S. missiles in Europe. If the Soviets could be shown to be behind truly atrocious crimes, European public protests might be stilled and the introduction of new U.S. intermediate-range weapons could find a more hospitable climate.

Two years later, after Haig's dramatic charge, the international scientific community came to suspect that honeybees, which apparently swarm in huge numbers in several parts of Asia, also deposit yellow spots on leaves and grass, "identical in size, color and general appearance" as the toxic Yellow Rain. For more than five years, scientific evidence mounted: Yellow Rain was simply bee feces. But the Defense and State Departments doggedly asserted that there had been a Soviet transfer of bacteriological weapons to their Asian clients.[34] Only as the U.S. gradually became more serious about arms control negotiations did the issue of mycotoxins begin to be met by embarrassed shrugs.

KAL 007

On September 1, 1983, in the days leading up to reengagement of the Soviets at the conference table in Geneva, a Korean commercial airliner (KAL 007) crossing the Pacific between the Sino–Soviet coastline and Japan, was shot from the sky. All 269 passengers perished, including one U.S. Congressman. The Boeing 747 had just finished an hour long fly-over of a sensitive Soviet test facility.[35] The Soviets, according to their conversations between pilot and Soviet ground control, believed the "target" was a surveillance craft. A U.S. KC 135 did, it seems, make passes over the same territory only a few hours earlier.[36]

The Korean airliner incident came at the moment when Soviet General Secretary Yuri Andropov had proposed a nuclear testing moratorium. A similar kind of initiative had been proposed by the United States in the early 1960s and had, eventually, led to the first real arms control agreement, the atmospheric Test Ban Treaty of 1963. At the time KAL 007 passed over the tip of the Sakahalin Island "exclusion zone," there had been quiet and unpublicized explorations by the secretary of state, with the approval of the president, for cultural exchanges and opening new consulates in Kiev and San Francisco.[37]

Despite the delicate overtures that were underway, the fact that the Russians were just returning to the INF talks, and that Reagan's foreign policy planners and campaign strategists had hoped for a summit before the 1984 election, the Reagan administration began to flail away at the Soviets. Members of the administration decided to play the KAL 007 hand for all the anti-Soviet leverage that could be mustered, and no voices of restraint were heard.[38] "Real-time" intelligence had made it clear that the Soviet command had mistook the Boeing 747 for a military espionage plane. There was also, at least in the State Department and CIA, the still-fresh memory that the last time a commercial airplane had penetrated deep within Soviet airspace, Soviet officers had suffered unusually harsh reprimands. The opportunity to portray the Soviets in the worst, even if inaccurate, light proved irresistible. Using as a platform the Point Magu Naval Air Station tarmac, Larry Speakes, the presidential spokesman, read a statement, according to one NSC aide, drafted in large part by the president himself:

> While events in Afghanistan and elsewhere have left few illusions about the . . . Soviet Union. . . , all of us had hoped that certain *irreducible standards of civilized behavior*, nonetheless, obtained. . . . What can we think of a regime that so broadly trumpets its vision of peace and global disarmament and yet so callously and *quickly commits a terrorist act* to sacrifice the life of innocent human beings? What can be said about *Soviet credibility* when they so *flagrantly lie about such a heinous act? What can be the scope of mutual disclosures* with a state whose values permit it to commit such atrocities?[39]

Not surprisingly, the intense invective, portraying the incident as deliberate mass homicide — when, in fact, U.S. officials know it to be a horrible accident — was destructive of the very initiatives the State Department and the president had been quietly pursuing. The way the charges were phrased — that the Soviets were a piratical state, residing in the outlands of international society, beyond civilization — made it seem that *any* agreement, much less one on such a critical question as limiting the national means of self-defense, would seem folly or worse. To the vice president, George Bush, and to the secretary of state, whatever their private beliefs, the KAL 007 incident had the saving grace of providing them rhetoric with which to prove themselves as hardliners. To administration civilian defense officials, the downing of KAL 007 was an irresistible opportunity to put the Soviets on the defensive. Especially for the true Reaganites, such as Richard Perle in the Defense Department, who had been characterized by his bureaucratic antagonists at the State Department as the "Prince of Darkness,"[40] the tragic KAL

007 incident was a vehicle that could carry the reinflated defense budget a substantial distance while delaying negotiations.

Opponents of arms control were well aware of allied concern about management of East–West relations and the domestic pressure for a nuclear freeze, and they knew that, eventually, competing fiscal pressures would be felt. One day, there would be an audit, and the budgetary piper would have to be paid. The defense budget could not claim sanctuary in perpetuity. Then, in the "out years," Reagan hardline planners who demanded a manifest and incontestable strategic superiority, were hopeful that the President's Strategic Defense Initiative might be more than a series of experiments in the desert and complicated models capable of being run on only the world's largest computers. Then, strategic superiority would be palpable. The Navy would have its much-coveted six hundred ships. With a bit more time, U.S. war-fighting strategies envisioned at almost every conceivable level, from insurgency through massive strategic exchanges, would find real, "prompt" and responsive forces. If time could be purchased, and the initial funding surge maintained, keels would be laid and missiles implanted; space research would yield results; and visibly capable and usable instruments of policy would flourish.

To the new "irreconcilables," the KAL 007 incident was, therefore, all opportunity. KAL 007 could help put off the day when the Soviets would be engaged diplomatically and the bills for the defense buildup would have to be paid. A price beyond money and time came with this. An unhappy tradition of corrupting the public debate in foreign affairs was perpetuated. And, to that extent, democratic processes and the public's ability to make informed decisions were left out of the calculus altogether.

KAL 007 capped off two and a half years of charges regarding Soviet bad faith in maintaining international commitments. With the regularity of a fine spring rain, a drizzle of newspaper articles and memos came down, indicating Soviet lapses in observing SALT. There was news that, in February of 1983, the Soviets had flight tested a "new missile," the SS-25. In July of 1983, the administration told Congress that the Soviets were building a battle management ABM facility. In the immediate aftermath of KAL 007, it would have been surprising indeed for the Senate to have done anything other than pass, by a vote of ninety-three to zero, a bill requiring the president to submit a report on the "record of Soviet compliance and non-compliance with the letter and spirit of all existing arms control agreements to which the Soviet Union is a party."[41]

The Soviets responded to this full-court press of accusation, pres-

sure, and buildup with real alarm. There seemed to be a belief that
the United States really might be preparing for war. The chief of the
London KGB station noted a virtual panic on the part of Soviet intelligence.[42] Extensive KGB "watches" were established for signs of nuclear
attack. The "alert" was not lifted until Gorbachev came to power. According to one careful analysis, as 1981 unfolded, Soviet defense minister Nikolai Ogarkov prepared to place Soviet forces on a war-footing.[43]
At a rate that exceeded four times their usual pace, the Soviets practiced "surging" submarines into the Baltic. One Russian submarine was
embarrassingly run aground in Sweden, and other submarines were said
to be lost. Inexperienced Russian submarine commanders, working at
a more rapid clip in augmented numbers, apparently were attempting
to reduce Soviet vulnerability to attack by U.S. hunter–killer submarines detailed to sink Soviet subs in Soviet home waters in the early moments of any conflict.[44]

The "Game Plan"
for Strategic Nuclear Policy

The early Reagan years were marked by a strange insouciance regarding nuclear war. At Secretary of State Haig's confirmation hearing, the
former NATO commander referred to the possibility of a nuclear "shot
across the bow" to warn the Soviets that an invasion of Europe would
have substantial nuclear consequences.[45] A few months later, a deputy
undersecretary of defense, T. K. Jones, told Los Angeles Time reporter
Robert Sheer, "If there are enough shovels to go around, everybody is
going to make it [in a nuclear war]. . . . It's the dirt that does it. With
a little bit of dirt, just about anybody could survive a nuclear war."[46]
The European antiwar movement, if it needed energizing, was motivated mightily, and the U.S. nuclear freeze movement gathered momentum; the movement's congressional resolution would be subsequently
supported by many Democrats.

The window of budgetary opportunity, the Reagan planners believed, was merely eighteen months. After that, the new defense consensus could not be guaranteed. One of the most influential Reagan
defense planners, Richard Burt, wrote to the new secretary of state,
Alexander Haig, that the "defense rhetoric — 'essential equivalence' —
and [the] policy of the past" was "no longer appropriate to our purposes in the 1980s." He continued, "The question before us now is how
to meet the strategic nuclear requirements of extended deterrence." But,
"war-fighting" strategies, including language about "prevailing" after a
protracted nuclear conflict, was largely derivative of Carter's planning.
Even the much-vaunted Reagan administration theory of "horizontal

escalation" was not new. In preparation for a fully funded and "robust" strategic posture, war-fighting strategies were elaborated. War-fighting strategies helped give the buildup a logical coherence, and they were seen as useful in bedeviling the Soviets. The first-term Reagan administration's nuclear bellicosity was aimed at fixing a new consensus revolving around America's refurbished leadership position. In the long run, this posture was believed capable of making the Soviets more pliable. In the meantime, the full-tilt nuclear procurements and harsh rhetoric* were directed at throwing the Soviets off guard and putting them on the defensive in as many aspects of the relationship as possible. Later, when the Soviets were engaged again — if for no other reason than the allies as well as the public would demand it — they might be more pliant, yielding to a logic of nuclear preponderance. Some Reagan enthusiasts went even further. Richard Pipes, the senior Soviet specialist at the National Security Council argued that, if the Reagan arms buildup were to prove successful, the "Soviet leaders would have to choose between peacefully changing their communist system . . . or going to war."[48]

To the Soviets, the unfolding strategic picture seemed to indicate the possibility of American planning for a surprise attack.[49] Visitors to Moscow in the early 1980s were pointedly directed to Reagan-era disaster planning. The Federal Emergency Management Agency (FEMA), in the Reagan years of domestic budget cutting, was not fixed on self-help measures to deal with hardships of wind and flood. Rather, FEMA focused on the need for states to develop mechanisms for coping with nuclear war. States wanting planning assistance and expertise in the event of disaster had to present plans for "surging out into the countryside" if war threatened and, at the same time, keep most essential services intact. While the Reagan team cut food stamps, school lunch programs, public housing, and even the Coast Guard by over fifty percent, sums exceeding $9 billion were spent in designing "post–nuclear attack" scenarios.[50]

Out of office, Reagan administration defense intellectuals prepared papers for the Joint Chiefs with titles such as "Exploiting Soviet Vulnerabilities." Once in power, the issue was how to keep the Soviets off balance and, if possible, push back what were seen as Soviet gains in the Third World and Armaments. As Burt explained to Secretary Haig,

---

*Projected attacks on such Soviet targets were a centerpiece of the Reagan navy's maritime strategy based on naval superiority. But the policy did not originate with the Reagan administration. The navy, in Congressional testimony on "the advantage of aircraft carriers" during the Carter administration, emphasized their power projection capability using an illustrated map of East Asia; the target zone was Vladivostok.[47]

the U.S. government "want[s] to continue to feed Soviet insecurities about long term strategic potential with vigorous implementation of the President's strategic program." The State Department had a great deal of autonomy and authority in the early days of Reagan administration defense planning, and it was a firm advocate of a posture that did not admit negotiations.[51] To be sure, bureaucratic opposition existed. Undersecretary of State Laurence Eagleberger, for instance, believed that even if the United States pressed ahead on strategic programs, it should at least "steer clear" of such terms as *superiority*. The argument Eagleburger made was that if the policy became known to the allies, it would create nothing but problems for them.

The United States knew the allies were concerned and that the Soviets were nearly panicked. But as the State Department action officer in these matters, Richard Burt, told Haig, "It would be ironic if we could not even decide . . . on an explicit and far sounding strategic policy because of [allied] concerns." If the Reagan defense modernization program could be driven forward, however, the State Department was confident that the United States could get through the inevitable rough spots of allied protests and would emerge with "significant long term leverage" even under a "substantial reductions regime." The object, meanwhile, was to give the appearance of interest in negotiations to avoid giving fodder to critics, but, at the same time, to avoid substantive overtures. Therefore, proposals crafted and presented to the Soviets were believed to be, in Secretary Haig's words, "non-starters."[52]

The Reagan administration had come to office charging that a period of great danger was ahead in U.S. defenses in which the Soviets would exploit a "window of opportunity," because of a combination of superior Soviet missile "throw weight" and improving Soviet warhead accuracies.[53] From the onset, these measures were known to be illusory. The real opportunity, in the mind of the early Reagan administration defense planners, was the chance to move from what Senator Sam Nunn called, in the last year of the Carter administration, "clinging parity" to, as the State Department put it, a new "edge in force effectiveness." A substantial price accompanied this seizing of the moment of defense budgetary permissiveness. Few in Congress or in the permanent bureaucracy wanted to be on the side of slighting the military, because the price of purported weakness had been electoral defeat. But the cost of the absence of Congressional challenges to the sums given to the military was staggering. Moreover, an amazing percentage of the increase was given through inadvertence. Budget Director David Stockman, for instance, noted a "calculator error" by which, in the late hours, he underestimated the Carter defense budget by 56 percent.[54] After Reagan's eight years, given what the Carter force structures had basically obtained throughout the Reagan years, there was some substantial mystification about where all the "excess" 56 percent, or, as it was to total, $1 trillion, had gone.

What divided the Reagan administration from the Carter administration was the sheer fiscal exertion on the one hand and the verbal bats employed to pound out the anti-Soviet message on the other. President Reagan began to issue formal "noncompliance reports" to the Congress. Compliance issues were, in part, some of the dust and fog generated to allow the Reagan grand strategy of maximizing strength and allowing time for the defense production base to expand sufficiently to add significant quantitative and qualitative numbers to the U.S. weapons inventory. Some of the charges seemed somewhat frivolous. Others, however, had to be taken seriously. They included the accusation that the Soviets had deployed a new class of missile, the SS-25; that the Russians had built a battle management ABM radar in violation of the 1972 ABM treaty; and that the Soviets were encrypting or otherwise hiding the flight tests of missiles and warheads.

The worry in the U.S. intelligence community was that some new system might come on line and that the United States would be bereft of warning. Carter's CIA director, Stansfield Turner, had argued long and hard that the treaty might be sustainable in the intelligence community if the Soviets used "scrambled" radio signals to broadcast data on their missile tests. Admiral Turner never believed there was any immediate danger,[55] but some potential for an innovative Soviet strategic "silver bullet" was always possible. In response to these American concerns, the Soviet defense minister, Dimitri Ustinov, stated in 1979: "As far as telemetry goes, I don't think there is any sense in discussing this problem. The information essential to verification will not be encrypted. Agreement in this has been reached."[56]

Although it was claimed during the Reagan years that Soviet encoding of missile tests "impeded" detection, no U.S. official would claim that Soviet tests could go unmonitored or that the Soviets succeeded, in effect, in camouflaging missile tests. For many years, the Soviets apparently tested their missiles "in the clear," and the question of telemetry was never broached. Discussions of Soviet encoding in Geneva at the Standing Consultative Committee were routine in the late 1970s. A U.S.–Soviet accord on encryption was formulated by the less-than-satisfactory mutual declarations attendant to the SALT II agreement. However, throughout the 1980s, a puzzling pattern of periodic Soviet encryption emerged.[57] The most plausible statement was hardly earth-shaking: The practice seemed only to correlate to Soviet bargaining behavior. It was not a practice designed to confound U.S. intelligence and develop a strategic "winning card."[58]

Another charge arose when Richard Perle told a House Committee that the development of a "new" mobile missile (the SS-25) in early 1983 was a violation of one of the "most important provisions of the SALT II treaty."[59] But in the SALT II agreement, the United States had reserved the right to deploy a mobile missile itself: the much-debated MX.[60] A significant group of U.S. experts intimate with the SALT process, such as chief negotiator Ralph Earle, argued that the United States had been aware for years that the Soviets were preparing to develop a single-warhead, mobile ICBM and that this was anticipated in the language of the treaty; and, indeed, the inevitable Soviet counterpart mobile missile—when it was deployed—would be the "trade off" for the U.S. insistence on developing the MX.[61]

The third charge was that the Soviets were in the process of deploying a modern ABM radar at Krasnoyarsk. If, indeed, the Krasnoyarsk facility was a battle management system, it was prohibited by the ABM treaty. Soviet Ambassador Anatoli Dobrynin had offered to allow western inspection of the Krasnoyarsk radar facility in 1985, but neither Congress nor administration took the offer seriously. However, as the process of meaningful agreements once again appeared as a presidential priority during the second Reagan administration, the offer was revived. In September 1987, a group of congressmen and journalists, in what one congressman called an unprecedented act of "military glasnost," arrived at the forbidding structure located near the geographic center of the Soviet Union. The visitors saw a cavernous, half-finished, "crumbling" facility. The enormous structure was all but bereft of equipment. Work had obviously been halted on it for months. In some sections, it appeared that no work had been done for years.

If the Krasnoyarsk radars had been installed, they would certainly have fit within the technical prohibitions of the 1969 treaty. But there seemed little reason to doubt Soviet host assurances that the facility would not be completed. Even the harshest critics of arms control yielded the point that the Krasnoyarsk white elephant could add nothing to either Soviet defenses or offenses. The most that could be said was that Krasnoyarsk was symptomatic of a cynical attitude on the part of the ebbing Brezhnev regime toward the unratified SALT II treaty.[62]

Charges of Soviet bad faith in carrying out international agreements of all kinds, much less arms control accords, had become, by the last two years of the Reagan administration, almost liturgical. The president was obliged to continue the practice even when it undercut support for both old agreements that he had begun to embrace along with his own initiatives at the end of his administration. Hence, only six days before Reagan and Gorbachev met in Washington on Pearl Harbor day,

December 7, 1987, Reagan blasted Soviet perfidy and lack of seriousness in international agreement making since Yalta.[63] The casualties of
this rote campaign of invective were substantial. The broad constituency that had favored arms control gradually became accustomed to
the idea that the Soviets were not reliable in negotiations with the United
States and could not be trusted to carry out their agreements. The re-
emergence of an arms control agenda in the latter years of the Reagan
administration was riven by suspicions of Soviet motives. By making
"distrust of the Soviets" part of the cant of East–West relations, im-
pediments were created to the acceptance of documents that the Reagan administration had arduously endeavored to conclude in the waning
months of its last term.

Beginning in 1985, the State Department tried to reverse the logic
of accusation. At a Senate Armed Services hearing in early 1985, after
a parade of first-term Reagan administration stalwarts had tossed up
a great wall of invective regarding Soviet "intentional" noncompliance,
Lt. General John Chain, a State Department adviser to Secretary of
State George Shultz, interjected:

> Mr. Chairman, if I may, I think with all due respect . . . I would hate
> to see this body walk out of here at the end of the day thinking arms
> control [is] no good because the Soviets always cheat. This is not the po-
> sition of the administration. It is certainly not the view of the State
> Department.[64]

In 1987, the Soviets began to play back, with a certain diabolical suit-
ability, longstanding U.S. proposals for instrusive "on-site inspections"
and verifications of treaties. A completely open verification regime had
a real military cost for the United States. Most U.S. military and intelligence agencies privately protested that the Soviet proposals not only
were too intrusive, but, equally, they could damage real secrets of U.S.
warhead manufacture and deployment patterns.

There were costs to using "verification" and adherence to arms control treaties as part of a complex strategy for delaying real engagement
of the Soviets until a position of superiority defined in terms of a viable counterforce and war-fighting inventory of weapons could be
achieved. First, it exaggerated a view of Soviet perfidy already widely
held in the American body politic—a view that we now know had a
limited factual base. At the beginning of 1986, the administration allowed, begrudgingly, in a report on Soviet "noncompliance," that violations of arms control agreements were not an overall "pattern of Soviet
behavior." The "Soviets had adhered to many if not most of the provisions to which they were a party." The loss of cows and sheep and ter-

rible illness in humans in the area of Sverdlovsk apparently occurred from animals' eating grass from soil to which inadequately treated fertilizer, bone meal, had been applied.[65] The Reagan portrayal of Soviet behavior was more caricature than analysis. Second, institutions useful in tempering superpower relations withered, furthering delay beyond what had become, by 1985, desirable. In fact, institutions such as the Standing Consultative Commission that, according to experts, were the most innovative and useful means of exchanging information on the most tension-filled and potentially difficult feature of U.S.–Soviet relations were bypassed. If a prolonged period of relaxed tensions were to eventuate, something like these dormant and abused institutions would have to be reconstructed.

Finally, because arguments about strategic systems were themselves heavily laden with symbolism that seemed to far exceed their real substance, a kind of cynical view of the management of controversy and debate in the most critical areas of public life was perpetuated. There was the private agenda of the bureaucrats who supported arms control but felt obliged to "sound tough." There was the real agenda of bureaucrats, some of whom were specifically charged with negotiations, who sounded reasonable in public but managed to advance every obstacle they could to arms control.[66] There was a set of functionaries who were privy to the calculations of the last two years of the Carter administration but were so intent on putting the Reagan administration in harsh light that even when the Reagan team followed a well-worn path — albeit with substantially more energy — the Carter exiles labeled the Reagan behavior irresponsible or worse, when they, in fact, had put forth the same plans and shared the same doubts. The dominance of symbols over substance in the political discourse 1980s was a bipartisan achievement.

Carter administration plans for war fighting were really hoary affirmations of the "stroking" process required by European allies, Germany in particular, for more than thirty years. Arms control and weapons programs in the late 1970s and early 1980s were means of deflecting Europeans' and Americans' questioning of the Carter administration's competence and steadfastness of purpose. In the Reagan years, public discussion of administration war-fighting doctrines and capabilities was an attempt to integrate highly accurate strategic and tactical nuclear weapons into the emerging notions of extended deterrence. In part, the Reagan nuclear doctrines were seen as counters to Soviet capabilities. And the Soviets were themselves acquiring a war-fighting doctrine and capability.[67] It was true the stridency of the Reagan years had not been heard since the days of John Foster Dulles. And, because the doctrines were harsh and a certain number of critics seemed to believe they were truly new and dangerous, the Soviets appear to have been genuinely unnerved. But the Reagan policy was not, in any real sense, fresh. It was wholly consistent with U.S. policy as it had developed since 1947 and, equally, with that of the Carter administration.[68]

An accelerating velocity characterized U.S.–Soviet relations in the last thirteen months of the Carter administration. Not for nothing did George Kennan despair that he smelled the powder of Sarajevo again. Congress and out-of-work high-level functionaries might not have liked the Reagan declamations that the Soviet Union was an "evil empire" and the "focus of evil" in the modern world, but John Foster Dulles had made liberal use of these kinds of epithets before. The Reagan foreign and defense policy did not have as its origins the newly minted lines of radical right-wing thought. Rather, the anlaysis and responses that connected contemporary policy led back to the Truman doctrine with the directness of a mariner's lodestone.

In public, those who believed American defenses should be better funded argued that the Soviets had raced on past "parity." In contrast, the private analysis of the CIA and most of the bureaucracy remained stubbornly consistent with the testimony of the Joint chiefs in the late 1970s, who had expressed "confidence" in the balance of forces.[69] By the end of its first term, the Reagan administration—bending to the logic of the president's own independent commission headed by General Brent Scowcroft—had virtually dropped the argument about the United States facing a "window of vulnerability." The president had appointed the commission in response to congressional rejection of his administration's initial proposal for basing the MX. With the chairman of the Joint Chiefs of Staff testifying that most of the chiefs were skeptical of the proposal, the Congress rejected it and directed the president to come up with a new basing mode by March of 1983.[70] The commission went far beyond consideration of the MX and delivered an analysis of the entire strategic posture of the United States that undercut Reagan's rhetoric concerning American strategic vulnerability and the need to move away from a strategic posture based on deterrence.[71]

The Scowcroft Commission concluded that, although the ICBM leg of the strategic triad was increasingly vulnerable, U.S. strategic capability as a whole was adequate to the task of deterring a first strike against the United States. Moreover, rather than base U.S. strategic posture on war-fighting capability, the Scowcroft Commission reaffirmed the notion of stable deterrence as the only sound basis for the Soviet–U.S. strategic relationship. Concerning the future of the ICBM, however, the commission managed to sit on two stools. On the one side, they argued for the limited deployment of the MX in existing Minuteman silos as an incentive to the Soviets to continue negotiations and maintain the flexibility of the ICBM leg of the triad. At the same time, the commission urged that this step be viewed as transitional, because they also proposed that the United States develop a new, much smaller, mobile, *single* warhead missile as the ultimate means for modernizing the ICBM force while maintaining a stable balance with the Soviets. The hope behind the new missile — immediately christened *Midgetman* — was that, by moving away from strategic arsenals deploying many large missiles armed with multiple and highly accurate warheads, neither side could credibly threaten a first strike against the other. Insofar as the fear of a first strike, and thus the need to contemplate a preemptive strike of one's own, was diminished, the entire relationship could become far more stable.

The Scowcroft Commission relied in large measure on the same data used in the 1980 estimates. Then, the CIA had held that the loss of U.S. ICBMs in a first strike would be around 18 percent of the U.S. retaliatory capability, assuming a high level of confidence in Soviet missile performance.[72] But the commission's recommendation that the MX be based in silos is otherwise inexplicable unless one assumes that there will be a relatively high level of survival of those silos. In other words, the "window of vulnerability" — like the bomber gap of the mid-1950s, the missile gap of the 1960s, and vanishing naval superiority alleged by Mr. Weinberger in budget presentations in the early 1980s — was manifestly not an analytic statement but a symbolic assertion with a domestic and overseas political objective.[73] In retrospect, it seems apparent that the rhetoric was used for the United States to race itself; and most high-level "players" in the competition for U.S. defense dollars knew it.

Strategic Defense

Perhaps the ultimate substitute of symbols for policy was the President's Strategic Defense Initiative — "Star Wars." In a speech on March 23, 1983, appealing for support of his arms buildup, the president offered the American people a "vision" that provided, in his view, a way out of the paradox of "deterrence of aggression through the promise of retaliation; [t]his approach to stability through offensive threat."[74] Rather than "rely on the specter of retaliation, on mutual threat," the president urged "that we embark on a program to counter the awesome Soviet missile threat with measures that are defensive."[75] Reagan offered no details for his defensive system, but it was clear to most observers that what he had in mind was a resurrection of the idea of ballistic missile defense that had been ostensibly severely restricted in the 1972 treaty on antiballistic missile defenses because of its potentially destabilizing effects.

The new technologies that the president seemed to have in mind were to be based in space rather than around U.S. ICBM sites, although the latter certainly was not excluded. The president was apparently persuaded that the more than $50 billion that the United States had invested in the development of military space applications since 1958 was on the verge of paying off with a new generation of weapons.[76] The effort under the Reagan administration had been impressive: the Department of Defense's space budget had grown from $6.4 billion in fiscal year 1982 (when it was larger than the National Aeronautical and Space Administration's budget of $5.9 billion, almost 25 percent of which was for military applications) to more than $14 billion in fiscal year 1984, when the military applications of NASA's budget are included. Moreover, in September of 1982, the Air Force had established an independent Space Command responsible for coordinating and developing space applications for the new technologies.

United States programs were not designed to be exclusively reactive. Although defensive applications were under study, General Robert T. Marsh, the commander of the Air Force Systems Command, made it clear in 1982 that "we should move into war-fighting capabilities, space-to-space, space-to-ground."[77] And consistent with its strategic posture, the administration's 1984–1988 Five Year Defense Guidance admonished the development of capabilities to "wage war effectively" and "vigorously pursue" technological applications that would allow the United States to "project force in and from space."[78] The air force, echoing Reagan's rhetoric, called for "space superiority" to ensure that the U.S. would "prevail" in any conflict.[79]

These preparations for "space combat," as the air force put it, left many questions concerning the president's notion of "defensive" systems and a stable future. The immediate objective of all this spending was the development of antisatellite capability superior to that which the Soviets could develop. Purportedly on the horizon, however, were laser and particle-beam applications that proponents saw as justification for the president's optimism. But would such applications (assuming that they would work, an assumption that many scientists and engineers rejected) ensure the hoped-for era of stability? Many analysts thought not; rather, the prospect was for extending the strategic arms race into yet another dimension where stability and arms control could become even more problematic.[80]

The president acknowledged that "defensive systems have limitations and raise certain problems and ambiguities. If paired with offensive systems, they can be viewed as fostering an aggressive policy; and no one wants that." Was the president proposing that the United States eliminate its offensive systems — its triad of ICBMs, SLBMs, and bombers? In fact, of course, the United States was modernizing and expanding its offensive capability for the 1990s and beyond. Furthermore, the defense establishment's programs for space emphasized war-fighting applications. Finally, it was clear that the administration had no intention of restraining the development of such ambiguous developments through existing or future arms control arrangements. Indeed, even when, later in the administration, strategic arms control did become the subject of meaningful negotiations with a new Soviet leadership, the President doggedly refused to surrender his vision of a space-based strategic defense system.

The proponents of SDI have had, however, another agenda. While building up U.S. offensive capabilities, SDI was, quite simply, a way of inhibiting agreements like SALT II. Publicly, SDI came to be viewed as a means of restoring credibility to the U.S. deterrent. It was, to the President at least, an alternative to mutual assured destruction, the very basis of mutual deterrence for two decades. To his opponents, however, SDI became a kind of shorthand for the ascendence of defense requirements over other social priorities in the Reagan years. In a sense, the Soviets collaborated with the Reagan administration in giving enormous weight to strategic defense in their negotiations with the United States. So intense was the Soviet focus on the administration's plans, that Ronald Reagan, like Harry Truman at Potsdam, may have believed that he possessed, in one weapons system, a "master card" for dealing with the problem of Soviet power. Potentially, strategic defenses degraded mutual deterrence because there would be, in Gorbachev's words, a shield, from behind which a sword could be drawn with impunity. At a minimum, SDI was an expression of what Yuri Andropov, General Secretary at the time, called a "flippant" attitude toward war and peace.[81] The "danger in U.S. policy" said one Politburo adviser, "was that politics are being carried out as if there was no danger of war."[82]

Strategic Defense Initiative could, the Soviets feared, involve them in a dimension of the arms race for which they had little preparation. Of course, this is exactly what some in the administration had in mind. As early as 1982,[83] Reagan was reported to have held the "private conviction" that the declining Soviet economy would eventually force the Russians to terms. Occasional hints suggested that it was this meld of defense strategy and economic warfare that drove the second-term

Reagan administration analyses of Soviet strategic behavior and of why negotiations seemed on track.[84] Believers had invested almost transubstantial powers and possibilities to SDI, arguing that it was the technological spear that had prodded the Soviets to the negotiating table. SDI was, in this light, a kind of expensive instrument by which the Soviets had been goaded into yielding to the logic of some of the United States' bargaining positions.

But after five years and $4 billion of research, few physicists could understand how the technologies would interact to perform the required mission of shielding significant portions of the U.S. population from an extensive attack in the absence of a wider arms control regime. For that matter, it was unclear how SDI could help save many U.S. population centers and significant military targets. Many administration stalwarts, including Secretary Shultz, were reduced to arguing that SDI's best use was against limited accidental attack in a world of vastly reduced ICBMs and as a "bargaining chip" with the Soviets. In 1986, one NSC aide close to arms control issues told one of the authors, "Just about every senior member of the administration, including the JCS [Joint Chiefs of Staff], have recommended, at one time or another a 'grand compromise' that would use SDI as a bargaining chip." Even Richard Perle, a professional antagonist of arms control, once out of office began to indicate that a goal of missile defense was "not realistic."[85]

The Strategic Defense Initiative was, however, meaningful to a gaggle of weapons laboratories where serious physicists and engineers could conduct research on an extensive program of lasers, mirror optics, computing and software puzzles, "imaging," and guidance techniques. Enormous resources were available, with little need for immediate results. It was a sweet ride for many of the research physicists, mathematicians, and computer programmers who have felt underfunded for much of the 1970s. Researchers at Lawrence Livermore Laboratories reverently labeled the artifacts of SDI the "Weapons of Life," as SDI consumed 48 percent of the Defense Department's research budget by fiscal year 1988.[86] By 1986, one well-positioned corporate observer of defense technology claimed that SDI "became an act of faith" with an autonomous "spiritual life."[87]

Even the most visionary advocate of SDI strained to explain how the system might also be coordinated to work against depressed trajectory weapons fired at close range to targets (either cruise missiles fired from virtually anything or ballistic missiles fired from submarines). A host of new weapons technologies was in the offing: supersonic, "stealthed" cruise missiles with pinpoint accuracy, hypersonic SLBMs and cruise missiles. SDI promised relief from the oldest, and what was generally believed to be the most obsolete, systems, ICBMs, at a cost that was generally believed to exceed $700 billion. SDI might have been more cost-effective than building replacements for ICBMs, but few would argue that these were the systems of choice in any realistic strategy for finding the road to deterrence of tomorrow.[88]

In the early fall of 1987, the Soviet press began to stress the myriad of technical difficulties in SDI as well as to claim that they were subjecting their own programs to cost-effectiveness criteria and to relax their near-hysteria about SDI.[89] The Soviets may have concluded congressional insistence on strict adherence to the antitesting provisions of the ABM treaty and fiscal constraints would likely hold down the United States' SDI program to what Richard Perle called "realistic levels" of expectation and expenditure.[90] The Russians may also have discovered from their own considerable efforts in strategic defense research, including laser technologies and space tracking,[91] that there were no practical solutions to the problem of "strategic vulnerability." Or, the Soviets might have merely done their sums and discovered that there simply was not enough money to fund fully Reagan defense buildup targets in the 1990s and, at the same time, manage to go forward with any serious deployable SDI as well. As the money began to run out and as the military had to make one painful choice after another, this latter interpretation seemed the most compelling. In that context, the chairman of the Joint Chiefs, Admiral William Crowe, informed Reagan that Soviet proposals for arms control would not interfere in any substantive way with any of the SDI tests before 1995.[92] By mid-1988, an operational SDI was being pushed further and further into an indefinite future.[93]

What some skeptics never considered more than space dust had finally been cleared from the U.S.–Soviet dialogue. The cost had been the energies of thousands of U.S. research scientists and huge portions of the Department of Defense's discretionary income between 1983 and 1988. The pity would be that the Reagan administration stalwarts and others as well would come to believe that it was the threat of SDI that had made agreements possible in the first place. SDI was delivered to the world without any notice to the secretary of defense or the Joint Chiefs. SDI's futuristic parts were yet to be specified, much less designed or tested. When there was a time of defense largesse, SDI was a great gravy train, at least for the Air Force, whose ICBMs were threatened and whose bombers seemed an increasingly anachronistic weapons platform. For the Defense Department as a whole, however, SDI assumed excessive proportions. Star Wars became a black hole into which resources were irretrievably drawn. In time, most military professionals hoped, it would quietly recede back into the remote labs from which it was conjured.[94]

The Reagan
Administration and NATO Policy

The 1979 NATO decision to bring new Pershing II missiles and ground-launched cruise missiles to Europe grew as a "hardware" response to complaints generated both in Europe and the United States that the United States was being delinked from European defense. The Soviets had developed a new class of missile, the SS-20. It was an impressive weapon: It could be MIRVed; it was mobile; and it had an all-terrain tractor carrier that could move the missile caisson, thereby immensely complicating Western attempts to locate the weapons. It had substantial accuracy, and each of its three warheads had very high yields of over two hundred kilotons. By the early 1980s, the Soviets had some two hundred of these weapons available for the European theater. The "novel" element of the U.S. response was the deployment of the Pershing IIs. They had real war-fighting potential, because they had prompt-firing capability, were mobile, and had sufficient range to strike command and control facilities in the Western part of the U.S.S.R. in less than twelve minutes.[95]

When the NATO decision to modernize INF weapons was reached in 1979, the issue had been carried beyond the point of any calculations about the relative balance of forces between NATO and the Warsaw Pact. Instead, the INF deployments became an emotion-laden "test" of the continuing relevance of the alliance (under pressure of concerned citizens in the West and an alarmed Soviet Union). Hence, symbolism dominated substance in an issue that was to consume U.S.–European relations for more than a decade. Many U.S. analysts were, in fact, basically satisfied that the Soviets were in no position to overrun Western Europe, given the extant NATO–Warsaw Pact force ratios and equipment. Just as importantly, the assertion that Soviet policy had, as a matter of doctrine, demanded a blitzkrieg assault much like the Nazis mounted in June of 1940 was not a certainty. Indeed, there were some important indications that the Soviets, by 1987, had come to believe that such an effort was "bound to fail."[96] The ensuing debate became not only sterile and mechanical but ethereal as well. Few analysts could specify any credible scenario that would provoke the Soviets to mount a serious assault in Europe.

The INF debate, nevertheless, had real and unhappy consequences for no less than the man who first raised the issue in public, West

German chancellor Helmudt Schmidt. In his last days in office, trying to salvage his diverse party from the ravages of the INF decision, Schmidt assessed the situation in the 1980s as being not unlike those in the summer before the Great War seventy-five years before. Chain-smoking even as he dipped snuff, the tired chancellor hammered the table with remarkable force and asserted:

> It was I who made the speech in 1977 [pointing out the danger of Europe's being divorced from the American deterrent]. . . . It was I who pursued it at [NATO summits]. . . . It was I who pressed INF on the Italians, Belgians, and Dutch. . . . I understood the issue and indeed had formulated it. The [levels of the Pershing and cruise missile deployments] are too high. The final levels — whether 400, 300 or 250 . . . must be negotiable. . . .
>
> You must appreciate that it is my soil that is at stake. Germany is the size of the state of Oregon and . . . there are some 6 to 7000 warheads in that small area. Imagine the concern if there were a similar area of land based missiles between Boston and New York or New York and Washington. . . . The trend is toward a world like Europe faced in 1914.[97]

As the December 1983 deployment date approached, European public distemper was brought into the streets. Throughout 1983, hundreds of thousands of antinuclear activists demonstrated in West Germany, France, Britain, and Holland. The antinuclear group captured the British Labor Party and, by 1983, became the dominant voice in the German Social Democratic Party. The Reagan administration's rhetoric was not helpful to the European policy elites now trying to contain the public protests. Eugene Rostow, Reagan's first director of the U.S. Arms Control and Disarmament Agency (ACDA), testified in confirmation hearings, "It may be that a brilliant light will strike [our] officials. . . . But I do not know anybody with whom I have talked on this problem who know what it is we want to negotiate about; what kind of measure we want."[98] President Reagan compounded the anxiety when he seconded Secretary of State Haig's Senate Foreign Relations confirmation testimony by musing in public that "you could have the exchange of tactical weapons against troops in the field without it bringing either of the major powers to pushing the button."[99]

In mid-November of 1981, Reagan tried to neutralize emerging European discontent by a "zero-option" arms reduction proposal. The United States would not deploy their 572 Pershings and cruise missiles if the Soviets would dismantle 600 of their comparable systems including all their SS-20 models. But the proposal was always a "nonstarter" as an arms control proposition. The Soviets were asked to give up systems already in place for U.S. weapons that, if there were enough

European public pressure, might not be deployed in any case. The Reagan initiative was, therefore, an invitation to the Soviets to apply pressure to European governments and publics.

Negotiations were begun in late November of 1981, but these INF talks quickly stalemated. As the deployment deadline approached, the Soviets advanced a proposal that would have them reduce their SS-20 models to numbers roughly equal to the missiles and/or warheads deployed by the British and French in the latter countries' national nuclear arsenals (162 launchers, mostly in submarines). The United States, Britain, and France rejected the idea, arguing that these systems were not under the control of NATO and were therefore not subject to U.S.–Soviet negotiations. Earlier it had been revealed that the U.S. and Soviet negotiators had, in private conversations in July of 1982, informally developed a proposed reduction of Soviet systems to between fifty and one hundred in return for a similar U.S. deployment. Both the Soviet Union and the United States had, however, quickly and unequivocally rejected the proposal of their negotiators.[100] In the case of the Soviet Union, it was speculated that the terminal illness of Leonid Brezhnev had perhaps paralyzed the Soviet decision-making process. In Washington, it seemed that there was simply no desire for an agreement.

The deadlock persisted until 1985 and the arrival of Mikhail Gorbachev, a new and vigorous Soviet leader, whose domestic policy agenda centered on a restructuring of Soviet society that required as a precondition a relaxation of tensions with the west.[101] Within a two-year period, Gorbachev succeeded in projecting an entirely new image of a more open Soviet Union. By 1987, Gorbachev had captured the diplomatic initiative from the Reagan administration by turning its proposals back onto the United States. The zero-option proposal originally and consciously advanced by the United States as a "nonstarter" was now accepted by the Soviet Union. The Reagan administration, perhaps realizing that acceptance of their own proposals would exacerbate and reawaken West European fears of being decoupled from the American nuclear deterrent, tried to deflect Gorbachev's initiatives with demands for on-site inspections. Historically, American demands for extensive and instrusive on-site verification arrangements had been unacceptable to the Soviet Union. But U.S. demands were suddenly accepted by the Soviets, and the Soviets asked for reciprocity in any "verification regime." Confronted with a Soviet Union that would not take no for an answer, the president who had stridently denounced the Soviet Union as an "evil empire" and the "source of evil" in the international system now entered into a series of summit meetings in Geneva in 1985, Reykjavik in 1986, and Washington in 1987, which culminated in a treaty eliminating intermediate-range nuclear forces from Europe and Asia and establishing an unprecedented on-site inspection and verification regime. By the time of a Reagan trip to Moscow in the spring of 1988, far more difficult negotiations on approximately 50 percent reductions in strategic weapons were making sound progress according to the principal negotiators.

In March of 1988, fifteen European heads of state and President Reagan posed together, displaying tight-lipped smiles giving the inevitable post hoc blessing to the Soviet–American accord on the INF. The missiles, so painfully employed, now would come out. But, from the European perspective, it could have been worse. During the November 1986 summit at Reykjavik, Iceland, the U.S. deterrent itself nearly disappeared. Reagan had attended the summit apparently expecting a repeat of the largely ceremonial meeting with Gorbachev the year before in Geneva, which might give a boost to Republican candidates in the 1986 elections. An unprepared Ronald Reagan had become engaged in a disarmament dialogue with Gorbachev that had wandered almost casually over the terrain of nuclear policy, with the president at one point seemingly agreeing to radical reductions in all nuclear weapons. All of this transpired with no prior consultation with the NATO allies. Subsequently in the meeting, Reagan stubbornly insisted on preserving SDI and thereby brought the talks to an impasse. However, although no agreement was reached at Reykjavik, the summit had major repercussions for the alliance.

The implication of the agenda established at Reykjavik and the subsequent INF agreement was that the Europeans might, within about ten years, have to make do with a NATO far more dependent on conventional forces and perhaps their own, in Henry Kissinger's words, "delegitimized" nuclear weapons. Perhaps the Europeans were grateful for deliverance from nightmares such as Reykjavik, but the fact remained that weapons so painfully placed in Europe had proved disposable. Senior members of the NATO bureaucracy protested having been cavalierly displaced from the U.S. nuclear shelter. With U.S. conventional forces shrinking in any case by as much as 40 percent, and growing demands from the Congress and Pentagon for augmented "burden sharing,"[102] the future of NATO's defense seemed to rest increasingly with the Europeans themselves.[103] No small augury was the response to all of this by archconservative West Germany politician Franz Joseph Straus, who made his own way to Moscow. On arriving home, Straus announced that Gorbachev was a more reasonable man for European affairs than Reagan. Europeans evinced a weariness with incessant modifications in American strategic planning, from U.S. naval policy to overall nuclear policy. Indeed, the ephemeral nature of U.S. strategic plans has become not only embarrassing but disruptive. Memories of Rapallo, the first separate German–Soviet accord, stirred in European chanceries.[104]

CONCLUSION

Congressman Jack Kemp spoke for many on the radical right, increasingly isolated from the second-term Reagan policies. INF and Reykjavik were "nuclear Munichs." On the other hand, arms control advisers within the administration took the successful negotiation of an INF agreement signed on December 8, 1987, as vindication for the massive build-up. As Richard Burt wrote in 1988:

> . . . [T]he President's Strategic Defense Initiative has served as a key instrument in persuading the Soviets to accept, at least in principle, a 50 percent reduction in strategic arms. Even glasnost itself, . . . can be understood to some extent as a Soviet response to the Reagan administration's emphasis on military preparedness.[105]

Of course, Gorbachev may have had his own agenda in Europe and with his own military. Arms control followed a dramatic turn in Soviet politics for which no administration could take credit. The Soviets had yet to be "spent into the ground," as Undersecretary of Defense Fred Ikle once expressed the Reagan team's plan, by SDI or U.S. strategic programs. Indeed, Soviet military spending had consumed, even with Afghanistan, about the same proportion of Soviet GNP as it always had. To be sure, prospects loomed for a dramatic slowdown in Soviet capital formation and the like. But the United States could hardly take credit for the inefficiencies of the Soviet economy. No administration, however, that had augmented real growth of the U.S. defense budget by over 50 percent and assigned more than $2 trillion to the Defense Department during its tenure was likely to entertain in public the notion that any new turn in Soviet–American relations was unrelated to a militant, even bellicose "position of strength."[106]

NOTES

1. Steven V. Roberts, "Return to the Land of the Gipper," *New York Times*, March 9, 1988.
2. Mr. Reagan's famous line from his film "Kings Row" and also the title of his biography.

3. See William Broad's observation in Philip M. Boffey, et al., *Claiming the Heavens: New York Times Complete Guide to the Star Wars Debate* (New York: New York Times Books, 1988).

4. Martin Tolchin, "An Inattention to Detail is Getting More Attention," *New York Times*, January 14, 1987, p. A16.

5. Steven Roberts, "Ex-Reagan Spokesman Roils Capitol with Book," *New York Times*, April 8, 1988, p. A7.

6. Lou Cannon, *Reagan* (New York: G. P. Putnam and Sons, 1982), p. 373.

7. Report by Brian Nailor, National Public Radio, "All Things Considered," May 3, 1988; Paul Houstin, "Reagan Denies Using Astrology in Decisions," *Wilmington News Journal*, May 4, 1988, p. A3.

8. See Donald Regan, *For the Record: From Wall Street to Washington* (New York: Harcourt, Brace, Jovanovich, 1988), pp. 3–4; Owen Ullman, "Reagan Based Decisions on Astrology, Insiders Say," *Philadelphia Inquirer*, May 3, 1988, p. 1.

9. Louis Gottschalk, et al., "Presidential Candidates and Cognitive Impairment Measured from Behavior in Campaign Debates," *Public Administration Review*, March/April 1988, pp. 613–619. Lou Cannon and Fred Barnes of *The New Republic* (October 2, 1987) claim the president's memory was astoundingly clear. Others have said that the president nodded off to sleep during significant meetings and even confused countries when talking to their heads of state.

10. The best summary of this, although a bit overwrought, is in Andrew Lang, "The Politics of Armageddon: Reagan Links Bible Prophecy with Nuclear War," *Convergence* (Washington: The Christic Institute, Fall 1985), pp. 3, 12. A National Public Radio program entitled "Ronald Reagan and the Prophecy of Armageddon" was broadcast in mid-1985.

11. To a high school audience in Florida. *Time* (Asian edition), July 10, 1987, p. 27.

12. Cited by Philip Geylin, "The Reagan Crisis in Foreign Affairs," *America and the World: 1986*, Foreign Affairs, Vol. 65, No. 3 (1987), p. 452.

13. As his former press secretary, Larry Speakes, put it, "The buck stopped with him but it did not necessarily start with him." Roberts, "Ex-Reagan Spokesman Roils Capitol with Book," *New York Times*, April 8, 1988, p. A20.

14. Roberts, "Ex-Reagan Spokesman."

15. Regan, op. cit., p. 142.

16. Haig, *Caveat: Realism, Reagan and Foreign Policy* (New York: Macmillan, 1984), p. 85.

17. House Report 100-433, 100th Congress, 1st Session; Senate Report 100-216, *Iran Contra Affair*, November, 1987, p. 271.

18. For a scathing review of this behavior, see Theodore Draper, "An Autopsy," *The New York Review of Books*, December 17, 1987, pp. 67–77.

19. A good way to follow these events is the well-written Joint House and Senate Committee Document, HR 100-43, and Scott Armstrong, et al., *The Chronology*, The National Security Archive/Fund for Peace (New York: Fund for Peace, 1987).

20. HR 100-43, p. 26.

21. "Face the Nation," November 16, 1986, and cited in HR 100-43, p. 262.

22. HR 100-43, p. 298.

23. *Financial Review* (Australia), September 25, 1987, p. 8.

24. See Steven Emerson, *Secret Warriors: The Covert Operations of the Reagan Era* (New York: G. P. Putnam, 1988).

25. Bill McAllister, "Reagan Hails Superpower Cooperation," *Washington Post*, April

22, 1988, p. 1; and "Reagan U-Turns, Gives Soviet Pat on the Back," *Wilmington News Journal*, May 5, 1988, p. A3.

26.   Haig, op. cit., p. 220.

27.   The B-1 had shorter range, carried fewer and lighter bombs, and was not much good at penetration because its avionics and stability apparently were designed deficiently.

28.   John H. Cushman, Jr., "Air Force is Facing Critical Gap in Combat Readiness," *New York Times*, April 6, 1988, p. A16. See also Bernard E. Trainor, "U.S. Concludes NATO Can Deter Soviet Attack," *International Herald Tribune*, December 1, 1987, p. 1; and *Arms Control Today*, Vol. 15, No. 9 (November/December 1985), p. 24.

29.   William W. Kaufmann, *A Reasonable Defense* (Washington: Brookings Institution, 1986); Barry R. Posen and Steven Van Evera, "Reagan Administration Defense Policy: Departure from Containment?" in Kenneth Oye, et al., *Eagle Resurgent? The Reagan Era in American Foreign Policy* (Boston: Little, Brown, 1987), pp. 75–114; and Congressional Budget Office, *Defense Spending: What Has Been Accomplished?* (Washington: CBO, 1985).

30.   R. Jeffrey Smith and Philip J. Hilts, "Soviet Deny 1979 Outbreak Involved Germ Lab," *Washington Post*, April 13, 1988, p. A4.

31.   Donald Bruce Johnson, *National Party Platforms of 1980* (Urbana, Ill.: University of Illinois Press, 1982), p. 211.

32.   Julian Robinson, Jeanne Guillemin, and Matthew Messelson, "Yellow Rain: The Story Collapses," *Foreign Policy*, No. 68 (Fall 1987), pp. 108–109. See also the "Report to the Congress on Soviet Non-Compliance with Arms Control Agreements," cited in ibid.

33.   Ibid., p. 109.

34.   Ibid., p. 105.

35.   Alexander Dallin, *Blackbox* (Berkeley, CA: University of California Press, 1985).

36.   Seymour Hersh, *The Target is Destroyed* (New York: Random House, 1986). Hersh claims that "Reagan felt no immediate need to denounce or in some other way seek vengeance. . . . He didn't need to prove that he could stand up the Soviets. Responding to the cacophony on his right, he did denounce the Soviets for deliberate downing of the aircraft, even after U.S. intelligence was clear that the Soviets believed it to be a military and not a civilian craft." This account is not correct according to one of the closest military advisers to the president on this issue.

37.   Dallin and Gail Lapidus, "Reagan and the Russians: American Foreign Policy Toward the Soviet Union," in Oye, et al., op. cit., p. 23.

38.   General Secretary Andropov apparently feared that this incident was a frightening indication of the seriousness with which the United States was approaching the nuclear abyss: "If anyone had illusions as to the possible evolution for the better in the policy of the American administration, the latest developments have dispelled them. . . . [The U.S.] is going so far that one begins to doubt whether it has any brakes preventing it from crossing the mark before which any sober minded person would stop." See Raymond L. Garthoff, *Detente and Confrontation: American–Soviet Relations from Nixon to Reagan* (Washington: Brookings, 1985), pp. 1015–1017. The statement was a major announcement read on radio and television and then widely reprinted. See the *New York Times*, September 29, 1983 and Dallin and Lapidus, op. cit., p. 232.

39.   Hersh, op. cit., p. 130, emphasis added.

40. Strobe Talbott, *Deadly Gambits* (New York: Knopf, 1984).

41. See the McClure Amendment No. 2188 to Senate Bill No. 1342, Authorization for FY 1984 for the Department of State, the U.S. Information Agency, and the Board for International Broadcasting, *Congressional Record*, Vol. 129, No. 123 (September 22, 1983), pp. S12679–S12680.

42. See John Vanocour, "The KGB Goes on the Offensive and the West Strikes Back," *New York Times*, July 24, 1983; cited by MccGwire, *Military Objectives in Soviet Foreign Policy* (Washington, D.C.: Brookings Institution, 1987), p. 303.

43. MccGwire, op. cit., p. 303.

44. See Linton F. Brooks, "Naval Power and National Security: The Case for the Maritime Strategy," *International Security* (Fall 1986), Vol. 20, No. 2, p. 80, ftn. 69. Ferreting out Soviet submarines thought to be loitering in bastions or sanctuaries seems to have been a part of the U.S. Navy's analysis of Soviet planning since 1972. See James M. McConnell, Report No. CRC 2757 prepared for the Office of Naval Research and the Chief of Naval Operations, Arlington (VA: Center for Naval Analysis, 1974). Within the Navy, the belief that the Soviets were wedded to their bastions became virtual dogma after a three-day convocation on the subject held at the Office of Naval Intelligence, Department of the Navy, Office of the Chief of Naval Operations. *Report of the Annual ONI Symposium* at Annapolis, Md., Document No. OP 009J2/2 Unclassified. But the former commander of the Atlantic fleet, Admiral Harry Train, challenges the "illusion" of a Soviet submarine "honey pot." See Admiral Train's commentary in James L. George, ed., *The Soviet and Other Communist Navies: The View from the Mid-1980s* (Annapolis: Naval Institute Press, 1986), pp. 284–286.

45. See Richard Barnett, "Reflections," *New Yorker*, March 9, 1987, p. 78.

46. Robert Scheer, *With Enough Shovels: Reagan, Bush and Nuclear War* (New York: Random House, 1982), p. 18.

47. See MccGwire, op. cit., p. 289.

48. U.S. Congress, House, Hearings on *Military Posture, Department of Defense Authorization for Appropriations for Fiscal Year 1980* before the House Committee on Armed Services, 96th Cong., 1st Sess., 1979, p. 941 and MccGwire, op. cit., pp. 176ff.

49. Tim Weiner, "Planning for World War IV," *Philadelphia Inquirer*, February 9, 1987.

50. Fred Hiatt, "States Pushed to Improve Nuclear War Readiness," *Washington Post*, July 26, 1986, p. A14; and Hiatt, "Building a Force for World War IV," *Washington Post*, July 28, 1986, p. 11. The plan to survive a nuclear war was projected to cost $40 billion.

51. In contrast to the Carter years, see Garthoff, op. cit., p. 790.

52. Haig, op. cit., pp. 223ff.

53. U.S. land-based missiles were at risk, it was argued, of being extirpated by a Soviet preemptive salvo that would leave the U.S. with only its slower responding and less accurate bombers and SLBMs. But see *New York Times*, July 19, 1985, p. A1, for an article that concludes that U.S. estimates of the accuracy of the Soviets' SS-19 missile have been off by one third, or three hundred meters.

54. David Stockman, *The Triumph of Politics* (New York: Harper and Row, 1986), p. 108; also see George C. Wilson, "Defense Budget Disaster Ahead, Weinberger Told," *Washington Post*, August 22, 1986, p. 22. It was a product of "haste" and late hours, Stockman explained to a PBS audience. The Reagan DOD transition

team knew quite well what the figures meant, however. The result was that a second-or third-level group of ultra-hardline defense intellectuals "cooked the books" for the greatest peacetime spending spree in history.

55. See Alan Krass, *Verification* (Lexington, Mass.: D. C. Heath, 1985), p. 189; and Brzezinski, op. cit., pp. 330ff.

56. S. A. Cohen, "The Evolution of Soviet Views on SALT Verification: Implications for the Future," in W. C. Potter, ed., *Verification and SALT* (Boulder, Col.: Westview Press, 1980), note 18, pp. 50–51.

57. Eric Uslaner, "The Soviets Test a New ICBM," *Air Force Magazine*, Vol. 67 (March 1984), p. 15.

58. John Pike and John Rich, "Charges of Treaty Violations: Much Less than Meets the Eye," *FAS Public Interest Report*, Vol. 37 (March 1984), p. 15; and Krass, op. cit., p. 191.

59. "Soviets Test Launch Small ICBM," *Aviation Week and Space Technology*, Vol. 118 (February 21, 1983), p. 16.

60. Fifty of the MX missiles were eventually based in silos for economic and environmental reasons. But in the first year of the Reagan administration, debates still were waged about "mobile modes," the variations of which seemed as infinite as the human imagination: bombers, commercial airliners, cargo planes, trucks, railroads.

61. U.S. Congress, Senate, *Soviet Treaty Violations*, Hearings before the Armed Services Committee, March 14, 1984 (Washington: GPO, 1984), p. 5; and Robert Earle, "America is Cheating Itself," *Foreign Policy*, No. x (Fall 1986), pp. 7ff.

62. Matthew Bunn, "Congressional Delegation Visits Controversial Radar," *Arms Control Today*, Vol. 17, No. 8 (October 1987), pp. 26–27. See also Michael Gordon, "U.S. is Questioned on '79 Arms Pact," *New York Times*, August 12, 1986, p. A6; and Gary Lee, "Gorbachev's Rein on Military," *Washington Post*, July 29, 1986, p. A10.

63. R. Jeffrey Smith and Don Oberdorfer, "Reagan Charges a New Violation of Soviets of 1972 ABM Pact," *International Herald Tribune*, December 1, 1987, p. 1; and R. W. Apple, "Reagan Seeking the Offensive," *International Herald Tribune*, August 28, 1987, p. 2.

64. *Soviet Treaty Violations*, pp. 43–44; and Krass and Catherine Girrier, *Disproportionate Response* (Cambridge, Mass.: Union of Concerned Scientists, 1987), p. 73. A former CIA Director under presidents Nixon and Ford, William Colby told the Congress: "There were a few ambiguous situations that arose in SALT I which we took up with the Soviets, and we have been satisfied that the activity was explicable and not in violation of the treaty. The record is that the Soviets essentially complied with the treaty." U.S. Congress, Senate, *Military Implications of the Treaty on the Limitation of Strategic Offensive Arms and Protocol Thereto*, Part III, hearings before the Armed Services Committee, July–August 1979, p. 1018.

65. Walter Pincus, "U.S. Issues New Warning of Soviet Arms Breeches," *Washington Post*, March 8, 1986, p. 19A.

66. See R. Jeffrey Smith, "Perle Urges Senate to Change INF Pact."

67. The Department of State had been excluded from the interdepartmental discussions of that new doctrine. PD 59 was announced publicly in a speech delivered by Harold Brown at the Naval War College on August 20, 1980. When Secretary Vance resigned, his replacement, Edmund Muskie, was not even aware of the new doctrine. In the Carter years, earlier decision documents, PRM 10 and PD

18, endorsed a nuclear employment strategy. PD 18 led directly to an increase in attention to civil defense issues and command and control questions. See Garthoff, op. cit., p. 799, esp. ftn. 126. The increasingly formalized discussion of nuclear employment doctrines were further codified by Brzezinski in PD 62, which was issued in January of 1981. This legacy was one of his proudest endowments to the policy kit bag of the new administration. See ibid., p. 790; and Brzezinski, op. cit., pp. 177–178, 469.

68. Brzezinski, op. cit., p. 335.

69. Moreover, CIA estimates of broad Soviet push into a greatly enhanced strategic weapons inventory proved unduly pessimistic. See the CIA briefing paper entitled "USSR Economic Trends and Policy Developments" in *Allocation of Resources in the Soviet Union and China, 1983*, part 9, Hearings before the Subcommittee on International Trade, Finance, and Security Economics of the Joint Economic Committee, 98th Cong., 1st Sess., 1984, p. 306.

70. Richard Halloran, "3 of 5 Joint Chiefs Asked Delay on MX," *New York Times*, December 9, 1982, p. 1; and Steven R. Weisman, "Reagan Gives Way, Agrees to Freeze on Money for MX," *New York Times*, December 15, 1982, p. 1.

71. The text of the Commission on Strategic Forces' report is available in *Survival*, 25 (July/August 1983), p. 177–186.

72. See Garthoff, op. cit., p. 798.

73. Even the assertion that greater Soviet lift capability—the "heavy missile" problem—that bothered Reagan strategists until the Scowcroft commission dispelled it turns out to be a probable overreaction. According to two U.S. researchers writing in *Scientific American*, "Warhead yields of the two countries bear marked similarities." Apparently, the Air Force Technical Application Center commissioned another study to look at both the classified and unclassified data, and it too indicated that the power of the Soviet warheads had been substantially overrated. See R. Jeffrey Smith, "Pentagon May Overrate Soviet Nuclear Weapons," *Washington Post*, December 25, 1986, p. A10.

74. Ronald Reagan, "Peace and National Security," Address to the Nation, March 23, 1983, Current Policy No. 472 (Washington: Bureau of Public Affairs, Department of State, 1983).

75. Ibid., p. 7.

76. The following budgetary data were taken from the Center for Defense Information, "Militarizing the Last Frontier: The Space Weapons Race," *The Defense Monitor*, 12 (1983), p. 2.

77. Quoted in ibid., p. 1.

78. Ibid.

79. Ibid.

80. See, for example, David Andelman, "Space Wars," *Foreign Policy*, No. 44 (Fall 1981), pp. 94–106; and *Arms Control Today*, 13 (December 1983). The latter source contains an excellent bibliography on space-based weapons and technologies.

81. Cited by MccGwire, op. cit., p. 363.

82. Cited by Charles Kielyak, "Round the Prickly Pear: SALT and Survival," *Orbis*, Vol. 22 (Winter 1979), p. 833; and MccGwire, op. cit.

83. Cannon, *Reagan*, p. 415.

84. See Paul M. Doty, "Comments" in *Reykjavik and Beyond* (Washington: National Academy of Sciences Press, 1988), p. 21.

85. R. Jeffrey Smith, "Pentagon Scales Back SDI Goals," *Washington Post*, March 23, 1988, p. A24.

86. Fred Reed, "The Star Wars Swindle," *Harper's*, May 1986, p. 43; and Smith, "Pentagon Scales Back SDI Goals."

87. Cited in Reed, op. cit.

88. *Washington Post National Weekly Edition*, April 4–9, 1988, p. 10. Two experienced analysts with extensive experience, Barry M. Blechman and Victor A. Utgoff, in a report commissioned by the Institute for Defense Analysis, estimated that the system would cost over $700 billion. See Charles Mohr, "Study Says Missile Defense May Cost $770 billion," *New York Times*, July 23, 1986, p. 1.

89. Gary Lee, "Arms Experts See Impact of Gorbachev in Treaty," *International Herald Tribune*, December 2, 1987, p. 1.

90. This was Perle's judgment after he had left office. See *Newsweek* (Asian Edition), September 28, 1987, p. 103.

91. See William J. Broad, "Civilian Satellite Details Soviet Laser Technology," *International Herald Tribune*, October 24–25, 1987, p. 3.

92. See "U.S. Officials Decide Limits on SDI Test Aren't Major Hurdle," *International Herald Tribune*, December 2, 1987, p. 1.

93. Michael Gordon with John H. Cushman Jr., "Pressure Rises for U.S. Flexibility on 'Star Wars,'" *New York Times*, May 25, 1988, pp. A1, A14.

94. Smith, "Pentagon Scales Back SDI Goals," *Washington Post*, March 23, 1988, p. 1.

95. The development of W86 "earth penetrator" warhead for the Pershing IIs seemed to confirm the counterforce potential of the planned NATO deployments.

96. See Christopher N. Donelly, "Ground Force," in David R. Jones, ed., *Soviet Armed Forces Review Annual*, Vol. 3 (Gulf Breeze, Fl.: Academic Press, 1979), p. 18; and MccGwire, op. cit., p. 65.

97. For Brzezinski's version of this statement, see his memoirs, *Power and Principle* (New York: Farrar, Straus & Giroux, 1983), pp. 310ff.

98. U.S. Congress, Senate, Hearings before the Committee on Foreign Relations, *Nomination of Eugene V. Rostow to Director, Arms Control and Disarmament Agency*, 97th Cong., 1st Sess., 1981, p. 45.

99. Remarks to a group of national news editors, October 1981; and cited by I. M. Destler, "The Evolution of Reagan Foreign Policy," in Fred Greenstein, ed., *The Reagan Presidency: An Early Assessment* (Baltimore: Johns Hopkins University Press, 1983), p. 144.

100. See Bernard Gwertzman, "U.S. Aide Reached Arms Agreement Later Ruled Out," *New York Times*, January 16, 1983, p. 1.

101. See Jerry Hough, *Russia and the West: Gorbachev and the Politics of Reform* (New York: Simon and Schuster, 1988); and Mikhail Gorbachev, *Perestroika: New Thinking for Our Country and the World* (New York: Harper and Row, 1987).

102. Stephen Milligan, "Congress Is Up In Arms Over Allies' NATO Spending," *London Sunday Times*, April 24, 1988, p. 18.

103. See Bernard E. Trainor, "U.S. Concludes NATO can Deter Soviet Attack," *International Herald Tribune*, December 1, 1987, p. 1.

104. See the comment by Joseph Joffe, "Two Zeros Two Many in Gorbachev's Offer," *International Herald Tribune*, May 30–31, 1987; and James Reston, "A Visitor Finds Europeans Exasperated With America," *International Herald Tribune*, May 28, 1987, p. 11, for hints of another Rapallo. Germany's most prestigious newspaper called the American treatment of Chancellor Kohl concerning defense matters "rape," *International Herald Tribune*, June 6, 1987, p. 1.

105. Richard Burt, "Strength and Strategy: U. S. Security in the 1990s," *The Washington Quarterly*, Vol. 11 (Spring 1988), p. 7.

106.   See Michael Gordon, "INF: A Hollow Victory," *Foreign Policy*, No. 68 (Fall 1987), pp. 159–179; and Lian Svec, "Removing Gorbachev's Edge," *Foreign Policy*, No. 69 (Winter 1987–1988), pp. 187–188.

Chapter 11
Hawks on an
Unsteady Perch

President Reagan's global confrontation with communism was prosecuted with all the assertiveness and activism of the 1960s. Especially in Latin America, conflict was understood to be the result of the Soviets and their clients pushing forward the perimeters of the communist world empire. The administration's response was proclaimed in the idiom of Truman and Dulles and implemented with the instruments of Kennedy and Johnson. Not since the presidency of John Kennedy had an administration so involved itself economically and militarily in the western hemisphere.

GETTING A "WIN"

Carter, like his predecessors and his successor, was preoccupied with Fidel Castro. In September of 1979, Carter signed a presidential directive to "devise strategies for curbing Cuban activities and isolating it politically."[1] By the end of the 1970s, Cuba had become a serious bedevilment, with Cuban advisers in Zaire, Angola and Ethiopia working against U.S. interests. The Mariel boatlift had brought 129,000 Cuban refugees to Florida, including a good number from Castro's jails and mental hospitals. The Cuban presence in Nicaragua, Salvador, and Grenada was equally unwelcome. A personal sense of effrontery was shared by Vice President Mondale and the White House staff, as well as Secretaries Vance and Edmund Muskie, resting on the belief that Castro had made it hard to normalize relations and had provided such copious ammunition to the enemies of detente.[2]

Notwithstanding their evident disdain for the substantial baggage the Carter administration had left at the foot of the hill of U.S.–Latin American affairs, the Reagan administration picked much of it up and energetically charged ahead. Reagan's closest advisers were convinced that pressure on Cuba would ameliorate instability in the hemisphere. Hence, they were prepared, they said, to strike directly at Cuba if Castro did not reverse himself. Speaking on February 27, 1981, Secretary of State Alexander Haig said: "Cuban activity has reached a peak that is no longer acceptable in this hemisphere. . . . [I]t is our intention to deal with this matter at its source."³ Wayne Smith, Chief of the U.S. interests section in Havana from 1979 to 1982, recalled "blockade, surgical air strikes, invasion . . . no option was excluded."⁴

The Reagan administration's concern had several dimensions. First, there was the intrinsic and growing interest of the United States in its neighboring region's instabilities. Second, the problem seemed something manageable. Central American interests were less hypothetical than those in Southeast Asia a generation earlier. They offered a seemingly manageable opportunity for the United States to turn back at acceptable costs what the Reagan administration gauged was a tide of declining U.S. influence. And, third, because the world view of the Reagan administration was steeped in nostalgia for the golden age of U.S. foreign policy — the Truman Doctrine and Marshall Plan era — the same rationales prevailed: the image of Soviet power in a world in which symbols of influence were as important as the substance of power, especially in a world of nuclear weapons. A challenge to any part of the fabric of American commitments threatened the whole cloth. Nearby, disorder was threatening not because of dependence on Central American coffee and bananas, but because of concern about the demonstration effect of a successful revolution, supported by Castro, elsewhere in the hemisphere. And, more fundamentally, disorder was seen by the administration to be potentially damaging to the extended formal and informal U.S. guarantees issued worldwide since the beginning of the cold war. As Secretary Haig explained:

> We must demonstrate to everyone — the Russians, our allies, the Third World — that we can win, that we can be successful. We must move decisively and quickly to turn things around in the world or be nibbled to death by the Soviets.⁵

In winning the presidency, Ronald Reagan accused the Carter administration of being virtual collaborators in establishing a Soviet beachhead in Nicaragua. The 1980 Republican presidential platform proclaimed, for example, "We deplore the Marxist–Sandinista takeover of Nicaragua . . . we will support the efforts of the Nicaraguan people to establish free and independent government."⁶ Privately, however, Haig believed that the Sandinistas were a "sideshow" and that the United States should strike the source of revolutionary and terrorist problems of the hemisphere, Cuba. In this, however, he had virtually no support within the regular bureaucracy nor from the Joint Chiefs. The Chiefs demonstrated that Haig's idea of a blockade would consume substantial ground and air assets from Europe, require much of the Sixth Fleet, and perhaps require bringing naval forces in from the Seventh Fleet as well.[7] And, if the island did not soon buckle, the only option might be invasion and a long war. Cuba had a large, combat-hardened army of more than 200,000. Even without Soviet participation on behalf of Cuba, and even if the U.S. public opinion were behind an assault on the island, an invasion and occupation of Cuba presented endless possibilities for disaster. Haig backed off the idea but argued that, in any case, the administration needed to "roll back" communism in the region. President Reagan concurred. He told associates, "I want to win one."[8]

Prolonged attention focused again on Nicaragua throughout the 1980s, but, in the interim, the Reagan administration went for its "win" on the tiny island of Grenada. From October 25 to 27, 1983, more than six thousand marines, army rangers, and navy personnel invaded Grenada ostensibly to protect the lives of some one thousand Americans, many of them attending medical school on the island. A bloody coup had taken place earlier in the month, leading to the displacement of one Marxist regime by another more radical group. This evident political instability led, in turn, to the small East Caribbean neighbors of Grenada — with, it appears, some American encouragement — to invite the United States to act. This political uncertainty and the East Caribbean invitation provided the pretext for the invasion, which encountered somewhat stiffer resistance than expected from seven to eight hundred armed Cuban construction workers and several hundred Grenadans. As resistance crumbled and some ten thousand mostly small arms and several captured documents outlining Cuban and Russian military assistance were put on display, the administration's rationale shifted to an emphasis on the political and strategic importance of the invasion. For months, the administration had been pointing out the "threat" posed by the construction of a ten-thousand–foot runway on the island, dismissing the claims of Grenada and the British construction company building the facility that the runway was to improve the prospects of tourism on the island. Captured arms and documents and the presence of more Cubans than anticipated allowed the administration to portray Grenada as a nascent communist base for the support of insurgency and instability throughout the region. The invasion itself could be read by the Soviets, Cubans, and Nicaraguans only with anxiety, a clearly desirable outcome for an administration that had been straining for almost three years to reestablish an American reputation for toughness and a willingness to use force.

Apart from the tiny East Caribbean states that had invited the

United States to invade their neighbor, however, no other support was garnered in Latin America for the act. Hemispheric and international legal norms were seen as violated.[9] El Salvador, practically an American satrapy, condemned the act in the Organization of American States, echoing the concern throughout the region that the step marked a return to the days of gunboat diplomacy and Yankee intervention. In the UN, the United States had little support. America's European allies deserted the United States on the issue. Especially in Britain, the Reagan administration's invasion of a commonwealth country against the express wishes of the Thatcher government proved embarrassing. Not only had the British opinion been ignored, but the invasion occurred at precisely the moment when the first U.S. cruise missiles were being moved to their bases in Britain in the face of large antinuclear and anti-American demonstrations. The Grenadan invasion precedent would be difficult to explain away for Margaret Thatcher and for all European governments scheduled to receive the missiles and trying to convince their parliaments and people that the United States was a restrained, dependable, and predictable ally willing to consult with and be guided by the advice of its allies.[10]

At home, there was ambivalence as well. As is common in times of crisis, there was a surge of support for the president, if not initially for the invasion itself. As the captured documents and arms were displayed and grateful American students were paraded before the television cameras, public and congressional support for the invasion coalesced. Undoubtedly of assistance to the administration in this regard was the inability of the press to cover the fighting itself because the administration refused to allow the press into the combat zone until the fighting was virtually over. Thus, unlike Vietnam, Americans were subjected to the official version of events with no alternative accounts' being available. Most Americans seemed to support this action by the administration. Perhaps the idea of a clear-cut American "win" after decades of confusing and frustrating global engagement — with all the ambiguity in these long years of trial underscored by the press — was at least momentarily more important than the larger implications of the administration's manipulation of the flow of information. In any event, the Reagan administration enjoyed a surge of support in the days immediately after the invasion.

Whatever public relations success the invasion achieved in the United States, however, the brief expedition in Grenada did not seem to inhibit the revolutionary enthusiasm of the insurgents in El Salvador or their patrons in Nicaragua.

NICARAGUA AND
THE REAGAN DOCTRINE

As the 1970s drew to a close, the Carter administration had searched for alternatives to Nicaraguan Dictator Anastasio Somoza. In a fore-shadowing of events to occur throughout the Reagan years, the Carter administration hoped to expel a tyrannical head of state who had been the focus of boiling grievances while preserving the pro-American pos-ture of his successor. The Carter administration was hopeful that Somoza's National Guard could remain intact, even after the Somozas themselves had departed.[11] The Carter administration calculated that the National Guard could become a centerist antidote to the broad, communist-led coalition that had fought the Somozas for years.

This view of the National Guard was, however, illusory. Professor Richard Millet, a long-time student of the Somoza regime, has described the Guard as "one of the most corrupt military organizations in the world." The National Guard and the Somoza family had stolen vast sums from funds donated by many countries to rehabilitate Nicaragua after a severe earthquake had leveled Managua in 1972. The National Guard had been responsible for more than fifty thousand deaths in the last years of the civil war and were known by most of the rest of Nica-raguan society as "los Bestias" — "the Beasts" — a title of opprobrium that some of them, perversely, wore with pride.[12] In the last weeks of the Somoza regime, President Carter's newly appointed ambassador, Lawrence Pezzullo, tried to make plain to the old tyrant the Carter administration's case: "You have become . . . the core of the problem," Ambassador Pezzullo told him.[13] Somoza replied with evident bitterness:

> I have thrown many people out of their natural habitat because of the United States . . . so let's talk like friends. I threw a goddamn Communist out of Guatemala (in 1954) and so did I [try to] do the same thing with the Cuban Bay of Pigs [in 1961]. I am being victimized.[14]

With his guards fleeing to safe havens in Miami and elsewhere as the rebels entered Managua, General Somoza in his real-life, banana republic version of Wagner's *Goetterdamerrung*, ordered the capital bombed and strafed. The result was more than a half billion dollars of damage to Managua. Hundreds of thousands of people were left home-less. Ambassador Pezzullo cabled, nonetheless,

> I believe it ill-advised to go to Somoza and ask for a bombing halt. Air power is the only effective force the [national government] has to com-bat the [Sandinistas] which is [capturing] more towns daily and clearly has the momentum.[15]

Meanwhile, Puzzullo was instructed to "explore ways of preserving some kind of effective but reconstructed Guard presence so as to avoid leaving the FSLN [the Sandinistas][16] as the only organized military force." Finally, on July 16, 1979, Somoza and his family fled to Miami in what was a rivulet of unsavory dictators to have been ousted within a ten-year period, including Iran's "Kings of Kings," the shah; Haiti's much-hated "Baby Doc" Duvallier; and, the bogus World War II hero, Philippine president Ferdinand Marcos. The last-minute U.S. change of allegiance away from Somoza came too late to satisfy most of the disaffected who had entered Managua to claim power. The U.S. assistance in the departure of dictators looked too tentative to supporters of change, on the one hand, and, on the other, a betrayal of trust and obligations to the ruling elements through which the United States had operated and now abandoned.

It was in this context that the Carter administration attempted "to create stability out of revolution"[17] and advanced a $15-million reconstruction package to the new Sandinista regime. At the same time, a $75-million aid package was rapidly moved through Congress. But there was another track. Two days after the Somoza family landed in Miami, the CIA evacuated the leadership of the National Guard. Several score of the Guards were taken to Miami with their families, where they almost immediately began to organize for a return. Meanwhile, President Carter signed an intelligence "finding" authorizing "several hundred thousands of dollars" to keep alive domestic opposition to the Sandinistas. As the reports mounted of Sandinista enthusiasms for the Soviet bloc, Carter suspended, four days before he left office, the last installment of the $75 million authorized by Congress.[18]

During the interregnum between Carter's defeat on November 4, 1980, and Reagan's inauguration on January 21, 1981, Carter received reports that Cubans were managing the Nicaraguan intelligence service, and that Bulgarian, Soviet, and even PLO personnel were assisting the new regime. There were reports that the Sandinistas had been assisting a Marxist insurgency in El Salvador. U.S. intelligence, however, was poor, because it relied largely on the instruments and informants of the National Guard. When the National Guard fled, the list and details of U.S. intelligence "assets" — like similar lists left behind by the Iranian Savak and in the U.S. embassy in Tehran and by the CIA station in Saigon — had fallen into the new regime's hands. From a U.S. intelligence point of view, the United States had been all but "blinded."[19]

Not all the reports were hair-raising. Robert White, the U.S. ambassador to El Salvador at this time, noted that the Sandinista regime was not excessive by the standards of the region.

[We] saw the mildest revolution that Latin America has ever experienced. . . . Unlike the Mexican revolution earlier this century, the Sandinistas [had] not persecuted the Church and [had] not expropriated large foreign enterprises. Unlike the Cuban revolution of 1959, the Nicaraguan rebels have not resorted to drum-head trials, summary executions, repudiated debt, . . . [nor] quit the Organization of American States.[20]

Meanwhile, Argentine military intelligence units made contact with a remnant group of Somoza's National Guard located in Tegucigalpa, the Honduran capitol. The Argentine military were directed by individuals who, in the years up to 1982, had "disappeared" tens of thousands of their own citizens and jailed an equal number. Argentine inventiveness in torture had become a perverse Latin standard of cruelty. Buenos Aires is 3,700 miles from Managua by air. But to the Argentine military, there was a threat that their archfoes, the much-hunted Argentine guerrillas called "Monteneros," had in fact been given safe haven and training by the new Sandinista regime. Indeed, at the second anniversary of their victory over Somoza, on the Sandinista reviewing stand, Monteneros in Sandinista uniforms stood shoulder to shoulder with their Sandinista supporters.[21] More importantly, perhaps, the Argentines worried that leftists in Argentina might be inspired by the example of the Sandinistas' success.

After a few months of training, in early 1980, one group of young guards were sent by their Argentine advisers to Costa Rica, where their assignment was to blow up a liberal radio station. Meanwhile, guards had begun training in Miami. Some guards who made their way to Guatemala worked with Guatemalan "death squads" and supported themselves by kidnapping and bank robbery. In El Salvador, some apparently worked with the extremist Arena party. Using their Salvadoran base, guards were able to send assassination teams into Nicaragua. Their targets included Cuban and Nicaraguan teachers working on literacy campaigns.[22] A few unsponsored, low-ranking guards remained scattered throughout the region, where they lived, as they described it themselves, by rustling cattle and stealing chickens.[23] For some eighteen months, this appears to have been the major activity of all the guards. In mid-July 1982, the Sandinista Government reported forty-five gun battles with insurgents and 234 cases of cattle theft.

To Haig, CIA Director Casey, the Latin Americanists at the National Security Council, and Ambassador Jeane Kirkpatrick, it seemed clear that the civil war in Nicaragua and the guerrilla campaign in Salvador were part of a "well-orchestrated international communist campaign" to disrupt the region from Panama to Mexico.[24] Haig, after being rebuffed on the military option in Cuba, even while confessing the peripheral nature of the Nicaraguan "threat," suggested that U.S. forces might go into Nicaragua. Haig argued that it would be a salutary lesson to the Cubans and the Soviets, and might well cow them in the future in the western hemisphere and perhaps elsewhere. But an invasion of Nicaragua proved no more acceptable to military planners within the administration than did an invasion of Cuba. The Joint Chiefs of Staff believed it would require a substantial portion of at least one fleet and considerable U.S. ground forces. Two possibilities remained. One was to make life as difficult as possible for the Sandinistas so, at a minimum, they might "self-destruct" from the pressure. The other was attempt to find a modus vivendi with the new regime.

The new Reagan assistant secretary for Latin American Affairs, Thomas Enders, an Asian veteran of the U.S. Foreign Service, was charged with the job of pressuring the Sandinistas. Enders, however, was hardly a run-of-the-mill "negotiator." Enders' diplomatic experience was shaped in managing the forces of Lon Nol in Cambodia during the Vietnam War. Enders had a peremptory personal manner and, at over six feet, seven inches tall, was a presence known to be unaccustomed to contradiction. Enders arrived at the U.S. Embassy in Managua and delivered, ex cathedra, his explanation of the "two-track" options he believed available to the Sandinistas. The Sandinistas could negotiate with the United States a conciliatory treaty or pay the price of their intransigence. *Washington Post* investigator Bob Woodward offers a lively description:

> Pezzullo thought Enders was a stuffed shirt . . . [but he] had control of administration policy. . . . Enders said maybe diplomacy could still work. . . . Enders complained that they were harassing the Church, the press and the labor Unions. . . . Internal matters, the Sandinistas replied. . . . Enders blew his stack, telling [the Sandinistas] their country was a god damn flea that could be knocked off by the United States with its hands tied. . . . Don't be silly. . . . You must commit yourself to limiting your military buildup [and] . . . you have to get out of El Salvador. [Daniel] Ortega said "No. The Salvadoran revolution is our shield — it makes our revolution safer."[25]

Enders came to Nicaragua as a kind of latter-day Roman Proconsul. The Sandinista leader, Daniel Ortega, in his early thirties, looked like a small, excessively serious graduate student. He had fought for years in the jungle against enormous odds, losing a brother in the process. He himself had been arrested and tortured by Somoza's National Guard. He had probably not met many bigger men, but he had undoubtedly met bigger bullies.

Nicaragua and the Reagan Doctrine

Ender's reference to the Guards training in the United States was a good indication of the "or-else track" the administration had in mind. Six weeks into the Reagan term, on March 9, 1981, the White House transmitted a "finding" to Congress authorizing the funding of "moderate" opponents of the Sandinistas. The finding secured discretionary monies to sweep Soviet influence from Afghanistan, Laos, Cambodia, Grenada, Iran, Libya, and Cuba in what became known, in the second administration, as the Reagan Doctrine. The Nicaraguan activity, or "project," had special emphasis in the CIA. To the "operations" side of CIA, the Reagan Doctrine was deliverance from a long, dark night of falling budgets, massive layoffs, and dispiriting revelations about excesses ranging from assassinations to the use of experiments with LSD on mental patients. William Casey, the new Director of Central Intelligence (DCI), and a member of President Reagan's "Kitchen Cabinet," was known as one of the "great buccaneers," in the language of an admiring deputy. By 1984, CIA operations worldwide had increased 500 percent from the Carter years[26] and their real budget had more than doubled.[27] Half of the operations were said to be in Latin America. Nicaragua, therefore, from the start, was a "test case" of overall U.S. policy on at least three levels:[28]

First, at the strategic level, the Nicaraguan element of the Reagan Doctrine was to sweep from the board Soviet "gains" of the 1970s and to reestablish uncompromised U.S. primacy in global affairs. At a minimum, it was calculated, the Soviets would be chastened by an exercise of systematic confrontation in the Third World, and, where possible, "beaten at their own game" in mounting externally funded insurgencies. It was hoped Soviet resources would be so depleted in trying to defend their clients that they would not be able to sustain the central competition in the arms race or to advance an activist policy in the Third World. The most sanguine hope was that the Soviets would be faced with the prospect of managing a deteriorating economy, and perhaps domestic unrest, or contemplating withdrawal altogether from the competition as it became too expensive and too unmanageable.[29]

In short, this renewed application of the black arts of intelligence was yet another "stage" of the cold war, as dangerous as the threat to Europe and the earlier exertions required of the United States. Undersecretary of Defense Fred Ikle, whose office was "tasked" for much of the effort, expressed the challenge in language that would have been familiar to Truman, Acheson, Eisenhower, Dulles, Rusk, Kennedy, and Johnson.

. . . [S]mall wars . . . are not just a collection of self-cancelling insurgencies. . . . There is a driving, organizing force behind it all: here it stirs up and feeds an insurgency, there it exploits a coup d'etat, here it instigates terrorism to weaken democratic governments, there it provides police forces and Pretorian guards to perpetuate a regime beholden to it, it diligently, ruthlessly expands its dominance through the world. We in the West . . . [have] checkmated . . . Soviet expansion. But . . . primarily [in] the so-called Third World, . . . the cold war [is being] followed by insurgency warfare.[30]

Second, at the tactical level, the opportunity existed to develop techniques of managing, as the military would put it, the "most likely contingencies": subnational violence, revolution and terrorism. The need to deal with this new threat held great promise as a source of new missions, men, and material for commanders of units that had languished since Vietnam. The prospects for fuller funding convinced the army, after some initial reluctance, that "low-intensity warfare" and "light mobile infantry," and not the stale arguments of "burden sharing" and the prepositioning of stocks, would help invigorate U.S. ground capabilities. The Army became vigorous converts to the "new strategy."

Finally, a successful "roll-back" campaign, in a place that was manageable and most "congenial" to U.S. strength, would help rid the United States of what was seen by the Reagan administration as a debilitating institutional immobilism and persistent public doubts and hesitations about the cost and use of U.S. power. If there could be success or, better, a series of successes, then, in some of Reagan's favorite language, "America would be back" and "standing tall."

To those with a memory, little of this seemed new nor convincing. It was very much like programs given priority in the early Kennedy years. And when "low-intensity efforts" failed in the 1960s, the alternative was bringing in a heavy, formal commitment or, ultimately, abandoning the interest and those foreign nationals who had been engaged in the service of U.S. policy. Many at the level of the Joint Chiefs and in service command schools believed the real lesson of the Vietnam War was to hit hard and overwhelmingly, but only after a national commitment could be secured. Grenada, they believed, not the emerging Central American operation, should be the model for future applications of American power.[31]

Some senior military professionals and experienced intelligence analysts, such as the chairman of the Joint Chiefs of Staff and Casey's deputy director of the CIA, Bobby Inman, a legendary career analyst, despaired.[32] One CIA intelligence analyst subsequently described the emerging plan. The operations would:

provoke cross-border attacks by Nicaragua and possibly call into play the Organization of American States provisions [for self defense]. . . . [T]he Nicaraguan government would clamp down on civil liberties. . . . [T]here would be reaction against United States' . . . diplomatic personnel.[33]

Despite the foreboding, CIA Director Casey apparently hoped that as a consequence of incursions and resultant counterattacks—perhaps across the Nicaragua–Honduras border—there might be found sufficient justification for open and direct action at clearing the Sandinista "flea" from the Americas—if not unilaterally, then by some combination of contra, regional, and American forces.

Flea Bites

The administration at first turned a blind eye to National Guards training camps in Texas, California, and Miami. In May of 1981, the CIA had given a $50,000 grant to help facilitate the Argentine effort to integrate the different contra groups under a single leadership.[34] By midyear, newspaper reporters on guided tours of contra camps, both in the United States and in Central America, found retired U.S. military personnel organizing "counterinsurgency" training. From the remnant Somoza Guards, a five-hundred–man "action team" of special commandos was set up in Honduras.[35] Another group of one thousand exiles received training from Argentine military intelligence. By winter 1981, some fifteen hundred men were given $19.5 million in "seed money" by the CIA.[36] At first, it was believed the Argentines, who had their own agenda in fighting communists in exile, were good "cutouts" to disburse the funds because the contras themselves were too disreputable to be seen with American officers.[37]

The United States never broke diplomatic relations with Nicaragua, and ambassadors were retained in Managua throughout the Reagan years. Title 18, paragraph 960 of the U.S. criminal code makes it a criminal offense to participate in a group that takes armed action against foreign property or nationals. It also prohibits assistance to "'armed expeditionaries' begin[ing] or set[ting] foot or provid[ing] for or furnish[ing] the money [to] any expedition" with any nation with whom the United States is not in a formal state of war.[38] By early 1982, there were reports that the Argentines were no longer being funded by Buenos Aires but directly from Langley.[39] Because, in part, of the evident contradiction with extant legislation, and because it seemed that the things that were going on in the shadows (about which the executive would allude but would not specify), Congress was never enthused about the effort.

Meanwhile, the United States put together a number of action teams for special duty inside Nicaragua itself. Some units of Americans organized suppressive fire and provided lift for the contras.[40] Other CIA personnel from Salvador, Honduras, Chile, Argentina, Ecuador, and Bolivia received training in Panama to sabotage ports, bridges, and refineries—most built with U.S. aid dollars during the Somoza years— and make it appear that the contras were an effective fighting and commando force.[41] In December of 1981, a Nicaraguan civilian aircraft was destroyed in Mexico City.[42] In the following eighteen months, the contras caused, according to Nicaraguan statistics, ten thousand casualties.

Several human rights groups began documenting stomach-turning contra atrocities.[43] Contra behavior was not a secret to the U.S. government, nor, for that matter, to those U.S. lawmakers who troubled themselves to read assiduously the press or ask the CIA direct questions in closed committee. The CIA's Duane Claridge was forthright. He told the House Intelligence Committee in 1983 that the contras had assassinated "the heads of cooperatives, nurses, doctors and judges. . . . After all, this is war."[44]

The U.S. armed forces, indeed the armed services of virtually all advanced countries, are instructed in the laws of war. Civilians are not proper targets of war, unless armed and an immediate threat and, indeed, making them a target is a prosecutable offense. If ordered to injure a civilian directly, a soldier is legally obliged to disobey a superior officer. The profession of arms is based on coherence, discipline, and honor. If it behaves wantonly, discipline is lost. The regular U.S. army is very much aware of this "lesson" in Vietnam, and, in general, has a proud history of professionalism. Claridge's characterization of war was a profound, even insulting, contradiction to people who have conducted themselves and sacrificed themselves with restraint and dignity; and, indeed, it sullies the profession of arms everywhere. At the time of Claridge's testimony, an American Catholic priest witnessed an attack in his parish in Nicaragua:

> 20 peasant people were assassinated by the contras, including women and children. Some of them were terribly tortured first. After decapitating one little girl about fourteen years old, they put her head on a stake at the side of a trail, to strike terror into people.[45]

The contras' conduct and the character of the contra military activities were an enduring problem. To dignify the contra activity and to widen its base, a number of more substantial Nicaraguan exiles were gathered into a ruling political structure. In January 1983, the CIA actually hired a Miami-based public relations firm, on a retainer of $600 thousand, to project a more "positive image" of the contras. At the same time, President Reagan signed a National Security Decision Directive (NSDD-77) that authorized a far-reaching public relations campaign to be directed under the Department of State's new Office of Public Diplomacy. In the Reagan bureaucratic argot, the State Department was being assigned "nontraditional white" propaganda operations.[46] Television ads supporting the contras were reviewed by Elliot Abrams, the Assistant Secretary of State for Latin American Affairs. Other monies were raised by briefings held in the Executive Office Building at which President Reagan appeared several times to "pitch" wealthy donors to support the "freedom fighters" with purchases of specific weapons. Wealthy donors were led to believe they were purchasing specific items from surface-to-air missiles to light attack aircraft.

> "Public diplomacy" was simply tax-supported public relations. . . . The office arranged speaking engagements, published pamphlets and sent material [op-ed pieces] to editorial writers. In its campaign to persuade the public and the Congress to support appropriations . . . the office used Government employees and outside contractors. . . . Later the Comptroller General would find that "White Propaganda" [was] "prohibited" . . . and violated "a [legal and historic] restriction . . . prohibiting the use of federal funds . . . for propaganda purposes. . . ."[47]

One White House–inspired, private group called the "American Anti-Terrorism Committee" used the "excess" profit realized from the bizarre sale of arms to Iran[48] and ran a television campaign that was helpful in defeating one Democratic House of Representative member's bid for a Senate seat in what would normally have been a "safe" seat.[49] A bogus Roman Catholic priest was paid $2500 by Lt. Col. Oliver North. The phony priest, Thomas Dowling, after disputing, in congressional testimony, contra human rights abuses, was then photographed with President Reagan and was commissioned to write a pamphlet describing the contras' virtues.[50] The monies in the safe of Colonel North's White House annex were apparently related to the "profits" generated from U.S. weapons sold "privately" to Iran.

In the spring of 1983, President Reagan had begun referring to the U.S. support for the contras in public, calling the contras "freedom fighters" and the "moral equivalent of the founding fathers."[51] In a rare joint session of Congress, the president said:

> . . . [L]et us be clear as to the American attitude toward the government of Nicaragua. We do not seek its overthrow. Our purpose, in conformity with American and international law, is to prevent the flow of arms to El Salvador, Honduras, Guatemala and Nicaragua.[52]

Unhappy reminders of the worst features of the Vietnam years resurfaced. From coast to coast, groups involved in protesting the administration's policies in Central America, had their offices ransacked and burglarized. Maryknoll nuns, members of the United Auto Workers, academics, and Martin Luther King's old group, the Southern Christian Leadership Council, were put on custom service and FBI "watches." Antiwar groups' activities were noted, and members, as well as their associates, were put under surveillance. Academics returning from Central America had their notes and telephone books confiscated. So furious was the determination and the momentum to aid "the democratic resistance" that there seemed an almost willful effort to avoid American laws and constitutional processes.

After several years, the White House and the NSC despaired of ever being able to manage, within the normal channels of the bureaucracy, a new counterinsurgency war that would show any meaningful, near-term payoff. Their despondency took its warrant from a series of leaks; legislative fund cut-offs; contra aid prohibitions; and the revelation that the CIA had first produced a manual for the contras that included instructions on hiring criminals, assassinating contra personnel and blaming the Sandinistas as well as "neutralizing" (i.e., assassinating) Sandinista officials.[53]

In January and February 1984, Nicaraguan harbors were secretly mined by CIA "contract" personnel. Ten ships, six belonging to U.S. allies, were subsequently damaged. The Congress, and especially the leadership of the Senate Intelligence Committee were in a white fury. Senator Moynihan tendered his resignation[54] and Republican venerable, Barry Goldwater, wrote Director Casey a letter stating "frankly" that he was "p--d off" that an "act of war" had been casually committed without customary consultation.

The concern about the legality of the act was well founded. The mining of harbors was defined as an act of war by the Treaty of Paris of 1856 (which settled the Crimean War) and the Hague Conventions of 1899 and 1907 (to which the United States is a party); and, therefore, falls within the clear logic of the War Powers Act of 1974.[55] Internationally, the mining seriously undermined the U.S. position. Britain and France offered to send mine sweepers to the Nicaraguans. France and the Netherlands backed a UN-sponsored Security Council resolution condemning the United States for "escalation of acts of military aggression." Britain abstained. The United States cast a veto. The vote was thirteen for, one against, one abstention.

Director Casey had, in fact, briefed the Senate Intelligence Committee twice on these plans to interrupt Nicaraguan commerce. But

Casey mumbled badly, speaking in almost inaudible tones, and read more than eighty pages of testimony with bewildering haste. Not one member of the Senate oversight panel heard him. When news of the mining was brought to the attention of the House and Senate Intelligence Committees by some congressional staffers (and the next day was reported in the press), the Senate Intelligence Committee members were outraged.[56] The Republican-controlled Senate passed a "sense of the Senate" resolution condemning the mining by a vote of eighty-four to twelve. The House passed an identical measure by 218 to 111. The nearly $24-million-dollar appropriations request for the contras was defeated.

Apparently, this was the moment when CIA Director Casey decided to "privatize" the Reagan doctrine.[57] On March 27, 1983, NSC adviser Robert MacFarland testified, the DCI "proposed a plan for third country support . . . for Contra assistance . . . as well as funding alternatives" to the U.S. Congress and CIA monies. The Sultan of Brunei gave money. The Taiwanese and the Koreans apparently antied up. Taiwan, Chile, Guatemala, El Salvador, and Honduras contributed some combination of weapons, money, and logistic support, to the "enterprise," as it became known. The Saudis had been giving monies for many of the countries in which the United States was running covert operations. They had been doing this since 1981 as part of an apparent quid pro quo for the sale to them of eight AWACs. By 1985, the Saudi contribution to the contras was estimated by MacFarland to have exceeded $31 million. According to MacFarland, the Saudis had munificently insisted that their help to the contras "was only a gift."[58]

The aid and resupply effort for the contras had many convoluted pathways. There were, for example, odd reports of Japanese personnel assisting the Miskito Indians, who were in rebellion against the Sandinistas.[59] An Israeli team apparently air-lifted supplies to the contras in Honduras from Israeli stocks. The Israelis had huge stocks of weapons; and Israeli military prowess, intelligence service, and ability to keep secrets were greatly admired by CIA and NSC. At one point, virtually the whole supply operation was being run by Israelis. On the return leg to the United States of some of the "private" contra supply support teams were said to have ferried cocaine to the U.S. market. The point man in Central America in much of this two-way guns and cocaine traffic was, apparently, Panama's General Manuel Noriega. Supervising the American interest in supplying the contras in this phase of the enterprise was Felix Rodriguez. Rodriguez, sometimes called Max Gomez, reported to Vice President George Bush's security adviser, Donald P. Gregg.[60]

To help the contras and undo Marxists elsewhere in Angola, Ethiopia and Afghanistan, the World Anti-Communist League (WACL) was enlisted through its head, retired General John Singlaub. But WACL's policies were unsavory, at best. In Mexico, WACL's "correspondent group" were the Tecos, an association of anti-Semites and neo-Nazis. In Honduras, the local WACL correspondent was in intimate association with the death squads. The Guatemalan WACL representative was Mario Sandoval Alacaron, who had been reliably linked with drugs and organized mayhem, such as kidnapping and bank robbing, to finance his party's activities. In El Salvador, the League's affiliate was managed through Roberto D'Aubuisson, a man who former Ambassador Robert White called a pathological killer.[61] The administration's view of these private supporters of the contras could not have been clearer. "What's kept the resistance alive," said Assistant Secretary Elliot Abrams on October of 1986, "has been private contributions. Some very, very, brave people have been willing to actually bring this material into Nicaragua. God bless them." Senator Patrick Leahey characterized this kind of encouragement of "private" funds as "a wink and a nod" in support of the activities and violation of the law. Abrams retorted, "a wink and a nod, hell. We think it's been fine."[62]

Much of Central America had been stitched together into a vast intelligence site, training redoubt, and arms depot to support the war against the Nicaraguans. Costa Rica had been virtually compelled to compromise its nonmilitary tradition and its neutral position in Latin America. Costa Rica still was without a "formal" army, but it raised a well-armed, fifteen-thousand–man militia that began with U.S. "Green Beret" training,[63] to patrol the countryside. Costa Rican civil guards were armed with U.S. infantry gear, including M16s, grenade launchers, eighty-millimeter mortars, and M-60 machine guns.[64] The small country was also enlisted to support a former Sandinista hero, Eden Pastora, and his commandos.[65] Costa Rican airstrips had been used with the connivance of police and intelligence officers in Costa Rica while assurances had been given to the political authorities that no such thing had occurred. When an ammunition-laden plane was stuck in the middle of an airfield, and had to be towed out with trucks borrowed by the U.S. embassy,[66] a barrage of recriminations began among the traditionally moderate Costa Rican ruling coalition. When the airstrip incident became public, the NSC attempted to find ways to "punish" the Costa Ricans.[67] Costa Rican politics, for years run by a centerist coalition, began to crack.

There was an attempt to make Honduras a secure redoubt and basecamp for much of the contra venture. Huge airstrips were cut, and massive amounts of military material and men were brought to Honduras in August of 1983 in Operation Big Pine II. One hundred fifty million dollars of electronic intelligence equipment powerful enough to reach "anywhere" and to hear "anything" was put into place. The Honduran navy of five hundred men and eight coastal patrol craft exercised with an unusual armada of American ships: two carriers, thirty-two other combatants, and the battleship *New Jersey* were sent up and down the Atlantic and Pacific coasts of Nicaragua. The operation involved over 37,000 U.S. naval personnel and 6,000 American troops lifted in by C-5As and other transports. In late 1983, it was announced that Big Pine II would be followed in mid-1984 by Big Pine III; and, in early 1984, the administration announced that up to twelve hundred American military personnel would be permanently stationed in Honduras.

These exercises were both a practice run at testing the U.S. capability of blockading Nicaragua and an attempt to intimidate the Nicaraguan government, Castro, and even the Russians. As Undersecretary Ikle proclaimed, "Let me make this clear to you, we do not seek a military defeat for our friends. We do not seek a military stalemate. We seek victory for the forces of democracy."[68] The pursuit of victory over Nicaragua with American-backed rebels operating out of Honduras and Costa Rica, and escalating conflict between Salvadoran rebels and the Salvadoran government threatened to engulf the whole area in strife. Moreover, by defining the region as vital and the stakes as critical, the promise of maximum involvement seemed ineluctable.[69]

Honduras became, therefore, an increasingly uneasy "patsy" for the U.S. secret war in Central America. But in March 1986, then U.S. ambassador John Ferch had to plead with Honduran president Azcona to ask for emergency U.S. aid to counter a purported Sandinista border incursion against contra bases inside Honduras. It was Easter weekend. Azcona saw no crisis and was heading to the beach when the U.S. request came in. "You have to tell them to declare there was an incursion," a high-ranking State Department official from Washington shouted over the phone to the U.S. embassy in Honduras. Azcona resisted. Finally, Ambassador Ferch, who was in bed with the flu, waylaid Azcona. "Mr. President," Ferch said, "let me give you a personal opinion: you don't have any choice now." Azcona relented, and Ferch and Azcona drafted the Honduran request for U.S. troops and assistance.[70]

Hondurans, perhaps the least nationalistic people in Central America, started to become resentful. The matter came to a head when the U.S. virtually put out a contract, with the elements of the Honduran military, to retrieve a notorious drug dealer who had been involved in the torture and murder of a Drug Enforcement Agency agent in Mexico. Hondurans of all classes seemed incensed by the high-handed bypassing of the judicial procedures, such as warrants, arrest, and extradition. A broad section of Honduran society seemed to relish the resultant riot and burning of the U.S. embassy, causing some $6 million in damage.[71] The group closest to the contras, the Honduran naval and army intelligence units, had been reportedly involved in the cocaine traffic from the onset of the contras' locating themselves in Tegucigalpa. But the DEA in Washington quashed efforts of the Honduran DEA field office to investigate; and, in 1983, the sole DEA office in the country was closed down.[72]

In El Salvador by the end of the Reagan administration, $3 billion had been spent to buttress democratic processes and defeat the communist rebellion. In the election of 1988, those Salvadorans who showed up to vote elected the extreme right-wing faction, one part of which was led by Roberto D'Aubuision, a man who is reliably reported to have considered murdering two U.S. ambassadors and who actually seems to have been behind the assassination of the archbishop of San Salvador.[73] Meanwhile, the Salvadoran economy was a shambles, the GNP actually declined 25 percent in eight years. Since the birth rate is one of the highest in the world, the Salvadoran per-capita income was the lowest in a century. The guerrillas (Farabundo Marti National Liberation Front), although declared by the U.S. embassy in San Salvador to have been reduced to a "nuisance," almost trebled the scope of their operations. Death squads that operated for years and were then suppressed for a time continued, and, by 1986, more than forty thousand noncombatants had been killed or "disappeared." Some 750,000 Salvadorans had fled and another 500,000 were refugees in Salvador itself.[74] Great sections of the Salvadoran countryside were made into fire zones to "separate the people from the guerrillas."[75] The nub of the problem was that the very army and security apparatus that had been funded to pursue a guerrilla war was not only corrupt but also characterized by endemic, criminal violence. As the U.S. Senate Committee on Intelligence reported: "Numerous Salvadoran and security forces and other official organizations have been involved in encouraging or conducting death-squad activity or violent abuses. This has included many middle-level officers and a few higher ranking officials; a large number of low-ranking personnel have been involved."[76]

In the Reagan years, the market in illicit drugs shipped from the Caribbean basin and Central America virtually exploded. Strong evidence existed as far back as 1972 that Panamanian military leader Manual Noriega, a U.S. intelligence "asset," was involved in drug deals through the peculiarly lax Panamanian banking system, which accepted dollars as the national currency, without references or explanations. By the mid-1980s, a conclusive case had been built by prosecutors in the U.S. Department of Justice and the CIA that the Panamanian strong man, the effective ruler of Panama, had been involved not only in the cocaine traffic but also in arms deals with Cuba. The Panamanian Defense Force—"down to the levels of captains and majors"—was involved in drug running. But, as the former deputy assistant secretary of state for Intelligence and Research testified, a decision was made to put Noriega "on the shelf until Nicaragua was settled."[77]

When Noriega was finally indicted by a Florida grand jury, the State Department decided to make him, if not his confederates in Panama, an example. The State Department attempted to manufacture Noriega's ouster by "constitutional" means, encouraging the putative president of the country to "fire" General Noriega by means of a prerecorded videotaped message.[78] When Noriega defied his U.S.-backed internal opponents, the United States virtually embargoed the use of dollars. But even with the Panamanian economy imploding, Noriega hung on, portraying himself as the heroic defier of Yankee imperialism, and even gained support. The result so harmed the Panamanian economy that massive civil unrest resulted. The damage from the embargo on currency was so disruptive to banking, Panama's major source of middle class employment, that a once-independent partner of the United States had been transformed almost over night into a seething and resentful charity case. It was, Reagan officials conceded, a "strategic mistake."[79] Panama teetered on anarchy and suffering a sudden 80 percent unemployment as a result of the U.S. dollar embargo. The State Departments' Latin American expert, Elliot Abrams, in handling the administration response to the Florida warrant for the arrest of General Noriega, groused one U.S. diplomat in Panama, "ruined a healthy economy, weakened the pro-American middle class and created the conditions in Panama for growing communist influence. . . . You've got to give yourself credit. That's a hell of achievement for diplomacy."[80]

As the Reagan administration wound down, options were few. There were three possibilities: Noriega would see the benefits of exile; he would give the effort up; or the United States would invade and "liberate" from a corrupt military a nation that was home to more than forty thousand U.S. citizens and that contained the most valuable political and military asset the United States had in the area, the Panama Canal.

In the end, the administration relented, and the dollar embargo was lifted. Noriega stayed on as the administration undertook ignominious negotiations involving an offer to Noriega to lift the indictment if he would leave the country until after the next election in Panama. This apparently one-sided "plea-bargaining" led one U.S. senator to observe that, in this case, the accused, Noriega, was bargaining and the prosecutor, the United States, was "plea-ing."[81] As the U.S. position deteriorated, both Democratic presidential candidates began to hammer the Republicans to such effect that Vice President Bush was forced to disassociate himself publicly on the issue from the Reagan administration. Ultimately, the administration withdrew from the negotiations, leaving Noriega, for the moment at least, victorious in his confrontation. The administration had acted in Central America without any sense of the consequences of success or failure. There are only two possible isthmus passages: Panama and Nicaragua. Both nations, by the end of the Reagan administration, seemed on the verge of irreparable alienation.

Virtually any guerrilla campaign, if it is to be successful at all, collects taxes and controls territory. The contras never had the ability to stay in a village for even twenty-four hours. The Viet Cong, Chinese Communists, Fidel Castro's small band, the Afghans—all the successful peasant-based revolutions of recent times—mounted a sustained military presence in the countryside. The Sandinistas did it, and the Salvadoran revolutionaries still move as a feature of the landscape that the government forces must either decimate or win back. But the contras had their Guard's heritage. Even if they could shake that legacy and stigma, they had been trained in an American tradition of meeting fire power with superior fire power. And in this, both they and their U.S. trainers, knew they would almost always be out-gunned.

The United States knew, from the onset, it was not a winning force regardless of what strategy it adopted. U.S. Army General Paul F. Gorman, chief of the Southern Command in Panama, testified, after hundreds of millions of official and off-the-books monies had been raised, the contras could not win and the U.S. knew it: "I did not see," he recalled ". . . a combination of forces that could lead to the overthrow of the Sandinistas. . . . The training of the Contras, when I last saw them, was abysmal. . . . I didn't regard it as a very effective military organization."[82]

It did not take any great ability at soothsaying to see how events would unfold. As the chairman of the Joint Chiefs, Admiral William Crowe, suggested, the contras' persistent lack of unity and absence of military successes would, inevitably, drive Americans to "back out from under the commitment."[83] The new White House national security team, after Admiral Poindexter left, could see the inevitable. On January 5, 1987, Frank Carlucci, in his incarnation as National Security Assistant, told associates, "I don't see how the Contras can win."[84] Nobody could. The contras had been failures in 1979. And although ten years later their numbers had swollen to fifteen thousand, the U.S. government was nearly unanimous in its judgment that they were failures still. Even the great enthusiasts of the war, in their private moments, would confess this dark truth to each other. Robert Owen,[85] the "buffer" between the White House/CIA and the contras, wrote, in a sad, tired, but affectionate valedictory to "B and G" (for "Blood and Guts"), Lt. Col. Oliver North, at the NSC, that the contras were simply "a creature of the U.S. [government]." The leadership of the contras, Owen wrote, is filled with "liars and greed[y] people." "In fact," Owen despaired, "the FDN has done a good job of keeping competent people out of the organization." Owen concluded, in bold letters: "This war has become a business" to the contras: "There is still a belief the marines are going to have to invade, so let's get set." In Owen's opinion, more money was not the issue. The fiscal year 1987 contra aid package, totaling $100 million, Owen believed, "would be like throwing money down a sink hole."[86]

While privately well aware of the limits of the army of their own creation, the president's National Security adviser, Admiral John Poindexter, and his young marine deputy, Lt. Col. Oliver North, on a secret inspection, toured the Sandinista encampments and told the contras: "We intend to pursue a victory." Accommodation with the Sandinistas, they told the rebels, would not be tolerated by the U.S. government.[87] In this way, by a process of deluding others while retaining privately remarkably clear-eyed and even cynical views of contra capability, the administration sought to perpetuate the fighting even when there were opportunities for negotiation, and even when the parties themselves had visibly lost their stomach for the quarrel. At least four senior Ambassadors of Career, the Foreign Service's highest rank, who believed a negotiated peace was possible in the region, were relieved from their posts. When Ambassador Philip Habib, for instance, reported to Secretary Shultz and the White House, in the summer of 1987, that a Central American peace process was a live possibility and could yield progress, he was "withdrawn." Habib, who had come out of retirement, and, indeed, had left a sickbed at the secretary's personal urging, was not allowed to return to the area after expressing a belief in a negotiated settlement.[88]

In sum, neither the contra leadership, nor the NSC believed the former could ever win.[89] Few of the Reagan administration policy makers disagreed with the formulation of Jeane Kirkpatrick,[90] which held that left-wing "totalitarian regimes" could not, by their nature, give way to democracy except by being virtually undone. Given that there were slim prospects for a contra victory and that the administration believed that die-hard Marxist–Leninists could not tolerate dissent, much less the most repressive and corrupt elements of the old regime, the administration's prescription for a peaceful conclusion to the war—"power sharing"— was a kind of oxymoron. The exact purposes of the contras and the Reagan administration, therefore, seem perplexing beyond the symbolic utility of bedeviling an extraordinarily poor society of three million whose leaders had chosen Marx and Lenin for their standard bearers.

The administration was apparently waiting for a miracle of deliverance from a course that was never viewed with support in the region, in Congress, or among the U.S. Joint Chiefs. A regional grouping of states—the Contadora group[91]—worked unsuccessfully against American opposition and Sandinista suspicion throughout the decade in an attempt to fashion a settlement. Eventually, the contras' war would end. But the war could not be won by the contras, the administration knew, because the contras lacked the numbers and the popular base. Nor did the administration believe the contras could exact a viable compromise or settlement. Any arrangement between the contras and the Sandinistas was precluded by the very nature, the administration believed, of the Sandinista regime and the administration's own efforts to thwart negotiations. In the private considerations of the U.S. administration (if there was any reflection at all on more than proximate goals in Central America), it was believed that the Sandinistas would never tolerate any return of the contras or, for that matter, any real opposition. The contras could not win, but their numbers and military stores had grown to the point where, for at least the life of the Reagan administration, they could not be defeated either.

As long as they could stay in their redoubts in Honduras, the contras would linger on. The "disposal" problem, as John Kennedy had referred to the survivors of the Bay of Pigs operation, would come later. It was the widespread, but largely private, belief shared by both the administration and the Congress that the contras would, eventually, dissolve. Honduras would accept some, but, like the Costa Ricans, Honduras would stop tolerating their presence in armed formations. Some would go into exile, some would be reintegrated back into the rural economy of Nicaragua, and some would simply be crushed in battle. Whatever contra remnant bands remained would probably bear their defeat bitterly, feeling that, at the end, they were let down in their hour of need. Then, the choice for U.S. policy makers would be to arrange somehow for their safe passage to the United States or abandon them to their fate. The contras would have to be compromised. The date and time the dues finally would have to be presented were matters of surmise. Although failure did not loom with any immediacy, it was, the administration knew, unavoidable. The best that could be hoped, by those who had funded the contras — no matter how reluctantly — and by those who had encouraged the contras' lost enterprise, was that when collapse or capitulation came, it would be "on a different watch."

After Lt. Col. North's bizarre linkage of the arms-for-hostages deal with Iran and secret funds for the contra enterprise was exposed and discredited, nobody in Washington had any idea how the contras could be sustained in perpetuity. Yet, when the president of Costa Rica came to Washington to discuss a settlement of the war, Assistant Secretary Abrams announced that he was "intensely displeased" that the Costa Ricans were "lobbying" the Congress for a peace plan for which Costa Rica's President Arias had just won a Nobel Prize.[92] An opportunity existed in the Arias plan for a circumspect, albeit not entirely graceful, U.S. exit. But in August 1987, President Reagan declared the Arias Peace plan "fatally flawed." In January of 1988, yet another U.S. National Security Assistant, General Colin Powell, toured Central America, offering "advice" that U.S. economic and military aid to the area be conditioned on support of the contras.[93] Congress, however, in the wake of the Iran–contra hearings, administered the coup de grace by refusing another round of aid. The contras, however, no matter how venal, inefficient, and brutal, could see the inevitable. Even if subsequent monies could somehow be extracted from Congress, they would be at a much-reduced level; and funds would be disbursed not by sympathetic CIA personnel, but by the OAS or the Red Cross. Funds for arms would, eventually, cease. More and more members would trickle back to their farms or villages or attempt to find a more comfortable exile in North America. Meanwhile, the contras suffered relentless military pressure. Seeing an inevitability to the end of their capacity to find arms, supplies and safe haven, the contras finally accepted a cease-fire and the offer of negotiations from their old foes in Managua in early 1988.

The Sandinistas suffered more than 27,000 dead[94] in their war with the contras. The Nicaraguan economy was in ruins. The new Gorbachev regime had not been as forthcoming in arms and economic support as Brezhnev and his immediate successors had been.[95] Indeed, in 1987, Gorbachev made it clear that oil deliveries would be scaled back and the much-hoped-for MIG fighter planes would probably never arrive. The Soviets had extended over $275 million in credits and $50 million in grants, plus a huge amount of oil. The East Europeans had also made substantial contributions, including those who were desperate for hard currency themselves.[96] Soviet priorities now ran to arms control agreements with the West and "perestroika," the restructuring of the internal economy of the Soviet Union and gaining access to Western capital and technology.[97]

But when the process of a cease-fire and reconciliation began in the area, American officials were, at best, churlish. As mortifying to the Reagan administration as the signal that their creation had lost faith in the creator was the news that the United States was, for all practical purposes, excluded from the emerging negotiations and settlement. First the Contadora and then the Arias proposal had offered a means for the United States to maintain some leverage on the peace process. But both had been rejected and actively resisted by the Reagan administration. It was surprising, then, that the administration was shocked when, in March of 1988, the contras signed a cease-fire and began negotiating their difficult integration into the "new order" of the Sandinistas' Nicaragua.

THE BALANCE SHEET
ON THE "ENTERPRISE"

The U.S. policy focus on the war in Central America was perhaps one of the largest failures not only of Reagan's presidency but in the whole course of the cold war. In terms of invidious effect, if not in expenditure of money and blood, it may have exceeded Vietnam. Every feature of the misbegotten effort to undo the Sandinistas was either misanalyzed, mishandled, or misrepresented. U.S. foreign policy in Central America, from Panama to Mexico was a tabloid of disaster. Nowhere in Central America did people have a better life. By the end of the 1980s, the fine-sounding phrases surrounding the "Caribbean Basin Initiative" and the Kissinger Commission[98] had gathered the same dust that covered the Good Neighbor Policy of the 1940s and the Alliance for Progress in the Kennedy years. The Mexicans, the great worry of the Reagan years, were floundering and had been projected by Casey as the next Iran.[99] But Mexican problems, beyond their fiscal problems of debt and the official abetting of narcotics traffic, were never addressed.[100] The Mexican middle class was decimated by devaluations and inflation. Mexico remained in an unhappy brew of bursting urban ills and social shocks from narcotics, corruption, repression, and the real dislocations from one of the worst urban earthquakes in Mexican history.

The Reagan administration had invested much hope and rhetoric in a coalition of bankers and investors that had cooperated in trying to support new, conservative, free enterprise voices in the area. Jamaica was singled out as a manageable case for revitalization. But there too, stubborn problems of high unemployment, crime, and low commodity prices marred the new paint of slick advertising, loan infusions, and parades of White House "photo opportunities" for Prime Minister Edward Seaga with President Reagan. In the face of it all, Jamaica, the corner stone of the CBI, emerged by the middle of the Reagan administration as the third-largest marijuana producer in the world.[101] Panama remained led by an army that had funded itself by smuggling, transshipping drugs, gun running, and other criminal interposes. Honduras was seething with discontents. Costa Rica, the once shining example of a demilitarized democracy in the hemisphere, indeed, unique in the world, had found itself with a U.S.-trained militia with every outward manifestation of a standing army. The contras had joined a heart-rending roll call of ostentatiously U.S.-supported peoples in Latvia, the Ukraine, Hungary, Vietnam, Cuba, and Kurdastan[102] who had been compromised or abandoned because their cause had become inexpedient or untenable.

A library shelf of American laws was broken and yet another president, in his last years in office, faced twin burdens of ineffectiveness.[103] First, there was the natural withdrawal of support that comes with any "lame duck" presidency. And, second, there was the self-imposed weight of a perception that, at the core of U.S. policy, decisions were made without much heed to their consequences. The evidence of illegality was inescapable. Monies were raised outside the law by "private" individuals, virtually working on commission from the White House. The National Security Council staff and CIA used a practice harkening back to letters of marque, a power expressly reserved to the Congress in the Constitution.[104] A war was fought while it was asserted that the United States was attempting to peacefully resolve disputes. Funds were expended for purposes expressly forbidden by the Constitution in knowing contradiction in article I, section 9, "No monies shall be drawn from the treasury but in consequence of appropriations made by law and a regular statement and account of the receipts and expenditures of all public money shall be published from time to time." Claims were asserted, and to some extent accepted by the Congress, that the president and his staff could construct clandestine treasuries designed to support a hidden intelligence apparatus and private wars, while also pursuing private schemes and private profits, because, it was argued, legislation had excluded every branch of the executive except the NSC and the president himself.[105]

The enterprise in Central America was a piece of a foreign policy of sham and symbol. There was heady enthusiasm on the part of politicians and policy makers for a war for which there had been little comprehension and for which there had not been much fundamentally at stake. The President's lawful responsibility, spelled out in article II, section 3 of the Constitution and in the President's very oath of office, that he "take care that the laws be faithfully executed," was disregarded. Presidential authority, which had begun to see the sun again in the Reagan years, disappeared once more behind a cloud of disappointment.

NOTES

1. Zbigniew Brzezinski, *Power and Principle* (New York: Farrar, Strauss, Giroux, 1983), pp. 351ff.
2. Ibid., pp. 348–352; and Philip Brenner, "The Unchanging Agenda in U.S.–Cuban Relations," paper delivered at the 11th Congress of the Latin American Studies Association, Mexico, September 1983. Brenner's forthcoming book on Cuban–American relations promises to be definitive.
3. Cited by Wayne S. Smith, "U.S. Policy: The Worst Alternative Syndrome," *SAIS Review*, No. 3 (Summer–Fall 1983), p. 17.
4. Ibid., pp. 17–18.
5. *New York Times*, March 4, 1982, p. 4. Haig was quoted by an unnamed aide.
6. Bob Woodward, *Veil* (New York: Simon and Schuster, 1987), p. 193.
7. Ibid., pp. 116–117ff.
8. Ibid., p. 136.
9. On the legality of the American action, see the exchange between Abram Chayes and Eugene Rostow in *New York Times*, November 15, 1983, p. A35.
10. See the interview with Prime Minister Thatcher in *New York Times*, January 22, 1984.
11. See Peter Kornbluh, "The Price of Intervention" (Washington: Institute for Policy Studies, 1987), p. 15.
12. Richard Millet, *Guardians of Destiny* (Maryknoll, New York: Orbis Books, 1977), pp. 2237–2238. See also Jack Anderson, "World's Greediest Dictator," in Robert S. Leiken and Barry Rubin, eds., *Central American Crisis Reader* (New York: Summit Books, 1987), p. 141. The Guard sold looted goods after the earthquake leveled Managua.
13. Somoza secretly taped his conversations with U.S. officials. See Anastasio Somoza and Jane Cox, *Nicaragua Betrayed* (Boston: Western Islands, 1980), pp. 329–330; also cited by Kornbluh, *Nicaragua The Price of Intervention* (Washington: IPS Books, 1987). Much of this narrative is indebted to Kornbluh and the Iran–contra hearings.
14. See Kornbluh, op. cit., p. 16.
15. See World Bank, *Nicaragua Credit*, 9655-NI, June 24, 1983, p. 3; John A. Booth, *The End of the Beginning* (Boulder, Col.: Westview Press, 1982), p. 181; and Kornbluh, op. cit., note 4, p. 96.
16. The cable is reproduced in Kornbluh, op. cit., p. 17, and is dated June 30, 1979. The Sandinistas take their name from a figure from the 1920s who waged a guerrilla war against an American occupation force.
17. Kornbluh, op. cit., p. 18.

18. See Christopher Dickey, *With the Contras* (New York: Simon and Schuster, 1985), p. 55; and Kornbluh, op. cit., p. 190.

19. Bob Woodward, op. cit., pp. 112–164ff.

20. See the Honorable Robert White, "U.S. Security and Central America," *San Francisco, The Commonwealth*, November 3, 1987, p. 525.

21. Catesby Leigh, "Argentina Backs El Salvador Firmly," *The Times of the Americas*, March 31, 1982.

22. See Dickey, op. cit., pp. 82–88; and *Newsweek*, April 11, 1983, p. 46.

23. John Prados, *Presidents' Secret Wars* (New York: William Morrow, 1986), p. 400.

24. See "Early Decision to Counter Marxism Led To Nurturing Rebels," *Washington Post*, January 1, 1987, p. A24.

25. Ibid., p. 165.

26. According to CIA Deputy Director of Operations Claire George, in House Report 100-433, 100th Congress, 1st Sess.; Senate Report 100-216, *Iran Contra Affair*, November, 1987; U.S. House, Select Committee To Investigate Covert Arms Transactions with Iran, and U.S. Senate, Select Committee on Secret Military Assistance to Iran and the Nicaraguan Opposition, chap. 2, p. 34.

27. Prados, op. cit., p. 386.

28. HR 100-433, p. 33.

29. See the study commissioned by the Army training and Doctrine Command cited by James Adams, *Secret Armies* (New York: The Atlantic Monthly Press, 1987), pp. 204–205.

30. Fred Ikle, a speech to the Inland Empire of Southern California World Affairs Council, January 30, 1986; cited in ibid., pp. 204–205.

31. See Col. John D. Waghlestein, "Post Vietnam Counter Insurgency Doctrine," *Military Review*, May 1985, p. 46; cited by Michael Klare in Michael Klare and Peter Kornbluh, *Low Intensity Warfare* (New York: Pantheon, 1988), p. 50, ftn. 50. Also see Marc S. Millar, "Ambiguous War," *Technology Review*, August/September, 1987, pp. 62–67.

32. See Woodward, op. cit., pp. 174–175, 192, 206. Shortly thereafter, both men retired.

33. See testimony before the World Court, September 8, 1985, cited by Kornbluh, "Nicaragua" cited in Klare and Kornbluh, op. cit., p. 138.

34. There are, to be fair, several reports of where this $50 thousand came from. See Scott Anderson and Jon Lee Anderson, *Inside the League* (New York: Dodd Mead, 1986), chap. 17, ftn. 3. It is clear that the intermediaries or "cutouts" were Argentines and not, as it was to be later, U.S. CIA personnel. See Kornbluh, "Test Case of the Reagan Doctrine," *Third World Quarterly*, January 1988, p. 5.

35. Pursuant to a Presidential Directive (NSDD 17, dated November 23, 1981).

36. Prados, op. cit., p. 397; Shireley Christian, *Revolution in the Family* (New York: Random House, 1985), p. 198; Kornbluh, "Test Case for the Reagan Doctrine," p. 5; and Woodward, op. cit., p. 172. See also Scott Anderson and Jon Lee Anderson, op. cit., p. 245, ftn. 3. The monies seem to have been transferred out of contigency funds. If the funds had been granted by any agency directly, they would have clearly violated several congressional injunctions that had banned assistance to the Argentine regime.

37. See "Early Decision to Counter Marxism."

38. See Jules Lobel, "The Rise and Decline of the Neutrality Act: Sovereignty and Congressional War Powers in United States Foreign Policy," *Harvard International Law Journal*, Vol. 24, Summer 1983.

39. Anderson and Anderson, op. cit., p. 245.
40. Steven Emerson, *Secret Warriors* (New York: Putnam, 1988), p. 150.
41. Kornbluh, "Test Case for the Reagan Doctrine," p. 12.
42. Prados, op. cit., p. 401.
43. America's Watch, *Human Rights Nicaragua* (Washington, D.C.: America's Watch, 1985).
44. Cited in Klare and Kornbluh, *Low Intensity Warfare*, p. 142, ftn. 16.
45. David Siegel, M.D., "Nicaraguan Health: An Update," *LASA Forum* (Winter 1984), pp. 30–31; and note 101, p. 229, in Kornbluh, "The Price of Intervention."
46. Cited in HR 100-433, p. 34. In the end, up to $97 million was raised, and more than $20 million could not be accounted for.
47. See Jeff Garth with Stephen Engleberger, "Cash for Contras Far Exceeds Sum They Had Sought," *New York Times*, April 8, 1987. HR 100-433, p. 34.
48. See Chapter 12, *infra*.
49. Michael Barnes, op. cit. See HR 100-433, p. 99.
50. See Prados, op. cit., p. 434.
51. Cited in Prados, op. cit., p. 427.
52. On April 27, 1983, cited in HR 100-433, p. 33.
53. Prados, op. cit., p. 406.
54. He later rethought the matter.
55. It requires prior authorization by Congress for acts of war or acts that are likely to lead to war.
56. Prados, op. cit., p. 414; and Woodward, op. cit., pp. 319–328.
57. Woodward, op. cit., pp. 328–329.
58. See Select Committee Reports, p. 38. Secretary Shultz, who regularly handled relations with Saudi Arabia, had not been told about these monies until eighteen months later. MacFarland stated it was an "oversight."
59. Prados, op. cit., p. 409.
60. See Steven Engleberg with Jeff Garth, "Officials Say Bush Heard '85 Charge Against Noriega," *New York Times*, May 8, 1988, p. A1. Tom Wicker, "Bush and Noreiga," *New York Times*, April 29, 1987, p. A39. The latter sentence is from the sworn testimony of Gregg, a CIA official who served through 1988 as Bush's National Security adviser. See the Iran–Contra Hearings HR 100-433, pp. 502–503, for Bush's and the contras' support activities. See Jim McGhee and David Hoffman, "Rivals Hint Bush Understates Knowledge of Noriega's Ties," *Washington Post*, May 8, 1988, p. A16. See also Bill McCallister, "Model Citizen Adopted Life of Smuggling Drugs," *Washington Post*, April 15, 1987, p. A1; see also Stephen Engleberg "3 Nicaraguan Rebels Tell Senators of Refueling Drug Planes For Cash," *New York Times*, April 8, 1988, p. A6. See also Dan Morgan, "Testimony of Bush Aides Point to Big Latin American Role," *Washington Post*, May 1, 1988, p. A4. Bush was head of the Reagan antidrug task force in this period and claimed that his close attention to the details of that operation were his proudest achievement. But Bush had been CIA director when Noriega first became a CIA asset, and there were reports that Noriega was involved in drugs throughout the early 1980s. This was noted by veteran Washington reporter Daniel Schorr on National Public Radio's "All Things Considered: Weekend Edition," May 1, 1988.
61. Anderson and Anderson, op. cit., p. 86. See also Jack Anderson and Joseph Spear, "Anti-Communist League Unleashed," *Washington Post*, August 9, 1986, p. F11. See also Robert White's testimony before the House Committee on Foreign Affairs, February 6, 1984; reprinted in Leiken and Rubin, op. cit., pp. 562–567.

62. Cited by Doyle McManus, "Dateline Washington," *Foreign Policy*, No. 66 (Spring 1987), p. 158.

63. For a good review, see Joel Millman's report, "The Narcotics War: Going For the Gold," Institute of Current World Affairs, Hanover, N.H. (March 8, 1988), pp. 4–5.

64. Morris J. Blachman and Ronald G. Hellman, "Costa Rica," in Blachman, et al., *Confronting Revolutions* (New York: Pantheon, 1986), pp. 178–179.

65. "Comandante Zero," as Pastora was called, had a high command that was deeply implicated in drug smuggling. In the end, because he had no taste for integrating his band under Somoza's Guard, which had been his nemesis for years, and because, perhaps, there had been two suspicious assassination attempts on his life (one apparently carried out by anticommunist, Miami-based Cubans) in Costa Rica, Pastora gave up the struggle to write his memoirs.

66. HR 100-433, p. 68.

67. Ibid., p. 76.

68. "Central America Military Victory Called Necessity," *Washington Post*, September 13, 1983, p. A12.

69. For example, see Weinberger's statement of September 6, 1983, in Panama in *Washington Post*, September 7, 1983. The move to support the El Salvadoran government and topple the Sandinistas was a boon to the CIA Operations directorate. Almost every covert agent "riffed" in the 1970s — over six hundred under retirement age — returned. The operations budget was doubled and was augmented by separate arms and drug enforcement intelligence units. *Washington Post*, August 23, 1983, p. A6.

70. See Roy Gutman, "A Competition of Blunders Between the U.S. and Nicaragua," *Washington Post, National Edition*, March 28–April 3, p. 23.

71. See James LeMoyne, "Stark Anti-Americanism in Honduras," *New York Times*, April 9, 1988, p. 6. Apparently, the Honduran military delivered the fugitive in the hope it would forestall implicating the minister of defense, the director of Military Intelligence, the chief of the Armed Forces and the director of the Military Command school, who were all suspected of having an intimate relationship with drug trafficking while assisting with the contra–American struggle against the Sandinistas on their southern border. The Honduran government had been made a reluctant redoubt for the contras. The $6-million figure is the amount of liability assumed by Honduras; see Reuters report in "Current News," Departmet of the Air Force, April 26, 1988, p. 18.

72. Elaine Sciolino and Stephan Engleberger, "US Security Interests Thwart War," *New York Times*, February 18, 1988, p. A3. A 1986 law required certification that countries in which drugs are produced or transshipped "cooperated fully" with the United States in suppressing narcotics traffic lest they lose American economic assistance.

73. See the testimony of Robert White in Hearings Before the Committee on Foreign Affairs, House of Representatives, February 6, 1984; reprinted in Lieken and Rubin, op. cit., pp. 562–567.

74. The figures are from Martin Diskin and Kenneth E. Sharpe, "El Salvador," in Morris J. Blachman, op. cit., p. 86.

75. See Jim Leach, George Miller, and Mark Hatfield, "Bankrolling Failure United States Policy in El Salvador and the Urgent Need for Reform, November 1987, and U.S. Aid to El Salvador: An Evaluation of the Past, A Proposal for the Future," a report prepared for the Congressional Arms Control and Foreign Policy

Caucus, February 1985. The quotation is from Colonel Sigrifiedo Ochoa as reported in Martin Diskin and Kenneth Sharpe, "El Salvador" in Morris Blackman, et al., *Confronting Revolution* (New York: Pantheon, 1986), p. 88.

76. U.S. Congress, Select Committee On Intelligence, "Recent Violence in El Salvador," October 5, 1984; cited in Blachman, op. cit., p. 381, ftn. 84.

77. Stephan Engleberger, "Ex-Aide Describes Ties to Noriega," *New York Times*, April 15, 1988, p. A1. The real journalistic ferret of the Noriega story was Seymour Hersh, who underscores the point that Noriega was a bipartisan scandal given his long history of involvement with the CIA and drugs, stretching back to the Ford administration. See his "Why Democrats Can't Make an Issue of Noriega," *New York Times*, May 4, 1988, p. A27.

78. See the letter to the *New York Times* dated April 11, 1988, from Ambler H. Moss, Jr., the former ambassador to Panama until 1982 in the April 20, 1988, *New York Times*. The observation is that of Moss quoted in David E. Pitt, "Did U.S. Tactics in Panama Backfire?" *New York Times, Week in Review*, May 1, 1988, p. E2.

79. Ibid.

80. See James LeMoyne, "Hope Fades for Panama Economy," *New York Times*, May 8, 1988, p. 14.

81. Senator Kerry quoted in LeMoyne, "Hope Fades," p. 14.

82. Cited by HR 110-443, p. 49. On January 28, 1987, Gorman told the Senate Armed Services Committee: "A sound, unconventional warfare campaign does not involve people with guns up front. It involves a lot of patient preparation. . . . Unless and until you have got the ability to move at will in the society. . . , you are not going to be effective. They [the contras] are not that kind of force. . . . [They] are a cross border raiding force."

83. Elaine Sciolino, "Joint Chiefs Head Warns Contras; Shultz in Aid Plea," *New York Times*, February 13, 1987, p. A3.

84. Jack Anderson and Dale Van Atta, "Carlucci Signals New Policy on Contras," *Washington Post*, January 14, 1987, p. C11.

85. A citizen employed on a contract basis with "Project Democracy" out of the Office of Humanitarian Assistance in the State Department.

86. See trip report dated March 28, 1986, and report dated March 17, 1986, in Byrne et al., "An Annotated Document Sampler on U.S. Covert Operations in Nicaragua from the Iran Contra Collection," Washington, D.C.: The National Security Archives, March 17, 1988; and Engleberger, "In Private, A Dark U.S. View of Contras," *International Herald Tribune*, May 22, 1987, p. 7. About half of fiscal year 1986 contra aid was, according to a GAO report "unaccounted for"; see Jamme Mang, "Half Of Contras' Aid Unaccounted For, GAO says," *Washington Post*, December 6, 1986, p. A19. Henry Kissinger shared the Reagan administration's private incredulity: "It cannot be that such a vital interest . . . can be solved with 100 million dollars." See "Off Record, Kissinger Talk Isn't," *New York Times*, April 26, 1986, p. 20. Also see on this, Arey Neier, "The Contra Contradiction," *The New York Review of Books*, April 9, 1987.

87. See HR 100-433, p. 63.

88. Francis J. MacNeil, a former ambassador to Costa Rica and widely regarded as a model Foreign Service Officer, had directed INR reports questioning the military effectiveness of the contras. He was passed over for promotion and endured humiliating investigations about whether he was a "security risk" and "disloyal." Finally, he quit, charging Assistant Secretary Abrams a McCarthyite. See John Goshko, "Top Aide Retires Assails Abrams; Latin Expert Says He Was Victim of

'Exercise in McCarthyism,'" *Washington Post*, February 11, 1987, p. A19. John Ferch, a twenty-seven–year career ambassador, was fired from his post as ambassador to Honduras because he claimed he believed a negotiated settlement was not being pursued. For the restrictions on Habib, see Roy Gutman, "U.S. is Said to Seek Military Solution In Nicaragua," *Washington Post*, July 15, 1987, p. A25. Former Assistant Secretary Thomas Enders had proposed a two-track policy of negotiation and support for the contras. But Jeane Kirkpatrick, closer to the president's ear, opposed him, arguing the contras would bring the regime down. Enders was then sent to Spain for a last tour before he was retired. Robert White was brought back after a year in El Salvador when he objected to acceptance of the right-wing Arena party who had attempted his own assassination and had murdered the archbishop of Salvador but were given U.S. visas and lavish reception in Washington. See McManus, op. cit., p. 160. For the decision of Pezzullo, see Woodward, op. cit., pp. 115–116; and Emerson, op. cit., p. 125.

89. The senior Contra military commander with contra numbers at their peak, nearly seventeen thousand, in 1986, Enrique Bermudez, acknowledged that since the contras could not defeat the Sandinistas militarily and since he did not believe the Sandinistas could be pressured into democratic reforms, the contra goals had to be "to heighten repression," and thus make it more likely the United States would send troops to defend a people groaning under a Sandinsta tyranny made worse by war and terror. See Roy Gutman, "A Competition of Blunders Between the U.S. and Nicaragua," *Washington Post, National Edition*, March 28–April 3, p. 23.

90. Jeane Kirkpatrick, "Dictatorships and Double Standards," *Commentary*, November 1979, pp. 34–45.

91. Consisting of Mexico, Colombia, Panama, and Venezuela and named for the Panamanian island on which they originally met in January of 1983.

92. Arias and his Ambassador protested they had done no such thing. See Roy Gutman, "A Competition of Blunders." This account is much indebted to Gutman's work now published as *Banana Diplomacy: The Making of American Policy in Nicaragua 1981–1987* (New York, Simon & Schuster, 1988).

93. See "For the Contras 'There was no help left in the US,'" *New York Times*, March 26, 1988, p. 4; and Julie Johnson, "At White House, Some Discomfort," *New York Times*, March 25, 1988, p. 1.

94. In absolute figures, about half the deaths the United States suffered in Vietnam.

95. Tad Szulc, "A Gorbachev Signal on Nicaragua," *New York Times*, September 6, 1987, p. E15; and "Moscow Signs Checks but Watches its Words," *New York Times*, March 23, 1986, p. E2.

96. In Poland and Romania, populations were groaning under the weight of food shortages, freezing from lack of heat, and pitched into darkness from brownouts and blackouts installed to save fuel. See Stephen Kinzer, "For Nicaragua, Soviet Frugality Starts to Pinch," *New York Times*, August 20, 1987, p. 6. Under Secretary of Defense Fred Ikle claimed the amount given the Sandinistas by the Soviets actually was $750 million.

97. See chapter 13, *infra*.

98. Report of the National Bipartisan Commission on Central America (New York, 1984). Portions are excerpted in Leiken and Rubin, op. cit., pp. 556–562.

99. Woodward, op. cit., pp. 340, 342.

100. Mexico was forced to liquidate its debt in exchange of "equity" positions sold to U.S investors at distress prices and guaranteed in a novel formula, by the issu-

ance of U.S. treasury instruments. In October 1988, a $3.5-billion U.S. loan was forthcoming.

101. Joel Brinkley, "Drug Crops Are Up in Export Nations, State Dept. Says," *New York Times*, February 15, 1985, pp. A1, A4.

102. The Kurds are a fiercely independent hill people who live in the border areas shared by Iran, Iraq, and Turkey. Between August 1972 and 1975, the United States, at the instigation of the Shah of Iran, passed $16 million to the Kurds so that they could harass his Iraqi enemies. When the Shah was ready for a political settlement with Iraq, the Kurds were suddenly cut off by the United States at the request of the Shah. The dying old leader of the insurgency, Mustafa Barzini, had sent a gold and pearl necklace to Kissinger in gratitude for the help to his people. Barzini was forced to leave his lands and, dying from cancer, was denied a visa for medical treatment. The fullest account is given in the "Pike Report" of the House Intelligence Committee Investigating Intelligence Activities. The report was never released officially but was leaked to the *Village Voice* on February 12, 1976; see Tad Szulc, *The Illusion of Peace* (New York: Viking, 1978), pp. 584–587. One Intelligence official commented about the Kurds with icy indifference, "Covert action should not be confused with missionary work"; see introduction to the Pike Committee Report, p. 85.

103. For example, there were several "Boland Amendments" prohibiting assistance to the contras. The "antideficiency act," made it a crime to spend monies owed the Treasury as well to spend improperly receipted funds. There was section 501 of the National Security Act (requiring Congressional notification) and the Arms Export Control Act, title 188, section 1505, prohibiting arms sales to Iran. There was section 18 USC 10001 against making fraudulent and false statements under oaths to Congress. There was the "Presidential Records Act," making it a crime to destroy embarrassing or incriminating documents. See Chap. 27 of HR 100-433, pp. 411–429.

104. Article I, section 8: "Congress shall have power . . . to declare war, grant letters of marque and reprisal, and make rules concerning captures on land and water."

105. See also HR 100-433, pp. 395–410; and the Minority report on the Boland amendment, pp. 499ff; see also Lawrence H. Tribe, "Irangate: A Constitutional Crisis?" *International Herald Tribune*, May 23–24, 1987, p. 11.

Chapter 12
The Reagan
Doctrine
Elsewhere

By the start of Ronald Reagan's second term, the effort to reinvigorate global containment became more formal. In his 1985 State of the Union message, the president uttered words that would have found resonance with Woodrow Wilson or Thomas Jefferson:

> Freedom is not the sole prerogative of a chosen few, it is the universal right of all God's children . . . Our mission is to nourish and defend freedom and democracy . . . wherever we can. [W]e must not break faith with those who are risking their lives on every continent . . . to defy Soviet-supported aggression and secure rights which have been ours from birth.[1]

As Robert Tucker, the Johns Hopkins–based editor of the conservative journal, *The National Interest*, noted, "breath-taking optimism"[2] characterized this assertion of interests in what Reagan's supporters began labeling the Reagan doctrine.[3] Reagan seemed to be conjuring an image of success derived from the experiences of Harry Truman and the first years of the Eisenhower administration in driving the Soviets and their associates from Third World footholds. The Reagan doctrine rested on three sets of beliefs: (1) the Soviets were overextended in the Third World; (2) history was working against the appeal of collectivism; and (3) enough money and will could confront and roll back the Soviets directly virtually anywhere outside of Eastern Europe.[4]

But, even if all these conditions were met, it did not follow that a new containment could be sustained. First, there was the problem of ever-escalating bills for the wherewithal. It was true, for instance, that there was an amazing recrudescence of enthusiasm for an "unleashed" CIA and "low-intensity conflict" (pronounced *lick* by aficionados). "Black budgets" for "operations" escalated by a factor of eight, and special operations personnel expanded from their Vietnam high by a factor of ten, to 34,000.[5] But the search for "quick wins" was based more on historical memory fixed somewhere between the years of 1953 and 1964. "Success" of a kind could, still, be gleaned from application of the "black arts" and the external sponsorship of exiles. But the problem with exiles storming the palace or coming in "over the beach" was that, in the world of the 1980s, even backward regimes had at their disposal sophisticated weapons superbly adaptable to their defense. Further, the global intelligence regime, especially when it came to U.S.-sponsored activities, was less opaque than it had been twenty-five years before. There was in the 1980s, therefore, a higher risk of finding proteges and surrogates "beached." Then, the choice for the United States would be direct military assistance, disavowal of the failure as an effort not of the United States's doing, or a humiliation. Even if externally based groups could change events, almost any new regime that came to power as a result of CIA assistance would require long-term financial aid, an unpopular political choice that a budget-cutting Congress seemed unwilling to commit except for historically favored clients.

Ultimately, the business of changing regimes calls for more than back-alley talents and "secret wars." First, adequate men and equipment would be required, and the military and Congress would have to be convinced that a fight "made sense." Libya might be punished for putative harms by a show of American naval force in the Gulf of Sidra and a midnight air raid.[6] But the Joint Chiefs believed that the real undoing of the Mohamar Ghadaffy regime would require ninety thousand U.S. servicemen on the ground.[7]

Second, some of those who accept covert monies inevitably prove to be adventuresome, unreliable, or worse. In Cambodia, Casey approved $5 million a year to help the anti-Vietnamese resistance that was dominated by the Khmer Rouge, a group that had outdone Ghengis Khan and Stalin in pure savagery and mindless bloodletting.[8] The Khmer Rouge had hacked, tortured, and starved to death one third of Cambodia's population in less than four years.[9] To help fight the PLO, Phalangist leader (*phalange* literally means *fascist*) Bashir Gemeyal's militia was passed tens of millions of dollars by the Casey-Reagan CIA, presumably to buy weapons that were used with a gruesome ferocity in the Lebanese civil war.[10] In one instance, a CIA-funded Lebanese group, in March of 1985, set off a car bomb that missed its intended victim but did kill eighty Lebanese, mostly passing civilians.[11] Both Washington and Beirut were rife with rumors that other CIA "hit squads" had begun to "free-lance."[12]

Finally, special operations in themselves were perhaps as much a prelude to engagement as a panacea to disorder in the Third World. As the new operations guidelines for special forces reads, "Special operations capability . . . project[s] power where the use of conventional power would be *premature,* inappropriate or infeasible."[13]

The "hidden agenda" in the Reagan administration's carrying freedom's flag to far-flung corners was, inevitably, the belief that, whenever the American standard was successfully unfurled, a great price was exacted from the Soviets. But clients extracted from Soviet influence were usually burdensome wards, at best. Whatever harm a "loss" of Soviet influence in a given region might do the America's principle adversary, the consequences for the United States could be substantial too. Perhaps a Libya or an Iran could pay their way; but then Libya had shifted back and forth already in the cold war; and Iran's example, after the U.S.-inspired coup of 1953, would give pause to any sojourner into the uncharted terrain of liberation.

The fact of the matter was that no matter how much one sought to cast regional conflicts in terms of an overarching Soviet–American conflict or believed that by applying American power within a context of a "doctrine," local or regional dynamics remained as a fundamental constraining factor. Whether in Central America, the Middle East and Southwest Asia, southern Africa, or East Asia and no matter how overt or subtle the effort, the Reagan administration, like its predecessors, encountered limits imposed by local conditions. In some instances — e.g., in the cases of Afghanistan and the Philippines — there were momentary successes; in others, e.g., Lebanon, bitter frustration and failure. In all these cases, once American activism and the interplay of Soviet and American interests and power receded, hard local and regional realities remained.

THE AFGHAN SUCCESS

If there was one plausible success of the Reagan doctrine to offset Central America, it was Afghanistan. When the Soviets invaded Afghanistan in 1979, the Carter administration felt both betrayed and afraid that the Soviets had launched a new course of assertiveness in the most flammable area in the world. Within a month, the Carter administration — with the Chinese, the Saudis, the Egyptians, and the Pakistanis — were sending arms to the Afghans, who were regrouping in Pakistan.[14] In the end, nearly $2 billion of U.S. funds were spent assisting the Afghans. The Saudis donated an equivalent sum. Large amounts of arms and ammunition came from the military stores of Egypt and China. The Soviet force, which rarely fell below a hundred thousand was harassed mightily and eventually lost more than thirteen thousand men to the Afghan resistance.[15] When, after a considerable debate and great pressure from Congress, the United States shipped "Stinger" shoulder-fired antiaircraft weapons to the Afghans, the stalemated battle began to turn away from the Soviets. Perhaps as many as four hundred aircraft were lost due to a weapon that was said to have over an 80 percent kill ratio.[16]

Perhaps the U.S. aid and the Stingers turned around the tide of battle. But it should be recalled that, since the 1840s, manuals on irregular and guerrilla warfare have contended that for every partisan, ten regular soldiers must be prepared to stand and hold ground. By that logic, the Soviets would have needed more than six hundred thousand troops. It was a price Gorbachev was not ready to pay. In the end, as U.S. commanders in Vietnam and the civilians who later looked at the effect of U.S. bombing of Germany and Vietnam have understood, wars are won or lost on the ground. Air power counts, to be sure; but rarely have bombers and, by extension, shoulder-fired antidotes been war-determining weapons.

Outcomes and Implications

Other ambiguities surround the end of Russian involvement in Afghanistan. In February of 1988, the Soviets agreed to abandon their position and bring their troops back with few conditions and less ceremony. By the time the Soviet withdrawal began in May of 1988, the Soviets had displaced nearly half the population, and about a third of all Afghans were residing in Pakistan or Iran. The Soviets were bled, humiliated, and eventually expelled from Afghanistan. The Soviet retreat was achieved at an unacknowledged and unforeseen price. Without a Soviet presence, the conflict would become an unmitigated civil war. The vast refugee population would remain stranded in Pakistan or Iran.[17] Those who returned would come home to scorched lands and festering hatreds. And that was not all that had to be included as the price for driving the Soviets back to their frontiers.

The victorious rebels were largely fundamentalist mujahedeen, "holy warriors." Groups that had been politically marginal before the civil war achieved new standing and status in the early 1980s. One major spokesman for the rebels was Gulbuddin Hekmatyar, who, at Kabul University before the Soviet invasion, was reported to have thrown acid in the faces of female students who failed to wear the chador, or the traditional veil.[18] The mujahedeen saw no need and felt no obligation to make any deals with a Kabul government ignominiously abandoned by the Soviets. The fundamentalists were supporters of the Ayatollah

Khomeini and felt little gratitude to the United States for a Soviet withdrawal that did not place them in a position of power. Some of the mujahedeen rebels described the U.S.–Soviet–Pakistani accord, which paved the way for a Soviet withdrawal, a "conspiracy"; while others suggested to their followers that, in any case, the United States and the West were "enemies of Islam." Neither the remnant regime in Kabul, abandoned by the Soviets, nor any successor regime in Afghanistan was liable to have cordial relations with the United States. Whatever the shape of the successor regime in Kabul, there was a prospect that there would be another state about to involve itself in an emerging fundamentalist Moslem league.[19]

Other regional leaders were uneasy. Indian Prime Minister Rajiv Ghandi was known to be fearful, for instance, that a fundamentalist Kabul would funnel weapons to Sikh separatists and inflame the situation in the perpetually restive Moslem border province of Kashmir.[20] The Russians had always been worried that fundamentalism might spread across their frontiers into their Asia republics. A new Soviet intervention could not be ruled out, therefore, if there were either a change in Moscow or another radical turn of events in Kabul.

All through the 1980s, India's old enemy, Pakistan, had demanded a quid pro quo for supporting the Afghan insurgency.[21] President Carter had cut off aid when Pakistan's "Islamic bomb" was near the assembly stage. But after the huge effort to support the Afghans began, pressure on the Pakistanis to drawback from nuclear capability became fitful. The Pakistanis made diligent and generally quiet progress in assembling a significant nuclear capability. The administration, shorn of leverage, fretted, but it took only episodic administrative actions to slow the Pakistani atomic armaments program.[22] While President Zia al-Haq was becoming a U.S. intimate in the region, he ruled by martial law. There were frequent riots and protests led by the daughter of an old political foe he had publicly executed, Banisar Bhuto. Since Zia's rule was personal and extraconstitutional, it would be only a matter of time until a successor regime emerged. Then, the previous U.S.–Pakistani cordiality could hardly seem assured.

In addition to its regional political effects, the Afghan war seemed likely to influence conventional military balances locally and beyond. According to former CIA director Stansfield Turner, only some 20 percent of the monies and weapons intended for the mujahedeen were used by the Afghan fighters. A great quantity of weapons found their way to the bazaars and warehouses of Pakistan and Iran.[23] In the summer of 1987, within a year of the first Stinger shipment to the Afghan resistance, Iranian revolutionary guards began firing these same missiles at

U.S. helicopters and gunboats patrolling in the Persian Gulf. John J. McMahon, deputy director of the CIA, had fought against the Stinger supply mission. But it was futile in the face of opposition from Congress and his superior, DCI, William Casey.[24] The Soviets and a number of their clients were said to have acquired the Stinger missile technology as a result of the inevitable leakage of war materials in combat. Not an inconsequential number apparently were sold, and others literally "fell off the back of the truck." About half of the U.S. defense budget is devoted to the production and development of U.S. tactical air power. All four U.S. services are dependent on air support for ground and sea missions. U.S. aircraft typically cost from $20 to $100 million a copy, while the Stingers used by Iranian Revolutionary Guards were released from U.S. stocks with a "ticket" of $36,000. Soon knock-offs or reasonably well-functioning replicas of Stingers were appearing in the weapons marketplace. An acceleration to the spread of a cheap antitactical air missile was one more cost to be counted when totaling the expense of the one real "success" of the Reagan doctrine.

The Afghan war was not just expensive for the Soviets and Afghans. At a minimum, the war exacerbated the growing stalemate between offensive and defensive power in the world[25] and tied the United States more closely to a near-nuclear Pakistani regime of dubious staying power. The relationship of the United States and the region's dominant democratic power and historic adversary of Pakistan, India, became thereby even more problematic. In addition, there was concern that the world's supply of illicit drugs might be increased. An area of the world that had produced almost no heroin or opium for export for some time was producing and transshipping more opium, heroin, and hashish than the rest of the world combined by the time Soviet columns began to assemble for what was hoped to be at least an orderly retreat.[26] Finally, the Soviet withdrawal seemed likely to lead to an expanded arena of legitimacy for Moslem fundamentalism. The Soviet Union now faced a southern crescent of Islamic fundamentalism bordering, in the east, the Armenian and Azerbaijhan Republic — where religious and ethnic disputes between Christians and Moslems led to massive demonstrations and rioting in early 1988 — and, in the west, the Moslem-majority republics of Turkmen, Uzbek, and Tadzhik.

The end of the long war would not bring an easy peace. The plain fact was, of course, that when the Soviets entered Afghanistan in force, almost no U.S. analysts thought they would leave.[27] Most of the U.S. funding of the Afghan war, was seen, as in Nicaragua, not as a road to victory but as a means of making clients of the Soviet Union and the Soviets themselves as uncomfortable as possible. In sum, while the

Soviet withdrawal was an unabashed and remarkable Soviet defeat, it could hardly be called an unmixed blessing for the U.S.[28]

Technological Fixes
and the Reagan Doctrine

Stingers became a kind of technological totem of the Reagan doctrine. Congress and administration alike were enthused by the Afghan success. As a result, the United States supplied Chad in its war with neighboring Libya in November of 1987. France, the traditional power in the region, had supported arbitration between Chad and Libya, but the United States believed Ghadaffy might be undone if Stingers were supplied.[29] Chad in fact won the dessert war not because of Stingers, but as the result of employing daring tactical mobility — using Toyota trucks — against oasis-bound Libyan forces.

In Southern Africa, the U.S.-supported Angolan rebels were led by Jonas Savimbi. Savimbi's 65,000-man rebel group, called UNITA, was backed by South African troops and material. They fought Angolan regular troops and were buttressed by Soviet and Cuban forces, who, ironically, also stood guard over the largest cash resource of Angola, the U.S.-operated Gulf Oil refinery. By early 1988, Savimbi's groups had acquired Stingers from the CIA.[30]

In short, the minimum cost of the Reagan doctrine was a diffusion of some of the most advanced elements of the U.S. "technological edge," shoulder-fired antiaircraft technology. At the outside, there was the cost of supporting, in the Angolan case, a self-styled Maoist backed by South Africa and thereby undermining American legitimacy in the eyes of the black states in the region who were the targets of South African intervention and aggression. In Cambodia, there was the cost of supporting an opposition that was manned largely by former members of the Khmer Rouge. On the other hand, fixation on the goal of diminishing Soviet gains and influence in the Third World was an open-ended claim on U.S. resources wherever and whenever the Soviets supported insurgencies. However small the increments in material and low the cost in at least U.S. life, these interventions exacted penalties. Insurgencies with virtually no chance of winning on their own, such as in Angola, were perpetuated because they distracted U.S. adversaries. In addition, few members of Congress wished to open themselves up to the charge they either favored Marxist regimes or had assisted in abandoning U.S. clients, even when those clients were, at first, signed up in secret. Perhaps all the costs would be acceptable in the end. Perhaps many of these insurgencies might prosper and turn the tide against regimes whom had been Soviet clients. But it was no guarantee they would be assets to the United States or associates who fit the historic vision of America as the "City on the Hill."[31]

THE MIDDLE EAST

The primary interests of the United States in Southwest Asia and the Middle East include maintaining a flow of oil to the West. This objective requires, in turn, a U.S. commitment to stability in the region, especially as instability affects the vital shipping lanes through the Persian Gulf and Arabian Sea as well as the areas where pipelines are in place. Logically, these objectives are closely linked to an American concern that stable and predictable regimes remain in place in the region and that they not engage in frequent or prolonged wars with one another.[32]

Throughout the 1980s, oil flowed from the region. Indeed, it flowed at such a rate that OPEC found it impossible to maintain stable and high prices on the world market. At the same time, however, anxiety about the maintenance of this condition was intense, as other American objectives proved difficult to achieve. A major state in the region, Iran, was dominated by a regionally activist and avowedly revolutionary Moslem fundamentalist regime. Major wars raged between Iraq and Iran in the Gulf and between Israel, the PLO, and Lebanese Moslems who were themselves divided between those sympathetic to Iran on the one hand and Syria on the other and who fought one another when they were not fighting the Israelis. "In the Middle East, more than any other part of the world," Barry Rubin has argued, "the Reagan administration's policy was constrained by regional forces and long-standing American commitments."[33] The Middle East required diplomatic finesse, a careful balancing of interests, sober application of power, and the coherent administration of policy more in order. At times, however, policy in the Reagan years seemed as if it was designed and staged by silent screen slapstick artists such as Max Sennet or the Three Stooges. Nowhere was this more evident than in the Gulf and with respect to the Iran–contra scandal.

Iran Redux

Secretary of State George Shultz claimed, credibly, that he had believed the Iran–contra operation had closed down. But it was also plain that he did not want to know if it had continued, perhaps so he could be in a position later to best his bureaucratic adversaries by saying "I told you so." To that end, apparently, he asked the National Security Advisor, Admiral John Poindexter, not to "be put in the loop." When Secretary Shultz did try to inform himself of what happened to the opening gambit in the weird arms-for-hostages, contra-aid scandal, White House Chief of Staff Donald T. Regan refused to confirm or deny the matter to the frustrated Secretary of State, who was trying to get Western leaders to condemn Iran as the sponsor of state terrorism.[34] Neither Secretary of State Shultz, nor his great bureaucratic adversary, Secretary of Defense Weinberger, were aware that there was an "intelligence finding" authorizing the diversion of funds (from the sale of military goods to Iran, against whom the United States was in the process of trying to organize an international embargo on military sales) to the contras.[35]

Secretary Weinberger was also not informed that the Saudis had given more than $32 million to the contras in what now appears to have been, for them, at least, part of an elaborate quid pro quo for the $8.5-billion sale of the AWACs surveillance aircraft.[36] The AWACs were sold to the Saudis to protect them from Iranian attack. Obviously, the new missiles the United States sent Iran after 1985 increased Iranian capability not only against Iraq, with whom they were militarily engaged, but also other powers in the region. These putative enemies included, of course, the Saudis who were supporting the Iraqis.[37] None of these balance-of-power considerations seemed to have had much effect on the calculations of the purportedly "realist" Reagan policy makers.

The Reagan administration set up a series of procedures in 1982 that required eight signatures before any intelligence "finding" would have effect. Subsequent to a finding being reached, Congress was to be notified in a "timely fashion," as previous legislation puts it.[38] Of the prescribed eight signatures, only four were obtained in the matter of the Iran arms sales. An astonished defense secretary learned that the Iran arms sale had gone forward when he read a third country's intelligence report mentioning it. Weinberger testified that he had believed, contrary to the news that later crossed his desk, that the Iran arms sales had been "strangled in its cradle."[39] Meanwhile the Joint Chiefs were kept in the dark. The chairman of the Joint Chiefs, the one group that at least had a consistent vision of what U.S. purposes and capabilites were in the Reagan years, testified that they were "the ones who are supposed to provide military advice. . . . I didn't appreciate having 'zero' knowledge" about military shipments to Iran.[40] The United States ambassador in Beirut, John H. Kelley, repeatedly met with NSC figures involved in the arms-for-hostages arrangements and did not report back to Secretary Shultz but rather to Lt. Col. North and Admiral

Poindexter. Shultz's public reaction was, "to put it mildly, shocked. . . . There is supposed to be—I say supposed to be—a chain of command."[41]

The CIA was "blacked out" in the sale of weapons to Iran and the transfer of funds to the contras. Those who were told of the undertaking with Iran seem to have been DCI Casey, Lt. Col. North, the two successive National Security assistants MacFarland and Poindexter, and, perhaps, the president, who signed at least one finding but apparently did not read it and, in any case, "forgot" its substance. According to Attorney General Edwin Meese, the nation's highest law enforcement officer, it did not matter that legal justification for U.S. arms shipments to Iran in 1985 could not be found in any document because the President had already made a "mental finding."[42]

While weapons were being sold to Iranian "moderates," Iran's dissidents and emigres overseas were encouraged by some in the CIA to overthrow the Khomeini regime. Meanwhile, other elements of the CIA gave reliable information to Iran regarding Soviet penetration of these same groups, which were, in turn, rounded up and executed. Meanwhile, Iraq, which started the prolonged war with Iran and, indeed, initiated most of the first four years of attacks on Persian Gulf shipping, was given targeting information by a U.S. general stationed in Baghdad. When asked to explain a portion of this bewildering chain of events, one official said, "You had to have been there."[43]

Finally, when the United States did send a flotilla, essentially to trump a Soviet offer of assistance to escort Kuwaiti vessels in the gulf, an Iraqi plane accidentally attacked and severely damaged the *U.S.S. Stark.* The United States responded by sinking Iranian assets and announcing a series of changes in the rules of engagement that gave local commanders the right to sink virtually anything Iranian when U.S. ships seemed to be menaced. After another *Perry* class U.S. frigate was damaged in April of 1988 by an Iranian mine, the United States retaliated by sinking most of the small Iranian navy and announced yet more "flexible" rules of engagement. As a consequence of the new "flexible" rules of engagement, on July 3, 1988, a regularly scheduled Iranian "air bus" with 290 passengers was shot down just after take-off by one of two missiles launched from the billion-dollar *Vincennes*, an Aegis class command cruiser.[44]

American policy towards the Iran–Iraq War was ostensibly tilted toward Iraq. When Richard W. Murphey, U.S. assistant secretary for Near East and South Asian affairs, testified to the House Foreign Affairs Committee on October 8, 1986, he said:

We continue to press our three-year-old decision to prevent arms from getting to Iran. We do this because of our desire to see the war wind down. We target Iranian procurement because Iran is the most intransigent party to the war.[45]

Three weeks after Murphey told Congress that the United States was pressing its allies to embargo Iran, the seventh shipment of U.S. arms, consisting of five hundred TOW missiles, arrived in Iran.[46]

The Iran–contra scandal also revealed inconsistencies in American antiterrorism policy as well. The United States was prepared to use military force against Libya for supporting attacks on American military personnel in Europe and for hijacking the Italian cruise ship *Achille Lauro*. Within months, however, the same administration was ransoming hostages by selling arms to the state it had accused of being the biggest state terrorist of all. For bargaining with terrorists, the French, Italians and Algerians had been publicly labeled virtually spineless by the United States. Yet, the United States used intense pressure to pry some 735 Shiite prisoners from Israeli jails to secure the release of a hijacked American plane.[47]

America's stated goal in sending combatants to convoy reflagged vessels in the Persian Gulf was, originally, to protect the oil lines for the west. But the tanker war, at the time, had inhibited less than one percent of all tanker traffic, and, with the construction of new pipelines, most of the region's oil would be piped, not shipped, through the Gulf, some eleven million barrels a day. The ostensible threat to Kuwait had been said by the United States to be Iran. In reality, it was the threat of Soviet power that the Kuwaitis wanted to balance. The decision to go to the gulf to protect reflagged Kuwaiti convoys was made in response to Kuwaiti request to the Soviets to escort three of their vessels. It was a classic case of manipulation of the threat of communist penetration in order to extract U.S. assistance and perhaps "balance" the Soviets. But the U.S. response caused visible Kuwaiti embarrassment: "a Hollywood reaction" Kuwaitis acidly observed. As the Kuwaiti undersecretary for foreign affairs rhetorically put it: The Soviets had been "quietly sailing in the gulf for some time. So what has [suddenly] changed?"[48]

Prior to the appearance of the U.S. fleet, Iraq had initiated most of the attacks on gulf shipping. And, indeed, Iran had asked that there be a cease-fire in the tanker war several times. A year after the U.S. gulf fleet had been on station, tanker attacks — most initiated by Iraq — almost tripled. Lloyds of London raised the price of insurance more than 200 percent. Although the price of petroleum remained stable, so much production was shut in, blockaded, or unable to find a carrier willing to run the risks associated with the gulf that production and future rise in demand or reduction in supply would inevitably have an exaggerated effect on price.[49]

American policy in the gulf was, in sum, characterized by executive inattention, confusion, and distraction. Until the attack on the *Stark*, White House chief of staff Howard Baker never, by his own admission, focused on the political risks in the gulf. The navy never was enthused about the mission, which drained resources by as much as $2 billion a year from the navy's budget. The professionals wanted to make a point about naval power and get out. As the exiting secretary of the navy, James Webb, wrote:

> Now that we have demonstrated our naval capabilities to Iran, and, at the same time destroyed much of its navy, [we can] declare victory and reduce our naval structure . . . and then disappear back into the sea . . . [so as to allow] diplomacy to be tested without offering up our naval assets as convenient targets.[50]

But the Reagan administration, instead of declaring victory and departing with grace, put the area on notice that new U.S. naval units were destined for the gulf with orders to protect whomever was there that might be in the line of fire.[51]

The Arab–Israeli Conflict

Military instrumentalities became central to the Reagan administration's approach to the Arab–Israeli dispute as well. Here again, the perception that the Soviet Union was the ultimate source of the conflict within the region was crucial to the administration's understanding of American objectives. Although the local sources of conflict and the expansionist policies of the Begin government in Israel forced the administration to focus for a time on the indigenous causes of instability, the confrontation of American and Soviet influence initially dominated the American image of Middle Eastern reality in the early 1980s. By the end of the administration, local forces controlled the initiative, as U.S. policy was thwarted by continuous conflict in Lebanon that was contained, if at all, by Syrian power, weak Arab governments incapable of responding to American peace overtures, and a coalition Israeli government and deeply divided nation transfixed by the nightmare of Palestinian revolt in the Israeli-occupied territories of the West Bank and Gaza and growing Arab disaffection within Israel itself.

Initially, the administration sought to pursue the development of what Secretary of State Haig termed a "strategic consensus"[52] directed against Soviet influence and power in the region even as the United States lent its support to the ongoing Camp David process of negotiations between Israel and Egypt. By the time Reagan took the oath of office, however, the Camp David process was already in deep trouble. Although negotiations concerning the return of all Egyptian territory in the Sinai were proceeding reasonably well and were consummated in April of 1982 with the withdrawal of the Israelis from Egyptian territory, the discussions of Palestinian autonomy on the West Bank and in Gaza were deadlocked. In the meantime, conditions within the region began deteriorating rapidly, as Israeli-backed Christian forces and Syrian-backed Moslem forces in Lebanon escalated their fighting to the most intense levels since 1976. By late April 1982, the Israeli air force was launching air strikes into southern Lebanon and the Syrians were moving surface-to-air missiles (SAMs) into the Bekaa Valley, leading the Israelis to threaten military action against the Syrians unless the SAMs were removed. U.S. diplomatic intervention via special envoy Philip C. Habib's shuttling between Israel and the Arab countries throughout the summer was instrumental in avoiding major fighting, although Israeli attacks in Lebanon continued, including a strike against PLO positions in Beirut that resulted in three hundred deaths and eight hundred injured.

The pursuit of an anti-Soviet strategic consensus in the Middle East continued throughout this hardening of regional animosities. United States policy included an administration plan to sell the Saudi Arabians equipment to upgrade their F-15 fighter aircraft as well as provide them with five airborn warning and control system (AWAC) aircraft. At the same time, the administration sought an agreement on strategic cooperation with the Israelis including some joint maneuvers, medical stockpiling in Israel, and joint security planning. As anti-Soviet measures, such steps might appear reasonable, but within the deteriorating regional context, the regional actors — the Israelis and the Arabs — could be expected to react skeptically. The regional antagonists quite predictably viewed each American move in terms of its effect on their conflicts and the regional balance. Accordingly, they attended to their own agendas and not that of the Americans.

In the case of the Israelis, the Syrians, and the PLO, this activity focused on the strategic situation in Lebanon, where the Syrians and PLO were seeking to consolidate their control. Israeli strategic concerns extended to the entire Arab world, as was dramatically evident on June 8, 1981, when they bombed and destroyed an Iraqi nuclear reactor that the Israelis contended was on the threshold of providing the Iraqis with nuclear weapons. The Osirk reactor was bombed just hours after Begin and Anwar Sadat were photographed smiling in the shade of a tent at the tip of the Red Sea. Sadat's days were numbered; within a year he was gunned down by fundamentalist Egyptian troops at a military review. The raid on the Osirk Reactor and the Israelis' contemptuous rejection of the condemnation that followed underscored both the toughness of the Begin government and also its relative strategic freedom in the wake of the Camp David agreement with Egypt.

Freed from military concerns on its Egyptian flank, the full weight of Israeli military superiority could be turned on the rest of the Arab world. Furthermore, if the Reagan administration hoped that the Camp David process might restrain Israeli belligerence and cool the regional conflict, those hopes were dashed when, on October 6, 1981, with President Sadat removed, an essential actor in the negotiating process had been eliminated. If the Reagan administration believed that the agreement on strategic cooperation could constrain the Israelis, they were jolted yet again; two weeks after signing the agreement with Prime Minister Begin, the Israelis extended Israeli law to the Golan Heights captured from the Syrians in 1967, a move widely viewed in the Arab world as tantamount to annexation. Although the United States suspended the agreement with Israel, the Saudis extended their full support to Syria even as the Israelis attacked the United States for treating them, in Begin's words, as a "vassal state."

With diplomatic efforts frozen, the Israelis, Syrians, and PLO slid toward war. In April and May, Israeli aircraft attacked PLO positions in Beirut, and the PLO shelled Israeli settlements in northern Israel. On June 6, the sixth Arab–Israeli war began, with thirty thousand Israeli ground troops invading Lebanon and moving within a week to positions around Beirut—cutting off, in the process, some seven thousand PLO and two thousand Syrian troops—as the Israelis laid siege to the city.[53] In their march north, Israeli forces inflicted significant casualties on the Syrians, including the destruction of seventy-nine Syrian MIG-21 and MIG-23 aircraft and nineteen SAM sites. Only one Israeli aircraft was lost in this embarrassing defeat of Soviet military hardware. But this would not result in the decline of Soviet influence; within a year, Syrian forces were completely replenished by the Soviets and buttressed by the presence of five to seven thousand Soviet miltiary personnel training the Syrians or actually operating their new and more effective air defense system.

The extent of American knowledge of Israeli intentions is disputed. Former Secretary of State Haig denies that the Israelis had informed him of their intention to move north. Israeli sources insist, however, that months before the attack, Washington was informed of Israel's intention to invade Lebanon.[54] In any event, Israeli actions demonstrate clearly that Prime Minister Begin and Defense Minister Ariel Sharon were seeking the elimination of the PLO, a decisive defeat of Syria, and a responsive regime in Beirut. By mid-August, after massive air and artillery attacks on Beirut itself, all sides accepted an American proposal for the insertion of a small multinational peacekeeping force (MNF) made up of U.S., French, and Italian troops that would supervise the withdrawal of Syrian and PLO forces. As the last of the PLO and Syrian troops left Beirut, President Reagan launched his own peace plan for the region.[55] On September 1, he proposed "self-government" for the Palestinians on the West Bank of the Jordan River "in association with Jordan," as well as a freeze on further Israeli settlements on the occupied West Bank. Jerusalem was to be an undivided city with final political arrangements to be negotiated. Although Arab leaders in a meeting in Fez, Morocco,[56] as well as Jewish leaders outside Israel found the proposal, if not entirely acceptable, at least useful as a point of departure for future negotiations, the Israeli cabinet rejected it outright. Indeed, four days after the Reagan proposal was announced, Israel allocated funds for three new settlements on the West Bank and began planning seven more.

In Lebanon, the peace-keeping force had begun withdrawing on September 10. Four days later, Bashir Gemayel, the newly elected, right wing, Israeli-backed Phalangist Christian president of Lebanon, was assassinated, and the Israelis moved their troops into and took control of central Beirut. By September 18, reports began to appear of hundreds of Palestinian civilians being massacred by Christian militia allowed into refugee camps in south Beirut by the Israelis. In the midst of international outrage, the multinational force was hastily reinserted (supplemented by about one hundred British personnel), and the Israelis withdrew from Beirut by the end of September.

American policy now focused on negotiating a withdrawal of Israeli and Syrian troops from Lebanon while supporting the government of Lebanon, now under the presidency of Amin Gemayel, Bashir Gemayel's brother. The latter task was complicated by the fact that Gemayel, like his brother, was seen as representing but one faction of the fractured Lebanese political setting. The government's political base was narrow and its political control did not extend much beyond the embattled Beirut suburbs. Because the United States was identified with Gemayel, the Americans inevitably became participants in the Lebanese civil conflict rather than being viewed as neutral peacekeepers. From the winter of 1982 through the spring of 1983, the marines composing the U.S. contingent of the MNF had to manage a relationship not only with extremely testy Israelis but also with the contending militias in and around the city. In April of 1983, the American embassy was bombed and destroyed by terrorists weeks before Secretary of State Shultz finally negotiated an agreement in principle on the ultimate withdrawal of troops. In the end, it was the steady increase in casualties suffered by the Israelis that led to their decision to withdraw to more secure southern Lebanon in September rather than to come to any agreement. Ironically, by that time, the Americans were encouraging them to remain in the Beirut area to serve as a stabilizing force.

With the Israelis gone, fighting intensified between the Lebanese Army, which sought to reoccupy the areas vacated by the Israelis, and the Syrian-supported militias. Furthermore, the sixteen hundred U.S. marines stationed around the difficult-to-defend Beirut airport as well as the French elements of the MNF were attacked with greater frequency and effect. By the fall, a large U.S. naval force consisting of two aircraft carriers, the battleship *New Jersey,* and more than thirty other ships had been assembled off the Lebanese coast and sporadically turned its firepower on the militia in the hills above the airport in support of the marines and also the Lebanese Army. By late summer, support of the Gemayel government — reportedly over the opposition of the Joint Chiefs of Staff, who feared retaliation — had become a rationale for the use of U.S. firepower equal to that of protecting the marines. Yet, none of this could prevent another successful terrorist attack on the American presence, this time a building at the Beirut airport in which hundreds of marine and naval personnel were sleeping on the night of October 23. (Almost simultaneously a French barracks area was hit as well.) Two hundred forty-one Americans died in the huge truck-bomb explosion detonated by a lone terrorist suicide who raced his vehicle into the courtyard of the multistory building used by the marines for a barracks. As the names of the dead were released in newspapers and newscasts, the American people underwent a kind of macabre deja vu as they contemplated the prospect of American involvement in a Lebanese civil war ten years after their painful exit from Vietnam.[57]

The Reagan administration seemed unable, however, to convince the public or a frustrated Congress, which had granted an eighteen-month mandate for American participation in the MNF, that exit from Lebanon was in the immediate future. Rather, the president warned of a "force" — the Soviet Union through their Syrian surrogates — poised to take over the region and the international repercussions of a withdrawal of American forces. In the wake of the October 23 tragedy, a full-scale review[58] of American policy was completed, with a decision being made to reinvigorate the strategic cooperation arrangement with the Israelis and force the Syrians out of Lebanon. Reportedly, the administration had virtually given up hope that moderate Arab leaders could any longer influence the Syrians, if they ever could.

In Lebanon itself, the administration tied itself to the fate of the Gemayel regime with the American navy providing episodic support of the Lebanese army's attempts to reassert government control over strategic points around Beirut. Gemayel refused, however, to broaden the base of his government, with the result that, by February of 1984, Druse and Shiite Moslem forces, heavily supported by the Syrians, launched an all-out assault on government forces. As the fighting escalated, the Italians and British announced that they would be withdrawing their forces in the MNF. The Reagan administration followed suit and announced: "the Marines are being deployed 2⅓ to 3 miles to the west," i.e., off shore, a move, they insisted, that had been planned for weeks — even as they attacked those in Congress who were proposing such a step as wanting to "surrender."[59] The naval task force would remain in the area, however, until sometime in 1985, supporting the Lebanese government. What precisely the Americans would support was problematic, because while Reagan was insisting that the Lebanese army had been transformed into a viable military force, it was, in fact, disintegrating. As forces supporting Gemayel broke rank, control vaporized, leaving the beleaguered marines almost totally surrounded at their Beirut airport base. By late February, the marines began their withdrawal as the secretary of state, for the first time, conceded that American policy in Lebanon had failed. The president and vice president, however, asserted that most of America's objectives had been accomplished. Reagan went so far as to hint in a news conference on February 23, 1984, that the marines might be sent back into Lebanon "if they could improve the possibility of carrying out their mission" — though the mission remained as unclear to most Americans as ever.[60]

In the wake of this collapse of the American position, U.S. policy became relatively quiescent. Syrian influence in Lebanon became ascendant, although sectarian violence remained the order of the day in that tortured land. Israel underwent domestic convulsion as its polity reacted to the political and moral costs of the Lebanese invasion. Out of this turmoil emerged a coalition government led first by the more moderate Labor prime minister, Shimon Peres, but followed by a return to Likud leadership under Yitzak Shamir in late 1986. Jordan's King Hussein seized this moment of moderate Israeli leadership to try to fashion an agreement with the PLO that would allow Jordan to serve as representative of Palestinian interests in negotiations with the Israelis.

American policy during this period was to support and try to facilitate Jordan's initiative through low-key intermediation between the Arabs and Israelis.[61] The effort ultimately failed, however, as Hussein proved unable to gain PLO consent to a Jordanian initiative. With the dissipation of the regional diplomatic effort in 1986, the focus shifted to the military action against Libya. By 1987, of course, cover on the arms deal with Iran was blown and diplomatic movement ceased with the return of a more conservative Israeli government.

As the administration's policy in the region drifted toward its last year, a new crisis erupted when Palestinians on the West Bank and Gaza launched a campaign of massive resistance to Israeli occupation. In December of 1987, rioting broke out in Gaza in protest over the handling of an automobile accident in which four Arabs were killed. The unrest quickly spread throughout Gaza and the West Bank and culminated on December 21 with a general strike that included not only the occupied territories but Arabs inside Israel as well. For weeks, demonstrations, boycotts, and stonings of Israeli police and military personnel were responded to with tear gas and beatings, hundreds of shootings, and thousands of arrests—all played out on world television. The occupation policy became, by early 1988, extremely harsh. It included expulsions of people from the West Bank without trial, a policy of systematically breaking the hands and arms of rioters and stone throwers by police and army, and the blowing up of homes of those suspected of being in league or, indeed, in sympathy with demonstrators in the occupied territories. At the same time, the Israeli government began denying the media access to the West Bank and Gaza. Finally, by the spring of 1988, the Israelis were resorting to cutting off the flow of food into the towns and villages of the area.

In this atmosphere, Secretary Shultz journeyed into the Middle East and bravely pushed for settlement of the question of the disposition of the territories Israel occupied. Once again, the United States pushed, in an echo of the Carter years, for an international conference during which the 1982 Reagan plan would be advanced as the basis of a settlement. King Hussein was to speak for the beleaguered Palestinians of the West Bank. But the year before, King Hussein, a long-time ally of the United States, expressed his frustration with U.S. policy and its evident willingness to deal with Iran:

> [W]hat . . . happened [in the Iran–contra affair was] in complete contradiction to everything that we've been assured was the United States policy at the highest levels. I do not believe it was a question of hostages

for arms. I believe it was a strategic decision which places in jeopardy the future of this entire area.[62]

When, therefore, Shultz came back empty-handed from his 1988 foray into Middle East peace making, it could not have been a great surprise that Jordan, at least, no longer wanted to get out in front of any new U.S. initiative. Indeed, within weeks, Hussein dropped the West Bank, literally, into the hands of the PLO, declaring it theirs to administer, and arguing that it was for the Palistinians and the Israelis to find a solution.

When Shultz arrived back in Washington, after having been stonewalled by the Israelis on any settlement, there was news of an assassination, apparently by the Israelis, of the second in command of the PLO, presumably an individual and an organization that would have been involved in any substantive negotiations on the future of the tortured West Bank. Within days of this occurence, however, the United States endangered its place as an interlocutor or honest broker in the area by a symbolic act of great importance: the signing of a formal five-year agreement codifying existing U.S. military, intelligence, and economic relationships with Israel. Israel had been, as King Hussein was well aware, the major supporter of Iran and, indeed, had helped promote the clandestine U.S. overture to Iran.[63] Nonetheless, less than two weeks after they had refused the opening gambit of Shultz's peace plan, the Israelis released the news that they had finally been given a formal, public undertaking in which the United States underwrote their security in much the same fashion that NATO was inscribed in the forefront of U.S. commitments.

In an area where symbols and words have great meaning, Prime Minister Shamir of Israel went on Israeli television, signed the agreement, and spoke proudly about having personally forged with the United States a "unique partnership in common values and interests and in the desire for peace." Against the advice of virtually his whole national security establishment, President Reagan signed the document. A top Reagan adviser complained, "Why do we want to reward Shamir? What has he done for us? . . . Why are we giving him a freebie?" Unlike Shamir, President Reagan signed the document in what was for him uncharacteristic seclusion, without press releases, cameras, or, indeed, any formal announcement whatsoever. Reporters who wanted the text of the agreement had to phone the White House Press Room and ask for a copy.[64]

Of the Saudis, William Quandt, the respected Middle East expert,

Brookings Senior Fellow, and key Carter adviser at the time of the Camp David negotiations, has said:

> Few countries will rival Saudi Arabia in their importance to the United States in the 1980s. At stake is the economic well being of much of the world, energy supplies, and the containment of Soviet expansion into the Persian Gulf region.[65]

By 1988, the Saudis seemed to be backing away from the United States. The Saudis turned down U.S. requests for joint relief efforts to the Afghans stranded in Pakistan and backed away from the Reagan doctrine in Chad and the Sudan, pleading that they no longer could help with financing U.S. interest in an era of budgetary stringency. At the same time, however, the Saudis managed to purchase long-range Chinese surface-to-surface missiles and to sign a $30-billion order for new fighter planes, military construction, and tanks with the British.

"Despite their wealth the Saudis are not very powerful," Quandt has said. "Aware of their own limitations and vulnerabilities, the Saudis move cautiously in foreign policy. They are not leaders. At best, they are consensus builders."[66] Was the Saudi weathervane signaling a shift in the Middle Eastern wind? The answer was unclear as the Reagan administration wound down. It was plain that the U.S. constituency in the Middle East had narrowed.[67] An undeniable cost of the Iran–contra affair and the incessant mismanagement of the essentials of foreign policy was that the United States was left in the sun at the end of the Reagan day, with yet more commitments but poorer in influence.

GLOBALISM AND
AFRO-ASIAN REGIONAL POLITICS

The Reagan administration's preoccupation with the vestiges of the predetente world, the Soviet Union, and its presumed clients tended to dominate its approach to regional politics. Thus, in Asia and Africa as in Latin America and the Middle East, the attention of the administration's policy was never specifically focused on the internal dynamics of the region. The source of regional instabilities was presumed to be the external influence of the Soviet Union. Even when the Soviet Union could not be construed to be at work—the president could not seem to disentangle his approach and policy from what he assumed were the constraints of past commitments.

The Old Triangle—
China, U.S., and the Soviets

President Reagan's ambivalence concerning the triangular diplomacy of the 1970s was, of course, in evidence even before he assumed office.[68] Throughout the late 1970s and as a candidate, Reagan insisted that, notwithstanding the normalization of relations with the Beijing government, some kind of "official" relationships with Taiwan should be maintained. Reagan's strident anti-Soviet rhetoric and rearmament posture received applause on the mainland, but this insistence on selling arms to both Beijing and Taiwan was regarded by the Chinese as unacceptable. Not until the administration was intent on consolidating its anti-Soviet position vis-á-vis the Polish crisis did it accept most of the Chinese position concerning a reduction and eventual elimination of arms sales to Taiwan. Not coincidentally, it would seem, the Chinese were applying pressure of their own, as they played European, Japanese, and American business suitors against one another as they all sought to benefit from the post-Mao modernization of the potentially massive Chinese internal economy.

Finally, the Chinese always had available their own "Russian card" to play against the United States. Thus, hints of and real improvements in Sino–Soviet relations of the sort that seemed to develop in 1983 and accelerated somewhat after Gorbachev's ascendancy in 1985 constituted a useful stick with which to prod the Americans toward policies more responsive to Chinese interests. By the early 1980s, it was clear to military analysts that it would take decades before China could develop a full range of military capability beyond self-defense. China's utility as a military make-weight was, therefore, dubious. In the final analysis, therefore, it would seem unrealistic to expect that Sino–American relations could move much beyond the kind of difficult pseudoalliance that had emerged by the 1980s.

In the meantime, it was evident that politico-economic issues had displaced strategic priorities in the Sino–American relationship. After Reagan visited China in 1984, talk of "playing China cards" against the Soviets virtually disappeared. Concern about a Chinese rapprochement with the Russians was still present, but questions of high technology sales, trade, and investment—in short, development and modernization—had come to dominate the agenda of Sino–American relations by the end of the Reagan administration. Even the Taiwan issue seemed to be moving more clearly into an exclusively Chinese context as the passing of Chiang Ching-kuo marked the onset of a liberalization of the domestic regime on Taiwan and some marginal relaxation of contacts between the residents of the province and the mainland. By 1988, there were estimates that Taiwanese entrepreneurs and the Chinese government had found ways to circumvent Taiwanese trade obstacles to the tune of $1.3 billion. Taiwanese-owned factories on the mainland operating through Hong Kong were estimated to be worth $15 to $50 billion.[69]

Relations with the entire region have come to center more and more on economics. Of course, the collapse of the Marcos regime in the Philippines and its replacement by a government under Corazon Aquino was fraught with security implications for the United States. The United States had served as midwife during the birth of the Philippine democracy, but the infant remained threatened by supporters of the deposed dictator and those who were ambitious in their own right. The massive U.S. base complex at Subic Bay was still viewed by the Pentagon as central to the American security posture in the region, and negotiations with the Aquino government for future lease rights proved no more easy than with her predecessor. But the central question in the future of Philippine security was economic development and the role U.S. aid would play in that process. As negotiations on the U.S. bases got underway, talk of a lease extension in exchange for a U.S. "mini-Marshall Plan" of more than $10 billion for the Philippines gave way to budgetary realities. The base argreement was renewed for just three years at a "rent" of just over $1 billion a year. The issue, plainly, was put on hold for the next administration.

Given the presence of more than thirty thousand American troops in South Korea, the continuing deadlock on the Korean peninsula remained a central security issue throughout the 1980s. The surge of democratic sentiment in South Korea during the late 1980s seemed to be ushering in internal changes in the direction of democratization similar to those to the south. In view of the history of military intervention and violence in the country, one could not rule our further instability. But by the end of Reagan's presidency the old irreconcilables, North and South, were starting to come to terms with each other.

The emergence in Singapore, Hong Kong, Taiwan, and South Korea of low-cost steel production and light manufacturing has proved more significant for the United States than any security issue in the region. If, as seems possible, China follows the economic lead of these countries, economic developments will likely prove far more consequential for the future of U.S. relations with the region than whether the Soviet-backed Vietnamese evacuate Cambodia and Laos, whether the Japanese assume more of the American regional defense burden — a major concern of the Reagan administration — or whether Soviet naval forces operate out of Cam Rahn Bay in Vietnam. Indeed, one recent comparative analysis of the Chinese and Soviet break with their centrally planned pasts concludes that the Chinese are more likely than the Soviets to pursue the labor-intensive industrial development of export-oriented goods that proved so effective for their Asian cousins. The "Asian approach," however, is hard act for the Soviets to follow; Asians

> start with simple manufacturing, such as textiles and toys, and gradually work their way up to more sophisticated products like radios and televisions, and ultimately VCRs and computers. It is hard to see how the Soviet Union can duplicate this pattern, or what other route it can take that will bring similar results as rapidly.[70]

In sum, throughout Asia, the United States has gained ground through far-sighted developmental aid practices, aggressive U.S. lending, and relatively open U.S. markets. These policies were largely independent of security undertakings, yet they have worked so well that the Soviets, by the end of the 1980s, were all but irrelevant in the region, except as the benefactor of regimes harboring rigid ideologies that wandered between the antiquated and the pernicious. And even if the Soviets themselves tried to follow the Asian model of development, they would, by the nature of their own planning and financial processes, fail. The U.S. position in Asia, as well as the Asian nations themselves, despite the augmented Soviet fleet in the region and despite declining U.S. military influence, was more secure than it had been since the Cold War began.

In Africa, the focus of the Reagan administration's policy was, as in the Carter administration, on the south. However, rather than attempt to pressure the South Africans into a resolution of conflict along their northern borders and with respect to Angola over Namibia, the administration chose to pursue a policy of "constructive engagement" emphasizing inducements to the South Africans including warmer relations and even relaxation of restrictions on economic contacts. In return, the administration assumed that the South Africans could be eased toward a resolution of regional conflicts with their black neighbors as well as a liberalization of their internal apartheid policies.[71] Moreover, from the administration's perspective, the overriding problem in the region was Cuban influence and presence in Angola, therefore, any resolution of regional conflicts centering on Namibia and Angola were to be predicated on Cuban withdrawal.

The South Africans, understanding the U.S. concern for the regional presence of Soviet power and surrogates, transformed the Americans into de facto patrons in the region. Indeed, South Africa's attacks into Angola, Zimbabwe, Botswana were increased as were attacks into Mozambique, from which guerrillas of the black opposition African National Congress were operating to greater effect in South Africa during the 1980s. In 1984 there was some progress on regional security arrangements between the South Africans and their neighbors as the latter were forced to confront superior South African military capability. Furthermore, all parties needed a respite from armed conflict if their own internal developmental needs were to be met. Nonetheless, even as the South Africans were signing a nonaggression agreement with Mozambique in 1984, they were continuing to support a brutal insurgent group in the country.[72] Similarly, in Angola, South Africa continued to actively support Joseph Zavimbi's UNITA in its attacks on the Cuban supported Angolan government. Here, U.S. military assistance to the insurgents was very much evident. Ironically, South Africa's activity in Angola included an unsuccessful attack on Gulf Oil's operation in 1985.

By the end of the Reagan administration, it was not clear if the threefold objectives of regional stability, Cuban and Soviet withdrawal, and internal South African reform were any closer. South Africa's foreign policy and domestic policy were predicated on brute force. Yet, after seven and one half years, a patient U.S. Assistant Secretary of African Affairs, Chester A. Crocker, had succeeded in hammering out an agreement for the South Africans to withdraw their forces in Angola while the 50,000 Soviet-backed Cuban troops also withdrew. It was possible, as the Reagan administration wound down, that one of the oldest conflict in the cold war, in Angola, was on its way to a settlement. But the parties had been at the edge of peace before. In 1983 and 1987, the Reagan administration believed it had a settlement of the South African occupation of Namibia and the end of Cuban support of the Angolans. But in both previous cases, the South Africans demanded to see the Cubans depart before they removed their own troops. Chester Crocker may have been an important facilitator in badgering the parties to the peace table in 1988. As important, one suspects, were the losses the South Africans suffered on the battlefield because of the beefed-up Cuban presence. Moreover, the U.S. position, linked so closely for so long with South Africa, was not much improved. Indeed, the Reagan administration insisted that it would continue to support UNITA. Nor was there any prospect for reform of the internal repression of South Africa's majority population.

In 1985, the South Africa government under the leadership of P.W. Botha suspended the right of assembly, clamped down on the press, and began to arrest and hold without warrant suspected dissidents. By 1988, some 800 children under the age of 11, according to Nobel laureate Desmond Tutu, were being held without any prospect for their release.[73]

Opposition in the United States to South Africa grew rapidly. The Reagan administration could head off congressionally imposed sanctions only by issuing its own milder version through executive order. The administration had been forced, therefore, to abandon the essence of its policy of "constructive engagement" and return to at least the rhetorical confrontation with the racist regime adopted by its predecessor, President Carter. To the extent that the United States had supported South Africa in the past, the administration's position vis-á-vis South Africa's neighbors and the opposition within South Africa was problematic. And now, at the end of Reagan's tenure in the wake of the imposition of sanctions, the adminsitration's contacts with the Botha government were strained.

The possibilities in South Africa were, therefore not promising. Regional peace agreements in the past have been, at most, ceasefires. Moreover, the South African regime, based on apartheid, was under intensifying black assault from within. American policy had either been unable or unwilling to lend significant support to the black opposition led by the African National Congress thereby creating an opportunity for more radical external influence. Another possibility was that South Africa, armed now with nuclear weapons might threaten to cut its own deal with the Soviet Union, perhaps offering them port privileges in Simonstown, unless the United States and others accepted the continuation of apartheid. Even the favored solution of many in the United States and Europe — some sort of concerted economic pressure brought to bear by governments and international organizations — seemed of questionable utility unless European, Japanese, and American private investors and creditors of the South African regime could be enlisted in the effort. In the meantime, it seemed likely that the internal violence and repression would continue — even escalate — as a distressingly regular feature of apartheid.

AMERICAN ECONOMIC RECOVERY
AND THE WORLD ECONOMY

International economic policy receded somewhat from the position of prominence it had occupied during the 1970s. In part, this was due to the declining fortunes of OPEC noted earlier. As the exercise of petropower proved more constrained than feared in the middle and late 1970s, the broader concern with international economic interdependence lost much of its urgency. The international political economy of the early 1980s was dominated by the consequences of the intense politicizing of international economy in the 1970s: global economic depression, massive debt problems in the Third World and Eastern Europe that threatened the international financial system, aggravated global poverty, and a lingering concern about the security of energy supplies. By the later 1980s, a modest recovery was underway in the industrialized west, and neither energy or inflation dominated the headlines. Debt and poverty remained a central economic reality outside the industrialized core, but it was as though they had become routine.

Initially, the Reagan administration regarded these problems as less the result of interdependence that must be actively managed internationally than as the result from *American* economic distress. It followed, therefore, that international economic difficulties, whether they afflicted the industrialized or developing nations, were best attacked through the reinvigoration of the American economy. The theme was set forth explicitly in the president's 1982 *Economic Report:*

> The successful implementation of policies to control inflation and restore vigorous real growth in the United States will have a profound and favorable impact on the rest of the world. . . . More generally, the Administration's approach to international economic issues is based on the same principles which underlie its domestic programs: a belief in the superiority of market solutions to economic problems and an emphasis on private economic activity as the engine of noninflationary growth.[74]

The principles of international coordination of economic policies received deference in the summit conferences of the major industrial powers at Versailles and Williamsburg in 1982 and 1983.[75] It was clear, however, that the United States was not prepared to make concessions to the Europeans and Canadians on those issues that concerned them most—i.e., high American interest rates that were pulling money out of their stagnant economies—if it meant weakening in any way what the administration regarded as an instrument of its domestic recovery program. Insofar as the American economy was perceived as the engine of global recovery by the administration, the American priorities would become the priorities of the industrialized world, notwithstanding the difficult accommodation to a more multilateral perspective during the 1970s.

The same policy held with respect to the developing world.[76] At the summit meeting of leaders from twenty-two industrialized and developing countries in October of 1981 in Cancun, Mexico, President Reagan repeated the message that he had delivered at the meeting of the International Monetary Fund the month before. Development would occur, the president asserted, when the Third World was opened up to the "magic of the marketplace" and the American economy was fully recovered. The latter was the essential precondition for eliminating poverty in the Third World, but in the meantime, these countries could prepare the way by reducing government controls on their own economies and opening themselves up to more outside investment.[77]

"We did not waste time on unrealistic rhetoric or unattainable objectives," Reagan noted on his return from Cancun.[78] Thus, the Third World's calls, during the 1970s, for a new international economic order were dismissed by the Reagan administration. Nor were significant increases in foreign aid forthcoming for the poorest of the poor. Aid levels for Africa were maintained at the levels that had been granted in the late 1970s, but for a region beset with staggering debt—$65 billion in 1983 versus $5 billion in 1970—and with virtually no prospect for growth during the 1980s, such aid levels would prove inadequate. Indeed, the World Bank reported in 1987 that Sub-Saharan Africa experienced negative 3.4 percent growth between 1980 and 1986 in per capita incomes, lower than those of the 1960s and early 1970s.[79] The administration was prepared to ask for significant aid levels, but they were for the Caribbean Basin countries—especially El Salvador—Turkey, Israel, and Egypt, countries undoubtedly afflicted with poverty but whose primary qualification for American attention was their strategic importance.

By 1983, the American economy emerged from its deep recession and entered a period of recovery that lasted through the Reagan administration, but the benefits that the administration had assured the other members of the international economy would accrue to them were less striking. Whereas the United States had growth of about 3.7 percent and Japan experienced 4 percent, the rest of the industrialized world experienced 2.9 percent growth, with the Germans at about 2.2 percent. Unemployment appeared to be dropping in the United States to levels well below those that had existed at the onset of the recession. Meanwhile, however, European unemployment rates were at the highest levels since World War II. Among the major industrialized economies, only Canada and the United Kingdom had declining unemployment rates by 1988. Japan, France, Italy, and Germany saw their unemployment increase or remain virtually unchanged over the course of the recovery.[80]

Very high U.S. interest rates—the result of the U.S. Federal Reserve's concern about a resurgence of inflation stemming from the enormous deficits built up by the Reagan administration as the result of its tax cuts in 1981 and its defense expenditures—had attracted a flow of dollars from abroad throughout the recovery, thereby keeping the dollar strong throughout the first part of Reagan's tenure. Europeans, undoubtedly conveniently ignoring many of their own domestic economic rigidities, placed much of the blame for their sluggish "recovery" on these high rates. During the second Reagan term, however, the dollar's value began to decline as confidence in the deficit-ridden American economy began to weaken. Although responding more slowly than many had expected, the decline in the value of the dollar did have a salutary effect on the United States' enormous trade deficit. In 1988, U.S. exports were higher than they had been during the previous year.

From 1985 on, with the Treasury Department, now under the direction of James Baker, American international economic policy became increasingly accepting of more international coordination if not management. Thus, beginning with the economic summit of 1985 held at the Plaza Hotel in New York, continuing through the Tokyo and Venice summits in 1986 and 1987, and reaffirmed at the December 1987 summit held at the Louvre in Paris, fiscal and macroeconomic policy coordination became the watchword. Structural changes in economies, especially in Europe, proved far less responsive, however. Nowhere was this problem of greater concern than with respect to trade.

European, Japanese, and American trade has been increasingly afflicted by protectionism in the 1980s as all parties resorted to more and more bilateral arrangements, such as quotas, to manage their trade relations. Nontariff barriers to trade also became more important as tariffs were reduced after completion of the Tokyo round of trade negotiations between 1974 and 1979.[81] By the mid-1980s, one observer estimated that the percentage of "managed" trade in what was ostensibly a free-trading world had reached 30 to 40 percent and seemed likely to increase. Indeed, World Bank data reveal that during the ostensibly free-trade Reagan administration, the United States had been as guilty as any of the industrialized nations in applying nontariff and other restrictions on trade.[82] "It remains an open — and valid — question," OECD trade expert Sylvia Ostray observed in early 1984, "whether creeping protectionism can just continue to creep or whether slow erosion, on reaching some invisible and unpredictable threshold, will abruptly transform the world trading system."[83]

Of Banks and Debtors

The combination of the second oil shock in 1980, resultant global recession, and dramatic increases in real interest rates had led to another transformation of the system that was hardly creeping and held the possibility of a dramatic and catastrophic collapse of the international financial structure: the international debt crisis. As the price of oil and money soared and their economies collapsed into recession, a number of newly industrializing countries in the Third World, several East European countries, and virtually all less-developed countries found their debt burden escalating dramatically. Whereas total outstanding debt had stood at $130.1 billion in 1973, this amount had increased to $614.2 billion by the end of 1982, with more than $100 billion of it owed to American banks. Latin American countries accounted for more than half of the total. By the end of 1982, the IMF estimated that the debt was equivalent to 246 percent of the annual export earnings of the non–oil-producing countries of Latin America. Argentina, for example, had an average debt in 1983 as a percent of its export of goods and services of 424 percent, Brazil stood at 359 percent, Chile 290 percent, and the oil-producing countries of Mexico and Venezuela stood at 275 percent and 196 percent, respectively.[84] The entire structure of international banking seemed threatened, and the U.S. economic recovery offered little solace. In fact, the high interest rates that seemed an inevitable part of the recovery exacerbated the problem.

As in the case of the oil crises that had brought on the debt crisis, ad hoc initiatives followed by an increasing degree of multilateral management emerged as the systemic response. Since most of the debt was held by private banks, bank debt restructuring increased dramatically, especially during 1983, when some twenty countries negotiated refinancing, rescheduling, or deferment of debt totaling more than $59.2 billion. By 1986, twenty-four countries had once again renegotiated some $71.1 billion in debts with government creditor private banks within a multilateral framework.[85] Official creditors, working closely with the IMF and the Bank for International Settlements, worked together within the so-called Paris Club to restructure debt resulting from various bilateral and multilateral foreign aid arrangements. Significantly, the IMF did not come to this process of private and official debt restructuring as a mere supplicant. In most instances, the Fund refused to offer its loan guarantee facility and its services as an agent for planning and administering the often "brutal" domestic adjustment programs in the debtor countries unless the private banks cooperated through the extension of more credit.[86] The Reagan administration was compelled in the end to pressure Congress into increasing the American government's participation in the Fund's exercise in international regulation—an ironic outcome for an administration ideologically committed to diminishing regulation of all kind and reliance on the market.

Economic Conclusions

It would, of course, be a mistake to conclude from these developments either that the international system had once again "dodged the bullet"

of international economic catastrophe by resorting to increased centralized, if ad hoc, management of the system or that the Reagan administration had accepted the process. Rather, it seemed likely that the
debt-restructuring process would become a recurring crisis in that most
of the arrangements worked out in 1982 and 1983 were scheduled to
end by the end of the decade. By 1987, the overall ratio of debts to
exports improved for the first time since 1980 and seemed likely to continue improving through the end of the decade. However, the total external debt of developing countries in 1987 remained at about $1.2
trillion, and, even if the ratio of debts to exports continued to improve
as projected, the ratios would remain higher by the end of the decade
than they were in 1982 when the major problems began.[87]

SUMMING UP

In his advocacy of his domestic economic program, President Reagan
sought to reverse what he understood to be fifty years of ill-conceived
social activism. In his most central foreign policy conceptions and actions of the early 1980s, it is evident that he sought a no less radical
reversal or redirection of America's international relations away from
what he regarded as the failed policies of accommodation and detente
developed during the 1970s. In its intensely conflictual and bipolar view
of international structure, the Reagan world view was not unlike that
of Dean Acheson and Paul Nitze in NSC-68. President Reagan's emphasis on strength, even superiority, as the basis of negotiations was the
idiom of that early strategy for prosecuting the cold war. Indeed, Reagan frequently indicated a desire to break out of what he believed was
a debilitating "Vietnam syndrome" that overemphasized international
complexity and limits on American power and thereby enfeebled American will. The buildup of U.S. strategic forces, the exercise of military
power in the Caribbean and the Middle East, and the vigorous pursuit
of the Reagan doctrine all within a framework of strident and moralistic rhetorical attacks on the Soviet Union and the legitimacy of its political and social order became, therefore, the instrumentalities of this
renewed American nationalism and activism.

But this posture also included an often explicit denial of developments of the Vietnam era that, as we have seen, involved a great deal
more than the defeat of American power in Southeast Asia. No less important, we have suggested, were the onset of strategic parity, the emergence of new political economic forces as American postwar hegemony
declined, a new configuration of political and economic capability in

both East Asia and Europe, and an intensification of nationalism that tended to lend primacy to local forces and conditions in understanding instability in the Third World. Notwithstanding their subordination to the superpower focus of the Reagan administration's renewed cold war, these forces and conditions retained their capacity to shape international politics and frustrate a foreign policy that ignores them.

By the end of Reagan's second term, the frustration and even failure were quite evident. The colossal bungling and frightful callousness towards the law and the Constitution associated with the Iran–contra scandal left an image of incompetence, incoherence, and illegality. But another underlying reality was obscured. In Central America and the Middle East, American initiatives were either at an impasse or edging toward bankruptcy as local dynamics asserted themselves and moved beyond American control. Even where, arguably, the administration had been successful, outcomes seemed increasingly ambiguous — as in the case of Afghanistan when superpower engagement lessened or in the Philippines when local economic realities reasserted themselves in the wake of successful democratic revolution aided by the U.S. assistance. American economic recovery paralleled some improvement in the international economy during the middle and late 1980s, but deep structural problems remained in place, as some sentiment for trade protectionism remained and the international debt and American deficit problems persisted. Here too, the administration had been forced by the end of its tenure to adopt a more pragmatic acceptance of international cooperation and management than its original ideology seemed to allow.

Similarly, in Soviet–American relations, the administration closed on a far more pragmatic note than it had begun. From enthusiastic bashing of the "evil empire," the administration moved to a series of summits with the new leader of the Soviet Union, Mikhail Gorbachev. Out of these negotiations emerged the first significant arms reduction agreement of the post–World War II era, encompassing innovative approaches to the old problem of verification of agreements. However, there was a sense that the Reagan administration had lost the initiative. Although his diminished band of admirers insisted that the Russians had been driven to the negotiating table by Reagan's toughness, little in the record of the Reagan administration demonstrated any underlying enthusiasm for negotiations. In fact, the administration's "negotiating" positions were advanced so confidently only because it was assumed they would be rejected. And so they were until 1985 and the arrival of Gorbachev, who not only accepted the American gambits, but converted them into advantageous positions from which he might pursue his own agenda. Indeed, as the United States entered its electoral season with the foreknowledge that there would be a new president in 1989, the questions pressed insistently forward: "Was the Cold War now finally over?" "Did the ascendancy of Gorbachev provide an opportunity to transform fundamentally the Soviet–American relationship?"

NOTES

1. Cited by Roger D. Hansen, "The Reagan Doctrine and Global Containment: Revival or Recessional?" *SAIS Review*, January 1987, p. 40.
2. Robert W. Tucker, "Exemplar or Crusader: Reflections on America's Role," *The National Interest*, Fall 1986, pp. 64–75.
3. The term is from Charles Krauthhammer, "The Poverty of Realism," *The New Republic*, February 12, 1986, pp. 16ff.
4. Jeffrey Record, "Jousting with Unreality: Reagan's Military Strategy," *International Security*, Vol. 8 (Winter 1983–84), pp. 6–10ff.
5. Marc S. Miller, "Ambiguous War: The United States and Low Intensity Conflict," *Technology Review*, Vol. 90, No. 6 (August/September 1987), p. 62.
6. Carried out April 14, 1986, on the capitol with collateral damage that, it apparently was hoped, would include Ghadaffy.
7. Woodward, p. 420.
8. Ibid., pp. 216, 384.
9. "The Reagan Doctrine and Containment," *SAIS Review*, Fall 1986, p. 57.
10. Woodward, op. cit., pp. 204–205.
11. Emerson, op. cit., p. 199.
12. Some of these activities are being chronicled by the former Washington Editor of *Harpers*, James Hougan, in a book in progress.
13. Anderson and Van Atta, "Special Forces Story Remains Untold," *Washington Post*, May 2, 1988, p. C9; emphasis added.
14. The best account is the major work by Raymond L. Garthoff, a member of the Carter administration at the time, *Detente and Confrontation* (Washington, D.C.: Brookings, 1985), p. 96.
15. This figure is the official Soviet estimate. The United States has estimated as many as 25,000 lost by the Soviets. For the latter estimate, see the State Department report prepared by Craig Karp, "Afghanistan: Eight Years of Occupation," The Department of State, Bureau of Intelligence and Research, Washington, D.C., 1988, reprinted in *Current News*, (Washington, D.C.: Department of the Air Force), Special edition, April 26, 1988, Number 1718, p. 8. Also see Philip Taubman, "Relief Comes to Russians as End of Combat Nears," *New York Times*, April 15, 1988, p. 1.
16. See David Evans, "A Deadly Weapon: Afghan Tribesmen Carrying A Stinger," *Chicago Tribune*, April 8, 1988, p. 27.
17. Selig Harrison, "On Afghan Peace," *New York Times*, March 29, 1988; and Richard M. Weintraub and Jonathan C. Randel, "Returning Afghans Would Face Many Problems," *Washington Post*, March 30, 1988, p. A19.
18. David Ottaway, "Kabul's Women See Threat to Status," *Washington Post*, May 4, 1988, p. A27.

19. See George Arney, "Afghan Refugees' Rally Assails Geneva Accord," *Washington Post*, April 17, 1988, p. A33.

20. See Steven Weisman, "After the Russians; South Asia Tries to Refigure Its Future," *New York Times*, April 17, 1988, p. 2E; and Steven R. Weisman, "Afghanistan Chief Visits India Today," *New York Times*, May 4, 1988, p. A11.

21. See Stephen Engleberg and Bernard Trainor, "Stinger Missile Parts On Iranian Ship were Sent by U.S. to Afghans," *International Herald Tribune*, October 19, 1987, p. 6. See also Michael Getler, "Stingers Alter Face of Afghan War," *International Herald Tribune*, October 15, 1987, p. 1.

22. See John H. Cushman Jr., "Pakistan's Nuclear Effort Worries U.S.," *New York Times*, March 17, 1987, p. A3.

23. Tim Weiner, "The CIA's Leaking Pipeline," *The Philadelphia Inquirer*, February 28, 1988, p. 1.

24. See Robert Pear, "Arming Afghan Guerrillas: A Huge Effort Led by the U.S.," *New York Times*, April 18, 1988, p. A11.

25. Evans, op. cit.

26. Karp, op. cit.

27. Including James Nathan, see his "Don't Arm the Afghans," *New York Times*, September 6, 1980.

28. Selig Harrison, "What Next for Afghanistan?" *Washington Post*, April 17, 1988, p. C2; and Henry Kamm, "Afghan Rebel Alliance Leader Outlines his Cause," *New York Times*, April 20, 1988, p. A3. The leader, Gulbuddin Heckmatyar, called the negotiations that led to the Soviet pull out part of a Soviet–American "conspiracy."

29. See Elaine Sciolino, "U.S. Decision to Send Stinger Missiles to Chad is Seen as Raising Ante," *International Herald Tribune*, November 7–8, 1987, p. 9.

30. See Andrew Alexander, "U.S. to Triple Aid to Rebels in Angola," *Des Moines Register*, March 8, 1988, p. 4; reprinted in *Current News* (Washington, D.C.: Dept. of the Air Force), March 25, 1988, p. 8.

31. See Samuel Huntington, "Will More Countries Become Democratic?" *Political Science Quarterly*, Vol. 99, No. 2 (1984), pp. 218ff; and Hanson, op. cit., p. 61.

32. For an elaboration of these arguments, see Barry Rubin, "The Reagan Administration and the Middle East," in Oye, et al., *Eagle Resurgent? The Reagan Era in American Foreign Policy* (Boston: Little, Brown, 1987), esp. pp. 432–434.

33. Ibid., p. 431.

34. See Walter Pincus and David Hoffman, "Regan Sought To Conceal Arms Role from Shultz," *Washington Post*, January 24, 1987, p. A1.

35. "Secret Saudi Funding Aids U.S. Policy Goals," *International Herald Tribune*, June 22, 1987, p. 1.

36. Jeff Garth, "'81 Saudi Deal: Aid to Contras for U.S. Arms," *New York Times*, February 4, 1987, pp. A1, A6.

37. Bernard Weinraub, "Thwarting U.S. Policy," *New York Times*, November 11, 1986, p. A10.

38. HR 100-433, p. 377; and 22 USC Sec. 2422. Congress was notified a year later; Walter Pincus, "Reagan Side Stepped '82 Security Order," *Washington Post*, December 11, 1982, p. 1.

39. *Time Magazine, Asian Edition*, August 10, 1987, p. 51.

40. See David Rodgers, "Iran Contra Plans Excluded Military Chiefs," *Asian Wall Street Journal*, October 15, 1987, p. 20.

41. See "Excerpts From House Testimony Before the House Committee on Foreign Affairs," *New York Times*, December 9, 1986, pp. A12–A13.

42. *The Tower Commission Report* (New York: Times Books, 1987), pp. 172ff, 228; and the references in HR 100-433, p. 379. Also see Walter Pincus, "CIA Bypassed In Iran Arms Supply," *Washington Post*, November 8, 1986, p. A1; and HR 100-433, p. 379.

43. Stephen Engleberg, "U.S. Disinformation Reportedly Sent to Iran and Iraq," *New York Times*, January 12, 1987, p. A1; and George C. Wilson, "U.S. May Widen Umbrella In Gulf," *Washington Post*, April 21, 1988, p. 1.

44. Bernard Trainor, "Error by a Tense U.S. Crew Led to Downing of Iran Jet, Inquiry to Find," *New York Times*, August 3, 1988, p. 1.

45. Richard W. Murphey, "Supporting U.S. Interests in the Middle East," Current Policy No. 874, U.S. Department of State, Bureau of Public Affairs, Washington, D.C.

46. Scott Armstrong, et al., eds., *The Chronology: The Documented Day by Day Account of the Secret Military Assistance to Iran and the Contras* (New York: Warner Books, 1987), pp. 531ff.

47. Adams, op. cit., p. 273.

48. Foreign Broadcast Information Service, Daily Report, Near and South Asia, June 30, 1987, p. j2; cited by Barry Rubin, "Drowning in the Gulf," *Foreign Policy*, No. 69 (Winter 1987–88), p. 125.

49. The best academic source is the one we have relied on, Professor Roy Nursessian of Monmouth College, N.J., interview, May 9, 1988.

50. James Webb, "At Least the Navy Knows What It Is Doing in the Gulf," *Washington Post*, April 20, 1988, p. 17.

51. Robert Pear, "U.S. Will Increase Its Gulf Defense of Merchant Ships," *New York Times*, April 23, 1988, p. A1.

52. See Christopher Van Hollen, "Don't Engulf the Gulf," *Foreign Affairs*, Vol. 59 (Summer 1981), p. 1067 *passim;* and Stephen S. Rosenfeld, "Testing the Hard Line," *America and the World 1982 – Foreign Affairs*, Vol. 61 (1982), p. 499.

53. For a brief overview of the war, see International Institute for Strategic Studies, *Strategic Survey, 1982–1983* (London: IISS, 1983), pp. 64–78.

54. See "Sharon Misled Cabinet on Beirut Advance," *The Jerusalem Post*, January 29–February 4, 1984, p. 2.

55. "A New Opportunity for Peace in the Middle East," Current Policy No. 417 (Washington, D.C.: Department of State, 1982).

56. See the partial text of the Fez summit communique in *The Times* (London), September 11, 1982.

57. See the survey, "The Marine Tragedy: An Inquiry Into Causes and Responsibility," *New York Times*, December 11, 1983, pp. 49–52.

58. For an account for this policy review and an overview of Middle East policy during the early Reagan administration, see Bernard Gwertzman, "Reagan Turns to Israel," *New York Times Magazine*, November 27, 1983, pp. 62–65, 82–88.

59. See Secretary of Defense Weinberger's description of the "redeployment" in Lou Cannon and John Goshko, "Troop Move Timetable Is Uncertain," *Washington Post*, February 10, 1984, pp. 1, 23.

60. "President's News Conference on Foreign and Domestic Issues," *New York Times*, February 23, 1984, p. A12; and an interview with pollster Louis Harris of American opinion on Lebanon on "Morning Edition," National Public Radio, February 23, 1984. See also the Gallup Poll results reported in Steven Weisman,

"President Asserts Marines in Beirut Still Have a Role," *New York Times*, February 23, 1984, p. A13.

61. See U.S. State Department, Current Policy No. 683, April 4, 1985 and Current Policy No. 726, June 27, 1985.

62. Anderson and Van Atta, "U.S.–Iran Deal Bruised Ties with Jordan," *Washington Post*, December 19, 1986, p. E7. Jordan had seen a $1.9 billion arms sale blocked in Congress because of intense Israeli pressure. At the same time, Israel had been supplying arms to Jordan's fundamentalist antagonists, Iran.

63. The Iranians, although vocally anti-Semitic, basically left their Jewish population in peace, while fomenting fundamentalist radicalism in the region. To the Israelis, the Iranians were long-time non-Arab confederates who served to weaken Israel's enemies, especially the Iraqis. There were, however, uncertainties in all of this for the Israelis, because the military and terrorist activities of the militant, Iranian-backed Hizbollah ("Party of God"), operating out of Lebanon were clearly anti-Israeli in thrust.

64. James McCartney, "Reagan Signs Israeli Friendship Pact Despite Aides' Reported Objections," *Philadelphia Inquirer*, April 22, 1988, p. 20A.

65. William B. Quandt, *Saudi Arabia in the 1980s: Foreign Policy, Security, and Oil* (Washington, D.C.: Brookings, 1981), p. 155.

66. Ibid.

67. Jim Hoagland, "The Turtle Snaps Back," *Washington Post*, April 13, 1988, p. 2.

68. For good overviews of regional developments in Asia from which this discussion is drawn, see Banning Garret, "China Policy and the Constraints of Triangular Logic," in Kenneth Oye, *Eagle Defiant* (Boston: Little, Brown, 1983), pp. 237–271; Garret and Bonnie S. Glaser, "From Nixon to Reagan: China's Changing Role in American Strategy," in Oye, et al., *Eagle Resurgent?*, pp. 255–296; Chalmers Johnson, "East Asia: Another Year of Living Dangerously," *America and the World, 1983 — Foreign Affairs*, No. 62 (1984), pp. 721–745; Stephen P. Gibert, "Reagan's Asian Policy: The Past is Prologue," *Asian Perspective*, No. 7 (Spring–Summer 1983), pp. 51–72; and Marshal I. Goldman and Merle Goldman, "Soviet and Chinese Economic Reform," *America and the World, 1987/88 — Foreign Affairs*, No. 66 (1988), pp. 551–573.

69. Susan Chira, "For Taiwan, China Looms Ever Larger," *New York Times*, May 22, 1988, p. 15.

70. Goldman and Goldman, op. cit., p. 572.

71. For an elaboration of "constructive engagement" by its chief architect and subsequently Assistant Secretary of State for Africa in the Reagan administration, Chester Crocker, see "South Africa: Strategy for Change," *Foreign Affairs*, No. 59 (Winter 1980–81), pp. 323–351. Useful critiques and overviews of the Reagan administration's policy in Africa are Jennifer Seymour Whitaker, "Africa Beset," *America and the World, 1983 — Foreign Affairs*, No. 62 (1984), pp. 746–776; Donald Rothchild and John Ravenhill, "From Carter to Reagan: The Global Perspective on Africa Become Ascendant," in Oye, et al., *Eagle Defiant*, pp. 337–365; and Rothchild and Ravenhill, "Subordinating African Issues to Global Logic: Reagan Confronts Political Complexity," in Oye, et al., *Eagle Resurgent*, pp. 393–430.

72. In April of 1988, the State Department reported that Mozambique National Resistance or RENAMO (the group's initials in Portuguese, the colonial language of Mozambique) was guilty of perhaps 100,000 murders. Oliver North was reportedly sympathetic to the group but sufficiently preoccupied with other matters that no aid was provided. In the Congress, Senator Jesse Helms unsuccessfully pressed

the Reagan administration to support RENAMO, which did receive some assistance from right-wing private groups in the United States. See Robert Pear with James Brooke, "Rightists in U.S. Aid Mozambique Rebels," *New York Times*, May 22, 1988, pp. A1, A14.

73. John M. Goshko, "After Seven-and-a-half Years, Africa Expert's Goal Is Near," *Washington Post*, August 11, 1985, p. A25.

74. Council of Economic Advisers, *Annual Report, 1982* (Washington: Government Printing Office, 1982), p. 167; and cited in Benjamin Cohen's overview of the administration's international economic policy, "An Explosion in the Kitchen? Economic Relations with Other Advanced Industrial States," in Economic Relations with Other Advanced Industrial States," in Oye, K., *Eagle Defiant*, pp. 105–130. For a useful survey of the effects of this policy, see Sylvia Ostry, "The World Economy in 1983: Marking Time," *America and the World, 1983*, pp. 533–560.

75. See the communiques of the Versailles and Williamsburg summits in *New York Times*, June 7, 1982, and May 31, 1983, respectively.

76. Richard E. Feinberg, "Reaganomics and the Third World," in Oye, op. cit., pp. 131–165.

77. The IMF speech can be found in *New York Times*, September 30, 1981, p. D22; and the President's assessment of the Cancun summit in *New York Times*, October 25, 1981, pp. 1, 12.

78. "Text of Reagan's Statement on Cancun Talks," *New York Times*, October 25, 1981, p. 12.

79. See World Bank, *World Development Report 1987* (Washington, D.C.: World Bank, 1987), p. 26.

80. International Monetary Fund, *World Economic Outlook* (Washington, D.C.: IMF, April 1988), table A.2, p. 112, and table A.4, p. 115.

81. See the discussion of nontariff barriers in World Bank, op. cit., pp. 133–153.

82. World Bank, op. cit., pp. 139–143, esp. fig. 8.1 and table 8.5.

83. Ostry, op. cit., p. 548.

84. See ibid., pp. 549–551; and E. Brau, et al., *Recent Multilateral Debt Restructurings with Official and Bank Creditors*, Occasional Paper No. 25 (Washington, D.C.: International Monetary Fund, 1983). For the background of the Latin American situation, see Pedro-Pablo Kuczynski, "Latin American Debt," *Foreign Affairs*, No. 61 (Winter 1982–83), pp. 344–364; and Kuczynski, "Latin American Debt: Act Two," *Foreign Affairs*, No. 61 (Fall 1983), pp. 17–38.

85. Brau, op. cit., table 8, p. 22, and World Bank, op. cit., pp. 20–21.

86. See ibid., pp. 9–10, 13–14, 23–24. The characterization of the Fund's "adjustment" arrangements as "brutal" is Ostry's, op. cit., p. 551. On the Fund's leverage on the entire restructuring process, see Ostry, op. cit., pp. 551–552.

87. IMF, op. cit., pp. 18–19. Only in the high-growth countries of Asia would this pattern not hold.

Chapter 13
Conclusion

Throughout the Reagan administration, Soviet–American relations were the centerpiece of American foreign policy. There was nothing new in this because, except for a brief interval in the Carter years, it has been so since World War II. But perhaps more so than in the past, Soviet–American relations were played out by U.S. policy makers as if they were political theater. Part of the performance was aimed at distracting the attentive public, part was played out to secure funding levels for much desired military programs. As a result, public debate grew stale, studied, formalized, and familiar. The arguments were presented with the detailed and obscure subtlety of the ancient Japanese Kabuki theater. In consequence, not only were nuclear weapons moving toward physicists' abstractions, but the arguments peeled off into the abstruse world of things that stood for something else but could not be argued *sui generis*. Hence, even for the "expert" and "cleared" analysts, the "policy debate" became little more than a combination of public passion play and Punch and Judy show in which the good and the bad took their whacks. Staging occurred partly to give moral sustenance to believers outside the Beltway and for the players inside to simply let off steam.[1]

In the meantime, there was the long-running melodrama of seemingly endless indictments and investigations of Reagan administration officials culminating in the sordid confused morass of Iran–contra. Mr. Reagan's last years were a time of soap opera politics. "Issues" were equated with personalities, especially those who had memoirs on the best-seller list. But as the president promised, he saved his best for the last act: There was a virtual parade of Soviet–American summits. The president who had labeled the Soviet Union the "evil empire" and seemed destined to go down in history as the only president of the post–World War II era to have not held a meeting with his Soviet counterparts, suddenly in his last three years strung together a series of meetings with the new Soviet First Secretary, Mikhail Gorbachev. It did not seem to matter that, in three of the four meetings held between November of 1985 and mid-1988, little of substance took place. The photo opportunities were great: Gorbachev and the president before the fire in Geneva; Gorbachev, to the dismay and horror of the KGB and the Secret Service, plunging into a Washington sidewalk crowd to press the flesh; a grim Reagan walking away from the Reykjavik failure; the president and Mrs. Reagan, again to the dismay of the KGB, greeting crowds on the Arbat in Moscow. Moreover, there was the diversion of "style wars," as the often prickly interaction of Nancy Reagan and Raisa Gorbachev was dubbed by the press. The president reportedly regarded Gorbachev as a friend; indeed, it was said that it was "Mikhail" and "Ron" when they were together privately, even when they struck "sparks" on issues such as human rights.[2] And all this normalcy had come about, it was argued, because the president had "hung tough" in the early days of his administration.[3]

Reagan had been superbly well equipped, by virtue of his gifts of communication and because of the nature of his following, to go further than Nixon and Kissinger in approaching the world with a new realism cognizant of the limits of both Soviet and American power and aware of the fluid nature of international politics. The last year of the Carter administration and almost all of Reagan's years offered, instead, an insistent vision of, on the one hand, America hobbled, and on the other, a Soviet Union attuned to every opportunity to chisel an advantage. Most of the world was seen through the kind of prism John Foster Dulles had used to squint out at the world. There was a world "permanently enslaved" and a world of free or potentially free states. The latter was a target of opportunity for the Reagan doctrine. And then, at the end, the Soviets were driven to their knees by American toughness and renewed military strength. Absent in the Reagan team's vision was not only a decent respect for the virtues of quiet diplomacy and, if diplomacy were not possible, a respect for really informed debate, but also a vision of where it all might lead.

Ill served by this tendency to present U.S.–Soviet relations as a kind of morality tale was the public who, in the end, would have to live with the consequences of a gross misperception about the nature of Soviet and American power and American purpose. The proximate aim of U.S. policy since World War II has been containment. The ultimate aim, however, has been, it should be recalled, to position the United States for the inevitable day when the Soviets would become a "normal" power.[4] Measured by the standards of the near term, the Reagan policy was a success. Arms control agreements were achieved, and others were possibly at hand. The United States had advanced its military superiority by any yardstick. But, if what was wanted was a settlement of the great issues of the previous forty years, then the Reagan policy, by denying until late in the day the possibility that fundamental changes could well be in the offing in Soviet society, needlessly deferred, if not lost, a substantial opportunity. At a minimum, a less confrontational and accusatory approach might have prepared the domestic groundwork for a break with the past.

THE FUTURE OF
AMERICAN FOREIGN POLICY

In the view of many analysts, there was indeed a break with the past, at least in the Soviet Union.[5] In his seminal examination of Soviet–American relations, "The Sources of Soviet Conduct," George Kennan sought to find a basis for American foreign policy in the post–World War II era. Out of that analysis came the public statement of the doctrine of containment that, amended by NSC 68, guided American foreign policy into the 1980s. Forty-one years later, questions concerning the new sources of Soviet conduct and what they might mean for American foreign policy were asked once again with real urgency.[6]

Glasnost *and* Perestroika

By 1988, two Russian terms — *glasnost* and *perestroika* — had become in the West a kind of shorthand for the changes under way in the Soviet Union. In these developments, one can begin to discern the new sources of Soviet behavior since the arrival of Mikhail Gorbachev in 1985. In that behavior might also reside the opportunity for transforming the Soviet–American relationship foretold by George Kennan at the dawn of the cold war.

Glasnost, the Russian word for "openness," seems the more general of the two terms in that it refers to an opening up of discourse on public and, to a lesser extent, political affairs in the Soviet Union. The precise meaning of *glasnost* is not clear. *Glasnost* seems to embrace a process whereby freer criticism of many aspects of the Soviet system is allowed to develop and is even encouraged. But the full extent of *glasnost* cannot be known *a priori*, because *glasnost* is a process whereby limits are sought and tested. It seems reasonable to conclude, however, that there are limits. Soviet citizens might be encouraged to criticize inadequate delivery of goods and services — e.g., food, housing, and medical care — but not core political processes and institutions — i.e., the central role of the Communist Party of the Soviet Union and its internal debates or the validity of socialism.[7] Thus, the West learned a great deal in the months after Gorbachev's ascendancy about various problems in the economy but the U.S. still had to rely on leaks, rumor, and very creative journalism to get any details concerning the demotion of Boris Yeltsin when he criticized the pace of reform as moving too slowly, or struggles between Gorbachev and more conservative party officials such as Yegor Ligachev, who challenged reform for moving too quickly and was demoted.[8]

Perestroika, or "restructuring," may be the more significant of the new concepts, because it refers to the restructuring of the Soviet political economy. Gorbachev has defined the term for us:

> Perestroika is a word with many meanings. But if we are to choose from its many possible synonyms, the key one which expresses its essence most accurately, [is that] perestroika is a revolution. A decisive acceleration of the socio–economic and cultural development of Soviet society which involves radical changes on the way to a qualitatively new state. . . .
>
> In accordance with our theory, revolution means construction, but it also implies demolition. Revolution requires the demolition of all that is obsolete, stagnant and hinders fast progress. Without demolition, you cannot clear the site for new construction. Perestroika also means a resolute and radical elimination of obstacles hindering social and economic development, of outdated methods of managing the economy, and of dogmatic stereotype mentality.[9]

This has led to the "Law on the Socialist Enterprise" that took effect in January of 1988. The resulting "new economic mechanism" is seen as leading to greater autonomy for state enterprises, including self-management and less control from the center, reform of the price structure, staged movement toward international convertibility of the ruble, rationalization of investment credits, and greater entrepreneurism in the service sector. Small-scale cooperatives are to be encouraged that will engage in what is essentially free-enterprise activities. Moreover, by mid-1988, Gorbachev was aggressively pushing for some measure of democratization of the Communist Party itself.

But perestroika seems to mean much more than domestic restructuring. Amost half of Gorbachev's book, Perestroika, is devoted to foreign affairs, and the book is subtitled New Thinking for Our Country and the World. Clearly, perestroika has major implications for the rest of the world and especially the United States. "There is no getting away from each other," he says of the Soviet Union and the United States. Restructuring must, in his view, extend to this most central of international relations.

In Gorbachev's formulation, the security interdependence of the United States and Soviet Union is the central reality of international relations, transcending other considerations, including one of the hoariest of Marxist axioms, class conflict.[10]

The new political outlook calls for the recognition of one more simple axiom: security is indivisible. It is either equal security for all or none at all. . . . Would it, for instance, be in the interest of the United States if the Soviet Union found itself in a situation whereby it considered it had less security than the U.S.A.? Or would we benefit by a reverse situation? I can say firmly that we would not like this. So, adversaries must become partners and start looking jointly for a way to achieve universal security.[11]

Perestroika implies, therefore, a shift in the definition of Soviet interests and behavior that: (1) seeks a reduction of confrontation and conflict with the United States and (2) reduces the extent and intensity of Soviet politico–military commitments elsewhere in the world, especially in the Third World.[12]

Evidence of these shifts is present in Soviet behavior since April of 1985. First, of course, is the decision to withdraw from Afghanistan. In addition, however, the Soviets have refused to expand their levels of support to the Sandinistas. Similarly, there have been reductions in Soviet support for the Cuban economy, including encouragement that the Cubans undertake some *glasnost* and *perestroika* of their own (the suggestion was apparently not well received in Havana).[13] Finally, there has been a slackening of enthusiasm for continued open-ended support for Angola and the Cuban presence there.[14] In sum, the period since Gorbachev's emergence has seen an overall reduction of Soviet optimism concerning and enthusiasm for liberation struggles in the Third World.[15]

In his relations with the communist world, Gorbachev has reopened a dialogue with China in an effort to establish a more normal relationship if not a full-fledged rapprochement. Even more striking is the tone of relations with Eastern Europe. Here, Gorbachev has declared acceptance of much greater diversity, including vague references to the development of a communist "commonwealth."[16]

In East-West military issues, the evidence of change is more ambiguous but no less tantalizing for being so. Thus, the Soviet concessions on the INF Treaty included acceptance and even some extension of the U.S. position especially regarding verification. In the related area of Soviet defense doctrine, Soviet military publications show evidence of a shift toward a more defensively oriented posture. Similarly, the Soviets have expressed a greater interest in conventional arms control. No less intriguing is the view expressed by some Soviet writers that their defense procurement has, in the past, been driven by a combination of bureaucratic politics and crude attempts to emulate the West. Moreover, concern has been expressed publicly that Soviet procurement may lead to fear and overreaction in the West. Uncertainties here lie in the fact that no changes have yet been introduced into the Soviet force structure in Europe. Nonetheless, there is little disagreement that a major debate is underway concerning *perestroika* and its implications for defense spending and doctrine.[17]

Perestroika *and Soviet–American Relations*

The possible significance of these changes for U.S.–Soviet relations lies in the underlying conditions giving rise to the need for *perestroika:* economic stagnation. Between 1981 and 1985, Soviet GNP grew at only about 2 percent versus 4.7 percent to 5.0 percent in the 1960s. Furthermore, in 1986, Soviet GNP had dropped to a 1.2 percent growth rate, which put the Soviet Union behind *all* of its East European communist brethren in that year.[18] In light of this economic slowdown, Gorbachev and his reform-minded associates perceived the necessity for major changes in the Soviet system requiring a prolonged period during which new resources would be found and then infused throughout the economic infrastructure of the Soviet Union. This process, according to most informed observers, is necessary for the Soviet Union to maintain not only its position of parity with the United States and the rest of the industrialized West but also its position vis-á-vis its own camp.

The Soviet Union can acquire these new resources in at least four ways:

1. Reallocation of resources internally away from existing expenditure—e.g., defense—and toward investment in economic infrastructure.
2. Earning new resources via increased trade with the West that can then be reinvested internally.
3. Retaining and reinvesting profits and technology generated via outside investment and joint ventures with American, European, and Japanese companies.
4. Borrowing capital from the West.

All these approaches have the same precondition: they require an open, nonconfrontational relationship with the West in general and the United States in particular. The *opportunity* for internal reallocation will not be available unless the Soviet relationship with the United States shifts to a more normal one. Similarly, *access* to Western capital, trade, and investment will not be available unless the tensions of the cold war are relaxed. Moreover, from a Soviet perspective, a temporary relaxation would not seem sufficient given the magnitude of the restructuring that Gorbachev and the reformers claim is necessary. If true, the Soviet Union's behavior under Gorbachev does not constitute a short-term tactic designed to lure the West into complacency.

Of course, even if the reforms continue and take root, enormous uncertainties exist as to whether Gorbachev and the reformers can sustain the political support to pursue prolonged *perestroika*. Gorbachev has conceded that there is tremendous anxiety, even "panic," within the Soviet Union at all levels concerning these changes in the political economy. "The panic has reached such a level — and this is very serious — as to question whether perestroika is something destructive, which is denying the value of socialism . . . and leading to the destabilization of society."[19] Nonetheless, even as Gorbachev prepared for and then entertained Reagan in Moscow, intense preparations were underway for the first national party conference in decades to ratify and further *perestroika*. Moreover, Americans who met with him noted Gorbachev's sensitivity to the political mine field through which he was venturing.[20]

More fundamental, however, the conditions underlying the need for reform are present and will persist whether Gorbachev or someone else leads the Soviet Union. The problems facing the Soviet Union are deeply structural and systemic and not merely the result of personalities, although individual leaders — their styles, intelligence, and creativity — can have significant impact on how the Soviet Union — and the United States — responds to the challenges and opportunities inherent in the situation.

THE FUTURE OF THE
SOVIET-AMERICAN RELATIONSHIP

Perestroika and *glasnost* may, therefore, herald the onset of the opportunity forecast by George Kennan forty years ago. Kennan argued then that if the United States and the West would undertake a posture of containment, the Soviet Union would — because of its internal structural, political, economic, and social tensions — be forced to adopt a "far greater degree of moderation and circumspection." Containment could, therefore, "promote tendencies which must eventually find their outlet in either the break-up or the gradual mellowing of Soviet power."[21]

It was Kennan's view at the time that once the "moderation and circumspection. . . , the mellowing" manifested themselves, the United States should be prepared to respond positively and pragmatically. American policy, he admonished, should have "nothing to do with outward histrionics: with threats or blustering or superfluous gestures of outward 'toughness.'"[22] As our review of the early years of the cold war suggests, Kennan's approach was not taken, and American policy became increasingly oriented toward the very confrontation that he cautioned against. This contributed, in his view, to a number of missed opportunities during the ensuing cold war when there may have been openings for better relations, e.g., after Stalin's death. In any event, there is good reason to believe that another opportunity — perhaps the greatest of all — is now before the United States and the Soviet Union. To seize opportunities, however, entails choices as to approaches and policy.

The United States might, for example, adopt a neo-Dullesian approach of pressuring the Soviets and trying to take advantage of their needs to extract from them concessions. Little in the history mapped in this book suggests that the Soviet Union would prove pliant in the face of such a policy. Indeed, the reverse seems likely, if the events of 1947 through 1949 and 1953 through 1955 — perhaps the closest parallels to the late 1980s — are any indiciation. On the other hand, Kennan's approach was not concerned with changing Soviet society or extracting concessions. Kennan never presumed that the United States can or should seek to "reform" the Soviet Union. Rather, he argued, U.S. objectives should be the establishment and maintenance of the necessary conditions for a more normal relationship with the Soviet Union.

In general, therefore, it seems in U.S. interests for the United States to be receptive to Soviet overtures for more normal relations. Certainly, the preoccupations of past U.S.–Soviet relations remain. Strategic and conventional arms and arms control are no less important in the late twentieth century than they were at mid-century. Likewise, what have come to be known as "regional" issues will inevitably shape a more normal bilateral discourse. But these traditional foci of relations need not exhaust the agenda. To the degree that *perestroika's* progress and the moderation of Soviet society entail acquiring capital and technology from the West, Kennan's prescription would also imply that, at a minimum, the United States should move to eliminate much of the residual cold war apparatus of economic warfare that has impeded that access in the past.

Specifically, the United States might repeal the Jackson–Vanick and Stevenson amendments to American trade-negotiating authority that rigidly link the granting of liberal trade concessions, e.g., access to U.S. credits, to human rights liberalization within the Soviet Union — in these cases, Jewish immigration. Substantial evidence suggests that these restrictions are counterproductive in two senses. First, it cannot be demonstrated that they have increased immigration. Indeed, the reverse seems to be true: After these restrictions were imposed, Jewish immigration declined; it increased when the overall political relationship between the United States and the Soviet Union improved.[23] Second, the existence of such restrictions provides advantages to American commercial competitors in exploiting any Soviet market that has developed or might develop. Of course, NATO mechanisms exist to restrict such trade by America's allies, but it seems likely that both the Germans and the Japanese will, as in the past, circumvent such restrictions if there is commercial advantage to be gained in doing so. Beyond trade, there might also be a process of treating the Soviets as they insist, with some of the verbal obeisance to Soviet power they so manifestly yearn for. It is a cheap "price" to pay for a more normal relationship. Patience and civility cost very little.

Political difficulties are likely to be associated with such policy changes. However, an ascending spiral in Soviet–American relations might also be encouraged by *not* doing certain things. Here again, Kennan's advice seems as relevant today as at the onset of the cold war:

> But when the Soviet power has run its course, or when its personalities and spirit begin to change (for the ultimate outcome could be of one or the other), let us not hover nervously over the people who come after, applying litmus papers daily to their political complexions to find out whether they answer to our concept of "democratic." Give them time; let them be Russians; let them work out their internal problems in their own manner. The ways by which peoples advance toward dignity and enlightenment in government are things that constitute the deepest and most intimate processes of national life. There is nothing less understandable to foreigners, nothing in which foreign interference can do less good.[24]

The American proclivity to moralize about other people's domestic poltics and institutions was very much on display during Reagan's mid-1988 visits to Moscow and Leningrad. One could understand — and by now, the Soviets expect — that, if for no other reason than U.S. domestic imperatives, human rights concerns will be manifest in Soviet–American relations. But there are times and places and limits to U.S. effectiveness in these matters. If the decibles decline and the dialogue enters the just-resurrected world of diplomacy, the results may be less flashy but perhaps more real. As important, they could well be longer lasting. Nothing could further the cause of the historic American interest in freedom than to pursue it abroad by quiet persuasion and at home by dent of its own example.

NOTES

1. Allan S. Krass, *How Much Is Enough?* (Boston: Lexington, 1985), p. 212.
2. Steven Roberts, "Reagan Aides Call Human Rights 'Agenda Item No. 1' at the Summit," *New York Times*, May 29, 1988, pp. 1, 14; and Roberts, "Reagan and Gorbachev Begin Summit Parley in the Kremlin; 'Strike Sparks' on Rights Issue," *New York Times*, May 30, 1988, pp. A1, A6.
3. See the comments by William Hiland and Richard Pipes, former associates of Henry Kissinger and Ronald Reagan, respectively, on Public Broadcasting System, *The McNeil/Lehrer Newshour*, May 27, 1988. Only Joseph Nye, a former member of the Carter administration, demurred to any degree from this analysis, ocidly observing that "the sun does not rise because the rooster crows." See also Adam Ulam, "Russian Openness and Reagan's Tenacity," *Los Angeles Times* in the *Wilmington News Journal*, May 27, 1988, p. A14.
4. See chap. 2, *supra.*
5. See for example, Jerry Hough, *Russia and the West: Gorbachev and the Politics of Reform* (New York: Simon and Schuster, 1988); and Seweryn Bialer, *The Soviet Paradox: External Expansion and Internal Decline* (New York: Vintage, 1986). See also the consensus—notwithstanding their very different political positions—among Hiland, Pipes, and Nye in PBS, op. cit.
6. See for example, Ulam, op. cit.; C. Robert Zelnick, "Dare We Hope that the Cold War is Ending?" *The Christian Science Monitor*, May 16, 1988, p. 14; Charlotte Saikowski, "A New 'Detente' for the 1980s," *The Christian Science Monitor*, May 24, 1988, p. 1; Don Oberdorfer, "U.S.–Soviet Experts Suggest Steps to End 40-Year Cold War," *Washington Post*, May 6, 1988, p. A28; and Christopher Walker, "Defense Chiefs Bury Cold War," *The Times (London)*, March 17, 1988, p. 7.
7. See David Remnick, "Glasnost: A Dissenting View," *Washington Post National Weekly Edition*, May 30–June 5, 1988, p. 10.
8. On the other hand, very complete pictures often can be constructed and much faster than in the past. See, for example, Timothy J. Colton, "Moscow Politics and the El'tsin Affair," *The Harriman Institute Forum*, Vol. 1 (June 1988).
9. Mikhail Gorbachev, *Perestroika: New Thinking for Our Country and the World* (New York: Harper and Row, 1987), pp. 49–50, 51–52.
10. Ibid., pp. 146–147.
11. Ibid., p. 142.
12. For a superb review of Gorbachev's foreign policy thinking, see Marshall D. Shulman, "The Superpowers: The Dance of the Dinosaurs," *America and the World, 1987/88 — Foreign Affairs*, Vol. 66 (January 1988), pp. 499–506.
13. Clyde H. Farnsworth, "Soviet Said to Reduce Support for Cuban Economy," *New York Times*, March 16, 1988, p. A13.
14. James Brooke, "Angolan Settlement Moves Higher on U.S.–Soviet Agenda," *New York Times*, May 29, 1988, p. E3.
15. Shulman, op. cit., p. 501.
16. John Tagliabue, "Gorbachev Offers a 'Europe for All,'" *New York Times*, March 16, 1988, p. A3; and Shulman, op. cit., p. 500. See also his interview in *Washington Post National Weekly Edition*, May 30–June 5, 1988, esp. p. 8.
17. See Dimitri K. Simes, "'New Thoughts' Remaking Soviet Military Doctrine, but Consequences Unclear," *Los Angeles Times*, March 18, 1988, p. 7.

18. Ed A. Hewett, *Reforming the Soviet Economy: Equality Versus Efficiency* (Washington, D.C.: Brookings, 1988), *passim;* and Central Intelligence Agency, *Handbook of Economic Statistics, 1987* (Washington, D.C.: U.S. Government Printing Office, 1987), table 3, p. 25.

19. "Gorbachev Says Soviet Reform Program is Causing Turmoil, Panic at Top Levels," *Wall Street Journal,* May 11, 1988, p. 17.

20. *Washington Post* interview, op. cit.; and Robert G. Kaiser and David Remnick, "A Careful Juggler in the Kremlin," *Washington Post National Weekly Edition,* May 30–June 5, 1988, pp. 6–7.

21. George Kennan, "The Sources of Soviet Conduct," in Kennan, *American Diplomacy, 1900–1950* (Chicago: University of Chicago Press, 1951), p. 127.

22. Ibid., p. 119.

23. See Robert Cullen, "Soviet Jewry," *Foreign Affairs,* Vol. 65 (Winter 1986/87), pp. 252–266.

24. Kennan, "America and the Russian Future," *Foreign Affairs,* Vol. 24 (April 1951), pp. 351–370; reprinted in ibid., p. 136.

Index